THE MYTH OF SOVIET MILITARY SUPREMACY

For my beloved wife
Wendy

THE MYTH OF SOVIET MILITARY SUPREMACY

TOM GERVASI

1817

HARPER & ROW, PUBLISHERS, New York
Cambridge, Philadelphia, San Francisco, London
Mexico City, São Paulo, Singapore, Sydney

FIRST EDITION

Designer: Sidney Feinberg

Library of Congress Cataloging-in-Publication Data

Gervasi, Tom.
  The myth of Soviet military supremacy.

  Bibliography: p.
  Includes index.
  1. Soviet Union—Armed Forces.   2. United States—
Armed Forces.   3. Arms race—History—20th century.
I. Title.
UA770.G42   1986   355'.033047   85-45809
ISBN 0-06-015574-4

---

86 87 88 89 90 RRD 10 9 8 7 6 5 4 3 2 1

"By simplifying the thoughts of the masses and reducing them to primitive patterns, propaganda was able to present the complex process of political and economic life in the simplest terms. We have taken matters previously available only to experts and a small number of specialists, and have carried them into the street and hammered them into the brain of the little man."

—Joseph Goebbels, *Wesen und Gestalt des Nationalsozialismus,* 1935.

"Ever bought a fake picture, Toby? The more you pay for it, the less inclined you are to doubt its authenticity."

—John Le Carré, *Tinker, Tailor, Soldier, Spy,* 1974.

"The greatest evil . . . is conceived and ordered . . . in clear, carpeted, warmed and well-lighted offices, by quiet men with white collars and cut fingernails and smooth-shaven cheeks who do not need to raise their voice."

—C. S. Lewis, *The Screwtape Letters,* quoted by Ronald Reagan before the National Association of Evangelicals, 1983.

"Time after time our national security choices have been misdirected by false argument, concealed assumptions, and hidden agendas. Some of the best options have been ruthlessly suppressed. We have all so far paid for that with our wealth and our well-being. If we don't restore integrity to our government, we may well pay for it with our lives."

—Richard L. Garwin, IBM Fellow, Thomas J. Watson Research Center, and former member, President's Science Advisory Committee and Defense Science Board, 1984.

Contents

I

MYTH
AND ITS ROLE
IN THE ARMS RACE

1 Expanding America's Defense

I am a citizen who believes that our nation must have a strong defense. What I have found is that we already have one. America has had a strong defense throughout its history. We have a strong defense today, and we had one five years ago, when a new administration gained office chiefly by claiming we did not, and by promising to rearm America. To that end, it has imposed needless and incalculable costs upon the American people, who have suffered these with all good will, and who would suffer more were there but reason. There is not.

Nor do we need weapons in space. In 1983, President Reagan announced a new program to expand our defense into space. This will contribute nothing to our security. It will not eliminate the threat of nuclear weapons. It will not reduce the risks of war, but increase them. It will only compound the staggering costs of defense.

The President offered "a vision of the future," in which "free people could live secure" in the knowledge that a new generation of nonnuclear weapons, based in space, "could intercept and destroy strategic ballistic missiles before they reached our soil or that of our allies," thereby "rendering these nuclear weapons impotent and obsolete." He acknowledged that "it will take years, probably decades" before America might achieve this capability, but later added that "whenever that time came," a future President "could offer" to share it with the Soviet Union.[1]

While he was careful, then, not to suggest that this capability be offered to the Soviets until after we had achieved it, the President nevertheless seemed to wish that the Soviet people could also be made secure from the nuclear threat. He reinforced this impression in 1985, when he instructed his arms negotiators in Geneva "to try to persuade the Russians to join in the evolution to a superpower balance based on defense," though he did not clarify whether he meant that their common pursuit of this goal should be a joint effort or two independent ones.[2]

The President seemed to expand his vision, declaring: "Our moral imperative is to work with all our power for that day when the children of the world can grow up without the fear of nuclear war."[3] It seemed, then, that he wanted all people freed from the nuclear threat. So nuclear weapons of every kind, not only strategic ballistic missiles, would have to be rendered "impotent and obsolete."

But the President's plan is only to build a defense against strategic ballistic missiles, intercepting them as they rise through the earth's atmosphere and prepare to loft their warheads into trajectories high above it. This defense would do nothing to eliminate the threat from cruise missiles flying close to the earth's surface, from tactical missiles fired in low trajectories at short ranges, from nuclear weapons delivered by bombers, or from the components of nuclear weapons brought secretly to their targets and then reassembled. It is only a plan for a limited defense, not a complete one.

There was no less fear of nuclear war in the 1950s, when ballistic missiles did not yet exist but bombers did.

Moreover, this limited defense is an imperfect one. Even if it could perform as well as its advocates ask us to believe, it still would not protect us from all the ballistic missiles it was designed to destroy. Those scientists whom the President pays to advise him admit this. Edward Teller, one of the plan's earliest advocates, who may have persuaded the President to adopt it, himself acknowledges: "I do not believe we can look forward, in the foreseeable future, to a 100 percent perfect defense."[4]

So some cities still could be hit. We still will not be secure from that threat. And our children still will grow up in fear.

These limitations and flaws in the President's plan were emphasized by several experts, including former defense secretary Robert McNamara, on a special Public Television program, *Shielding America: Can Star Wars Make Us Safe?*, sponsored by AT&T and broadcast the week before the President's Geneva summit meeting with Soviet Secretary Gorbachev. The program concluded, however, by interviewing Edward Luttwak, another advocate of the President's plan, who did not acknowledge any of its limitations and flaws. Instead, as though in summation, he offered an analogy for the present strategic situation. He likened the two superpowers to "two principalities" sharing a common border, with "no barriers, no trenches" between them. Either nation, he said, could send its cavalry to "seize the other." He called this an "unstable situation."

Luttwak's analogy was misleading. The superpowers already hold each other hostage, without a shot being fired. Neither could unleash its nuclear weapons against the other like cavalry, without risking immediate retaliation. Luttwak could not show how the President's defensive shield in space might protect us, either from an initial attack or from a retaliatory one. Then he could not show how this shield might make the strategic situation more stable, or how it could make the world safe.

Moreover, there is no reason to believe this defensive shield could be more than marginally effective. There is every reason to think it could not be. Its greatest prospect of success is against the smallest number of targets. So it must concentrate its efforts on intercepting Soviet missiles in the few minutes between their launch and the moment their boosters burn out and they begin releasing their warheads.

After that moment, the number of targets the system must destroy will have been multiplied several times. Without booster flames to reveal their positions, it will be almost impossible even to locate them in free flight through the darkness of space, let alone distinguish several thousand warheads from what is sure to be an even larger number of decoys. Consequently, the administration's own Defense Technologies Studies Team, led by Dr. James C. Fletcher, concedes that unless the major portion of the Soviet missile force is destroyed before it releases its warheads, no defense of our population is even theoretically possible.[5]

But for most of the time before that moment occurs, these missiles would still be moving through the earth's atmosphere. Two of the weapon systems proposed for our defensive shield, X-ray lasers and neutral particle beams, would be wholly ineffective in the atmosphere, which quickly absorbs X-ray energy and charges neutral particle beams by coupling their neutrons with air molecules.[6] Once a particle beam is charged it cannot be aimed, because its particles are steered off course by the earth's magnetic field.[7]

A third weapon system, interceptor rockets released from satellites, and equipped with infrared sensors to seek out the heat of Soviet booster flames, would also be ineffective in the atmosphere. The friction of moving through it at the high speeds the rockets would have to sustain in order to overtake their targets would form a layer of heated air around them, blinding their sensors and making guidance impossible.[8]

Once Soviet missiles had risen well above the atmosphere, all of these weapon systems could be highly effective against them. But long before we could deploy such systems in space, the Soviets would be able to refit their missiles with more powerful engines that burned fuel more quickly, so that they gained sufficient momentum in less time and at a lower altitude. The boosters would then burn out, and the missiles would begin releasing their warheads, before they had even fully cleared the atmosphere.

Then none of these weapons would ever have the opportunity to attack Soviet missiles above the atmosphere. And all these components of our defensive shield would be useless.

The technology to accelerate the boost phase of missile flight and complete it within the atmosphere already exists. A Soviet SS-18 missile booster would presently take five minutes before it burned out above the atmosphere at an altitude of 250 miles; but our MX missile has been designed to burn out in only three minutes at half that altitude. The Fletcher Panel found that with further improvements our MX booster can burn out in only fifty seconds, well inside the atmosphere at an altitude of only 56 miles, and begin releasing its warheads ten seconds later.[9]

We may make these improvements in the MX, and similar ones in our *Minuteman,* precisely in order to eliminate the possibility of interception by the same set of weapons in space, should the Soviets deploy them. We do not need ever to take such steps, of course, because we could agree with the Soviets never to deploy any weapons in space. But if we do not agree to that, and make these improvements in our missiles instead, then the Soviets are going to make the same improvements in theirs.

The only proposed components of our defensive shield whose contemplated use in the atmosphere does not openly contradict the basic laws of physics are chemical and excimer lasers. But because these appear to perform in theory does not mean they will ever perform in fact.

While a laser may concentrate energy into a powerful beam at very close range, this beam diffuses and its intensity rapidly diminishes as it spans greater distances. Even in low orbits, satellites equipped with lasers would have to be able to fire pulses into the atmosphere at ranges of up to 2,000 miles. Each laser would have to dwell on each missile long enough to rupture its casing. The greater its distance from the missile, the more time this would take; the weaker its power, the more time it would also take. The longer it had to dwell on each target, the fewer Soviet missiles it would have time to intercept.[10]

Presidential science adviser George Keyworth exploits public ignorance of these contraints on our use of lasers when he claims that if the Soviets "multiply their missiles by 10, we can multiply the pulses sent against those missiles by 10 at infinitely less cost."[11] This suggests that a given number of lasers could destroy any number of missiles, either by taking whatever amount of time was needed to intercept them all, or, if the interception time were limited, by firing more rapidly.

In fact, the interception time would be severely limited: it would end when the Soviet boost phase ended. If we fired our lasers too rapidly, they would not dwell on any missile long enough, and would destroy no missiles at all. Lasers of sufficient power certainly could reduce their effective dwell time on each missile, but an increase in the number of Soviet missiles could force a further reduction in average dwell time to the point where it became ineffective. The only countermeasure to this would be to add more lasers.

The Union of Concerned Scientists estimated that a 25 megawatt laser would have to dwell on a Soviet missile for at least two seconds to rupture its casing, and that if the boost phase of the Soviet missile force lasted for a hundred seconds, then at least thirty lasers with this level of power output would have to be within range of the Soviet missile fields to achieve average dwell times of two seconds each on the 1,400 missiles those fields presently can launch. Each laser, then, would be assigned to fewer than fifty missiles.[12]

But these scientists also realized that to ensure that this number of lasers is within range of the Soviet missile fields at any given moment, ten times as many of them, or a total of three hundred laser stations, would have to be orbited around the earth. Then we would have to deploy at least one laser station for every five Soviet missiles deployed.[13]

If the Soviets shortened their boost phase by half, to only fifty seconds, then each laser would have time to strike at only half as many missiles, and twice this number of satellites with lasers of equivalent power would be needed. So we would have to deploy a total of six hundred laser stations, at least one for every three missiles the Soviets deployed. We would have to add another for every three missiles the Soviets added.

Then the reverse of Keyworth's claim is true. To increase the number of laser pulses against a larger missile force would not cost us infinitely less than the missiles would cost. It would cost infinitely more.

Cost, though a formidable and possibly insurmountable problem, is not even the major problem in building a laser defense. The major problem is that a 25 megawatt laser does not exist; not even a 5 megawatt laser exists. According to the Union of Concerned Scientists, the most powerful lasers we can build "are more than a million times below the power level that would be needed" to do any damage to more than a small fraction of the Soviet missile force in the time available and over the ranges required.[14]

Excimer lasers produce ultraviolet light of a shorter wavelength than the infrared light emitted by chemical lasers. One consequence of this is that they retain more energy over longer ranges. But again, to have any effect at these ranges, they would need a supply of electrical power equivalent—the same scientists note—to as much as "60 percent of the entire power output of the United States."[15] This much power can neither be stored nor drawn at one time from the nation's commercial grid. A vast system of power plants therefore would have to be built for no other purpose than to deliver this power if needed.[16]

Nor do the problems end there. Even if such lasers could be built and supplied with all the power they needed, they would still be unable to hit anything without optically perfect focusing mirrors, absolute precision in aiming, and a battle management system of flawless efficiency, which would instantaneously select the nearest new target for each laser each time. Not only are all these capabilities beyond the current reach of technology; they are beyond its foreseeable reach.[17]

The mechanical and electronic data processing standards that would have to be met to provide them are staggering. Computer software alone would require between 10 million and 100 million lines of error-free programming.[18] David L. Parnas, a computer expert at the University of Victoria in British Columbia, resigned in 1985 from a Defense Department advisory panel studying the feasibility of software development for such a program, after he reached the conclusion that it "would be impossible to produce."[19] He added that even if such a program ever is produced, "there will never be a day when we will trust it," and that consequently "we will get no benefit from it."[20]

Other leading experts have also resigned from major research programs investigating the use of lasers for missile defense. After conducting a test of X-ray laser beams generated by an underground nuclear explosion in Nevada early in 1985, scientists at the Lawrence Livermore National Laboratory announced that they had succeeded in increasing the brightness, and hence the power, of the beams by "six orders of magnitude."[21] But they later "discovered that key monitoring equipment had been improperly calibrated" during the test, so that it was unclear how much brighter the beams really had been. A "new defect in beam collimation" had also been found, so that it remained unclear whether the beams could be focused to produce sufficient destructive power.[22] After these failures were revealed, Roy D. Woodruff, chief of nuclear X-ray laser research at Livermore, resigned.[23]

Moreover, there are countermeasures to lasers, too. The Soviets, who certainly would have adopted new boosters that burned out as quickly as possible in order to cut interception time to a minimum, could also be expected to produce new rocket casings coated with highly reflective material, to deflect laser energy as harmlessly as a mirror does. They could be expected to add skirts shielding their booster flames, so that our defenses could not easily acquire them as targets, and to launch flares so that we acquired false targets.[24]

Moreover, our defenses could be attacked. Like all other satellites, they would be far more vulnerable to attack than missiles are.

The Soviet *Galosh* missile, designed to intercept other missiles, is no more effective against them than our own *Spartan* and *Sprint* missiles were before it. It is no more effective than similar missiles we develop today. A single successful test we conducted in 1984 intercepted a *Minuteman* reentry vehicle unaccompanied by the decoys and chaff that certainly would not be absent in a real attack.[25] Three other tests failed to intercept the same target.[26]

But the *Galosh* burns out its booster in the atmosphere, as our *Spartans* and *Sprints* were already able to do years earlier, and it cannot easily be tracked and targeted thereafter. It has the range, as our own missiles did and do, to reach satellites in low orbit. Consequently, like so many antiballistic missile systems, the *Galosh* has a dual role. It can also perform as an antisatellite weapon—and it is far more effective in that role. Armed with nuclear warheads, *Galosh* missiles could destroy large portions of our space defenses.

Then the President's defensive shield, no more than a limited defense which could not protect all of our cities to begin with, cannot be counted on to protect any of them at all, even if it could be built. The technology it promises could be useless even if it were at hand. "There would be no advantage," Great Britain's Foreign Secretary Sir Geoffrey Howe concluded, "in a new Maginot Line of the 21st century, liable to be outflanked by relatively simple and demonstrably cheaper countermeasures."[27]

Retired General Daniel O. Graham, a prominent advocate of the President's plan, appears to believe it is "a strange moral and political logic that argues that because we cannot save everyone we should abandon all efforts to save anyone."[28] It is an even stranger logic which asks that we undertake so monumental an effort, without any evidence that it will save anyone. It is a suspect logic which asks this, but abandons any effort to pursue the most practical means of saving everyone: an international agreement to ban nuclear weapons of every kind.

The loss of a single American city would be an unprecedented catastrophe. The loss of two cities was such a catastrophe to the Japanese. It is clear that under the President's plan all our cities still could be lost. Then all of our children still will grow up in fear.

2   Strengthening Deterrence

Administration officials insist that we must try to build a defensive shield in space anyway. When reminded that it cannot fulfill the mission the President claimed for it, they substitute a different mission. They admit that it could not protect our cities, but say that its purpose will be to protect our *Minuteman* missiles instead, thus "strengthening deterrence" by making the results of a Soviet attack "too unpredictable."

The results of a Soviet attack are already too unpredictable. That is why our *Minuteman* missiles need no protection. That is why deterrence needs no "strengthening" of any kind.

The Soviets cannot predict how many *Minutemen* they might destroy in an attack. Their own missiles, like ours, would have to be "fired from launchers never before used, over polar trajectories never before tested, for which the catalog of even the known uncertainties is lengthy," as the United States Strategic Institute's Arthur Metcalf points out. They would have to be fired, he adds, "in numbers never before launched, and within a time frame for which no shred of statistical information on operational reliability exists."[1] Indeed, "nothing has been put forward which technologically supports the belief that we or the Soviets could, with any degree of confidence, expect to hit one silo at ICBM range, let alone 1,000 of them."[2]

This means the Soviets cannot predict how many *Minutemen* might survive to retaliate against them. They cannot risk any retaliation. The loss of a single city would be no less catastrophic for them than for us. Their attack would place hundreds of their cities at risk.

The Soviets cannot even be sure they would destroy a single *Minuteman*. All of our *Minutemen* can be launched after an impending attack is confirmed, but long before it could hit them.[3] Even if we chose not to launch them in the face of an attack, and not to launch any of those that survived an attack, the Soviets would still face wave after wave of certain retaliation from our bombers and missiles at sea.

A single *Poseidon* missile can destroy Leningrad.[4] In response to a Soviet attack, a dozen *Poseidon* submarines, each with sixteen missiles, could destroy the two hundred largest cities in the Soviet Union, and with them a third of the Soviet population and three quarters of its industry.[5] Twenty of our *Poseidon* and *Trident* submarines could destroy all of this and almost every military installation in the Soviet Union that might still pose a nuclear threat to the United States.[6]

We keep this number of submarines, with more than 4,000 nuclear weapons, on station at all times.[7] We keep sixteen more submarines, with another 3,000 nuclear weapons, ready to go to sea.[8] By contrast, the Soviet Union keeps no more than ten ballistic missile submarines with no more than eight hundred nuclear weapons at sea.[9]

Our submarines cannot even be attacked, because they cannot be located. George Keyworth warns that "the day may come" when advances in signal-processing technology make it possible to locate them.[10] He does not add that nothing suggests this day will ever come. Nor does he add that if it did come it would threaten Soviet submarines long before it threatened ours, because we hold the lead in this technology.[11]

Kosta Tsipis, a director of the Program in Science and Technology for International Security at MIT, concludes that "the bulk of the ballistic missiles aboard strategic submarines are immune to surprise attack," both "at the present time and for the foreseeable future." But he adds that given our "superiority" in antisubmarine warfare technology, and given "the small number of Soviet ballistic missile submarines deployed at any one time," the probability that we may ever detect all Soviet submarines at one time is larger than the probability that they may ever detect all of ours at one time.[12]

Nor could most of our bombers be destroyed in a Soviet attack. The Congressional Budget Office estimates that 95 percent of them could be fully alerted before an attack, that 73 percent could survive one even if it came from Soviet submarines at close range, and that as many as 75 percent of these could penetrate Soviet air defenses and deliver their weapons to their targets.[13] So these bombers could deliver between 1,500 and 2,000 nuclear weapons to their targets in the Soviet Union.

Then either by air or by sea, we could destroy hundreds of military and industrial targets in the Soviet Union, and hundreds of Soviet cities, in response to an attack. Our surviving land-based *Minutemen* might well do the same. The Soviets cannot risk any one of these responses, let alone all three; yet any attack of their own would risk all three. These risks are unacceptable; yet they are inescapable. In 1983, the President's Commission on Strategic Forces, chaired by General Brent Scowcroft, recognized that our existing retaliatory forces, and the risks they pose, "guarantee deterrence."[14]

This conclusion flatly contradicted earlier administration assertions that America faced a "window of vulnerability" in which deterrence was not guaranteed. Those assertions were used, at the time, to justify "strengthening deterrence" by building the MX and *Trident II* missiles, the B-1 bomber, and a whole generation of new strategic weapons we do not need, because those we already have "guarantee deterrence." We are building the new weapons anyway, despite the Commission's findings.

Once administration officials acknowledged that the President's defensive shield in space could never "replace deterrence," as he had promised, they could find no other justification for it but as another measure to "strengthen deterrence," instead. This required them, once again, to ignore the findings of their own Commission that deterrence needed no strengthening because it was already "guaranteed." It required all proponents of a defense in space to repeat the same assertions about America's "vulnerability," which the Commission had shown were unfounded.

This they now do. The entire argument insisting that America does face a "window of vulnerability" has been recycled in support of the President's plan. The central propositions in this argument remain unchanged. One of them is that after a Soviet attack our only choices would be either to retaliate against Soviet cities, dooming our own cities to retaliation in kind, or to save our cities by not retaliating at all. The choice is between surrender and suicide.

This view of our options has been presented repeatedly. In 1979 the Coalition for Peace Through Strength, arguing for "strategic modernization" and against ratification of the SALT II Treaty, suggested that it was "most unlikely that any U.S. President would retaliate after a Soviet first strike," when "the Soviets would still have enough strategic nuclear forces to destroy 60 percent of all Americans."[15] In 1983 the National Strategy Information Center, arguing against a nuclear freeze, surmised that "given the choice between the destruction of our urban areas or acquiescence to Moscow's demands, it is hard to believe that a U.S. President would choose the former course."[16]

In 1985, arguing for the President's defensive shield in space, Max Kampelman, head of our arms negotiating team in Geneva, former National Security Advisor Zbigniew Brzezinski, and Robert Jastrow, founder of the Goddard Institute for Space Studies, warned that "an American President, knowing that a strike against our cities would inevitably follow our response to a Soviet first strike," would be faced with "having to choose either annihilation or submission to nuclear blackmail."[17]

Such a view rests on a number of assumptions that are either dubious or wrong. It assumes that at first the Soviets would attack only military targets, and would not attack cities at the same time. It assumes that few or none of our cities would be destroyed anyway in such an attack. It assumes that we could not retaliate first against military targets rather than cities, or that we could not retaliate against both at the same time. It therefore assumes that our retaliation could not diminish the Soviet capacity to launch a second attack, and so diminish the damage we would sustain from it.

Most important of all, this view assumes that since the Soviets could be willing to launch a first strike, they would be willing to risk the destruction of their cities in response, whereas we would not be willing to risk the destruction of ours. Then it assumes that any action that raises such risks would deter us but would not deter them. This is a double standard.

Ronald Reagan reinforced this double standard in 1980 when he told *Los Angeles Times* correspondent Robert Scheer that "we have a different regard for human life than those monsters do."[18] Kampelman, Brzezinski, and Jastrow reinforced it again in 1985 when they warned that the Soviets might launch a first strike, despite the destruction they would suffer in response, because "some Russian leader could someday well consider such a potential cost bearable."[19]

This certainly was not the view of the Scowcroft Commission on Strategic Forces. Our weapons could only "guarantee deterrence" if they posed risks that Soviet leaders could not find "bearable."

The purpose of this double standard is to deny that deterrence works both ways. Such a denial has played a fundamental role in the arms race. It has repeatedly been used to dismiss all the weapons we have had as inadequate to deter attack, and to justify any number of new weapons and bold new defensive plans as measures to "strengthen deterrence," even though all of these, in turn, could later be dismissed as inadequate too, and often were, for precisely the same reason.

In this way, each new generation of weapons can always be found to fall short of its promise. For otherwise, the arms race could not continue. Advocates of the President's new defense in space are merely trying to repeat this cycle.

In fact, though the Soviets have been able to attack us for more than thirty years, ever since they first developed the means to deliver nuclear weapons to targets in the United States, in all this time they have never attacked. Then either they have no desire to attack or they are deterred. If they are deterred, it can only be the weapons we have that deter them. So the weapons we have protect our cities far more effectively than a defensive shield in space ever could.

In fact, in response to a Soviet attack, we would not be limited to a choice between "annihilation" or "submission." We would not first retaliate against Soviet cities. "Contrary to what many believe," our Defense Department notes, "the U.S. has always aimed a majority of its strategic weapons at military—not civilian—targets."[20] This has been our stated policy since 1962, when Defense Secretary Robert McNamara first declared that our retaliatory objectives would be "the destruction of the enemy's military forces, not of his civilian population."[21] The only reason more people do not know this is because those who claim we are "vulnerable" have done their best to obscure it.

Our first priority, then, is to strike at Soviet military forces, precisely in order to minimize further damage to the United States by minimizing the Soviet capacity to launch further nuclear attacks. We could not eliminate that capacity. The Soviets keep missiles at sea just as we do, and we could no more destroy them than they can destroy our missiles at sea. But we could destroy most of their other remaining nuclear weapons and strategic bases.

Since these facts contradict the impression of "vulnerability" which advocates of military expansion must promote, they vigorously deny them. They deny that our weapons are accurate enough to strike at military targets. They invent new threats. Kampelman, Brzezinski, and Jastrow, for example, claim that "many Soviet missile silos are reloadable" and "are set up for launching three salvos to our one."[22] Congressman Thomas Downey of New York points out that this Soviet capability "doesn't exist."[23] The Defense Department comments that even if it did exist, "U.S. retaliatory capabilities could destroy any ICBM reload facilities long before a second Soviet salvo could be fired."[24]

Our weapons do not lack the accuracy to attack such targets. Many of the reentry vehicles on our missiles at sea are capable of striking within 900 feet of their aimpoints.[25] This makes them nearly as accurate as the most accurate Soviet land-based missiles.[26] Many of the reentry vehicles on our *Minutemen* are far more accurate than any of those on Soviet land-based missiles. Since 1978 they have been capable of striking within 600 feet of their aimpoints.[27] What is almost wholly ignored is that our bombers can deliver most of their nuclear weapons with equal accuracy.[28]

Some of the weapons our bombers deliver are the most accurate of all. Our Air-Launched Cruise Missile is capable of striking within only 100 feet of its aimpoint.[29] This level of accuracy almost guarantees the destruction of even the hardest targets, including Soviet missile silos and military command and communications centers.[30] The prospect of such a guarantee raises the promise of further minimizing damage to the United States, by striking the Soviet Union first, crippling the Soviet command system, and eliminating many Soviet land-based missiles before they can even be launched. This possibility has not been overlooked by our military planners.

Downey notes that in their argument for a defensive shield in space, Kampelman, Brzezinski, and Jastrow "assume that (1) United States bombers can't get safely away from their bases in time to escape Soviet ICBM attack, (2) our cruise missiles aren't accurate enough to destroy Soviet ICBM silos, and (3) the threat of annihilation by our missile submarines is no deterrent to Soviet attack. All these assumptions are incorrect."[31]

But just as all of these weapons, which the Soviets cannot eliminate, effectively deter Soviet attack, so those Soviet weapons we cannot eliminate, though many times fewer in number, no less effectively deter an American attack. Then no matter how devastating these weapons become in Soviet and American arsenals, neither nation can use them against the other with impunity. While this is a far better guarantee against their use than a missile defense in space would be, it is by no means a perfect guarantee. As long as these weapons exist, children will continue to grow up in fear.

If the President truly desires to banish that fear, and to render all nuclear weapons obsolete, the best way to do so, instead of trying to build a defense against some of them, is to dismantle them all.

The President and his advisers may not believe all other nations would agree to this solution. But how do they know? They have never asked. If they agreed to participate in this solution on more equitable terms than America offered in the Baruch Plan of 1946,[32] they might be surprised at the response.

The administration undoubtedly would claim that compliance with an agreement eliminating all nuclear weapons and the further production of fissionable material could not be verified. But verification only requires a political agreement. The technology to make it work already exists. The technology to make the President's plan work does not exist. No evidence suggests it ever will. If it ever did, the most it could produce would be an imperfect and incomplete defense that was highly vulnerable and easily circumvented.

The President tells us, nevertheless, that he wants to eliminate "the fear of nuclear war." He knows we support that goal, but he makes no comprehensive attempt to achieve it, even though the means of achieving it are at hand. He asks our support, instead, for an effort not even designed to achieve it, because it is meant to protect against only one kind of nuclear weapon, and its proponents acknowledge that it cannot even succeed at this. So the President does not want to eliminate the fear of nuclear war; he and his advisers do not "work with all our power" to that end.

His supporters hailed the President's announcement of his new defense plan as the moment the "old theory" of deterrence "died forever."[33] Deterrence is not merely a theory—it is an inescapable risk. It may certainly fail to prevent nuclear war, but it will not disappear until the weapons do. The President has no plans for that. On the contrary, he has authorized programs to build a total of 17,000 new nuclear warheads; only 6,000 of these are intended as replacements for those now deployed. Thus America's arsenal is scheduled to expand by a net increase of 11,000 warheads.[34]

If all of this seems familiar, that is because it has happened so many times before. Every new generation of strategic weapons has been more costly and complex than the generation before it. The history of the arms race has been a history of the search for new ways to expand military investment, and of the search for new areas where public knowledge is too weak to challenge official policy. Almost every new weapon has been presented as a defensive measure, but perceived as an offensive one. It has been introduced as a means of "strengthening deterrence," but it has often destabilized the balance of power and risked the failure of deterrence instead.

The President's plan is no different. Weapons deployed on satellites will threaten other satellites long before they threaten ballistic missiles. One nation could use these weapons in an attempt to gain a critical advantage before its attack on another, by first destroying the other's early warning and communications satellites. That is why Defense Secretary Caspar Weinberger finds the idea of a Soviet system of weapons based in space "one of the most frightening prospects" imaginable.[35]

But that is exactly how the Soviets view America's plan for such a system, exactly how they must assume we might use it. Administration officials point to Soviet opposition to this plan as proof that the Soviets believe it can achieve its stated goal, and suggest that we should therefore believe it too. It is merely proof that the Soviets believe it may achieve its *unstated* goal.

The Soviets know we are well ahead of them in space-based weapons and antiballistic missile (ABM) technology. We have frequently denied this, in order to justify our own programs as an effort to catch up with theirs. But we know otherwise.

John Pike of the Federation of American Scientists called administration assertions that the Soviets were ahead of us in these technologies "laughable," and added: "There's no doubt that there's an ABM gap, but it's in our favor."[36] This was confirmed by Robert Cooper, director of the Defense Advanced Research Projects Agency, who told the Senate Armed Services Committee in 1984 that "I don't think the Soviets are far advanced as to where we are in many, if not most, of these technologies."[37]

The Soviets do not want another arms race in which they are once again threatened, and once again must try to catch up with us. They returned to Geneva chiefly to persuade us out of it. But the Reagan administration declared its main purpose was to persuade them into it, and the President told his negotiators that his new defense plan was "non-negotiable."

Inflexibility of this kind recalled a familiar pattern in the Reagan administration's arms negotiating techniques. These techniques usually involved a "two-track" approach: heavily publicizing our willingness to reduce existing weaponry, while deemphasizing the specific details of our proposals, which invariably called for greater reductions in Soviet arms than in our own; and simultaneously committing ourselves to programs for the development of new weaponry, the technology for which lay much closer at hand for us than for the Soviet Union. Then the Soviets could either refuse to accept our proposals, or they could refuse to accept unrestrained competition in new arms development. They have usually refused both. Whenever they made either kind of refusal, we could point to Soviet intransigence as the cause for failure to achieve arms control.

Thus, the President's "Zero-Option" proposal of 1981 asked the Soviets to dismantle or withdraw all of their SS-20 and other nuclear missiles of intermediate range targeted on western Europe, without proposing that comparable British *Polaris,* American *Poseidon* and French M-20 and SSBS-2 missiles targeted against eastern Europe be dismantled or withdrawn too. Simultaneously, he warned that if the Soviets did not accept this proposal, we would deploy a new generation of far more sophisticated Cruise and *Pershing II* missiles, which could be targeted on the Soviet Union. The Soviets naturally refused, and we proceeded with our new missile deployments.

In the same way, the President's START (Strategic Arms Reduction) proposal of 1982 asked for what seemed equivalent reductions in Soviet and American nuclear arsenals to a level of 5,000 ballistic missile warheads each. Less publicized was the fact that it also asked the Soviets to achieve their reduction by eliminating 75 percent of their force of SS-17, SS-18 and SS-19 missiles,[38] the most modern weapons they had developed, while it did not even include the most modern weapons we had developed, long-range Air-Launched Cruise Missiles, or the very large arsenal of nuclear gravity bombs our strategic aircraft also deploy, even though these two categories of weapons perpetuate a sizeable numerical and qualitative United States lead in strategic power over the Soviet Union. The Soviets, of course, did not agree to these terms.

In the summer and fall of 1985, as the Geneva summit meeting between President Reagan and Soviet Secretary Gorbachev approached, the Soviets made a number of significant new arms proposals, including a 25 percent reduction in the number of nuclear warheads each superpower could target on the other's territory,[39] a reduction of all such warheads to the level of 6,000 each,[40] and, beginning in August, 1985, a comprehensive test ban, which the Soviet Union would unilaterally observe through the end of that year, and which it would continue to observe thereafter, as long as the United States refrained from further tests too.[41]

The Reagan administration rejected the Soviet offer of a test ban,[42] arguing that tests were needed, among other purposes, in order to develop an X-ray laser for the President's defensive shield in space. X-ray lasers were still planned as a principal component of this shield, even though they could only be produced by nuclear explosions, and even though plans to deploy nuclear weapons of any kind in space violated the Limited Test Ban Treaty of 1963 and the Outer Space Treaty of 1967, both of which the United States signed and ratified.[43]

For that matter, however, every component of the proposed defensive shield violates the ABM Treaty of 1972, Article V of which unequivocally states that "Each Party undertakes not to develop, test, or deploy ABM systems or components which are sea-based, air-based, space-based, or mobile land-based."[44] The administration likes to quote from Agreed Statement D of the treaty that "specific limitations" on systems "based on other physical principles" are "subject to discussion."[45] The administration does not like to quote the remainder of that statement, which adds that such limitations are subject to discussion "in accordance with Article XIII and agreement in accordance with Article XIV of the Treaty." Article XIV provides for "Agreed Amendments" to be added to the treaty, after consideration of proposals for such amendments by the Standing Consultative Commission established by Article XIII.[46] Without prior agreement by both parties, then, the treaty simply forbids the President's plan. No such prior agreement has been reached by the Standing Consultative Commission.

President Reagan has promised "to stay within a strict definition of the treaty.

And what we are doing with regard to research—and that would include testing—is within the treaty."[47] But Article V of the treaty clearly states that testing—including our underground X-ray laser test in Nevada in 1985—is not permitted.

"I would characterize our arms-control position," the President stated in one press briefing, "as deep cuts, no first-strike advantage, defensive research . . . and no cheating."[48] His own administration has already cheated.

Having violated one treaty, and having repeatedly insisted on proceeding with a plan that will violate this treaty again, as well as violate two more, the administration responded, one month after the Soviets proposed a reduction of all strategic warheads to the level of 6,000,[49] with a counterproposal of its own to reduce strategic warheads to the same level—but in a different way. As *Time* magazine noted, "the U.S. proposal applies the 6,000 figure only to warheads on strategic missiles (submarine ballistic missiles and land-based ICBMs) and on cruise missiles launched from planes. The Soviets would like to lump gravity bombs and short-range attack missile warheads into that category; the U.S. has a significant lead in these weapons."[50] *Time* did not add that the Soviets also included in their proposal all nuclear weapons based in Europe and targeted on Soviet soil.[51]

Once again, as in so many previous negotiations, the United States was exempting large numbers of its own weapons from its proposals.

But the primary obstruction to any agreement was that the Soviets did not want the President's plan for a new defense in space to proceed beyond the basic laboratory research permitted by the ABM Treaty, while the President did.

To prevent the public from understanding that his inflexibility over his new defense plan was really intended to ensure that no agreement was reached on reductions in nuclear arms, the President frequently repeated his idea of "sharing" space-based missile defense technology with the Soviet Union. This delighted columnist William Safire, who exulted that the President's "shield-sharing" idea "pulverized" Soviet "propaganda about our destabilizing intent."[52]

Safire had to acknowledge, however, that the President had been rather vague about how and when we would go about "sharing" this technology, "making it seem," in one interview with Soviet journalists, that "he predicated shield-sharing on elimination of offensive weapons."[53] Administration officials subsequently acknowledged that they could not expect the Soviets to disarm before sharing our technology, and were quick to remind the public that we had no intention of eliminating all of our own nuclear weapons either.

But the President soon grew more precise about how he meant to share our technology. "I don't mean we'll give it to them," he told a group of foreign journalists. "They're going to have to pay for it—but at cost."[54] In his 1985 Voice of America broadcast to the Soviet people before his Geneva summit meeting with Secretary Gorbachev, he became even more precise: "If and when our research proves that a defensive shield against nuclear missiles is practical, I believe our two nations and those others that have nuclear weapons should come together and agree on how *gradually* to eliminate offensive nuclear weapons as we make our defensive system available to all."[55]

The meaning is clear. If the Soviets cannot afford or do not wish to pay for our new technology, whose cost will be staggering even "at cost," then we will not share it. If the Soviets do not "agree" on "how gradually to eliminate" nuclear weapons—which is to say, if they do not accept our terms for reductions in nuclear arms, whether these terms are equitable or not—then we will not share our technology. If the Soviets do not want our technology, and do not want us to develop it, then we no longer have to agree to any reductions in nuclear arms. We can take the same position we have always taken in past negotiations: we have made our proposals "in good faith." We have shown a willingness to bring the arms race to a halt, and it is only Soviet intransigence that carries it forward.

In this way, by making his new defense plan "non-negotiable," the President made arms control non-negotiable.

Since weapons in space can help us to launch a first strike more effectively than they can protect us from one, by deploying such weapons we increase the threat of such an attack on the Soviet Union. If we increase this threat, yet cannot eliminate the threat of Soviet retaliation, then we only increase the threat to ourselves. Merely by planning to build such weapons, we increase the risk of a Soviet attack to prevent us from building them. The administration claims that the Soviet return to the negotiating table is a triumph of American diplomacy. This is the kind of triumph a terrorist feels at getting others to do his will because he threatens to blow himself up along with them.

3   Limiting the Framework of Debate

The President has taken research initiated thirty years ago and never abandoned since, and called it his own Strategic Defense Initiative. For decades, scientists have searched for a feasible means of building the defensive shield he now calls his "vision," but found none. Nevertheless, insisting a means may yet be found, he has shifted the world's attention away from steps that might be taken now to eliminate the nuclear threat, and focused it instead on a distant prospect "years, probably decades" away, that is so remote it probably never will come to pass, and that would not eliminate the nuclear threat if it did.

Immediately after the President announced his plan, most administration officials acknowledged that it could never do more than provide an imperfect and incomplete defense. But the President did not acknowledge this. He had committed himself to the goal of rendering ballistic missiles "impotent and obsolete," and to the larger goal of eliminating "the fear of nuclear war." His plan could accomplish neither one of these goals; yet they were the sole justification for the plan. So he was urging support for his plan by using false promises.

Since the President did not acknowledge any of this, no one could ignore his plan. There is no better demonstration of American presidential power. His administration proceeded to make his commitment to this plan the primary issue in dispute at Geneva, and the primary subject of public debate on arms control throughout the West.

Meanwhile, the weapons the President still insists his plan will protect us from, and all of the other weapons no one even pretends it will protect us from, go ignored. The threat that these weapons will always pose as long as they exist, and the many more feasible means already at hand of eliminating this threat, go ignored. The vast amounts of money we already spend for defense, and the premises on which we spend it, go ignored too.

Yet the spending continues. In its military budget for fiscal year 1986, the administration plans to spend $3.7 billion on research for the President's defensive shield in space. But in the same budget it plans to spend $153 billion on investment in new conventional and strategic weapons. That is triple the amount spent on weapons in 1980. It is nearly half the military budget.[1] While the public and press debate the merits and costs of a defense in space, this larger expenditure is taken for granted.

Since gaining office, the Reagan administration has spent more than $1 trillion on defense; it plans to spend another $1.7 trillion on defense through 1990.[2] Our military budgets now run at an annual average of $300 billion. As a share of all federal spending, defense has risen from 23 percent in 1980 to 29 percent in 1986.[3] This percentage includes only costs charged to the Department of Defense. When costs are added for the Department of Energy's nuclear warhead production, NASA's military Space Shuttle flights, veterans' benefits, federal administrative overhead, and interest on war-related debt, our actual military burden is 57 percent of all federal spending.[4]

"We are spending more on weapons and on military might this year," noted Congressman Jim Wright of Texas, the House majority leader, "than we spent in any year during the Vietnam War, in any year during the Korean war, and yes, in any year during World War II."[5]

Though President Reagan continues to insist that he is devoted to a balanced budget, columnist Tom Wicker notes that a "major cause" of the nation's record deficits "is increased military spending, which has risen by 60 percent in the Reagan years, against only a 28 percent increase in nonmilitary spending."[6]

This pattern of spending has made a shambles of social programs that were the cornerstone of America's efforts to build a just society. In its first year in office, the administration authorized cuts of $44.4 billion in domestic social programs. According to the Congressional Budget Office, it made further cuts totalling $75.8 billion in these programs from 1982 through 1985. It plans further cuts of $65.5 billion in these programs from 1986 through 1988.[7] If that does not suffice to pay its military bills, then with or without a budget "compromise" to reduce deficits, it may run the government further into debt.

This extraordinary shift in the nation's priorities has barely been questioned. As the administration began to appropriate the enormous sums it said were needed to rearm America, there was extensive public debate about how the money might be spent and what its possible effects on our economy might be. There was no discussion at all of whether we really needed to spend it. Columnist Anthony Lewis observes that "hardly anyone in the political mainstream challenges the proposition."[8]

For its first several months in office, the administration did not even explain how the money it had taken for defense would be spent, until budget director David Stockman revealed that no one in the administration had yet decided how to spend it.[9] Then a list of the weapons we would purchase and the forces we would expand very promptly appeared, in the administration's *Fiscal Years 1984–1988 Defense Guidance.*

But this document did not explain how these weapons and forces would be used to counter the threat we presumably faced. It did not explain precisely what threat they would meet that could not be met by weapons and forces we already had. Then what were the answers to these questions? How much more military power, if any, did America really need? How should we use it? What should it cost?

These questions should guide our assessment of any plan to rearm the nation. They should be at the heart of every debate on increases in military spending. In this debate, over the largest increases in military spending the nation had seen, they played no role at all. They were only asked by public interest groups, and by some Democratic Party candidates who tried, but failed, to make them a major issue in the 1984 election campaign. The administration did not respond to them. The press responded to the administration's silence by deciding these questions were not a major issue. No one else in the "political mainstream" even raised them.

The President's emphasis on his plan for a new defense in space has made these questions seem even less relevant in current debate on military policy. That debate is now wholly preoccupied with the question of whether it will ever be possible to build such a shield, rather than whether it would ever be prudent to build one, when the most it could do, instead of protecting us from nuclear weapons, would be to make existing weapons more dangerous. Advocates of this new defense reward blind faith in the President's plan, and in the false promises on which it is based, by calling it optimism. They dismiss the most optimistic assessment of the plan's limitations and liabilities as pessimism.

Meanwhile, the only defense that is not "years, probably decades" away, and whose enormous costs we already bear, is almost forgotten. This is the administration's continuing program to rearm America. Its costs continue to multiply, but in all this time its premises have gone unexamined.

4 Rearming America

Nor has the nation been rearmed. There has been no expansion of America s military power. In most cases, the promised improvements and additions to our arsenal have not been made. Our armored battalions, air wings, and fleets have received fewer new tanks, aircraft, and ships than even the Carter administration had planned.

Heritage Foundation analyst George W. S. Kuhn discovered this in 1983. "The increased spending secured by President Reagan," he noted, "should afford significant improvements in force size. It does not. The acquisition account is buying less this year in many programs than former President Jimmy Carter's 1979 plan had projected."[1]

This situation has not changed. In 1985, the Defense Department reported continuing late deliveries from many of the leading contractors responsible for this equipment, among them General Dynamics, Lockheed, Hughes Aircraft, McDonnell Douglas, and Martin Marietta.[2] Senate investigators found that most defense contractors were taking as much as "10 times longer" than they had projected to complete their work.[3]

If we truly needed all the weapons this administration had prescribed, and which it was spending unprecedented sums to purchase, we were not getting them.

Then where was all this money going? In 1983, an advisory commission, the President's Private Sector Survey on Cost Control, traced where the money was going. It found that out of $390 billion the administration had spent on defense since 1981, $92 billion had been wasted. It found that all of this money could have been saved without any reduction in planned force expansions to meet our presumed security needs.[4]

The Commission, headed by J. Peter Grace, was promptly discredited by the administration that had appointed it for using poor methodology to arrive at such a conclusion. But in 1984, Air Force management systems deputy Ernest Fitzgerald told a Senate subcommittee that at least 30 percent of the money paid in most military contracts was wasted.[5] Former Deputy Secretary of Defense Paul Thayer estimated that the same percentage could be saved in almost every contract for weapons procurement. This meant that $30 billion a year could be saved in the costs of weapons alone.[6] For the period of three years the Grace Commission had studied, that came to almost exactly the same amount it had cited.

In 1985 the Senate Budget Committee, whose Republican members outnumber its Democrats, reached nearly the same conclusion the Grace Commission had. It voted 18 to 4 to cut $79 billion from the administration's military budget over the next three years.[7] It seems that a growing consensus shares the Commission's methodology.

"We must never again abuse the trust of working men and women by sending their earnings on a futile chase after the spiraling demands of a bloated Federal establishment," President Reagan affirmed in his second inaugural address. He would not want any American, then, to think that his administration's policies were only bloating that establishment further, increasing the burden of its demands, and making the chase more futile.

Yet this seems to be precisely what those policies are doing. Senior citizens face the prospect of cuts in Social Security so that we might continue to buy more tanks and aircraft. We are not even getting all the tanks and aircraft. Those we are getting frequently fail to perform as advertised, and almost always cost far more than promised.

In 1982, the Pentagon announced that the cost of forty-four major weapon systems had increased over prior projections by $114 billion.[8] In 1983 Murray Weidenbaum, former chairman of President Reagan's Council of Economic Advisers, reported that the costs of some of these weapons were running over original estimates by as much as 320 percent.[9] All the major defense contractors the Pentagon accused of late deliveries in 1985 it also accused of high costs, poor quality, and excessive profits. Pentagon Inspector General Joseph Sherick acknowledged that "the taxpayers are being ripped off by excessive charges."[10]

When a weapon costs more than we planned, the funds set aside for it cannot buy as many. Small wonder, then, that we have not seen all the weapons we thought we had paid for. We have been paying more, but getting less. This is indeed an abuse of our trust.

The problem goes deeper. The Pentagon's budget for operations and maintenance has not been expanded to accommodate the larger arsenal this administration promised. Instead, it has shrunk. While weapons procurement rose from 37 percent of the Pentagon's budget in 1980 to 49 percent in 1984, the allowance for operations and maintenance dropped from 32 percent of that budget in 1980 to only 26 percent in 1984.[11]

This is important. It means that even if we now had all the new weapons we paid for, we could not operate most of them anyway. They would have no fuel or ammunition; no one would have been trained to fly the new aircraft or drive the new tanks or repair them. In their *Fiscal Year 1985 Military Posture Statement,* the Joint Chiefs of Staff confirm that "shortfalls in authorized end strength, senior grade enlisted personnel, spare parts, ammunition, training funds" and other support capabilities "continue to inhibit readiness."

This means the administration has had no intention of deploying all the weapons it said we needed. Then the administration does not really believe we need them. This should come as no surprise. David Stockman pointed out that at first the administration did not even know what weapons it wanted; it only knew how much money it wanted. For its military budget, he said, it was "so goddamned greedy" it wrote itself "a blank check."[12]

So the administration has been subjecting us to two kinds of military waste. It has been making us pay more than weapons should cost, and doing nothing to control their cost. It has also been making us pay for countless weapons we do not even need.

Yet the administration said we did need these weapons. It made quite a point about that. In justifying a military budget of unprecedented size, it made a series of unprecedented claims. One of these was that the weapons it wanted were urgently needed to redress an "adverse imbalance" of military power. Another was that the Soviet Union held a definite margin of strategic "superiority" over the United States.

Both of these statements were lies. The latter must rank as one of the largest lies ever told. The Soviet Union did not have a margin of strategic superiority over us. It never has had one. It does not have one now, and it probably never will.

Some Soviet missiles are larger than ours. Some Soviet warheads have greater explosive force than ours. Both of these facts have been used to suggest that the Soviets held a margin of superiority.

We could have had larger missiles too, had we wished to build them. We did not wish to build them. We could have built warheads with even greater explosive force than those the Soviets have, had we chosen to do so. We did not choose to do so. Our missiles are far more accurate than Soviet missiles. As a result, with a fraction of the explosive force some Soviet warheads can produce, our warheads threaten far greater damage to targets in the Soviet Union.

Then if any more significance can be found than the Scowcroft Commission could find in a "window of vulnerability," through which one nation's missiles presumably threaten another's, those who continue to warn of it must acknowledge that this "window" looms far larger, and has loomed far longer, for the Soviets than for us.

Just before Thanksgiving in 1982, the President appeared on television to count the numbers of missiles and bombers the superpowers deploy to deliver strategic warheads. He showed that the Soviets had more missiles than we did. This, too, was meant to substantiate the administration's earlier claim that the Soviets held superiority.

But the President did not point out that our missiles were more accurate; he did not mention that our bombers could deliver weapons with greater accuracy than most missiles could; nor did he show how many warheads our missiles and bombers could deliver. Had he done so, and compared them with deliverable Soviet warheads, he would have revealed that our forces can strike 4,000 more targets in Soviet territory than Soviet forces can strike in ours.[13] No expert can be found who will disagree with our Defense Department that this is by far "the most significant indicator of strategic strength."[14]

Yet Americans could not be expected to know this, or to know that they had been given only some of the facts. The administration made sure not to give them the rest. One of the ways it made sure of this was to cease publishing estimates of the balance of nuclear warheads between the Soviet Union and the United States, as our government had done every year since 1967.

These figures had appeared regularly in the Defense Department's *Annual Report.* In its *Fiscal Year 1983 Annual Report,* released early in 1982, the figures on nuclear warheads were no longer there. They have not been there since. This was one way of eliminating information which contradicted the administration's claims of Soviet superiority.

Of course, former government officials quickly came forward to contradict the administration's claims. They had long had access to exactly the same information the President had, and they knew that since their departure from government the strategic balance of power could not possibly have changed enough even to give the Soviets parity with us, let alone superiority.

Yet their comments were given little attention in the press, nor did the mainstream press itself challenge the administration's claim. Most of the press, in fact, accords a surprising degree of respect to administrations in power. It seems reluctant to publish information that official sources will not confirm, even though official sources clearly are not about to confirm information that contradicts official views.

Thus the testimony of former officials, and much other information the press could easily verify, but which contradicted the new administration's claims of Soviet superiority, simply did not appear. How could the press be so naive? Or if it was not so naive, how could it do such disservice to the public, and so abdicate its responsibility to seek out and present the truth?

As a result, the administration's claim of Soviet superiority has gone almost unchallenged. Yet this claim has been the primary justification for hundreds of billions of dollars in military spending beyond any level of established need, whose effects on our economy and on global security have been far from benign. This claim has been used to persuade Americans that an agreement with the Soviet Union to freeze further testing, production, and deployment of nuclear weapons would leave America "in second place." It has been used to justify an arms-negotiating posture in which this administration takes credit for seeking arms reductions without ever having to offer an equitable proposal for reductions.

The administration has also taken action to silence the voices of former officials who might contradict its claim, whether the press pays them any attention or not. Early in 1983, the President issued a directive requiring nearly 120,000 federal employees with access to special categories of classified information to sign an agreement consenting to prepublication review of all of their writings even after they leave government—indeed, for the rest of their lives.[15]

When Congress complained that this provision was an "unwarranted infringement of open debate on matters of national importance,"[16] the President withdrew it. What his administration did not publicize was that it had already made all of the same employees, because of their access to additional categories of classified information, sign forms agreeing to exactly the same provision only six months after it first took office.[17] The General Accounting Office estimates that by the end of 1983 nearly 225,000 current and former employees of the government or private contractors with access to such information had signed agreements consenting to lifetime prepublication review.[18]

This could not affect officials who had left government before such agreements were signed; thus it could not affect the use of their testimony in this book. Their statements are an important source of information—though by no means the only source—to demonstrate that the administration's claim of Soviet superiority is a lie.

However, if the directives authorizing these agreements are allowed to stand, and Congress and the courts do not challenge their constitutionality, what will we do some years hence when a new administration may more plausibly claim that the balance of power has changed? Former officials may no longer be able to use the information available to disprove such claims. Government censors will be empowered to withhold it. In that case, deprived of a major source of reliable testimony to challenge official statements, the public will be denied its right to an informed role in the decisions of government. We will not know what we give our consent to. How long will it be reasonable to call this condition democracy?

5   Exploiting Conventional Wisdom

Nor could most Americans be expected to understand that the very concept of military superiority is meaningless in describing the balance of power between two nations equipped with nuclear arms. While some measures of strategic power are more significant than others, the nation which holds an advantage by these measures still cannot hold a decisive one. While we can deliver many more warheads to Soviet territory, and while the greater accuracy of our weapons increases their likelihood of destroying their targets, it cannot guarantee that they will destroy them.

Consequently, even if the reverse were the case, and the Soviets—as the administration claims—really held such advantages instead, this still would not warrant a program of unlimited spending in order to catch up.

All of this, however, runs counter to the conventional wisdom, which continues to hold that numerical and other advantages can be decisive. This thinking has changed only slowly to take account of the new realities nuclear weapons have introduced. As a result, misconceptions still prevail in the nuclear age about the significance of numerical leads and qualitative advantages reflected in comparisons of military power.

These misconceptions can still be exploited to gain support for increased military spending, or to block efforts at arms control, by using comparisons which suggest the Soviets are "ahead." If fair and accurate comparisons fail to reflect this, partial comparisons can be devised, or false comparisons can be created, largely based on what their inventors will not explain, unless they are asked, is a series of "worst-case assumptions" rather than verifiable facts.

William Arkin, director of nuclear weapons research at the Institute for Policy Studies, certainly understood all this when he told a meeting of peace activists in 1984 that "the Soviet Union has now surpassed us in every measure of military might, from warheads to tanks," and then added that this news could "blow the peace movement and arms control out of the water," because the conventional wisdom played such a powerful role in the politics of arms control that no effort to restrain military expansion could succeed in America unless the public remained secure in "the belief that the United States is superior."[1]

Arkin went on to suggest that these activists would prefer to deny any evidence which might be taken to mean the United States had fallen behind, rather than teach the public it really meant nothing of the kind. For when many of them took issue with his assertion that the United States no longer held the numerical lead in nuclear warheads, he dismissed their objections by saying "you just cannot believe that the Soviet Union is ahead,"[2] as though it were a proven fact that the Soviet Union was ahead, and as though their refusal to accept his word for this merely confirmed their reluctance to face a political obstacle, not their knowledge that the best evidence about the military balance contradicted him.

What this does confirm is that numerical comparisons of military strength have enormous political significance. If advocates of arms control really are inclined to deny evidence that the Soviet Union is ahead, this hardly proves such evidence exists, as suggestions of this kind seem primarily intended to imply. It means, instead, that by the same token advocates of military expansion are inclined to deny evidence that the United States is ahead. It means that just as long as fair comparisons show the United States is ahead, advocates of military expansion have a powerful incentive to misrepresent the military balance with false comparisons in order to suggest that the reverse is true.

Consequently, some numerical comparisons have another kind of significance: fair and accurate comparisons are meaningful because they reveal the existence of false ones, and expose the political intent behind them. That is why it is important to determine what the best evidence about the military balance shows. For then it is clear when advocates of military expansion are lying to us.

But even fair and accurate numerical comparisons have little military meaning in the nuclear age. The margin of "superiority" we presumably gain from our greater number of more accurate strategic nuclear weapons does no more for us than it could do for the Soviets if they had it instead. As physicist and former presidential science adviser Richard Garwin points out, deterrence "doesn't require superiority. It doesn't require equality."[3] It doesn't matter which superpower has more warheads or whose missiles are the more accurate. This ceased to matter once both nations had developed the means to inflict unacceptable damage in retaliation after an attack.

An attack can only be successful if retaliation can be avoided. That can only be done by eliminating all retaliatory forces. But in 1968, the Soviets began to deploy ballistic missiles on submarines at sea.[4] At that moment, they created an invulnerable retaliatory force. This gave them the same assured retaliatory capability we had had since 1960, when we first placed ballistic missiles at sea.[5]

Since that time, it has been impossible for either nation to assure that all retaliatory forces could be eliminated, no matter how massive or accurate the attack. It is impossible to be certain one's own weapons will behave predictably. It is impossible to be certain the nation under attack will behave predictably, and allow its weapons to be destroyed before it launches them. Nothing has ever changed these uncertainties; nothing ever can. Nor can anything change the uncertainties surrounding conventional, nonnuclear war between nations equipped with nuclear arms. It is impossible to be certain that such a war can be limited and controlled, avoiding escalation to a nuclear exchange.

All of this was perfectly clear at the dawn of the nuclear age. It was perfectly clear that war of any kind between nuclear powers risked suicide. As they watched the first nuclear explosion at Alamogordo in 1945, many scientists and government leaders believed that this moment signalled the end of war. Now, they believed, the human race must bring an end to its instincts for power and aggression, or those instincts would bring an end to the human race.

It was not the end of war, of course. The old instincts still could be unleashed. War still could be fought. It could be fought between nations which did not possess nuclear weapons. It could be fought by one nation which possessed nuclear weapons against another which did not, and which therefore could not retaliate in kind. That is why America was able to use nuclear weapons against Japan. And, indeed, terrible wars continue to be fought. The only kind of war that has not been fought is war between two nuclear powers.

The only certain reason for this is that uncertainties which have never been resolved have posed unacceptable risks for any nation that has considered launching a nuclear attack. This inescapable reality has enforced deterrence between the superpowers ever since both were able to retaliate to an attack. Since these uncertainties can never be resolved, they will always pose unacceptable risks.

This does not guarantee that a nuclear war will never be fought. As long as nuclear weapons exist, nothing can guarantee they will never be used. But unremitting uncertainties and inescapable risks have certainly minimized the likelihood of their use. That is all that deterrence has ever meant and the most it could ever mean.

Advocates of military expansion have always been quick to point out that this does not make the world entirely safe from the nuclear threat. Indeed it does not. They have always laid claim to the goal of a safer world, yet everything they have done has only made the world more dangerous. The only way to make the world safer would be to eliminate all nuclear weapons, yet they have never prescribed this solution. Instead, they have always insisted on building more nuclear weapons, either to expand or to "modernize" existing arsenals. But deterrence, as Richard Garwin points out, "doesn't need modernization,"[6] any more than it needs "superiority" or "equality."

For forty years, then, advocates of military expansion have tried to ignore the lessons that were clear at the dawn of the nuclear age. Rather than clarify those lessons for the public, they have only obscured them. Rather than teach the public that greater numbers of weapons and other presumed advantages have no military significance, they have publicly warned that such advantages might enable an adversary to overcome uncertainties and eliminate risk, and they have privately promised that the advantages we already possessed might enable us to do the same, when they knew there was no evidence that any nation could ever eliminate risk.

To gain support for each new generation of strategic weapons, those who called for them have always used the same warnings in the public arena, and the same promises in the inner circles of policymaking, to justify what they wanted as an urgent measure to "strengthen" deterrence, when they knew deterrence was already strong enough because there was never anything feeble about an unacceptable risk. They have applied double standards to suggest that every risk was always acceptable to an adversary, but never acceptable to us. If they could not show how some new weapon was needed to strengthen deterrence, then they said it was needed to strengthen "perceptions" of our firm intent to use nuclear weapons, when nothing we said we intended could possibly affect those perceptions more than they were affected by what the weapons we already had could do.

This is how the conventional wisdom has been exploited, and public opinion manipulated, in order to win support for an increasing investment in strategic weapons, continuing a nuclear arms race that might have ended long ago.

6   Ignoring the Real Danger

America might have stopped building nuclear weapons in the 1950s, by the time it had built several hundred warheads and the means to deliver them. This was more than enough to deter aggression. The Soviet Union might have stopped in the late 1960s, by the time it had done the same.

But they did not stop. Neither nation made any attempt to curb the momentum of technology, or the expansion of an industrial base prepared to utilize it. They designed new weapons, improving their accuracy and increasing their destructive power. They did this not because such refinements met any military need, but because technology had made them possible.

But simply because technology had made new weapons possible did not mean their inventors had to proceed to build them. It was enough to know how to build them, and avoid technological surprise. Before building them, each nation might have considered whether the other had done anything, or was doing anything, to warrant building them. To know what the other was doing was not nearly as difficult as advocates of military expansion have implied. They have naturally implied this in order to argue that since we could not be sure what our adversary was doing, it was only prudent to prepare for the worst. A much greater investment in new strategic weapons could be based on "worst-case" assumptions than on the evidence usually at hand to contradict them.

But, in fact, each nation was quite sure what its adversary was doing. Each closely monitored the other's weapons-testing and development activities. Each could easily determine whether the other was about to deploy a major new weapon system, just as each could determine whether the other was violating any agreement to limit deployment of new weapon systems. Admiral Noel Gayler, former director of our National Security Agency, confirms that "no conceivable Soviet violation big enough to tip the nuclear balance could escape our intelligence."[1]

Yet neither nation ever paused to consider whether the weapons it was building were really warranted by the weapons the other was building. Both had already committed ample resources to weapons production. Because those who managed these resources sought only to justify and perpetuate their work, and because the military advantages they promised always seemed to present an irresistible lure, both nations went ahead and built new weapons anyway.

That, of course, answered the question each might have asked first about what the other would do. What the other did was often used, in turn, as the public rationale for weapons each had already decided to build anyway. Each claimed it was merely building its weapons in response.

Yet weapons were seldom built simply in response. Aside from deploying a very large number of air defense weapons, which remain largely ineffective against our bomber force, the Soviets have not responded to the weapons we have built. They have not even attempted to duplicate our offensive capabilities. They never built a large intercontinental bomber force comparable to ours. They made their major investment in land-based missiles, while we made ours in missiles more safely based at sea.

But it didn't matter what weapons were built, or how many. One nation might deploy more weapons than the other, or it might deploy more accurate weapons, or weapons of greater destructive power. None of these weapons reduced in any way the risks both nations continued to face. None, therefore, was needed to "strengthen" deterrence.

Sadly, it was America which took almost every new step in the arms race first, and thereby gave the Soviet Union the opportunity to claim, each time, that it was forced to respond. We introduced multiple warheads in 1970; the Soviets first deployed them in 1975.[2] We introduced long-range cruise missiles in 1982;[3] the Soviets will eventually deploy them too. We already acknowledge regret at having taken the first of these initiatives; we will eventually regret having taken the latter.

America took each new step first because technology had usually made that step possible for us, long before the Soviets could follow suit. For us, there were incentives too. Each new step required a greater investment, and thereby raised the expectation of a larger return on investment. Each time this expectation was realized, the design and production of weapons became more desirable. As the margin of profit from this activity grew, the activity itself seemed to grow more necessary. Meanwhile, the lure of gaining a critical military advantage never disappeared.

As these arsenals of weapons grew, theory was needed to explain them. Strategies of nuclear war fighting, escalation dominance, and counterforce targeting soon evolved. The new weapons were said to be needed to fill the requirements of those strategies. But the strategies were being created to justify the weapons. Counterforce targeting of an adversary's nuclear forces and chain of command was emphasized because it required greater accuracy and larger numbers of warheads, thereby justifying the more accurate missiles and multiple warheads which technology had already made it possible to design.

Accompanying these strategies were corresponding myths of survival in the post-attack environment. Because it implied that cities could be saved, a policy of counterforce strikes at military rather than civilian targets was portrayed as more humane, in order to discredit the policy of mutual assured destruction it was now obliged to replace. But mutual assured destruction was not a policy. It was a fact. It will always remain a fact, even in planning for the most limited counterforce strike. Today there are eighteen military targets in New York and sixty in Moscow.[4] War between nuclear powers risked suicide thirty years ago. It risks suicide today.

One of the most significant implications, though largely ignored, of the work of Carl Sagan, Paul Ehrlich, and other leading scientists who have warned of the long-term atmospheric and biological consequences of nuclear war is the near certainty that any nuclear attack, even if it could achieve the impossible and eliminate risk and uncertainty itself by destroying all of an adversary's retaliatory forces, would only expose the earth to sufficient radiation and toxic gas, and deprive it of sufficient warmth and light, to damage its ecosystem beyond repair, so dooming the attacker along with the rest of humankind to extinction.[5]

Then destruction no longer has to be mutual to be assured. In nuclear weapons, we have already invented our doomsday machine.

Nevertheless, all of the theories and policies each nation proclaimed were presented either as an effort to win a nuclear war in precisely this way, by eliminating all of an adversary's retaliatory forces, or as an effort to prevent an adversary from doing the same. Clearly, no effort of either kind was needed if all of them continued to fail. Clearly, nothing would really be gained if any such effort should ever succeed. All of them failed. All of this theory, and all of the weapons it served to justify, did nothing to reduce the risks and uncertainties that have persisted since the first nuclear bomb was detonated at Alamogordo.

So deterrence has worked, and nuclear war has been avoided, not because of this vast undertaking but *despite it*. Far from reducing the risks of nuclear war, the policymakers, weapons makers, planners, politicians, and scientists who have presided over the growth of our nuclear arsenals have succeeded only at increasing those risks.

They continue to increase those risks. By continuing to increase the numbers of weapons in our arsenals, and to improve their accuracy and lethality, they steadily increase the margin of probable destruction an attack will cause, though without ever guaranteeing there will be no retaliation. By placing these weapons closer to their targets, as we have placed our *Pershing IIs,* and so reducing the time they need to reach their targets, they increase the burden on early warning and communications systems in identifying and responding to an attack. By threatening to destroy military command and communications centers, they threaten to cripple an adversary's capacity to respond to an attack, though without ever guaranteeing there will be no response.

While none of this eliminates or even appreciably reduces the risks an attacker would face, and while none of it therefore makes winning a nuclear war by avoiding retaliation any more possible than it ever has been, it still makes a significant change. It gives an attacker much more to gain, and a defender much more to lose.

Consequently, in the event of a crisis that might seem to lead to war, neither superpower may any longer be inclined to wait until the other strikes first, though waiting until an attack is confirmed remains the only declared policy of both. Instead, each now has a growing incentive to strike first itself, both to avoid the devastation it might expect to suffer if the other strikes first, and to minimize the damage the other could inflict in retaliation.

Because military and political leaders of both nations would be highly vulnerable to a nuclear attack, and because the communications equipment they rely upon to maintain contact with their nuclear forces is inherently fragile, journalist and nuclear energy specialist Daniel Ford appears to believe that a first strike could reduce not only the magnitude but even the "likelihood" of a retaliatory attack, and recommends that America therefore "build a more robust command-and-control system, and so eliminate a weakness that could make the Soviets think there was much to gain from a first strike."[6]

This seems to state the case for a new "window of vulnerability." It suggests that the Soviets might be able to carry out a first strike without the risk of retaliation, but does not acknowledge with equal emphasis that if the Soviets could do this, so could we.

It is probably impossible to build a system for the command and control of nuclear forces that could ever fully protect our leaders and their communications from nuclear attack. A MITRE Corporation study concluded that protecting communications in a nuclear war was "an almost insurmountable problem."[7] Nor would a sturdier system, even if it could be built, necessarily reduce the Soviet incentive to strike first. The greater likelihood is that it would only provide our leaders with a stronger incentive of their own to strike first, in the belief that they could survive a retaliatory attack and remain in better control of their nuclear forces to exploit the advantages they had presumably already gained.

Nor is there necessarily any need for a communications system that is sure to survive a nuclear attack. A retaliatory attack does not have to rely on such a system. Since no such system exists or is ever likely to exist, it also isn't too likely that the retaliatory plans both nations have certainly made do rely on one.

There is no way of knowing what retaliatory plans exist, or how they would be executed. There is no reason why national leaders, in order to execute these plans, must maintain contact with their nuclear forces once under attack themselves. Before the first warheads of the initial attack detonated, all the commands needed to launch a retaliatory attack could already be transmitted. This could be done in thirty seconds.[8] Consequently, the likelihood of a retaliatory attack remains as high as ever, posing the same inescapable risks it has always posed.

Political scientist Paul Bracken notes that "the Soviets do not know precisely who [in the USA] has nuclear authority in an emergency and, more important, how this authority would flow from the highest levels of government." He adds that the Soviets "also cannot easily know whether a long-dormant commercial satellite is actually a disguised 'dark satellite' containing coded firing messages for ICBMs and bombers that could be activated from any one of numerous secret transmitters located on innocuous military posts or civilian locations."[9] Any of the satellites we have spent hundreds of millions of dollars to place in orbit and then "failed" to activate in recent years may well have been designed for this purpose.

For all that either superpower knows, any disruption of the other's command and communications system may be precisely what automatically triggers a maximum retaliatory attack. It is this uncertainty, Bracken concludes, "rather than any hardening of command and control systems," which creates "a deterrent against a command-structure attack," and indeed "a deterrent against any sort of nuclear attack on the United States."[10] It creates the same deterrent against any kind of attack on the Soviet Union.

Nevertheless, the only result of all the refinements the superpowers have made and continue to make in their nuclear arsenals is that once they believe war is bound to occur, both nations have an increasing incentive to strike first. This is not because either nation thinks it can avoid damage from a retaliatory attack if it strikes first. It is because both nations hope to prevent the much greater devastation each has now given the other good reason to expect from being struck first. It is not because either nation hopes to win a nuclear war. It is because neither nation believes it could otherwise survive one.

Our readiness to strike first has always been reflected in official American policy, but has not been publicly acknowledged since the Soviets first developed the capability to retaliate. Before that time, as former Pentagon analyst Daniel Ellsberg recalls, the "only mission" of our Strategic Air Command "was to threaten or carry out a U.S. first strike."[11] After that time, we encouraged the public notion that striking first was morally indefensible, and always denied our readiness to carry out such a plan. But the readiness exists, and the plans to carry out a first strike exist too. Enough has now been placed on the public record, most of it originally classified, to confirm this.

At a top secret briefing in 1954, General Curtis LeMay, then chief of our

Strategic Air Command, declared: "If the U.S. is pushed far enough, we would not hesitate to strike first," and added: "That's what I'm going to do."[12] In 1977, Defense Secretary Donald Rumsfeld acknowledged that in order to "limit the damage" we would suffer in a nuclear war, the most effective strategy "dictates a first-strike capability." He denied that we had already developed this capability, but suggested we might not be able to avoid doing so "much longer."[13]

At a Senate hearing in 1980, when asked if the United States held plans to carry out a first strike, Defense Secretary Harold Brown confirmed: "There are options that cover that situation."[14]

That same year, discussing strategy in a memorandum to Francis Kane of TRW, a prominent defense electronics firm, General Bruce Holloway, who had been chief of Strategic Air Command in the early 1970s, wrote that "striking first would offer a tremendous advantage," by "degrading the highest political and military control to the greatest possible degree."[15] He did not appear to consider how we might negotiate an end to a war we had won by eliminating everyone who could negotiate.

In 1981, at a symposium sponsored by the MITRE Corporation, Richard DeLauer, Under Secretary of Defense for Research and Engineering, remarked that the *Trident II D-5* missile soon to be deployed on our submarines had been designed with "a preemptive capability."[16]

There is every reason to assume that the Soviets have prepared plans for similar "options," and that they, too, have had only a growing incentive to carry them out.

Deterrence, then, is not threatened by either superpower's desire for the other's destruction, whatever role such desires may play in formulating policy. It is threatened by progressive refinements in nuclear weaponry. These may soon deprive both nations of any choice in trying to avoid their own destruction. The certainty of retaliation will always deter either one from attacking the other, as long as its leaders believe they will not otherwise be attacked. But once they believe they will be attacked anyway, and that war is unavoidable, they may abandon their declared policy of waiting for that attack.

In the judgment of leaders of both nations, advances in weapons technology may already have given them too much to lose if they wait for an attack. When striking first seems to offer the only chance of surviving a nuclear war, they will certainly feel they have no other choice. When the damage they hope to avoid seems so much greater than the retaliatory damage they know must follow, they will accept retaliation. Then retaliation, hitherto unacceptable, will no longer deter them. That is how deterrence can collapse.

In a crisis, normal safeguards on the use of nuclear weapons will be rapidly removed. Absolute priority will be given to maximum readiness. Nuclear forces will be primed to react as quickly as possible. Subordinate commanders will expect disruptions in communications, and will prepare to act on their own authority even if no disruptions occur. Each nation's preparations will be scrutinized by the other. Defensive preparations may be misread as offensive preparations. Prudence may no longer dictate restraint: it may demand that each nation assume the worst. Each level of alert set for one nation's forces may provoke the other's to a higher level of alert. This mutually reinforcing pattern of misinterpretation and overreaction may be impossible to break before it ends in war.

The real danger, then, in having created so powerful an incentive to strike first, is the danger of nuclear war by sheer miscalculation. We have already created this danger. We have forced ourselves into hair-trigger postures. This is all we have done. All the improvements and refinements we have made in our nuclear arsenals over the years, ostensibly in order to "strengthen" deterrence, have only risked its collapse, and thereby made the world an infinitely more dangerous place.

It was time to stop many years ago. Now, as America prepares to deploy a new generation of even more accurate nuclear weapons with "a preemptive capability," the danger increases, and the problem of controlling it takes on a new urgency. Some former officials realize this. Such prominent architects of nuclear war fighting theory as Robert McNamara now renounce it.

But there are many more officials who continue to perpetuate the deception that we have no plans for a first strike, that only the Soviets do, that deterrence is threatened only by Soviet aggression and not by refinements in nuclear weaponry, and that Soviet aggression can only be met by more refinements. Perhaps these officials believe that because governments have managed increasing levels of risk for forty years, they can continue to do so indefinitely. We must understand such arrogance. The road from deception to self-delusion is short.

7   The Dynamics of the Arms Race

Perhaps these officials also really believe that they can continue to trust the Russians. For this is what they privately do in relying on Soviet forbearance in the face of the growing threat our new weapons pose, even while they publicly insist that we cannot trust the Russians and must build these weapons for that very reason. We must understand this kind of duplicity. It means that many of our officials may not have been deluding themselves. Over the years they may have known exactly what they were doing; certainly, they were encouraging our belief in the need for more weapons to strengthen deterrence. But they may not have done this because they really thought it would reduce the nuclear threat. Indeed, they would have known that the presence of more nuclear weapons, and of a more complex and dangerous theory of deterrence to justify them, helped to sustain that threat.

They may have wanted to sustain that threat. For these officials may have recognized that nuclear weapons also served a political purpose. They would have known, of course, that nations equipped with nuclear arms could threaten nations not so equipped, for political purposes. America has put nuclear weapons to this kind of use with some regularity, as Daniel Ellsberg and others have testified. But equally some of these officials also understood that the key political use of nuclear weapons by those governments that control them is against their own people.

Nuclear weapons terrorize. Terror creates the conditions of emergency which rally political support and enforce political consensus. At least, it does so when it is accompanied by the appropriate myths to direct our attention to a common enemy. If we can be persuaded to agree that this enemy exists, then we will unite against it. If we can be persuaded that this enemy poses an immediate threat, then the continuing use of our resources to meet that threat seems urgently needed, and the increasing risks we suffer seem unavoidable.

But why continue to prepare for a threat if there is already more than sufficient force on hand to meet it, and nothing more is required? Why would a government so deceive and manipulate its people into supporting a wholly gratuitous effort?

Because there is no other way it can meet the demands of a military-industrial establishment that has become the most powerful institution in our society. President Eisenhower warned that this would happen—and it has. This establishment is powerful not merely because it lays claim to our patriotism and exploits our desire for security. It is powerful most of all because it dispenses wealth. The more wealth it can control, the more dependent on it do business and labor and government become. The more dependent they become, the more they will applaud its mission and accommodate its needs.

With control of a budget that currently averages $300 billion a year, this establishment has gained unprecedented power, exactly as it meant to do by insisting on budgets of this size. "There is no similar concentration of disposable wealth anywhere else in our economy," notes economist John Kenneth Galbraith.[1]

Business is chiefly interested in this wealth as a source of profits. Profits are chiefly what business means to create, whatever else it may create. The defense industry has always been the most profitable sector of our economy. Its profits are highest because the complexity of its products and the urgent need always claimed for them justifies any price. So the price is paid—paid no matter how far it exceeds expectations.

The companies which charge such prices are almost entirely free of the normal constraints that help to control prices in every other sector of our economy. There is virtually no competition for military contracts. There is no capital risk. Every penny of investment capital is provided by the American taxpayer. There are few limits on overhead costs. Cost overruns are routinely charged, and they are routinely reimbursed. They are reimbursed even if they are fraudulent.

And they are frequently fraudulent. The Pentagon has lately taken to publicizing the fraud it discovers. It does this to assure the public that fraud is being punished. But most fraud is not being punished. In 1984 the Pentagon announced that it had found more than four hundred military contractors guilty of overpricing and other abuses, and had debarred or suspended them all from future work.[2] But none was a major contractor; all were suppliers of spare parts. The combined total of all the money they overcharged was no more than a fraction of the sum that suppliers of major weapon systems were overcharging.[3]

Fed by military appropriations that far exceeded the limits of plausible need, the margin of profit in military contracting was bound to grow. So it has. In 1984 the nation's ten largest military contractors averaged profits of 35 percent. This was three times the corporate average for the economy as a whole.[4] It would have remained more than twice the national average after taxes, had these contractors paid their taxes. But most of them had not. They were deferring their taxes. They have been doing this for years. General Dynamics has not paid any taxes since 1972.[5]

Our government once considered such profits "unconscionable."[6] Former Navy attorney Morris Amchan recalls that the Vinson-Trammell Acts of 1934 and 1939 "sought to limit the profit on defense contracts to 10 percent of the contract price." This legislation, he adds, was "permitted to expire in the late 1970s."[7]

As the defense industry's profits increase. so do its claims for cost overruns, reaching the unprecedented levels the Council of Economic Advisers recorded.[8] There is no evidence that defense corporations with access to higher levels of funding suddenly encounter higher levels of unanticipated costs; there is evidence only that they have access to higher levels of funding. As the number of claims for cost overruns increases, so does the proportion of false claims. None of this contributes to our national security. It contributes only to waste, as the Grace Commission, the Senate Budget Committee, the Deputy Secretary of Defense, the Pentagon's cost analysts, and its own inspector general found.

As the margin of fraud increases, so does the scale of waste. In 1984, the Joint Economic Committee of Congress released evidence showing that General Dynamics had falsified claims for $500 million in cost overruns to build submarines.[9] In 1985, the Pentagon announced it had suspended General Electric, the nation's fourth largest military contractor, after learning the company had falsified claims for work on missile reentry vehicles.[10] It also demanded that General Electric refund $168 million in profits "significantly in excess of those negotiated by the government."[11]

But the suspension was only temporary; it did not affect other General Electric contracts the Pentagon had already signed. Nor was any action taken against other major corporations. No fewer than forty-five of the nation's one hundred leading defense contractors were under criminal investigation in 1985.[12] Several of them, including Boeing, the Ingalls division of Litton Systems, National Semiconductor, McDonnell Douglas, and Sperry, had even admitted submitting false claims or pleaded guilty to criminal violations. Yet none of these was suspended.[13]

The corporations that have enjoyed these unusual privileges, and whose increasing abuse of them has been for the most part tacitly condoned, have set themselves the same goal set by every business enterprise: they must grow. They have no alternate economic model to follow, and none is imposed on them. If they are making missiles, then the easiest and most profitable way to continue growing is to make more missiles, even if missiles are no longer what we need. To justify their growth, they exaggerate the need for weapons by exaggerating the threat they are meant to counter.

The military establishment, in turn, legitimizes this growth by supporting the same view of the threat, because it is deeply committed to the support of an industry it must rely upon in time of genuine need, and whose prosperity consolidates military power and expands its influence throughout society. In step with these expediencies, government magnifies the threat to rally support for continued growth in military spending and a continued acceleration of the arms race.

Those administrations that do the least to obstruct this process, and that impose the fewest controls on the conduct of business and the military, are the least challenged by them. Those politicians who best serve the interests of business and the military are best rewarded with their support, which is usually decisive at election time.

It is important that we understand this process, and recognize that it is nothing more than a simple set of human venalities, which most of us have long accepted, that has produced such extraordinary inhumanity and terror. For it has sustained the growth of a vast infrastructure of weapons research and design laboratories, test ranges, training schools, production plants, procurement agencies, subcontractors, think tanks, strategic planners, consultants, lobbyists, sales and distribution networks, political action committees, and investment banking groups, all of whose work long ago surpassed the bounds of rational need, and today threatens their own survival as surely as it threatens everyone else's.

Several of the same institutions exist in the Soviet Union; many of the same processes are at work there. By needlessly warning of imminent threats to the national security, Soviet leaders can gain support and consolidate their political power as easily as our own leaders do here at home. Soviet weapons design and production bureaus want no more to reduce output or convert to meet civilian needs than American corporations do. Both nations can point to each other's advances in military technology as though these were proof that the military expansion they urge is needed. In this way, the arms race creates its own false logic in order to perpetuate itself.

8 Enforcing Political Consensus

We will always need to maintain some of the weapons and forces we now have, to provide for an adequate national defense. We will always need to sustain some facilities for arms research, in order to keep abreast of developments in military technology and anticipate those that might destabilize the balance of military power. But that is very different from developing new weapons themselves. Both of these real needs can be met with only a fraction of the funds now appropriated for defense. The problem is that addressing only the real needs would support no more than a corresponding fraction of the immense military-industrial establishment we now have, whose expansion the current administration has only accelerated.

If it were clear that we are already prepared to meet the military threat any adversary can pose, that we could easily anticipate and prepare for any future threat well before it materialized, and that we have always been lavishly prepared to do whatever military power still can do, then public support for the continuing growth of our defense establishment would collapse. Business would be accused of perpetrating monstrous and wasteful fraud for its self-perpetuation. Government would be accused of telling the people dangerous lies for the sake of political expediency.

For administrations chiefly guided by expediency—as most have been—the only solution has been to tell larger lies, and to tell them more frequently. To the first set of lies that increased military spending was urgently needed, they added lies about how military spending did not harm but helped the economy.

Military spending harms the economy. It is inflationary. It raises the costs of goods and services by diverting raw materials and technical expertise away from civilian sectors of production. It pays labor for production, increasing consumer demand, but produces no corresponding supply of goods and services to meet that demand. This further raises the costs of existing goods and services. It diminishes our ability to compete with foreign goods, adversely affecting our balance of trade.

Military spending creates fewer jobs than any other kind of spending. According to the Congressional Budget Office, every $10 billion spent on the military creates 40,000 fewer jobs than if it were spent on anything else.[1] The Coalition for a New Foreign and Military Policy points out that every $1 billion spent on the military would create almost twice as many jobs if it were spent on mass transit, and almost three times as many jobs if it were spent on day care.[2] Lockheed Aircraft, the nation's sixth largest military contractor, whose contracts with the Defense Department rose in value from $2 billion in 1980 to $2.6 billion in 1982,[3] reduced its labor force almost by half, from 30,000 to 16,000, in the same period.[4]

The Reagan administration attempted to obscure this reality by making military spending the only source of new jobs. Diverting all of the funds it had stripped from domestic social programs to defense, it promised to make our military budget a national public works program that would confer a variety of benefits on all the ailing sectors of our economy.

But if it planned to enforce a defense consensus among those in need by eliminating all but a single source of hope, the administration failed. It raised only false hopes. According to Employment Research Associates, the nation spent $41.5 billion more on the military in taxes than it earned back in contracts and salaries in 1983. While fifteen states and the District of Columbia recorded a net gain of $29.9 billion, thirty-five states lost a total of $71.4 billion.[5] The administration could only support its claim that it had put more Americans to work since gaining office by including 2 million military personnel in its 1984 employment figure, but not including them in the 1981 figure with which it was compared.[6]

To their lies about the economic benefits of military spending, most administrations have added reassurances that the expansion they urged of America's military power would never threaten world stability, because we were in the hands of responsible leaders who would always avoid conflict. Since the end of World War II, and through several additional conflicts that were not avoided, these lies, together with systematic reminders of the Soviet threat, have helped to sustain the continued growth of America's war economy.

Nor has the threat ever diminished. It has only grown larger. We have had a bomber gap and a missile gap and a military spending gap and a window of vulnerability—none of which ever existed. Yet we never learned that they didn't exist until after the political objectives they were designed to achieve had already been accomplished. After the missile gap helped elect President Kennedy, we learned there hadn't been one. After the military spending gap helped elect President Reagan, we learned there never was one. Time after time, Americans have had to accept each gap, each set of lies, and each cycle of military expansion.

Occasionally, there were bursts of outrage. There was outrage in the early 1960s over the effects of fallout from nuclear tests. Mothers grew concerned about strontium-90 in milk. A movement to ban the bomb and outlaw all tests gained momentum. Fear in the aftermath of the Cuban missile crisis helped. The superpowers responded with a limited test ban treaty, which eliminated fallout by taking tests underground but did not eliminate the tests themselves.

There was outrage in the 1960s over the risks of building an antiballistic missile system. Its advocates promised that once such a system worked, the nation that deployed it would no longer be vulnerable to nuclear attack. This was exactly the same promise the Reagan administration makes today for its defensive shield in space. The promise was false for all of the same reasons. If it worked at all, an antiballistic missile system would remain an imperfect and incomplete defense that could be easily circumvented.

Scientists joined to demonstrate that nothing could guarantee a defense against nuclear attack, and to reason that any defense that was not complete was futile. They also warned that a nation which thought it was no longer vulnerable to attack would no longer be deterred from initiating one, and that nations which began to build such systems would only invite each other's preemptive attacks to prevent their completing them. They concluded that antiballistic missile systems would solve no problems and only create new, more dangerous ones. This prompted exactly the same debate we are having all over again today.

In the 1960s the superpowers realized that the public saw the logic of the arguments against an antiballistic missile defense. Since they were giving up only one of a multitude of possible paths of military expansion, they agreed to calm public fears with a treaty that limited deployment of such systems. The United States deactivated the one hundred antiballistic missiles it had, and the Soviet Union kept the sixty-four it had. Neither nation built new ones.

But the Reagan administration has now revived the plan for an antiballistic missile defense. The only difference between its proposal and those of the 1960s is that it plans to base its system in space. This would make it far more costly and far more vulnerable. While its vulnerability lengthens the list of arguments against such a system, its costliness may be exactly what guarantees that those arguments will go ignored. For of all the paths of military expansion this administration pursues, space offers the greatest potential for future investment, whether military expansion is needed there or not.

As the world becomes more dangerous and the economic burden of military expansion increases, Americans grow more cynical. But the arms race breeds different kinds of cynicism. There is that of its key beneficiaries, the corporate and financial owners and managers who continue to believe America can afford it, or who may not care if America cannot afford it because they know they will be the last to feel the effects of economic decline. The benefits they meanwhile accrue give them a larger investment in the belief that military expansion can be safely managed indefinitely.

But there is another kind of cynicism. This is the cynicism of large numbers of Americans who feel that the burden has grown too heavy and the risk too great, and that it is time to do something about it, but that no one in a position to do anything about it cares. They find no persuasive evidence that the administration cares. They feel their interests are no longer represented by Congress and that they are dealing with a largely unsympathetic press. A majority of them wants a nuclear freeze but has not achieved it. They wonder why their efforts have not had the same kind of effect the civil rights and antiwar movements of the 1960s had. They feel disenfranchised from the political process.

That is because everything possible has been done to ensure that they are disenfranchised. We no longer live in the 1960s, but those concerned with the problems of sustaining political consensus paid close attention to what happened in the 1960s, and learned a great deal. They did not want the press again opposed to administration policy, as it was during much of the Vietnam War. They did not want an administration again unable, as the Nixon administration was in its negotiations with Hanoi, to achieve its political objectives abroad merely because of dissent at home. To prevent those conditions from recurring, the impact of dissent had to be limited and controlled. To ensure this, government had to play a larger role in shaping public opinion and in managing information, both at home and abroad.

So it has played a larger role. The Reagan administration has embarked on an unprecedented effort to push information control to its logical extreme. Not only has it told whatever lies were needed to gain support for its policies. It has also taken every available step to ensure that the press and the public draw the desired conclusions from these lies, that their attention is continuously fixed on the issues it chooses, and that they examine and debate these issues within the framework it sets, so that options of policy it deems unacceptable are already closed off in the public mind.

The administration has made every effort to see that its own views are favored while opposing views are minimized or ignored, and that those who offer opposing views are challenged or discredited, so that its own interpretation of events prevails to reinforce its policy goals. It has done all it could to see that information which challenges these goals or contradicts its views is withheld from the public so far as the law permits this, and that the law, if it does not permit this, is changed.[7]

9   Exploiting the Myth in America

The largest of the lies the Reagan administration told was its claim that the Soviets held strategic superiority. No administration had gone that far before. Former officials who immediately knew it was a lie, and the larger body of citizens who heavily depend on those officials to keep them reliably informed, were at first too stunned to react. What did the administration have in mind? How did it think it could get away with this? By the time they began to protest, their voices were too late and too few. In psychological warfare, as in every other kind of war, surprise affords the attacker a critical advantage.

The announcement that the Soviets held strategic superiority served several functions at once. A number of Americans who assumed it was true also assumed it described a genuine threat. They naturally believed America must act to counter that threat. Many of them said so, when polled on the question. Consequently, the administration could claim it had widespread support for its military buildup. It was able to make this claim without even specifying how its buildup would counter the threat. It has never specified that, and it probably never will. This matter has been left to specialists, though the money came from everyone.

In this remarkably vague way, an undefined remedy for an unproven threat was used to justify the largest shift of America's resources to military investment since World War II.

The vision of Soviet strategic superiority also helped to silence the administration's critics. It made the goal of a nuclear freeze seem dangerous and irresponsible; it made the administration's proposals for strategic arms reductions seem far more equitable than several of its officials have since acknowledged they really were. By focusing on alleged Soviet advantages, it helped obscure the blatant contradiction between the administration's stated desire to reduce arms and its admitted intent to increase them in order to gain advantages of its own.

This contradiction has been almost entirely overlooked. That has been one of the administration's most significant accomplishments in manipulating public opinion. It has taken credit for seeking to reduce the nuclear threat to both nations through negotiations with the Soviet Union, while at the same time it has not even hidden the fact that it seeks to increase the threat to the Soviet Union by achieving America's military "superiority." It has insisted, in fact, that no serious negotiations be undertaken with Moscow until after we have achieved "superiority." Moscow, it said, would not negotiate seriously until the United States was the stronger.

This means that throughout the current period of alleged Soviet superiority, the administration has had no intention of negotiating anything.

Yet it said otherwise. In May, 1982, only two months after he told Americans that the Soviets held "a definite margin of strategic superiority," President Reagan announced his offer of a new series of Strategic Arms Reduction (START) Talks, and proposed that the Soviet Union and the United States each reduce their arsenals of missile warheads by one third.[1]

In our nation's mainstream media, the arena for public debate, no one asked why the President was making this proposal if he did not believe the Soviets would negotiate seriously at that time, and when he had already said that he himself would not negotiate seriously at that time. No one asked how, if the Soviets could not be expected to negotiate seriously as long as they held the "lead" in strategic power, we could be expected to negotiate seriously once we held it.

Nor did anyone closely examine the proposal itself. No one pointed out that it took up only one category of strategic weapons, exempting others in which America held an extravagant lead both in numbers and technology, or that in this single category the President's figures substantially overstated the number of warheads Pentagon officials reported the Soviets had.[2] No one seemed to notice that requirements in the proposal's finer print would have left many fewer

Soviet than American warheads, and would have eliminated entirely those missiles in which the Soviets had made their largest investment.

Finally, no one pointed out that the President seemed to have no intention of following through with reductions in our own arsenal. The Soviets must look at his deeds, not words, as carefully as he tells the world he looks at theirs. Far from planning the reductions his proposal implied, he had already authorized programs for a net increase of 11,000 warheads in America's arsenal.[3]

These programs were not widely reported. When they were reported, the obvious conclusions were not drawn from them. The obvious questions were not asked. All that was emphasized repeatedly was the administration's claim that the Soviets held a strategic lead. This combination of emphasis and omission drew more attention to Washington's policies and views than to facts which contradicted them. As a result, the President's sincerity in making this proposal went virtually unchallenged.

The proposal, of course, like many American arms proposals before it, was simply one more offer the Soviets had to refuse. That was because Washington was not really negotiating with Moscow. It was negotiating with the American people, to a substantial portion of whom it has always had to demonstrate a commitment to arms control, while at the same time avoiding any commitment that might curtail military expansion.

The most valuable purpose the START proposal served was to preempt the initiative of the nuclear freeze movement in calling for genuine efforts at arms control. When Moscow inevitably refused this proposal, Washington could say it had tried in good faith. Advocates of military expansion were never alarmed. They knew that Moscow had to refuse the proposal. They also saw that the President's deeds, if not his words, were continuing to fulfill his campaign promise that America would achieve military superiority.

The press has allowed this duplicity to proceed without noticeable complaint. Nor has it examined the larger question of why America seeks military "superiority." That is surely a step well beyond restoring the "parity" we claim we lack. Many Americans must wonder what we intend to do with "superiority" when we get it. Yet no one has offered to answer this question.

Perhaps that is because those who know the answer know there is no longer any such thing as military superiority, that in the modern world military power can only be continuously expanded, but that no matter how great its expansion it will never enable one nuclear power to force another to do its will. Perhaps they know that no matter how much more military power we acquire, we will never be able to do any more with it than we can already do with the multiple and redundant advantages in military power we have long possessed.

Perhaps those in the administration who advocate "superiority" know this too. But they appear to be more dedicated than any administration before them to serving the interests of our defense establishment, and preserving its freedom to use America's resources and decide its economic future as it sees fit. They may be equally dedicated to protecting America's access to resources and markets throughout the world. If one benefit of freedom to manage resources at home is a measure of expanded military power, that power can be used to better control resources abroad.

East and West, then, are engaged in two wars, one of resources, the other of ideologies. The latter war, justifying the moves taken in the former, is a propaganda war, concerned as much with gaining the support of our own people as with winning the allegiance of our allies.

The need to restore parity is a goal designed for Americans who can be persuaded that a Soviet military advantage threatens our security. The need to achieve superiority is a goal for the smaller number of Americans who believe that America has a right to any advantage it can get, no matter how much this threatens the security of other nations and peoples.

All that can actually be gained by winning support for either of these goals is a further redundancy in military power. This will do little to protect the advantages we already have; it will do nothing to give us new ones. The more our military power is used, and the more it threatens the security of others, the more it will lose respect and support for America throughout the world. The more America justifies its military deployments as part of a worldwide struggle with Moscow, the more it risks bringing that struggle about.

10 Exploiting the Myth in Europe

Expanding the myth of Soviet military supremacy to include the assertion that the Soviets hold the lead in conventional as well as strategic and theater nuclear power serves several functions at once. By claiming that Soviet conventional forces are superior to ours, it also suggests that those of the Warsaw Pact are superior to NATO's. This implies that NATO's conventional defense against the Pact is inadequate. That, in turn, justifies the presence of American nuclear weapons in Europe to remedy this imbalance. Moreover, it justifies America's refusal to renounce the first use of nuclear weapons, on the grounds that we would have no choice but to use them on Europe's behalf should a conventional defense fail. The added claim of Soviet theater nuclear superiority justifies a continuous expansion of NATO's nuclear arsenal to remedy that purported imbalance as well.

By creating the impression that Europe needs our protection, and that the only adequate protection is an extension of America's nuclear umbrella, we extend political control to Europe. First, we define a common enemy against which Europe must unite with us in a common defense. That polarizes opinion in Europe: its people must take sides. Next, we define nuclear weapons as the only possible defense. This creates the conditions of emergency in which support for a united defense is patriotic and dissent disloyal: Europeans must take our side. That is how nuclear weapons are used to enforce political consensus. The requirement for consensus, in turn, creates a strong bond of mutual obligation which protects our access to Europe as a market and source of investment.

Most Europeans realize that our nuclear weapons in Europe cannot be used without bringing about the destruction of what they presumably mean to defend. Most Europeans do not believe that nuclear-free zones or renunciations of the first use of nuclear weapons will prevent escalation to nuclear war should conventional war break out. They know that a weaker force may resort to nuclear arms just as soon as it is threatened with defeat. They know there is consequently nothing to gain by being stronger, that both the weak and the strong are equally subject to nuclear blackmail. Neither NATO nor the Warsaw Pact could precipitate any kind of war in Europe without risking suicide. Europe has had a deterrent to nuclear attack since 1952, when America first deployed nuclear weapons there,[1] ostensibly for deterrence. Since that time, all the nuclear weapons that have been added have done nothing for Europe's security but place it at greater risk.

Most Europeans also know that nuclear war cannot be restricted to Europe. They know that if America launched its missiles in Europe against the Soviet Union, the Soviet Union could easily retaliate against targets in the United States, and might do so. In fact, it has promised to do so. They also know that everything America can hit in the Soviet Union with missiles based in Europe it can hit with missiles based in the United States. It is patently clear, then, that no more nuclear weapons need be based in Europe for Europe's deterrence, and that the additional nuclear weapons America has now begun to deploy there serve no European purpose but only an American one, and have no effect on Europe but political coercion.

Consequently, growing numbers of Europeans want no part of these weapons. They feel that America has made them hostage to serve its own strategic interests.

Some of their governments do not feel the imminent threat from the Soviet Union that is supposed to make them grateful for America's protection. Others, namely Great Britain and France, do postulate a threat, but have built their own nuclear forces so that they need not depend on America's protection. The obstacle to full European independence from the United States is West Germany, which has not been permitted to build its own nuclear deterrent. Were it otherwise, America could make no case at all that Europe needs its protection.

The Soviets, of course, have encouraged Europe's desires for independence. We call this subversion. How dare they attempt to decouple Europe from America? Certainly, were Soviet missiles in Cuba today, and the United States unable to remove them, we would be doing all we could to decouple Havana from Moscow, reminding Cubans of the terrible risks to which they needlessly exposed themselves.

As it serves this political function, the myth of Soviet superiority in conventional weapons also enables us to exploit another of our several strategic advantages over the Soviet Union. This is Europe's proximity to Soviet territory. The ostensible need to rely upon nuclear weapons in Europe enables us to threaten targets in the Soviet Union at only a fraction of the range between Soviet nuclear weapons and their nearest targets in the United States.

We have long exploited this advantage. Since 1958, we have had aircraft based in Europe capable of penetrating Soviet air defenses and dropping nuclear bombs on Moscow. The Soviets call these forward-based systems. We don't like to use this term because it is a reminder that the Soviets have no comparable forward-based systems. That is because they have no forward bases where they might deploy them. Our blockade of Cuba in 1962, our recent invasion of Grenada, and our attempts to destabilize the government of Nicaragua all demonstrate our determination to prevent the Soviets from repairing this inequity, whether or not any governments aside from Havana's would even allow them to try.

The Soviets have always defined a strategic weapon as any weapon that could hit another nation's homeland, wherever it was based. We have always defined it as a weapon of intercontinental range. This is a convenient definition for us because it excludes weapons of much shorter range based in Europe which can hit the Soviet homeland. By excluding these weapons from strategic arms discussions with the Soviet Union, and calling them theater weapons instead, we have been able to protect this inequity and the additional strategic advantage it gave us, while fostering the public impression that no such advantage existed.

We continued to insist on our own definition of strategic weapons until the Soviets placed missiles in Cuba. Then suddenly we agreed with their view that weapons which lacked intercontinental range still could play a strategic role.

After these missiles were removed, we reverted to our own definition again. But one of the reasons why the Soviets placed missiles in Cuba was to confront us with the consequences of our definition, and require reciprocal action from us in eliminating forward-based missiles that threatened both superpowers.

It worked. In 1958 we had placed sixty *Thor* missiles in England; we followed them with forty-five *Jupiter* missiles in Italy and Turkey. These weapons threatened large areas of the Soviet Union in precisely the same way Soviet missiles in Cuba threatened coastal regions of the southeastern United States. Had President Kennedy not privately consented to remove our missiles, it isn't clear whether the Soviets would have agreed so quickly to remove theirs. For what is not commonly known is that the Soviets had made our agreement to remove ours a precondition for removing theirs.[2] This is not commonly known, because if it were better known we would no longer be able to teach our children that the Cuban missile crisis was a triumph of American resolve. In fact, in the words of Harvard historian Graham Allison, it was President Kennedy who "cracked and folded."[3] All of our *Thor* and *Jupiter* missiles were withdrawn in 1963.

We will never have to admit that many of the nuclear weapons we retained in Europe, as well as the new ones we have since been deploying there, pose a strategic threat to the Soviet Union until the separate negotiations we have always insisted upon for limits on theater and strategic nuclear arms are combined, as disarmament experts have long recommended, and until we do more than merely pretend to agree to this arrangement, which the Soviets demanded as a precondition of the Geneva talks early in 1985. After the first round of those talks, Soviet leader Mikhail Gorbachev remarked that Washington "refuses in general" to discuss all these weapons "simultaneously," and "thus violates the accord reached in January on the interconnection" of "nuclear strategic arms reduction and reduction of medium-range nuclear armaments in Europe."[4]

The reason both superpowers consider forward land-based missiles more threatening than forward-based bombers or missiles at sea is not because they are more accurate. Missiles at sea are becoming just as accurate. Bombers have always been accurate enough. Nor is it because land-based missiles are less vulnerable to preemptive attack. Missiles at sea are nearly invulnerable, and likely to remain so at sufficient ocean depths and at sufficient range from hostile shores. Bombers are vulnerable only if they are caught on the ground. Indeed, land-based missiles are the most vulnerable because they are fixed in place and cannot quickly be repositioned. That is why we had planned anyway to remove our *Thor* and *Jupiter* missiles from Europe—though not quite so quickly as the Cuban missile crisis required—and to replace them with missiles more safely based at sea aboard the *Polaris* submarines then entering service.

Forward land-based missiles are the most threatening because they take the least time to reach their targets. Without placing its submarines at too great a risk, neither superpower can bring them much closer than within fifteen minutes of flight time to their targets. Bombers take much more time, even though they are forward-based. An F-111E aircraft of our 20th Tactical Fighter Wing at Upper Heyford in England is only 1,500 miles from Moscow, but still would take over an hour to fly there with its six nuclear bombs. An F-4F *Phantom* of the West German Bundesluftwaffe's 74th Fighter Group at Neuberg is but 1,200 miles from Moscow, yet it would take as long as the F-111E to reach that city with its three nuclear bombs.

On the other hand, a *Thor* missile of RAF 77 Squadron stationed at Feltwell in England had the capability to reach Moscow in nine minutes. A *Pershing II* of our 56th Field Artillery Brigade at Heilbronn in West Germany is now able to reach Moscow in only six.

Why, when we once removed land-based missiles from Europe precisely because they were at once too vulnerable and too threatening, and replaced them with missiles at sea which are still in position today, have we introduced vulnerable and threatening missiles again? Aside from their political function, do they serve any other purpose?

Yes, according to the professional journal *Defense Electronics:* "With a range allowing strikes on Moscow from Germany, the removal of C2 [command and control] capability by a comparatively small number of *Pershings* would render much of the Soviet ICBM first strike and retaliatory forces impotent."[5] Then the *Pershing II* may not simply play its advertised role in support of NATO forces in the European theater; it could also play a major role in our strategic plan for a first strike of our own against the Soviet Union, which Defense Secretary Harold Brown acknowledged was one of our "options."

This is not what the public hears. The public has repeatedly been told that our new missiles are being deployed in Europe because Europe asked for them, and because they are needed to redress an "adverse imbalance" of theater nuclear power.

The claim that NATO suffers an adverse imbalance of theater nuclear power is based on comparisons of long-range missile warheads which include all of those deployed on Soviet SS-20s and other missiles, but do not include the much greater number of warheads deployed by the United States and other NATO nations on missiles at sea. The claim that Europe asked for our new missiles is based on a speech given in London in 1977 by West German Chancellor Helmut Schmidt.

In fact, Schmidt's appeal to NATO "to make available the means to support its present strategy"[6] was preceded, ten years earlier, by America's new doctrine of "flexible response," which did not discover an "adverse imbalance" of theater nuclear power, but instead defined the need for a new missile based in Europe with a longer range and greater accuracy than the *Pershing I*. In 1971, six years before Schmidt's speech, the U.S. Army formally approved and initiated the *Pershing II* program for a new missile to replace the *Pershing I* in Europe.[7] The *Pershing II* would have arrived there with or without the Soviet SS-20 or Helmut Schmidt.

Our government's undeclared mission for the *Pershing II* is no more plausible than the rationale it offers the public. It is merely a part of that elaborate web of war fighting theory which attempts to justify the funding and deployment of new weapons because technology has made them possible, profitability has made them desirable, and theory must find something for them to do. They cannot possibly do anything that does not risk retaliation. They are subject to all of the same operational uncertainties planners can never resolve. If one of our missiles misses its target, we risk prompt suicide; if none of them misses, we merely delay suicide, by minutes or hours at most.

Certainly, we realize all of this. But we are deploying our new missiles anyway, not only to raise the costs of political dissent in Europe but also to add to the general military pressure we place on the Soviet Union, in the belief that each addition to our arsenal will intimidate the Soviets a little more and make them hesitate a little longer to confront us on any issue, so that we might come a little closer to this administration's vision of an America that moves wherever it likes through the world with impunity.

What we appear to have forgotten since the Cuban missile crisis—or what we believe we can safely manage—is the real danger which missiles like the *Pershing II* have always posed. Because their time to target is so short, they place extraordinary pressure on an adversary's early warning system. The components of that system, be they human or mechanical, will barely have time to identify and evaluate an attack, and in fact may not have enough time. This raises the risks of false identification and premature response beyond any level such systems have previously had to endure.

Our own warning systems, incorporating far more advanced technology than the equipment the Soviets must rely upon, have processed false alarms countless times. We have always been able to determine that each alarm was false, but the time it has taken to do so has sometimes exceeded the time it would take for a *Pershing II* to reach Moscow.

Consequently, we must now live with a risk of nuclear war by accident or miscalculation that is infinitely greater than the risk we had to bear before. It isn't simply the Soviet Union which faces this risk; the United States faces it in exactly equal measure. Forward-based missiles are pointed only in one direction, but the dangers are shared. Of all of the steps the United States has taken in the arms race, deployment of the *Pershing II* is probably the most reckless, myopic, and suicidal.

The final purpose served by claims of Soviet conventional superiority is preparation for the growing possibility that public demands for a nuclear freeze may one day be met. Our defense establishment has no intention of losing the scale of investment it has secured in nuclear weapons research, development, and production, most of which would cease with a freeze. What better way to retain that investment than shift all of it to conventional weapons research and manufacture, on the grounds that we can only free ourselves of dependence on a nuclear defense if we build a stronger conventional one?

The impression that we need a stronger conventional defense has already been reinforced by a group of former officials, among them George Kennan and Robert McNamara, who would like to see NATO renounce the first use of nuclear weapons. While they concede that "there has been some tendency, over the years, to exaggerate the relative conventional strength of the USSR," they nevertheless propose that "new levels of effort," though not "excessively high" ones, be undertaken to ensure "strengthened confidence in the adequacy of the conventional forces of the Alliance."[8] Thus, despite their careful qualifications, these officials do not directly challenge the administration's contention that the Soviets, already purported to hold the lead in strategic and theater nuclear arms, hold the lead in nonnuclear arms as well.

11 Disseminating the Myth

How has the Reagan administration persuaded America that the Soviets hold the lead in military power? Chiefly by saying that it does, and by systematically misrepresenting the balance of military power to reinforce its assertions. It simply selects whatever information best supports the conclusions it wishes the public to draw, and omits whatever information contradicts those conclusions. This means that a great deal of information must be omitted. Most of the information the administration presents is perfectly accurate; it is just incomplete. The result is a wholly different conclusion from the one that all of the facts would provide.

Thus, the administration talks of the number of Soviet strategic missiles, which exceeds ours, but not of the number of strategic warheads available to us, which exceeds theirs. It talks of the threat posed by Soviet heavy missiles, but not of the much larger threat that has long been posed by our much lighter but more accurate missiles. It talks of the greater throwweight of Soviet missiles, implying they could carry more warheads than they do, but does not point out that several provisions of SALT II—a treaty both nations continue to honor—forbid their carrying more, and that our ability to monitor Soviet tests and verify their compliance with such provisions would tell us they were planning to disregard them months before they could deploy any missile that did, and well in time for us to take countermeasures if any were truly needed. It talks of the greater explosive force of Soviet warheads, but not of the greater accuracy of our missiles, whose warheads could thereby destroy the same targets with even less explosive force than they currently possess.

To raise doubts about whether our missiles are really the more accurate, the administration has vaguely warned of the growing accuracy of Soviet missiles, while simultaneously doing as much as the law will allow to remove responsible estimates of their accuracy from public access, so that few comparisons reflecting our greater accuracy can be made.

Sometimes, when no facts are available to support the conclusions it prefers, the administration will fabricate them, overstating Soviet strengths and understating ours. Thus, when it had to concede that warheads, not the means of delivering them, are the most significant measure of strategic power, it had to confront the dilemma that by this measure we held a substantial lead. So in May, 1982, when the President announced his START proposal for equal reductions in strategic warheads, he offered a comparison of Soviet and American strengths which implied the proposal was fair by showing both arsenals at parity.[1] To create this comparison, not only did the President eliminate a large portion of our lead in warheads by excluding all of the bombers that would deliver them. He also went on to make the number of Soviet missile warheads seem equal to ours by giving the Soviets 1,200 more warheads than officials from his own Defense Department, in sworn testimony to Congress one week earlier, reported the Soviets had.[2]

When it talks about the nuclear balance in Europe, the administration talks only about land-based missiles of intermediate range, as if this were the only significant category of nuclear weapons in the region. If that were so, why have we continued to develop and deploy so many other types of nuclear weapons there, from nuclear gravity bombs to artillery projectiles?

On arriving in office, administration officials began to talk of the threat which Soviet SS-20 missiles had posed to western Europe's cities since they were first deployed in 1977. This implied that western Europe's cities had not been threatened before, and that consequently the SS-20s posed a new threat that had to be countered. These officials insisted that only land-based missiles of comparable range, namely, the *Pershing II* and *Tomahawk* cruise missiles they planned to deploy in Europe, could counter such a threat and end the Soviet monopoly in this category of weapons.

The officials did not remind the public that all of the same cities in western Europe had been threatened by Soviet SS-4 and SS-5 missiles since 1959, and that far from insisting on land-based missiles of comparable range to counter them, we had withdrawn those we had from Europe in 1963. They did not publicly recall that for the next eighteen years Europe lived with the same threat they now pronounced to be "new," and with the same "adverse imbalance" of power that now appeared suddenly to alarm them.

Nor did the Soviets hold a monopoly of missiles of intermediate range in Europe. This impression, too, was false. The administration could only sustain it by refusing to place British and French missiles of equal range in the same category, and by ignoring missiles of even greater range which America has long committed to Europe's defense from its *Poseidon* submarines at sea.

The administration presumably excludes our *Poseidon* missiles because they are not based on land. This is supposed to make them inexact candidates for a category it has deliberately defined as narrowly as possible. But they are missiles; there is no defense against them; they are capable of intermediate and far greater ranges. The fact that they are based at sea only makes them superior weapons, because they cannot be targeted and destroyed by preemptive attack as land-based missiles can be. That is precisely why we had already planned, before the Cuban missile crisis, to shift our missiles of intermediate range in Europe from land to sea.

The administration excludes French and British missiles on the grounds that they are autonomous weapons of last resort, and that NATO has no control over how they are used. Yet the possibility that they may not be used cannot very well eliminate the possibility that they may be used. They exist. They are aimed only at the Soviet Union. Therefore, their effect on Soviet security should have been taken into account by our negotiators in Geneva.

Had the Soviets given such weapons to East Germany and Czechoslovakia, or encouraged those nations to build and deploy comparable weapons of their own, and then claimed that these were autonomous forces over which neither Moscow nor the Warsaw Pact had any control, we would have laughed at them. Had they further claimed that, inasmuch as they had no right to offer proposals to reduce these weapons, we should negotiate as though the weapons did not exist, we would have been outraged.

By imposing such an outrage on Soviet negotiators, we forced them once again to refuse an offer we knew they could not accept, because it was based on a deliberate distortion of the European balance of power.

French President Mitterand made his own contribution to this exercise in sophistry, proclaiming: "French arms cannot be taken into account in the Geneva negotiations" because "France would lose a decisive element of its deterrent capability."[3] This implied that the Soviets had proposed to reduce French forces. Mitterand knew perfectly well they had done nothing of the kind and could not expect to do so. The Soviets had requested, instead, that French and British forces be acknowledged to exist, and that their existence be taken into account in negotiations over American forces. American forces, after all, were only a portion of those NATO deployed against the Soviet Union.

By deliberately misinterpreting the Soviet request, Mitterand made our refusal to accede to it seem like a rescue of France's arsenal when that arsenal had never been imperiled. This diverted public attention from the truth, and helped sustain support in the West for a false balance sheet that reflected a monopoly the Soviets never had, further justifying new Euromissile deployments.

Sometimes the administration has a specific pretext for its asymmetric comparisons. It increases the number of Soviet ground combat personnel in eastern Europe by including construction workers in its count because they are uniformed, even though they are not armed. By contrast, personnel assigned to American and other NATO engineer units are heavily armed. The administration reduces the number of NATO ground combat personnel by excluding French forces from its count on the grounds that France withdrew them from NATO command in 1966, even though France remains a member of NATO, committed to its collective defense, and the 51,200 ground combat troops it maintains in West Germany and Berlin are not there as tourists.

Sometimes the administration attempts no pretext at all for its asymmetries. When it compares the number of aircraft available to NATO and the Warsaw Pact to carry out nuclear strikes, it counts on NATO's side only those aircraft specifically assigned to this role, while it simply assumes that every aircraft capable of carrying a nuclear bomb for the Warsaw Pact will do so. That is more than 3,000 aircraft, well over half of those flown by the Pact. If so many of its aircraft were reserved for this purpose, the Pact would have too few remaining aircraft to perform reconnaissance, fighter escort, ground support, combat air patrol, deep strike, early warning, and other missions, and would forfeit air supremacy to NATO.

The administration warns that the Soviets have almost one hundred divisions with which to reinforce Warsaw Pact forces in the event of war. It does not add that NATO has prodigious reinforcements too, and that Soviet reinforcements are at such a low state of readiness that there would never be a time, in successive stages of mobilization, when the Warsaw Pact could muster more ground combat troops than NATO would already have opposing them.

When it compares the balance of tanks between NATO and the Warsaw

Pact, the administration counts all the tanks the Soviet Union and other Pact nations have ever produced, even though large numbers of them have been exported abroad, placed in reserve, stored, or assigned to southern and far eastern military districts of the Soviet Union, while on NATO's behalf it counts only those tanks assigned to active NATO units deployed in Europe. Substantial NATO tank reserves, pre-positioned American equipment, and tanks accompanying other NATO reinforcing units are left out.

Even when all of NATO's tanks are included, or course, and the figure for total Warsaw Pact tank production is replaced by the number of tanks truly available to the Pact for combat in Europe, the Pact continues to hold a substantial numerical lead. That lead, however, is more than offset by NATO's overwhelming lead in the number, variety, and lethality of its antitank systems. It is further offset by the intrinsic advantages of NATO's presumably defensive role. Nor does it reflect the superior quality of NATO's own tanks. NATO, in fact, has a larger number of more advanced tanks than the Pact, with better armored protection, greater maneuverability, far more lethal offensive weaponry, and more highly sophisticated ranging and sighting equipment.

12 The Real Value of Numbers

Numerical comparisons, then, no more reflect real advantages in conventional military capability than they reflect real advantages in strategic nuclear capability. By themselves, they seldom clearly represent the balance of any kind of military power, or reflect those factors that will determine the outcome of war.

This is often pointed out by the same people who select and present incomplete information, and who use it to make the misleading numerical comparisons that misrepresent the balance of military power. When the information they had excluded is restored, and the equivalent forces and weapons they would not juxtapose are compared, they are often the first to suggest that nothing can be learned from it. Whether comparative figures are correct or not, they say, the result of a war will depend less on one side's numerical advantage than on how quickly it mobilizes its forces, how long it can sustain them in battle, how well it maintains communications between them, the quality of their weaponry, their skill in using it, the judgment of their leaders, and their care and foresight in operational planning.

All this is perfectly true; therefore, they conclude, numbers do not really matter. They belittle numerical comparisons by calling them "bean counts." But they do not say this when the numbers favor the Soviet Union. They say it only when the numbers favor America and the West.

Nor is a war what we have. If we are careful, we will not have one. What we do have, instead, is the single most intensive and prolonged campaign in America's history by its government and its defense establishment to create a mythical threat to our security, in order to justify an unparalleled shift in the use of our nation's resources. In creating this threat, false comparisons and misleading statements have played an indispensable role. And numerical comparisons have played the most prominent role of all. In fact, the administration's rationale for all of its military appropriations rests almost entirely upon them.

When numerical comparisons of military power are as accurate and complete as circumstances permit, the real value of the numbers they display is that they quickly reveal and correct the distortions created by incomplete or false comparisons. The real value of analyses that go beyond the numbers to examine the actual capabilities of forces and weapons is that they reveal the advantages which static comparisons fail to reflect even when they are accurate and complete, and which static comparisons are consequently utilized to hide. Both of these exercises are critical in determining the real balance of military power; to what extent the Reagan administration has distorted it; and whether there is any justification at all for its continuing program to rearm America.

Circumstances may not permit fully accurate numbers to be established. It may be impossible, for example, to determine how many additional SS-20 missiles the Soviets are deploying each month during periods when they are adding any at all. Our intelligence services certainly know these numbers, but do not make them available so frequently. Cumulative totals are available intermittently, as public officials release them for their own purposes.

This inability to know the precise numbers of weapons deployed at any time is often cited to discredit comparisons that attempt the highest possible level of accuracy. But the people who usually discredit such comparisons are the same people who present false or incomplete comparisons, and who would prefer not to have these challenged.

Absolute precision is not even needed; it is enough to know how many SS-20s all the available sources report each year. This information is always available annually, and the sources that provide it almost invariably agree on the numbers they give. The occasional variances between them, and the occasional rise or fall in the rate of a weapon system's deployment before they next report it, represent quantities too small to be of any significance.

It is enough to establish a weapon system's initial deployment date, and its rate of deployment thereafter, based on the evidence all of these sources provide. Then the probable number of such weapons deployed at any given time may be based on the assumption that, barring any evidence to the contrary, it continues to be deployed at the rate these sources already have established. If this assumption is used, however, that should be clearly explained.

It is more important to understand how these sources present their information, and how public officials present it. Are they reporting all of the SS-20s deployed throughout the Soviet Union as if all of them were within range of Europe, even though a third of them are deployed in the Far East, well beyond range of Europe? All sources acknowledge this, but several do their best to obscure it. Some may assume that because SS-20s are mobile, those in the Far East could eventually be moved within range of Europe. But if they assume this, they do not explain that assumption. Nor do they acknowledge that we would know when this move took place, and that until it takes place, there is no justification for including these missiles in the European theater nuclear balance.

Most important of all is to determine what weapons and forces should be compared. Those who point out that the numbers used in numerical comparisons can never be absolutely accurate do not offer more accurate comparisons themselves when they fail to compare Soviet SS-20s with NATO's missiles at sea. Not only are the comparisons they offer less accurate; they are intentionally misleading.

If we are to know whether this administration deserves our support, we must know whether the basis of its claim for support is true. We must have a means of evaluating what it says. It is not enough to be suspicious simply because we see that it tries to deny us this means, with legislation that increasingly curbs our access to information. We must know in our own minds whether what it says is reasonable or fair. If it is spending our money to prepare for a threat we have long been able to meet, and if its military buildup raises rather than reduces the risks of our survival, then it is wasting our money and gambling with our lives, and it must stop.

Growing numbers of Americans fear that this is happening. In the startling shift in this administration's budget priorities, they see our nation's resources diverted away from the public interest to satisfy private interests. They see that this has not at all preserved our security, but has undermined it. They do not believe the administration has justified its use of our money. They suspect they have been misinformed about the urgency of the Soviet threat, but they lack the information to prove it. They need to inform themselves and to educate others. They cannot refute the administration's arguments, or demonstrate that it has misled the public with false comparisons and incomplete information. Before they can settle these questions, they need the information that has been missing from public debate.

One purpose of this book is to restore such missing information, using the best evidence available from public sources. This task may be performed by any competent researcher. All of the information needed is in the public domain, though it is often not easily accessible to the general public; time must be taken to learn where to look in order to find it. This book may save some readers time, because it lists where every scrap of its information was obtained. It lists sources that inflate the threat and sources that deflate the threat. For the first important lesson to learn is that all sources work with essentially the same information. All that matters is how they present it.

For this reason, I do not recommend that you simply take for granted what this book tells you, any more than I could possibly recommend that you take for granted what the Reagan administration tells you. I urge you to check its sources, and to check those sources against other sources, to find out for yourself whether the information presented here is presented as you would present it yourself, whether the comparisons made are appropriate and fair, and whether the conclusions reached are relatively free of bias. For the facts themselves are not the danger. The danger is in how the facts are presented.

Indeed, there is little dispute about the facts. Where facts are not available and estimates must be made, some analysts will accuse other analysts of exhibiting bias because the estimates they make are too high or too low. But it is perfectly clear when there is no basis for an estimate of any kind. What is comforting is that most of these disputes are artificial. We seldom need rely on estimates anyway. Most of the facts are known.

The Soviets seldom try to hide their weapons or disguise major military units. They make little effort to do this because they know it would not succeed. Our government learns what it knows, and continuously verifies it, through a variety of intelligence collection systems which it sometimes refers to as "national technical means." These include satellites, a vast network of ground intercept stations, and large fleets of intelligence ships and reconnaissance aircraft. This book fully describes their capabilities, and defines exactly what our government learns from them. It demonstrates that our government knows exactly what weapons and forces the Soviets do have, and what their capabilities are. It is just that this administration, like many before it, does not make all its knowledge available to the general public.

The administration has not yet been able to prevent the information it tries to withhold from surfacing in military and technical publications, industry journals, and congressional testimony. Nor has it yet been able, though it has tried, to prevent officials who do not agree that the public should be denied such information from leaking it to the press, or to prevent former officials from using it freely to support their disagreements with current policy. That is why all this information can still appear in these pages.

13 The Best Evidence

This book does not offer a comprehensive review of every category of military power; if it did, it would be impossibly unwieldy. It has taken up only those categories in which the administration has focused its claims of Soviet military supremacy, and where it has found most success in misleading the public. The administration has had only modest success, for example, in magnifying the threat from Soviet conventional air and naval power. This is not because the public is more aware of the severe limits geography imposes on the movements of the Soviet fleet, or of the West's substantial numerical lead in surface combat ships, its parity in numbers of combat aircraft, and its significant qualitative lead in both these categories of power. Nor, by any means, did the administration concede these facts or refrain from misrepresenting them. Rather, it concentrated its efforts elsewhere.

Those categories on which the administration focused its claims were the balance of strategic nuclear power between the Soviet Union and the United States, the balance of theater nuclear power in Europe, and the balance of ground combat personnel and ground combat equipment—especially tanks—in Europe. These are also the categories on which the most significant efforts at arms control have focused in the past several years, from the separate negotiations between the United States and the Soviet Union on strategic and theater nuclear arms in Geneva, to the Mutual and Balanced Force Reduction talks between NATO and the Warsaw Pact in Vienna.

This book therefore concentrates on those same categories, and on statements the administration made about them from its campaign for office through the end of its first term in office, during all of which time it never stopped campaigning for increased military spending.

In each of these categories, the book documents the most significant claims the administration has made to misrepresent the balance of power, whether by omitting information, misinterpreting it, fabricating it, or combining these manipulations in various ways. It traces how each of these key misrepresentations was disseminated, often appearing first in official publications or in the statements of administration officials, and how each was then repeated by the press and private organizations until it became established in public debate as the truth.

The book compares these established truths with the evidence available from a broad range of public sources. These include former government officials, prominent scientists, government agencies, military and technical publications, academic studies, West European governments, congressional sources with access to classified data, specialized military research groups, and private individuals highly respected for their expertise in the field. All are identified. The reader will find no reference in this book to "certain sources," or to "officials who spoke on the condition that they not be identified."

The book's appendixes document how the evidence drawn from all of these sources was compiled. They take careful note of each time these sources achieve a general consensus, and of each time no evidence can be found to contradict that consensus on the number of weapons of any type deployed, or on its rate of production or conversion, or on its speed, range, or other characteristics. They also take careful note of any discrepancies between sources, and of how these were resolved.

Many sources, when they present information comparing the numbers or characteristics of weapons deployed, will list their own sources without identifying which piece of information came from what source. It is impossible, in this situation, to know where a particular piece of information came from, or whether any of the sources listed really provided it. Care has therefore been taken, in the major appendixes in this book, to go the needed step further and identify precisely what information came from which source.

These appendixes create an independent estimate of the strategic balance of power, and of the balances of theater nuclear and conventional ground combat strength in Europe, based on the best evidence from all of these sources. They provide a startling contrast to the impression the Reagan administration has tried to sustain. Here are the major conclusions that may be drawn from them:

- Contrary to what the administration says, it is the United States which holds the lead in strategic power over the Soviet Union, by every significant measure of that power. This lead, however, affords us no advantage over the Soviet Union that may be utilized. Neither superpower can have sufficient confidence in its ability to carry out a first strike on the other's territory without incurring retaliation. Each has assured means of inflicting unacceptable retaliatory damage upon the other.
- Contrary to what the administration says, each alliance in Europe is capable of mounting a successful conventional defense of its territory against the other's attack. Given the increased lethality of modern conventional

weapons, a war fought exclusively with these weapons in Europe would wreak unprecedented devastation. As soon as either side feared defeat in such a war, the danger promptly exists that it would resort to nuclear weapons, whose use might escalate beyond control. Consequently, neither alliance can risk a conventional war in Europe.

• Contrary to what the administration says, in almost every category of military equipment the United States and its Western allies hold a substantial numerical lead and an enormous lead in quality over the East. In the few categories where the East holds a numerical lead, as in numbers of tanks, that lead is more than offset by the West's lead in quality, and by its lead in other types of equipment, as in the number, variety, and lethality of its antitank weapons. Nevertheless, while the West may be able to use its superior military capabilities to considerable coercive effect in other parts of the world, it has little to gain from them in Europe, where they remain largely gratuitous.

14 The Machinery of Coercion

What emerges from the comparisons of statements about the military balance is that, even though these statements are drawn from a wide variety of sources, they fall into only two groups. One group presents only information supporting administration claims, or presents no information conflicting with them. The other group presents a great deal more information which wholly contradicts them. Those citizens exposed only to the first group's statements are bound to conclude that the Soviet Union holds the lead in military power. Those citizens exposed to additional information from the second group will draw conclusions similar to mine.

The first group cannot deny the validity of the information the second group provides. There are witnesses; there are records. Too many people serve in the military units the first group ignores, or have designed and developed and built and operated and seen and described and photographed and counted and authorized the purchase of the equipment the first group does not count. Our B-52 bombers cannot be made to disappear.

What the administration and its supporters can do, however, is claim that the B-52 is irrelevant, and inadmissible for the purposes of their comparison. Thus when the President, in May, 1982, compared the balance of strategic warheads and excluded all of the warheads our bomber force carries by excluding our bomber force, I asked one editor whose newspaper printed the incomplete comparison why the bombers had been left out. He said they were not important because they were obsolete and could not penetrate Soviet air defenses.

In that case, I asked him, why do we continue to deploy them? Why do we plan to keep them operational through the late 1990s? Why have we already spent $3.4 billion to rebuild and improve them, and why do we plan to spend another $7.7 billion to continue improving them, adding sophisticated electronic countermeasures and other equipment precisely in order to ensure that they *could* penetrate Soviet air defenses?[1] Why does the Congressional Budget Office estimate that as many as 75 percent of our bombers *would* penetrate Soviet air defenses?[2]

The editor could not answer these questions. He had no excuses for leaving the bombers out, and he knew it. His explanation was disingenuous. Most probably, magnifying the Soviet threat was a harmless old game to him.

The game is not harmless. This may be the last time it can be played. What is disquieting is that the group which plays it, wittingly or not, consistently includes all of the nation's major media: its news weeklies, television networks, and most influential daily newspapers. In shaping public opinion, they have far more influence than the media that provide more complete information.

For the most part, this additional information is restricted to publications of small circulation or public and local television. Occasionally, additional information appears in a major newspaper's letters column or op-ed page, where it comes to the attention of only a fraction of those exposed to the articles that appear day after day on its front page. It is as though America lived in two worlds: that of the inadmissible, and a much smaller world of the rational and pertinent.

How does this happen? How is information in an open society so perfectly partitioned? How does a free press dismiss truth as though it were irrelevant, when the facts it dismisses are the most pertinent? This would be simple to understand if the press were dealing only with rumor. But it is dealing with demonstrable fact. Its refusal to deal with it, then, seems no accident.

This phenomenon has also been critical to the administration's success. For it really could not justify shifting several hundred billion dollars from public programs to private industry simply by making a series of misleading statements about the balance of military power, when every one of those statements could be disproved with information in the public domain. It had to ensure that its statements would not be disproved on a wide scale. It had to ensure that only the smallest number of Americans would learn the truth, while its own misrepresentations reached the vast majority, and were repeated to that majority without challenge until they became accepted as truth.

This could not be done without the participation, or at very least the acquiescence, of America's major media. The media had to accept and disseminate the administration's statements, repeat them as often as possible, and ignore or minimize the importance of contradictory information. This is exactly what the media did. Why did they do it? What did the administration do to ensure that they did it?

Another purpose of this book is to shed some light on those questions, and to examine the process by which the Reagan administration gained the cooperation it needed to mislead the American people on an issue so fundamental to their welfare and security. We must understand this process before we can ever bring it to a halt or prevent it from recurring.

The last section of this book, then, examines the issues that prevailed in the press and in public debate as the administration announced its program to rearm America. It finds that the press has enormous power to limit the terms of debate, focusing public attention on those issues it selects, and that government has even more power to influence the press.

Government holds a variety of levers of influence over the press. It can keep the focus of national news fixed steadily on its own policies and views with a continuous schedule of press conferences and major policy statements. It can influence how the news is covered by flooding the press with guidelines on how its policies and views should be interpreted. It can place the press on the defensive by complaining of unfair coverage whenever its own interpretation of events does not prevail. It can limit unfavorable coverage by alternately rewarding reporters and threatening to deny them access to their sources. It can shape the tone and direction of news coverage from within the press by using its influence with corporate directors who sit on the boards of major news organizations and control news management.[3]

The Reagan administration certainly used all of these means to help establish its myth of Soviet military supremacy. But to dissuade the press from challenging its misinformation, and to encourage skepticism in the press toward critics who did challenge it, the administration also had to create a general atmosphere of emergency and distrust of the Soviet Union, in which acceptance of its statements would seem at once more loyal and more responsible.

The administration's announced intentions to build the MX missile and deploy *Pershing II* and Cruise missiles in Europe sustained the necessary atmosphere of emergency. But distrust had to be created by focusing public attention on the adversary whose threat to our security was said to require these weapons in response. If questions remained about Soviet capabilities, then Soviet intent had to be portrayed as unremittingly malevolent. This would create the sense of a permanent threat which could never subside but only increase, thereby justifying a limitless expansion of military power in response.

A critical element of the administration's campaign, therefore, has been a broad series of accusations, regularly repeated, of Soviet expansionism, Soviet violations of arms treaties, Soviet intransigence in arms negotiations, Soviet initiatives in the arms race, Soviet planning for nuclear war, Soviet use of inhumane weapons, Soviet violations of human rights, and Soviet support of violence and terrorism throughout the world.

The book examines these accusations and finds that, apart from Soviet human rights violations, which our press heavily emphasizes over serious violations that occur in other parts of the world,[4] almost all of the remaining charges are wholly without foundation. It finds that many of these accusations are used not only to create a general atmosphere of lasting distrust, but also to suggest a Soviet initiative where America took one, as in planning for nuclear war, or to suggest a Soviet initiative where America plans to take one, as we now plan to produce a new generation of chemical weapons and to expand into the lucrative but highly dangerous field of weapons in space. It also finds that focusing public attention on the Soviet record has served to obscure the American record, which in almost every area save human rights has been far more reprehensible.

In sustaining its campaign, the administration has also had to deal with its critics, who have continued to grow in number and authority. When they have contradicted its misinformation, it has called the information they use for this purpose disinformation, even though it is usually incontrovertible fact. The administration also implies that such facts have been fabricated by Moscow, and that in using them its critics are either Moscow's agents or Moscow's unwitting dupes.

But the B-52 bomber was not fabricated in Moscow, and the real disinformation in our debate over national security comes not from the Kremlin but from the White House.

The administration has also deliberately misinterpreted its critics. Those who support a mutual freeze on further production, testing, and deployment of nuclear weapons by the Soviet Union and the United States are portrayed as seeking a freeze on America's weapons alone. Those who believe we must have a strong defense, and can therefore only disarm in mutual, equivalent stages with the Soviet Union, are portrayed as seeking complete disarmament on America's part alone. All are portrayed as though they would rather be red than dead, when surely most would rather be neither, and none accepts the idea that such a choice should ever be required, or that any government has the right to make it for them by declaring war.

The administration and its supporters have questioned the right of many critics to involve themselves in the nuclear policy debate, though if they had no right to join in this debate they would no longer have any right to a role in formulating policy. That role is constitutionally guaranteed.

When this is pointed out, the administration is quick to qualify its complaint. It claims it has no desire to deny the people their constitutional rights, but only questions the right of those not competent to judge such issues. The administration would rapidly improve the general level of public competence, of course, if it less zealously attempted to limit public access to information about the issues. Yet despite such efforts, many critics, if their appreciation of the risks of our policy is any measure of their competence, seem to have reached a higher level of competence on nuclear weapons policy than almost anyone in the administration.

The administration has warned that opposition to our policy is irresponsible, and has even implied that it is disloyal, because it can damage America's efforts to achieve its policy objectives. The single purpose of this opposition, of course, is to change America's policy objectives. If growing numbers of Americans believe that our government's policies are doing the nation more harm than good, then they have more than a right to oppose those policies. They have a duty. They do not serve the nation by keeping silent and loving America, right or wrong; they only serve politicians momentarily in power.

The administration has complained that dissent can adversely affect our national security, because it demonstrates a lack of political consensus at just those times of crisis when consensus is essential to preserving national security. It appears that dissent itself may now be essential to preserving national security. Yet this administration would prefer to suppress dissent. It seems perfectly willing, then, to turn our system into the very kind of society it tells us it condemns.

15 The Power of Information

America's people are the only hope for America. They always have been. When the people have known what they wanted, they have often been able to obtain it, or at least obtain some part of it. When they wanted a comprehensive test ban, they got a limited test ban, but that was at least a step in the right direction. When they wanted America out of Vietnam, we got out. Now they want some assurance of peace. President Eisenhower once remarked that the people want peace so much that one day governments had better get out of their way and let them have it. Now is that time.

Knowledge is what our people need. It teaches them what problems they truly face, and how they must focus their efforts to solve them. It is the necessary precondition of change. That is why so much effort is made to deny them knowledge.

A stunning example of this occurred in November, 1983, when the ABC Television Network broadcast *The Day After,* a film depicting the results of a nuclear war in a midwestern American city. Before the film was shown, administration supporters were denouncing it as Soviet propaganda, and demanding that it be taken off the air. Their complaint was that it weakened support for our policy of deterrence by depicting a situation in which deterrence had failed. They did not want anyone to believe this could happen. Presumably they did not believe it could happen themselves.

Yet obviously there are those who do believe it could happen. Surely they have a right to say so.

After the film was shown, the administration naturally suggested that support for its policies was the best way to continue to ensure that deterrence would never fail. Yet many believed that its policies were precisely what might cause deterrence to fail. If the administration wanted deterrence to succeed, they argued, then wouldn't it be better to leave deterrence alone? Why introduce new weapons that risked its failure? Why continue to twist and contort deterrence theory in an attempt to justify those new weapons by showing how they might serve deterrence, when the problem was that they might not, and when deterrence already worked without them, because it was already based on mutual risks that neither superpower could eliminate?

While the administration and its supporters were distracted with a defense of their policies as the best way to avoid a nuclear war, they seemed to overlook, or tacitly to accept, what the film actually accomplished. This was to teach more than 100 million Americans that a nuclear war *had* to be avoided, because it could neither be won nor survived.

Before *The Day After* was shown, the administration was saying that a nuclear war could both be won and survived. It had been saying this ever since it first arrived in office. The administration's *Defense Guidance* was leaked to the press to suggest its belief in the former point. The Federal Emergency Management Agency was given $4.2 billion of our money to suggest its belief in the latter point, and to deflect charges of the administration's indifference to our fate.

The administration had to sustain the impression that it believed in both of these points, because its declared policy of planning for the conduct of a nuclear war "over a protracted period," and of "prevailing" in such a war, would not otherwise make sense. This policy would seem irresponsible and dangerous if the administration intended to pursue it without believing that a nuclear war could be won and survived.

Probably, the administration believed nothing of the kind. But it had to say so. That was the only way it could justify its new policy of "prevailing," and its new policy was the only way it could justify the new generation of nuclear weapons it intended to build.

But after *The Day After* was shown, the administration ceased saying that a nuclear war could be won or survived. It never made either such statement again. President Reagan even declared that a nuclear war "cannot be won and must not be fought." For it had now become eminently clear to a large majority of the electorate, and clear for the first time, that all of the statements the administration had previously made to the contrary simply were not true.

Of course, the administration did not publicly renounce its policy of "prevailing" in a nuclear war. Nor, certainly, did it abandon its plans for a new generation of nuclear weapons. But the sudden absence of a plausible justification for them has not been explained to this day.

An editorial in *The New York Times* complained that *The Day After* told us nothing new. Perhaps it told the editorialist nothing new. It told the few hundred thousand readers of Jonathan Schell's book *The Fate of the Earth* nothing new. It told those who have listened to Helen Caldicott or Jack Geiger or Carl Sagan nothing new. But all of those people who already knew this were only a fraction of the 100 million who know it now.

Today, those 100 million no longer believe a nuclear war can be won or survived; they no longer delude themselves that they are safe. Now they are concerned with avoiding nuclear war. So they have moved on to the question of how that may be best assured. Where they had accepted the administration's policies before, they are now critically examining them. They are beginning to ask why this administration is building a new generation of nuclear weapons specifically designed to fight a nuclear war, when a nuclear war "cannot be won and must not be fought." This is the power of information.

The administration would have preferred that these people still believe what they used to believe. Then they would have remained politically passive. They would not have threatened a challenge to the consensus in support of administration policies. That is the real reason why those who support these policies would have preferred that *The Day After* never be shown.

That is also why a group of former government officials tried quickly to contain the threat of this challenge on network television, in a special ABC Nightline program immediately following *The Day After,* by recreating the decision-making process during a fictional superpower confrontation. This was designed to demonstrate that our leaders are prudent and responsible, want no war, and that we may therefore safely place our fate in their hands, and not concern ourselves with issues of policy.

If our leaders do not want war, why have they given us so much war? Why, if they are always prudent and responsible, have more than 25 million people died in over 150 armed conflicts of one scale or another since the end of World War II? Why, if we speak only of the world's current leaders, are thirty-seven major or minor conflicts involving more than 8 million people in uniform being fought today on every continent except Australia? Or, if we speak only of America's leaders, then why does America now find itself participating or assisting, so far as we know, in nine wars, in Lebanon, Afghanistan, Cambodia, Ethiopia, Morocco, Chad, Angola, El Salvador, and Nicaragua?

Our leaders are too frequently prisoners of the system they serve, whose momentum they have done nothing to stop, even though it leads them closer to their own destruction. Of course they do not want their own destruction, however tolerable or even necessary they may find destruction elsewhere. They are too often the victims of their own rationalizations. As they publicly continue to insist we cannot trust the Soviet Union, how long will they privately continue gambling our survival on the assumption that the Soviet Union will not overreact to the increasing threat our weapons pose? It will take only one miscalculation of how far we may push them to risk the end of human consciousness.

Or what if our leaders begin to believe their public distortions of Soviet character? Then they will lose their ability to see events as the Soviets see them. They will no longer be able to predict how the Soviet leadership may respond. Then it may be the United States, not the Soviet Union, which overreacts and risks human extinction. What if they begin to believe in the Soviet threat? Those who lie must sooner or later begin to believe their lies or begin to hate themselves. When the threat becomes real to them, it is easier for them to make enemies than friends, and easier to make war than keep the peace.

It is going to be up to the people, then, to keep the peace. And to do that, they need information. They must make themselves as competent as possible on every issue of nuclear weapons and conventional arms policy. They must make the best effort they can to understand how information about these issues is presented to them, and to take careful note of what they are being asked to do in response, so that they can evaluate what they are told. This book means to be a contribution toward that effort.

II

THE MYTH
OF SOVIET STRATEGIC
SUPERIORITY

16 Announcing the Myth

"The truth of the matter is that on balance the Soviet Union does have a definite margin of superiority—enough so that there is risk and there is what I have called, as you all know several times, a window of vulnerability."[1]

These were the words spoken by Ronald Reagan at his news conference on March 31, 1982. It was a historic occasion: the first time an American President had told his people they no longer held the lead in the arms race.

Americans had been warned many times, of course, that they were about to lose a military lead of one kind or another. Leads had been diminishing, new trends emerging, windows of vulnerability opening, gaps looming, and balances shifting steadily against the West for almost forty years. Yet never once was it said they had shifted so far as to place America behind. It was always conceded that America remained ahead. The moment when we might fall behind was always placed at some point in the future—a point unspecified in time and hence subject to infinite revision by those who warned of its eventuality.

We were always promised we could prevent that moment's arrival if we took decisive action. Invariably, this meant undertaking a major expansion of American military power. Invariably, the decision to take that step had already been made by our leadership; we were merely being asked to accept it. Invariably, that step was taken, with or without our approval, with or without a Vietnam syndrome, with or without the defeatism which was always said to be at the heart of any resistance to increases in military spending. A major increase in military spending was always granted. It was always followed by a decline in America's productivity; often it was followed by a decline in America's world reputation too. The hope of avoiding these consequences, of course, had always been at the real heart of resistance to excessive military spending. But, at least, each time the money was spent it presumably purchased the military power we were told we needed to secure America's lead.

Now we were told we had already lost that lead. This was "the truth of the matter," according to President Reagan. Yet how could it be the truth of the matter, when every administration over the past forty years had assured us we would always be able to keep that lead so long as we gave it the money it wanted, and when it had always gotten the money it wanted?

This made some Americans skeptical. Presidents had lied in the past. Was another one lying now? Or did this one believe what he said? He delivered his statement with the simple conviction he had always displayed. The impression this made had always inspired public trust and that trust had always served as a powerful inducement to accept whatever he said as true.

But even if he believed what he said, did that necessarily mean it was true? In the past, Presidents who deceived their people had often been deceived themselves, or else had made themselves believe in their own deceptions in order to convey the sense of inner conviction these required. Speculation over whether Ronald Reagan believed what he said this time, then, did nothing to help determine whether it was true.

Most Americans, it seemed, did not believe any President would lie about a question of such paramount importance to the nation's security. Few could be expected to appreciate that this was no longer a question of any importance at all. It had long since ceased to matter. Both superpowers had long possessed nuclear weapons invulnerable to a first strike. This meant that each had the capability to inflict unacceptable levels of damage upon the other, in retaliation for a first strike. No additional strategic forces had ever been able to change that fundamental fact. None in existence or contemplated held any promise of ever being able to change it, frequent though such promises were.

Additional strategic power was therefore redundant. Which nation had more of it, and thereby could be said to hold a lead, no longer mattered. No lead in any category of strategic power could provide either one of them with a single military advantage; consequently, it could not provide either one of them with any political advantage. The quest for strategic superiority had become obsolete. Nor did any further attempt by either nation to acquire it strengthen that nation's economy or improve its reputation. It only further injured both.

Since injuries of this kind were systematically denied or overlooked by advocates of military expansion, it was difficult for most Americans to realize how urgent it had now become to avoid inflicting deeper ones. Since warnings of military emergency were seldom challenged, and were always assumed to rise from concern for the national rather than private interest, they always gained greater attention and greater respect than warnings of any other kind.

So most Americans were well prepared to assume that military emergencies, though always imminent and never yet at hand, were more important than emergencies of any other kind. Since advocates of military expansion still enjoyed the reputation of knowing best each time they insisted theirs was the only means of preventing such an emergency, it seemed most Americans were inclined to believe them.

It seemed they believed this each time a new emergency arose, despite the fact that not a single one of those predicted in the past had ever materialized. Each time a new alarm was sounded, a growing number of Americans pointed to the unbroken record of false alarms before it. Each time they did so, they were discredited as agents or victims of disinformation, as though only Moscow could have informed them instead of the indisputable record that did. Since that record could not be disputed, it was ignored.

Yet each new predicted emergency never arrived. Each new prediction turned out to be a mistake. Each mistake was always officially acknowledged, though only years after it was made. It turned out, each time, that there had never been a bomber gap or a missile gap or any other gap. Each new expansion of American military power to close these gaps had therefore been unwarranted. It had always been impossible, however, to appreciate this fact until long after each expansion had already taken place.

Nevertheless, advocates of military expansion continued to enjoy the public trust. It was still presumed that they would never ask for what they wanted unless they truly needed it. Consequently, most Americans, it seemed, were still inclined to give it to them.

At least, so it seemed. Some Americans were frankly puzzled by the impression they always received of what most Americans were still inclined to do. How had so many learned so little, they wondered, from so perfect a record of forty years of false alarms? This puzzled them until they remembered that they didn't really know what most Americans were inclined to do. They knew only what their government told them and what they learned from the press—and much of the time what they learned from the press was only what their government told them.

If many Americans still believed the nation could afford each expansion of military power, and that each was urgently needed, this was only because that was always what their government told them. After it told them, it took polls of their opinion. Then it held up the results, for the rest of the world and not least the people themselves to see. It called these the will of the people. It told the people it had their support. Consequently, most Americans believed it did.

What government had, of course, was the acquiescence of the people, many of whom lacked the knowledge to challenge what it told them. Few of them, however, had any trouble remembering the past, and most of them yearned for an alternative. So government used their acquiescence to create the false impression of a broad consensus in support of official policy. Its persistent claims of such a consensus demoralized those who sought an alternative, and often succeeded in dissuading them from further pursuit of one, while still preserving the comforting surface impression that the voice of the people was being heard.

When the Reagan administration took office, the polls showed less positive results. A majority accepted the administration's insistence that the Soviet Union posed a threat, but doubted that a military expansion of our own was any longer a solution that would make us more secure. The administration ignored public reluctance to accept an increase in military spending, and instead took public belief in the Soviet threat as a full endorsement for that increase.

A very large majority believed more nuclear weapons would only increase the threat of war, and wanted a freeze on their further production and deployment. It did not get one. The will of the people was ignored. This failure of democracy had to be denied, just as the record of false alarms had always been denied. Commentators therefore began to refer to that majority as a fringe; its dissenting views were given a minimum of attention. The press appeared to lose interest in them. For the most part, Americans heard about their own opinions only when these favored administration policy.

It was in this climate that the President's announcement came. It came as a shock. If the Soviet Union now held a margin of strategic superiority, then the emergency was no longer imminent but already at hand. That made it a larger emergency than any before, and implied it was a more genuine one. This shock cannot have been unintended, for it perfectly suited the administration's request for a larger peacetime military budget than any before it. In fact, it was to be the only justification ever offered for that request.

The shock also came at the best time to subdue congressional resistance to the administration's budget request. This resistance had steadily grown since David Stockman, director of the Office of Management and Budget, three months earlier called the Pentagon a "swamp" of waste and mismanagement, and the administration's entire economic plan a "Trojan horse" to protect the rich.[2]

Thus, whether or not there was a real military emergency, there was a real fiscal one. The President's statement indisputably resolved the latter crisis in his administration's favor.

But this unprecedented claim of Soviet superiority could not simply be asserted; it had to be carefully reinforced. Measures of strategic power which seemed to support it had to be repeatedly emphasized, while those which threatened its credibility had to be minimized or ignored.

It also carried with it a new disadvantage. While previous claims of emergency had been difficult to refute because they always predicted what would transpire at some future point in time, this one described the present moment. It could be disputed, then, with facts already at hand. Consequently, it was essential to do whatever could be done to make such facts unavailable.

The new assertion's flexibility somewhat compensated for this problem. Most previous claims had focused on a single aspect of strategic power, predicting a threat, for example, from many more bombers of intercontinental range than the Soviets ever produced, or from much more rapid deployment of Soviet land-based missiles than ever took place, or from much greater progress in the development of antisatellite weapons than the Soviets ever made.

The new claim, however, avoided specifying the nature or the scale of the threat. Statements supporting it could therefore move between a variety of suggestions without fear of self-contradiction, emphasizing whatever information seemed most persuasive and least in dispute at the time. If the claim was contested, evidence of an American lead by one measure of strategic power could be disqualified simply by shifting public attention to another, while insisting the latter had always held greater importance.

Yet there were only so many elements of strategic power, and only so many ways of measuring them. First of all, there were the nuclear weapons themselves. These were the warheads mounted in missiles, and the nuclear gravity bombs and other weapons loaded on bombers. Then there were the missiles and bombers which delivered those weapons to their targets; they were sometimes called delivery vehicles.

The number of weapons each bomber or missile could carry varied according to its size and the size and weight of each of its weapons. There was a maximum possible number of weapons it was capable of carrying. Then there was the somewhat lower number of weapons it normally did carry, due either to operational limitations imposed on its range by larger loads, or to political limitations imposed by arms control agreements.

The number of bombers or missiles of each type produced by the Soviet Union and the United States was known. The number of each type operationally deployed by either nation at any given time was known. The much larger number of weapons they all carried was also known. A variety of reconnaissance satellites and other intelligence systems monitored every stage of their production, testing, and deployment, and gave immediate notice of any change in their deployment.

Their numbers were known with a very high degree of certainty, which meant that they could be counted with a very high degree of accuracy. The total number of delivery vehicles each nation possessed could be counted. Bearing in mind the number of each type of vehicle operationally deployed, the maximum number of weapons each could carry, and the minimum number it was certain to carry, the much larger total of all the nuclear weapons carried by all these delivery vehicles could be counted too. A count could be made of the maximum possible number of nuclear weapons in each nation's strategic arsenal. Another count could be made of the minimum number of weapons each nation was bound to have deployed.

Given sufficient information, all of which was available, even a child could add up these totals. Even a child would know that comparing the maximum possible number of strategic weapons one nation might have with the minimum number the other was bound to have was misleading.

A count could also be made of the total weight of all these weapons, including the weight of every bomb with its casing, and the throwweight of every missile. A missile's throwweight was the weight of its final stage, thrown into a ballistic trajectory by its earlier stages. This included the entire post-boost vehicle, its protective nosecone, all the reentry vehicles it carried, the warheads within them, guidance equipment, and any decoys or other devices that may have been added to help the reentry vehicles penetrate an adversary's defenses.

The sum of the weights of all a nation's strategic bombs and the post-boost vehicles lofted by all its strategic missiles comprised its aggregate strategic throwweight, and could be measured in millions of pounds. Again, a nation's aggregate throwweight could either be a measure of the maximum potential load capacity of all its delivery vehicles, much of which went unused, or a measure of the actual load they normally carried.

There was also a weapon's explosive yield: the destructive energy it released on detonation. This was measured in kilotons or megatons, the thousands of tons or millions of tons of TNT required to release an equivalent amount of energy. The total of megatons of explosive power possessed by all the weapons in each nation's arsenal could be counted.

Finally, there was the destruction each weapon might actually cause. This varied according to its yield, the nature and size of its target, and its distance from the target when it exploded. A highly accurate weapon might bring all of its energy to bear on its target. A less accurate weapon might not; in that case, much of its energy could be wasted—though certainly this did not mean it might not cause a great deal of unintended destruction.

The likelihood that a given weapon would destroy its intended target could be computed as a function of its probable accuracy, its probable reliability, its anticipated yield, and the resistance of its target to blast overpressures. Technological improvements might steadily raise this likelihood, though they could never transform it into a certainty.

It was clear that if the accuracy of a weapon could not be improved sufficiently to bring it within lethal range of its target, that target might still be destroyed at the same range by increasing the weapon's explosive yield. Conversely, if its accuracy were substantially improved, it might need only a fraction of its former yield to destroy the same target. In fact, increases in a weapon's lethality were far more responsive to improvements in accuracy than to increases in yield. "The overriding importance of accuracy," former missile systems engineer Robert Aldridge had pointed out, "can be illustrated by saying that if we cut the miss distance in half we would need a bomb only one eighth as powerful to retain the same hard-target kill capability."[3]

Consequently, if one weapon's yield was higher than another's, this did not mean that it would be more lethal against a given target. Indeed, the weapon with the lower yield might be more so. In the same way, if one nation's arsenal held a higher aggregate megatonnage than another's, this did not mean its weapons held the greater capability to destroy their intended targets. The nation with more accurate weapons might well hold that capability with only a fraction of the other's aggregate megatonnage.

The higher a weapon's yield, the more plutonium and other materials it used in its fission tamper and fusion core, and the more it weighed. The less efficient a weapon was in producing a desired yield, the greater the proportion of such materials it wasted, and the more of them it had to use to assure that it achieved that yield. This further increased its weight. If two weapons produced the same explosive yield, but did so with different degrees of efficiency, the more efficient one could weigh substantially less.

Two weapons of equal destructive power could also vary in weight according to the weight of their guidance, arming, fuzing, and other mechanical or electronic components. The more these were miniaturized, and the lighter the materials used in their manufacture, the less the weapon they equipped would weigh. The lighter and smaller weapons became, the greater the number of weapons a nation's force of bombers and missiles could carry. Or if this force carried lighter weapons but did not increase their number, it reduced their aggregate throwweight without any reduction in their aggregate destructive capacity.

As a result, the nation with more efficient and better miniaturized weapons might have many more of them in its strategic arsenal than its adversary had, even though they weighed less in the aggregate. If its adversary's weapons were larger and less efficient, it might have fewer of them, even though they weighed more in the aggregate. If some of these weapons were larger because they were built to produce higher yields, they might still be less effective against their intended targets than more accurate weapons with much smaller yields.

A nation's higher aggregate throwweight, then, meant neither that it had more weapons nor that it had more effective ones. Higher aggregate throwweight no more meant that its possessor held the greater military capability than higher aggregate megatonnage did.

In assessing how much destruction each superpower's arsenal could wreak upon the other's territory, and hence which nation's capability for destruction was the greater, some measures of strategic power were thus more important than others. The number of targets each nation could destroy was not limited by the number of delivery vehicles it possessed; it was limited only by the much larger number of weapons they could deliver to separate targets. Consequently, a count of the total of independently targetable warheads and bombs a nation could deliver was a far more significant measure of strategic power than a count of the bombers and missiles which delivered them.

Neither aggregate megatonnage nor aggregate throwweight could indicate how many targets a nation's arsenal could attack, let alone how many it might destroy. Only a count of its independently targetable weapons could indicate the number of targets it could attack. Only an assessment of the lethality of various weapons in this arsenal against various targets could indicate how many targets all of them might destroy, and in this assessment accuracy played a much more important role than yield.

Nevertheless, the Reagan administration consistently refrained from making comparisons of strategic power based on a count of the total of nuclear weapons in each nation's arsenal, even though every administration before it had emphasized that this was the only significant comparison to make.

When the administration took office in 1981, the Defense Department had just released its *Annual Report* for the following fiscal year. This report, like every one before it for many years, included a comparative count of the nuclear warheads and bombs in American and Soviet strategic arsenals. That year, it offered the following count of the minimum total of these, which it called force loadings,[4] operationally deployed on each nation's strategic bombers and missiles:

USA	USSR
9000	7000

The Reagan administration never once referred to this comparison. It even attempted to remove such comparisons from the public record. For the first time, such figures did not appear in the Defense Department's *Annual Report* issued in 1982. They did not appear in the *Military Posture Statement* issued by the Joint Chiefs of Staff that year. They appeared in neither volume the year after that, or the year after that.

As a result, when the President claimed the Soviets had achieved a definite margin of superiority, such figures were no longer available from these sources to dispute him. Defense analysts Anthony Cordesman and Benjamin Schemmer complained about these and other omissions from both documents. "With almost Orwellian timing," they noted, "Secretary Weinberger has removed virtually all of the useful data on the balance from the Defense Department's two main defense policy and budget statements," with the result that "the truth about the balance is missing from his defense of the nation's defense budget."[5]

Defending these omissions, Secretary Weinberger even went so far as to say that comparisons of strategic warheads were "not a very accurate measure" of strategic power,[6] though he apparently found the figure for Soviet strategic warheads important enough to include it in the Pentagon's publication *Soviet Military Power* in 1981. There, however, it appeared without benefit of comparison with the larger American figure.[7]

Physicist Edward Teller, a staunch administration supporter, moved to reassure those Americans who might learn they had been denied such information, by suggesting it had never been available in the first place. "Neither the United States nor the Soviet Union publishes information on its current arsenals," he told the readership of *Reader's Digest* in 1982, as though this had always been true.[8]

But it had only just become true. Until that year, the United States had regularly published information on the arsenals of both nations. Nor would it remain true. The United States had already published information that year on the Soviet arsenal, and would continue to do so in future editions of *Soviet Military Power*. The Soviet Union would soon publish information on the American arsenal in its booklet *Whence the Threat to Peace*. The following year the Soviet Union, but not the United States, would publish information on both arsenals.

Each government's information on the other's arsenal, of course, was considered less dependable than its information on its own. Americans were further obliged to consider information from Moscow more suspect than information from Washington.

But the implication of Teller's statement was still clear. The public was supposed to think it could not judge the relative strategic strengths of the superpowers, because it had no access to dependable information on which it could base such a judgment. It therefore had to rely on the word of those who said they did, and to trust that they had only the public interest in mind.

In fact, the public did have access to dependable information on the strategic balance, despite the efforts of the Reagan administration to withhold it. This came not only from random disclosures by former officials. It also came from regular and mandatory disclosures by current officials from the Pentagon and other agencies, before the Appropriations and Armed Services Committees of both Houses of Congress. These officials could heavily interpret the facts they presented, and often they did. But since they were under oath, the facts they presented were usually correct.

Certainly, the value of their testimony depended on what questions Congress asked. Certainly, this testimony was not widely distributed. Indeed, the more it conflicted with official policy, and the more the press understood how serious that conflict was, the less prominent it became. But it continued to form the heart of the official record on which all research institutions, specialized publications, and other sources of military information in the private sector closely depended for accuracy and authority. It continues—so far—to be a matter of public record today.

If this should ever cease to be the case, and public access to information about the strategic balance, already laborious to maintain, is one day wholly denied, as Teller implied it already had been, then we would have a very different situation on our hands.

We are now kept ignorant of critical facts about the balance in large part because government prefers us to be, and because the press and private institutions increasingly respond to that preference by growing increasingly reluctant to report whatever contradicts official statements and views.

If we were also kept ignorant because the courts refused to allow such information in the public domain, then we would have no basis at all for judging our nation's defense needs. We could no longer play any role, as our Constitution ordains, in formulating policy on this most critical of all issues. On this most critical issue, upon which our very survival depends, we would no longer have any semblance of government by the people, for the people. Teller did not comment on these wider implications.

17 Misrepresenting the Balance of Strategic Power

While it avoided warhead comparisons, and tried to minimize their importance whenever it was asked why it had removed them from the official record, the Reagan administration did its best to support the President's claim of Soviet superiority by making comparisons of other kinds. There were many of these. They were the same comparisons the administration had made in its original campaign for office. They could always be used to create the impression of a Soviet lead because they were based on existing asymmetries of force structure that *seemed* to favor the Soviet Union, as the table *Comparative Measures of the Balance of Strategic Power* (see page 92) shows. Those who did not know that these comparisons were irrelevant would always be misled by them.

So the President emphasized the greater number of Soviet bombers and missiles, even though they could deliver thousands fewer warheads than America's bombers and missiles could. "For example," he declared in a television address to the nation late in 1982, "the Soviet Union has deployed a third more land-based intercontinental ballistic missiles than we have. Believe it or not, we froze our number in 1965 and have deployed no additional missiles since then."[1]

We could believe it. By 1965 we had almost completed building all the land-based missiles we planned to deploy: we had built 854 of them by that time, but the Soviets had only 270. By 1967 we had built 1,054, and we stopped. The Soviets had only 460, so they did not stop. We "froze" our number because we finished our program. We finished our program before the Soviets finished theirs. Finishing first did not place us behind; it placed us ahead.

Certainly, we could have built many more land-based missiles, had there been any advantage in doing so. There wasn't. Why build more missiles, when instead we could place more than a single independently targetable warhead on each? The Soviets could not yet do this, so they continued to build their missiles. That did not mean they were going to surpass us. It meant they were trying to catch up.

Nevertheless, Ronald Reagan could look at any arms race in which the Soviets were trying to catch up, and say that we were "already in an arms race, but only the Soviets are racing,"[2] while neglecting to add that we had already *won* that race and were starting a new one.

For, as *New York Times* correspondent Leslie Gelb observed, "each administration since then has elected to increase the number of nuclear warheads on each missile rather than the number of missiles themselves, a choice that American experts say was deliberately made for strategic reasons."[3]

Indeed it was. The Soviets finally did build more land-based missiles than we had. But by the time they completed their program in 1970, they would have had to build *three times* as many such missiles before they could compensate for the advantages we had meanwhile accrued. For in the interim we had introduced multiple warheads. By 1970, our strategic forces could deliver a total of 5,522 nuclear warheads on targets in the Soviet Union, while Soviet forces could deliver no more than 1,914 on targets in the United States.[4] We have never lost our lead in deliverable warheads.

If the greater number of Soviet missiles provided no advantage, then the administration and its supporters focused on the size of those missiles and talked of their greater throwweight. Retired General Daniel O. Graham, a leading light of the ultraconservative wing of our defense establishment, emphasized that the

Soviets held a "4 to 1 advantage in missile throwweight,"[5] because many of their missiles were so much larger than ours.

The President's Commission on Strategic Forces concluded that Soviet heavy missiles, because of their greater throwweight, presented a "one-sided strategic condition," which our planned MX missile was needed, of course, to "redress."[6]

The administration's START proposal, which purported to offer an equitable plan for mutual reductions in strategic arms, demanded in its finer print the elimination of almost three quarters of the Soviet force of heavy SS-17, SS-18, and SS-19 missiles, from a total of 818 such missiles to only 210, though its authors could not have been unaware that the Soviets never would agree to dismantle so large a portion of what they considered the mainstay of their deterrent capability. Certainly they would not agree to it without a corresponding sacrifice on America's part that this administration had not offered to make.[7]

This reduction in Soviet missiles was needed, the administration claimed, to eliminate a Soviet advantage in throwweight. It explained that the greater throwweight of larger Soviet missiles could enable them to carry a greater number of multiple warheads than smaller American missiles could.

In other words, an administration that scrupulously avoided offering full warhead comparisons by saying it made no difference which nation had the larger number was saying, at the same time, that the nation which had more throwweight could have more warheads as a result, and that this was precisely the reason, and the *only* reason, why throwweight made such a difference.

But, of course, the larger size of some Soviet missiles had not provided them greater numbers of multiple warheads than American missiles carried. America was far more advanced in miniaturization; it was far more advanced in accuracy. This meant an American warhead of much smaller yield could destroy the same target that a less accurate Soviet warhead would need a much larger yield to destroy. Which meant, in turn, that America's warheads needed less fissile material to perform the same amount of destruction. That further reduced their size.

America was so far ahead of the Soviet Union in the efficient miniaturization of warhead components that it had placed fourteen warheads on a single *Poseidon C-3* submarine-launched ballistic missile as long ago as 1970. It was not until 1977 that the Soviets were able to place eight warheads on some of their SS-18 missiles. They managed to flight-test the SS-18 with ten warheads before SALT II was signed, and many SS-18s with ten warheads are operational today.

But today the United States can mount as many as seventeen Mk 500 Maneuverable Reentry Vehicles (MaRVs) or Mk 600 Precision Guided Reentry Vehicles (PGRVs) on the *Trident II D-5* missile,[8] or as many as twenty on the MX, a missile larger than the *Minuteman* but a good deal smaller than the Soviet SS-18.[9]

Consequently, America does not need more throwweight, or larger missiles to deliver it. If we did, we would have built them. Certainly, there is no question that we *could* have built them. What is not remembered is that we once did build larger missiles than any the Soviets have operational today.

The largest Soviet missile, the SS-18, is 120 feet long; our *SLV-5C Titan IIIC* was 127 feet long.[10] The next largest Soviet missile, the SS-19, is 80 feet long and 8.5 feet in diameter. Our *SM-65 Atlas D,* first operational in 1959, was 82.5 feet long and 10 feet in diameter. We had 129 of these missiles operational in thirteen squadrons at ten Air Force bases until 1966.[11]

We could have continued to build such missiles, had they offered us any advantage. They didn't. By then we had developed solid fuels, which were far more efficient and powerful than the older liquid fuels they replaced. When they burned they produced more energy, and consequently more thrust, for each pound of fuel consumed. This reduced the amount of fuel a missile required, and the sizes of rocket stages containing it, to carry a warhead the full distance to its target.

"With the new solid fuel," one missile engineer noted, describing the early stages of *Polaris* missile development, "it became possible to build an IRBM small and safe enough to be suitable for submarine launching, yet powerful enough to carry a warhead a long distance."[12]

At the same time, the smaller the warheads themselves became, the greater the number of them our new, smaller missiles could carry without any sacrifice in range.

All of America's missiles but *Titan IIs,* now undergoing retirement, use solid fuel. By contrast, almost all Soviet missiles, including all of those large ones over which the Reagan administration professes such concern, use liquid fuel. That is one reason why they are so large.

It is also why Soviet missile forces are kept at a state of readiness so much lower than ours, need so much more time to be brought to alert, and continue to suffer so many more accidents of the kind our *Titan II* squadrons experienced in 1978 and 1980. Liquid fuels are highly volatile and dangerous. Each missile must be fueled to prepare for launch. It must be defueled if it is not launched. Solid fuels are much simpler and more dependable to use.

Hardly, then, did larger Soviet missiles present a "one-sided strategic condition," least of all when we chose to create that condition ourselves. What more perfect hypocrisy than to claim—as the Reagan administration now did—that an asymmetry in missile size we had done all we could to accelerate now endangered us?

While America no longer needs large missiles, the Soviets still do. Larger missiles, with room for larger warheads with larger explosive yields, and with sufficient capacity for the fuel required to carry that greater throwweight the necessary distance, have been the only way they could attempt to compensate for the inferior accuracy of the reentry vehicles carrying those warheads.

In time, of course, the Soviets would catch up in both miniaturization and accuracy. Thus, though the administration had to concede the Soviets could not *now* place as many warheads on their missiles as we could on ours, it still could argue that one day they would be able to do so, utilizing their greater throwweight to maximum advantage, and surpassing us in the number of strategic warheads deployed.

The administration did not point out that this need never occur. One of the purposes of SALT II was to prevent it from occurring. The treaty did this not only by limiting the number of missiles each nation might deploy, but also by limiting the number of reentry vehicles each nation might deploy on each type of missile it possessed. It limited this number to the maximum number deployed on each missile type at the time the treaty was signed, or to the maximum number flight-tested a sufficient number of times on a given missile at that point to consider it an operational capability. And it fixed the number of such flight tests at twenty-five.[13]

Thus, for example, though the Soviet Union had not yet begun to deploy its SS-18 Mod 4 with ten warheads when the treaty was signed, it had flight-tested the Mod 4 enough times to consider it, by the treaty's standard, an operational system. Consequently, SALT II allowed the SS-18 up to ten warheads, but no more than that number. It allowed the SS-17 a maximum of four warheads, and the SS-19 a maximum of six.[14] The whole purpose of this, as Secretary of State Cyrus Vance confirmed, was to "prevent the Soviet Union from fully exploiting the larger throwweight of its ICBMs by increasing the number of its reentry vehicles" beyond those limitations.[15]

SALT II has already been signed by both heads of state; both governments have pledged themselves to continue honoring its terms. We have needed only to ratify it to make it binding law. While the administration states that this treaty has been "withdrawn" from consideration by Congress, Congress has needed only to vote its advice and consent to ratification, without any further action of any kind from this administration or any other authority, and SALT II would be ratified.

Nor is it widely understood that SALT II's limitations on warheads place America in a position to deploy more warheads on its missiles more quickly than the Soviet Union can. The treaty allows each *Poseidon C-3* fourteen warheads, each *Trident C-4* seven, and each *Minuteman III* not the three warheads it currently carries, but seven.[16] That is because the *Minuteman III* has been flight-tested a sufficient number of times with seven reentry vehicles to qualify it, so loaded, as an operational system.

When SALT II was signed, no existing Soviet missile had been flight-tested sufficiently with a greater number of warheads than the treaty specified to qualify it as an operational system. The treaty banned further flight testing of existing missile types with greater numbers of warheads than it specified.[17] Of all the missiles possessed by both superpowers, then, only the *Minuteman III* could be immediately deployed with a greater number of warheads than it now carries.

We have pledged not to deploy the *Minuteman III* with more than three warheads "during the term of the Treaty." But SALT II will have expired at the end of 1985. Should both governments choose to express their intent to continue to honor it after that time, we could cite the treaty's allowance of seven warheads on each *Minuteman III* in order to justify deploying that number, and disregard our pledge to deploy fewer, even more easily than we have already disregarded some of this treaty's other provisions. Every proposal to base the MX in other than existing silos has violated Article IV, Paragraph 1, of SALT II. Current plans to deploy both the MX and a single-warhead *Midgetman* violate Article IV, Paragraph 9, of SALT II.

In either case—whether we abandon SALT II entirely or continue to honor some of its provisions, interpreting others as we choose—before either superpower could deploy a missile of any new type, or deploy a larger number of missiles of any existing type, America could deploy more warheads on its missiles than the Soviets could. If all the missiles now deployed by both nations were fitted with the maximum number of warheads specified by SALT II as the limit of their current, flight-tested operational capability, the Soviet missile force could have no more than 8,637 warheads, while ours could have 10,690. The missile forces of both nations would be composed as follows:

Soviet Union

Missile Type	Number	Warheads on Each	Total Warheads
SS-11	520	1	520
SS-13	60	1	60
SS-17 Mod 1	150	4	600
SS-18 Mod 4	308	10	3080
SS-19 Mod 1	360	6	2160
SS-N-5	57	1	57
SS-N-6	400	1	400
SS-N-8	292	1	292
SS-N-17	12	1	12
SS-N-18 Mod 3	208	7	1456
Total:			8637

United States

Missile Type	Number	Warheads on Each	Total Warheads
Titan II	42	1	42
Minuteman II	400	1	400
Minuteman III	600	7	4200
Poseidon C-3	320	14	4480
Trident C-4	224	7	1568
Total:			10,690

The Soviets do not yet have this number of missile warheads; neither do we. They may eventually build up to this number; so might we. There is really no need, however, for either nation to do so. Both already have several times the number of warheads they would need in order to obliterate each other's cities, industries, and military machines entirely.

Of course, the Soviets could utilize the excess throwweight of their missiles if they were willing to violate SALT II limitations. But before they could deploy any missile with a greater number of warheads than the treaty allows, they would have to test it. They could have little confidence in its performance unless they did so. And whenever they did so, we would be watching them.

We observe every Soviet missile test; we identify the type of missile being tested; and we count the number of reentry vehicles it releases in its terminal stage of flight. If these tests indicated the Soviet Union was planning to deploy a missile in violation of SALT II limitations, is there any doubt that we would begin taking measures immediately to counter the threat this posed, if it posed any threat at all, and if any measures to counter it truly were needed?

In view of the time it would take to complete a new missile's tests and begin deploying it in meaningful numbers, is there any doubt that in the meanwhile we would be able to complete countermeasures of our own? There are several immediate steps we could take that would more than offset any Soviet effort to increase their inventory of deliverable strategic warheads beyond the limits of SALT II.

We could reconvert and reload eight *Polaris* submarines that were never scrapped when they were retired, but instead have undergone conversion for use as attack submarines.[18] We could add four more warheads to each *Minuteman III* missile, a configuration already flight-tested sufficiently to qualify it, by SALT II standards, as an operational system.[19]

We could even deploy more *Minuteman IIIs*. To those we now have deployed, General Alton Slay, former Air Force Chief of Research and Development, pointed out that "we already have on the books some 123 *Minuteman III* missiles that we could deploy if the occasion should arise."[20] There is no shortage of silos in which to place them. We could reactivate and convert for the *Minuteman III* any of 177 former *Atlas* and *Titan I* silos located across the United States.

We could do all this in much less time than it would take for the Soviets to deploy a new weapon system. The Soviets already expressed their concern in 1975 about the "possible reactivation time" for *Atlas* and *Titan I* silos, which had not been dismantled in accordance with procedures defined in the Interim SALT Agreement in 1972. But the United States took the view that these silos were "deactivated prior to the Interim Agreement and were not subject to that agreement or to accompanying procedures for dismantling or destruction."[21]

Nevertheless, there was considerable public doubt about how quickly we could respond to new Soviet strategic weapons developments. There was even doubt about how well we could *observe* them. That was because the Reagan administration had done its best to raise such doubts, and to exploit public ignorance of our real capabilities for monitoring and verifying Soviet compliance with the provisions of SALT II and other treaties. This allowed the administration to suggest that the Soviets might violate those provisions without our being aware; that, in turn, validated the concern with Soviet throwweight, and enabled it to imply that Soviet throwweight still posed a potential threat.

In fact, as Representative Les Aspin has pointed out, "the verification capabilities of the U.S. are excellent" for "observing Russian missile tests," or any other stage of weapons development and deployment in the Soviet Union. That is because these capabilities are based on "national technical means" of surveillance that are "multiple, redundant and complementary."[22]

These include *Big Bird,* KH-9 and KH-11 photographic and multispectral scanning satellites, which produce and instantaneously relay a continuous flow of detailed images of every square inch of Soviet territory by day or night, and active imaging radar satellites, which produce the same images, at almost the same level of detail, when clouds obscure the view for the others. They include a network of over-the-horizon radars that have been tracking and measuring Soviet missiles in test flights at ranges of thousands of miles since at least 1955. They include more than 4,000 electronic ground intercept stations, a large fleet of intelligence ships, and a force of more than 400 specialized reconnaissance aircraft to perform photomapping and collect radar, signals, and telemetry intelligence from every border of the Soviet Union. They include electromagnetic satellites, from orbiting *Ferrets* to geostationary *Rhyolites,* which record and instantaneously relay every electronic signal broadcast anywhere in the Soviet Union.[23]

No object of military significance moves in the Soviet Union that we do not see. No sound is made on Soviet airwaves that we do not hear. That is why Harold Brown, President Carter's Secretary of Defense, could say of SALT II: "We are confident that no significant violation of the treaty could take place without the United States detecting it."[24]

Finally, the Reagan administration and its supporters talked of the higher aggregate megatonnage in explosive yield produced by the weapons Soviet strategic forces could deliver. The Soviets "outnumber the United States," General Graham announced, by "5 to 1 in deliverable megatonnage."[25] That, too, was an exaggeration. The actual Soviet lead, by this measure, was 3 to 2.[26] But even if it had been as high as General Graham claimed, it had no military significance. It provided Soviet forces with no more advantages than higher throwweight did. It did nothing to counter the lead in numbers of warheads America possessed.

Weapons of higher yield merely provide an excess of destructive capability.

Comparative Measures of the Balance of Strategic Power, December, 1982: What Different Comparisons Imply and What They Hide

Type of Comparison	Example USA	Example USSR	Impression Created and Underlying Assumptions	What Comparison Hides
Delivery Vehicles	1924	2502	USSR either has more weapons, or it has the means to carry them to more targets.	Smaller US force of bombers and missiles carries 10,880 weapons, 4235 more than larger Soviet force carries. All can be delivered to separate targets. US can therefore attack 4235 more targets.
Throwweight (millions of lbs)	10.4	13.2	USSR has more weapons, or bigger weapons, or both. Bigger weapons are better weapons.	US has more weapons, and can attack 4235 more targets. Bigger weapons are not necessarily more effective, and may only be less efficient. US weapons are more efficient and better miniaturized. Consequently, they are smaller and lighter than Soviet weapons of equivalent power.
Megatonnage	3847	5825	USSR has more weapons, or more powerful ones, or both. Their higher aggregate yield in megatons gives Soviet forces the greater destructive capacity.	US has more weapons, and can attack 4235 more targets. Destructive capacity depends more on accuracy than on explosive yield. US weapons are more accurate. US can deliver a minimum of 3356 weapons whose individual lethality against the hardest targets is rated at 50% or higher; USSR has only 320 weapons of equivalent lethality. Higher yields of Soviet weapons are an unsuccessful attempt to compensate for their inferior accuracy.
Ballistic Missiles	1596	2367	Missiles are better delivery vehicles than bombers, and USSR has more of them.	US bombers are the most effective delivery vehicles in either nation's arsenal. The individual lethality of every one of the 2456 weapons they carry is rated at 87% or higher against the hardest targets. By eliminating all bombers, comparison omits 20% of all US weapons but only 3% of Soviet weapons, understating US strength more than it understates Soviet strength, and thus artificially reducing US lead. Smaller force of US missiles still carries 1979 more warheads than larger Soviet missile force, and can therefore attack 1979 more targets. Full US force can attack 4235 more targets.
Missile Warheads	8424	8337	US leads by only 87 warheads. This minimal lead must be assumed, as USSR may have exploited its full potential capacity to add	Comparison is asymmetric, juxtaposing maximum hypothetical Soviet capacity for additional warheads with actual number of US missile warheads deployed. Verification capability is more than adequate to determine actual number of Soviet warheads deployed. USSR has not utilized its maximum capacity. USSR deploys no more than 6445 warheads on its missiles at this time. US continues

to lead, with 1979 more missile warheads. If US were to exploit the full capacity of its own missiles, and the maximum hypothetical number of warheads they could carry were compared with the hypothetical Soviet number, the US lead would only further expand to 2287 more missile warheads.

Parity did not exist 10 years ago. US had already built 41 strategic ballistic missile submarines before that time. US continues to hold the large lead it has always held in the number of nuclear warheads deployed by the missiles aboard its submarines. US missiles at sea deploy 4631 more warheads than Soviet sea-based missiles do at this time. While more Soviet submarines are newer, they are not better. Readiness rate of all US submarines is 66% or higher, while that of even the newest Soviet submarines is no more than 33%. Reliability rate of US missiles at sea is 80% or higher, while that of Soviet missiles at sea is no more than 75%. US has not failed to modernize. In past 10 years, it has introduced 8312 newer, more accurate and more lethal nuclear warheads and bombs as replacements or additions to its strategic forces.

While US leads in accuracy and reliability suggest US forces are more likely to destroy a greater proportion of the targets they attack, the outcome of any attack can never be certain, and the risks of failure will always be too high. Neither the nation can ever be sure it will destroy a sufficient number of targets to avoid receiving unacceptable levels of damage in retaliation.

			more warheads to its missiles, and US verification capability is inadequate to assure otherwise.
			Parity existed 10 years ago. As a result, USSR now has more weapons, and it has better ones since none of them are newer.
Newer Equipment (strategic submarines built in last 10 yrs)	2	33	
All Deliverable Strategic Nuclear Weapons	10,880	6645	US can attack 4235 more targets than USSR can. Therefore, US can *destroy* 4235 more targets.

Sources

Figures for the numbers of delivery vehicles, ballistic missiles, and deliverable nuclear weapons in American and Soviet strategic forces are taken from the table *Composition of American and Soviet Strategic Forces, December, 1982,* in Appendix A: Summary and Analysis. This appendix develops the author's estimate of the strategic balance, based on a consensus of available estimates from public sources, and on critical information overlooked by those sources but also available in the public domain. Figures for aggregate throwweight and megatonnage of American and Soviet strategic forces are taken from the table *Comparative Measures of Strategic Power* in Appendix A.

Hypothetical figures for maximum loads not yet attained on Soviet and American ballistic missiles are from the table *Hypothetical Composition of American and Soviet Strategic Forces, December, 1982* in Appendix A: Summary and Analysis. This table shows the number of nuclear weapons American and Soviet strategic forces could deliver if all operational aircraft were loaded to maximum capacity and all missiles fitted with the maximum number of warheads allowed by SALT II, or with any higher number already deployed.

Lethality ratings of American and Soviet nuclear weapons are computed on the basis of formulas provided by Kosta Tsipis, *Offensive Missiles:*

(continued)

Comparative Measures of the Balance of Strategic Power, December, 1982: What Different Comparisons Imply and What They Hide (*cont.*)

Stockholm Paper 5, Stockholm International Peace Research Institute (Stockholm: Almqvist & Wiksell, 1974), page 18. Reliability rates for all Soviet and American missiles are from the Senate Armed Services Committee, *Hearings, Department of Defense, Fiscal Year 1981*, Part 2, page 459, and from Robert Aldridge, *First Strike!* (Boston: South End Press, 1983), page 56. Readiness rates for all Soviet and American submarines are from the Congressional Budget Office, *Modernizing U.S. Strategic Offensive Forces*, May, 1983, page 95.

For America's ability to determine the actual numbers of Soviet missile warheads and other weapons deployed, and its capability to verify Soviet adherence to the provisions of SALT II and other treaties, see the sections in this book on *Violations of Salt II, Verification, On-Site Inspection*, and *Telemetry*, and the table *United States Military Satellite Systems* in Appendix I: Verification.

By releasing greater blast forces and higher amounts of heat over larger areas, they might produce greater levels of *unintended* destruction more quickly than weapons of lower yield. But in even a limited exchange of nuclear weapons, the radioactive fallout from those of much lower yield would eventually—and inexorably—take just as high a toll of human lives. The higher yield of many Soviet weapons, like the higher Soviet missile throwweight to which they contributed, was simply an attempt to compensate for their inferior accuracy. In this, it was no more successful than larger missiles had been.

"In megatonnage, the Soviets are way ahead," Paul Warnke, director of the Arms Control and Disarmament Agency in the Carter administration, agreed. But he added that "it doesn't make a damn bit of difference," because "we have roughly 10,000 strategic nuclear warheads," whereas "the Soviets have 7,000. We're way ahead."[27]

Indeed we were. Here are the maximum numbers of warheads Soviet strategic forces could deliver, and the minimum numbers American forces could deliver, in the period of Soviet "superiority" President Reagan had promised:[28]

Year	USA	USSR
1981	10,330	6203
1982	10,733	6521
1983	10,973	6769
1984	11,657	7370
1985	11,857	7865

18 Misrepresenting the Balance of Strategic Warheads

As the greater significance of comparative warhead counts over all other measures of strategic power became increasingly evident, the administration's refusal to provide such counts grew increasingly suspect, and threatened the credibility of its claim that the Soviets held a margin of superiority. It had to begin to offer such counts, yet it also had to support its claim. The only way to do both was to offer counts which did not reveal that it was America that held the lead. The only way to do that was to offer incomplete comparisons, counting weapons only in some categories, while justifying the exclusion of weapons in others.

The most useful category of weapons to exclude, in order to create the impression of a reduced American lead, was bomber weapons. Bomber weapons comprised over 20 percent of America's strategic arsenal, but only 3 percent of the Soviet Union's.[1] Eliminating bomber weapons would therefore understate America's strength far more than it understated Soviet strength. Their elimination from warhead comparisons could be justified by the familiar claim that they were obsolete, a claim already used to justify development and production of a new bomber, the B-1.

President Reagan was fond of saying that "our B-52 bombers are older than many of the pilots who fly them."[2] This neglected the fact that almost every piece of every one of our B-52s had been replaced by new parts that were a good deal younger than any of the pilots who flew them. As a result, Strategic Air Command officials acknowledged, "the B-52s will be structurally sound through the late 1990s."[3]

Over the past twenty years, we had spent more than $3.4 billion to upgrade the offensive avionics, weapons delivery, and electronic countermeasures systems for our B-52s. Over the next fifteen years, as our new B-1 bombers grew "older" than the pilots who would eventually fly them, we would spend another $7.7 billion on our B-52s.[4] This money was not going to be spent on "obsolete" aircraft; it was going to be spent to modernize existing aircraft and keep them from becoming obsolete. The new B-1 was not a "force modernization." It was a force expansion.

The result of all the money we continue to spend on our B-52s is that, despite the administration's emphasis on the formidable power of Soviet air defenses, at least half of the B-52 force, armed with Cruise missiles, is expected to penetrate them.[5]

The best-kept secret of all, as the Reagan administration moved to minimize the importance of our bomber forces and exclude them from force comparisons, was that they were the most effective weapon system we had. Certainly, our missiles were effective. Certainly, they were more effective than Soviet missiles. Against Soviet missile silos hardened to withstand 3,000 pounds per square inch of blast overpressure, the lethality of each of our most accurate reentry vehicles, the MK-12As mounted on our *Minuteman IIIs,* was rated at 55 percent.[6] Against American missile silos hardened to resist 2,000 pounds per square inch of over-pressure, the lethality of each of the most accurate Soviet reentry vehicles, those mounted on the SS-18 Mod 4 and the SS-19 Mod 1, were rated, respectively, at 40 and 42 percent.[7]

However, against the same Soviet targets, the individual lethality of every one of the weapons carried by America's bomber forces was rated at 87 percent or higher; most of them were rated at 99 percent.[8] The reason was accuracy.

Our bombers could deliver their nuclear gravity bombs with the same precision achieved by our most accurate reentry vehicles.[9] Our air-launched missiles were even more accurate. The AGM-69A Short Range Attack Missile (SRAM) could strike within 300 feet of its target. The AGM-68A Air-Launched Cruise Missile (ALCM) could strike within 100 feet of its target.[10]

At the end of 1982, our bomber forces carried a total of 2,456 nuclear weapons, all of them more lethal than any missile warhead.[11]

These were the weapons the Reagan administration excluded in all the comparative counts it initially offered of strategic warheads. The problem was that even when it excluded them, counting missile warheads only, America *still* led by a wide margin, with 8,233 missile warheads in mid-1982 compared to 6,321 such warheads at that time for the Soviet Union.[12] A means had to be found for creating the impression that America's total of missile warheads was lower, and that the Soviet Union's was higher.

The most promising means of lowering America's total was to continue to overlook some or all of the 1,216 *Poseidon* warheads that were added to the fleet ballistic missile force between 1980 and 1982. They were added as 10 older *Polaris* submarines were retired, removing the equivalent of 160 targetable warheads from the fleet inventory, and as newer *Trident I* missiles, with fewer warheads but longer ranges, replaced 192 *Poseidon* missiles on 12 *Poseidon* submarines.

Until that time, *Poseidon* missiles had carried an average of ten warheads each;[13] the newer *Trident I* missiles carried only eight.[14] This caused a further net reduction of 384 warheads in the fleet inventory.

So, in 1980, the Defense Department announced it was increasing the number of warheads carried by each remaining *Poseidon* missile "to 14 from 10," and that this increase "more than offsets the effect" of other reductions in the fleet inventory.[15]

The decision was not surprising. Former missile systems engineer Robert Aldridge noted that "*Poseidon* missiles were originally deployed with two warhead 'mixes': the full load of 14 on some missiles to reach targets within 2,500 nautical miles, and a reduced load of 10 warheads on others to achieve greater ranges for destroying targets farther away. Since the longer range *Trident I* missiles have been backfitted into twelve *Poseidon* submarines and can cover the farther targets, it seems logical that the remaining nineteen *Poseidon* submarines would carry a full load."[16]

With a full load of fourteen warheads, the *Poseidon* missile's range was indeed only 2,880 statute miles, the equivalent of the range Aldridge gave in nautical miles. With only ten warheads, the *Poseidon* was able to expand that range to 3,200 statute miles. But the *Trident I* did eliminate this requirement for a reduced payload on *Poseidon* missiles to reach more distant targets—it had a range of 4,870 miles.[17]

A total of 304 *Poseidon* missiles on 19 submarines would remain in the fleet. Before their loads were increased, they had disposed a total of 3,040 warheads. But after their loads were increased from 10 to 14 warheads each, they would dispose a total of 4,256 warheads. The Stockholm International Peace Research Institute (SIPRI) noted that this increase "will add a total of 1,216 warheads to the US SLBM force in the early 1980s."[18]

These 1,216 warheads were duly added. This was confirmed by the Deputy Chief of Naval Operations;[19] it was confirmed by the House Appropriations Committee of Congress;[20] it was confirmed by the House Armed Services Committee.[21]

Yet even though this addition had been officially and repeatedly confirmed, it went virtually unreported. Out of 26 major reporting sources surveyed between 1980 and 1983, from the Department of Defense to the International Institute for Strategic Studies and major news organizations, 19 ignored this addition entirely, reporting 1,200 fewer warheads than we had in the fleet at the time, while the remaining 7 sources only partially acknowledged it, reporting 400 to 600 fewer warheads than our fleet then possessed.[22]

Thus, in the first comparative count of warheads the Reagan Administration offered, it acknowledged only some of our added *Poseidon* warheads, giving America a total of 7,450 missile warheads on land and at sea, rather than the 8,233 we had at the time. The occasion for release of this figure, in May, 1982, was a press briefing by administration officials, accompanying the President's announcement of his START proposal for strategic arms reductions.[23]

At the same time that it gave America 7,450 missile warheads, the administration gave the Soviet Union 7,400, almost exactly the same number.[24] This was an important admission, though only a temporary one, that the Soviets did not lead in numbers of missile warheads, and that an impression of Soviet superiority could not be built on the claim that they did.

However, the figure the administration gave for Soviet missile warheads could only be achieved by assuming the Soviets had placed many more multiple warheads on their missiles than any evidence indicated. At the same time, the administration had to create the public impression that we could only make estimates based on such assumptions, because we had no way of knowing how many warheads the Soviets actually *had* deployed. That, in turn, once again required exploiting public ignorance of the fact that we *did* know.

Every missile tested with different numbers of MIRVs (Multiple Independently targetable Reentry Vehicles) had observable differences in size, shape, weight, and the materials used in its construction. These were noted when it was tested, and noted when it was deployed. "U.S. analysts already know from extensive observation," Les Aspin points out, "which Russian missiles are MIRVed." He adds that "future MIRV-capable ICBMs and SLBMs can be detected at the test stage." He also notes that "Russian silos that contain MIRV-capable missiles are significantly different in appearance from those that contain un-MIRVed missiles," and that "MIRVed launchers require different command-and-control systems, support equipment and other facilities, all of which are observable with existing U.S. satellites."[25]

We knew every type of missile deployed. Each modification of the Soviet SS-18 or SS-19 or any other missile had observable differences. We knew the number of each type deployed. From the number of reentry vehicles a particular missile type released in its tests, we knew the number of warheads it would carry when it was deployed.

Although no evidence supported an "estimate" of Soviet missile warheads so high as the one the administration now gave, a great deal of evidence contradicted it. And the most significant evidence of all was testimony given by Defense Department officials in Congress only a week before the President announced his START proposal.

While these officials did all they could to give the highest possible figure for deliverable Soviet strategic warheads, including in that figure the weapons ostensibly carried by Soviet Tu-22M *Backfire* bombers, even though the State Department acknowledged the *Backfire* was limited only to the "theater and anti-ship role," and that we could verify any change in its deployment "with confidence,"[26] the maximum number of warheads they could attribute at that time to Soviet missiles, both on land and at sea, was 6,300.[27]

This was 1,100 fewer Soviet warheads than administration officials would claim in press briefings a few days later.

It was also an important official acknowledgment that the Soviet MIRV program was proceeding no more rapidly than it ever had since it first began five years after our own. The Defense Department's figure of 6,300 Soviet missile warheads in May, 1982, almost perfectly matches the estimate of 6,321 Soviet missile warheads in June, 1982, given in this book.[28]

According to this estimate, in the four years examined from 1979 through 1983, the Soviets have increased the numbers of MIRVed warheads on their missiles at an average rate of 325 per year. If they were to continue at that rate, it would take them until 1989 before they had fitted all their existing missiles with the maximum number of 8,637 warheads allowed by SALT II.

Nevertheless, early in 1983 President Reagan announced that "over the past year," since his administration told the press it had counted 7,400 Soviet missile warheads, "the Soviets have deployed over 1,200 intercontinental ballistic missile warheads."[29] That came to a total of 8,600 warheads.

In less than a year, it seemed, the Soviet Union had increased its inventory of missile warheads by almost 17 percent over the administration's previous figure, and by almost 40 percent over the maximum number the Defense Department could substantiate at that time. It now had 2,300 more warheads than the Defense Department said it had only ten months earlier. In less than a year, it had placed on its missiles the maximum number of warheads allowed by SALT II, a number it normally would have taken another six years to reach.

Not only did this strain credibility. Once again, all the evidence contradicted it. The President's statement could only be true if all of the following conditions prevailed: no Soviet SS-17, SS-18, or SS-19 missile could any longer exist with a single warhead. Every SS-18 had to be of the Mod 4 variety with the maximum of ten warheads each allowed by SALT II; none of the Mod 2 variety with only eight warheads each could any longer remain. All 208 of the SS-N-18 submarine-launched missiles then in service had to be of the Mod 3 variety with seven warheads each; none with only three warheads each could remain.

But of those sources which offered breakdowns of the numbers of missiles of each type deployed by the Soviet Union from 1979 through the date of the President's statement in 1983, only four reported any SS-N-18s with seven warheads.[30] The International Institute for Strategic Studies (IISS) reported half the SS-N-18s with seven warheads each, but the other half with only three warheads each.[31]

Only three sources offering breakdowns of land-based missiles in the same period reported SS-18s with ten warheads, and they only reported a very few. All reported a preponderance of SS-18s with eight warheads.[32] The IISS based its estimate "on the assumption that the bulk of SS-18 are Mod 2," with eight warheads each.[33] Almost all sources reported substantial numbers of SS-18s and SS-19s with a *single* warhead.[34]

This was not surprising. Until the Soviets had made significant advances in missile technology not now within their reach, there was every reason to think they would keep their missiles with single warheads, especially their newer and somewhat more accurate SS-18s and SS-19s.

A single warhead could reach targets out of range of a multiple payload, because it weighed less. The more warheads a missile carried, the more their weight reduced its range. This consideration was not critical for missiles at sea; most of the time, they could move within range of their targets. But missiles on land, for the present, were fixed in one place.

This consideration was no longer critical for any of America's missiles: our land-based missiles could reach any target in the Soviet Union. What went wholly ignored, however, was that many Soviet land-based missiles could *not* reach any target in the United States. Soviet SS-18s with multiple warheads had a maximum range of 5,500 miles. Every one of America's 1,000 *Minuteman* missiles had a range of 8,000 miles.[35]

If the Soviet land-based missile force was to have any flexibility in retargeting, a significant portion of it would have to be dedicated to achieving the maximum possible range. The best way to ensure that was to limit its throwweight to a minimum. This meant single warheads. A single warhead on the SS-18 Mod 3 raised its range to 6,500 miles;[36] that was the best any Soviet missile could do. It was no match for the capabilities of American missiles, but it was a distinct improvement.

Until their ranges could be increased by improvements in their propulsion systems and reductions in their size and weight, Soviet SS-18s and SS-19s with single warheads were more than likely here to stay.

That is why Defense Intelligence Agency officials, more than a year after the President's announcement of an unprecedented increase in Soviet missile warheads, told researchers William Arkin and Jeffrey Sands that a number of Soviet missiles "are still configured to carry single warheads," and that "current force loading is actually below" the level of Soviet warhead estimates the Pentagon was offering at the time, "taking into consideration actual single warhead deployments."[37]

The Soviet Union had no more fitted its missiles with the maximum number of multiple warheads allowed by SALT II than America had. Ronald Reagan's figures for Soviet missile warheads were no more correct in 1984 than they had been in 1983.

For the most part, of course, the general public remained unaware that the administration had heavily inflated the figures for Soviet missile warheads. The public was more often exposed to publications like *Soviet Military Power,* compiled annually by the Pentagon and widely quoted and reproduced by the mainstream media, than it was to the work of independent analysts like Arkin and Sands, which gained relatively little attention. The 1984 edition of *Soviet Military Power,* like each edition before it, neglected to mention that a number of Soviet missiles capable of being fitted with multiple warheads were still deployed with single warheads. The Defense Department explained that this information had been omitted due to "space considerations."[38]

The public was aware, however, that the administration's figures comparing the warheads in Soviet and American strategic arsenals omitted bomber weapons, just as all of its negotiating proposals omitted them. A portion of the public was also aware that our bombers carried a formidable arsenal of such weapons, whereas the Soviet bomber force did not.

The administration had to respond to criticism that it had left out of its comparisons the most important component of our strategic arsenal. It also had to challenge that evaluation by minimizing the importance of this component. In quantitative terms, America's bomber weapons should not be too numerous, or they would reveal the true extent of America's lead. In qualitative terms, the true range and potential lethality of the Cruise missiles deployed on our bombers should not be too well publicized, or these capabilities would reveal the extent of our technological edge, and of the new military threat we posed, to which the Soviet Union simply had no counterpart.

So the administration gave the range of the Air-Launched Cruise Missile (ALCM) as 1,553 miles,[39] whereas in fact the range of the current second-generation ALCM is already 2,473 miles,[40] and will soon be nearly 3,000 miles.[41] Meanwhile, it warned of impending Soviet "long-range" cruise missile development. That development would surely come, just as the Soviet Union has promised, in response to deployments we have already made.

By giving a lower range than the true one for our current generation of cruise missiles, the 1984 edition of *Soviet Military Power* was able to make their range seem lower than the anticipated range of Soviet cruise missiles with which it compared them, though it had to concede that these Soviet missiles were only "in development." The range it gave for the Soviet missiles was 1,864 miles.[42] That was approximately the range our first generation of cruise missiles had.[43] Meanwhile, the longest range reported for any Soviet cruise missile now deployed was 620 miles.[44]

In its official briefings, the administration reduced the size of the nuclear arsenal America's bombers carried from 2,392 in 1980 to only 1,500 in 1982,[45] whereas this force carried a minimum of 2,456 weapons in 1982, and was capable of carrying as many as 3,892.[46]

At the same time, the administration revived the threat of the Soviet *Backfire* bomber, even though it knew the *Backfire* was neither equipped nor deployed as a strategic bomber. It loaded the *Backfire* with more weapons than it was capable of carrying, including an extra AS-4 air-to-surface nuclear standoff missile. And it published a photograph of the *Backfire,* announcing that it could carry "two wing-mounted AS-4s on the pylons visible in the photo."[47]

The photo showed the wing pylons, but it did not show any AS-4s mounted on them. It showed only one missile, mounted under the aircraft's fuselage. No photo can be found that does show more than one. There is an excellent reason for this: the *Backfire* can carry only one.

The AS-4 missile weighs 12,100 pounds.[48] The load capacity of the *Backfire* is 17,500 pounds.[49] Two AS-4 missiles would exceed that. Of the AS-6 missile, which the *Backfire* may also carry,[50] one aerospace analyst notes that "the weapon appears to be larger than first reported, and is more suited to a single installation, like that of the AS-4 on the Tu-22. Armament of the *Backfire*," he concluded, "is likely to comprise a single AS-4 or AS-6."[51]

Nevertheless, the administration continued to claim that the *Backfire* carried two such missiles, or as many as four nuclear gravity bombs on "long-range missions," even though out of nineteen sources surveyed between 1979 and 1983, only five reported the *Backfire* as a strategic bomber at all, and only five reported more than two weapons of any kind carried by any Soviet aircraft, including those with greater load capacities than the *Backfire* had. The International Institute for Strategic Studies reported no more than two; not even the Joint Chiefs of Staff reported more than two.[52]

By including the *Backfire* among strategic bombers, and by inflating the load it could carry, the administration was able to raise the total of weapons carried by the Soviet strategic bomber force from 300 in 1980 to 1,000 in 1982.[53] It did this in the same briefings it had used to reduce America's bomber weapons, by that time, to 1,500. In strategic power, the Soviet bomber force began to look as though it could match our own. That was the whole idea. In fact, it was doubtful whether the actual force of one hundred prop-driven Tu-95A *Bear* and thirty-five MyA-4 *Bison* aircraft would carry any more than two hundred nuclear weapons to intercontinental ranges.[54]

Seventy of the Soviet Union's Tu-95A *Bears* carry the AS-3 *Kangaroo* nuclear standoff missile.[55] The AS-3 is an even larger missile than the AS-4; *Jane's Missiles* notes that it is "of much the same size" as a fighter aircraft.[56] In fact, as William Koenig notes, it is "derived from the SU-7 *Fitter A* aircraft."[57] It weighs 24,200 pounds.[58] No Soviet aircraft but the *Bear* can carry it. When it does, it can carry only one, and nothing else; a single AS-3 takes up 96 percent of the *Bear*'s load capacity.[59] Consequently, only sixty-five *Bears* and *Bisons* remain to carry more than a single weapon to targets in the United States.

The question also arose of whether the *Backfire* really could be considered a "long-range" aircraft. Though the Stockholm International Peace Research Institute had pointed out that the *Backfire* "has been publicly recognized in US intelligence estimates as having less than intercontinental range,"[60] the administration and its supporters did their best to imply that it did have such a range, while at the same time they implied that one of our own bombers, the FB-111A, did not.

They did this by misinterpreting data about each aircraft's range, as the table on page 106 shows. The combat range of the FB-111A, well established at 4,700 miles before the administration took office, soon appeared in many sources as 4,700 kilometers, the equivalent of only 2,920 miles. The combat range of the *Backfire,* originally established as 3,600 miles on the basis of a McDonnell Douglas study commissioned by the CIA in 1975, and reconfirmed as the aircraft's true range by the White House in 1976,[61] was soon reinterpreted as its combat radius. In 1983, *Air Force Magazine* gave it a combat radius of 3,400 miles. An aircraft's combat radius is only half its range, so this implied that the *Backfire*'s range was double that distance, or 6,800 miles.[62]

In this way, the *Backfire* was qualified as a strategic bomber, so that the inclusion of more weapons than it could carry in comparative counts of the balance of strategic weapons seemed justified. At the same time, the exclusion of the FB-111A and its weapons from such counts also seemed justified, even though the FB-111A's speed of 1,650 miles per hour, higher than that of any other strategic aircraft, and the accuracy of the Short Range Attack Missiles it normally carried, made it one of the most lethal weapon systems in our arsenal.[63] "Due to its high speed, small size and low level terrain following capability," several researchers noted in summarizing a Senate Armed Services Committee evaluation of this aircraft, "the FB-111 will remain a better penetrator than the B-52 through the 1990s."[64] If 50 percent of our B-52s would penetrate Soviet air defenses, then a higher number of FB-111As would penetrate them.

For those who were able to learn that the *Backfire*'s range was only 3,600 miles, and doubted that it could then pose any strategic threat, the administration had a fallback position: with aerial refueling, the bomber could still be used on "one-way missions" against targets in the United States. By that token, however, hundreds of additional American aircraft not now deployed as strategic bombers, but with much greater load capacities than any Soviet bomber, could do exactly the same. Which nation was the more capable of refueling its bombers in flight? The United States had 615 KC-135 tanker aircraft;[65] the Soviet Union had 48.[66]

Early in 1984 the administration tried again to create the impression of a Soviet lead in warheads, by releasing an estimate of the total of nuclear weapons in the Soviet stockpile. This estimate, presented to the House Appropriations Committee by Assistant Secretary of Defense for Atomic Affairs Richard Wagner,[67] included short-range and "tactical" weapons, most of which could not even be delivered by Soviet strategic forces.

But even as a count of all the nuclear weapons the Soviet Union possessed, the estimate was heavily inflated. That was because it had been based on a variety of assumptions which all the available evidence only contradicted. The most serious of these was that the Soviets had built much larger numbers of *reload* weapons than America had, though no evidence of this existed. Nor could the Soviets have thought that building so many reload weapons was a sensible investment. They knew as well as we did that in a nuclear war few weapons delivery systems were likely to survive long enough to be reloaded.

The estimate was further inflated by its assumption that all Soviet missiles had been fitted with multiple warheads to the maximum allowable extent, even though the Defense Department knew and concurrently acknowledged that this was not the case, and by the assumption that large numbers of nuclear gravity bombs had been built to arm every Soviet aircraft deemed capable of carrying them.

The Soviets could not have assigned a much larger portion of their available strike aircraft to nuclear weapons delivery than we had assigned of our own, without neglecting other missions aircraft must perform. A similar assumption about our own stockpile would have added several thousand more nuclear gravity bombs to those we already had.

Nevertheless, by these means Assistant Secretary Wagner produced an estimate of 34,000 nuclear weapons in the Soviet stockpile.[68] Though only a fraction of this number could ever be used against strategic targets at intercontinental ranges, and though no evidence supported the claim that a very large portion of it even existed, the administration could hope that release of this figure would *imply* a Soviet strategic lead.

It was not disappointed. "Soviets Leading in Warheads, Pentagon Claims in Reversal," an article in *The Washington Post* announced.[69] "Soviets Said to Lead U.S. by 8,000 Warheads," *The New York Times* proclaimed.[70] *Times* correspondent Richard Halloran had arrived at this margin for the Soviet Union's lead by comparing Wagner's estimate of 34,000 weapons in the Soviet stockpile with a figure frequently quoted for the United States. "The United States, by comparison," he wrote, "had 26,000 warheads."[71]

The United States had a good many more than that. Halloran's figure was close to the number of *deployed* American warheads—those that could be launched as first rounds from available silos, gun tubes, and other launchers, and those that could be delivered in an initial sortie by available aircraft assigned to carry out nuclear strikes. But this figure did not include more than 12,800 additional warheads in America's stockpile that year.

When *deployed* weapons are compared, it is the United States which leads, by more than 11,500 warheads. When *stockpiled* weapons are compared, the United States leads again, this time by 20,000 warheads, as the accompanying estimates of both categories of weapons in Soviet and American arsenals show.[72]

These estimates allow weapons in the Soviet stockpile exactly the same margins of increase over weapons deployed as they allow weapons in America's stockpile, on the assumption that in both nations' arsenals these margins will provide sufficient spares to maintain the deployment levels shown.

Greater numbers of weapons for reloads are likely to have been provided only for air-launched and artillery-fired systems. That likelihood, too, is reflected in these estimates, though the likelihood of opportunities for the use of such weapons is barely more plausible than it is for nuclear reloads of any other kind.

Articles like Halloran's, of course, created the public impression of what researchers William Arkin and Jeffrey Sands called a "Warhead Gap." They found Wagner's estimate no less "contrived" than previous gaps and "past misrepresentations" that reflected a Soviet lead. They recalled that only a month before Wagner had presented his estimate, the Joint Chiefs of Staff, in their

Manipulating Perceptions of the Strategic Balance, 1975–83: The Reinterpretation of Range Characteristics to Qualify the Soviet Tu-22M/Tu-26 Backfire as a Strategic Bomber, and to Disqualify the American FB-111A

Tu-22M/Tu-26 *Backfire*

Combat Range in Statute Miles	Source and Date	Reinterpretation	Source and Date	Equivalent Combat Range in Statute Miles
3600	IISS 1975	Combat *radius* of 3400 statute miles	Air Force Magazine 1983	6800
3200	Sweetman 1981			

FB-111A

Combat Range in Statue Miles	Source and Date	Reinterpretation	Source and Date	Equivalent Combat Range in Statute Miles
4700	USAF 1977	Combat range of 4700 *kilometers*	IISS 1983	2920
4700	Tsipis 1983			

Sources

For the Tu-22M/Tu-26 *Backfire:* International Institute for Strategic Studies (IISS), *The Military Balance, 1975–1976* (London, 1975), page 72; Bill Sweetman, *The Presidio Concise Guide to Soviet Military Aircraft,* (Novato, Calif.: Presidio Press, 1981), page 177; *Air Force Magazine* (March, 1983), page 81. Sweetman gives the *Backfire* a maximum combat radius of 1,600 statute miles. For the FB-111A: United States Air Force proposals to extend the range of the FB-111A "to 5,700 nautical miles from the present 4,100," or to 6,550 statute miles from the present 4,700, quoted by Bernard Weinraub, "Air Force Urges Revival of FB-111 As a Long-Range Nuclear Weidenfeld & Nicolson, 1978), page 249. Here, a range of 3,570 miles is given.

In October, 1985, the Defense Intelligence Agency announced it had lowered its estimate of the *Backfire*'s range, claiming that it had originally estimated the aircraft had no more than an "unrefueled combat range of about 3,000 miles." See Michael R. Gordon, "Pentagon Reassesses Soviet Bomber," *The New York Times,* October 1, 1985. Gordon notes that "Officials were reluctant to give specific estimates of the bomber's revised range, but one ventured it could be about 20 percent less when fully loaded

Bomber," *The New York Times*, Sept. 7, 1977, and again by Weinraub, "Substitute for B-1 Sought in Addition to Cruise Missile," *The New York Times*, Sept. 20, 1977; Kosta Tsipis, *Arsenal: Understanding Weapons in the Nuclear Age* (New York: Simon & Schuster, 1983), page 152; IISS, *The Military Balance, 1983–1984* (London, 1983), page 120.

The Tu-22M *Backfire* range had originally been established at 3,600 miles on the basis of a McDonnell Douglas study commissioned by the CIA in 1975. This was reconfirmed as the aircraft's true range by the White House in 1976. See *Aviation Week & Space Technology*, Sept. 13, 1976, page 13. It is further confirmed not only by Sweetman but also by Michael J. H. Taylor and John W. R. Taylor, *Encyclopaedia of Aircraft* (London:

than the previous military intelligence figure." This would reduce the aircraft's range to 2,400 miles. "Pentagon officials," Gordon adds, "said the new projections indicated the plane could not carry out a round-trip mission against the United States without midair refueling. They also said the new estimates implied that it would be very difficult, if not impossible, for the aircraft to carry a large payload on a one-way mission and then land in Cuba after dropping its bombs. The intelligence reports also show that the *Backfire* lacks special probes needed for in-flight refueling. The officials added that the Soviet Union in any case did not have enough aerial tankers to refuel the *Backfire* and other aircraft on very long-range missions."

The Balance of Strategic Warheads, 1981–84: What Different Statements Imply and What They Hide

Date	Source	Example		What Statement Describes and Impression Created	What Statement Hides
		USA	USSR		
Sept. 1981	DOD		7000	Deliverable strategic warheads. USSR has a large number, possibly more than USA.	USA has 3875 more deliverable strategic warheads at this time, with 10,277 to 6402 for USSR. US can therefore attack 3875 more targets.
Mar. 1982	*NY Times*	6902	7400	Strategic missile warheads. USSR has more of them.	Comparison inflates Soviet figure with 1100 more warheads than DOD will substantiate two months later, and excludes from US figure more than 1300 warheads, most of which US Navy acknowledges were added to *Poseidon* fleet between 1980 and 1982. USA has 1912 more missile warheads at this time, with 8233 compared with 6321 for USSR.
May 1982	Reagan Admin.	7450	7400	Strategic missile warheads. Parity now exists. This is the only important measure of strategic power.	Parity does not exist. These figures restore only half the US warheads the Navy acknowledges were added to the *Poseidon* fleet between 1980 and 1982, and cite 1200 more Soviet missile warheads than *concurrent* DOD testimony substantiates. Corrected figures show that USA has 1912 more missile warheads at this time, with 8233 compared with 6321 for USSR. Missile warheads are not the only significant measure of strategic power. US bomber weapons are more effective. The individual lethality of every one of the 2500 weapons US bombers carry at this time is rated at 87% or higher against the hardest targets. By eliminating all bomber weapons, comparison omits 20% of all US weapons but only 3% of Soviet weapons, understating US strength more than it understates Soviet strength, and thus artificially reducing US lead. Full US strategic arsenal has 4212 more warheads at this time, with 10,733 to 6521 for USSR.

Date	Source				
Nov. 1982	NY Times	7100	7500	USSR leads in most important category of strategic power.	USA leads by 1979 warheads in this category alone, with 8424 missile warheads at this time to 6445 for USSR. This is not the most important category of strategic weapons. Bomber weapons are, and they have been excluded here. When they are restored, US leads at this time by 4235 deliverable strategic warheads of all types, with 10,880 to 6645 for USSR. US can therefore attack 4235 more targets.
Dec. 1982	NY Times	9100	10,000	Missile warheads and strategic delivery vehicles. USSR leads in all categories of strategic power.	Figures do not include all categories of strategic power. They omit bomber weapons, and in their place substitute delivery vehicles, adding 2500 Soviet bombers and missiles to 7500 Soviet missile warheads, and 2000 US bombers and missiles to 7100 US missile warheads.
					USA at this time has 1979 more missile warheads, with 8424 such weapons to 6445 for USSR. If delivery vehicles were added to these totals, US would have 10,348, the USSR 8947. If bomber weapons were then restored, USA would have a total of 12,804 weapons and vehicles, the USSR 9147. If delivery vehicles are excluded, as they should be, then US leads by 4235 deliverable strategic warheads of all types, with 10,880 to 6645 for USSR.
Apr. 1983	Reagan Admin.	8600		USSR has commanding lead over USA, whose last reported inventory of missile warheads was 7100 in 1982.	Figure is 2300 higher than number of Soviet missile warheads substantiated by DOD in 1982. Represents growth of almost 40% in entire Soviet missile warhead inventory in a single year. It is almost full total USSR could have if all missiles were fitted with maximum possible number of warheads allowed by SALT II.
					If all US missiles were fitted with maximum possible number of warheads allowed by SALT II, then US would lead USSR by 2053 missile warheads, with 10,690 to 8637 for USSR. Actual Soviet growth has been normal, with 269 more missile warheads in 1983 than total of 6300 DOD substantiated in 1982. That, however, is still 1756 fewer warheads than US total of 8325 at this time.

(continued)

The Balance of Strategic Warheads, 1981–84: What Different Statements Imply and What They Hide *(cont.)*

Date	Example				What Statement Describes and Impression Created	What Statement Hides
	Source	USA	USSR			
June 1984	*NY Times*	26,000	34,000		All nuclear warheads in stockpiles. All *might* be deliverable. USSR shows commanding lead of 8000.	Figures include warheads for tactical and theater as well as strategic systems. All could *not* be delivered by strategic forces. No more than 12,500 could be delivered by US strategic forces at this time, while fewer than 7000 could be delivered by Soviet strategic forces. Comparison is also asymmetric, almost doubling the number of weapons in Soviet stockpile by estimating many more reload weapons than evidence shows USSR has built, and many more than USSR could ever have the opportunity to use, and comparing this hypothetical figure for warheads in Soviet *stockpile* with a figure only slightly higher than number of US warheads *deployed*. If stockpiled warheads are compared, US leads by 20,001, with 37,657 to 17,656 for USSR. If deployed warheads are compared, US leads by 11,568, with 24,783 to 13,215 for USSR.

Sources

Statements are taken from the Department of Defense, *Soviet Military Power* (September, 1981), page 3; *The New York Times*, "Three Ways to Measure Strategic Forces," March 21, 1982; *The New York Times*, "Precise Arms Figures Difficult to Pin Down," May 10, 1982; *The New York Times*, "The Nuclear Balance Without MX," Nov. 28, 1982; *The New York Times*, "Nuclear Missiles and Bombers: A Balance Sheet," Dec. 22, 1982; Ronald Reagan, statement on the Report of the President's Commission on Strategic derived by the methods shown and based on the sources provided in Appendix A: The Strategic Balance. See the table, *Recapitulation: The Balance of Deliverable Strategic Warheads, 1979–85*, in Appendix A: Summary and Analysis.

Lethality ratings of American and Soviet nuclear weapons are computed on the basis of formulas provided by Kosta Tsipis, *Offensive Missiles: Stockholm Paper 5*, (Stockholm: Almqvist & Wiksell, 1974), page 18. The

Forces, reprinted by *The New York Times*, April 20, 1983; and Richard Halloran, "Soviets Said to Lead U.S. by 8,000 Warheads," *The New York Times*, June 18, 1984.

The Defense Department estimate of May, 1982, is from "U.S. and Soviet Strategic Arsenals," published by *The New York Times* on May 2, 1982. All other figures for the actual numbers of deliverable strategic warheads compared with the statements cited above are the author's estimates, individual lethality ratings, computed on this basis, of all significant Soviet and American nuclear weapons currently deployed may be found in Appendix D: Accuracy and Lethality.

Figures for totals of Soviet and American nuclear weapons of all types stockpiled and deployed are the author's estimates, derived by the methods shown and based on the sources provided in notes to Appendix F: Nuclear Weapons Stockpiled and Deployed by the Superpowers, 1982–84.

Fiscal Year 1985 Military Posture Statement, had reiterated that "the United States has more warheads."[73]

Arkin and Sands noted that Wagner's estimate "necessarily depends on an assumed high level of reloads," even though the Strategic Air Command had acknowledged that Soviet reload missiles would not be "compatible with existing silo launchers," the Defense Department had estimated that "reloading a significant fraction of the ICBM force" might take the Soviets "up to several weeks," and the Defense Intelligence Agency had informed them that reloading missiles at sea, as well, was "unlikely, if not impossible, during a nuclear war."[74]

They concluded that a more realistic estimate, based on no more reloads than the Soviets would have had any reason, let alone the resources, to build, and on the number of multiple warheads actually deployed on Soviet missiles, not on a hypothetical maximum figure the Pentagon has admitted was incorrect, could produce an estimate "as small as 18,000."[75] That is close to the estimate provided in the accompanying tables in this book.

19 Disseminating the Myth

Our government, because it controls the intelligence apparatus which collects our basic information about Soviet military forces and their capabilities, may claim the highest authority for whatever information it presents. So it does. That authority is recognized. "Official sources" are recognized as superior to all others.

Our government also wants to use the information it has to support its policies in whatever way it can. It will therefore *interpret* that information, shaping the way it is presented to emphasize certain facts over others, while excluding whatever facts contradict the conclusion it wishes the public to draw.

The Reagan administration's initial exclusion of all of our bomber weapons from its comparative counts of strategic weapons deliverable by the superpowers is a perfect example of this. Had all of our bomber weapons been included, the resulting comparisons would have led to conclusions the very *reverse* of what the administration intended.

This exclusion of relevant data may be noticed and even criticized, but that presents no lasting problem. So long as our government does not deny that we have a bomber force, or deny the truth of any other conflicting data, it can insist on its right to make whatever interpretations and selective presentations of existing data that it likes. So it makes them. If necessary, it is usually ready to explain why it makes them, and why incomplete comparisons are still "meaningful" and "fair."

That is why President Reagan repeatedly emphasized the age of our B-52s. This had no other purpose but to justify the absence of the weapons they carried in the administration's comparative counts. But often such explanations, even oblique ones of this kind that do not acknowledge why they are really being given, are not needed. It is usually enough to demonstrate that everything has at least been considered; many will then assume that the resulting comparison must be fair.

A problem can arise when there is no information to make the case government desires. An even larger problem arises when there is a great deal of information to contradict that case. In claiming the Soviet Union held military superiority, the Reagan administration faced both these problems. It nevertheless had to solve them, because its claim had to prevail, since it could not otherwise gain support for its massive increases in military spending. And that was the single objective to which this administration seemed most dedicated; indeed, that appeared to be its whole *raison d'être.*

There would be little problem if its claim were to go unchallenged. But, of course, that would not happen. This claim could not simply be made without what at least appeared to be evidence of some kind to support it. Government's word for it was not enough. History had painfully taught that government could not always be taken at its word. The impression of sincerity President Reagan conveyed was not enough, frequent though the administration's efforts were to tell the public that the public *thought* it was enough. So the administration embarked on the most intensive campaign this nation has seen to persuade the public by carefully chosen facts and figures that its claim was true.

But the numerous selective statements and incomplete comparisons with which it invaded the public consciousness throughout that campaign remained inconclusive. There emerged no clear measure by which the Soviets could be shown to hold that "definite" margin of superiority the President had claimed. This threatened to weaken his claim, and to throw his own credibility into question. It became tempting, therefore, to suggest that his claim was based on information to which the public had no access.

So that is exactly what the administration did suggest. When one of a group of students challenged the President, and questioned whether the Soviets really held military superiority, "he suggested," she reported, "that he as President had access to information that I don't have access to."[1]

The administration could only have such privileged access if it had failed at the same time to keep the public properly informed. But it soon became clear that it had no intention of keeping the public properly informed; instead, it did its best to make its suggestion of privileged access come true.

Because so much information existed to contradict its claim of Soviet superiority, the administration tried to ensure that the public would not have access to it. It strengthened the secrecy requirements, tightened the censorship laws, and maximized the penalties for all but the highest officials who failed to observe them.

Such actions gave the illusion of control over information. They encouraged the administration to lie freely in support of its claim, as it did by inflating the inventory of Soviet missile warheads, in the belief that no information would now surface to contradict it.

Yet this did not stop Congress, in 1982, from eliciting testimony by Defense Department officials who did contradict it. They could not substantiate the existence of 1,100 missile warheads the administration claimed the Soviet Union then possessed. It did not stop Defense Intelligence Agency officials, in 1984, from contradicting the administration again, by acknowledging that a number of Soviet missiles "are still configured to carry single warheads."[2] These were direct challenges to the administration's credibility.

The administration predictably responded by questioning the competence of the intelligence apparatus that collected our information. It relied again on public ignorance of the fact that our intelligence systems provided more comprehensive and detailed information on Soviet force levels and capabilities than estimates of this kind even needed.

We had a problem, the President now suggested, in "trying to verify what is going on" in Soviet missile development and deployment.[3] In this way, the administration deflected these challenges to its credibility, by suggesting there really was no means of knowing whether the Pentagon's figures or its own were the more correct, though by the same token its claims of Soviet superiority were weakened, for they now seemed based more on suspicion than certainty.

Those who subsequently disseminate the information government provides, from private research institutes to the press, bear many of these same risks, and some greater ones, in maintaining a reputation for the balance and authority of their work. Their enterprise would suffer without that reputation, but there are many pressures upon them to present work that is not balanced at all.

Chief among these is the pressure imposed by the primary source on which they rely so heavily for their information. For when government provides this information, it has already shaped it so that it will best support its policies and views. That is the shape in which government wants to see its information remain, in order to produce its desired effect on the wider public it means to reach.

For the most part, those who receive this information are perfectly well aware when it is unbalanced or incomplete. They know perfectly well that the purpose of this is to misrepresent the balance of power. For the most part, they are quite capable of finding and restoring missing information, or giving all facts their due prominence, to make what government gives them more balanced and complete. But when doing so contradicts official statements, as it would certainly do in this case, it also jeopardizes support for official policies.

When this happens, those responsible for it immediately find themselves in official disfavor. Their access to government as an information source is immediately threatened. News organizations in particular, if they lose access to that source, are placed at a serious disadvantage in the competition for news. They may certainly still collect the information they need, but the task of doing so is made much more difficult.

Government exerts a powerful *political* pressure, then, on those who rely upon it for information. They must support and disseminate its views.

Nor is the pressure from government equal to pressure from government's critics. Those who oppose official views, unless they may one day take their own place in government, have little influence over the press or private research organizations. It is much easier to minimize or ignore the information they emphasize. In this way, the acceptance of official views over those which contradict them becomes the more "responsible" course.

At the same time, the press and private research institutions cannot afford to present too little information. They cannot be accused of incompetence, and must demonstrate their competence, especially to their competitors. Without earning official disfavor, they must publish as much information as they can find and know to be accurate. Because they do not control the flow of information at its source, they cannot hope, as the Reagan administration has, to succeed in suppressing it. They cannot deny what they know to be true. They cannot omit information that is all too likely to surface elsewhere. Nor can they be accused of lacking "balance."

For all of these reasons, then, they must make the best effort they can to include information that *does* contradict official views. That is the paradox. But it is a simple one to solve. All they must learn to do is present this information as inconspicuously as possible. It is simply a matter of emphasis. Then, if called to account, they can demonstrate that they have not neglected conflicting information. But, of course, that is precisely what they have tried their best to do.

The weaker the government's case for its policies and views, the more the burden of making that case falls to the press and private institutions, and the greater the pressure on them to emphasize information supporting it and to suppress information contradicting it. This can lead to misrepresentations no less flagrant than government's own. That is precisely the situation the Reagan administration has produced among the most prominent and respected news and military research organizations in the West.

No private research institution specializing in military affairs has a higher reputation for authority, or a greater impact on public opinion in the West, than the London-based International Institute for Strategic Studies (IISS). One of its publications, *The Military Balance,* presents information at a high level of detail. It is highly compact, which makes it far more accessible than most other publications reporting the same information. It is updated and published on an annual basis. Consequently, it is used more than any other single source by news media throughout the West for current information on military force levels.

Much of the information *The Military Balance* provides *is* accurate. It can be a valuable source if the numerous qualifications it makes in its footnotes for the information it presents are carefully noted, and the substantial adjustments they call for are then made. But, of course, most of those who use it, especially in the press, have neither the time nor the inclination to examine its premises so carefully, certainly not when it has already found useful ways of misrepresenting the balance of power that only make their own task of supporting official views that much easier.

For that is what *The Military Balance* does. Its subtle emphasis and omissions, as Milton Leitenberg of the Swedish Institute of International Affairs observed, "have a clear bias. They uniformly *under*state the capabilities of the United States and of the West, and *over*state those of the Soviet Union."[4] The misrepresentations disseminated in *The Military Balance* have always played a central role in exaggerating the *conventional* threat posed to NATO by the Warsaw Pact, in order to gain public support for increased NATO military spending. Now they played a central role in supporting the Reagan administration's claim of Soviet *strategic* superiority. As always, they were widely repeated throughout the Western press.

The Institute's support of this new claim became evident the moment the Reagan administration was elected to office. In its 1978–79 edition of *The Military Balance,* published at the end of 1978, it had reported 11,000 deliverable strategic warheads for the United States, and 4,500 for the Soviet Union.[5] In its 1979–80 edition, it had again reported 11,000 for the United States, and 5,000 for the Soviet Union.[6] But in its 1980–81 edition, which appeared after the 1980 presidential election, it reported 7,301 warheads for the United States, and gave no figure for the Soviet Union, suggesting only that an increase of 1,000 warheads in the Soviet total "could potentially result" from the replacement of older missiles by newer ones.[7]

This reflected a very sudden and dramatic reduction in America's warhead inventory. Yet the Institute reported a loss of only 364 warheads in America's total, which it attributed to "a reduction in *Polaris A-3* and B-52 strengths." The loss of an additional 3,335 warheads from America's total the previous year went unexplained. Those who consulted this edition gained the impression that America possibly led the Soviet Union by only 1,301 warheads. Only a year earlier, it had led by 6,000.

The 1981–82 edition of *The Military Balance* restored some, though not all, of America's missing warheads. reporting a total of 9,000. But at the same time, it took the previous year's "potential" increase of 1,000 warheads for the Soviet Union to be accomplished fact, and reported a new increase of 1,000 additional Soviet warheads, for a total of 7,000. This time the Soviet increase, representing twice the growth rate the Institute had reported in 1978 and 1979, was said to be the result of "introducing MIRVed launchers to replace single-warhead launchers,"[8] though in fact the Soviets had begun to introduce MIRVed launchers six years earlier.

In its explanation for the sudden, though incomplete, restoration of American warheads missing the previous year, the Institute explained that the previous year's count had been of "missile-warheads only."[9] However, the previous year's count had not said that. In fact, it had implied that its count was not of missile warheads only, because it had explained a reduction in that count as the result of reductions in *Polaris A-3* and "B-52 strengths." The B-52 is not a missile. Mention of the B-52 in that edition gave those who consulted it no choice but to assume that bomber warheads were included in its count, and that 7,301 warheads were all the warheads America possessed that year.

In its current edition, the Institute reported a loss of only 272 American warheads. That still left the loss of another 1,364 warheads since 1979 unexplained.

In its 1982–83 edition, the Institute reported a loss of 304 American warheads, and other increases for a net total of 9,268; the loss of 1,060 additional warheads since 1979 still went unexplained.[10] If they had been restored at this point, the Institute's estimate would have been reasonably close to the estimate given in this book for the minimum number of America's deliverable strategic warheads at that time.

For the Soviet Union, the Institute reported the same total of 7,000 missile warheads it had reported for the previous year, remarking that Soviet missile warheads had only increased "marginally" since 1981. Including bomber weapons, it gave the Soviet Union a total of 7,300 deliverable warheads of all kinds. It did not include the *Backfire* among Soviet strategic bombers.[11]

In the 1983–84 edition, the Institute reverted to reporting missile warheads only, though this time it said that was what it was doing. That served to deflect subsequent criticism that it had created confusion, but did nothing to make it more possible to obtain a full total of strategic warheads, including bomber weapons. Bomber weapons had been omitted, and that was that.

The Institute reported a net gain in America's missile warheads that year, for a total of 7,297. It reported a small gain of 171 Soviet missile warheads over the previous year's total of 7,000, with "marginal" increases. We could now expect the current year's total to be 7,171, with "marginal" increases. But it was not. It was 8,342.[12]

This implied that the current year's increase of 171 warheads should be added not to the figure of 7,000 for the previous year, but to a figure of 8,171 for the previous year. But the previous year's edition had not *said* that 8,171 was the figure for that year; it had said that 7,000 was the figure for that year. That was 1,171 warheads fewer than the Institute was now saying that figure was.

Of course, the Institute had said that the previous year's figure was "marginally" increased over the total for the year before it. But an increase of 1,171 warheads, higher than any other the Institute had ever attributed to a single year's growth in the Soviet warhead inventory, could hardly be called a "marginal" increase.

There was no way to reconcile this sudden, retroactive, and unprecedented increase of 1,171 Soviet missile warheads in a single year. There was no way to understand it. At least, there was no way unless it was recalled that some months before the Institute had gone to press with this edition, President Reagan had declared that the Soviet Union had added more than 1,200 warheads to its missile force "over the past year."

The administration's statements were adhered to no less closely by the press. In 1982, in its issues of March 21, May 2, and June 29, respectively, *The New York Times* reported a decline in America's strategic bomber weapons from 2,500 to 2,100 to 1,500, and a simultaneous rise in Soviet strategic bomber weapons from 600 to 900 to 1,000.[13] The Soviet bomber force could not have carried so many weapons unless *Backfire* bombers were included in it. But later that year, in its issue of December 22, the *Times* did not include *Backfires*.[14]

Nor could the *Times* decide that year, any better than the administration could, how to explain the large inventory of Soviet missile warheads, which the administration had fixed at 7,400 in March and raised to 7,500 by November. In its issue of March 21, the *Times* included 1,900 sea-based missiles in this total. By June 29, the sea-based component had risen to 2,400, while the land-based component dropped by 400, from 5,500 to 5,100. But by November 28, the sea-based figure suddenly fell to only 1,500, *below* its March level, while the land-based figure rose straight to 6,000.[15]

The total increase the *Times* reflected in the Soviet missile force through that year, however, was only 100 warheads. This was the year in which we would *later* be told, first by President Reagan and then by the International Institute for Strategic Studies, that Soviet missile warheads had actually increased by 1,200. Each year we would be told of small increases; each subsequent year we would be told that these small increases had really increased by ten times as much or more. No one was supposed to notice.

Significant evidence contradicting the administration's claims was easily dismissed by the press. The Defense Department's report of 1,100 fewer warheads than the administration claimed when it made its START proposal could have been a major political setback, showing that the reductions the administration proposed would not be made from a level of mutual parity at all, but from two very different levels, the higher of which was America's.

The *Times* handled this by simply noting that precise arms figures were "difficult to pin down."[16] It made no attempt of its own to pin them down, even though the justification for hundreds of billions of dollars in excess American military spending hung entirely in the balance, resting as it did on nothing but the impression the public gained of which nation held the strategic "lead."

By suggesting precise figures were "difficult" to pin down, the *Times* implied that pinning them down was beyond its competence. All it could do, this suggested, was report the conflicting figures given. It noted that estimates vary "considerably, as for example, older submarines are placed in dry dock before new submarines are commissioned."[17] But, of course, at a specific time those older submarines either have been placed in dry dock or they have not. If they have been, estimates which take account of that fact are more accurate than estimates which do not.

Both the administration's figure and the Pentagon's were given at the same specific time: within the span of a single week in May, 1982. It was possible to find out a great deal more about what the precise figures were at the time, for example by interviewing those who gave the conflicting estimates, and asking them to explain the extraordinary discrepancy between them.

But the *Times* did not do this. It dismissed this issue in six column inches and did not bring it up again, whereas it continued to devote page after page, day after day, to assembling every scrap of evidence as to whether, for example, the Drug Enforcement Agency could or could not do a better job of keeping drugs out of the country, or whether the New York City Transit Authority could or could not improve that city's subways, or whether John DeLorean was or was not telling the truth—over all of which issues, important though some of them were, a good deal less hung in the balance than the economic priorities and fundamental security of an entire nation.

Editors were ready with a variety of excuses. They could say they had already covered a story, when in fact they had covered it up. But if they had so much as mentioned it once, as the *Times* did in this case, that would give them this excuse. They could say the public was no longer interested in a story, even though no issue held more intense, abiding interest than this one did, as the polls unmistakably reflected.

However, the polls ceased asking questions about our strategic policy and the desirability, for example, of a nuclear freeze, just as the press ceased covering the freeze movement itself, for several months until the Democratic candidates forced these issues back to their attention only weeks before the 1984 election.

Editors would also cloak themselves in the mantles of "balance" and "objectivity," complaining that they could not be expected to engage in "advocacy journalism" by examining official statements and policies too closely, when all they might be expected to advocate by so doing was the public interest.

Official statements and policies, of course, were already what chiefly took up the news. The press was never accused of advocacy journalism, or of an "adversarial" viewpoint, if it simply reported them. It was only accused of these failings if it questioned official policy, or brought up information that contradicted official statements. Then it was very quickly accused.

No administration before Ronald Reagan's had made a more intense effort to impose its views upon the press, to guide press coverage of its policies, and to suppress criticism by complaining that it was "unfair."

It had inundated the major media with press releases instructing journalists on how its policies should be interpreted and reported. This had been done before; but as one reporter noted, "the Reagan administration seems to have carried the practice to new heights," with "a continuous effort to spoon-feed material to reporters" that would ensure its actions were described in the manner it chose.[18]

It had alternately flattered and threatened the Washington press corps, rewarding favorable coverage with more intimate access and "unsympathetic" treatment with the loss of accreditation. It had consulted with the major television networks on a daily basis "about an hour and a half before their final deadline to find out what they were going with" and "to influence what they were doing."[19] It not only recommended how the leading items in the news should be covered, but also complained whenever past coverage had not been to its liking.

CBS News anchorman Dan Rather acknowledged that his network had received "relentless" criticism from the administration for its unsatisfactory coverage of official policy, and that this was "certainly pressure" to produce more favorable coverage.[20] White House communications director David Gergen insisted that "we are not asking for favorable stories. We are asking them to be fair."[21] But the administration only found them fair when they were favorable.

In most news organizations, the response to this pressure, as well as to growing internal pressure from ownership and management that increasingly favored the administration's views, was simply to report whatever the administration said or did without commentary or challenge. This meant suppressing a considerable amount of information. That suppression had to be denied, or it would become apparent to the public that the press in America was not really free.

The frequent assertions of editors, then, that they must strive for "balance" and "objectivity," were simply an effort to hide the lack of any attempt at either, to justify wholly uncritical acceptance of official views, and to deny that a great deal of information was missing from public view. There was no comparable pressure upon news organizations to *produce* the information they omitted. The struggle was unequal. For the most part, the general public had no idea it wasn't getting all the facts.

It was outrageously simple to claim "balance" while avoiding it. Late in 1982, *The Washington Post* published an administration chart of the balance of strategic nuclear forces, showing 7,100 missile warheads for the United States and 7,500 for the Soviet Union. The chart included bombers, but omitted the weapons they carried. Its implication was either that the Soviets held the lead in deliverable strategic warheads, or that even if we had enough bomber weapons to surpass their total, the Soviets still held the lead in the most important *category* of strategic weapons. Neither implication was true.

All the *Post* had to do was *observe* that the chart "omitted a basic measure" by excluding bomber weapons. Then it went right ahead and omitted that basic measure itself. The omission had been noted, so the *Post* could claim it had achieved balance. But it had not corrected that omission. It had indicated bomber weapons should be added, but it had not added them and shown the resulting totals. It simply published the chart as it was, repeating and disseminating the misleading impression it had been designed in the first place to convey.[22]

When Paul Newman, a board member of the Center for Defense Information, wrote to *Newsweek* complaining that a chart it had published on the nuclear balance had omitted a large portion of America's strategic forces, and that "the bottom line is that the United States can already explode 12,000 nuclear weapons on the Soviet Union. They can explode 8,000 on us," the magazine published his letter and replied that its chart was only "intended to be a selective repre-

The Balance of Strategic Warheads, 1979–82, According to *The New York Times*, Compared with Data Released by the United States Department of Defense

| | NY Times | | DOD | | |
Date	USA	USSR	USA	USSR	Comments
May 1979	9200	5000	9200	5000	DOE source is *Annual Report, FY 1980*, January 25, 1979.
Dec. 1980	7301	6000	9200	6000	DOE source is *Annual Report, FY 1981*, January 29, 1980. The *Times* issue is that of December 7. It lists the International Institute for Strategic Studies (IISS) rather than DOD as its source. A year will pass before IISS announces that its figures for 1980 were of "missile-carried warheads only," and excluded bomber weapons.
Oct. 1981	9000	7000	9000	7000	DOD source is *Annual Report, FY 1982*, January 19, 1981. The *Times* now follows DOD and lists it as source. DOD had recently repeated its figure for the USSR in *Soviet Military Power*, published in September, 1981.
Mar. 1982	9402	8000			*Times* issue of March 21. It lists the Arms Control Association, IISS, USAF, DOD, and the Center for Defense Information (CDI) as sources. At this time, no information is available from DOD, which has ceased publishing warhead totals. No information is available from IISS until several months later, when its figures for 1982 give the USSR 7300 rather than 8000 warheads. One CDI estimate for 1982 does give the USSR 8000 warheads, but at the same time it gives the USA 12,000.
Apr. 1982	6902	7400			*Times* issue of April 2. First impression of a Soviet lead. DOD still offers no information which might dispute it. The *Times* uses the same figures it published the previous month for missile warheads; notes number of bombers on each side, but this time omits bomber weapons; gives no source.
May 1982	9300	7200	9300	7200	*Times* issue of May 2. Reports recent DOD testimony in Congress. Bomber weapons are restored, but those for the USA are reduced from 2500 to 2100, while those for the USSR are increased from 600 to 900. This wrongly presupposes that the Soviet *Backfire* bomber has been deployed in the strategic role, and thereby demonstrates an intent to exaggerate the

Soviet threat. Even so, DOD can still attribute only 6300 missile warheads to the USSR. That is 1100 fewer than the *Times* stated one month earlier.

May 1982	9000	8500	(9300	7200)	*Times* issue of May 16. Now follows Reagan administration's assertion that each nation has about 7400 missile warheads. This gives the USSR 1100 more missile warheads than DOD officials testified existed only a week before. It also further reduces US bomber weapons from 2100 to 1500, and further increases Soviet bomber weapons from 900 to 1000. The Soviet bomber force begins to seem comparable to our own. The *Times* lists "Official U.S. Briefings" as source.
June 1982	9000	8500	(9300	7200)	*Times* issue of June 29. Repeats assertions of May 16, and again lists "Official U.S. Briefings" as source.
Nov. 1982	7100	7500	(9300	7200)	*Times* issue of November 28. Returns to practice of omitting all bomber weapons, and simultaneously reduces US missile warheads by a further 400. These two steps create new impression of a Soviet lead, with a larger total for Soviet missile warheads than DOD gives for *all Soviet* weapons. A *Times* reporter, queried by author, cites retirement of *Polaris* submarines as cause of new reduction in United States warheads. But final *Polaris* submarine was retired in March, 1982, two months before the *Times* first published Reagan administration figures giving the USA 7450 missile warheads.

The *Times* has also ignored the promised, and confirmed, addition to the fleet of more *Poseidon* warheads, all of them independently targetable, than *Polaris* warheads retired. The US total of sea-based warheads was never reduced; it was increased.

The *Times* lists "U.S. Government Estimates" as source, and refers the author to *The Washington Post*, where the same statement first appeared on November 24, attributed to "U.S. Government Unclassified Sources." These, according to a *Post* reporter, were briefings by the Arms Control and Disarmament Agency. The *Post* noted that this statement "omitted a basic measure" by excluding bomber weapons, but published it nevertheless.

(continued)

The Balance of Strategic Warheads, 1979–82, According to *The New York Times*, Compared with Data Released by the United States Department of Defense (cont.)

NY Times			DOD		Comments
Date	USA	USSR	USA	USSR	
Dec. 1982	9000	8500	(9300	7200)	*Times* issue of December 5. Published as a correction, after author complained to the *Times*. Repeats original Reagan administration assertions published by the *Times* on May 16 and June 29, giving the USA 300 fewer warheads, and the USSR 1300 more, than does DOD.
Dec. 1982	9100	10,000	(9300	7200)	*Times* issue of December 22. This extraordinary comparison first adds together the vehicles that *deliver* nuclear weapons, including both bombers and missiles, on each side. It arrives at 2000 for the USA and 2500 for the USSR. It then adds to these totals the *warheads* that missiles deliver, though it does not correspondingly add the weapons that bombers deliver. This is a double distortion. It adds apples and pears, and does not add all the pears. If all the pears *were* added, the US figure for the combination of both categories would still be much larger than the Soviet figure, though such figures would still be as meaningless as those published here by the *Times*.

Those insulted by such comparisons may fail to appreciate how artful this one is. It repeats a distorted comparison of missile warheads, which ignores remaining *Titan* warheads and more than 1200 *Poseidon* warheads added to the US fleet, and which raises the figure for Soviet missile warheads by 1200 beyond the DOD total. It magnifies this distortion by adding to it the sum of strategic delivery vehicles, the least significant category of strategic power, but one in which the USSR holds a lead. It further magnifies this distortion by omitting bomber weapons, a very significant category of strategic power in which US weapons predominate by an overwhelming margin.

By stating that only missile warheads are included, the *Times* of course acknowledges that bomber weapons have again been omitted. Why include the bombers themselves in that case?

But to readers whose eyes are drawn to the totals in boldface type, passing over the finer print, the US total, close to the familiar figure of 9300 last quoted by DOD, gives the *impression* that bomber weapons have been included, and that the comparison is complete and fair. The result is a quick, persuasive impression of a commanding Soviet lead.

The *Times* lists IISS, the State Department, and DOD as sources. IISS at this time gives the Soviet Union 500 fewer missile warheads; DOD gives the Soviet Union 1200 fewer.

Among Soviet delivery vehicles, the *Times* comparison includes only 150 bombers. It therefore excludes *Backfire* bombers, even though the *Times* was only able previously to obtain the very high figures it cited for Soviet bomber weapons by *including* 200 *Backfires*. The new comparison may be taken as an admission by the *Times*, though only a temporary one, that the *Backfire*, as our State Department confirmed in August, 1979, is not even deployed as a strategic bomber, but is limited to the "theater and anti-ship role."

On January 4, 1983, the *Times* printed a letter from Benjamin Abelow which noted that its comparison of December 22 was "at worst, deceptive," and asked: "Could it be that the *Times* was duped by the Pentagon?" But the Pentagon was not responsible for the figures published by the *Times*. Its own figures, quoted earlier that year, still showed a commanding US lead.

Changing Inventories of Strategic Weapons, 1982, According to *The New York Times*

United States Strategic Bombers and Bomber Weapons

	March 21	May 2	June 29
Bombers	316	400	400
Bomber Weapons	2500	2100	1500

Soviet Strategic Bombers and Bomber Weapons

	March 21	May 2	June 29
Bombers	150	350	350
Bomber Weapons	600	900	1000

Soviet Intercontinental Ballistic Missile Warheads

March 21	June 29	November 28
5500	5100	6000

Soviet Submarine-Launched Ballistic Missile Warheads

March 21	June 29	November 28
1900	2400	1500

sentation of the missiles involved in the European theatre, with an emphasis on ground-launched missiles, rather than a comparison of the entire Soviet and American arsenals."[23]

This chart was not a representation of the missiles "involved in the European theatre." It included several Soviet and American strategic missiles, and even labeled them as such. Few of those shown, except for America's *Poseidon,* had any role in the European theater. It was certainly a "selective" chart, because it did not show all strategic missiles, or all of anything else.[24]

But if the chart was intended to represent missiles involved in the European theatre, then it could not give a balanced representation of them by placing an emphasis on "ground-launched missiles." It could only represent Soviet missiles, almost all of which happened to be ground-launched. But most of the West's missiles "involved" in that theater were at sea. These included not only the missiles aboard four American *Poseidon* submarines, but those aboard four more British and five French submarines. It was precisely by focusing solely on "ground-launched missiles," and ignoring those at sea, that the Reagan administration misrepresented the balance of European theater nuclear power in the first place, to justify bringing in more missiles. Now *Newsweek* chose to repeat what it conceded to be this "emphasis."

If all Soviet missiles targeted against Europe were painted silver, but none of ours were, the Reagan administration would have aroused NATO allies to insist on reductions in silver missiles. It was that simple. It was as though our missiles at sea did not exist. Yet there they were, as the Soviets well knew. Nor were they inferior weapons, compared with Soviet land-based missiles; they were superior, and the West knew it perfectly well. They could not be targeted, as land-based missiles could be, in a preemptive strike. That was why the West had originally moved its missiles to sea.

In the article this chart accompanied, *Newsweek* carefully noted that "the Soviet Union would like to include" the British and French missiles in European theatre arms negotiations. Small wonder. But *Newsweek* did not include them in its own chart; it offered no explanation of why they were not included, nor of why it had chosen this "emphasis on ground-launched missiles." Undoubtedly, it felt no explanation was needed. This was the same emphasis the Reagan administration had established. What was good for the Reagan administration was good for *Newsweek*.[25]

Nor did this chart exist in limbo. It accompanied an article which discussed strategic as well as theater nuclear arms, and it did not offer the full warhead totals Newman had given. Once again, its figures, following the administration's own, were for missile warheads only, and repeated all the familiar omissions in America's warhead inventory and all the familiar inflations in the Soviet inventory, arriving at a count of 7,200 for the United States and 7,500 for the Soviet Union. This was one of the fundamental distortions Newman had written to correct, and which *Newsweek*'s article and chart served primarily to convey. But all the magazine had to say was that it had not "intended" to convey it. What else *could* it have intended?

20 The Myth of Soviet Missile Accuracy

If the Reagan administration could not truthfully claim that the Soviet Union held anywhere near the number of deliverable strategic nuclear warheads America possessed, and if it could not control information well enough to make false claims of a Soviet lead in warheads prevail, then it could not use this measure of strategic power, even though it was the most decisive one, to support its claim of Soviet strategic superiority.

If the larger number of Soviet missiles could be shown to have little importance when a smaller number of American missiles delivered so many more warheads to their targets, and if the higher aggregate throwweight and megatonnage of Soviet forces had no more importance compared to the much higher number of targets America's warheads could attack, then neither could any of these measures of strategic power persuade the public of Soviet strategic superiority.

Consequently, the administration lost little time in exploiting one of the few significant measures of strategic capability remaining: missile accuracy. If it could persuade the public that Soviet missiles were more accurate than ours, this would certainly support the President's claim that the Soviet Union held a "definite margin" of superiority. Even though we had more warheads, the Soviets still might be portrayed as capable of destroying more targets.

Here, too, was an area where the administration might better control the flow of information, for missile accuracy had been shrouded in secrecy, and relatively little information about it could be found in the general media, though there was no shortage of it in the public domain.

The paradox of secrecy in the nuclear age, of course, is that it may do more harm than good. Before the advent of nuclear weapons, military advantages were gained by guaranteeing surprise. Surprise now only posed unacceptable risks. Nuclear powers no longer enhanced their security by hiding their military capabilities. Now, hiding them only prevented them from serving as a deterrent to war.

But, of course, that was not what the Reagan administration wanted secrecy for. It wanted only to be able to select and present the information it chose without fear of contradiction.

Its campaign followed the familiar pattern. First came the flat lies. "Soviet missiles are now much more accurate than ours," Defense Secretary Casper Weinberger told the press.[1] Next came the official "estimates" in background briefings, and the emphasis in congressional testimony on only the most successful Soviet tests. All of this information was duly disseminated from specialized to general media.

The record of America's missile accuracy was obscured. When the Reagan administration took office in 1981, the accuracy of our *Minuteman III* seemed to be well established with a CEP of 600 feet. CEP, or Circular Error Probable, was the distance from a specific aimpoint within which half of the reentry vehicles of a specific type, for example, the Mk 12A on the *Minuteman III,* were expected to fall. But by 1982, *Minuteman* accuracy appeared to have declined. CEPs of as much as 1,312 feet were reported.[2]

At the same time, of course, Soviet missile accuracy appeared to improve. In 1981, CEPs of 1,215 feet were reported for the most accurate Soviet missiles.[3] But in 1983, Theodore White reported to readers of *The New York Times Magazine* that according to unnamed sources Soviet missiles were accurate to within 450 feet.[4]

This was, in fact, a characteristic reversal of the truth. For it was quite close to the current accuracy of our Mk 12A reentry vehicle, with improvements in guidance that had been reported as "the current U.S. advanced technology capability" as long ago as 1978.[5]

America's missiles were far more accurate, which made them far more lethal. The *Minuteman III* had been capable of placing its reentry vehicles within 600 feet of their aimpoints since 1979, when an improved INS-20 guidance system had first been installed on the missiles. It was the combination of this level of accuracy and the Mk 12A's yield of 335 kilotons which made that reentry vehicle so lethal. Its likelihood of destroying a hardened Soviet missile silo in a single shot was rated at 55 percent.[6]

By contrast, the most accurate Soviet reentry vehicles, those fitted on the SS-18 Mod 4 and SS-19 Mod 1, were given a likelihood rated at 40 and 42 percent, respectively, of destroying an American missile silo in a single shot.[7] This was despite the fact that their explosive yields were substantially higher, and that American silos are not hardened to the extent that Soviet silos are presumed to be.

The reason for this lower lethality rating was that Soviet missiles are *not* as accurate as Theodore White was told. They can strike within 850 feet of their aimpoints, and that is the best that any Soviet missile can do. Nor was it officially reported that they could even do that until 1981,[8] by which time America's guidance was already improving.

As this example demonstrates, accuracy contributes far more to lethality than yield does. That is one more reason why the greater aggregate megatonnage of Soviet strategic forces is wholly irrelevant.

All of these facts gradually emerged, though they did not often come to prominent public attention. The same unintended leaks occurred; there were the same contradictions. Shortly after Secretary Weinberger announced that the Soviets held the lead in accuracy, Pentagon officials told one reporter that he "overstated Soviet capabilities," and that "no intercontinental ballistic missile the Soviet Union has deployed is as accurate as the latest U.S. *Minuteman III* now on the line."[9]

The implications of greater accuracy cannot be ignored. As missiles grow more accurate, the explosive force of the weapons they release will matter less and less. If it explodes on its target, a weapon with a yield of less than 40 kilotons will destroy it.

It will not matter how well that target has been hardened to resist blast over-pressures, nor whether it really is true that missile silos and other structures can be hardened beyond the 3,000 pounds per square inch of resistance that Herbert Scoville, former deputy director of the CIA, reports is the maximum strength "believed possible."[10] The weapon will simply excavate and vaporize whatever is there. Once its CEP, its probable radius of error, has become smaller than the crater it excavates, it has reached what some analysts call a level of "maximum lethality."[11]

Several American weapons have already reached this level, as subsequent tables in this book describing weapons now in development or entering service show. The Soviets have been able to reach a comparable level of lethality only with weapons of enormous explosive force, and the consequent increases in weight and sacrifices in range they impose. The much larger investment these very large Soviet weapons require has also kept their deployed numbers to a minimum. That, too, has been a disadvantage of the Soviet Union's inability to match American levels of accuracy.

Thus, our lead in accuracy has also led to a lead in *numbers* of highly lethal weapons. Both of these leads have been the result of our sizable lead in the technology of precision guidance. With mid-course guidance from our NAVSTAR/GPS (Global Positioning System) satellites, six of which are already deployed, the MX missile, if it is also deployed, will be able to make precise navigational adjustments in pitch, yaw, and velocity while in flight. These will bring its warheads to within 300 feet of their aimpoints.[12]

Our *Pershing II* and Cruise missiles can already strike within 100 feet of their aimpoints. The Mk 600 Precision-Guided Reentry Vehicle, which may be deployed on our *Trident II D-5* submarine-launched ballistic missile, will add terminal homing to its NAVSTAR/GPS guidance. That will bring its accuracy down to 30 feet.[13] The "countermilitary potential" of these weapons, capable of destroying whatever targets they attack, is frightening.

What also began to emerge, however, was the realization that not even weapons as formidable as these, sad testaments to the human genius for destruction, made any military difference. They made a first strike no more feasible. The risks of undertaking such a strike remained insurmountable. A variety of random and systematic uncertainties continued to govern every stage of operational planning for the offensive use of nuclear weapons.

The effects of one weapon's explosion might destroy other weapons at random before they could detonate. This was called fratricide. Continuously changing effects of weather and polar magnetism might systematically shift large numbers of ballistic missiles off course, destroying the perfect timing required to avoid fratricidal effects. These uncertainties would always make it impossible to predict the outcome of any nuclear attack.

These uncertainties prevailed even over the outcome of an attack against another nation's most vulnerable targets, its force of land-based missiles. Because the success of such an attack remained unpredictable, the possibility of retaliation from missiles left undestroyed in that attack could not be eliminated. Nor could even a fully successful attack against those missiles prevent the possibility of retaliation from other forces which could not be eliminated even in theory.

Since 1968, when the Soviets first placed ballistic missile submarines in the oceans, they have had the same assured retaliatory capability we have had since 1960.[14] Missiles at sea cannot be targeted and destroyed with any certainty. That condition will continue to prevail as far into the future as any honest expert can see.

Consequently, each superpower now has an invulnerable force that will survive a first strike. With it, each will always be able to inflict unacceptable levels of damage upon the other in retaliation for a first strike.

Even if a time were to come when these forces, too, became at least theoretically vulnerable, the operational uncertainties which jeopardized the success of any nuclear attack, and the unacceptable levels of risk those uncertainties incurred, would *always* remain.

These risks cannot be avoided. Even the President's Commission on Strategic Forces recognized this. Chaired by General Brent Scowcroft, this Commission recognized that land-based missiles had grown increasingly vulnerable to attack. However, it also recognized that attacking them would always incur unacceptable levels of risk. That is all deterrence is: inescapable risk.

By acknowledging this, and conceding that our own retaliatory capabilities more than sufficed to deter an attack on our own land-based missiles, the Scowcroft Commission closed the "window of vulnerability."

It did so, of course, only as part of a more manipulative exercise to concede the existence of retaliatory capabilities America had had for more than twenty years, and so strike the note of sanity that arms control advocates were meant to reward by supporting its recommendation to build the MX. It did so even though these capabilities could have been acknowledged just as easily six years ago, when warnings of our vulnerability were first sounded as part of an earlier exercise in manipulation to establish the need for the MX.

Nor had the window of vulnerability ever loomed larger for us than it had for the Soviet Union. "My own view," Henry Kissinger confessed, "was that the Soviets were more vulnerable to a first strike than we since most of their strategic force was land-based and fixed."[15]

The weapons will grow more sophisticated and lethal; the threat they pose will increase. International tensions will rise with that threat, and the world will become a more dangerous place. New weapons will not provide a solution that can eliminate this danger, because they can never eliminate uncertainty or risk. They can only increase both.

The Reagan administration's Strategic Defense Initiative, or "Star Wars" proposal, to find a solution by placing laser and particle-beam weapons in space as a defense against ballistic missile attack, can only add new uncertainties and new risks.

Every reputable organization of independent scientists in America, from the Union of Concerned Scientists to the Federation of American Scientists, has warned that such weapons could never be more than marginally effective, and that when they were less than 100 percent effective they failed to improve our security at all. Physicists Hans Bethe, Richard Garwin, Kurt Gottfried, and Henry Kendall noted the "questionable performance" of such weapons, and "the ease" with which a defense based upon them "could be overwhelmed or circumvented."[16]

Even the Office of Technology Assessment found the prospect of an effective defense by these means "so remote that it should not serve as the basis of public expectation or national policy."[17] Yet that was precisely the expectation this grandiose scheme was intended to create. To physicist George Rathjens, its hollow promise of eliminating uncertainty and risk was "like offering laetrile to patients afflicted with cancer."[18]

But those who conceive and design and build and otherwise benefit from these weapons and weapons of every other kind will continue to try to persuade the public that other nations are striving for the decisive military advantage no nation can ever gain, and that even though no nation can gain it, we must continue to exhaust our resources and accept higher levels of terror in order to prevent them.

All that those who warn of this eventuality can ever hope to do is achieve this advantage themselves. All that can ever happen is that one nation will persuade itself it *has* achieved it, or that its adversary has, or that its adversary soon may. All that this can lead to is the war no nation wants and no part of the earth is likely to survive.

Yet those who benefit from the arms race are there, and they are persuasive and determined. If the Reagan administration is any example, they will grow more sophisticated in manipulating opinion and more ruthless in controlling information. If they can fully control information, they can win. If no one can *see* that the emperor wears no clothes, the world will believe he wears clothes. This is a war they are waging now, and it is a war we must fight. If we wish to secure government by the people, for the people, we must work to secure open government, an independent press, and our access to the truth.

21 The Record

Several of the appendixes to this book further document the foregoing observations and conclusions. Some provide a record of significant facts in the public domain on the size, composition, and capabilities of the Soviet and American strategic arsenals. Others provide a record of many statements made over the past four years, from 1979 through 1983, contradicting those facts and thereby, wittingly or not, misrepresenting the balance of power.

There are six appendixes dealing with strategic weapons. The first of these, The Strategic Balance: Author's Estimate, collects the information the author has used to make an independent estimate of the balance of strategic warheads as it evolved over the period under study, from 1979 through 1983. That estimate is consistent with the Defense Department's estimate for Soviet missile warheads in 1982. It is also close to Defense Department estimates for the total of warheads in both Soviet and American arsenals in all the years under study. It is even closer to the estimates offered in SALT II testimony for the total of warheads in America's arsenal in those same years.

The Strategic Balance: A Chronology of Estimates reviews estimates made of Soviet and American land-based and sea-based missile warheads, bombers, and bomber weapons throughout the four years under study. These estimates have been drawn from a variety of sources, some of them official and many in the private sector. Of those in the private sector, some were research institutes, some independent authorities, and many were news media. All were influential in shaping public opinion.

These estimates are also compared with the author's estimates for concurrent inventory levels. Substantial differences between the two sets of estimates are frequently apparent. It is also apparent, from a sequential review of the estimates quoted, how quickly and frequently official estimates were repeated by other sources. From a review of all the estimates, it is apparent which sources regularly took the lead in repeating official estimates.

Missile Accuracy: A Chronology of Estimates reviews estimates of Soviet and American missile accuracy during a period of growing American superiority in precision guidance, and evaluates the influence these estimates exerted on public opinion. It is again simple to note the emergence of trends supporting official policy, as American missiles seemed to grow less accurate over this period while Soviet missiles seemed to grow more so, and to note which sources were most responsible for establishing these trends. Sources which understated America's capabilities were most often the same sources which overstated Soviet capabilities.

The Quest for Certainty: The Future of Nuclear Weapons examines the proven capabilities of nuclear weapons, and the continuing effort to increase their accuracy and lethality, in order to increase the likelihood that they will destroy whatever targets they attack. It examines weapons in current inventory as well as those now in development, and demonstrates how their increasing accuracy has already brought some of them to the level of maximum lethality, where their probable radius of error in striking their aimpoints has become smaller than their radius of lethal destruction. A number of America's weapons, it notes, have either reached this point or are closer to it than those the Soviet Union now possesses.

But this study also concludes that no matter how far these improvements progress, and despite the inevitability of a time when the Soviets will match them, improved lethality can never *guarantee* that every target a nation attacks will be destroyed. The only successful first strike is one which renders the nation first struck incapable of retaliating. Any retaliatory action may inflict unacceptable damage upon the attacker. Because success will always remain uncertain, and there is no guarantee of preventing retaliation, the risks of failure will always remain too high.

Thus, all our continuing efforts in the strategic arms race, from the development of more lethal weapons and more reliable command and communications systems to current activities ostensibly designed to move war into space, are attempts to eliminate risk by achieving certainty, when certainty never can be achieved. The decisive advantage does not exist. The goal of strategic superiority is unattainable. Strategic planning which ignores this is irrational; public declarations of strategic policy which appear to ignore it are either irrational or insincere.

Yet it has only been the cruel promise that certainty can be achieved, and the prospect of achieving it ourselves, or the alternative claim, put forth as convenience warrants, that a potential adversary may achieve it, which have continued to justify all these efforts, and to justify the appropriation of larger proportions of public money and irretrievable resources each year to support them.

The Strategic Arms Race: The Record Since 1945 provides a historical record of initiatives in the strategic arms race up to the present time, and a record of the operational deployment of strategic weapons of every kind, weapon by weapon, year by year, from 1945 to 1983.

Nuclear Weapons Stockpiled and Deployed by the Superpowers provides an estimate of all of the nuclear weapons, both "tactical" and "strategic," deployed by Soviet and American forces, and all of those stockpiled in Soviet and American arsenals, from 1982 through 1984. It serves as the basis for the estimate provided in a subsequent appendix of all of the nuclear weapons stockpiled and deployed in the European theater by NATO and Warsaw Pact forces.

III

THE MYTH
OF SOVIET NUCLEAR SUPERIORITY
IN EUROPE

22 Contradictions in Declared Policy

As the record demonstrates, official statements purporting to evaluate the capabilities of nuclear weapons, and to weigh their effect upon the balance of strategic power, frequently contradict one another in their effort to manipulate public perceptions in support of official goals.

When the public had to be persuaded that the MX missile was needed, it was presented as a mobile missile, safer than fixed targets. The vulnerability of fixed land-based missiles was emphasized. The existence of an invulnerable retaliatory force of missiles at sea, which held the power to deter any threat to land-based missiles, was conveniently ignored.

When it was revealed that the MX would not be mobile after all, but would be placed in the same fixed silos whose vulnerability had originally been presented as the only reason for building the MX in the first place, the existence of our missile force at sea was suddenly recalled, and the Scowcroft Commission decided that it did deter any threat to our missile force on land.

When this left no apparent reason to build the MX, the Commission declared that the missile was needed to "redress" the "one-sided strategic condition"[1] presented by larger Soviet missiles, which it said could eventually deliver larger numbers of multiple warheads than American missiles could. Though smaller American missiles now held many more warheads than Soviet missiles did, so that no such "one-sided strategic condition" existed yet, the Commission warned that larger Soviet missiles still held the *potential* for carrying greater numbers of warheads in the future.

But the MX was not going to be as large as those Soviet missiles. Therefore, it would not "redress" this hypothetical imbalance. Nothing stopped us from building missiles as large as those the Soviets had. We had already built, and once deployed, missiles larger than any the Soviets ever had. We could do this again. But we were not doing it. Therefore, we were not even trying to "redress" this condition now.

Moreover, the Commission noted, the greater the number of multiple warheads the superpowers deployed on their land-based missiles, the greater the number of warheads each could use to attack the other's land-based missile force. A larger number of warheads targeted on each such missile made its destruction more likely, though they never could make it a certainty. A larger number of warheads carried by each such missile raised its value as a target, and made its destruction more desirable.

All of this seemed to increase the risk of preemptive attack by one nation's land-based missile force upon the other's, in an effort either to eliminate the other's or to avoid the elimination of its own. That, in turn, seemed to increase the vulnerability of missiles we had already been told were vulnerable because they were fixed in place.

At least, these conditions *might* have increased the vulnerability of land-based missiles, were it not for the continuing existence of an invulnerable force of missiles at sea, whose retaliatory threat continued to make the risks of a first strike of any kind unacceptable.

The Commission had begun its report by recognizing that our missiles at sea deterred all such strikes. With this reminder, it closed the "window of vulnerability" our land-based missiles faced. But now, as it warned again of their vulnerability to the hypothetical threat posed by larger Soviet missiles and the greater numbers of warheads they could carry, the Commission appeared to ignore that our missiles at sea deterred this threat as surely as they deterred all others. It appeared to ignore that our missiles at sea existed.

There was no way the Commission could avoid this contradiction. It had both to justify building the MX and to show that the MX would be safe based in *Minuteman* silos originally deemed vulnerable. It could only show that *Minuteman* silos were safe by recollecting that our missiles at sea deterred any strike against them. But if our *Minuteman* silos were safe, then so were the *Minuteman* missiles already based in them. No new missile was needed.

The Commission could only justify building a new missile by finding a new threat to which it was responding. The only new threat it could find was that posed to land-based missiles by a potential increase in the number of multiple warheads targeted against them. And this threat could only be said to require a response if nothing existed to deter it. Therefore, the existence of our missiles at sea, which *did* deter it, now had to be ignored.

Thus, in the space of a single report, the Scowcroft Commission first closed and then reopened the window of vulnerability, by first acknowledging and then denying the existence of our deterrent force at sea.

Nor was the Commission's business finished. If our *Minuteman* silos were vulnerable again, then so would be the MX missiles based in them. Since the MX would carry more warheads than the *Minuteman,* though never a sufficient number of warheads to "redress" the imbalance the Commission said it feared, then the MX was all the more threatening, and all the more desirable as a target. Consequently, it was all the more likely to be targeted in a preemptive attack.

The Commission now emphasized this threat, and continued to ignore the presence of missiles at sea that no less surely deterred it, in order to recommend development of a new *Midgetman* missile with a single warhead, whose vulnerability would be reduced because it posed less of a threat and therefore held less value as a target.

Since the Commission judged the *Midgetman* less vulnerable than the MX, one might assume it would recommend that the *Midgetman* be built instead of the MX. On the other hand, since it would have only a single warhead, the *Midgetman* could do even less than the MX to "redress" the imbalance the Commission now used to justify building the MX. Since neither of these new missiles would fully redress that imbalance, neither had adequate justification to be built. And since missiles at sea deterred all threats to missiles on land, neither new missile needed to be built. Nevertheless, the Scowcroft Commission recommended building both.

All of these contradictions were unavoidable. The Reagan administration, and the defense community it served, wanted both missiles to be built, whether building either one of them could be publicly justified or not. It could not.

Weapons that have no acceptable justification cannot be made to seem justifiable. Attempts to justify them are merely declaratory policy, what Paul Nitze, when he was Deputy Secretary of Defense in 1956, called "policy statements," made to the public for their "political and psychological effects," and not to be confused with the real policy, which "will in fact govern our actions."[2]

If an acceptable justification exists for a weapon, the public will hear it. If no acceptable justification exists, that does not mean the weapon will be cancelled. It simply means the public will not hear the real reasons why it may be built anyway. A variety of unacceptable reasons for building it remain. The most common of these is that industry wants to build it, because it will profit from doing so. Industry usually promises that the weapons it wants to build will provide a decisive military advantage; government usually believes this is possible. The lure of gaining such an advantage is the next most common reason for building new weapons.

Neither of these reasons is publicly acceptable, so they are not offered to the public. They become part of government's *private* rationale for its programs. Its public rationale is then bound to seem inadequate.

That is why neither the MX nor the *Midgetman* seem justifiable. The real reasons for building them are simple, though quite unacceptable. The MX offers a five-fold increase in the accuracy of America's intercontinental ballistic missiles. These are currently capable of striking within 490 feet of their aimpoints; the

MX will bring them initially with 300 feet, and eventually within 100 feet of their aimpoints.

That does not mean this improvement offers a decisive military advantage. Nothing can provide such an advantage, nor does deterrence require it. It doesn't matter which superpower deploys the more accurate missiles; it doesn't matter how accurate missiles become. The risks of retaliation after their use in a first strike remain unavoidable and unacceptable, as those who promote the MX would realize with but a moment's reflection.

Nothing suggests that those who promote the MX permit themselves such moments. The MX simply represents an "improvement" in capabilities; it is a "better weapon." It seems that is all it needs to promise in order to ensure that it is built.

The *Midgetman,* by carrying a single warhead rather than several, is designed to appease a growing constituency which considers it less threatening than the MX, and consequently a more stabilizing influence on the strategic balance. It would have such an effect, however, only if it were not deployed in excessive numbers, only if it were deployed to replace existing missiles with multiple warheads, and only if additional missiles with multiple warheads were not being planned for deployment at the same time.

But an additional missile with multiple warheads *is* being planned for deployment. That missile is the MX. There are no current plans to retire existing *Minuteman* missiles with multiple warheads. Nor is there any guarantee of a limit on the number of *Midgetmen* to be deployed.

The ingenuity of the *Midgetman* proposal is that, like the Reagan administration's Strategic Defense Initiative, it claims to promote stability by an expansion rather than a curtailment of military research and development, funded by an increase rather than a reduction in military spending, even though it promises only to create new instabilities rather than to eliminate existing ones. Thus, while failing to accomplish its stated objective, it accomplishes the real objectives that have always been behind the momentum of the arms race.

Since there is no guarantee that the Soviets will follow suit with a new single-warhead missile of their own, and every likelihood that they will not, the *Midgetman* also promises to reinforce the existing "one-sided strategic condition" of larger Soviet missiles, providing the rationale for an unknown number of additional future programs in an ostensible effort, always well short of the mark, to "redress" this growing imbalance.

The *Midgetman* proposal also claims to avoid vulnerability by offering a mobile basing system, though the feasibility of that system has no more been proven than it ever was for any attempt to provide mobile basing for the MX.

The *Midgetman* is one more well-planned redundancy in military power, which has won support by exploiting the desire for greater stability, when stability can only be achieved through major reductions in strategic arsenals, not major additions.

23 Extending Deterrence to Europe

America's prescriptions for Europe's security contain no fewer contradictions, and obscure a private agenda no more acceptable to the public. To gain support for declared policy, officials have had to navigate with equal care between these contradictions, emphasizing selected facts and subsequently denying them.

We promise Europe, on the one hand, that an attack on any NATO nation will be met by America's military response at every level of escalation, including nuclear war between the Soviet Union and the United States. We promise America, on the other hand, that escalation can be controlled, and a wider war avoided. As Christoph Bertram, director of the International Institute of Strategic Studies, noted: "The integration of theatre nuclear forces into West European defence has only been made acceptable in the past to Americans and Europeans alike by pretending to the former that the weapons would not entail the risk of an attack on the United States and to the latter that they deter because of that risk."[1]

When we want to expand our nuclear forces in Europe, we say we must rely on a nuclear deterrent for Europe's defense, because our conventional forces are inadequate to deter attack. We say that the credibility of our nuclear deterrent in Europe forbids our renouncing first use of nuclear weapons. We say that their use bears no risk to the United States because escalation from theater nuclear war to global nuclear war can be controlled.

When we want to expand our conventional forces in Europe, we say that we cannot rely on a nuclear deterrent, because the use of nuclear weapons in Europe does bear the risk of escalation, and that once the process of escalation has begun, it cannot be controlled. We say that reliance on nuclear weapons therefore must be avoided, by establishing superiority in conventional forces.

The Reagan administration has launched programs to expand both nuclear *and* conventional forces in Europe at the same time, ignoring its own assurances that an expansion of the latter eliminates any need to rely upon, let alone expand, the former.

This dual force expansion—based simultaneously on the admission and the denial that escalation is bound to occur—also ignores that as long as any nuclear weapons remain in Europe, the threat of their use remains too, and that renunciation of their first use provides no guarantee that they would not be used by either alliance, whichever one first found itself threatened with defeat in a conventional war.

The threat of nuclear war in Europe could not be eliminated, then, by a further expansion of conventional forces. It could only be eliminated by removing nuclear weapons.

When asked why such weapons could not be removed entirely from Europe, America's first response had always been that there was no guarantee that the Soviets would remove all their nuclear weapons from Europe. When reminded that it was America that had first introduced nuclear weapons in Europe, and consequently bore the greater responsibility for removing them, America's next response was to concede that this was true, but that it could not afford to mount a purely conventional defense of Europe, and that for this reason it had come to rely on nuclear weapons instead.

But if it could not afford a conventional defense of Europe, and its nuclear weapons were therefore in Europe to stay, then why did America keep conventional forces in Europe at all, at a cost so much greater than it paid for its nuclear deterrent?

The usual answer given to this was that America's troops in Europe were a symbol of its commitment to Europe's defense, which made our promises of extended deterrence more credible—though surely the presence of our nuclear weapons in Europe lacked no credibility in Soviet eyes. Another answer given was that conventional forces offered NATO and the Warsaw Pact an alternative to nuclear war—though surely this was an alternative neither alliance would choose unless it could guarantee victory without nuclear war. It could not.

Parity in conventional strength could not guarantee victory for either alliance; any lack of parity only revived the risk of nuclear war. The prospect of victory for one alliance was the prospect of defeat for the other. There was no guarantee that the weaker force would not resort to nuclear weapons once threatened with defeat. That was precisely what NATO, which claimed that it held the weaker force, threatened to do.

There was no way to resolve this paradox. Whether NATO's conventional forces were weaker or the reverse was true, both the weak and the strong were equally exposed to the threat of nuclear war. Consequently, conventional forces could no more be used in Europe than nuclear forces could be. Neither alliance could precipitate any kind of war there without risking suicide.

America's troops in Europe, then, could not be used; they seemed no more than a token of support for the NATO alliance. Yet they were more than a token force. According to the General Accounting Office, America paid $122 billion in 1982 alone to equip and maintain its forces in Europe. The greater portion of this sum by far was spent on conventional forces.[2] There was every good reason to question whether we could afford this.

But whether we could easily afford it or not, we were determined to keep our conventional forces in Europe, even though they had no feasible military role to play in Europe's defense. We *did* have a reason for this, but since it was publicly unacceptable it was seldom publicly declared.

Our conventional forces in Europe were never meant to perform a military role: they had a political role. This was to reinforce Europe's belief in a common enemy, and to dramatize NATO's need to remain united against it. The more urgent that need appeared to be, the more essential to Europe's security NATO seemed. This compelled a political consensus in support of NATO, and demanded allegiance to America's view of NATO's mission. It made dissent from that view seem disloyal.

Two West European governments, those of Great Britain and France, did not fully share this view. They had been capable of developing their own nuclear weapons, and had not been prevented from doing so. As a result, they had already done all they had to do for their defense. But the very presence of America's conventional forces in Europe, ostensibly poised for a mission they could not fulfill, implied that this mission too was needed, and thereby helped to enforce the consensus in support of America's view. In doing so, it helped to assert America's political control over Europe.

The Reagan administration did not invent this policy, inclined though it was to pursue it. This was the legacy of more than thirty years of an undeclared strategy to retain control over Europe. The Reagan administration simply inherited it, just as it inherited the program to expand America's nuclear forces in Europe by deploying the Cruise missile and the *Pershing II.*

Those missiles, too, were part of an undeclared strategy to place more military pressure on the Soviet Union from forward bases in Europe. This strategy, too, long preceded the Reagan administration. The Soviets could make no equivalent response to it. They had no stable forward bases where they might place weapons of their own within comparable range of targets in the United States.

There was no need for such a strategy. It was adopted simply to justify the more accurate weapons which technology had begun to provide, and which our control of bases in Europe gave us the opportunity to exploit. Yet these weapons gave us no decisive military advantage; they simply further threatened the Soviet Union. Moreover, by its proximity and short flight time to target, the *Pershing II* placed Soviet warning systems on automatic alert, further raising the risks of accidental war. These were risks the superpowers could not face but in equal measure.

None of this was publicly acceptable. So this strategy, too, remained undeclared. That is why the General Accounting Office, when it explained that the "need being addressed by Pershing II resulted in 1967 from a North Atlantic Treaty Organization change in tactical nuclear weapons strategy," had to add that the "nature of the change is classified."[3]

The nature of that change depended only on whatever technology had made it possible for weapons to do. An Army study completed early in 1971 anticipated that "improved accuracy for Pershing, coupled with a low-yield, earth-penetrating nuclear warhead," would mean that the weapon need be "no longer used for mass destruction," but instead could be held "for selective use against operating bases for fighters and bombers."[4]

Refinements such as these in the capabilities of weapons led to NATO's doctrine of "flexible response." The doctrine was publicly declared, though the new capabilities that had inspired it were not. The doctrine committed NATO's nuclear forces to strikes against military targets rather than targets of mass destruction. Because it rested squarely on the pretense that military targets, most of which were located in or near major population centers, could be destroyed without performing mass destruction, officials were quick to call it more "humane" than the doctrine they said it replaced.

That was the doctrine of "mutual assured destruction." Officials pretended that mutual assured destruction was merely a policy that might be discarded at will, not an inescapable fact that no nation could change unless every nuclear power disarmed. So they ignored that fact, and asserted their preference for "flexible response," as though the intention this implied to avoid the loss of civilian lives would save any.

The less publicized capabilities of the weapons themselves meanwhile improved. The Army wanted a missile that could attack Soviet and Warsaw Pact airfields. Late in 1971, it initiated a full-scale program to develop and produce the *Pershing II* for deployment in Europe.[5]

But the radar area correlation guidance for the *Pershing II* soon proved capable of much greater accuracy than planners had foreseen: it would be able to place the missile's warhead within 100 feet of its aimpoint.[6] This level of accuracy gave the *Pershing II* a far more significant capability. Not only could it attack airfields; it could attack the hardest targets, including Soviet command centers in Moscow.

The implications were not lost. "With a range allowing strikes on Moscow from Germany," *Defense Electronics* magazine duly recognized, "the removal of C2 [command and control] capability by a comparatively small number of Pershings would render much of the Soviet ICBM first strike and retaliatory forces impotent."[7] A Reagan administration official remarked upon "the efficiency of using Pershing IIs" for this purpose, and acknowledged that "the number of missiles required to do the job is very small."[8]

The *Pershing II* thus became a component of America's "decapitation" strategy to eliminate the Soviet military and political leadership, a strategy whose special risk—in addition to all of the unacceptable risks incurred by any decision to use nuclear weapons—was that by eliminating all those officials best able to see when nothing more could be gained by continuing to use them, it might also eliminate any possibility of bringing their use to a halt.

This strategy too was declared, as were most of the other elements of America's nuclear "war fighting" doctrine, which seemed to envisage a continuing series of "counterforce" strikes against military targets over a "protracted" period of time. It was useful to declare all of this, for it made the requirements of deterrence seem far more complex than they were, and thereby justified the continued development and deployment of new weapons, ostensibly to meet those requirements.

That a nuclear war might end within only a few catastrophic hours was denied. That we have already achieved deterrence once and for all, the moment we placed our first retaliatory missiles aboard submarines that remained invulnerable at sea, was carefully denied. All of the weapons we had added to our strategic arsenal since that time, we were told, had been needed in order to "strengthen" deterrence, as though the guarantee of annihilation needed any reinforcement.

But while these strategies were declared, the means for carrying them out were not. The real capabilities of our weapons were seldom described. If those capabilities appeared to have no place in declared strategy, then they were not described at all. Less threatening capabilities than these weapons possessed were attributed to them instead.

It was only in *Defense Electronics,* a magazine for defense industry professionals, that the *Pershing II* was acknowledged to have "a range allowing strikes on Moscow from Germany." The public had been led to believe it did *not* have that range. Consequently the public, though it certainly had heard of our "decapitation" strategy, was unaware that the *Pershing II* was one of the weapons intended to carry it out.

Nor was the public aware that the objective of this strategy was to "render much of the Soviet ICBM first strike and retaliatory forces impotent." We could render those forces impotent only if we struck first ourselves. The public had assumed "decapitation" was a strategy to end a nuclear war, though this strategy promised only to prolong one. What the public had not assumed was that it might be a strategy to *begin* one.

This was not to suggest that the public would never support our first use of nuclear weapons. It would—though only under certain circumstances. It would support their first use only in order to avoid defeat in a conventional war, and only if the Soviet Union or one of its allies had initiated that war, and only if our nuclear weapons could guarantee victory without escalation to a wider war. The public would not support our first use of nuclear weapons unless all of these conditions prevailed. It would never support their first use in a war which America initiated.[9]

The problem was that a force that could eliminate the Soviet capability to retaliate was a force that could do more than prevent escalation and the risk of nuclear attack on the United States. It was also a force we could use to initiate a nuclear war of our own. If we could build such a force, there was no guarantee that we would not use it in this way. If we had such a force, we might not wait for the Soviets to initiate hostilities before using it; we might use it first to disarm Soviet forces in a single strike.

Officials denied that we had such intentions, even as they endorsed "decapitation" and other strategies which fully relied on first strike capabilities. They defended those strategies even as they avoided confirming whether we were developing the means to carry them out. If we could build nuclear weapons which guaranteed victory without escalation, they suggested, then surely the threat of their use could only "enhance" deterrence. This, they insisted, was the only purpose for building them.

The Soviets could take no more comfort from these assurances than we had ever chosen to take from any statements of theirs. If we could build a first strike force, this would raise the same deep anxieties in the Soviet Union that the Reagan administration had tried to raise in America by claiming the Soviets were building a first strike force of their own, and by warning that our land-based missiles faced a "window of vulnerability."

If the Soviets ever became persuaded that we could *achieve* a first strike capability, nothing would be more dangerous for the United States. We would not have "enhanced" deterrence; we would have created the very grave risk of a preemptive Soviet strike on our forces in a Soviet effort to avoid our elimination of theirs.

Increasing the risk of a preemptive strike on its own forces is all either superpower's efforts to create a first strike force will ever do, just as this is all either nation's efforts to create a ballistic missile defense will ever do. The more effective their weapons become, the more they will increase each other's anxieties, thereby increasing the risks they face themselves.

Yet their weapons will never become effective enough to achieve a first strike capability, any more than they will ever achieve a perfect ballistic missile defense. A first strike is only successful if it renders the nation first struck incapable of striking back. A "decapitation" attack cannot guarantee the destruction of every command center, any more than the first strike of which it is part can guarantee the destruction of every missile silo. Even if all command centers were destroyed, the resulting silence between them and surviving forces might be precisely the circumstance that automatically prompts a retaliatory strike. We may never be sure how our weapons will perform. We may never be sure what our adversary may do.

In the same way, unless a ballistic missile defense can *guarantee* that not a single warhead, out of more than 7,000 Soviet warheads that might now be launched against the United States, would reach its target or detonate anywhere on American soil, millions of American lives could be lost. No scientist in America who does not serve the government or a government contractor believes such a defense can ever guarantee anything of the kind.

Thus, neither of these efforts—at a perfect defense or a perfect offense—can guarantee success. Moreover, if they *could* guarantee it, far from "enhancing" deterrence, they would only place us under the immediate threat of a preemptive attack. The objectives of both efforts, then, are suicidal. Both promise greater security, but deliver increasingly less.

President Reagan has promised to circumvent one of these risks by "sharing" ballistic missile defense technology with the Soviet Union, thus taking the "far more humanitarian" course of "destroying missiles instead of slaughtering millions of people."[10] The offer might seem significant if the technology could work. But even if it could work, we could not fully share it until we had achieved it. How much of it would we share before that time? Would we share everything we knew? And how would the Soviets know if we were sharing it all?

This promise is similar to one made in 1946, when our Baruch Plan proposed that every government, with the exception of the United States, share all of its nuclear technology immediately under a common authority, after which, it promised, the United States would share its technology too.[11] Most other governments of the world, including the Soviet Union, considered this an empty promise. Why should the United States be trusted if other nations were not to be trusted?

Would we trust the Soviet Union to share its technology with us? There was no better reason to trust Ronald Reagan. His promise to share the technology of a "perfect" defense was empty, too, just as the dream of such a defense was hollow. An empty promise, made merely to deflect criticism of a hollow dream, was not the "more humanitarian" course; it was the least so. It was insincere and cruel.

Not even a promise came, however, to "share" the technology of a perfect offense. Consequently, as evidence emerged of the growing offensive capabilities of our new weapons, there was no way to deflect growing concern over the threat they posed, and a growing awareness that the first strike strategies based upon them were impossible to achieve and suicidal to attempt.

Officials had already done their best to deny the public any knowledge of our first strike capabilities. Though the general public knew that our *Pershing II,* based in Germany, could reach its targets in much less time than our missiles based in the United States would take, it remained unaware that the *Pershing II* had the range to reach Moscow. It remained unaware that the Cruise missile could fly undetected at altitudes beneath the scanning lobes of Soviet radar defenses, so that it could attack those defenses in an effort to eliminate them, allowing our missiles based in the United States to attack Soviet targets with less prior warning.[12] It remained unaware that the accuracy of both these missiles greatly increased their likelihood of destroying the hardest targets.

Whenever reports of these capabilities did emerge, officials first tried to deny them; and if they could not deny them, they minimized their importance. Just because our weapons had such capabilities, they said, did not mean America was planning to build a first strike force. This, they said, was not our strategy.

But if this was not our strategy, why did our weapons have these capabilities? What strategy, in that case, did they serve? When had strategy, in any case, ever determined what the capabilities of weapons ought to be? It had always been the other way around. Strategy had always *adapted* to these capabilities. Once technology had shown what capabilities it could provide, strategy had always followed to exploit them. Whatever became possible, strategy quickly made necessary and right. If it seemed we could build a first strike force, then we would surely try, and we would soon enshrine its mission in the appropriate strategy.

Official denials that we had done this only left the purpose of our new weapons unexplained. An alternate purpose had to be found for them. This was done by reinterpreting the strategy they had unavoidably inspired. That is why officials next said that these weapons were intended only "to guarantee victory without escalation," should war of any kind occur in Europe or anywhere else in the world, by eliminating the Soviet capability to retaliate. That is why the public learned as much as it did about "decapitation" and other elements of our strategy—all of which were now presented as efforts to guarantee against escalation.

But since the capability to guarantee against escalation was exactly the same capability needed to guarantee the success of a first strike, the American public was no more satisfied with this assurance than the Soviet Union could be.

So officials went further. They acknowledged that the success of a first strike could never be guaranteed, and that efforts to build a first strike force were therefore pointless, irrational, and dangerous. "A nuclear war," President Reagan finally admitted, "cannot be won." If government acknowledged that efforts to achieve a first strike capability were irrational, then of course this implied that it had no strategy based upon that capability.

But if a nuclear war cannot be won, that is only because we cannot guarantee the elimination of all Soviet retaliatory forces, any more than the Soviet Union could ever be assured of eliminating ours. If we cannot guarantee against retaliation, then neither can we guarantee against escalation from a regional war. Yet the whole purpose of our new and more capable nuclear weapons, and the only surviving justification for their deployment, had been official claims that they would "enhance deterrence" because they *could* guarantee this.

Government had first promised that these weapons could do what no weapons could do. Then, in order to deny that these weapons had any undeclared mission, government had to contradict itself and acknowledge that they could not do what it had promised. If they could not perform their undeclared mission, then they could not perform the declared one; if they could not perform their declared mission, no rational justification remained for their deployment.

That did not mean they would not be deployed. The entire history of the arms race, whether of declared or undeclared policy, was a history of irrationality. This was but one more example.

24 Justifying Deployment of the Cruise and *Pershing II*

But it was important to make declared policy *seem* rational. To justify deployment of the *Pershing II* and Cruise missiles in Europe as a guarantee against escalation to a wider war ran the risk of exposing the emptiness of that guarantee; it ran the risk of exposing all of the contradictions and irrationalities that actually lay behind the development of these weapons. It was therefore best not to offer this justification to the public. An entirely different justification had to be found.

So the Reagan administration created a special cabinet-level interagency group, chaired by the National Security Advisor, whose "sole purpose" was to find that justification, "coordinating the Administration public relations abroad, with special emphasis on obtaining more favorable media coverage and influencing younger Europeans to adopt sympathetic attitudes toward the presence of nuclear weapons and U.S. nuclear policy in Europe."[1]

Authorized by National Security Memorandum 77, the group included Defense Secretary Caspar Weinberger; Secretary of State George Shultz; David Gergen, Assistant to the President for Communications; U.S. Information Agency director Charles Wick; and M. Peter McPherson, head of the Agency for International Development. Its special planning team was directed by former advertising executive Peter Dailey. This team "was established to develop a public relations strategy to sell" the deployment of *Pershing II* and Cruise missiles in Europe.[2]

The team's strategy was first to organize a new effort to obscure the true capabilities of these weapons, so that the risks and dangers they posed to both East and West would be less likely to emerge in public debate. The role these weapons played in developing our "nuclear war fighting" strategies of "decapitation," "counterforce" targeting, and "flexible response," and the role they were expected to play in carrying them out, could then be denied with little fear of contradiction.

As a result, public debate of such strategies could be limited to a discussion of land-based weapons of intercontinental range, and of sea-based weapons long considered components of each superpower's "strategic" forces. This would exclude land-based *Pershing II* and Cruise missiles in Europe from that debate, creating the impression that they had only a "theater" and not a "strategic" role to play. That, in turn, would obscure the advantage we sought to exploit of their proximity to targets in the Soviet Union, which *Pershing II*s could reach in so much less time than land-based Soviet missiles would take to reach targets in the United States. Our intention to exploit that advantage, after all, would not seem justifiable to the majority of the public.

Next, Dailey's team would develop a public justification for deployment of our new missiles in Europe which gave no hint of their true role.

It was simple to obscure the capabilities of the weapons. That the range of the *Pershing II* allowed "strikes on Moscow from Germany" could be denied simply by quoting figures for its maximum range that were insufficient to cover that distance. If the implications of such figures were lost on the public, they could be spelled out. *New York Times* columnist Flora Lewis carefully wrote that "the Pershing 2's range is 1,125 miles, 65 miles short of Moscow."[3]

The Reagan administration had given the *Pershing II* a range of 1,118 miles;[4] NATO followed suit by quoting the same range.[5] The International Institute for Strategic Studies quoted the same range.[6] *Time* and *Newsweek* further reduced the missile's range to 1,000 miles.[7] In fact, the *Pershing II* had a range of up to 1,242 miles,[8] well over the 1,190 miles needed to reach Moscow from its positions in West Germany, as the editors of *Defense Electronics* knew and confirmed.

Denying that our new missiles in Europe had any strategic role would be simpler if we could also deny that we had ever *conceived* such a role. What better way to do this, and at the same time deny America's responsibility for urging Europe to accept these weapons, than by claiming that it was Europe which first asked for them? For then the growing numbers of Europeans who did not want them could be made to feel they had only themselves to blame for getting them.

According to Strobe Talbott, Defense Secretary Weinberger privately offered other officials the following advice on how to manipulate European public opinion in order to create precisely this impression: "We've got to make them think that what we're doing is good for them. Not just that, but we've got to make them think that they're going to *like* it, and that it's what they've been asking us to do."[9] Weinberger denies having said this.[10]

The impression that Europe had asked for the weapons was not difficult to create. NATO did not make its decision to accept deployment of the *Pershing II* and Cruise missiles in Europe until 1979. Two years earlier, addressing the annual meeting of the International Institute for Strategic Studies, West German Chancellor Helmut Schmidt expressed his concern that SALT II negotiations, then in progress, would "neglect the components of NATO's deterrence strategy" because they dealt only with the "nuclear strategic weapons" of the superpowers, and did not take into account "the disparities between East and West in nuclear tactical and conventional weapons." He recommended that NATO "be ready to make available the means to support its present strategy."[11]

That was all the United States needed. "Schmidt's remarks," John Newhouse observed, "were read by some as soliciting a response to the SS-20," the missile the Soviet Union had begun to deploy that year in eastern Europe, and as recommending a response "in the form of an American make-weight based in Western Europe."[12]

At no point in his address had Schmidt defined the nature of the "disparity" in arms between East and West, or suggested that the SS-20 was its cause, or even mentioned the SS-20 at all. He had not specified what "means" NATO should take to "support its present strategy." If he thought that the SS-20 posed a new kind of threat, he never said so. If he thought that this threat required a new response, he never prescribed one, nor implied that it ought to be an American one, or that a "make-weight" could be the only appropriate one.

Schmidt never suggested that the "disparity" he perceived could be remedied by *any* additional NATO weapons "based in Western Europe." He told *The Washington Post,* in fact, that if new weapons had to be deployed at all, he preferred "sea-based deployment" to the deployment of additional weapons on European soil.[13] And in May, 1984, he told *Newsweek:* "I would find it difficult, given the German psyche, to tell the Germans that they need to add missiles to the 6,000 American nuclear warheads stationed in West Germany already."[14]

So Helmut Schmidt never asked for the *Pershing II* and Cruise missiles. His remarks more plausibly might have been taken to mean that the SALT negotiations should include not only "nuclear strategic" weapons but "nuclear tactical and conventional" weapons as well, so that the superpowers might properly take them into account and compensate for the strategic role which some of them, especially America's "tactical" nuclear weapons in Europe, played.

Our new nuclear weapons in Europe simply better enabled us to fight our own war, rather than Europe's, against the Soviet Union. Certainly, the Soviets understood this. Probably, when they first began deploying their SS-20s in 1977, justifying this to the West as a "force modernization," they justified it to themselves as a "counter" to the large number of nuclear weapons America already had in Europe.

Nevertheless, the remarks Schmidt made in 1977 were quickly interpreted as Europe's original request for the *Pershing II* and Cruise missiles. This interpretation was systematically repeated by the Reagan administration, and disseminated widely through the press, especially in the months leading up to our initial deployment of the missiles. The assertion that Europe first requested them was carefully included in almost every discussion of their deployment.

President Reagan assured reporters that it was only because Europeans appreciated the need for our new missiles that we were deploying them, "remember, at their request."[15] *New York Times* columnist James Reston discussed their forthcoming deployment "at the request of the allied governments."[16] Congressman Stephen Solarz even wrote that Schmidt had "urged the United States to deploy theater nuclear weapons in Western Europe," and that our NATO allies had "insisted on having a European-based counter to Soviet theater nuclear forces." He deplored the growing opposition to their deployment by Europeans who, it seemed, did not appreciate the need for them, and who "forgot that the original Pershing-and-cruise decision was a result of a European initiative."[17]

The public had no way of knowing that it was *not* a European initiative. The public was never told that America's decision to deploy the *Pershing II* in Europe was made in 1971, six years before Helmut Schmidt rose to deliver his address in London.

Because the public had no idea of this, nothing prevented officials from suggesting that our deployment decision was made many years *later.* Nothing prevented them from claiming, eight years later, after the Soviet SS-20 had already appeared, that our deployment decision was made for no other reason but as a response to it. So the threat allegedly posed by the SS-20 became our primary justification for deployment of both the *Pershing II* and the Cruise, as though both of our missiles had been designed solely to counter it, and as though neither one had really begun development so many years before the Soviet missile even existed.

Although Soviet advances in military capability appeared, 95 percent of the time, only after we had already achieved the same capability ourselves,[18] whenever a new Soviet weapon appeared, whether or not it incorporated such advances or posed a new threat of any kind, we always said that it did. We always said that it represented a "buildup," creating an "adverse imbalance of power." We always said, though 95 percent of the time it was not true, that we lacked an "equivalent" weapon to "counter" the threat this posed by posing a "comparable" threat to the Soviet Union—as though this were the only way threats could be countered, if they existed at all.

We always used the need to "respond" to this threat, whether any response was truly needed or not, as public justification for whatever new weapons we happened to have ready for deployment at the time, no matter how unsuitable a response those weapons might seem, and usually were. This served to obscure our true purpose, or the lack of any coherent purpose, in deploying them.

All of this was said about the Soviet SS-20, once the decision was made to use it as the primary public justification for deployment of the *Pershing II* and the Cruise. This justification was first offered by the Carter administration; the Reagan administration merely inherited and refined it. The argument served to conceal the belligerence, as well as the irrationality, that had actually inspired deployment of these weapons.

The editors of *The New York Times* had no trouble understanding this. In a rare aside to please those readers who already understood it too, the newspaper's editorialist wrote that the Reagan administration "seemed to want above all to deploy Pershing and cruise missiles in Europe, nominally to match the Soviet buildup but actually to trump the Russians by vastly complicating their defenses."[19]

Even the Reagan administration understood the irrationality of our real purpose in deploying the *Pershing II* and the Cruise. Richard Perle, Assistant Secretary of Defense for International Security, believed he was speaking off the record when he acknowledged that our new missiles in Europe were, as Alexander Cockburn reported, "militarily useless because they will be vulnerable to attack," and that they "have caused far more political damage to NATO than they were worth."[20]

The SS-20 was first offered as a public justification early in 1979, when Carter administration officials announced, in the aftermath of the Guadeloupe Conference, that the heads of state who had met there were "considering development of a new intermediate-range nuclear missile based in Western Europe" as a "possible response" to new Soviet weapons, most especially "a new Soviet intermediate-range weapon known as the SS-20," which they said "posed an unacceptable security threat to the West." They did not mention that the missile they were considering, which they said "would be developed by the United States," had already been developed by the United States.[21]

Toward the end of 1979, the NATO ministers met in Brussels and announced their "two-track" decision to proceed with plans to deploy a total of 572 *Pershing II* and Cruise missiles by 1983, while offering at the same time to negotiate reductions in that number in return for reductions in Soviet theater nuclear arms. In 1981, the Reagan administration refined this strategy into its "zero option" proposal. "The United States," President Reagan announced, "is prepared to cancel its deployment of Pershing 2 and ground-launched missiles if the Soviets will dismantle their SS-20, SS-4 and SS-5 missiles."[22]

This implied, of course, that the only reason we had for deploying our new missiles was to "offset" an "adverse imbalance" of power presumably created by existing Soviet missiles. The public would quickly doubt the sincerity of our offer to cancel deployment of our missiles if it learned that we had other reasons entirely for deploying them, and that consequently we had already decided to deploy the *Pershing II* years before the SS-20 ever appeared.

If this were discovered, it would be clear that we had no intention of cancelling their deployment. It would be clear that we could not have offered to cancel their deployment without first being certain that the Soviets would refuse to dismantle their own missiles. For we could not take the political risk of finding ourselves forced to break our word should the Soviets agree.

But we could only be certain that the Soviets would refuse if we knew that dismantling their missiles, far from restoring parity, would create an adverse imbalance of power for them. If we knew this, then we knew that the two alliances were really closer to parity without Soviet reductions or NATO increases.

This meant that we were asking the Soviets to reduce their nuclear arsenal in Europe without offering a comparable reduction in our own. If the Soviets refused to create this adverse imbalance for themselves, we would create it for them by adding more missiles of our own.

The "zero option" proposal, then, was never meant to appeal to the Soviet Union; it was meant to appeal to the public in Europe and America. It was meant as an offer the Soviets had to refuse, thereby creating the public justification for missiles we had already decided to deploy. When a reporter suggested that the proposal was just such a "ploy," an administration official insisted that "nothing could be further from the truth," and described it as "a genuine, serious effort" that was "being forwarded in good faith."[23]

To ensure that it would seem genuine and serious, the administration had to make it seem equitable. Not only did this require it to keep its real reasons for deploying our new missiles concealed; it also required it to find every possible means of representing the balance of theater nuclear power in Europe as "adverse" to NATO when it was nothing of the kind.

As always, we had to deny the advantages we already held if we were to gain new ones. As always, we had to pretend we had suffered an adverse imbalance before we could justify the measures we planned in order to impose one in reverse.

25 Refining Declared Policy

"The need for NATO modernization," our State Department duly announced, "stems from the fact that in the mid-1970s the Soviets began deploying the triple-warhead SS-20, exacerbating the threat to our European allies" by enabling the Soviets to hit "targets anywhere in Western Europe."[1] President Reagan had pointed out that these targets included all of "the great cities, Rome, Athens, Paris, London, Brussels, Amsterdam, Berlin and so many more."[2]

Yet every one of those cities, and indeed all of western Europe, had already been within range of the Soviet SS-5 since it was first deployed in 1961. That missile's range was 2,300 miles.[3] Most of those cities had also been within range of the Soviet SS-4 since it was first deployed in 1959. How, then, did the SS-20, first deployed in 1977, pose a new threat that western Europe had not already faced for the previous eighteen years?

The administration's reply was that the "triple-warhead" SS-20 could hit targets "in great numbers,"[4] and that it also had much greater range than the SS-5. What advantage greater range could afford over a missile already able to reach any target in western Europe was not immediately clear, since beyond western Europe lay only open ocean and portions of northern Africa not under NATO control. The administration soon clarified this. The SS-20's range, it said, would enable the Soviets to strike western Europe "from locations deep within the USSR and far beyond the range of any of NATO's European-based systems."[5] President Reagan said that SS-20s could strike western Europe "even if deployed behind the Urals," the mountain range 1,000 miles east of Moscow.[6]

The administration accordingly gave the SS-20 a maximum range of 3,100 miles.[7]

Was this true? Not according to most other sources. Before the Reagan administration took office, *New York Times* military correspondent Richard Halloran had given the SS-20 a maximum range of 2,750 miles, "slightly more than some older missiles."[8] Anthony Cordesman, a former national security analyst for the Defense Department, the State Department, and the Department of Energy, gave it a maximum range of 2,730 miles; and Defense Department consultant James Dunnigan gave it a maximum range of 2,670 miles.[9]

Jane's Weapon Systems pointed out, moreover, that this missile could reach its maximum range only with "offloading from the triple MIRV payload,"[10] when it carried the lighter throwweight of a single warhead. However, according to former strategic intelligence analyst John Collins, "there is no evidence any have been deployed in this mode."[11] Indeed, according to all sources, including the Reagan administration itself, the only version of the SS-20 deployed was the Mod 2 with three warheads. In that case, according to *Jane's*, its range was 2,300 miles.[12] Then its range was the same, and no more, than the range of the older SS-5.

Nevertheless, the SS-20's range was soon systematically exaggerated, and this exaggeration too was widely disseminated. The maximum range of 3,100 miles the administration had given the missile soon appeared in all official sources. It appeared in every edition of the administration's annual publication *Soviet Military Power;* it appeared in NATO's official reports and *NATO Review.*[13] It appeared in reports from the Stockholm International Peace Research Institute and the Carnegie Endowment for International Peace.[14] It appeared throughout the mainstream media.[15]

In a chart published shortly after President Reagan announced his administration's "zero option" proposal, *The New York Times* gave the SS-20 a maximum range of just 2,700 miles. This might have seemed to acknowledge the lower range most sources had given the missile originally. The problem was that the *Times* quoted its range in nautical miles. The figure was almost exactly the equivalent of 3,100 *statute* miles—the same range the administration now quoted.[16]

This exercise neatly bridged the gap between the familiar old figure and the administration's higher one, suggesting that the old figure might have been misquoted in statute miles, and that this had led to earlier underestimates of the missile's true range.

Two years later, *Jane's* reminded its readers that the administration's figure of 3,100 miles was nothing but an "estimate" itself, while the only range "that has been recorded" for the SS-20 was still just 2,300 statute miles.[17]

The exaggeration, however, went further. John Collins took the administration's figure of 3,100 miles to be the SS-20's *minimum* range, and gave it a higher maximum range of 4,000 miles. He then quoted both of these figures in nautical miles, making the missile's maximum range the equivalent of 4,600 statute miles. That, as Collins did not hesitate to suggest, was "sufficient to hit 60 percent of the United States."[18] It appeared that the Soviet Union had acquired a new intercontinental ballistic missile.

The Reagan administration had increased the maximum range of the "triple-warhead" version of the SS-20 by 800 miles, from 2,300 miles to 3,100 miles. Collins had now increased it by another 1,500 miles. The two increases doubled the only recorded range for the missile.

The International Institute for Strategic Studies duly reflected the new Collins figure of 4,600 miles in its edition of *The Military Balance, 1981–1982.*[19] It appeared again in the following year's edition of *The Military Balance, 1982–1983,* but was withdrawn from the edition published the year after that, which returned to reporting the administration's figure of 3,100 miles as the missile's maximum range.[20] By that time, after all, the higher exaggeration was no longer needed. Deployment of the *Pershing II* and Cruise missiles had already begun.

Lost entirely in the effort to portray the SS-20 as the new threat justifying our missile deployments was the fact that each of the three warheads on the Mod 2 version of the SS-20—the only version of the missile all sources agreed was deployed—had an anticipated explosive yield of 150 kilotons.[21] The aggregate yield of the three, then, was 450 kilotons. Each of the older SS-4 and SS-5 missiles the SS-20 had begun to replace carried a single warhead with a full megaton, or 1,000 kilotons, of explosive yield.[22] While its greater accuracy certainly enabled the SS-20 to do greater damage to the military targets at which it might be aimed, the warheads it carried, with an aggregate of less than half the destructive power of the older missiles, would cause less collateral damage. The SS-20 could hit no new targets on NATO territory. Far from posing a greater threat to Europe's cities, it posed a *smaller* one.

As President Reagan misrepresented the threat posed by the SS-20, he also suggested that "the only answer to these systems is a comparable threat," and went on to claim that "there is no equivalent deterrent to these Soviet intermediate missiles," because "the United States has no comparable missiles. Indeed, the United States dismantled the last such missile in Europe over 15 years ago."[23]

By "the last such missile," the President could only mean the last land-based missile of intermediate range the United States had deployed in Europe, which we had indeed withdrawn more than fifteen years ago. We still had many missiles in Europe of shorter than intermediate range; we still had many other weapon systems of intermediate range, such as aircraft and missiles based at sea, committed to European targets.

By carefully restricting his reference to missiles we had withdrawn at that time from Europe, whose only distinction from weapons we still had deployed there was that they were *land-based,* the President created the impression that the only weapons "comparable" to Soviet land-based missiles were land-based missiles of our own. It was an impression his administration would systematically reinforce, because it would heavily depend upon it for subsequent efforts to misrepresent the balance of theater nuclear power in Europe.

The land-based missiles the President had referred to were *Thor* and *Jupiter* missiles we had dismantled eighteen years earlier. We had first deployed them in 1958, when we activated three missile squadrons of our Strategic Air Command, one of them in Turkey and two in Italy, with a total of forty-five *Jupiter* missiles, and sent another eighty *Thor* missiles to England, sixty of which became operational under joint U.S. Air Force and Royal Air Force control in four RAF squadrons of fifteen missiles each at Feltwell, Driffield, Hemswell, and North Luffenham. Each missile of both types carried a single warhead with an explosive yield of 1.5 megatons. The *Jupiter*'s range was 1,500 miles; the *Thor*'s 1,750 miles.[24] The distance from the RAF bases to Moscow was 1,500 miles—a distance the missiles could travel in nine minutes.

We withdrew all these missiles in 1963. By pointing this out, the President meant to dramatize how long it had been that Europe lay vulnerable to Soviet missiles without "comparable" missiles of our own to act as an "equivalent deterrent."

But if withdrawing our missiles truly left Europe so vulnerable, then why did we withdraw them? Why, in all of the intervening time, did the Soviets, who were always presumed ready to exploit such vulnerabilities, never do so? Why, instead, had they waited until we were now about to repair the adverse imbalance we claimed? The President offered no explanation.

The explanation was simple. NATO was not threatened by an adverse imbalance of power; it never had been. Soviet missiles targeted on western Europe did not give the Soviet Union an advantage. NATO did have an "equivalent deterrent." It was not dependent on the United States for that deterrent. Other NATO nations did have missiles "comparable" to those deployed by the Soviet

Union; the United States had them too. Not only were these missiles "comparable"; in most respects, they were *superior*. That was why the United States withdrew its *Thor* and *Jupiter* missiles in 1963. It withdrew them to replace them with better missiles. One of the major reasons why they were better was that our new missiles allocated to NATO for the defense of Europe were not based on land, they were based at sea.

In 1961, the Joint Committee on Atomic Energy issued a report entitled *The Study of U.S. and NATO Nuclear Arrangements.* Among other matters, it studied the relative merits of land-based *Jupiter* and sea-based *Polaris* missiles. "Compared with the solid fuel Polaris missiles," it concluded, "the liquid fuel, fixed Jupiters are obsolete weapons" whose "retaliatory value is highly questionable." It recommended that "an alternative system such as Polaris submarines should be assigned to NATO."[25]

This alternative system was duly assigned to NATO. As military historians Bill Gunston and Ian Hogg later noted, "the Jupiters in Italy and Turkey were withdrawn and replaced by Polaris submarines."[26] Our *Thor* missiles were withdrawn for the same reasons. "The deployment of fleet ballistic missiles," Gunston and Hogg also noted, "soon made *Thor* redundant, especially as it was virtually unprotected from attack."[27]

Two decades later, Assistant Secretary of Defense Richard Perle would merely note that our new land-based missiles, the *Pershing II* and the Cruise, were "militarily useless" for exactly the same reasons.

To protect missiles from attack was an excellent reason to place them at sea. This did not make them inferior to land-based missiles; it made them superior, because it made them less vulnerable. They could not be located, targeted, and destroyed as land-based missiles could be. Even "mobile" land-based missiles were much more vulnerable than sea-based missiles. They took much more time than sea-based missiles did to prepare for launch, and could only be launched from a few pre-selected positions. The Union of Concerned Scientists pointed out that Soviet SS-20s "have only limited operational mobility: the missiles must be fired from pre-surveyed launch sites and thus can be easily targeted by NATO."[28]

After they had taken over the NATO deterrent mission first assigned to *Thor* and *Jupiter* missiles, the *Polaris* missiles on our submarines at sea were replaced, in the early 1970s, with newer, more capable *Poseidons.* The NATO mission was then reassigned to the newly equipped *Poseidon* submarines. Randall Forsberg, director of the Institute for Defense and Disarmament Studies, reported that "four U.S. Poseidon strategic submarines" had been "assigned to the North Atlantic Treaty Organization,"[29] patrolling in the North Atlantic and the Mediterranean Sea.

The International Institute for Strategic Studies reported this reassignment too, and concluded that as a result, "a total of 400 Poseidon warheads will be allocated to SACEUR [Supreme Allied Commander Europe]."[30] All of these warheads were independently targetable. This represented a sizable force expansion over the total of 105 warheads originally deployed on our force of *Jupiters* and *Thors*. That expansion would have been significant enough, had the Institute's figure included all the *Poseidon* warheads actually assigned to NATO. It didn't. The actual force expansion was larger.

As the Institute acknowledged, "the number of Poseidon warheads allocated to SACEUR is an entirely arbitrary figure which, given the redundancy of America's strategic second-strike systems which is generally believed to exist, could be raised to a substantially higher figure without difficulty."[31]

The number had been higher to begin with. Each of the four submarines assigned to SACEUR carried sixteen *Poseidon* missiles. From the outset, each of those missiles carried an average of ten warheads, as the Joint Chiefs of Staff later acknowledged.[32] As a result, these four submarines carried more than 400 warheads; they carried a total of 640 warheads, as Forsberg notes.[33]

It was that number which subsequently was "raised to a substantially higher figure without difficulty" when, at the end of the 1970s, the number of warheads on all of our *Poseidon* missiles was raised from ten to fourteen.[34] This raised the total of *Poseidon* warheads allocated to NATO from 640 to 896.

The Defense Department confirmed that recent improvements in "our current capability for theater-wide nuclear strikes" in Europe included "the assignment of additional Poseidon reentry vehicles to the Supreme Allied Commander Europe (SACEUR)."[35] Nevertheless, in its subsequent editions of *The Military Balance, 1981–1982* and *1982–1983,* the International Institute for Strategic Studies continued to report that just four hundred *Poseidon* warheads, less than half the true total, were "assumed to be available to SACEUR for NATO targeting."[36] The Carnegie Endowment for International Peace duly quoted the same figure, acknowledging IISS as its source.[37]

Far more serious, however, was that most other sources, in their tallies of the European theater nuclear balance, did not report any *Poseidon* warheads at all. Frank Blackaby, director of the Stockholm International Peace Research Institute (SIPRI), did not include them in his summary of SIPRI's 1982 annual report published in the *Bulletin of the Atomic Scientists;* they were not included in SIPRI's full report for that year.[38] *The New York Times* repeatedly excluded them from tallies of the balance it published after the President announced his proposal.[39] *Time* magazine did not mention them in its Special Report, "Playing Nuclear Poker."[40]

Of course, there was a reason for this. All of our *Poseidon* missiles had been included as "strategic" systems counted under the SALT agreements. Consequently, they were not subject to renegotiation in discussions between the superpowers on theater nuclear arms. Not even the Soviets included them in their own counts of theater nuclear arms.

When *The New York Times* published its tables of the theater nuclear balance, it frequently published America's official count alongside a separate Soviet count based on an estimate by Soviet Lieutenant General Nikolai Chervov. The *Poseidon* warheads were always absent from both counts.[41]

Why should we include *Poseidon* warheads in our counts of theater nuclear arms, we might well ask, when the Soviets did not even include them in theirs? This position seemed eminently fair, though *Poseidon* warheads were in fact assigned to NATO targets. By excluding them, and carefully noting that the Soviets had excluded them too, we were simply further exploiting a false distinction we had already made, and forced the Soviets to accept, by insisting long ago on separate negotiations for "theater" and "strategic" nuclear arms.

This distinction created what seemed two separate categories of weapons, and the illusion that no single weapon could play a role in both. It allowed us to obscure the strategic role for which some weapons, ostensibly committed to "theater" use, might actually be designed, as the *Pershing II* and Cruise missiles were. It allowed us to obscure the theater role which some weapons, already counted as "strategic" systems, might actually be assigned, as 896 of our *Poseidon* warheads now were.

The Soviets gained no comparable benefit from drawing such a distinction. There was no second "theater," as close to the United States as Europe was to the Soviet Union, where they might place nuclear weapons of their own, ostensibly in "defense" of that theater but within comparable range of targets in the United States.

Once two separate categories of weapons had been established, it seemed only fair that the same weapon not be included in both, and that limits on its permissible numbers not be negotiated twice, first in "theater" and then in "strategic" negotiations. By repeatedly drawing attention to this principle, we also promoted the view that the same weapon should not be counted twice, as though counting a weapon were bound to require renegotiating its numbers.

Yet many weapons, especially our own, had the potential for both theater and strategic use. Consequently, they affected both theater and strategic balances of power. Negotiations attempting to stabilize either one of those balances were fair only if they were based on an accurate assessment of that balance; and this assessment was accurate only if all of the weapons affecting that balance were counted. A weapon affecting both balances had to be counted in both assessments, whether its numbers were renegotiated or not.

Yet often such weapons were not counted. Our refusal to count them in each balance they affected, based on our feigned concern that this would subject them to renegotiation, had kept our forward-based aircraft in Europe from being counted as strategic weapons, even though they were capable of delivering nuclear weapons to targets deep in the Soviet heartland, and therefore held the potential for strategic as well as theater use. It had kept our carrier-based aircraft from being counted as strategic weapons, though they held exactly the same potential. It had once kept our *Thor* and *Jupiter* missiles from being considered strategic weapons, though they had held the same potential too.

All of this had helped to create a false impression of the strategic balance of power which persists to this day, reflecting a much smaller threat to the Soviet Union than American forces actually pose, and thereby justifying fewer reductions in American nuclear arms.

We were now preventing our *Pershing II* and Cruise missiles from being considered strategic weapons, by presenting them as theater weapons instead. We could plausibly portray them as theater weapons only because they had less than intercontinental range, and therefore did not fit our definition of strategic weapons, though they certainly fit the Soviet definition. We could justify their deployment only by creating the impression of an adverse imbalance of theater nuclear power in Europe. We could create this impression only if we refused to recognize that 64 of our *Poseidon* missiles, with 896 warheads, as well as additional French and British missiles with additional warheads, were part of the theater nuclear balance in Europe.

So we did refuse to recognize this. Even though sixty-four of our *Poseidon* missiles had actually been assigned a theater role, and the Defense Department had officially confirmed that assignment, we reminded the press in Europe and America that our *Poseidon* missiles had already been counted as "strategic" systems, and that consequently none should now be counted again as theater systems.

This was what had led most sources in the Western press to ignore our *Poseidon* warheads entirely. Those that mentioned them at all gave little information about them. When *Newsweek* first mentioned them in 1983, it did not give their number; it said, in fact, that the number of *Poseidon* warheads assigned to NATO was "classified."[42] As a result, its readers could not measure the effect those warheads had on the balance of theater nuclear power in Europe, and so determine whether that balance was truly "adverse" to NATO.

The next time *Newsweek* referred to them, it did so only obliquely. It listed four hundred sea-based warheads in NATO's arsenal, aside from those held by Britain and France, but did not identify them as *Poseidons*.[43] This figure was consistent with the estimate of four hundred *Poseidon* warheads first offered by the IISS, but that figure had been an *underestimate,* which also ignored the Defense Department's confirmation that "additional Poseidon reentry vehicles" had been assigned to NATO. Thus, more than half the *Poseidon* warheads long since allocated for NATO use remained deleted from *Newsweek*'s balance sheet.

French President François Mitterand used a similar form of manipulation to help keep French and British nuclear forces off the balance sheet as well. By feigning concern that his country's nuclear *Force de Frappe* might be bargained away by Soviet and American representatives at the Geneva negotiations, and that as a result, "France would lose a decisive element of its deterrent capability,"[44] he helped reinforce the attitude that French and British weapons should not be counted in an assessment of the balance that served as the context for those negotiations.

Mitterand knew perfectly well that French forces could not be bargained away or even touched at Geneva because they had never been a part of those negotiations, any more than British forces ever had been. The Geneva talks, he knew, had never been intended to deal with any but Soviet and American weapons. It was precisely because they exempted the nuclear forces of all other NATO nations, including his own, from discussion that the focus of the Geneva talks had been lopsided from the outset, artificially restricting the available remedies to any imbalance of theater nuclear power that might exist. Mitterand's concern, then, was simply a pretext for his declaration that "French arms cannot be taken into account in the Geneva negotiations,"[45] as though they were not a part of the balance these talks assessed, or as though there were some other balance, in some other separate theater, of which they were more properly a part.

But, of course, there was no other balance to which they belonged. French nuclear forces existed for the defense of France. They were not scattered halfway around the world; they were in Europe. They belonged, then, to no other nuclear balance of power but Europe's. French and British forces were a significant part of that balance, and their contributions to it *had* to be taken into account. The Soviets certainly took them into account.

But the Reagan administration wanted them counted no more than it wanted our *Poseidon* warheads counted. So they had to be discounted in Western opinion. Mitterand's false indignation made it seem unfair to count them, as though their absence from the negotiating agenda had also eliminated them from the balance of nuclear forces arrayed against the Soviet Union. It hadn't.

The Reagan administration found other pretexts for discounting French and

British nuclear forces from the balance sheet. It called them weapons of "last resort," as though NATO's other nuclear weapons were not also weapons of last resort, but might be used at some earlier stage of conflict. It called them "autonomous forces," as though they were not committed to NATO's defense, and consequently posed no threat to the Soviet Union, when the only reason they had been built was to pose such a threat, and when they had been fully integrated into NATO's operational planning. That was why the IISS had included both French and British missiles and aircraft among NATO's "Long- and Medium-Range Nuclear Systems for the European Theatre."[46]

Nevertheless, the American press obligingly took up these suggestions. *Newsweek* listed French and British forces in its summary of Europe's theater nuclear arms, but carefully listed them separately, referring to them as "independent nuclear arms," without adding them to the total of weapons in NATO's nuclear arsenal.[47] In this way, the magazine could not be accused of having ignored these forces, though at the same time, in its tally of the European theater nuclear balance, it had in fact ignored them.

This is a common technique for misrepresenting the balance of power of any kind. The mere mention of certain forces appears to take them "into account," while the reinterpretation of their role effectively excludes them from that account, and denies their contribution to the balance.

The New York Times always included French and British nuclear forces in its tables reproducing the "Soviet Count" of the European balance, but almost never included them in its tables reproducing the "U.S. Count."[48] This, of course, was "balanced" reporting. The *Times* was merely reporting the official counts both governments had presented. What could be more objective and fair?

It was clear that most American readers would always consider the Soviet counts, which showed an approximate parity even without America's *Poseidon* warheads, less "valid" and "credible" than the counts presented by their own government. To consider their own government's statements less "credible" would be disloyal. It was clear, in other words, that whenever the statements of both governments had to be taken on faith, most Americans were bound to feel a political bias favoring their own government.

These statements, needless to say, did not have to be taken on faith; there was more than enough information available to determine how accurate they were. Most Americans, however, would not have gone to the lengths required to find and absorb this information, as their government well knew, and as the press well knew. Consequently, they had little choice but to take such statements on faith. And whenever they did so, their natural bias would incline them to believe their own government's statements over those of the Soviet Union, whether these were more accurate or not. If they did not wish to take such statements on faith, then they were dependent on sources other than government to determine how accurate they were.

A major newspaper like *The New York Times* has more than sufficient means of finding and absorbing the information needed to determine just how accurate such statements are. There is even a school of opinion that it is the proper duty of the press to serve the public interest by presenting such information.

The *Times,* however, simply published the two separate counts of the theater nuclear balance in Europe side by side, as though most readers would lend equal credibility to each. It provided no accompanying assessment of how complete and accurate, and hence of how "valid" and "credible," each count was.[49]

Even in articles adjoining these tables, the newspaper seldom offered any information that might help provide such an assessment. On one occasion, *Times* correspondent Drew Middleton noted that French forces "would almost assuredly become an integral part of the Western defenses in the event of war."[50] That, of course, was almost assuredly why the Soviets had included French forces in their count. On another occasion, *Times* correspondent Leslie Gelb reported that "Washington wants to count all 270 Russian SS-20s, even though only two-thirds of them are deployed facing Europe, on grounds that those now facing China could be moved," and went on to note that "Washington does not take into account Moscow's need to confront China's nuclear arsenal of about 250 warheads."[51]

But these were the only indications that America's official counts might be less than accurate or complete. Readers who saw only the far more prominent figures in the tables themselves would have missed even these hints that all was not as the tables had made it seem.

Thus, the *Times* did next to nothing to prevent political bias from favoring America's official counts of the European theater nuclear balance as the more "valid" and "credible" counts, even though America's official counts had excluded French and British as well as our own *Poseidon* warheads.

"Balance" and "objectivity," then, are positions to which the press retreats when it does not wish to contest the validity of official views, even though it knows that in the absence of any effort to clarify or correct those views they will prevail, valid or not.

The Reagan administration certainly had an *ostensible* reason for excluding all of these warheads from its counts of the European nuclear balance. It had taken the position, after all, that "the United States has no comparable missiles," and that "there is no equivalent deterrent" which NATO could present to Soviet SS-20s, SS-4s, and SS-5s.

Yet if NATO's missiles were not "comparable," how did they fail to match the capabilities of these Soviet missiles? They had the equivalent ranges, and comparable yields. They could be placed within equal proximity of their targets. Consequently, they would take no longer to reach those targets, and were no less accurate. Indeed, some were more so. The *Poseidon*'s reentry vehicles were more accurate than those of the SS-20; even with its full load of fourteen reentry vehicles, the *Poseidon*'s range was 500 miles *greater* than that of the SS-20 Mod 2.[52]

The only difference between Soviet missiles and NATO missiles targeted against Europe was that the Soviet missiles were based on land, whereas all of NATO's, aside from eighteen French missiles, were based at sea. To say that they were not "equivalent" or "comparable" to Soviet missiles made them sound inferior, yet the reverse was the case. Not only were most of them superior in accuracy and range; all were superior by virtue of the single major difference between them and their Soviet counterparts. Because they were based at sea, they were less vulnerable.

But the Reagan administration relied on public ignorance of these facts to suggest, instead, that land-based missiles were superior to theater nuclear weapons of all other kinds, and that NATO faced an "adverse imbalance" of power because only the Soviets had any land-based missiles.

Accordingly, the administration's official "comparisons" of theater nuclear power frequently narrowed themselves to the category of land-based missiles alone. The State Department reprinted the text of President Reagan's "zero option" announcement with a chart entitled "Key Intermediate-Range Land-Based Systems." Naturally, it showed only Soviet systems actively deployed, with nothing on the NATO side but America's missiles yet to come.[53] This selective view of the balance was repeated in a variety of forms. *NATO Review* published a chart of intermediate-range nuclear forces in Europe entitled "Key INF Missile Systems," which again restricted itself to land-based missiles, listing Soviet SS-20s, SS-4s, and SS-5s, and again showed no NATO systems then deployed. The *Pershing II* and Cruise missiles yet to be deployed, it suggested, would only partially restore this "imbalance."[54] America's *Poseidons,* and British and French missiles, all of them already long since deployed, were nowhere to be found.

The administration's real reason for refusing to count any of NATO's existing intermediate and longer-range missiles, of course, was that it could not otherwise create the impression it needed of an "adverse imbalance," in order to justify deploying additional missiles. For, in fact, in this category of weapons alone, it was NATO which retained a clear lead over the Soviet Union, and it was the Soviet Union which therefore presumably faced an "adverse imbalance" of power. Here was the balance of such forces when Ronald Reagan declared that NATO had "no equivalent deterrent," at the end of 1981:[55]

NATO				Warsaw Pact			
Missile Type	Number	Warheads on Each	Total Warheads	Missile Type	Number	Warheads on Each	Total Warheads
Poseidon (USA)	64	14	896	SS-4 (USSR)	340	1	340
Polaris (UK)	64	3*	64	SS-5 (USSR)	40	1	40
MSBS M-20 (Fr)	80	1	80	SS-20 Mod 2 (USSR)	150	3	450
SSBS S-2/3 (Fr)	18	1	18	SS-N-5 (USSR)	57	1	57
	Total		1058		Total		887

* Each British *Polaris* missile was fitted, at that time, with three warheads that were not independently targetable, so that they are counted here, as they are in most sources, as a single warhead.

What may appear to be wrong with this count is that the figure for Soviet SS-20s is so low. The Reagan administration quoted a figure of 250 such missiles deployed at the time; most sources, in fact, agree that the figure was 230.[56] What the Reagan administration did not explain was that a third of this number were deployed in the Far East, as Leslie Gelb had pointed out. The IISS noted that only a third of the SS-20 force was deployed in the western districts of the Soviet Union, with another third "in 'swing-zone' in the Central USSR and with range to threaten NATO and the Far East,"[57] Consequently, as the editors of *Jane's Weapons Systems* concluded, "perhaps two thirds" of the total SS-20 force was "deployed for maximum effect in the European theatre."[58]

This pattern of deployment did not change. Late in 1983, the IISS reported that "an estimated two thirds of SS-20" were "within range of Europe."[59] Nevertheless, the administration frequently included the entire SS-20 force on its European balance sheet, as though all existing SS-20s threatened Europe.

The administration also frequently exaggerated the number of SS-20s deployed. Early in 1983, Defense Secretary Weinberger raised the total of SS-20s to 351. This would have meant that as many as 1,053 warheads had been added to the Soviet arsenal. All of them could be assumed to threaten Europe, if all were assumed to be within range of European targets. The Secretary said nothing to discourage that assumption.[60]

The total of SS-20s deployed at that time, instead, was 315.[61] Of this total, two thirds, or 210 missiles, were deployed within range of Europe. Assuming that none of these carried a single warhead, and that all were indeed of the Mod 2 variety with three warheads each, then SS-20s that year contributed at most 630 warheads to the Soviet arsenal threatening Europe.

The press, however, usually carried the administration's figures. Sometimes these figures were *doubled,* reflecting the additional assumption that all SS-20 launchers were accompanied by a reload missile.

The likelihood is slim that in a nuclear war many launchers, or any other delivery systems for nuclear weapons, from aircraft to artillery tubes, would survive long enough to fire their reloads or fly them to their targets if they had them, or that any information would be available to their crews indicating what targets survived. Nevertheless, this assumption was always made, together with the assumption that the Soviets, for reasons never explained, were bound to have more reload missiles than NATO had.

But NATO had reload missiles too, though certainly there was no greater likelihood that its forces would ever have the opportunity to use them. Though sixty of our *Thor* missiles had been operationally deployed in England, we had sent eighty. And though we planned to deploy only 108 *Pershing II* missile launchers in Europe, we were building a total of 384 missiles,[62] 228 of which would be deployed in West Germany as first rounds, reloads, and spares.[63] This number was sufficient to provide one reload missile for each launcher.

The same numbers of *Pershing 1* and *Pershing 1A* missiles had been kept for the 108 launchers deployed by American forces in West Germany since 1964.[64] The West German Bundesluftwaffe has had, and will continue to have, reload missiles for its own seventy-two *Pershing 1A* launchers.[65] United States and NATO forces have just 126 *Lance* missile launchers in Europe, but keep 360 MGM-52 *Lance* missiles with W-70 nuclear warheads stored there.[66]

NATO's reload missiles never appear on the official balance sheets prepared by our government; but Soviet reload missiles almost always do, often in exaggerated numbers. The press dutifully records and further disseminates this additional asymmetry. That leads to further distortions, which help to create the impression of an imbalance of power "adverse" to NATO.

The only fair way to deal with reloads is to count their known and plausible numbers among weapons *stockpiled,* while separately counting weapons available as first rounds among weapons *deployed,* and to follow this same procedure for the arsenals of both superpowers and both European alliances on the balance sheet.

Though the number of SS-20 warheads deployed was increasing, it was increasing more gradually than claimed, and that increase was also partially offset by the continued withdrawal of SS-4 and SS-5 missiles the SS-20 had been designed from the outset to replace. NATO continued to keep its lead in numbers of deployed missile warheads. There was no reason, any more than there was a scrap of evidence, to suppose that NATO did not also keep a comparable lead in numbers of stockpiled warheads, though the poor likelihood that any warheads not deployed as first rounds would ever be used made the latter lead far less significant.

In the category of intermediate and longer-range missile warheads deployed, here was the balance in successive years:[67]

Year	NATO	Warsaw Pact
1982	1058	887
1983	1245	978
1984	1510	1007

The initial deployment of *Pershing II* and Cruise missiles in 1983 was not the only reason for the growth of NATO's arsenal of missile warheads reflected here. That growth has been due even more to less publicized changes that would have retained NATO's lead *without* deployment of the *Pershing II* and Cruise.

What has been barely publicized at all is that the British began deploying their new *Chevaline* warheads aboard their *Polaris* missiles in 1983. Each of these missiles now carries six warheads;[68] the British force of independently targetable warheads at sea has consequently grown from the equivalent of 64 in 1982 to 384 today. Although the British Ministry of Defence concedes that the *Chevaline* has a "manoeuverable payload," it nevertheless claims it is not "a MIRVed system" with independently targetable warheads.[69] It is scarcely conceivable how it could be anything else, or that the British would otherwise spend the £1 billion it has cost them[70] to develop and deploy it.

That was but the beginning. The French will start replacing their M-20 missiles at sea with M-4s in 1985. Like the *Chevaline* reentry vehicles, those on the M-4 will carry six warheads each. This will raise the French force of warheads at sea from 80 to 496 by 1989. With the addition of a seventh submarine, *l'Inflexible,* that force will eventually carry 592 warheads, with only one submarine, *le Redoutable,* still carrying the old M-20s.[71]

With America's *Poseidon* warheads already assigned to SACEUR, the French and British force expansions will give NATO a total of 1,872 warheads safely based at sea. If parity in numbers is what our deployment of Cruise and *Pershing II* missiles was supposed to be all about—and that is all the public was ever told it was about—then they were never needed.

Aircraft, of course, were also "long and intermediate-range systems," capable of covering all the targets missiles could cover throughout the European theater. When the Reagan administration restricted itself to "comparisons" of "key intermediate-range systems," it excluded aircraft on the grounds that they were less threatening than missiles because they were slower. Not even this was always true.

America's F-111 bombers flew at 1,650 miles per hour; from their bases at Lakenheath and Upper Heyford in England, they could reach Moscow in less than an hour. America's Cruise missiles flew at 500 miles per hour; it would take a Cruise missile launched from Greenham Common Air Force Base in England three hours to reach Moscow. Both the missile and the aircraft were equipped with terrain-following radar,[72] and could fly beneath the search lobes of Soviet radar defenses. The Short-Range Attack Missiles (SRAMs) carried by the F-111 were almost as accurate as the Cruise.[73] If speed was any criterion of military capability, then our 156 F-111 aircraft, based in England for almost a decade, were *better* weapons than the new missiles we had just begun to deploy there.

Capabilities of this kind finally led the Reagan administration to concede that missiles were not consistently superior weapons, and that it should include aircraft in its counts of "long and intermediate-range systems" assigned to Europe's defense. It did so, and counts of aircraft were duly tabled at the negotiations on theater nuclear forces in Geneva.

But the counts that the two governments presented were startlingly different. The Soviet Union counted 824 NATO aircraft and 461 of its own. The United States counted 560 NATO aircraft and no fewer than 3,095 Soviet aircraft![74]

What had happened was that the Reagan administration, in order to sustain the impression it needed of an "adverse imbalance" of power in this larger category of theater nuclear forces, had availed itself of a means of inflating the Soviet threat used so often, for so many years, that it had become tradition. This was to assume that every existing Soviet strike aircraft capable of carrying nuclear weapons had been assigned to Europe, and accordingly to include them all, regardless of where they were actually based, on the European theater nuclear balance sheet, while including only a fraction of NATO's nuclear-capable strike aircraft, even though many more were based in Europe.

The administration did all of this. It reported only American aircraft, as though no other NATO nation had an air force. Even then, it did not report all of the strike aircraft America kept in Europe or within range of European targets. At the same time, it reported the entire inventory of tactical strike aircraft and medium-range bombers that the Soviet Air Force possessed.

According to the International Institute for Strategic Studies, the Soviets had 2,595 tactical strike aircraft that were capable of delivering nuclear weapons at that time;[75] they also had 500 medium-range bombers that were not assigned to Naval Aviation.[76] This made a total of 3,095 aircraft of both types—the same total the administration gave.

Yet the Institute also pointed out that only 365 of the Soviet bombers were based in the western USSR, within range of Europe.[77] It noted, further, that the

Soviet Union had "4 Tactical Air Armies (2,000 aircraft) in Eastern Europe," while twelve more Soviet Air Armies were based in the USSR, one in each of twelve Soviet military districts.[78] If those figures were correct, then the Soviets had a total of 2,365 aircraft of all types, including medium-range bombers, available for combat in Europe.

The figures seemed to be correct. According to Britain's *Journal of the Royal United Services Institute,* the Soviet Air Armies in eastern Europe had 1,975 aircraft in 1978.[79] According to John Collins, the Soviets had 2,020 tactical aircraft available for combat in central Europe and on both NATO flanks in 1980.[80] According to William Lewis, "about one-half" of the 4,600 aircraft of Soviet Front Aviation, or 2,300 aircraft, were "oriented against Western Europe" in 1982.[81]

These figures reflected a close consensus. The Reagan administration's total of 3,095 Soviet aircraft in Europe exceeded even the highest of them—that from the IISS of 2,365 aircraft—by 730 aircraft.

Moreover, the administration claimed its total was the total of only one aircraft type: strike aircraft capable of carrying nuclear weapons. Many Soviet aircraft did not have that capability. Many were not needed for that role. The Soviet Tactical Air Armies assigned to Europe needed a variety of aircraft types for the many missions they had to be prepared to perform. Strike aircraft could make up only a portion of their total number; strike aircraft that were also nuclear-capable would make up an even smaller portion.

If the entire inventory of 2,595 nuclear-capable tactical strike aircraft existing throughout the Soviet Union was distributed evenly among all sixteen Soviet Tactical Air Armies, then only 25 percent of that number, or 648 of this aircraft type, would be assigned to the four Air Armies in eastern Europe. If, as might reasonably be expected, higher numbers of strike aircraft were maintained in the four Air Armies in eastern Europe, there is still a limit to the number that could be drawn for this purpose from the other twelve Air Armies without compromising their combat effectiveness by leaving them too few of that aircraft type.

William Lewis estimates that 1,150 aircraft of Soviet Front Aviation are concentrated in those military districts of the USSR bordering the People's Republic of China.[82] Certainly, this force would include a number of nuclear-capable strike aircraft. Certainly, those aircraft could not simultaneously be assigned to Europe.

Nor, aside from the 365 bombers in the western USSR, could the proportion of strike aircraft be too high among the remaining 2,000 of all types which the IISS estimates comprise the full Soviet force in eastern Europe. Soviet aircraft formed more than half the Warsaw Pact's total. If too few of them were available for air defense, combat air patrol, fighter interceptor, fighter escort, close air support of ground forces, deep interdiction with nonnuclear weapons, early warning, reconnaissance, defense suppression, electronic countermeasures, and other missions, the Pact would forfeit air supremacy to NATO.

Of the 2,020 Soviet tactical aircraft of all types which John Collins estimated were available for combat in Europe, 1,075 were fighter interceptors, unable to *carry* nuclear weapons.[83] Nor were all of the remainder strike aircraft with that capability. In fact, the IISS estimates that "about 25 percent" of Soviet nuclear-capable strike aircraft are "generally deployed in East" against NATO.[84] Of the 2,595 such aircraft it estimates exist, this percentage does represent about 648 aircraft.

Adding 365 Soviet bombers in the western USSR, all of them certainly nuclear-capable, according to the IISS, the Soviet Union had a total of 1,013 aircraft capable of delivering nuclear weapons on European targets at the time.

Yet according to the Reagan administration, the Soviet Union had 2,082 *more* aircraft of that type assigned to Europe. Indeed, according to the Reagan administration, the Soviet Union had more aircraft of that type assigned to Europe than most other sources estimated it had of *all* types assigned to Europe.

Nor was this the end of the matter. Because aircraft were capable of delivering nuclear weapons did not mean they were assigned a nuclear strike role. The IISS estimated that "some 50 percent" of available Soviet bombers and "some 25 percent" of available Soviet tactical strike aircraft in Europe would be "retained in nuclear role."[85] Then just 182 of the 365 bombers available at that time, and 162 of the 648 tactical strike aircraft available at that time, would be assigned a nuclear strike role—making a total of 344 aircraft of both types.

This was 2,751 *fewer* aircraft than the Reagan administration implied the Soviets might use in nuclear strikes against NATO. Then could the IISS estimate be too low? Not according to other authorities. In 1984, the office of the Deputy Under Secretary of Defense for Policy estimated that the Soviets would retain only 201 aircraft on "nuclear withhold" for Europe.[86]

Nor was that the end of the matter. According to their varying load capacities, some aircraft were capable of carrying more nuclear weapons than others could as normal operational loads. Here the IISS, too, began to inflate the Soviet threat. In a table in *The Military Balance, 1981–1982,* it assigned greater numbers of nuclear weapons to Soviet aircraft than their load capacities could easily accommodate, while assigning NATO aircraft fewer weapons than they normally carried.

While it acknowledged that the British *Vulcan* bomber had a load capacity of 21,000 lbs, and that the Soviet Tu-22M *Backfire* had a load capacity of only 17,500 pounds, in its table the IISS assigned the *Vulcan* only two weapons but the *Backfire* four.[87] While it acknowledged that the Soviet Su-19/24 had a load capacity of only 8,000 pounds while the French *Mirage IIIE* had a load capacity of 19,000 pounds, in its table the IISS gave the Soviet aircraft two weapons but the French aircraft only one.[88] It assigned the American and NATO F-4 *Phantom* only one weapon, when it normally carried three.[89]

Three years would pass before the Institute would acknowledge, in its edition of *The Military Balance, 1984–1985,* that the *Mirage IIIE* could carry *two* AN-52 nuclear weapons, and that the American carrier-based A-6 *Intruder* and A-7 *Corsair II* strike aircraft normally carried, respectively, three and four nuclear weapons each, not two weapons each, which was all that its earlier table had allowed.[90] While its earlier table had assigned each Soviet *Backfire* four nuclear weapons, it was not until the *1984–1985* edition that IISS conceded that the *Backfire* carried but "1 or 2" such weapons at most.[91]

In the intervening three years, the period when it was most critical for the Reagan administration and the entire Western defense establishment to sustain the impression that NATO faced an "adverse imbalance" of power, the original table published by the Institute in its edition of *1981–1982* played an important role. By overstating the nuclear weapons loads of Soviet aircraft and understating those of NATO aircraft, it heavily distorted the balance of nuclear weapons all these aircraft carried.

But the IISS did not stop there. The same table further magnified this distortion by distorting the balance of aircraft themselves. Though footnotes to this table specified the guidelines the Institute recommended for determining the number of nuclear-capable strike aircraft in Europe, as well as the smaller number of these actually assigned to the nuclear strike role, and though according to these guidelines just 344 Soviet aircraft were so assigned that year, the table itself ignored these guidelines, and without any explanation reached a higher total of 819 Soviet aircraft allocated for nuclear strikes.[92]

At the same time, this table listed only 1,170 nuclear-capable NATO and American strike aircraft based in Europe, even though a total of 2,036 such aircraft was listed in the national entries in the same book.[93] The Institute offered no explanation for deleting 866 of them. It abruptly changed its criteria for determining their number, assuming in another footnote that American aircraft were available for nuclear strikes in Europe from only "2 carriers in US 6th Fleet (Mediterranean)," whereas earlier in the same book it had listed American aircraft available for such strikes from "6 carriers in European area."[94] The higher figure was understandable, since "4–5 carriers," as the Institute had noted itself, again in the same book, were also attached to the U.S. 2nd Fleet in the Atlantic.[95]

The IISS assumes that all *Vulcan* and *Mirage IV* aircraft, a third of all F-4 *Phantoms* and F-104s, and half the nuclear-capable NATO strike aircraft of all other types will be allocated to nuclear weapons delivery.[96] Its table—which follows these guidelines but ignores those for the Soviet Union—produces the totals of aircraft assigned to the nuclear strike role that year, and of weapons they are presumably capable of delivering:[97]

NATO		Warsaw Pact	
Aircraft Assigned	Weapons Carried	Aircraft Assigned	Weapons Carried
494	695	819	1167

However, if the 866 missing NATO aircraft are restored to this table, and if the guidelines the IISS specifies are followed to determine how many Soviet as well as NATO aircraft are assigned to the nuclear strike role, the total of NATO aircraft so assigned is considerably *higher,* and the total of Soviet aircraft drops to a level more consistent with figures provided by other sources, including the Department of Defense itself. If, furthermore, these aircraft are then assigned the number of weapons they normally carry, as most other sources confirm,[98] and as the IISS itself would confirm in most cases three years later, here were the numbers of aircraft assigned at that time to the nuclear strike role, and the numbers of weapons they could carry:[99]

NATO		Warsaw Pact	
Aircraft Assigned	Weapons Carried	Aircraft Assigned	Weapons Carried
846	1965	344	429

By ignoring the normal operational loadings of several aircraft types, as well as its own guidelines for the number of Soviet aircraft allocated for nuclear strikes, and other significant information it presented elsewhere in the same book, the Institute produced a table that substantially distorted the balance of theater nuclear power in Europe. Those who read it carelessly, or those who wanted to read it carelessly, could easily use it to substantiate their own misrepresentations of the balance of power.

The Reagan administration may have used this same table for that purpose. At the Geneva negotiations, it included a total of 3,095 Soviet aircraft in its count of Soviet theater nuclear systems in Europe. It is in this table, under the heading "Long and Medium-Range Nuclear Systems for the European Theatre," that the same total of 3,095 Soviet aircraft appears.[100]

This implies that all of those aircraft are available for the nuclear role in

Europe, even though the IISS had earlier acknowledged in the same book that this total was the total of all nuclear-capable Soviet strike aircraft that *existed,* and of all the medium bombers the Soviet Air Force possessed, and even though the IISS now estimated, in footnotes to the same table, that only 1,013 of all of those aircraft were available for combat in Europe, and that only 344 of these were assigned to the nuclear strike role.

The full inventory of 3,095 such Soviet aircraft therefore has no reason to appear under this heading. It appears there ostensibly as a "basis" for subsequent reductions to the lower numbers of Soviet aircraft actually available and assigned to the nuclear strike role. But no comparable figure for the full inventory of all the existing nuclear-capable NATO strike aircraft is given.[101]

Nor do the lower totals of Soviet aircraft actually available and assigned to the nuclear strike role appear anywhere in the table. These must be calculated by the reader, following the guidelines the IISS specifies only in the footnotes. Nor does the information developed in the table itself follow those guidelines. The table offers only percentages of the total inventory of each aircraft type.[102] When these are added, they produce a total of Soviet aircraft presumably allocated for nuclear strikes that is more than twice as high as the total the footnotes themselves specify.

Thus, the guidelines the IISS says it means to apply for determining the actual number of aircraft that should be included among "Long and Medium-Range Nuclear Systems for the European Theatre" appear only in footnotes. They can only be applied, and the number of aircraft properly included under that heading can only be determined, if the footnotes are read. Otherwise, the information in the table is bound to be *mis*read.

The most prominent total of Soviet aircraft in that table is the sole total the IISS chooses to provide: the total of 3,095 nuclear-capable strike aircraft and bombers. Only the reader who has read other passages in the book will know that this total represents the full Soviet inventory of such aircraft, and that it far exceeds the number of Soviet aircraft of all types available in Europe. Only the reader who has checked the NATO total against other passages in the book will know that the NATO total is incomplete, and that the comparison the table makes between these two totals is therefore grossly misleading.

Only the reader who checks the weapons loads of each aircraft, and who learns from other sources that they overstate Soviet and understate NATO loads, will appreciate the extent to which this further compounds the table's initial distortions.

Thus, the same source can both present and *mis*represent the balance of power at the same time. It is in the footnotes and other marginal passages of their publications that such sources, protecting their reputations for accuracy and authority, can demonstrate to one another that they are really aware of the basic facts on which all of them agree. This does not prevent them from simultaneously giving much greater prominence to information which wholly contradicts those facts. In this way, they can simultaneously serve political goals by misrepresenting the balance of power. That is all it seems the IISS has done here. It repeated the same exercise in the following year's edition of *The Military Balance.*[103]

Though the British have now retired their *Vulcan* bombers, additional *Jaguar* and *Tornado* aircraft have more than compensated for their loss. The number of F-16s in Europe, all of them nuclear-capable, continues to grow. It is NATO that has the advantage in nuclear strike aircraft. Not only does it have the advantage in numbers of such aircraft; most of its aircraft also have much greater ranges and load capacities than their Soviet counterparts. These advantages would have continued to offset Soviet SS-20 deployments without the deployment of the *Pershing II* and Cruise missiles, and without French and British expansion of their missile forces at sea.

Using IISS guidelines for the numbers of aircraft assigned to the nuclear strike role, using aircraft inventory totals obtained from subsequent IISS editions of *The Military Balance,* and using the number of weapons carried by each aircraft type as its normal operational load, here is the balance of nuclear weapons deliverable by aircraft assigned to the nuclear strike role in the European theater in successive years:[104]

Year	NATO	Warsaw Pact
1982	1965	429
1983	2305	473
1984	2087	433

Adding these to the totals of intermediate-range missile warheads deliverable in successive years, here is the balance of nuclear weapons of *both* kinds, all of them capable of striking targets throughout the European theater, in those same years:[105]

Year	NATO	Warsaw Pact
1982	3023	1316
1983	3550	1451
1984	3597	1440

These, then, were the nuclear weapons deliverable by aircraft and missiles of longest range in the European theater. There should have been nothing surprising about our lead in this category of weapons. The Defense Department was perfectly well aware of our strength in this category. "Our current capability for theater-wide nuclear strikes," it acknowledged, "is provided by carrier and land-based tactical aircraft, Pershing surface-to-surface missiles, Poseidon and United Kingdom Polaris submarine-launched ballistic missiles, plus other additional U.S. strategic forces."[106]

All that might have been surprising was that the Reagan administration had refused to recognize the existence of some of these forces, or the relevance of others, and grossly misrepresented the balance of nuclear strike aircraft by counting only some of ours and counting more Soviet aircraft than the Soviets even had available for Europe, let alone available for nuclear strikes. By 1984, when the administration published its third edition of *Soviet Military Power,* it counted a few more NATO aircraft, for a total of 700, but still continued to count "up to 3,000" Warsaw Pact aircraft "in nuclear role."[107]

Anthony Cordesman subsequently complained of this. "The US and NATO did fail," he wrote, "to provide any real explanation of the overall strength of NATO and Warsaw Pact theater nuclear forces and did focus on Soviet IRBMs without counting the total numbers of NATO nuclear capable strike aircraft and the SLBM warheads assigned to SACEUR."[108]

But this was the only way the Reagan administration could create the impression of an "adverse imbalance of power." And its efforts to do that did *not* fail: its figures were picked up repeatedly by the press. *The New York Times* published the administration's false aircraft comparisons within only a few weeks after the President announced the "zero option" proposal, and published a modified version of it in 1982.[109]

If it did not publish the administration's figures, the press published its own. But it almost always published figures showing a substantial Soviet lead, even though it was NATO which actually held the lead. In 1983, *Newsweek* gave NATO 604 nuclear strike aircraft, and the Warsaw Pact 1,085.[110] Then it gave NATO aircraft 1,380 deliverable nuclear weapons and the Warsaw Pact 3,485.[111] At that time, according to IISS data, IISS guidelines, and normal operational loads, NATO aircraft could deliver 2,305 nuclear weapons, while the Warsaw Pact's aircraft could deliver just 473.

Complaints like Cordesman's, though few and far between, did warn the administration that its attempts to create the impression of an adverse imbalance of power with false comparisons of longer-range theater nuclear forces would not go unchallenged. So it turned its attention to comparisons of all of the nuclear weapons both alliances held ready for use in Europe, including all weapons of shorter range, even though NATO had usually sought to avoid such comparisons because its overwhelming lead in shorter-range weapons only further emphasized NATO's overall theater nuclear advantage.

In 1981, for example, military historian William Koenig noted that NATO not only maintained superiority "in the longer-range deep-strike capability of its tactical air forces," but also "a considerable superiority in tactical nuclear warheads," with a total of 7,000 warheads of all types, compared with the Warsaw Pact's 3,500.[112]

Nevertheless, the administration maintained that the balance in short-range nuclear forces, while "traditionally an area of NATO advantage, also has shifted dramatically in favor of the Soviets in recent years";[113] and in 1984 it published a chart showing 1,600 Soviet short-range missile launchers and artillery tubes, compared with 1,300 such weapon systems for NATO.[114]

The administration's figures for the Warsaw Pact included 700 short-range missile launchers and 900 artillery tubes. These figures appeared to be roughly correct. Most authoritative sources, including David Isby and the IISS, agree that the Soviets, at division, army, and front levels, *have* added nuclear-capable artillery systems to their forces in Europe.[115] But to the 882 of those systems the Soviets have deployed, NATO has 2,234 nuclear-capable artillery pieces, and keeps more than 4,000 rounds of 155 mm and 203 mm nuclear artillery ammunition stockpiled in Europe.[116]

The administration's chart listed only 1,200 of these artillery pieces, and only 100 of NATO's 1,112 short-range missile launchers. Gone, it seemed, were the *Pershing 1A*s deployed both by the United States and West Germany, the *Honest Johns* in Turkey and Greece, the *Nike-Hercules* missiles that had not been included among those NATO had already withdrawn, and the French *Plutons*.[117]

If all the nuclear-capable missile launchers and artillery tubes available to both alliances were to fire a single round, without reloads, and all the aircraft they had assigned a nuclear role were to fly a single sortie—which is all that any of these systems would most probably ever have the opportunity to do—then here are the full balances of all such weapons, of long range and short, they had deployed and could bring to bear against European targets in successive years:[118]

Year	NATO	Warsaw Pact
1982	6777	2296
1983	7295	2819
1984	7315	2949

NATO's theater nuclear forces never had faced an "adverse imbalance of power." They did not face one now. Those of the Warsaw Pact did.

There was no military significance to this imbalance. Parity was not needed to ensure stalemate. The Warsaw Pact had more than enough nuclear weapons to deter any offensive operations mounted by NATO. But the political implications of this imbalance were perfectly clear: it was the very reverse of what the Reagan administration had claimed. Had the public been aware of this, the United States would have had no excuse for deploying the *Pershing II* and Cruise missiles in Europe. That is why such an extraordinary effort was made to keep the public unaware.

IV

THE MYTH
OF SOVIET CONVENTIONAL
SUPERIORITY

26 The Balance of Ground Forces in Europe

Of the $153 billion the Reagan administration plans to spend solely on weapons research and procurement in its fiscal year 1986 military budget, it has set aside $111.2 billion for conventional weapons.[1] While this administration has raised military spending of almost every kind to unprecedented levels, expenditures for conventional weapons have always consumed the major portion of military investment since its arms buildup began.

To justify this, as well as to help justify the presence of nuclear weapons in Europe and America's refusal to renounce their first use, the administration and its supporters have repeatedly sought to create the impression that America's conventional forces are inadequate, and that until they can be sufficiently strengthened, the West has no choice but to rely on nuclear weapons as a deterrent to attack by presumably stronger conventional forces of the East.

Since both superpowers, and both military alliances in Europe, now have nuclear weapons, neither can any longer safely use them against the other without risking retaliation and uncontrollable escalation. Consequently, the threat of their use, which is all that the policy of deterrence comprises, is fundamentally irrational. Nevertheless, the need to rely on nuclear weapons in view of alleged weaknesses in conventional military power has played a critical role in enforcing acceptance of an irrational policy.

Sometimes the alarmists who seek to create an impression of America's military inadequacy will only assert that we cannot match the Soviet Union, weapon by weapon, in every category of military power, as though this gave the Soviets advantages of certain kinds, and as though there were conceivable circumstances in which these advantages might be brought to bear. Introducing a recent study by John M. Collins of the balance of power between the United States and the Soviet Union, the congressmen who commissioned it write that it demonstrates "we are not doing well in narrowing the gaps between U.S. and Soviet capabilities that existed in 1980."[2] Which gaps were these? Was there ever any need to narrow them? Have we ever had any real intention of narrowing them? They do not say.

The congressmen add that the study shows "our military force structure is inadequate to meet our formal and informal worldwide commitments."[3] This, too, is a warning often repeated. Almost invariably, as in this case, it is unaccompanied by any specification of what our commitments are, or by any discussion of whether our "informal" commitments may ever conflict with the interests of other nations and peoples. Our military force structure may be more than adequate to meet all our formal treaty obligations, and these congressmen could still make the same statement, for they can presume any additional "commitments" they please. They can envisage America at war with the entire world, and some of them very well may.

Thus, statements about the inadequacy of a military force are meaningless without clearly defining the purpose of that force. But such statements are still effective in manipulating public opinion. Release of the Collins study was noted by *The New York Times* in an unsigned article entitled "Soviet Found Ahead in Arms."[4] The article further quoted from the book that "America's active all-volunteer force is too small to dispose of even one extensive contingency anywhere in the world' without stripping forces from the United States or bases overseas." This creates the impression that America is dangerously unprepared. But forces must be "stripped" from somewhere. How many wars can a nation prepare to fight? Almost every scenario for a conventional war in Europe presumes the commitment, at various stages, of the entire active Soviet Army of 1,825,000. This "extensive contingency" would certainly involve "stripping forces" from all of the other borders of the Soviet Union, leaving them undefended. Then the Soviet active army, too, appears to be "too small."

Most efforts to obtain support for greater expenditures on conventional weapons, however, involve numerical comparisons, designed to make NATO seem at a disadvantage. In 1982, for example, NATO claimed it had 84 divisions facing a total of 173 Warsaw Pact divisions.[5] In notes it explained that in this count, "both United States and Canadian trans-Atlantic reinforcements have been excluded on the one hand, while the Soviet Strategic Reserves from the Moscow, Ural and Volga Military Districts have been excluded on the other." However, it noted that in addition to Soviet forces stationed in eastern Europe, all Soviet forces "in the Leningrad, Baltic, Byelorussian and Carpathian Military Districts" of the USSR had been included in the count for the "Northern and Central Regional balance."[6]

According to David Isby, author of *Weapons and Tactics of the Soviet Army,* there are forty-nine Soviet divisions in various states of readiness in the four military districts of the Soviet Union NATO had cited.[7] According to the Reagan administration's booklet *Soviet Military Power,* however, there are ninety-four Soviet divisions "located opposite the Central and Northern regions of NATO."[8]

In 1983, NATO brought out new figures, giving itself 88 divisions and the Warsaw Pact 167.[9] This time, in explanatory notes, it included the "rapidly deployable" United States divisions, "whose equipment is stored in Europe and two-thirds of their personnel based in the United States,"[10] while for the Warsaw Pact it included Soviet forces in eastern Europe and the Leningrad military district, and "only the high readiness units" of the Soviet Baltic, Byelorussian, and Carpathian districts.[11] Why had more Soviet divisions been counted before? Why hadn't the United States divisions been counted the last time?

Including all Soviet divisions in the Leningrad district, and the "high readiness" divisions in the three other military districts NATO had cited, Isby's figures show a total of either twenty or thirty-eight divisions, according to whether NATO was counting only those units in the highest states of readiness or those in the next highest state as well.[12] In either case, the total of Warsaw Pact divisions confronting NATO did not seem appreciably reduced.

In 1984, NATO released a new study which reduced the estimate of Warsaw Pact divisions confronting NATO by one third, to only 115 divisions. It now excluded fifty-eight more Soviet divisions "not immediately available to fight because of low combat readiness or distance from prospective battlefields."[13]

It isn't too likely that these divisions were any more ready to fight, or any closer to prospective battlefields, in 1982. But in the intervening years, the public in West Europe and America was persuaded that NATO desperately needed to build its conventional strength.

Nor could the public assume, after NATO issued its lower estimate of Warsaw Pact strength in 1984, that the situation was very much better. How many people knew that the Warsaw Pact's divisions are substantially smaller than NATO's, with an average of 40 percent fewer troops?[14] How many people, then, would realize that if NATO's 1984 figures were correct, NATO's 88 divisions held more manpower than the Warsaw Pact's 115?

Nor had the manipulation of figures ended. Hard on the heels of NATO's 1984 estimate, John Collins, in his new study of the military balance—whose "statistical quality and coverage" was more "complete," its congressional sponsors promised, than any "other summary"[15]—found a new way of comparing the balance of "on-site" forces in Europe: lowering NATO's divisional total to 64, but adding 103 "brigades, regiments," without distinguishing how many there were of each, and raising the Warsaw Pact's divisional strength to 138, with another 48 "brigades, regiments" added.[16] The table providing this data refers the reader to notes at the back of the book, which reveal that included among the "on-site" forces are Soviet and Warsaw Pact "Category III divisions at estimated current strengths."[17]

According to David Isby, the Soviet Army's Category III divisions, those at the lowest state of readiness, are "not deployable until between 90 and 120 days after mobilization."[18] In that case, they can't very well be "on-site" beforehand. Nor is it possible to determine the total manpower of the various ground units Collins places "on-site," because in his notes he has only given a single total for each nation's ground and air force personnel taken together.[19]

Here, then, is how estimates of NATO and Warsaw Pact strengths in divisions have been presented in the past four years:

NATO			Warsaw Pact	
Estimate	Divisions	Smaller Units	Divisions	Smaller Units
NATO 1982	84		173	
NATO 1983	88		167	
NATO 1984	88		115	
Collins 1985	64	103	138	48

When the manpower of an American armored division averages 18,300,[20] and the manpower of a Soviet armored division is unlikely to exceed David Isby's estimate of 9,456,[21] comparisons of this kind between numbers of NATO and Warsaw Pact divisions are wholly misleading. That is presumably why they are used. Comparisons of the total manpower represented by all of these divisions would provide a far more accurate measure of the balance of power between the alliances.

Since that fact is reasonably obvious, NATO and other official sources, while emphasizing division comparisons, have had to provide manpower comparisons too. Since they have had to provide them, they have had to design incomplete comparisons which continued to support the impression that NATO suffers an adverse imbalance of conventional power. Here is one comparison of "total military personnel in place in Europe," provided by the Reagan administration in 1982:[22]

NATO	Warsaw Pact
2,600,000	4,000,000

These are meant to be figures for military personnel in all branches of service; but the administration acknowledges, in footnotes, that the figures for NATO "exclude French forces," because "France withdrew its forces from NATO's international commands in 1966," though it "remains a member of the alliance."[23] Another footnote acknowledges that the "above figures do not include Spain, which became a member of NATO on May 30, 1982."[24]

William Mako of the Brookings Institution points out that French forces are frequently "excluded from some assessments" of the European balance, "such as those by John Collins of the Congressional Research Service, apparently on the assumption that French forces could not easily be reintegrated into the NATO command structure in wartime. France has, however, continued to engage in joint exercises and planning with NATO since 1967."[25]

New York Times correspondent Drew Middleton notes that "although France since 1966 has not been integrated into the NATO military structure," there are "48,000 Frenchmen" stationed in West Germany nevertheless, and "military officials make it clear that France's position in a war would be one of full support."[26]

According to Robert Lucas Fischer, the presence of French forces in West Germany "is a political and military fact, and it seems reasonable to take account of it."[27] According to the West German government, "France has never left any doubt that she would honor her commitments to the Alliance in the event of a military conflict."[28]

"Including France in calculations of the balance," former Defense Department official Robert Komer told *Newsweek,* "can reverse an unfavorable manpower ratio for NATO to a favorable one." Komer added: "France is the key to a credible, cost-effective, conventional defense of Europe."[29]

According to the IISS in *The Military Balance, 1981–1982,* France had a total of 504,650 active personnel in all military services at the time the Reagan administration excluded them in its manpower comparison,[30] and Spain's entry into NATO added another 342,000 active military personnel in all services.[31] Restoring these personnel to the administration's comparison yields the following balance of NATO and Warsaw Pact military personnel:

NATO	Warsaw Pact
3,446,650	4,000,000

Are personnel still missing from this balance? Yes—personnel from both alliances are missing. The administration was careful to note that its figures were only for personnel "in place in Europe."[32] Presumably, therefore, it had excluded NATO and Warsaw Pact personnel not in Europe.

The administration's figures were exactly the same as those offered by NATO in 1982. NATO, too, was careful to note that its figure for its own personnel was only for personnel "stationed in Europe."[33] It did not say, however, that 4 million Warsaw Pact personnel were "in place in Europe"; it said that 4 million of them "face NATO in Europe."[34] It did not clarify from how far away some of these personnel faced NATO.

But in its notes, NATO had already explained that its count included not only Soviet personnel stationed in eastern Europe but also those in four military districts of the Soviet Union.[35] Military districts of the Soviet Union are not in Europe; they are in the Soviet Union.

NATO offered exactly the same count of personnel in both alliances in 1983,[36] even though its notes explained that its counts now included those "rapidly deployable" divisions "two-thirds" of whose personnel were "based in the United States," but only the "high readiness" divisions in three of the four Soviet military districts it continued to count,[37] and its Secretary General offered his opinion that this new count provided "a more realistic picture."[38]

NATO, too, excluded French and Spanish forces from its count, on the grounds that, though these nations are members of the alliance, "they do not participate in its integrated military structure."[39] "At their request therefore," NATO added, as though it really would have preferred to count these forces but had no choice in the matter, "no account of French and Spanish forces is taken in this comparison."[40]

According to the International Institute for Strategic Studies, the balance of all active NATO and Warsaw Pact uniformed military personnel in all branches of service stood thus in 1982:[41]

NATO	Warsaw Pact
5,275,889	4,788,000

Here is how the IISS counted the forces of each nation in both alliances that year:[42]

NATO		Warsaw Pact	
United States	2,049,100	Soviet Union	3,673,000
Belgium	89,500	Bulgaria	149,000
United Kingdom	343,646	Czechoslovakia	194,000
Canada	79,497	East Germany	167,000
Denmark	32,600	Hungary	101,000
France	504,630	Poland	319,500
West Germany	495,000	Romania	184,500
Greece	193,500		
Italy	366,000	Total	4,788,000
Luxembourg	690		
Netherlands	102,800		

Norway	37,000
Portugal	70,926
Spain	342,000
Turkey	569,000
Total	5,275,889

The Institute notes that only 273,729 U.S. Army and Air Force personnel, and 3,764 Canadian Army and Air Force personnel, were stationed in Europe in 1982.[43] Both the Reagan administration and NATO appear to have utilized these figures for the United States and Canada when they made their counts of alliance personnel "in place" or "stationed" in Europe. When they counted Warsaw Pact personnel "in place" in Europe, they should not have excluded the forces of any eastern European nation, since all of those nations are indisputably located in Europe. Here, then, is the only way it seems the administration and NATO could have produced their identical counts:

NATO		Warsaw Pact	
United States	273,729	Soviet Union	2,885,000
Belgium	89,500	Bulgaria	149,000
United Kingdom	343,646	Czechoslovakia	194,000
Canada	3,764	East Germany	167,000
Denmark	32,600	Hungary	101,000
West Germany	495,000	Poland	319,500
Greece	193,500	Romania	184,500
Italy	366,000		
Luxembourg	690	Total	4,000,000
Netherlands	102,800		
Norway	37,000		
Portugal	70,926		
Turkey	569,000		
Total	2,578,155		

Thus, to count a total of 4,000,000 Warsaw Pact military personnel "in place in Europe," the administration must assume that 2,885,000 Soviet military personnel are "in place in Europe." NATO, somewhat more ambiguously, must assume that 2,885,000 Soviet military personnel "face NATO in Europe" at some range or other.

The IISS does not offer a count in 1982 of the number of Soviet military personnel stationed in Europe. But in 1976 it offered a count of 460,000 Soviet Army and 45,000 Soviet Air Force personnel stationed in East Germany, Poland, and Czechoslovakia.[44] These figures appear to have grown only slightly through 1982. Lothar Ruehl, a West German Government official, counted 467,000

Soviet Army and 58,000 Soviet Air Force personnel in the same three countries in 1982.[45]

Soviet forces are also stationed in Hungary. In *The Military Balance, 1984–1985,* the IISS offers a somewhat larger count of Soviet ground forces in Europe, including 65,000 in Hungary.[46] It offers no estimate of the numbers of Soviet Air Force personnel in Europe. David Isby, however, estimates the numbers of tactical aircraft flown by each of the four Soviet Tactical Air Armies stationed in Europe; and Ruehl provides figures for the number of Soviet Air Force personnel in three of those armies.[47] Using both of their estimates, which show an average of forty-two personnel per aircraft flown, it is possible to make a reasonable estimate of the number of Soviet Air Force personnel in Hungary:

Soviet Tactical Air Army in	Isby's Figures for Tactical Aircraft	Ruehl's Figures for Air Force Personnel*
East Germany	975	40,000
Czechoslovakia	100	5,000
Poland	350	13,000
Hungary	275	11,550

* Except Hungary, which is estimated.

Assuming that Soviet Army personnel in Hungary were no fewer in 1982 than the IISS estimates in 1985, and using the estimate derived above for Soviet Air Force personnel in Hungary, and Ruehl's figures for all other Soviet Army and Air Force personnel, it is possible to make a reasonably confident estimate of the total of Soviet military personnel stationed throughout eastern Europe in 1982:

Stationed in	Soviet Ground Forces	Soviet Air Forces	Total
East Germany	366,000	40,000	406,000
Czechoslovakia	73,000	5,000	78,000
Poland	37,000	13,000	50,000
Hungary	65,000	11,550	76,550
Total	541,000	69,550	610,550

If that is the case, then the administration and NATO have counted 2,274,450 more Soviet military personnel in Europe than are really "in place" or "stationed" there. This surplus exceeds the entire active Soviet Army strength by half a million. We know that a large portion of the Soviet Army is on the eastern Soviet border, facing China. The IISS tells us that 385,000 Soviet military personnel are in the Strategic Rocket Forces, and that another 550,000 are in the Soviet

Air Defense Forces.[48] They cannot all be stationed in Europe. In principle, all Soviet military personnel may "face NATO in Europe"; but in reality, most of them face NATO at an enormous, and tactically futile, distance.

If only U.S. military personnel "in place in Europe" are to be considered in such a balance, then only Soviet military personnel "in place in Europe" should be considered. If only the active personnel of both alliances "stationed in Europe" in 1982 are to be compared, then we are left with the following figures:

NATO		Warsaw Pact	
United States	273,729	Soviet Union	610,550
Belgium	89,500	Bulgaria	149,000
United Kingdom	343,646	Czechoslovakia	194,000
Canada	3,764	East Germany	167,000
Denmark	32,600	Hungary	101,000
France	504,630	Poland	319,500
West Germany	495,000	Romania	184,500
Greece	193,500		
Italy	366,000	Total	1,725,550
Luxembourg	690		
Netherlands	102,800		
Norway	37,000		
Portugal	70,926		
Spain	342,000		
Turkey	569,000		
Total	3,424,785		

The IISS has already shown what a static comparison of all the active military personnel of both alliances, regardless of where they are stationed, reveals. The Institute also noted in 1982 that the "mobilization strength" of West Germany's armed forces is "about 1,250,000"—a note that it made about no other NATO nation."[49] The IISS was not here speaking of reserves; West Germany has a territorial army which the Institute distinguishes from reserves, and whose strength Chris Holshek places at 450,000.[50] According to Milton Leitenberg, West Germany has "the ability to mobilize 1.2 million men in 60 hours in an acute crisis."[51] If the full strength of West German forces is 1,250,000, then 755,000 must be added to the figure of 495,000 "total armed forces" the IISS first provides. This raises the IISS static comparison of all uniformed military personnel of both alliances, excluding reserves, to the following in 1982:

NATO	Warsaw Pact
6,030,889	4,788,000

These figures are close to those given by the Center for Defense Information in Washington, D.C., for the total of all uniformed military personnel of both alliances in 1982:[52]

NATO	Warsaw Pact
5,900,000	4,800,000

Contrary, then, to the impression that NATO and the Reagan administration have sought to create, the manpower balance, whether of personnel "stationed in Europe" or elsewhere as well, substantially favors NATO.

Adding figures for reserves would raise the manpower totals of both alliances. The problem here is in making a reasonable estimate of what figures to add. While the estimates for NATO's reserves are fairly consistent and can be easily checked, those for the Warsaw Pact, and especially those for the Soviet Union, vary widely.

According to William J. Lewis, for example, the Soviet Army is "backed up by over 2,000,000 trained reservists."[53] The IISS, on the other hand, says that "total reserves" for all Soviet military services "could be 25,000,000."[54]

In light of David Isby's comments on the Soviet Army's reserves, it is doubtful whether the Soviets could muster or equip even a fraction of the number Lewis quotes. "The Soviets," Isby notes, "have no reserve units that meet for regular peacetime training, as does the U.S. National Guard, except for some small specialist units." He estimates that designated reserve units of the Soviet Army, "which have no peacetime existence," comprise at most fifty formations, and that no more than twenty of these have cadres of more than three hundred men. These units, he adds, would be given "civilian trucks" and equipment of "wartime vintage." Such formations, he concludes, "are unlikely to be deployable even for second-line duties before 180 days after mobilization."[55]

Assuming the Soviets could mobilize even as many as 2 million reserves for all branches of service, and accepting IISS figures for all other Warsaw Pact reserves as well as for all NATO reserves in 1982, here is the manpower balance between both alliances, including reserves, at that time:[56]

NATO	Warsaw Pact
8,229,013	5,032,500

Most important of all is to consider whether a nation's reserves will ever be used, and if so, under what conditions. NATO presumably exists only in order to defend itself from an attack by the Warsaw Pact. It does not anticipate, or does not acknowledge, the possibility that it might precipitate hostilities by invading Warsaw Pact territory itself.

Consequently, so far as the public knows, the fundamental premise of all NATO planning has been defense. If hostilities occur, it is NATO which will be attacked, not the Warsaw Pact. It is NATO, not the Warsaw Pact, which must defend its homeland. Reserves are far more likely, therefore, to be mobilized and brought into action by NATO than by the Warsaw Pact.

NATO has in fact planned for rapid mobilization of both active and reserve units. The IISS recognizes this, noting that "the most rapid build-up of any size would be that from the mobilization of reserves in Europe, which could occur within days. This applies particularly to Germany." It adds that "other European nations could also use mobilized reserves to strengthen units and, in certain cases, increase their number. Formations from outside the immediate area would come from Canada, Britain and possibly France, but principally from the United States," whose "personnel could be moved very quickly, using the very considerable airlift available." The Institute acknowledges that with "full reinforcement," NATO would "reach a better position."[57]

The utilization of large numbers of NATO reserves, and only the partial utilization of Warsaw Pact reserves depending on the readiness of existing units, are accordingly assumed in all relevant portions of this book.

Unfortunately, static manpower comparisons, no matter how carefully made, have only a limited value. Even when they eliminate asymmetries, and attempt to compare only truly equivalent forces, they give but a partial view of what would happen in the event of war. The corrected balances attempted here of all NATO and Warsaw Pact military personnel worldwide, both with and without reserves, show forces which might never play a role in the outcome of combat in Europe. The corrected balance of active NATO and Warsaw Pact personnel truly stationed in Europe does not include Soviet and American naval personnel, large numbers of whom would be engaged in combat off Europe's shores. The troops in this balance would be at varying distances from the initial zone of combat; those closer to the front line might take longer to get there than others further away. For example, if hostilities broke out in central Europe, large numbers of reinforcements would arrive there from the United States before those from Spain.

Consequently, more detailed analyses of what would probably happen have focused on where it would happen and in what sequence of events. Political boundaries, geographical features, and the resulting disposition of NATO and Warsaw Pact forces have made central Europe the most probable region where hostilities might first occur. Misrepresentations of the central European balance have thrown doubt not only on how much equipment and how many troops are stationed there, but also on how rapidly and in what sequence they could be reinforced.

There have been misrepresentations even of how the balance is represented. In an effort to stabilize that balance, NATO and the Warsaw Pact have been holding Mutual and Balanced Force Reduction talks in Vienna for fifteen years.[58] Apparently, for fifteen years they have been unable to agree on the number of troops they counted in the region. According to our State Department, the Warsaw Pact has 960,000 ground troops in the region; according to *The New York Times,* the Soviet Union counts only 830,000 Warsaw Pact ground troops in the region.[59] But according to the Soviet government, there are 979,000 Warsaw Pact ground troops in the region.[60] That is higher than our own State Department's count.

Here is how these statements compare:

Warsaw Pact Ground Forces in Central Europe

US Count in 1982	Soviet Count According to *NY Times* in 1982	Soviet Count According to Soviet Union in 1982
960,000	830,000	979,000

If the Soviet Union publicly provides a figure for Warsaw Pact troops in this region higher than the figure our own government provides, then it cannot very well get away with providing the lower figure quoted by *The New York Times* at the Mutual and Balanced Force Reduction talks in Vienna. Either the *Times* misrepresented the Soviet count, or its source did so and the *Times* did not correct it.

The following table shows the comparison the IISS gave, in 1976, of ground troops in central Europe, and of the smaller number of "combat and direct support troops available" in the somewhat larger region of "Northern and Central Europe":[61]

Ground Forces in Central Europe

Total Manpower		Combat and Direct Support Troops	
NATO	Warsaw Pact	NATO	Warsaw Pact
742,000	925,000	625,000	895,000

These figures, the Institute noted, "do not include French forces." Nor did they include "the men in the American dual-based brigades, because they are not physically present in Europe."[62] The figures, however, did include "on the Warsaw Pact side some 185,000 in, or in direct support of, divisions in the

Western Soviet Union, since these formations are clearly designed for operations in Central Europe, though they are at some distance in time and space from the area."[63] If French forces were added, then the Institute suggested the NATO totals should be raised as follows:[64]

Total Manpower	Combat and Direct Support Troops
NATO	NATO
800,000	675,000

The figure of 800,000 which the IISS gave in 1976 for NATO's total manpower in central Europe, including French forces, is the same figure our State Department quoted for NATO forces in the region in 1982.[65]

In 1978, however, the Institute published a new comparison of "manpower in combat units" in northern and central Europe. Though troops in combat units could only be a portion of the total of troops in combat and noncombat units, the figure the IISS now gave for the Warsaw Pact was above the larger figure it had reported for the total of Pact manpower in central Europe in 1976. NATO's figure, meanwhile, was barely larger than the lowest of the figures the IISS had given in 1976 both for NATO's "combat" and its "direct support troops" in northern and central Europe:[66]

Manpower in Combat Units
Northern and Central Europe

NATO	Warsaw Pact
626,000	943,000

Again, the IISS noted that the figures "do not include French forces."[67] *Time* magazine did not restore them when it reported that NATO remains "outmanned" in the "strategically crucial central and northern European regions. To the 626,000 troops fielded by NATO, the East Europeans have 943,000."[68]

Here is how Jeffrey Record counted the total of NATO and Warsaw Pact ground forces in central Europe in 1980:[69]

NATO		Warsaw Pact	
United States	193,000	Soviet Union	475,000
United Kingdom	58,000	Czechoslovakia	135,000
Canada	3,000	East Germany	105,000
Belgium	62,000	Poland	220,000
West Germany	341,000		
Netherlands	75,000	Total	935,000
Total	732,000		

As his source for the figures, Record gives *The Military Balance, 1979–1980,* page 110.[70] Numbers for active and reserve divisions appear on that page, but figures for manpower in central Europe do not.[71] NATO's total, Record notes, "excludes French forces in Germany," which "number some 50,000 troops." He also asserts that "Warsaw Pact negotiators claim significantly lower manpower levels."[72]

This does not seem, at least recently, to have been the case, since the Soviet Union publicly acknowledges higher manpower levels. What becomes clear, on closer examination, is that much of the Warsaw Pact's added manpower is not in major combat units, and that it would take time for the Pact to fully mobilize the troops that both sides count, and to bring up to strength all its units in eastern Europe. NATO, in the meanwhile, would have built up its strength to much higher levels. Here is an estimate of the manpower levels in place and in the first stages of mobilization and reinforcement in central Europe:[73]

	Manpower in Combat Units		Total Manpower	
Time	NATO	Pact	NATO	Pact
Prior to First Alert	470,023	390,607	886,835	574,422
24 Hrs After First Alert	697,120	520,810	1,297,830	765,895
After 10 Days	1,374,471	679,987	2,563,880	999,977

Even though the IISS had acknowledged, in 1976, that Soviet reinforcements for the Warsaw Pact, stationed in the western military districts of the USSR, were "at some distance in time and space from the area," it suggested, the following year, that the Warsaw Pact was "capable of a much faster build-up" than NATO, provided "surprise is achieved."[74] It had also acknowledged, however, that if the Soviet Union began to mobilize, "it would be impossible to conceal it on any scale."[75]

So it seems that surprise cannot be achieved. Indeed not. According to General Alexander Haig, when he was commander of NATO forces in 1977, NATO at that time could already "count on 8 to 15 days' warning of an attack by troops of the Soviet-led Warsaw Pact."[76]

In that case, NATO already would have built up its forces before the attack could begin. The IISS acknowledges that the "American ability to bring back the men of the dual-based brigades in days by air has been demonstrated on exercises," and that "the increase of manpower strengths of combatant units (as distinct from an increase in their number) could take place rapidly, both from the United States and from the European NATO countries."[77]

According to William Mako, by the end of 1981 the United States had pre-positioned equipment in Europe "for five divisions, an armored cavalry regiment, and other corps-level support units based in the United States."[78] Only the troops need to be airlifted in. Defense Secretary Harold Brown told NATO's defense ministers in 1980 that "in the event of any crisis in Europe the United States would double its army there in two weeks and triple its aircraft strength in a week."[79]

Before an attack by the Warsaw Pact could begin, West Germany's armed forces would be fully mobilized. The British would pour heavy reinforcements into Germany. According to Deborah Meyer, "with over 55,000 British army troops stationed in West Germany," Great Britain has "another 150,000 or more regular army, reserve army, or territorial army troops ready to be there within hours in a time of crisis."[80]

The French would quickly reinforce, too.[81] Stephen Canby notes that "in the critical central region NATO, including France, has 200,000 more men in its air and ground forces than the Pact. NATO's problem is not one of lack of resources."[82]

As the preceding estimate shows, there would never be a time when NATO did not have more troops in central Europe than the Warsaw Pact could have opposing them.[83] As the reinforcements schedules in the appendixes to this book make clear, the Warsaw Pact does not have many divisions at a high state of readiness with which to reinforce its front line in central Europe.[84] The IISS acknowledges that few of these are in a high state of readiness. It lists only ten additional Soviet divisions in Category I, and eight of these are airborne units without main battle tanks.[85] Isby lists a total of fifteen Category I divisions available throughout the Soviet Union. His higher figure is used in the estimates in this book. Many of these divisions, however, would have great distances to travel; one motor rifle division in this category, for example, is based outside Moscow.[86]

The IISS lists an additional fifteen Soviet divisions available in Category II, and a total of sixty-seven divisions in Category III.[87] According to Isby, however, Category II divisions are not deployable until "within 30 days of mobilization," and those in Category III are "not deployable until between 90 and 120 days after mobilization."[88] Many eastern European formations are also in Categories II and III.[89] The powerful establishment of second-echelon and third-echelon forces, always envisaged to follow up immediately after a front-line Warsaw Pact attack, simply doesn't exist, as NATO itself began to acknowledge in 1984.

Anthony Cordesman notes that "NATO's analysis of the land balance did fail to make any intelligent comparison of the readiness of divisions and buildup capability and did compare NATO's *forward deployed* combat equipment strength against the *total* equipment strength of Warsaw Pact units with no regard for readiness or the US' rapid reinforcement capabilities."[90]

Jeffrey Record has followed NATO's practice. He has excluded from his count several hundred thousand NATO troops which already would have arrived in central Europe, outnumbering Warsaw Pact troops in the region, long before combat began, and long before the Pact could build its manpower strength to the level he shows. Subsequent NATO reinforcements would continue to outnumber Warsaw Pact troops as long as conventional conflict endured.

27 The Balance of Tanks

The Soviet Union certainly has produced more tanks than the United States has. But the number of tanks it produces, the number of tanks it has the capacity to produce, and the number it actively deploys have all been exaggerated by the West.

According to the Reagan administration, in its first edition of *Soviet Military Power* in 1981, the Soviets produced tanks at the following rate from 1976 through 1980:[1]

1976	1977	1978	1979	1980
2,500	2,500	2,500	3,000	3,000

The Soviets, by this count, seemed to be producing tanks at an average of 2,700 per year. In 1983, the Reagan administration gave new figures for Soviet tank production from 1978 through 1982:[2]

1978	1979	1980	1981	1982
3,000	3,500	3,100	2,500	2,500

The Soviets now seemed to be producing tanks at an average of 2,920 per year. But in 1980, the Defense Department released figures showing the Soviet buildup in tanks and other equipment from 1964 through 1980. It placed 30,000 tanks in the Soviet arsenal in 1964, and 45,000 in 1980. This indicates an annual rate of production over sixteen years, including all of the years cited by the Reagan administration in its first edition of *Soviet Military Power,* of 937 tanks per annum.[3] The Soviets may have produced more and exported some, but this appears to be all they acquired themselves.

From 1976 through 1981, the United States was producing the M-60 tank at a rate of 120 per month;[4] that is an annual rate of 1,440 tanks per year. In 1977, before the M-1 tank entered production, we already had the capacity to produce 218 tanks per month, or 2,616 tanks per year.[5]

This may come as a surprise to those familiar only with the map of the Soviet Nizhniy Tagil tank plant imposed over Washington, D.C., in the first edition of *Soviet Military Power*.[6] The administration suggests that our only available tank production facilities comprise 93,000 square meters of space at Lima, Ohio, and 111,500 square meters at Warren, Michigan, and that these are dwarfed by the 827,000 square meters at Nizhniy Tagil.[7]

The Lima Army Modification Center in Ohio actually occupies 259,130 square meters, a rather more generous space than *Soviet Military Power* suggests.[8] The U.S. Army Tank Plant in Warren, Michigan, took up 111,500 square meters at one time, but 76,214 square meters more were added to it well before *Soviet Military Power* was published.[9] The true combined space of these plants still falls far short of the area occupied at Nizhniy Tagil. However, when the 701,176 square meters of space at the Cleveland Automotive Tank Assembly Plant in Brookpark, Ohio, are added, the area of the three U.S. plants exceeds Nizhniy Tagil's by more than 320,000 square meters. Representative Charles Vanik of Ohio calls the Brookpark plant "one of the best tank production facilities in the world."[10]

In addition to the Brookpark plant, *Soviet Military Power* neglected to mention other facilities existing at that time in the United States for the production and assembly of tanks, including the Michigan Army Missiles Plant in Sterling Heights, Michigan; the Anniston Army Depot in Anniston, Alabama; the North American Plant in Columbus, Ohio; the Chrysler Plant in New Stanton, Pennsylvania; the Colt International Plant in Dallas, Texas; the ExCello Corporation Plant in Highland Park, Michigan; the Alco Products Plant in Schenectady, New York; the Delaware Defense Plant; the Ford Motor Plant in Livonia; the Phelps-Dodge Brass Plant in South Brunswick, New Jersey; and the United States Steel Plant in Elwood City, Pennsylvania.[11]

More significant than how many tanks a nation produces, or how many it has the capacity to produce, is how many tanks it could bring into battle. Neither NATO nor the Warsaw Pact could bring all its tanks into battle in central Europe or anywhere else, as an appendix to this book attempts to demonstrate. General Samuel V. Wilson, when chief of the Defense Intelligence Agency in 1977, testified to the Joint Economic Committee of Congress that Soviet "logistical support" for a Warsaw Pact attack would be "hampered by deficiencies in rail and road transport."[12] He also explained that "Soviet tank strength in Central Europe includes a large number of tanks in storage."[13]

Here is an estimate of the numbers of main battle tanks which NATO and the Warsaw Pact could bring into battle in central Europe at successive stages of mobilization and reinforcement:[14]

Main Battle Tanks

Time	NATO	Pact
Within 24 Hrs	10,351	12,766
Within 10 Days	14,073	14,590
Within 30 Days	15,585	17,230
Within 120 Days	18,717	24,523

In each case, these numbers are only about half of all the tanks each alliance possesses:[15]

Main Battle Tank Holdings

NATO	Pact
33,577	49,407

It is clear that the Warsaw Pact can still bring larger numbers of tanks into combat in central Europe than NATO can. Lest this should be taken to indicate that the Pact enjoys the decisive military advantage such comparisons are so often quoted to suggest, it is time to realize that numerical comparisons are only one index of military capabilities—and seldom the best one. A better one is quality. NATO not only enjoys a comfortable numerical lead in most categories of military equipment; it also enjoys a significant qualitative lead in virtually all of them.

General Daniel O. Graham, former chief of our Defense Intelligence Agency, compared Soviet and American military capabilities this way when he testified before Congress in 1975: "I think that in almost all military technologies we do lead them."[16] More recently, Alexander Haig had this to say as Secretary of State in 1981: "In a contemporary sense, the United States is very, very strong and very, very capable," adding, "our systems are both more sophisticated and reliable and more technologically sound."[17]

Tanks are no exception. The IISS acknowledges that "NATO tanks are generally superior."[18] Indeed they are, being both more heavily armored and more maneuverable. They also have more sophisticated sighting and range-finding equipment. They carry more ammunition, and can fire it more quickly, with greater accuracy, at higher muzzle velocities and consequently with far more lethal effect, than their Soviet counterparts do.[19]

In 1980, Soviet factories began producing a modified T-72 tank whose most significant changes over its predecessor were the addition of smoke mortars and armored fabric side skirts to provide added hull protection against light-caliber fire. This was seized upon by the Reagan administration, and exhaustively publicized, as a major new weapon system which posed the most serious threat NATO had yet confronted. The administration called it the T-80.

A full-page photograph of this tank appeared in *Soviet Military Power* in 1983. "The most modern Soviet tank, the T-80, featuring collective nuclear/biological/chemical protection, enhanced firepower and survivability," the accompanying text read, "is in production, and at least several hundred have been deployed to the Soviet Groups of Forces in Eastern Europe." The administration warned that the impact of this "on the most critical area—the one opposite the NATO center—is particularly significant."[20]

Steven Zaloga, an authority on armored vehicles, calls "the latest version of the T-72" the T-74, and describes it as "fitted with fabric armour skirts on the side to protect the suspension and external fuel cells from auto-cannon fire." He adds that "the T-74M are also fitted with smoke mortar arrays," and that "the US Army calls this tank the T-80."[21]

America's M-60A3, our main battle tank for several years, carries sixty-three rounds of ammunition, and fires it at a rate of ten rounds per minute. The T-72, T-74, or T-80 carries forty rounds. It fires at a rate of two rounds per minute; it could fire at six rounds per minute if its automatic loader were safe to use, but it is not. The M-60's turret turns at a rate of 24 degrees per second; the turret on the T-72 or T-80 turns at a rate of 17. The DBL-12T 125 mm gun mounted on the T-72 or T-80 can fire BR-11 APFSDS (Armor-Piercing, Fin-Stabilized, Discarding Sabot) ammunition at a velocity of 5,298 feet per second to a distance of 2,185 yards. The M-60A3's M-68 105 mm gun can fire the M-833 APFSDS round at a velocity of 6,127 feet per second to a distance of 3,640 yards.[22] The M-60's turret armor is 250 mm thick; the thickest frontal armor on the T-72 or T-80 is 210 mm.[23]

Nor are the Warsaw Pact's tanks outmatched only by the preponderance of superior NATO tanks; the ammunition NATO tanks fire has also been improved. In combat with Syrian forces in 1982, the Israelis first tested "a modified 105 mm shell which pierced the honeycomb armor of the formidable Soviet T-72 main battle tank,"[24] and which is now in NATO inventory. NATO, in addition, has more than 400,000 highly lethal antitank weapons carried by infantry, mounted on helicopters, and fired by artillery units.[25]

28 The Balance in the Air and at Sea

A comparison of NATO and Warsaw Pact aircraft again reflects NATO's superiority. While the alliances have almost perfect parity in numbers, each with the capability to commit about 12,000 combat aircraft to the European theater, NATO again has many more advanced aircraft, including 144 carrier-based F-14 *Tomcats,* 96 F-15 *Eagles,* more than 250 F-16 *Falcons,* over 650 F-4 *Phantoms,* 80 *Tornados,* 105 *Mirage IIIEs,* and 150 *Jaguars*—all of them superior to anything the Warsaw Pact flies.[1]

By contrast, the Pact air forces still fly 775 obsolete MiG-15 and MiG-17 aircraft, as well as 944 MiG-21s. Soviet tactical air armies in Europe still fly about 200 MiG-21s, but only 125 newer MiG-27s. Only forty-eight newer MiG-23s are flown by other Warsaw Pact nations. Czechoslovakia and the German Democratic Republic have just one squadron of twelve of these aircraft each.[2]

NATO's aircraft have greater range, greater maneuverability, much greater load capacities, more lethal armament, and far more sophisticated electronics for navigation and weapons control. Many more are all-weather aircraft. Many more can be used in more than a single role.

In central Europe, each alliance could commit about 4,400 aircraft to combat. While America would triple its aircraft there in only one week,[3] the Pact could still build up its aircraft more quickly—to more than 7,000 in a month, compared with NATO's ability to build up its aircraft to just under 6,000 in that time. But this assumes what would never happen. It assumes that in the meanwhile NATO's air forces would not have used their substantial qualitative superiority to reverse this numerical imbalance by sheer attrition.

At sea, NATO holds even greater advantages, with 490 major surface combatants to the Warsaw Pact's 292.[4] NATO's surface fleet has an advantage of more than two to one in tonnage alone,[5] aside from the more sophisticated fire control, missile guidance, radar, antiaircraft, antimissile defense, and antisubmarine warfare systems these vessels deploy. All these are advantages which high technology continues to afford the West almost exclusively.

With little exception, then, the Reagan administration's claims—and NATO's claims—of Warsaw Pact superiority are false. In virtually every case, NATO has long possessed far more than deterrence requires, and can retain the substantial advantages it already has at a fraction of what the Reagan administration intends to spend. Consequently, few of the programs the administration has embarked upon to redress this fictional imbalance are needed.

Yet as Anthony Cordesman and Benjamin Schemmer observed, "comparisons of US and Soviet forces," precisely like those of NATO and Warsaw Pact forces, "have furnished the essential rationale for increased defense spending."[6]

V

CREATING THE MYTH

29 Renewing the Soviet Threat

America, then, never needed to be rearmed. The nation had never been disarmed; it was already armed to the teeth. Before the Reagan administration ever arrived in office, our forces already had more equipment and more military power than they needed to do whatever military power still could do. This equipment was not about to become obsolete; it was the most capable equipment technology could provide. If some of it failed to perform as advertised, that was not for want of resources or expertise. It was only for want of reforms to eliminate waste and fraud in military spending. The Reagan administration has done nothing to curb either of these practices. Its military buildup, instead, has become a monumental example of both.

It would have been enough to institute such reforms, to maintain a portion of the weapons and forces we already had, and to continue advance research programs already under way. This research was needed only to avoid techno-logical surprise. We did not need the knowledge it gave us in order to build new weapons: we needed it only to give us the capability to build them. That capability was deterrent enough. It was more than sufficient to bargain with at the nego-tiating table, without also building the weapons themselves, ostensibly as bar-gaining chips. For once they were built, their exorbitant costs would only gain them a life of their own in defiance of efforts at arms control.

We could have done everything we needed to do for the nation's defense at only a fraction of the costs the Reagan administration has made us pay.

In every category of military equipment, we already held, and were not about to lose, immense qualitative advantages over the Soviet Union. In almost every category of equipment, we also held a substantial numerical lead over the Soviet Union. This was of no military consequence. Without that numerical lead, and even if the Soviet Union really had held it instead, the United States and NATO still would have had far more military power than deterrence required, just as the Soviet Union now has more than enough military power to deter us despite our lead.

Nevertheless, if the Soviets had held a numerical lead in nuclear warheads or any other significant category of military power, an accurate comparison of their numbers with ours, no matter how little it told of real military capabilities, would have been the simplest and most effective means of suggesting that America was endangered and needed to build its military strength.

But because America held the numerical lead in every significant category of military power, the Reagan administration could not use comparisons of this kind to justify its military buildup.

Consequently, it resorted to false comparisons, juxtaposing numbers that were either fabricated or incomplete. It had to misrepresent the balance of power. Otherwise, it could not possibly have gained our initial consent to the massive increases it demanded in defense spending, ostensibly to fund a buildup. It had to be vague about how that buildup would restore America's power, because it could not possibly demonstrate what power America lacked.

False comparisons of numbers that misrepresent the balance of power have always been the simplest and most effective means of gaining support in America for increases in military spending. Administrations before this one had used them. Groups in America that sought political power had used such comparisons to gain it, and then used that power to gain the increases. If no administration before this one had used so many false numbers at once, or repeated them so often, that was only because no administration before this one had sought an increase in military spending on such a vast scale.

But this administration used many other means of gaining support for its buildup. It launched a broad campaign of accusations of Soviet misconduct and malevolent intentions throughout the world, ranging from hints of Soviet violations of SALT II and other arms treaties to claims of Soviet support of violence and terrorism, the better to deepen distrust of the Soviet Union on a permanent basis, whether it posed an immediate military threat or not. As often as it used false comparisons of the military balance, it also avoided comparing figures, and focused public attention instead on figures for Soviet weapons alone. This implied that Soviet military power posed a threat to the West without any evidence, accurate or contrived, to demonstrate that it did, the better to encourage the notion that Government's word for it should suffice.

Government's word for it was never hard to find. Defense Secretary Weinberger offered it repeatedly to argue against reductions of any kind in military spending. He would continue to do this right into his administration's second term, after the federal deficit, fueled almost entirely by four years of unlimited military spending, had risen beyond $200 billion. In May, 1985, Congress cut the Reagan military budget for the first time, restricting its growth to no more than the pace of inflation. But until that moment, Weinberger never ceased warning that "it was pushing fallacious thought to the point of danger" to believe that America's defense budget "should be based on anything but the size and imminence of the threat we are all facing."[1]

How large a threat? How imminent? He did not say. Could America already have more than enough military power to counter that threat? No one asked.

Yet this was the question that had to be asked to determine how large our military budget should have been. A clear assessment of the threat America faced, together with an assessment of the forces already on hand to meet it, was the only rational basis on which to prescribe whatever additional forces, if any, America might require.

The administration offered no such assessment. It never explained what the weapons and forces it had decided to build could do that existing weapons and forces could not. Congress made no such assessment. It never determined what weapons America might really need, nor how they could be used. The press made no such assessment.

The press, indeed, quickly limited the framework of debate over the unprecedented size of this administration's military budgets. It wondered how the money might be spent most *efficiently*. Should it be used to purchase smaller numbers of complex weapons or larger numbers of simpler ones? It wondered whether the nation could *afford* to spend so much. It wondered whether industry could provide what the Pentagon had ordered. *Time* magazine worried that industry would be "strained to meet demand."[2] *Newsweek* answered that the demand could be met, but that "sustained, well-planned spending is what it will take."[3]

What the press did not ask was whether all of this spending was really needed. That was simply assumed, just as the Soviet threat had been assumed.

As early as 1980, toward the end of the Carter administration's term, Roger Morris had already noticed "an assumption journalists seemed to take for granted: the huge size and menacing nature of the Soviet threat."[4] Three years later, Hodding Carter expressed understandable awe at the size of the latest military budget the Reagan administration had planned, "most of it," he explained, "to defend ourselves against the Soviets."[5] He did not question whether it was needed. If the threat went unquestioned, then the nature and size of the buildup presumably needed to counter it went unquestioned too.

Consequently, the administration could continue to use the Soviet threat to justify its military buildup, without ever having to demonstrate whether the threat warranted the buildup, whether the buildup would counter the threat, or whether, in fact, there was any real relationship between the two.

Former CIA director William Colby knew that the relationship between the two was all that really ought to matter. He knew it was misleading "to assess only the adversary, rather than to compare his capabilities against our own." He knew that only a "net assessment" of the capabilities of both nations could determine whether the Soviet Union posed any threat at all. "Had net assessment evaluations been entrusted to an independent body," he added, "the official view of the balance of power might have differed from the Defense Department's recitation of the 'hard facts' of Soviet weaponry and forces," because "more sober investigation revealed the facts to be considerably less threatening."[6]

30 Soviet Military Spending

Frequently, the administration did not even offer a count of Soviet military equipment. It found other ways of measuring Soviet military power, which implied it had grown even more than an inflated count of equipment could suggest. Its favorite way of implying this was to offer its estimate of Soviet military spending, based on the CIA's calculation of "what it would cost to produce and man in the United States a military force of the same size and with the same weapons inventory as that of the USSR."[1]

To make that calculation, the CIA obviously had to know what the size and weapons inventory of the Soviet force was. Then it might simply have offered its count of the personnel and weapons of each type which made up that force. Instead, it offered a "dollar cost" estimate based upon that count.

This was counting the shadows on the wall instead of turning around to count the objects that made them. But the numerous distortions such an exercise produced were of singular value in promoting the Soviet threat. Only the largest of these resulted from estimating the costs of Soviet military pay as though Soviet personnel were paid at American pay rates. Soviet military personnel were not paid at those rates; they were paid considerably less.

In 1979, a Soviet recruit earned 3 rubles and 80 kopecks a month.[2] At international exchange rates, that was the equivalent of $5.50 per month,[3] or $66 per year. In the same year, an American recruit earned $448.80 per month,[4] or $5,385 per year. The "dollar cost" estimate, then, paid each Soviet recruit $5,319 more than he ever received.

This was but the beginning of the distortion, which higher American pay scales only further compounded as grades above the rank of recruit were taken into account. According to Franklyn Holzman, a professor of economics at Tufts University who analyzed the dimensions of this distortion and all of the others the "dollar cost" estimate achieves, American military pay and allowance scales "average about $20,000 per person" per year.[5] The Soviet Union employed an estimated total of 3,658,000 military personnel in 1979.[6] If an average of

$20,000 each had been paid to them all that year, as the "dollar cost" estimate prescribed, then they were paid a total of $73.1 billion in 1979.

But the CIA also produced an estimate in rubles of what the Soviets actually did spend on their military each year. This estimate was almost unknown to the public, because the Reagan administration was careful never to quote it. According to this estimate, the Soviets may have spent just 58 billion rubles on defense in 1979;[7] at the same exchange rates, that came to $84.1 billion.

According to the Air Force, Soviet military pay and allowances in the 1970s "amounted to some 20 percent of the Soviet defense budget."[8] In that case, and according to the CIA's estimate of real Soviet military spending in rubles, Soviet military personnel were not paid $73.1 billion in 1979; they were paid $16.8 billion. In which case, the "dollar cost" estimate paid Soviet military personnel $56.3 billion more than they actually received in 1979.

Over a decade of equivalent spending, then, the "dollar cost" estimate created an imaginary fund of $563 billion that the Soviet Union never spent on defense.

But this amount was only the amount never paid to Soviet military personnel. The imaginary fund was larger, because the "dollar cost" estimate included other distortions. It chose to assume, for example, that the Soviets paid the same amount for each tank and aircraft that an American manufacturer would charge for the equivalent product.

When all these distortions were taken together, they enabled the CIA to estimate the "dollar costs of Soviet defense activities" at "about $165 billion" in 1979.[9] This, of course, well exceeded America's military budget of $115.2 billion that year.[10] But it also exceeded the CIA's ruble estimate of what the Soviets spent that year. It exceeded it by $80.9 billion. Thus, the "dollar cost" estimate *doubled* the Agency's estimate of real Soviet military spending. Its estimate of real Soviet military spending fell below America's military spending that year.

Here were the disparities between the two estimates in 1979 and 1980:[11]

CIA Estimates of Soviet Military Spending ($ billion)

Year	US Military Budget ($ billion)	"Dollar Cost" Estimate	Margin over USA	Dollar Equivalent of Ruble Estimate	Margin under USA
1979	115.2	165	49.8	84.1	31.1
1980	142.7	170	27.3	89.9	52.8

The CIA knew perfectly well that its "dollar cost" estimate exaggerated Soviet military spending. It acknowledged that "inherent in the dollar cost comparison" was an "overstatement of Soviet defense activities relative to those of the United States."[12] Other sources acknowledged this too. "Estimating how much it would cost to produce and man the equivalent of the Soviet defence effort in the USA," the International Institute for Strategic Studies observed, "tends to overstate the Soviet defence effort relative to that of the USA."[13]

Nevertheless, the "dollar cost" estimate, even though its originators admitted that it was inaccurate, and that it exaggerated Soviet military spending, was the only estimate the administration and its supporters used.

This illustrates an important technique of propaganda. First admit that certain statements can have a misleading effect: this implies that you will not use them for that purpose. It challenges suspicions that you might use them for that purpose, and it disarms opposition based on those suspicions. It implies that if you do use them, you will have some other purpose, and that since you have been so forthright, you will only use them for an honorable purpose. Then go ahead and use them. They have only one purpose.

The CIA's "dollar cost" estimates enabled President Reagan to claim, in his 1981 inaugural address, that over the previous decade the Soviet Union had "spent $300 billion more" on its military than America had.

The next step in threat inflation was to forget what earlier had been acknowledged: that a large portion of the Soviet military budget, calculated by the "dollar cost" estimate, did not exist. The imaginary fund never spent could then be applied to whatever expenditure seemed most threatening. The large fund never spent on Soviet military personnel, for example, could be presumed spent on equipment.

Captain Roger Villar provides an excellent example of how this assumption can be used. Writing an introduction to the highly influential *Jane's Weapon Systems,* he first acknowledges that only "25 percent, if as much" of the Soviet military budget "goes on personnel and their support costs." He then subtracts this portion of the 1980 Soviet military budget. The problem is that he subtracts it from the 1980 Soviet military budget calculated by the "dollar cost" estimate. That figure is $170 billion. It owes its magnitude in large part to the pretense that Soviet military personnel were paid much more than Captain Villar now allows. The captain concludes, nevertheless, that the remaining three quarters of this sum, or $127 billion, was "available for equipment and research and development" that year.[14]

The "dollar cost" estimate of Soviet military spending in 1980 exceeds the CIA's ruble estimate of real Soviet military spending that year by $80.1 billion. Even the remaining three quarters of the "dollar cost" estimate, which Captain Villar spends on equipment and research, exceeds the CIA's ruble estimate of *all* Soviet military spending that year by $37.1 billion.

Late in 1982, the CIA released figures to the Joint Economic Committee of Congress showing that the Soviets may have spent the equivalent of no more than $80 billion a year on the military between 1970 and 1980. This was the same decade in which President Reagan claimed the Soviets had spent $300 billion more than America had. It seemed, instead, that they had spent $300 billion less.[15]

In 1983, the CIA added that over the previous seven years Soviet military spending had increased at a rate of just 2 percent a year.[16] This was only half the rate it had previously claimed. America's military spending in 1983, meanwhile, had risen by 9.5 percent over its 1982 level. Throwing into doubt most of the counts of Soviet military equipment offered by the administration in annual editions of *Soviet Military Power,* CIA analysts explained that their lower estimate of Soviet military spending was "based on evidence that the Soviet Union has been producing less military equipment than was expected."[17]

Administration supporters were ready, of course, with a reverse bit of sophistry. If the Soviet Union spent less on its military than the United States did, they suggested, then this only proved that the Soviets got "more bang for the buck." That presupposed, however, that somewhere along the line the size of the Soviet bang had been established. It hadn't. The whole purpose of the "dollar cost" exercise, indeed, had been to circumvent any accurate measurement of that bang, for fear that the public would learn how small it really was.

Nor did the Soviets get more bang for the smaller buck they spent. Franklyn Holzman pointed out that "machinery and equipment, especially high-tech weapons, are many times more expensive in the Soviet Union than in America."[18] The Soviets were getting less bang, and the bang they had was much too small to justify *any* expansion of America's military power, let alone the unprecedented expansion that was taking place.

31 The Common Wisdom

The administration, however, had so often repeated its warnings of rising Soviet military power and America's growing vulnerability to it that belief in these notions, despite the absence of any evidence to warrant it, came to dominate the general media and public consciousness. Both the press and the public came to accept the Soviet threat—without asking for any measure of its size—as full justification for the nation's enormous increases in military spending. The common wisdom had been established. Whenever experts like Franklyn Holzman or former officials like William Colby came forward to challenge or contradict it, they drew little attention.

This common wisdom had been established well before President Reagan took office. Indeed, it played a decisive role in placing him there. Early efforts to establish it were launched even as President Carter began his own term in office. Among the powerful organizations leading this campaign was the Committee on the Present Danger, a group of prominent conservative businessmen, academics, and public officials formed in 1976. Its policy committee chairman was Paul Nitze, a New York investment banker who had been a member of the American delegation to the Strategic Arms Limitation (SALT) Talks until 1974. He had also worked for earlier administrations, "and those that he has not worked for," remarked New York Times correspondent Charles Mohr, "he has tended to work tirelessly against."[1]

One of Nitze's earliest efforts to raise official and public awareness of the Soviet threat, and a highly successful one, was NSC-68, a National Security Council memorandum "cited by many as one of the opening trumpet calls of the cold war."[2] According to Fred Kaplan, "Nitze drafted most of the paper in the early spring of 1950."[3] In it, Nitze warned that recent Soviet military developments had "greatly intensified the Soviet threat to the security of the United States," while at the same time our own military strength was "becoming dangerously inadequate." He warned not only of Soviet capabilities but also of Moscow's intentions, describing the "Kremlin's design for world domination," which he asserted "required" nothing less than the "ultimate elimination of any effective opposition," principally that posed by the United States, "whose integrity and vitality," in what he seemed sure was the Soviet view, "must be subverted or destroyed." To encounter this "limitless" threat, Nitze urged "a rapid buildup, sufficiently advanced by mid-1954" to "wrest the initiative from the Soviet Union."[4] His advice was heeded. Our defense budget was raised from $13.5 billion that year to $48.2 billion in fiscal year 1951—an increase of 357 percent.[5] Only the previous year, General Omar Bradley, chairman of the Joint Chiefs of Staff, had reminded Congress that "obviously, if war is thrust upon us, the American people will spend the amount necessary to provide for national defense." Historian John Lewis Gaddis, recalling Bradley's testimony, concluded: "What NSC-68 did was to suggest a way to increase defense expenditures without war."[6]

It was Nitze, again, who wrote the report of the Gaither Security Resources Panel in 1957.[7] He was familiar with a RAND Corporation report which studied the growing strategic capabilities of intercontinental ballistic missiles (ICBMs),[8] and with Air Force Intelligence estimates predicting the Soviets could deploy as many as five hundred ICBMs by 1961, at which time the United States was scheduled to have only sixty-five missiles deployed.[9] Taking this information into account, but ignoring concurrent National Intelligence Estimates predicting the Soviets would have no more than ten missiles by that time,[10] Nitze warned in his report that "the dynamic development and exploitation" of missile technology in the Soviet Union had "probably surpassed us," posing "an increasing threat" from Soviet ICBMs that would leave us "almost completely vulnerable" to attack. This time he urged additional appropriations of $44.2 billion for civil defense and a crash missile program aimed at deployment of six hundred ICBMs by 1959.[11]

When President Eisenhower ignored this recommendation, it was Nitze who, with the help of the Gaither Panel's Robert Foster, arranged to leak his report to the press, including Chalmers Roberts of *The Washington Post*.[12] The article Roberts based upon it brought the "missile gap" to the American public.[13]

This led Henry Kissinger to write in 1961 that "there is no dispute about the missile gap as such. It is generally admitted that from 1961 until at least 1964 the Soviet Union will possess more missiles than the United States."[14] But on August 10, 1960, the United States had launched its first successful strategic reconnaissance satellite, Discoverer 13.[15] And the Discoverer series, repeatedly photographing every square yard of the Soviet Union for several months, could find only four operational ICBMs.[16] Former RAND and Pentagon analyst Daniel Ellsberg further recalls that they were "four soft, nonalert, liquid-fueled ICBMs, at one site at Plesetsk that was vulnerable to a small, slow U.S. attack with conventional weapons."[17] Fred Kaplan concludes: "there *was* a missile gap," and "the ratio in forces was nearly ten to one—but the gap was in *our* favor."[18] In 1976, reviewing the Gaither Report that had been released nineteen years before, a joint committee of Congress termed it "unduly alarmist."[19]

If Nitze had been unduly alarmist about Soviet capabilities, what about Soviet intentions? Did our government agree with him about Moscow's "design for world domination"? In 1949, just before he joined the Department of State and before NSC-68 had even appeared, John Foster Dulles declared: "The Soviet Union does not contemplate the use of war as an instrument of its national policies. I do not know any responsible official, military or civilian, in this Government or any government, who believes that the Soviet Union now plans conquest by open military aggression."[20]

Then why be "unduly alarmist?" When there is no real evidence of a threat, why suggest one? Why allow it to justify the expenditure of billions of dollars which might be used to remedy more genuine problems? A common explanation, repeatedly offered, is that threats must be exaggerated or people will not respond to them. This begs the question of whether something requires a response. Christoph Bertram, director of the International Institute for Strategic Studies in London, felt that "the particular American problem with strategies" was that "they have to be over-presented, even over-sold, to gain political support."[21] But what if none of these strategies warrants support? Richard Perle, Assistant Secretary of Defense for International Security, claimed that "democracies will not sacrifice to protect their security in the absence of a sense of danger."[22] General Omar Bradley flatly disagreed with this idea in 1949, and he had the record of public support for our effort in World War II on which to base his opinion. What was the basis for Perle's opinion? Where is the record of America's failure to respond to a *genuine* threat? The only record we have is the one which Nitze helped to create: blatant misrepresentation as the sole basis for lavish overspending on defense. Why? When it meets no genuine need of national security, what are the benefits of such prodigality?

The primary benefit of excess military spending is the profit it provides in those sectors of our economy where it is spent. A 1971 study based on information from the Federal Renegotiation Board found 131 defense contractors with profits after taxes of more than 50 percent of their net worth, 49 with profits of more than 100 percent, 22 with profits of more than 200 percent, and 4 with profits of more than 500 percent.[23] A subsequent General Accounting Office study showed that between 1970 and 1980, American defense contractors averaged profits of 56 percent after taxes. Michael Parenti concluded that "military appropriations are the single most important source of investment and profit for corporate America."[24]

Nitze had been a vice-president of the New York firm of Dillon, Read & Company, the investment banker for a number of corporations engaged in defense manufacture, among them Grumman Aircraft.[25] He was a director of several other financial institutions, including Schroder's Incorporated, American Security and Trust Company, and Northwestern Mutual Life Insurance Company.[26] On the board of just one of these firms, Northwestern Mutual Life, he sat with directors who served on the boards and thereby promoted the interests of several other firms, including General Motors, American Telephone & Telegraph, North American Phillips, R. J. Reynolds Industries, Litton Industries, Cutler-Hammer, the Singer Company, and Control Data Corporation.[27] All of these were among the nation's one hundred leading defense contractors in 1975.[28]

Nitze had also married the granddaughter of one of the founders of Standard Oil Company of New York.[29] Standard Oil of California, Mobil, and Standard Oil of Indiana, the three largest of the thirty-eight independent companies formed after the Supreme Court dissolved the original firm and attempted to divide its assets in 1911,[30] were among the top fifty defense contractors in the United States in 1975.[31]

To expect Nitze to ignore the multiple interests to which he was tied, both professionally and personally, was to deny him almost every human inclination. Yet his interests were nearly always overlooked in evaluating what he had to say, even in the proven absence of any other explanation for it. Each time he had something new to say, his record of prior misrepresentations was usually overlooked too, or when it was not overlooked, it was discounted.

Thus, when Nitze was appointed adviser to Secretary of State George Shultz at the Geneva Arms Talks in 1985, a *New York Times* reporter did not entirely overlook his record. He did not identify Nitze as one of the principal architects of a missile gap America had never faced, or as the prophet of the Kremlin's designs for world domination. But he did acknowledge Nitze's long record as "an advocate of more military spending," and his "reputation of being tough toward the Soviet Union." Nevertheless, the reporter pronounced the appointment "acceptable both to conservatives and to liberals."[32]

Of course, there now appeared to be one mitigating factor on Nitze's record, whether or not this justified discounting the rest of that record. The *Times* reporter reminded his readers that Nitze was also "regarded as committed to equitable arms accords," because he had made "an effort in 1982 to end an impasse on medium-range missiles in Europe" by privately working out "a compromise proposal during a walk in the woods outside Geneva" with his Soviet counterpart.[33]

At least, it *appeared* that Nitze had made that effort, in which the two parties seemed to agree to propose that America limit deployment of its Cruise missiles in Europe to 300 of the 464 originally planned, and forego deployment of 108 *Pershing IIs* entirely, while the Soviets reduce their deployment of SS-20 missiles to 75, armed with a total of 225 warheads.

That Nitze seemed willing to deploy fewer missiles than his government wanted in Europe was certainly no small surprise. But we shall never know if he really was willing to do anything of the kind. It ran counter to every instinct his public record had ever displayed. He seemed to commit himself to the proposal without the official sponsorship of his government. If that was so, he could not have been unaware how unlikely it was that his government would accept it. His government rejected it the moment it was reported. The public was told that the Soviet government had rejected it too.

Has the public been told of every proposal that did not enjoy official sponsorship but was privately discussed by negotiators at Vladivostok in 1974, or in the years of talks that led up to the signing of SALT II? This proposal found its way into the press as quickly as Nitze's report for the Gaither Panel did in 1957.

Time magazine's diplomatic correspondent, Strobe Talbott, has since produced an entire book in which the episode of the walk in the woods occupies a position of singular prominence,[34] and in which, as Theodore Draper notes, "if there is a hero, it is Paul H. Nitze." In a review of the book, Draper finds himself "acutely troubled," because "more than any other book of its kind, it is made up of direct quotations attributed to its leading characters," as if Talbott knew "just what was said in the most unlikely places."[35]

Yet none of the sources for any of these quotations is identified. In fact, Draper later adds, "there is not a shred of documentation in the book," so that all it provides is a "pretension of omniscience."[36] How are we to know whether it is accurate?

Talbott explains in a foreword to the book that he "cannot, here or in the pages that follow, acknowledge the sources" on which he depends, because many are key "participants" in the events he describes, and they are "constrained from freely discussing their roles, for years to come."[37] Draper finds this explanation "somewhat disingenuous," because Talbott's book "reads as if the many participants were not at all constrained from freely discussing their roles with him." He wonders, for example, who told Talbott "just what was said before and during the celebrated 'walk in the woods' between Mr. Nitze and the Soviet negotiator, Yuli Kvitsinsky, on July 16, 1982. Only the two of them were there . . . our choices at this juncture are extremely limited."[38]

What worries Draper is that Talbott's book is one more example of the "collusion between anonymous officials and favored journalists, together engaged in surreptitiously feeding the public a version of events for which no one can be held accountable." He recognizes that this is how officials who make policy "also seek to control the history of their policy making."[39]

In this case, after Draper asked him to comment on the matter, Nitze, who otherwise might have appeared to have something to hide, made himself accountable, acknowledging that he was indeed a source for Talbott's book, and that he did his best "to help him get those sections dealing directly with me right."[40] We have only his word for it, however, that these sections are now right; we have only his word for it that during his walk in the woods with Kvitsinsky he helped formulate their joint proposal in good faith.

Without Nitze's word for it, the idea never would have entered anyone's mind that he was "committed to equitable arms accords." Once this impression was created, however, Nitze suddenly became a man of high importance to the Reagan administration.

By announcing that it had rejected the "walk in the woods" proposal, the administration demonstrated again, of course, that it was not committed to equitable accords. But the American people already had good evidence of that. So did America's NATO allies. So did the Soviet Union.

To confirm what the world already knew was a small price to pay for what the administration gained with Nitze's new reputation. He now had a reputation unlike any other it could hire; it could present him as "acceptable both to conservatives and to liberals." By appointing him arms adviser to a new round of talks in Geneva, it could claim it had indeed "turned over a new leaf." And it could more plausibly insist, both at home and abroad, that it was sincere, this time, in seeking substantial reductions in arms.

Thus, at a critical juncture in the Reagan administration's campaign to reassure the public of its benign intent, a man who had helped usher in the Cold War, and who since that time repeatedly has raised false alarms to precipitate the expenditure of billions of dollars that might have been saved on defense, became "acceptable" to represent the best interests of the majority of the American people, as well as the peoples of western Europe, merely on the strength of his own report of his equitability on a single day of a life which seems to have been dedicated only to warning of inequities that never existed.

In 1976, Nitze had begun again to warn of the Soviet threat. He "vigorously opposed" ratification of the SALT II Treaty, helped to popularize the concept of America's strategic "window of vulnerability," and urged that defense spending be increased by "an absolute minimum" of $260 billion over the next six years.[41] This time he did not write a report. That task was left to Norman Podhoretz, another member of the new Committee on the Present Danger, whose book *The Present Danger,* published a few months before the presidential elections in 1980, warned of "the Finlandization of America, the political and economic subordination of the United States to superior Soviet power."[42]

Many members of the Committee had their own financial ties to the defense community. John Lehman owned the Abington Corporation, a consulting firm for which Richard Perle also worked, and whose clients included Northrop, Boeing, TRW, Inc., the Finnish arms firm of Tampella, and Salgad, the marketing firm for the Israeli arms corporation Soltam.[43] David Packard, a former Secretary of Defense, was chairman of Hewlett-Packard, a leading manufacturer of electronic warfare equipment, and a director of Caterpillar Tractor and Standard Oil of California.[44] Melvin Laird, another former Defense Secretary, sat on the boards of no fewer than twelve corporations with multiple ties to leading defense manufacturers.[45]

Before the end of 1981, in what amounted to "a virtual takeover of the nation's national security apparatus," the Committee had placed 33 of its 182 members, including Ronald Reagan, in the new administration.[46] William Casey became director of the CIA, Jeane Kirkpatrick our ambassador to the United Nations, Eugene Rostow director of the Arms Control and Disarmament Agency, and Richard V. Allen Assistant to the President for National Security Affairs. Two more Committee members occupied key positions on the National Security Council, five in the Department of Defense, and no fewer than eight on the

President's Foreign Intelligence Advisory Board. Lehman became Secretary of the Navy, Perle an Assistant Secretary of Defense, and Nitze the administration's chief negotiator for Theater Nuclear Forces.

The Committee was but one of several organizations which sounded identical themes, mobilizing growing opposition to SALT II, and its membership frequently overlapped with theirs. Eugene Rostow was also a director, and Frank Barnett the president, of the National Strategy Information Center, whose activities, together with those of the National Security Program at New York University, had been supported since 1973 with approximately $6 million from the Sarah Mellon Scaife and Carthage Foundations.[47] In the same period these two foundations, largely endowed by Gulf Oil,[48] contributed roughly $360,000 to the Committee itself, while they also helped to support several leading conservative think tanks, among them the Hoover Institution with $3.8 million, Georgetown University's Center for Strategic and International Studies with $5.3 million, and the Heritage Foundation with $3.8 million.[49]

The Heritage Foundation and the American Enterprise Institute also received support from the Bechtel Foundation, which annually spent about $875,000 endowed by the Bechtel Corporation,[50] whose general counsel, Casper Weinberger, became Secretary of Defense in the new administration, and whose president, George P. Shultz, was to become its Secretary of State. Shultz too was a member of the Committee, as was Midge Decter, who sat on the board of trustees of the Heritage Foundation.

Committee members Clare Booth Luce and William R. Van Cleave were also members of another influential organization, the American Security Council, which organized an alliance of 106 conservative groups, the Coalition for Peace Through Strength, of which Van Cleave was a co-chairman.[51] The Council's membership included nuclear physicist Edward Teller, a key Reagan scientific adviser; former CIA counterintelligence chief James Angleton; and 2,465 retired admirals and generals, including former chairman of the Joint Chiefs of Staff Admiral Thomas Moorer, a director in 1976 of two leading defense corporations, Fairchild Republic and Texaco, Inc.,[52] and former commander of Air Force Systems Command General Bernard Schriever, a director that year of two more defense companies, Control Data Corporation and Emerson Electric.[53]

In the fiscal year ending in March, 1979, the Council held twenty-six press conferences, sent nine members of its Coalition to testify before Congress against SALT II, provided speakers for eight hundred local events, sent three million pieces of mail, and produced *The SALT Syndrome,* a documentary film opposed to SALT II which was shown before ten thousand groups and more than five hundred times on television. In that year it spent a total of $1.9 million on these activities,[54] while by contrast the Carter administration spent $1.2 million through all of 1978 and the first six months of 1979 in its effort to gain support for SALT II.[55]

32 The Concept of Linkage

That same year, 1979, opposition to SALT II sent Henry Kissinger to Congress, where he recommended the treaty's ratification be made conditional upon "linkage between SALT and Soviet geopolitical conduct," as well as on a guarantee of increased defense spending.[1] In 1976, however, during his tenure as Secretary of State, Kissinger had condemned Soviet actions in Angola as "irresponsible" and "dangerous," while at the same time he conceded that "the basic necessities of preserving peace in the nuclear age" were such that a "dual policy" must also be preserved, avoiding linkage between Angola and the SALT negotiations, so that the United States could "remain ready to work for a more peaceful world."[2]

"Linkage," then, appears to be a term used only in the absence of real links, and only when it is convenient to create artificial ones. It means to invoke opposition to a policy which otherwise would stand unopposed, and to demand support for another policy which otherwise would gain little favor, by suggesting there ought to be a link between the two when otherwise no link would exist, and even when it might be unwise to create one.

At that time, Kissinger had also asserted: "The United States has the military capacity" to resist "the expansion of Soviet political influence by military power."[3] Now he told Congress: "The military balance is beginning to tilt ominously against the United States."[4]

"Linkage" was the maneuver to which President Reagan resorted, before his 1985 Geneva summit meeting with Soviet Chairman Gorbachev, when he accused the Soviet Union, in an address to the United Nations General Assembly, of aggravating conflicts in Afghanistan, Angola, Cambodia, Ethiopia and Nicaragua.[5] "All of these conflicts," he said, "are the consequence of an ideology imposed from without, dividing nations and creating regimes that are, from the day they take over, at war with their own people."[6]

The President did not acknowledge that almost all of the delegates to whom he spoke represented governments which recognized the legitimacy of four of the five regimes he cited as truly representative of their people, and that none of the four had had its ideology imposed from without. He did not acknowledge that all of the delegates knew that in all of these cases the United States was itself involved in aggravating conflict, in an effort to destabilize regimes it didn't like by providing military support for movements which it hoped might set those regimes at war with at least a part of their people.[7]

Nor did the President mention many other regions of the world, from Southern Africa, the Spanish Sahara, Chile and El Salvador to Indonesia, South Korea and the Philippines, where the United States aggravated conflict by supporting regimes which were truly at war with their own people.[8]

Nevertheless, the President had partially achieved his goal. As *New York Times* correspondent Leslie Gelb noted, until the President had given his speech, there had been no question that the issue of "arms control" would "occupy center stage in Geneva," but that in his speech "Mr. Reagan had tried to shift the spotlight to regional disputes."[9] *Times* correspondent Bernard Weinraub noted that the President had now "linked progress in East–West relations to the resolution" of these disputes."[10]

"The President," NBC News correspondent John Chancellor concluded, "had changed the subject."[11] The administration did not try to deny this. Weinraub quoted a "ranking White House official," who said that the President's speech was "a deliberate attempt to shift the world's focus," and that Geneva should not be "merely" an arms control meeting.[12] The President himself tried to defend his maneuver, pointing out that "the indispensable elements of a true peace" included "the steady expansion of human rights for all the world's peoples," and "support for resolving conflicts in Asia, Africa, and Latin America that carry the seeds of a wider war."[13]

In a letter to The New York Times, Karen Cowgill pointed out that "it is foolish for the U.S. to make arms control contingent on Soviet human-rights policies. It is also hypocritical. The Russians could make a case for U.S. human-rights violations, pointing to our support of the Nicaraguan contras. Since neither country would acknowledge the other's accusations, linking human rights with arms control can only confound and retard nuclear arms control."[14] She had divined the true purpose of the President's maneuver.

33 An Adverse Imbalance of Power

The growth of Soviet military power became one of the leading themes of opposition to SALT II. But opponents of the treaty were seldom agreed on just when the military balance would tilt in favor of the Soviet Union, or on whether it had already done so. In November, 1978, two years after the Committee on the Present Danger first claimed that it had, Joseph Alsop still warned of a time when it would, "when overwhelming superiority passes to the Soviets, as it is now doing."[1] This time appeared to arrive two months later, when Foreign Policy Perspectives, a group of more than 170 retired admirals and generals based in Boston, announced in January, 1979, that "Russia has quietly passed us in military strength."[2] Yet in March, the Republican National Committee worried that America, rather than having already become secondary to the Soviet Union, was still "rapidly becoming" so.[3]

This conflicted with the views of the Coalition for Peace Through Strength, which announced in April that "an imbalance in both strategic and conventional military power" already favored the Soviets, and must have favored them for some time because it "has grown worse during the period of SALT."[4] But in June, Army Chief of Staff General Bernard Rogers declared that it still would not be until "the early 80s" that we "will lose our essential equivalence" with the Soviet Union.[5] Ben Wattenberg of the American Enterprise Institute seemed somewhat reluctant to agree with this assessment when he asserted in July that "the Soviet Union has at least caught up with the United States,"[6] implying that the Soviets might have advanced beyond parity. Three months later, columnist George Will doubted that they had quite yet. "Soon," he wrote in October, "the Soviets will have strategic superiority."[7]

Nor did it seem that this question was settled in the mind of the man who would soon become the nation's new chief executive. In March, 1980, candidate Ronald Reagan announced: "Today, we are not equal to the Soviet Union" in military power;[8] but in August he would complain that the Soviets still "seek a superiority of military strength,"[9] a superiority they would presumably no longer seek if they already had it. General Richard Ellis of Strategic Air Command had agreed with Reagan in March that we suffered "an adverse strategic imbalance";[10] but in August, chairman of the Joint Chiefs of Staff General David Jones agreed with General Rogers that the Soviets would not "gain an advantage" until "the early 1980s."[11]

Only a few days earlier, Defense Secretary Harold Brown had declared: "The truth is that we are second to none," and added that "those who mistakenly claim that the United States is weak" were "not only playing fast and loose with the truth, they are also playing fast and loose with U.S. security."[12]

Nevertheless, Edward Luttwak of the Georgetown Center for Strategic Studies wrote in September that "the great majority of the voices in our public life have come to agree" that American military power had declined "to a level of net inferiority" compared with the Soviet Union's.[13] If it seemed there was as much agreement on this point as Luttwak wished his readers to believe, that may have been because some voices, more heavily financed than others, were making more noise than others.

Nor would these voices cease, and the Soviet threat vanish, after the elections which swept so many of those who warned of it into office. In September, 1981, the new administration released its booklet *Soviet Military Power,* which Leslie Gelb noticed contained "no new information, no conclusion," and "no systematic comparison with American forces," though "its impression of relentless and almost overwhelming Soviet military power" was "fully consistent" with "Reagan's charge in the 1980 Presidential campaign that the Soviet Union had achieved military superiority over the United States."[14] Charges of that kind were frequently made during presidential election campaigns, but always dropped afterwards.[15] This time, however, they continued, and moved beyond the level of innuendo contained in *Soviet Military Power.* In March, 1982, President Reagan declared that "the truth of the matter is that on balance the Soviet Union does have a definite margin of superiority."[16] It was the first time a presidential contender had made such a statement *after* winning office. Did this mean that, for the first time, the statement was true? Or did it mean that this particular President was still campaigning?

In March, 1983, the administration published 300,000 copies of a new version of *Soviet Military Power,* at a cost of $585,000.[17] In a news conference broadcast live to Europe to discuss its "findings," Defense Secretary Weinberger estimated it would still take "a good five years to regain the strategic and conventional strength and readiness that I think we need."[18] Senator Edward Kennedy remarked: "Secretary Weinberger's exercise in excessive rhetoric and exaggeration, timed to coincide with the defense budget and nuclear freeze votes, is classic scaremongering."[19] All the same, it was clear that in the administration's view, our "adverse imbalance" would no longer be closed "in the early 1980s." Indeed,

Under Secretary of Defense for Policy Fred Ikle, another member of the Committee on the Present Danger, had already told Congress that even higher military spending than we now planned "would not close the gap in accumulated military assets between the United States and the Soviet Union until the early 1990s."[20]

34 "A Window of Vulnerability"

If the threat was to be prolonged, assertions of its existence could not always be quite so vague. To give them substance, pronouncements that seemed to be more specific were offered. "Soviet heavy missiles," the American Security Council declared, "give the Soviets a first-strike capability";[1] or more precisely, according to Patrick Buchanan, the Soviets have "the capacity to destroy 90 percent of the U.S. land-based missile force in a first strike."[2] The risk of such a strike was what Ronald Reagan referred to when he said, "there is what I have called, as you all know, several times, a window of vulnerability."[3]

A government interagency group, formed by the Carter administration to respond to these critics, reminded them that the capacity to carry out a first strike was at best a "theoretical capability," which they could attribute to the Soviets only "if they ignore our ability to launch under attack" and assume, moreover, that the Soviet attack "would work as planned."[4] They did ignore it, concluding that after such a strike the Soviets would still be able to destroy "60 percent of all Americans if the United States were to retaliate," while "the Soviets might lose no more than 4 percent of their population because of their active civil defense."[5]

The CIA, however, estimated that in such an exchange, "the Soviets would suffer over 100 million prompt casualties," not 4 but 40 percent of their population, before even taking into account the effects of radiation, famine, and disease that would follow, and that the "bulk of the general population" in the Soviet Union, far from having access to sophisticated civil defense measures, "must rely on evacuation from urban areas for its protection."[6] This, too, was ignored. The American Security Council concluded that even if we really did not risk war, we might still "expect greater coercion everywhere in the world,"[7] while the Coalition for Peace Through Strength warned of "accommodation with the Communist bloc."[8] Neither organization explained precisely *what* the

West might have to accommodate itself to if it did not choose to do so, or demonstrated how it might be coerced into doing so, in the absence of any real risk of a war that promised consequences no less catastrophic to the Soviet Union.

35 Strategic Modernization

If this argument seemed weak at the time, in the face of so many authoritative statements to dispute it, that was only because it had not yet been repeated enough. Repetition was an essential element of the campaign which began then and continues today. In March, 1980, Ronald Reagan said of the arms race that the Soviets were "already running as fast as they can and we haven't started running."[1] In August, he said: "We're already in an arms race, but only the Soviets are racing."[2] In November, 1982, in a televised address, he said: "The truth is that while the Soviet Union has raced, we have not." In that address he also said: "Many of our B-52 bombers are now older than the pilots who fly them."[3] In January, 1983, he said: "Our bombers were older than the pilots who flew them."[4] In March, 1983, Deputy Secretary of State Kenneth Dam said that "some of our B-52 bombers are older than the pilots who fly them."[5] In April, Reagan said: "Our B-52 bombers are older than many of the pilots who fly them."[6]

Complaints about the age of our bombers ignored the fact that the Air Force "has spent more than $2 billion on major modifications of the B-52 over the past 20 years—in structural design, improved defensive electronics systems, better avionics and newer weapons," and that Strategic Air Command officials "testify that the B-52s will be structurally sound through the late 1990s,"[7] at which time they could easily be rebuilt again, or the B-52 production line reopened, at a fraction of the cost a new bomber would require.

Other complaints, that while America had stood still the Soviets were "producing or testing *eight* new ICBMs,"[8] later corrected to "ten variants of three new systems,"[9] ignored modernizations of our own in the past decade, which aside from improvements to the B-52 force have included the addition of multiple warheads to 550 *Minuteman* and 496 *Poseidon* missiles, the replacement of 900 *Minuteman* warheads on 300 missiles with a more powerful warhead, the replacement of 192 *Poseidon* missiles with the *Trident* missile, delivery of the first *Trident* submarine, and the addition to the bomber force of 65 FB-111 bombers, 356 F-111 bombers, 1,140 short-range attack missiles, and most significant of all, the first of more than 3,400 Cruise missiles then planned.[10] We had also just completed a $1.4 billion Silo Upgrade program for the *Minuteman* missile. This, according to Representative Les Aspin, directly contradicting concurrent charges of *Minuteman* vulnerability, "delayed Minuteman vulnerability for at least six years." Aspin asked: "Is cost necessarily proportional to effectiveness?" Even if the Soviets did spend what they were said to have spent on improving their ICBMs, "our ICBM improvements," he pointed out, "have been more than six times as cost-effective."[11]

Nevertheless, these considerations were seldom offered, and received so little attention in the mainstream press that by March, 1983, Jed Snyder, who had served the Reagan administration in the State Department's Bureau of Politico-Military Affairs, was able to say without public contradiction that since 1972, "America has virtually ignored its strategic nuclear inventory."[12]

Numbers were also used, though they seldom matched, to suggest an adverse imbalance of strategic power. In March, 1980, according to candidate Reagan, the Soviets were "outspending us in the military field by 50 percent," or in June, 1982, according to President Reagan, "by 40 percent," or in February, 1983, by "85 percent."[13] They had a "6 to 1 advantage in missile megatonnage," or an advantage of "5 to 1 in deliverable megatonnage," or of "3 to 2 in strategic missiles,"[14] presumably both those on land and at sea, or a "3 to 2 numerical advantage over the U.S. in ICBMs" alone, excluding missiles at sea, or a "2 to 1 advantage in strategic offensive weapons," or simply: "the nuclear tilt is 3–2 against us."[15]

These statements were intrinsically difficult to assess. Did they deal with the most significant measures of strategic power? How was the public to know if they were accurate? And even if they were, how was the public to know whether they told the whole story? By the time it might be learned that some of them were untrue, or some of them true but misleading, they already would have made their intended impression, raising fear—whether or not it was warranted—of Soviet military supremacy.

36 Soviet Intentions

Lest anyone believe that no real threat was posed by the adverse imbalance of power variously alleged—by the Committee on the Present Danger and its several affiliated groups—as imminent or already at hand, it was equally important for them to disabuse the public of any notion that Soviet intentions were benign, and further, that the Soviets would approach the risks of military confrontation with the same caution shown by the rest of mankind.

Thus, as long ago as 1978, at an Israeli Bond dinner in Chicago, Ronald Reagan announced: "There is an evil influence throughout the world. In every one of the far-flung trouble spots, dig deep enough and you'll find the Soviet Union stirring a witches' brew, furthering its own imperialistic ambitions."[1] During his campaign for the presidency in 1980, he declared that "the Soviet Union is embarked on a goal that they have never retreated from, and that is to communize the entire world."[2] In 1981, he warned: "Let us not delude ourselves. The Soviet Union underlies all the unrest that's going on. If they weren't engaged in this game of dominoes, there wouldn't be any hot spots in the world."[3] And in 1983, he suggested that those who ignored the meaning of Soviet doctrine were reluctant "to see totalitarian powers for what they are," adding, "they are the focus of evil in the modern world."[4]

On the same occasion, speaking to the National Association of Evangelicals, Reagan cited an "elementary fact" of Soviet doctrine: that "the only morality they will recognize is that which will further their cause, which is world revolution." He added that "Soviet leaders have openly and publicly declared this," and that he was "only quoting Lenin" to that effect, as he had done in his first press conference as President.[5]

In that conference he had quoted from what he called the "Ten Commandments of Nikolai Lenin," one of which was that "promises are like pie crusts, made to be broken."[6] This sent the press on a search for the text of the "Ten Commandments." It could not be found. After two years, the White House acknowledged that "Lenin did not issue 'Ten Commandments' as such," and that "Mr. Reagan got the reference from a clipping sent by a friend."[7] Then it seemed the Soviets may never have "openly and publicly declared" their willingness to break promises after all. One witness to the search for the Commandments said he had "copied them off a German propaganda pamphlet, published during World War II."[8] If that was so, they had now been put to the same purpose they served more than forty years ago.

37 Soviet Expansionism

But Reagan had no need to find some other means of arousing public distrust of Soviet intentions. It had already been well ingrained. A multitude of warnings about every aspect of Soviet behavior had further intensified public suspicions throughout the period of SALT negotiations. Charges of Soviet imperialism and expansionism proliferated. These, it is clear, would have been raised with or without the Soviet intervention in Afghanistan. More than a year before that intervention, Reagan had already declared: "If the Soviet Union would simply go home, much of the bloodshed in the world would cease."[1]

The readiness of the press to adopt this view of Soviet behavior while avoiding the same view of our own much longer record of intervention around the world— which includes the open use of military force to intervene in the affairs of other peoples against their will no fewer than twenty-eight times since 1900, and the *covert* use of paramilitary force or other forms of violence for the same purpose on at least eighty-three known and documented occasions since 1946[2]— created a double standard which made it possible to suggest, at least to Americans, that the Soviet Union was more aggressive than the United States, and thereby posed a greater threat to world stability. Thus, on the death of Soviet leader Leonid Brezhnev, *The Washington Post* reviewed his conduct of "a foreign policy that in the end valued empire over detente in the American mode," and that "rationalized aggression."[3] Surveying the mood of American journalists at this time, Roger Morris concluded: "For most of the media, the meaning of the Iranian and Afghan crises seemed plain enough: the United States had become ominously weak, and its Soviet enemy defiantly, perhaps decisively, stronger."[4]

The theme of growing Soviet strength conflicted with another idea introduced by Reagan and his associates, who repeatedly emphasized that the Soviet system was on the decline, "that Communism is another sad, bizarre chapter in human history whose last pages even now are being written."[5] *Time* magazine capably resolved this contradiction, warning that "the Soviet Union could be less predictable and more dangerous when it is economically weak than when it is doing well."[6] *The Wall Street Journal* believed that on account of its "economic decline," Russia's "expansionism could become more urgent."[7]

Journalism professor William Dorman noticed this "shift in emphasis" by the press. "Russia," he remarked, "has been transformed from a hulking bully into a menacing failure." He also noticed that this reinterpretation "happens to coincide with a change in administrations and the election of a highly ideological president who has stressed that sanctions can hurt the Russians."[8] The Soviet threat had been preserved, even as the administration's new theme of Soviet economic doom was promoted.

Without the support of the press, that theme could have been undermined when the Joint Economic Committee of Congress issued a CIA report which found that the Soviet gross national product actually had increased at "an average annual growth rate of 4.7 percent" since 1950.[9] The press simply ignored this report or minimized its importance. *The New York Times* carried the story, but pointed out in its first paragraph that "in recent years, according to the report, the increase has dropped to less than 3 percent a year."[10] *Newsweek* ran a story entitled "The Soviet Economy: Down But Not Out."[11] These interpretations did more to confirm than challenge predictions of an eventual Soviet economic collapse.

What the *Times* chose not to publish was another finding in the CIA report: "The average annual growth rate of Soviet GNP is a full percentage point higher than that of the United States for the entire 1950–79 period."[12] If it was true, as *Time* had suggested, that the "economically weak" nation was "less predictable and more dangerous," then perhaps it was the United States, not the Soviet Union, which stood to be the more aggressive, and posed the greater threat to world stability. That likelihood was never raised by the general press.

Nor has the press in America ever examined another likelihood: that the more dangerous nation is the more *exploitative,* that the superpower which utilizes more of the world's resources, and holds the longer list of critical "interests," will build the longest record of worldwide intervention to protect them.

What better way to protect those interests than to "defend" them from aggressive intentions presumed of the other superpower? Thus, the administration could not concede that the Soviet Union might be any less aggressive because its economy was more stable. Months after the CIA's report, Reagan continued to claim that Soviet leaders could not leave "any vacuum of power unfilled,"[13] that they are "always" making their "final territorial demand," and that we must not "accommodate ourselves to their aggressive impulses."[14] He would have said this whether the Soviet economy was weak or strong, and whether the Soviets had invaded Afghanistan or not. How else could he justify *America's* much longer record of intervention, including its forthcoming "defense" of Grenada?

38 Soviet Planning for Nuclear War

Another means of focusing public fear on the Soviet Union was to dwell upon Soviet planning for nuclear war, which Soviet leaders consider "winnable," according to Amoretta Hoeber and Joseph Douglass, Jr.,[1] two more members of the Committee on the Present Danger, whose book *Soviet Strategy for Nuclear War,* published by the Hoover Institution, became the principal text for this theme while the authors themselves became, respectively, Deputy Assistant Secretary of the Army for Research and Development and assistant director of the Arms Control and Disarmament Agency in the Reagan administration.

Their book is filled with quotations which at first seem persuasively ominous. One of the most popular has been General A. S. Milovidov's comment: "There is profound error and harm in the disorienting claims of bourgeois ideologues that there will be no victor in a thermonuclear world war."[2] There are quotations, too, from former chief of the Soviet General Staff Marshal Vassili Sokolovskiy, whose book *Soviet Military Strategy* the authors concede is "the single most important text on these matters since World War II."[3]

The difficulty with these statements arises from when they were written. Milovidov's book was first published here in 1974,[4] when according to official records the Soviet Union had 2,500 deliverable strategic nuclear warheads to our 7,650.[5] Sokolovskiy's book was published here in 1968,[6] when the same records show that the Soviet Union had 1,100 warheads to our 4,200.[7] Both books were published earlier in the Soviet Union. If Milovidov believed, at that time, that a global thermonuclear war could be won, he obviously didn't believe his own country would win it. Sokolovskiy could have believed it even less. At best, these statements were an attempt on the part of their authors to build Soviet morale. Nowhere do Hoeber and Douglass suggest that likelihood.

Nevertheless, ten years after Milovidov's book was published in the Soviet Union, Leon Wieseltier quotes from it in *The New Republic* to support his contention that "there is a great divergence in nuclear doctrine between the

United States and the Soviet Union."[8] There is no divergence at all. Andrew Cockburn quotes from a *U.S. Army Field Manual* published in February, 1980, well before the Reagan administration took office and began to formulate policies of its own, which asserts: "The United States Army must be prepared to fight and win when nuclear weapons are used."[9] Injunctions of this sort—equally self-deluding whether they occur in American or Soviet texts—are common to the military literature of any nation that deploys nuclear weapons, and result from its institutional need to create doctrine justifying their existence.

Subsequent publication of the Reagan administration's *Defense Guidance,* disclosing its own nuclear war fighting plans and its intention to "prevail" in a nuclear war, was far more effective than military field manuals had been in publicizing American doctrine. Of course, it contradicted earlier contentions, which now had to be abandoned, that only the Soviets had such plans. But it was quickly justified as a necessary response to them. Thus, Wieseltier speaks of the "Sovietization of American strategy that is reflected in the *Defense Guidance,*"[10] implying that it was the Soviets who first brought such thinking into the world, and consequently the Soviets alone who must still bear the moral onus for public fears of nuclear war, even though news of our own plans had multiplied those fears.

The evidence is all to the contrary. It was in 1962 that Defense Secretary McNamara first discussed America's nuclear war fighting plans, announcing that "strategy in a possible general nuclear war should be approached in much the same way that more conventional military operations have been regarded," and that military objectives "should be the destruction of the enemy's military forces, not of his civilian population."[11] Attempts were made to incorporate nuclear weapons in tactical doctrine as long ago as 1965. An Army Field Manual issued that year, fifteen years before the one quoted above, gave the following instructions to company commanders planning fire support operations: "The company commander's responsibility for planning and employment of nuclear weapons is the same as for any other fire support means available to him. The company commander must insure that nuclear and nonnuclear fires are completely integrated. He does this whether the nuclear fires are requested by him or are planned and directed by higher authority."[12]

Not one of the Soviet military sources drawn upon by Hoeber and Douglass is dated as early as McNamara's speech. Nor is it clear whether many of the quotations they use are from texts discussing Soviet or Western doctrine. In a recent edition of *Strategic Review,* Leon Goure and Michael Deane unintentionally provide an insight into how misleading the use of such quotes can be. Introducing translated excerpts from an article by General V. Reznichenko in the restricted Soviet General Staff journal *Voyennaya Misl (Military Thought),* they say: "While discussing theater offensive operations largely in the context of a nuclear battlefield, the author uses the familiar Soviet technique of illustrating Soviet concepts with descriptions of alleged Western views and practices."[13] What if Reznichenko is illustrating Western concepts? Why would he engage in such subterfuge when other writings in *Voyennaya Misl* do not, and instead openly discuss Soviet concepts? Were there too few of the latter type of discussion to make an effective case of Soviet planning for nuclear war?

39 Arms Control: The Soviet Record

Soviet belligerency also has been repeatedly implied through a steady series of charges of Soviet refusals to accept proposals for arms control, Soviet violations of existing arms control agreements, and Soviet initiatives in new areas of military technology. The evidence, again, is all to the contrary.

Thus, in 1946, according to President Reagan, the United States "proposed the Baruch plan for international control of all nuclear weapons," but the Plan "was rejected by the Soviet Union."[1] What he neglected to mention was that the Plan was proposed after the United States was already producing atomic bombs but before the Soviets had even tested one. Yet it "required the Soviet Union and all other nations," Sidney Lens recalls, "to turn over control of their uranium mines, and open their doors to geological surveys immediately—whereas the United States would not have to end its bomb production or divest itself of its hoard until some vague point in the future."[2]

Similarly, according to President Reagan, "in 1955, President Eisenhower presented his 'open skies' proposal," recommending that the United States and the Soviet Union "permit aerial reconnaissance to insure against the danger of surprise attack. This, too, was rejected by the Soviet Union."[3]

Not quite. Reagan neglected, this time, to mention that Eisenhower's proposal was in response to what Alva Myrdal called "a detailed plan, the most comprehensive so far," prohibiting the use of nuclear weapons, their manufacture, and eventually their possession, proposed two months before by the Soviet Union. The Soviet plan developed proposals in an earlier Anglo-French memorandum which the United States supported. Myrdal recognized that "by declaring that it would accept in principle the British-French memorandum," the Soviet Union had "delivered the big surprise."[4] Sidney Lens quotes the U.S. delegate to the disarmament talks, who said he was "gratified" that Moscow had finally accepted "in large measure" concepts "which we have put forward over a considerable period of time."[5]

The United States demonstrated its gratification in an odd way. Instead of consummating the agreement then within reach, it suddenly presented its Open Skies proposal at the Geneva Summit Conference. It did so "without prior consultation," Myrdal notes, "with the Russians or even the Western allies."[6] This moved the talks in a new direction. Now, remarks Lens, "There would be a lot of inspection of each side's territory, but no disarmament."[7]

The Soviets barely had time to "reject" this plan. Their initial reaction had only been to reply "that ground inspection seemed preferable," which "could be interpreted as a positive response to Eisenhower's proposal."[8] One month later, it was not the Soviet representative but Harold Stassen of the United States who announced that his government was placing "a reservation on all of its pre-Geneva substantive positions."[9] It never subsequently lifted that reservation. The United States had reversed its position, rejecting concepts it had earlier called its own. Nor could Soviet reservations over the Open Skies proposal be used as an excuse for America's withdrawal. An agreement over Open Skies still might have been attained; and even without one, the United States "had been flying into Soviet air space with impunity since the end of World War II,"[10] using RB-47 aircraft. The Lockheed U-2 made its maiden flight in the same month Stassen made his announcement at Geneva.[11] Six months later, U-2s were flying regular secret reconnaissance missions over the Soviet Union.[12]

President Reagan's selective account of these negotiations—designed to suggest that the Soviet Union was reluctant to join in mutual steps toward arms control when the record shows only that America was—frequently adorns his speeches on arms control. He included it in his address to the United Nations Special Session on Disarmament in 1982, and repeated it to the Los Angeles World Affairs Council the following year.[13] It appears regularly in current State Department literature on arms control.[14]

40 Chemical and Toxin Warfare

It was at the United Nations that Reagan also made another charge. "The Soviet Union and their allies," he claimed, "are violating the Geneva Protocol of 1925," which bans the use of chemical and biological weapons in war.[1] This charge, too, has been repeated many times. It began to appear very promptly after the Soviet intervention in Afghanistan. Four days after the first airlift of Soviet troops to Kabul, *The New York Times* announced that, according to Afghan rebels, the Soviets had "already" used poison gas there, as though the world had always known that sooner or later they would.[2] Within a month, unidentified American "intelligence sources" announced to the press that they had reports "from Afghan Army defectors and refugees" that "the Soviets had used a lethal chemical vapor," a form of nerve gas identified as Soman, against the Afghan insurgents.[3]

This prompted an investigation of those reports by Professor Julian Perry Robinson of Sussex University, one of the world's leading experts on chemical warfare. Alexander Cockburn interviewed Robinson and found that "the authoritative reports winding through the world media" about Soviet use of Soman "are in fact based on the testimony of a single defecting Afghan army officer," who himself heard them "at second hand."[4] Robinson also wondered "exactly how Afghans unacquainted with chemical weapons had managed to identify Soman," when "even a trained chemist would have needed a well-equipped laboratory and a sample of the agent concerned to reach that conclusion."[5]

Nor were samples of such chemical agents produced or the bodies of any victims found. By November, 1981, Richard Burt, director of the State Department's Bureau of Politico-Military Affairs, conceded: "We do not, as yet, have physical evidence of chemical warfare in Afghanistan."[6]

This, however, did nothing to prevent reports of chemical warfare from continuing to gain wide publicity. Four months later, Deputy Secretary of State Walter Stoessel declared that in Afghanistan, "as a result of chemical attacks," presumably by Soviet forces, "3,042 deaths attributed to 47 separate incidents between the summer of 1979 and the summer of 1981 have been reported."[7] This was the same period for which Burt had lacked evidence. Had new evidence now come to light? Had some of the bodies been autopsied? It seemed not. One Pentagon aide, asked to corroborate Stoessel's report, "searched high and low, then conceded 'I've got nothing.' "[8]

Nevertheless, later that month Secretary of State Alexander Haig issued a major report, containing the same list of deaths, in which he announced that "evidence of chemical and toxin warfare has accumulated."[9] Although in its introduction the report claimed "this evidence has led the U.S. Government to conclude," among other certainties, "that Soviet forces have used a variety of lethal chemical agents, including nerve gases, in Afghanistan," it later admitted that "none of the agents being used in Afghanistan has been positively identified through sample analysis."[10] Then no evidence *had* accumulated. There were only more "reports"; 3,042 bodies were still missing.

All the same, Secretary Haig's report gained headlines throughout the nation.[11] This was because it successfully obscured the lack of evidence of nerve gas by shifting its emphasis to *new* charges that in Laos, Cambodia, and Afghanistan, the Soviets and their allies had been using "lethal" tricothecene mycotoxins.[12] Of these, which the State Department had earlier dubbed "yellow rain," the report now claimed to have solid evidence, and this time it offered its analysis of samples it said were taken from those countries. Again, there were lists of deaths from exposure to mycotoxins or "other combinations of chemical agents," including 4,606 deaths in Laos from 1978 through the winter of 1979–80, and another 276 deaths in Cambodia in the same period.[13] But, again, there were no bodies. In March, 1980, a Thai officer reported that "so far we have not heard of any deaths";[14] nor could the State Department produce evidence of any deaths from such causes. It could only produce samples of mycotoxins, and more "reports."

By November, 1982, Secretary of State George Shultz had issued another report containing "new evidence collected in 1982," which "reinforces the previous judgment that lethal chemical agents were used on the Afghan resistance."[15] What was this new evidence? Two "contaminated Soviet gas masks acquired from Afghanistan."[16] Did they indicate the use of nerve gas? No. They "showed the presence of several mycotoxins," which led the State Department to conclude that "mycotoxins have been used by Soviet forces in Afghanistan since at least 1980."[17] Inasmuch as the "previous judgment" had been that the "lethal chemical agents" used in Afghanistan through the summer of 1981 were not mycotoxins but nerve gases, the "new evidence" appears not to reinforce but to contradict that judgment.

It was Harvard biochemist Matthew Meselson, another leading academic expert on chemical warfare, who first pointed out that mycotoxins could be the result not of chemical warfare but of "natural fungal activity"; and it was Bruce

Jarvis, a chemist at the University of Maryland, who had found a Brazilian shrub which contained "tricothecene toxin that reached 200 to 300 parts per million, far higher than those found in the State Department's samples,"[18] contradicting the Department's assertions that even lower levels of concentration do not naturally occur. Meselson was also "puzzled by the reported toxin concentrations, which seem too low to cause death."[19] Though Reagan administration officials hoped their new evidence "would overcome public doubts about previous charges,"[20] Meselson noted that "in some respects, official Government statements have contained demonstrable and serious scientific errors."[21]

Still, the administration was not deterred. In January, 1983, six Afghan refugees, through their interpreter, Michael Barry, spoke at a news conference sponsored by Freedom House in New York to repeat State Department charges of chemical warfare and other "Soviet atrocities,"[22] as though live Afghans might prove what the absence of dead ones could not. In February, Under Secretary of State for Political Affairs Lawrence Eagleburger insisted again that there was "extensive evidence" that "toxin weapons are being used right now in Afghanistan and Southeast Asia."[23] But in May, at the annual meeting of the American Association for the Advancement of Science, Meselson, Julian Perry Robinson, and two other experts contended that "yellow rain" might be nothing more than bee excrement, in which spores from fungi commonly found in Southeast Asia subsequently grew and produced toxins. Similar fungi had grown in samples of bee droppings Dr. Meselson had collected in Cambridge, Massachusetts.[24] All nine samples of "yellow rain" that had been officially reported as tested for pollen "did in fact contain pollen."[25]

Secretary Shultz, in his report, claimed that his administration had "invited others to join us in examining the evidence."[26] Meselson now "challenged the Government to allow outside scientists" really to do so, and "to conduct further tests on yellow rain samples to establish the truth or falsity of the bee hypothesis," and hence, of administration claims.[27]

But what if the administration now produces further evidence? In the light of its singular persistence in publicizing its charges, despite an inability to prove them, wouldn't new evidence, suddenly emerging after more than three years, have to be weighed very carefully? If the State Department now began to publish photographs of chemical warfare victims, or produced samples of chemical warfare equipment or toxins that do not naturally occur, wouldn't it be necessary, at this point, to ask where the photographs were taken, the equipment found, and the toxins produced, and to see that the answers given are independently verified?

As one reporter acknowledged, these charges have "enormous political and military implications," because they raise doubts about the Soviet Union's "good faith in professing willingness to negotiate other arms control agreements."[28] Yet, even as the administration conducted its massive campaign to raise those doubts, charges of our own violations of the Geneva Protocol—including unexpected outbreaks of sugar cane rust, tobacco mold, and African swine and Dengue fever in Cuba[29]— were seldom given a fraction of the attention focused on "yellow rain." Nor was it often recalled that Napalm and Agent Orange, whose use we did not hide in Southeast Asia, were chemical weapons, or that the Soviet Union formally agreed to comply with the Geneva Protocol in 1928, while the United States did not sign and ratify it until 1975.[30]

In view of this imbalance of emphasis, Arnaud de Borchgrave's apparent fear that the press in America is vulnerable to Soviet "disinformation"[31] seems merely uninformed, and ignorant of where most disinformation afflicting our media may originate.

Even though the administration professed to seek "the moral high ground," it did not fail to use its charges of Soviet violations of the Geneva Protocol to justify building a new generation of binary chemical weapons in order to be able to "respond in kind," despite the fact that our possession of "300,000 tons"[32] of chemical weapons, "of which two thirds is nerve gas, including three million artillery shells,"[33] had long guaranteed our ability to do so. Nor is there any assurance that the new binary weapons, deemed safer to store because their chemicals are meant to unite and form a lethal mixture only after they have been launched at their targets, will not be subject to the same "microscopic weld defects" that were heavily publicized as "leaks"[34] in our existing stockpile, suggesting it was aging and needed replacement. These suggestions were made at exactly the same time as our charges of Soviet violations began.

41 Violations of SALT II

Raising further doubts about Soviet "good faith," the administration has also implied that the Soviet Union may have violated provisions of SALT II. President Reagan announced in March, 1983, that "there have been increasingly serious grounds for questioning their compliance" with the treaty.[1] In April, administration officials told the press "there was already a virtual consensus" that "a violation occurred."[2] Idaho's Senator James McClure declared there was "a clearcut pattern of violations," an "open-and-shut case."[3] His most specific charge was that the Soviets had tested "two new types" of intercontinental ballistic missile, though the SALT II Treaty permitted only one.[4]

In November, 1982, Moscow had duly notified Washington that a new missile it tested at that time was "the one permitted by the treaty."[5] But in February, 1983, it tested what the United States claimed was another. This turned out to be "a modified version" of the old "SS-13 missile permitted under the 1979 treaty."[6] However, the administration claimed that "analyses indicated" this particular SS-13 "exhibited characteristics that exceeded the modifications permitted under the treaty for an old missile—a 5 percent change in length, diameter, launch weight and throw weight, and a clear retention of a single warhead," and that therefore it "technically constituted a new missile."[7]

A change of more than 5 percent in the missile's size or weight, however, would violate SALT II only if it increased those dimensions. The treaty's provisions "do not preclude a decrease in launch-weight or throw-weight in excess of five percent."[8] The administration did not indicate which kind of "change" it had detected; nor did it indicate why it wasn't "clear" whether the newly tested SS-13 had only a single warhead.

During SALT II negotiations, officials had contended that "there is no way to detect whether a missile is fitted for more than one nuclear charge" once it has been deployed; and they consequently "agreed that once a new missile is tested with multiple warheads all others of that type will be considered to have that ability and will be counted as such under the treaty."[9] They further agreed that after May 1, 1979, neither nation would test or deploy any missile "with a number of reentry vehicles greater than the maximum number of reentry vehicles" with which a missile "of that type had been flight-tested as of that date."[10]

That is how SALT II, at the same time it limited the total number of missiles each nation might deploy, also limited the maximum number of reentry vehicles, and therefore warheads, that might be placed on each type of missile. The two nations never would have agreed to this means of establishing such limits unless they knew it allowed for their verification. Each knew that testing was a prerequisite of deployment; that the other could not deploy a missile with multiple warheads until it had tested that missile several times with that number of warheads to ensure that their reentry vehicles performed reliably. Each knew that whenever the other tested a missile it could be *observed* doing so.

This meant that whenever a missile released its reentry vehicles during a test, they could be counted. If they exceeded the number previously observed on that type of missile, the fact was noted. If the same number of warheads was tested on the same missile several times, this indicated how many warheads might be carried by that missile if it was later deployed. An agreement not to test or deploy existing missiles with greater numbers of warheads could be enforced by observing subsequent tests.

SALT II limited the SS-13 to one warhead because it had never been tested with more than one warhead when the treaty was signed. This fact seemed simple enough to establish at that time. Why wasn't it simple now? Was the government now claiming it was unable to do what it had found no difficulty doing four years earlier?

Yes. Officials claimed that "not all American intelligence-gathering equipment was functioning that day."[11] This implied that if all our equipment had been functioning, we would have been able to count any warheads released by the SS-13. Senator McClure also charged that there was increasing evidence of "camouflage, concealment and deception designed to interfere with the U.S. national means of technical verification."[12] If there is evidence of deception, then the deception did not succeed. This suggests that our means of verification, able even to detect *attempts* to obstruct it, has not been obstructed.

But could the Soviets be sure that we really lacked sufficient equipment, that day, properly to monitor the SS-13 test? Without being sure of that, would they really be willing to take the risk of being caught violating the treaty? If they really had attempted concealment, this meant they didn't want us to think they were violating the treaty, and that therefore they would be careful to avoid violations which might be observed. It isn't likely, then, that the Soviets would have tested the SS-13 with more than one warhead. In view of this, and of our admitted lack of evidence to prove otherwise, why accuse the Soviets of having done otherwise?

The administration never did. In discussions with Soviet representatives, it "stopped short of accusing Moscow of violating the treaty."[13] But this did not stop unidentified officials, in discussions with American journalists, from forming "a virtual consensus" that Moscow had violated the treaty. It did not stop President Reagan, at a press conference in May, from affirming his "very great suspicion" that Moscow had done so.[14] It did not stop Senator McClure from openly charging that Moscow had. Columnist Tom Wicker noted that McClure "has described the Soviet tests in such detail that his information is almost surely coming from the administration," which "appears willing to let this serious charge be aired in the Senate while Mr. Reagan remains more or less silent."[15] Once again, suspicions the administration could not substantiate had nevertheless gained nationwide attention.

Nor did the administration's refusal to substantiate its case against the new version of the SS-13 prevent Defense Secretary Caspar Weinberger from calling it a new missile, the SS-25, when it first began deployment in October, 1985,[16] just as he had called a new version of the Soviet T-72 tank the T-80 when it was first deployed. When we deployed a new version of the *Minuteman III* with a Mk 12A warhead in 1980, increasing the missile's throwweight by 35 pounds, we did not call it a new missile, even though it was deployed ten years after the *Minuteman III* was first deployed with the Mk 12 warhead.

In the same way, the administration claimed that a new Soviet phased-array radar at Abalakovo, near Krasnoyarsk in Siberia, was a "clear" violation of the ABM Treaty of 1972, which forbids the construction of such radars "for early warning of strategic ballistic missile attack except along the periphery of its national territory and oriented outward."[17] The Abalakovo radar is located 500 miles from the Soviet border with Mongolia, and is oriented inward.[18]

The Soviets maintain, however, that the Abalakovo radar is only capable of space tracking, and could never be used for ABM battle management. The Central Intelligence Agency seems to agree that this radar is "not well designed" to serve as an antiballistic missile radar, because it operates at the wrong frequency, has only a single face which is not at "the optimal angle to perform a battle management function, is not "hardened" as battle management radars are, is undefended by interceptor missiles, and "does not cover the path of incoming U.S. ICBMs because it is too far east and is pointing in the wrong direction."[19] A British Intelligence report also agrees with this assessment.[20]

It is certainly difficult to consider the Abalakovo radar to be located "along the periphery" of Soviet "national territory." But it is also difficult to consider the phased-array radar the United States deploys at Robins Air Force Base, Georgia, 260 miles inland, as located "along the periphery" of our "national territory." It is certainly impossible, as the Soviets have pointed out, to consider the phased-array radars the United States has begun to build in Thule, Greenland, and at Flyingdales in the United Kingdom as located "along the periphery" of United States "national territory."[21]

Yet even though President Reagan conceded "you can't go to court without a case" and "we don't have that,"[22] our very inability to make a case, far from restraining the administration's efforts to raise suspicions over the Soviet tests, was actually used to justify them. The President alluded to a problem he said we had in "trying to verify what is going on."[23] McClure, too, had charged that Soviet attempts to "interfere" with our national means of verification included "almost total encryption of the telemetry" data passed from missiles to Soviet ground engineers during tests.[24] All of this suggested that, even when every piece of our equipment was functioning, we still lacked the ability to verify SALT II compliance.

Not only, then, could Washington raise suspicions about Soviet compliance, but in justifying those suspicions by claiming we were unable to resolve them, it could also dramatize our own vulnerability. The administration had long contended that America was militarily endangered. It had also contended that America lacked "preparedness" to meet that danger. Now, by claiming we could not even fathom the danger's extent, it disclaimed responsibility for having to prove the first of these contentions even as it continued to publicize them both.

What is the truth? What "national technical means" do we have to monitor Soviet tests and weapons deployment? And how capable are these of verifying Soviet treaty compliance?

42 Verification

In 1960 Discoverer 13, one of our earliest photographic satellites, provided images which "could identify objects," according to Fred Kaplan, "as small as thirty-six inches on the ground."[1] By 1964, according to James Fusca, our SAMOS (Satellite and Missile Observation System) satellites had achieved "a ground resolution of 16–20 inches at altitudes between 100–120 miles."[2] In 1971, under a project coded 467, we launched a new series of satellites known as Big Bird. These, according to Richard Burt, provided "a clear photograph of a one-foot object from an altitude of 100 miles."[3]

Burt offered that estimate in 1979; Big Bird probably had already achieved much finer ground resolutions well before that time. Four years earlier, Bhupendra Jasani of the Stockholm International Peace Research Institute had calculated the ground resolutions obtainable by improving image resolution at the camera's lens. The image resolution of a photographic print is commonly measured by counting the maximum number of parallel black lines that may be reproduced on each millimeter of film surface without closing all the observable white space between them. The longer the focal length of the camera and the finer the grain of its film, the greater this number will be.

Jasani had analyzed a photograph of Chicago taken by Skylab 4 at an altitude of 275 miles, using a camera and film which produced a print with an image resolution of 40 lines per millimeter. He established the photograph's ground resolution at 82 feet, but pointed out that if it had been taken at an altitude of 95 miles, the height at which most military reconnaissance satellites orbited, its ground resolution would be 28 feet. He also knew that "modern film materials have resolutions considerably higher," and he reasoned that with such film, and with "lenses of long focal length," image resolutions of "at least 100 lines per millimeter" ought to be obtainable.[4]

Jasani postulated a camera with a focal length of 19.6 feet. This did not mean the camera body had to be that long. A series of mirrors could now be used to create "folded optics," in which the path of light was reflected at multiple angles, so that the camera's focal length, or the distance light traveled through the lens system, became "far greater," as John Noble Wilford observes, "than the actual length of the telescopic lens" itself. Wilford notes that "the greater the focal length of the camera, the greater the magnification of its images."[5] With the focal length Jasani envisioned, and with the image resolution of 100 lines per millimeter which he believed was obtainable, he showed that it would be "possible to get a ground resolution of 25 centimeters,"[6] or less than 10 inches.

We had already progressed further than Jasani knew. By the time his analysis was published, Itek had developed its KA-102A aircraft camera. Using 3414 film, it needed a focal length of only 5.5 feet to achieve an image resolution of 115 lines per millimeter.[7] The cameras mounted in our Big Bird KH-9 satellites were almost certainly larger and more powerful; according to James Bamford, these satellites themselves are 55 feet long and weigh 12 tons.[8] In view of the vast potential such dimensions raise, Bamford's own estimate that Big Bird's "superhigh resolution camera" was "capable of distinguishing objects eight inches across from a height of ninety miles"[9] may substantially understate its true capabilities. With film of the quality Itek revealed was available in 1975, and the much longer focal length Jasani had suggested, image resolutions of at least 175 lines per millimeter could already be achieved, yielding ground resolutions of less than 6 inches.[10]

What does all this mean? Thomas Karas learned from official testimony in Congress that it takes "15 feet of resolution to spot an airplane on the ground," 10 feet "to detect the existence" of a ballistic missile, 5 feet "to identify the missile," and "6 inches to describe the exact dimensions" of such objects.[11] We may have been able to do all of this by 1971; we were certainly able to do it by 1975. Indeed, since 1966 we had also been sending up "Close-Look" satellites,[12] whose more elliptical orbits brought them at times within only 77 miles of the earth's surface. At that height, equipment comparable to Big Bird's could achieve ground resolutions of just over 4 inches. That was in 1975. Today's Close-Look satellite, the KH-8,[13] may produce photographs with ground resolutions of less than 1 inch.

In 1976, under a project coded 1010, our first KH-11 satellite was launched.[14] Though the KH-11 orbits at higher altitudes than Big Bird, its cameras, according to Kosta Tsipis of the Massachusetts Institute of Technology's Center for International Studies, "in principle can see objects on the surface of the earth that are a few centimeters in size."[15] That, Wilford reports, is because the KH-11's cameras "do not use photographic film" any more. Instead, "light reaching the camera's focal plane forms images" on a silicon chip arrayed with photoelectric cells, "thousands of microscopic light-sensitive elements," each of which is electrically charged; and "when a photon, or unit of light, hits one of these," it frees an electron.[16] The escaping electrons form a beam whose intensity varies precisely according to the amount of light that has freed them. Each resulting electrical signal "is given a computer number in accord with its light magnitude."[17] The converted data bits are then transmitted to ground stations.

Electron beam conversion from photoelectric cells is the same technology used by the civilian Landsat program, whose satellites study the earth's resources for the National Aeronautics and Space Administration. The precision of ground resolution this system may achieve is limited only by the size of its cells and their sensitivity to light. Advances in microelectronics have continuously reduced their size and sharpened their sensitivity. According to Vincent Salomonson of the Goddard Space Flight Center, Landsat 4, the latest in this series, launched in July, 1982, has cameras with "four times the sensitivity to reflected light" of previous Landsats,[18] because each of its sensors now responds to 256 variations in light intensity, whereas earlier cells responded only to 64.

This technology has revolutionized military reconnaissance. "In addition to its greater resolution," Wilford writes, its "sensitivity to light" is far beyond "the rather limited perception of the human eye." It can "see more because it measures reflected light in six wavelengths, four of them infrared, as well as in a thermal channel for taking surface temperatures." Thus, "what is essentially invisible," including much of the infrared spectrum, "is made visible."[19]

Multispectral imaging of this kind, Karas points out, can "register wavelengths that photographic film can't see." It can "produce pictures at night," and can "detect military camouflage by differentiation between, say, live and dead or artificial and real foliage."[20] Bamford adds that multispectral sensors are "capable of detecting hidden, underground missile silos because the silos' temperature is warmer than that of the surrounding area."[21]

Moreover, "the technology that was cleared for use on the Landsats," Wilford notes, "was purposely not as good as it could have been, since it was intended as a basically non-military tool," and the "Pentagon did not want the Russians to know what the United States could actually see from space."[22] The first Landsat was launched in 1972.[23] This means that technology superior to that on the earliest Landsat was already in military use at least four years *before* the first KH-11 was launched in 1976.

Multispectral scanners are also carried by our Big Bird KH-9 satellites, yielding information photographs cannot provide. They were probably also carried by our earlier SAMOS satellites. As long ago as 1960, they were the principal sensors aboard our TIROS (Television and Infra-Red Observation Satellite) weather and reconnaissance spacecraft.[24] In fact, since 1956, according to Harry Martin, the editor of *Defense Electronics,* the United States has "kept under wraps" a "major sensor camera that optimizes heat sensitivity" so well that it can detect "missile-launching sites and troop movements that were completed in the past and camouflaged today."[25]

While photographic cameras eventually exhaust their film, electronic sensors simply produce a continuous stream of images; the result is unlimited coverage of the earth's surface. Wilford reports that the images from each Landsat, "taken along a 115-mile-wide swath, covered 13,000 square miles of land surface," so that with "some 30,000 images," a Landsat "could record the whole world every 18 days."[26] According to the Center for Defense Information, one such satellite can record "the entire territory of the Soviet Union in one week."[27] If necessary, it can observe the same area every ninety-two minutes.[28]

Because the information electronic sensors provide can be digitized, it can be processed by computers. This means it can be transmitted instantaneously. Benjamin Schemmer describes how the images produced by the Itek 2KL miniaturized electro-optical imaging system "appeared at a ground read-out station about 100 miles away" within "thousandths of a second after being taken."[29] It also means that images can be enhanced, using what Karas found were highly "sophisticated computer programs" to "sharpen the lines of resolution beyond the theoretical limits of the optical systems that took the pictures."[30] The Jet Propulsion Laboratory made impressive use of this technique, he recalls, in refining the images of Jupiter and Saturn transmitted by Voyager spacecraft.

Schemmer adds that computer processing can "provide even greater detail" than the images would otherwise show, by making them "brighter, lighter, or darker," by "sharpening the contrast," and by "filtering out smoke, haze, or smog." It can also "enlarge them" with "no degradation in resolution up to about 10 times magnification."[31] If that is so, then even the "few centimeters" of which Kosta Tsipis spoke have been resolved. Digital image enhancement may now allow us to see an object more clearly by satellite than with normal vision from only a few feet away on the ground.

What if that object is obscured by clouds? Then there is imaging radar, which provides pictures of ground terrain, as well as what *Jane's Weapons Systems* describes as "both moving and stationary" features upon it,[32] with such fine detail that they appear to be etched in relief. It does this by measuring the backscatter strength and range of microwave signals it beams down to earth, and then reproducing these measurements in light waves whose patterns it records on film. To the military, Jim Meacham observes, "radar is the ideal sensor," because "it can see through clouds and can be pointed."[33]

The first civilian use of imaging radar in space was aboard Seasat, the oceanographic satellite launched in 1978;[34] but according to L. C. Graham of Goodyear Aerospace Corporation, this technology was already in military use "in the mid 1960s." At that time, imaging radar could only achieve resolutions of 30 to 50 feet, but "more modern" systems, Graham reported, had improved "to the order of 10 feet."[35] That disclosure, however, was made in 1976. In November, 1981, an imaging radar system aboard the space shuttle Columbia was able to penetrate the Saharan Desert to reveal its subsurface contours at depths which, according to Wilford, who published a photograph of the result, could now be measured in single feet.[36] This was a nonmilitary system. Our newest generation of military spacecraft utilizing imaging radar is the RORSAT (Radar Ocean Surveillance Satellite), which is "so electronically refined," according to James Canan, that it can "spot bombers and cruise missiles in flight."[37] The first RORSAT was placed in orbit in April, 1983.[38]

Radar was used to take precise measurements long before its data could be converted to imagery. The unconverted information has proved no less valuable. In 1957, *Aviation Week* reported that an "extremely powerful long-range radar," General Electric's AN/FPS-17, had been operating "for more than two years" near Samsun, Turkey, to monitor Soviet missile tests at Krasny Yar, 810 miles to the north. Its presence was "well known to the Soviet Union." The radar "provided data on the type of Russian missiles being launched," as well as "their speed, altitude, track and approximate range," and could follow the "entire path of intermediate missiles" from their launch site, west of the Volga River between Volgograd and Saratov, to their impact area in the Kyzyl Kum Desert, 1,450 miles east of Samsun. Radars of that type, already "the most powerful sets now operating in the world," were being "modified to increase their range to 3,000 miles at extreme altitudes."[39]

Radar has undergone several generations of further refinement in the quarter century since that time. Soviet test sites have not moved further away. The Baikonur space center at Tyuratum on the Syr Darya River, northeast of the Aral Sea, is just 1,350 miles from Samsun. Plesetsk, the other key Soviet missile test site,[40] below the Aral Sea and northwest of Bukhara, is even closer. Nor was Samsun the closest site from which we could monitor tests. Peshawar, in Pakistan, was 880 miles from Tyuratum. Beshahr on the Caspian Sea, and Kabkan and Klarabad in northern Iran, were only 700 miles from Tyuratum. Nor did distance soon matter. Far more powerful radars were being developed. By 1970, RCA had produced the AN/MPS-36 missile tracking radar, accurate to within 2 inches per second in determining the speed of an object moving as fast as 60,000 feet per second—more than three times the speed of any ballistic missile—at distances up to 37,000 miles.[41] Three of these radars were delivered to the Federal Republic of Germany. From Wiesbaden, Tyuratum is only 2,450 miles away; from Bodö, Norway, it is just 2,000 miles away.

Nor did it matter that the Caucasus Mountains obstructed the line of sight from Turkish radars to Soviet test areas in Kazakhstan, as did the Kopet range from receivers in Iran and the Hindu Kush from those in Pakistan. In 1962, we began developing "over-the-horizon" radar, to send and receive radar energy reflected from the ionosphere, a series of ionized layers in the earth's upper atmosphere. The ionosphere served, according to *Jane's Weapon Systems,* "as a 'mirror' to bend the radiation round the Earth and direct it back towards the surface," reaching points "at great distances far beyond the 'line-of-sight' horizon."[42] The first of these radars became operational under Project Red Mill in 1968.[43] Several such radars, including Cobra Mist and Cobra Talon, were installed at additional sites, among them Orfordness in England; Cyprus; Dijar-Bakir in Turkey; Kokha in Thailand; Shemya in Alaska; and Chitose and Tokovozawa in Japan.[44]

By 1977, the giant Cobra Dane phased-array radar system had become operational in Shemya, Alaska, at the tip of the Aleutian Islands, to monitor the final phase of flight of Soviet test missiles of intercontinental range as they reentered the atmosphere over the Kamchatka Peninsula, 450 miles away, or over the Pacific Ocean north of Guam and the Marshall Islands. With a range of more than 28,000 miles, Cobra Dane provides "precise data on up to 20 targets," and can "track up to 100 targets simultaneously."[45] James Canan describes it as able to "spot a spaceborne basketball at 2,000 miles"; and while it is part of America's BMEWS (Ballistic Missile Early Warning System), its "chief mission," he says, "is to keep its eyes on missile tests."[46]

In 1961, the United States also began a program, which would continue for several years, of refitting a series of former naval freighters and tankers (some of them displacing more than 21,000 tons) as missile range instrumentation ships, and mounting on each the most powerful radar and other electronic equipment available at the time of its conversion. We produced a fleet of twenty-six such vessels, many more than are needed to track the performance of our own missiles in tests, and only nine of which are in fact listed in active service today, while the disposition of the remaining ships is far from clear.[47] Any of these vessels could as easily track Soviet as American missiles, and could be placed almost anywhere we chose, for example, in Turkish waters at the eastern end of the Black Sea, 1,100 miles from Tyuratum.

One of these ships, the *Observation Island,* was fitted in 1977 with Cobra Judy, a phased-array radar similar to Cobra Dane. One respected source has no more than this to say of the vessel's mission: "She is operated by the Military Sealift Command with a civilian crew for the Air Force Eastern Test Range."[48] But according to the *Proceedings* of the U.S. Naval Institute, the *Observation Island* functions not in support of our own test programs but "as a national technical means for collecting data on foreign strategic ballistic missile tests."[49]

Canan reports that this ship "prowls the neighborhood of the Soviets' Pacific test range," its radar working with Cobra Dane to monitor the terminal phase of intercontinental missile flights. As individual warheads separate from their post-boost vehicles, Cobra Judy is able "to track the warheads that land in that range" all the way to splashdown.[50]

Naturally, reentry vehicles used in tests are not fitted with nuclear charges, but they are necessarily identical in every other respect to designs planned for operational deployment. A nosecone's ballistic performance in flight can only be verified if tests which establish its flight characteristics use reentry vehicles whose size, shape, weight, and materials are precisely the same. Even a change in the design of a nosecone's interior can change its distribution of weight, shifting its center of gravity and altering its trajectory. Therefore, while the fission and fusion fuels are removed from the tampers and cores of test warheads, they are replaced by materials of the same density and weight. In their reentry vehicles aimed at Pacific test ranges, the Soviets use conventional high explosives for this purpose; they also retain high explosives in the lens shell surrounding the weapon's trigger, so that the warhead may still be electrically triggered and the nosecone destroyed after it completes its flight and sinks underwater.

Many of these warheads, however, have failed to detonate. In April, 1962, Roy Varner and Wayne Collier report, the United States began Operation Sand Dollar "to recover nosecones whose self-destructing warheads had not detonated as expected." The nosecones were easy to locate because we track them to their points of entry; sonar and magnetic anomaly detectors do the rest. The results have been "extremely successful." The actual dimensions of the recovered reentry vehicles not only confirm measurements already taken by optical and radar surveillance, but also confirm the validity of our measuring techniques applied to whatever else we do not already have in our possession. "Scientists analyzing the captured nosecones" have further been able to learn "how the Soviets designed and constructed each part," and can even "estimate the warhead's nuclear power based on the size of the compartment."[51]

To our radars, both on the ground and at sea, we added electronic intelligence (ELINT) equipment, to monitor the telemetry from Soviet missile tests and any other communications signals we could collect. Additional collection sites were established—at Sinop, Trabzon, Izmir, Anadolu Kavak, Dijar-Bakir, Pirinclik, and Karamursel in Turkey; at Dubai; at Takhli and Nakhon Phanom in Thailand; in Xinjiang Province in China;[52] at Sakata, Kamiseya, Sobe, Hanza, Kakata, and Futema in Japan;[53] and at Pine Gap and Nurrungar in Australia. While most of these stations collected their own intelligence, some also received information from satellites, and relayed it to stations in Great Britain and the United States.[54] They were only a portion of the network of "as many as 4,120 intercept stations around the globe" which David Shribman reports our National Security Agency has maintained since the late 1950s.[55]

In addition to ground sites, the United States has also converted more than one hundred naval vessels, including two former aircraft carriers, to communications relay ships, amphibious command ships, environmental and general technical research ships, and oceanographic, hydrographic, and surveying ships. Some of these certainly perform their designated functions; but any number of them, whether listed in active service, as only twenty-eight are, or stricken from the Naval Register, may perform ELINT or other intelligence missions instead.[56]

We know this was true of the *Liberty,* attacked for that reason by the Israelis in 1967, and of the six other ships in her class which *Jane's Fighting Ships* described as "intelligence collection ships classified as technical research ships,"[57] and which "performed their chores," according to Trevor Armbrister, "primarily for the National Security Agency."[58] We know it was true of the *Pueblo,* captured for the same reason by the North Koreans in 1968, and of her sisters *Banner* and *Palm Beach,* which according to *Jane's* were "the two surviving intelligence collection ships classified as environmental research ships."[59] We know it was true of the *Glomar Explorer,* classified, along with fifteen other vessels, as a miscellaneous auxiliary ship, but built expressly to carry out the CIA's Project Jennifer. Between July 10 and August 13, 1974, the *Glomar Explorer* successfully raised all the major sections of a Soviet Golf-II class strategic missile submarine, together with her navigational, fire control, and cryptographic systems, her torpedoes, and her three SS-N-5 missiles, from a depth of 17,500 feet 750 miles northwest of Hawaii, where she had sunk in April, 1968.[60]

Thus, from orbiting spacecraft, we use optical systems and radar to observe, precisely measure, and permanently record everything below. There is nothing of military significance that we cannot see. We see every missile, aircraft, tank, and naval vessel in Soviet territory—or, for that matter, anywhere else in the world. It is only the American public, left largely unaware of these capabilities, which might have been surprised when "officials suggested" that the photograph of a *Backfire* bomber in the first edition of *Soviet Military Power* "had been taken from a satellite."[61] We do rather better than that. We read the squadron markings on Soviet aircraft, the platoon numbers on their tanks. We have classified every major weapon in the Soviet arsenal and counted the number of each.

We also keep well abreast of changes. "U.S. surveillance satellites," Representative Les Aspin wrote in 1979, "currently provide complete photographic coverage of the U.S.S.R. at frequent intervals," so that "the U.S. can reliably identify by means of satellite photography such telltale activities in the U.S.S.R. as the construction of new ICBM silos and the transport of missiles to new deployment sites."[62] Not only do we know how many weapons there are; we also keep track of where they are. When a plane prepares for takeoff, or a ship leaves port, or an armored regiment forms convoy, we follow it. We follow what goes in and out of buildings whose contents we cannot see, and so we eventually learn what it does or did contain.

Multispectral scanning and electronic data processing have given us the power to see far more than the human eye can. Our ability to detect infrared wavelengths has enabled us to measure heat with enormous precision. We can do more than see through camouflage and into the earth. As our satellites watch missile tests, "the infrared sensors on these satellites," Aspin notes, "can identify the rocket-exhaust plume of a missile"[63]—if that missile has not already been identified by optical and radar measurements from space, by radar from sites on land and at sea, and by its telemetry signals.

There are further uses for infrared measurement. "Geological surveys from space," Karas points out, "tell what minerals are mined where."[64] That is because different minerals and other materials emanate different amounts of heat. The result is that almost every kind of raw material, and every kind of fabricated one, has its own place in the infrared spectrum of light. This helps us identify the materials delivered to factories. Measurements of the temperatures produced at different factory locations help, with visual analysis, to determine what manufacturing processes are going on inside. All of this information helps predict what will emerge completed from a factory, and in what quantity, when visual observation has not already told us. As a result, we have a "demonstrated ability," as Aspin observes, "to monitor the production of much smaller pieces of Russian military equipment, such as tanks."[65]

Not only do we use these techniques fully to monitor the testing, production, and deployment of Soviet weapons. We use them to monitor research and development, too. "We monitor the activity at the design bureaus and production plants well enough," testified William Perry, Under Secretary of Defense for Research and Engineering, in 1979, "that we have been able to predict every ICBM *before* it ever began its tests."[66]

The information we compile from space surveillance is complemented and further confirmed by information we collect from a multitude of ground sites and naval vessels that literally encircle the Soviet Union. It is reconfirmed yet again by physical examination of most Soviet weapons themselves, from strategic missile nosecones retrieved off the ocean floor to aircraft shot down, and tanks, electronic equipment, and tactical missiles captured during combat operations by Israeli forces in the Middle East.

In 1972, anticipating such technology, which would soon be operational if it had not already become so, John Taylor and David Mondey remarked that it would "give the West continuous almost-live surveillance of the territory of any potential enemy," making it "almost impossible for an aggressor to build, test and deploy" new strategic weapons "without the 'other side' being aware of every detail."[67] By 1976, all of this technology had become an accomplished fact, and had given us what Aspin called "multiple, redundant and complementary" surveillance capabilities.[68] This achievement led Ray Cline, former deputy director of the CIA, to declare in 1978 that "virtually no significant event can take place on the Earth's surface undetected."[69]

In 1979, even as opposition to SALT II mounted, based largely on the contention that Soviet compliance with the treaty could not be verified because such definitive capabilities did not exist, the Senate Intelligence Committee, after a thorough examination, concluded that they did, and that "our national reconnaissance system is complex and comprehensive."[70] At the same time, the Senate Foreign Relations Committee heard Arms Control and Disarmament Agency director George Seignious testify that "we can detect any violation by the Soviets which could pose a significant military risk or adversely affect the strategic balance."[71] Secretary of Defense Harold Brown told the Council on Foreign Relations that "no significant violation of the treaty could take place without the United States detecting it."[72] Inasmuch as "the verification capabilities of the U.S. are excellent," Aspin concluded, "it becomes evident that the much-touted problems of verification are more imagined than real."[73]

In January, 1981, as Washington prepared to receive a new administration whose success at the polls was due in no small measure to the success of its supporters in persuading the electorate to ignore all this testimony, so that America might still appear as vulnerable as they insisted, Edward Boland, chairman of the House Intelligence Committee, reminded his colleagues that "our nation is served by technical intelligence systems unsurpassed by any other nation."[74]

In May, 1983, as President Reagan continued to attack the nuclear freeze movement by asserting that a freeze "would be virtually impossible to verify,"[75] and after *Time* magazine had concurred that a freeze "almost by definition" could not be verified,[76] Senator Edward Kennedy pointed out that "an array of experts, including former Director of the CIA William Colby, former Defense Secretary Clark Clifford and former Chief Arms Control Negotiator Paul Warnke, have stated that a freeze is indeed adequately verifiable," and that, if anything, it is "more verifiable than many other arms control proposals, including President Reagan's START plan."[77]

Colby himself added that while a freeze would certainly "make it easier" to keep track of Soviet strategic weapons, "our intelligence will cover the Soviet Union's nuclear weaponry whether there is a freeze between us or not."[78] He also understood, it seemed, that the exhaustive efforts by the Reagan administration to raise suspicions about every aspect of Soviet intentions were wholly irrelevant. Even if the administration had been better able than it was to prove there was some cause for alarm over what the Soviets *intended* to do, we had always known exactly what they were able to do, and we would immediately know whatever they in fact did. Our absolute knowledge of Soviet capabilities meant that "we do not *have* to, nor should we, 'trust' the Russians."[79]

43 On-Site Inspection

There is no need, then, for on-site inspection by personnel sent to the Soviet Union. We are already on site. At each site, we can already see more than any inspector could, and whatever we cannot see, neither could he. Nor could that pose a significant obstruction to verification of treaty compliance. We can already verify treaty compliance. We are on site all the time, day or night, in all kinds of weather, at all sites at once.

Yet President Reagan claims that on site inspection is required as one of what he calls "the means to insure effective verification and compliance."[1] His administration, and many of those before it, could not have made this seem so urgent a necessity without suggesting that our existing means of verification were inadequate. To do that, they have had to hide our true capabilities. For eighteen years, they pretended that the most important of these did not even exist. It was not until 1978 that President Carter publicly announced that the SALT II Treaty we were then negotiating "would not rely on trust" because the United States had "photographic satellites" which would reveal any Soviet efforts to circumvent it.[2] Richard Burt noticed that "Mr. Carter's reference to surveillance satellites" was "the first official acknowledgement by an American President" that they existed.[3] They had existed since 1960.

Had we needed to hide this capability in order to prevent the Soviets from knowing "what the United States could actually see from space"?[4] Why? Wouldn't we *want* them to know what we could see? Wouldn't their knowledge that we can detect efforts to circumvent the treaty eliminate any incentives they might have to do so? Isn't that why improved means of verification "tend to be stabilizing influences on world affairs," as Wilford recognized, by "reducing the chances that one side will act hastily through miscalculation of the other's capabilities or intentions"?[5] Isn't that why President Carter, seeking support for SALT II, decided to reveal the existence of our satellites?

Had we needed to hide this capability in order to protect our "sources and methods"? These might require protection if revealing them gave an adversary some advantage in finding ways to compromise them. But the only way to compromise our surveillance technology is to destroy it. In an Interim Agreement signed in 1972, the United States and the Soviet Union agreed not to do that. Each party agreed "not to interfere with the national technical means of verification of the other Party."[6] This ban on interference was also included in SALT II.[7] In fact, the Soviets have known our methods and means of surveillance; even in 1957, our radar in Turkey was "well-known to the Soviet Union."[8]

It is only the American public that has not known how well we could verify Soviet compliance with SALT II and other treaties, and which has consequently been led to believe on-site inspection was necessary. Why has the public been deceived, when the Soviets have not been? Why has on-site inspection been presented as a critical precondition of our agreement to almost any arms control proposal?

Because, in the 1950s, the Soviets initially resisted on-site inspection. It was a time when they were painfully aware of our strategic superiority, and feared that inspection without disarmament would only give us a greater military advantage than we already posssessed. Any Western proposal for on-site inspection therefore seemed certain to be refused. Joel Wit, of Georgetown University's Center for Strategic and International Studies, notes that "tacking inspections on to an arms control proposal was seen as an almost sure guarantee that Moscow would find it unacceptable."[9]

Why would we want the Soviets to refuse the conditions of our arms proposals? Because for the most part we have not wanted to accept them ourselves. The actual stipulations of our Baruch Plan, which would have placed the Soviets at a greater disadvantage than they already suffered, and the actual record of negotiations over our Open Skies proposal, from which we withdrew as soon as it appeared that the Soviets might not reject it, demonstrates that even in the 1950s the United States had little genuine interest in disarmament. Yet our government still had to give the impression that it did.

It is time we realized that Washington has been negotiating not only with the Soviet Union but also with the American people. In order to sustain public support, successive administrations have had to demonstrate a continuing commitment to arms control. In order to accommodate the interests of business and the military in developing and producing new weapons, they have had to avoid any arms control measures which might too severely restrict these activities. They have had to make proposals that appeared to be in good faith, and they have had to appear willing to accept them. By proposing what they had made the public believe was essential, but which they were reasonably certain the

Soviets would refuse, they could disguise their own reluctance to submit to such proposals, yet blame the failure of negotiations on Soviet intransigence.

Publicizing Soviet intransigence has also helped to build general distrust of the Soviet Union, which in turn has helped to justify our continuing buildup of arms. It was only because SALT I did not substantially interfere with the development of new strategic weapons that we promptly dismissed the need for on-site inspection and agreed to it. It is only because SALT II does place some limits on their development and production—though it also leaves growth unrestrained in many areas of nuclear weaponry—that opposition to it grew.

The strategy of making an offer the Soviets had to refuse could only work, however, as long as Moscow responded predictably. As the Soviets began to learn more than the American public would know for many years about our true surveillance capabilities, and realized how little on-site inspections would add to what we already knew, resisting such procedures seemed less and less important to them.

Nor does the record reflect, as most Americans have been led to believe, that the Soviets always rejected on-site inspection, or even that they rejected it most of the time. In 1955, as an alternative to our Open Skies proposal, they actually suggested it.[10] In 1963, during negotiations toward a comprehensive test ban treaty, they announced their willingness to permit three on-site inspections annually. "The United States demanded seven," Fox Butterfield reports; as a result, "the two sides agreed to settle for an accord prohibiting tests in the atmosphere," but still allowing tests underground.[11] Thus, "there was a great opportunity lost in 1963," Jerome Wiesner, former science adviser to President Kennedy, recalls. "If a comprehensive test ban treaty had been signed," he believes, "it would have been more significant than SALT in arresting things."[12]

In 1976, Joel Wit recalls, "Moscow agreed to an inspection protocol in an agreement on peaceful nuclear explosions."[13] In 1979, according to Christopher Paine of the Federation of American Scientists, the United States, the Soviet Union, and the United Kingdom, in renewed negotiations toward a comprehensive test ban, "agreed that there could be on-site inspections in case of suspicious events."[14] In 1980, in their tripartite report to the United Nations on progress toward such a ban, the same three governments "formally agreed to the principle of on-site inspections," notes Eugene Carroll, deputy director for the Center for Defense Information.[15] The report itself recognized that the verification measures negotiated, "particularly the provisions regarding the international exchange of seismic data, the committee of experts, and on-site inspections—break significant new ground in international arms limitation efforts."[16]

In 1982, faced with the fact that no other government had at its disposal technical means of verification comparable to those employed by the United States—whose capabilities Representative Boland had already pointed out were "unsurpassed"[17]—Swedish Prime Minister Olof Palme's Commission on Disarmament concluded that "the possibility of on-site inspection of enemy facilities" must still be one of the verification procedures that "any major arms-reduction treaty must include."[18] Since the Commission endorsing this position included among its members Georgi Arbatov, who was also a member of the Soviet Central Committee, *Time* magazine accepted that "this could be an important breakthrough."[19]

Early in 1983, the Soviet Union announced that it wanted "to start talks this spring," Bernard Nossiter reported, "on opening some Soviet civilian nuclear plants to United Nations inspectors." This was "the first time Moscow had taken a step toward allowing foreign monitors inside Soviet borders," Nossiter was informed.[20] If so, he was misinformed. Those who so informed him, he said, were "disarmament specialists." If so, then they knew this was not "the first time," in which case they disinformed him. The impression of Soviet intransigence in refusing on-site inspection persists, because the administration and its supporters want it to persist. This impression has been so pervasive that, shortly before the Soviet government took its latest step, columnist William Safire was able to write that mere mention of on-site inspection in arms negotiations had become "taboo."[21]

Because these several Soviet endorsements of on-site inspection contradict official explanations so often given the public for the long series of failures in arms negotiations, the press has been encouraged to misinterpret their meaning, or to minimize their importance, or simply to ignore them, creating the impression that they never really occurred. In this way, the apparent record of Soviet intransigence can continue to play a significant role in establishing the view that we cannot trust Soviet intentions, even though William Colby pointed out that we do not *have* to trust them.

Meanwhile, though we continue to claim that on-site inspection has been an obstacle to arms agreements, we can no longer rely upon it to be one; other means have had to be found of ensuring that Moscow will reject arms controls we do not want ourselves. The Reagan administration has tried to achieve this by demanding reductions so much greater in Soviet than American arms as to jeopardize Soviet security, thereby virtually guaranteeing their refusal.

However, if the public saw these demands as excessive, Washington would no longer appear to be negotiating in good faith. Therefore, the administration has had to contend that the military balance of power favors the Soviet Union.

This makes it difficult for many to see whether our demands are disproportionate, for they would now seem merely to correct an existing imbalance. It makes a freeze seem unwise because it would seem to preserve that imbalance. It helps to justify the vast military buildup Americans have been required to fund by suggesting that it, too, was needed to help correct that imbalance, and that it will be all the more needed should negotiations fail.

44 Telemetry

Certainly, with the exhaustive knowledge supplied by its satellites and other intelligence resources, our government is capable not only of verifying Soviet compliance with arms limitation treaties, but also of making definitive assessments of the existing balance of military power—whether or not it makes those assessments available to the public. It can count the numbers of Soviet weapons of every kind. It can determine their measurements and other physical characteristics. Frequently, it can evaluate their performance.

Our government already knows the external dimensions of the Soviet SS-13 missile. That is how *Jane's Weapon Systems,* as long ago as 1975, was able to report the length of the SS-13 as precisely 20 meters, or just over 65 feet, 7 inches.[1] A change of 5 percent, or 3 feet, 3 inches, in the missile's length, let alone much smaller changes, would be immediately apparent to cameras in space capable of resolving objects "a few centimeters in size."[2] Its detection, at the time the Soviets tested an SS-13 in February, 1983, would have led not to President Reagan's "very great suspicion" that the Soviets may have violated SALT II, but to a very great certainty that they had.[3]

If a Soviet missile's external dimensions may be established with great precision, what about its launchweight and throwweight? Throwweight, or what Charles Mohr calls "the weight of warheads, guidance equipment, warhead dispenser and decoys that a missile can lift,"[4] may be determined simply by weighing the nosecones of warheads and dispensers we retrieve, and by measuring the external dimensions and using infrared scanners to determine the materials of those we do not retrieve. This can be done, as Roy Varner and Wayne Collier point out, with "surprising accuracy."[5] That is why precise figures for the throwweight of each Soviet missile are offered to the public by the leading sources of such specialized information, such as London's International Institute for Strategic Studies, which lists the throwweight of the SS-13 as 1,000 pounds.[6]

A missile's launchweight, or the total weight of all its stages including its reentry vehicles prior to launch, may be estimated, again, with very high accuracy by measuring its size and determining the materials used to build it and the type of fuel it carries. Just as different materials emit different levels of heat, which infrared sensors can measure, so different fuels burn at different temperatures. These temperatures, too, can be measured with great precision, and the types of fuel that produce them identified. That is how we can identify a missile whose fuel is already known, as Les Aspin pointed out, simply by identifying its "rocket-exhaust plume."[7]

Radar tracks the missile through its entire trajectory, from launch to impact, measuring its maximum altitude, its speed, and range. Its available space for fuel is estimated from measurements of the outer dimensions of each of the rocket stages. The total volume of fuel it is carrying can then be calculated. Because its fuel has been identified, the amount of fuel it carries deduced, and its rate of fuel consumption determined by timing the observable duration between ignition and burnout at each stage, the missile's maximum thrust can then be calculated. Finally, computers determine the total launchweight, including the weight of the fuel itself, which this amount of thrust may propel to the height observed in the time measured.

That is how we know the launchweight and throwweight of the SS-13 and of every other Soviet missile that has been tested. It is how we would know immediately whether changes in either of these weights exceeded those allowed by the SALT II Treaty.

Some of this information is reconfirmed by our interception of telemetry— the radio signals from instruments aboard the missiles, which Karas notes "report to the ground their measurements of acceleration, position, fuel consumption and other performance characteristics."[8] Data from fuel monitors reconfirm our own calculations of the amount of fuel the missile carries, as well as our measurements of the intervals of time in which it burns. This verifies our deductions of thrust and launchweight. Data from compasses and accelerometers reconfirm our own radar track of the altitude, speed, directional bearing, and range of the missile and its reentry vehicles. Other instruments report on malfunctions, telling us how reliably the missile's systems perform, and how frequently and with what degree of accuracy its reentry vehicles fall within range of their intended aim-points. This helps confirm our own estimates of accuracy, made by using radar and navigational positioning data from satellites to record variances in the landing pattern and positions of reentry vehicles released in previous tests. The precision with which we record these variances probably surpasses that obtained by the instruments the Soviets use, so that we may know better than they do how accurate their reentry vehicles are.

If the Reagan administration cannot plausibly claim, as it has tried to do, that it lacks the means to determine whether the SS-13 recently tested violates SALT II, it may still claim, as Senator McClure has, that Soviet encryption of missile telemetry during tests is a "militarily significant" violation of that treaty.[9] If the information telemetry affords was not already available to us by several other redundant means, its loss might hold some military significance. But that is not the case. Nor is it clear whether its encryption has denied us access to it.

Nevertheless, the encryption of some of this information may still be construed as a violation of one provision of SALT II, which specifically states that "neither Party shall engage in deliberate denial of telemetric information, such as through the use of telemetry encryption."[10] The Soviet government signed the SALT II Agreement in 1979. Even though "Mr. Reagan has refused," as Tom Wicker notes, "to ask the Senate to ratify the treaty,"[11] he did state: "As for existing arms agreements, we will refrain from actions which undercut them so long as the Soviet Union shows equal restraint."[12] The result has been that "the two sides have informally agreed to carry out the provisions" of SALT II.[13]

Therefore, even though we do not need the information allegedly denied us, mere evidence of a Soviet *attempt,* successful or not, to deny it through telemetric encryption suggests, at the very least, their *intention* to violate a treaty whose terms they agreed to observe. Consequently, Senator McClure may appear to be wholly sincere in publicizing it as an example of Soviet bad faith.

Or is it anything of the kind?

Is encryption necessarily a violation? No. The SALT II provision prohibiting denial of telemetric information adds that this prohibition must be observed "whenever such denial impedes verification of compliance with the provisions of the Treaty."[14] What about occasions when encryption does *not* impede verification of treaty compliance? Then it is not prohibited.

Richard Burt felt that because the full provision "still permits Moscow to conceal some missile-test information," it was "somewhat ambiguous."[15] Why? The treaty limits the number of strategic missiles and bombers each nation might deploy, and the number of warheads that may be placed on each missile. It limits the development of new missiles whose length, diameter, launchweight, or throwweight exceeds one or more of the same characteristics of any existing missile by more than 5 percent. Thus, telemetric information which might help confirm our measurements of such characteristics during missile tests, and which thereby might help verify treaty compliance, may not be denied by encryption or any other means.

But what about telemetry which reports the reliability and accuracy of the missile and its components? That is a large part of what telemetry does. Encryption of this data in no way "impedes verification of compliance" with treaty provisions, because there is nothing in SALT II which limits the accuracy of a missile or its reentry vehicles, and with which either party must therefore comply, and whose compliance must therefore be verified. Nor could there be any provision in any treaty setting standards of reliability for offensive weapons. Telemetric data on accuracy and reliability would certainly be "militarily significant" to a nation that did not merely use it, as we do, to confirm information already developed by other means. But under the provisions of SALT II the Soviets are perfectly entitled, as are we, to encrypt it.

Senator McClure was careful to qualify his charge that Soviet encryption of telemetry data had been "*almost* total."[16] Some administration officials, too, "said the Soviet encoding had not been total."[17] So it seems that some Soviet telemetry has not been subject to encryption.

In view of the persistence with which the Reagan administration continues to misread the record of arms control to find Soviet intransigence when most of the intransigence has been ours, and its equal persistence in charging that the Soviet Union has violated the Geneva Protocol without any evidence that it has, it is clear enough that if any evidence *did* exist of a Soviet violation of SALT II or any other treaty, Washington would promptly present it, lodge formal complaints, and give the widest possible publicity to its public condemnation of Moscow. This has not happened. If the administration claims this has not happened because it is working to improve relations with Moscow, then charges of Soviet intransigence and Soviet violations of the Geneva Protocol should be dropped. Again, this has not happened.

In light of these circumstances, and of our ability to detect violations of any treaty the moment they occur, as well as our acknowledgment that Soviet encoding of telemetry has not been "total," isn't it most likely that the Soviets have complied with the provisions of SALT II, leaving uncoded any telemetry which might otherwise impede verification of its compliance, and encoding everything else which does not, while the administration has taken advantage of public ignorance of the difference?

Senator Alan Cranston thought so, and charged the administration with "floating" suspicions of Soviet violations of SALT II as "a ploy conveniently timed" to help persuade Congress to approve MX missile funds.[18] Hedrick Smith reports that some conservative senators even wanted the administration to "publicly charge Moscow with violations" in order to "strengthen the Administration's case for the MX missile and spur 'a public campaign to increase the defense budget,' " as well as "to throw Moscow on the defense in arms talks and to counter pressure for a nuclear freeze."[19]

These, then, appeared to be the real reasons for making such charges. It seemed not to matter whether there was any truth to the charges themselves.

Complaints about our loss of access to Soviet telemetry are not new. "The Soviet Union," according to Robert Lindsey, "began encoding telemetry signals from its test missiles about six months after the arrest" of two Californians, Christopher Boyce and Andrew Lee, who had sold information to Soviet agents about satellites the United States was using to collect these signals.[20] The two were arrested in January, 1977,[21] so that by this account Moscow began encrypting its telemetry in the summer of 1977. Bamford reports the same date; so does Tad Szulc.[22]

Yet according to Richard Burt, the Soviets began this practice three years earlier. "Until 1974," he reported, we had had "fairly easy access" to Soviet telemetry; but "Moscow at that time began to transmit telemetry in many channels in undecipherable code."[23] This was well before Boyce and Lee are reported to have made their first contacts with Soviet agents the following year.[24]

If that is so, then Boyce and Lee, whose crime was publicized as a major compromise of America's intelligence resources, may have revealed to the Soviets little they hadn't already known and taken steps to counter. The CIA appears to have made a similar assessment, though it did so belatedly. While Assistant U.S. Attorney Richard Stilz charged at Boyce's trial that the information he sold caused "grievous" harm to our national security,[25] CIA spokesman Herbert Hetu remarked: "It wasn't that terrible."[26] This comment, however, did not come until two years after Lee had been sentenced to life imprisonment and Boyce to forty years.[27]

In any case, it appears that by 1977 the Soviets were already encrypting their telemetry. This was deemed no less "militarily significant" then than it is said to be today. Burt reported that it had "exacerbated" our job of collecting data on Soviet missile tests.[28] Szulc acknowledged that it "rendered monitoring more difficult."[29] Small wonder, if this data was being transmitted in "undecipherable code."

Yet we still seemed to place high priority on collecting it. For we revealed two years later, in February, 1979, that we had been continuing to collect it, from two listening stations at Kabkhan and Beshahr in northern Iran. However, after the shah's departure from that country in January, and the subsequent collapse of the military regime he left behind, we announced that "in the wake of the revolution there" the CIA had been "forced to abandon the Iranian stations," which had been used, according to Burt, "to intercept radio signals broadcast by missiles" launched from Soviet test sites. These signals, "known as telemetry," Burt explained, "provided data on key missile characteristics," and that information was "judged to be vital to verifying provisions in the new arms treaty" which would be signed later that year as SALT II, and to which, by this time, domestic opposition had grown quite intense.[30]

Yet how were the Iranian stations able to provide this "vital" information, if the telemetry they received was broadcast, and had been broadcast for at least two years, in "undecipherable code"? Perhaps that code had proven rather less of a challenge than this description suggests, for a nation whose cryptoanalytic resources included what Bamford calls "the largest and most advanced computer operation in the world,"[31] exploiting technologies that the Soviets, according to Kosta Tsipis, "simply do not have."[32]

This contradiction of earlier complaints by newer ones went ignored as the newer ones gained headlines across the nation. In a story on the front page of *The New York Times,* Hedrick Smith reported that "according to Congressional sources," CIA director Stansfield Turner had told a Senate committee that it would take four years "to restore fully the intelligence capability for monitoring Soviet missile tests" that was "lost with the shutdown of two electronic listening posts in Iran," because the data they obtained was "unobtainable through other means."[33] Senator Jake Garn of Utah helped drive home the point, warning that the "loss of our electronic listening posts in Iran has served only to reinforce" his conviction that "SALT II is not verifiable."[34] This became the leading theme of opposition to SALT II.

The Carter administration tried to remind the treaty's opponents that the information from Iran was in fact obtainable by other means. It planned to equip U-2 reconnaissance aircraft with ultra-high-frequency antennas and base them in Turkey, where they would be able "to collect much of the data on missile performance previously intercepted in the northern mountains of Iran."[35] This was quickly disputed by retired Lieutenant General Daniel Graham, an active member of the American Security Council, one of the leading organizations opposing SALT II. "Sending airplanes would be fraud," said he, "because they're not up for twenty-four hours and they can't carry the tons of equipment we had in Iran."[36] No, they can't; but ships can, and did. Graham also neglected to mention that the same equipment had already been based at hundreds of ground stations in other countries for several years. As a former director of our Defense Intelligence Agency, he knew better than most that these were but some of the means by which the same information was already being obtained, and had been obtained for years.

Administration officials attempted to point this out, too. Defense Secretary Harold Brown announced that surveillance was already "being exercised from unnamed ground stations, ships and aircraft flying in international airspace."[37]

These announcements, however, were often reported as if they described possible rather than existing capabilities. Thus, Richard Burt reported that Herbert Scoville, a former deputy director of the CIA, "maintained that the Iranian stations were not vital to verifying compliance" with SALT II, because "listening stations in Turkey" and elsewhere, "together with new satellites, ships and aircraft, could be used to collect missile telemetry and other test data."[38] So they could. But this gave the impression that such resources were not already being used that way. Scoville had pointed out that they were.

Reporting of this kind helped to sustain the impression that the loss of our listening posts in Iran had left a critical gap in our ability to verify SALT II compliance. Some of our existing means of verification, now reinterpreted as mere suggestions for closing that gap, were also discounted as ineffective. Thus, Burt worried that "American stations in Turkey are too far away to pick up line-of-sight radio broadcasts." He did add, however, that we were "still able to pick up the trajectory of experimental Soviet missiles" from "a new generation of 'over-the-horizon' radars, which bounce signals off the ionosphere."[39]

Didn't Burt know that other electronic signals bounced off the ionosphere in the same way, and that if Turkish stations picked up reflected radar energy, they could pick up telemetry too? Stations much further away had been doing this since at least 1973, when a former National Security Agency official disclosed that our station at Pine Gap, Australia, did more than receive and relay information collected by satellites; it also carried out "electronic interception missions" of its own. "Pine Gap and the antennas subordinate to it," he wrote, "are ideally suited from a global 'bounce back' point of view to monitor Russian high-frequency telemetry originating in the testing area near the Caspian Sea and in the down range at Tyura Tam."[40] American stations in Turkey, then, were not "too far away."

Other means of verification were discounted as unavailable for operational use until years later. Thus, Burt promised that "as early as 1983," the United States would have "a new satellite" in orbit, which would be "able to collect the entire spectrum of telemetry communications,"[41] including "the missile test data formerly obtained by the monitoring sites in Iran."[42] This meant, of course, that we would not have such a satellite *until* 1983.

We had had satellites capable of picking up Soviet telemetry since 1962. In March of that year we launched the first of a series of electronic and signals intelligence (ELINT and SIGINT) satellites to gather everything that could be overheard in space. They picked up signals throughout the radio spectrum, from voice communications to the pulses of Soviet radars. They regularly passed over Soviet missile test sites. And whenver they did so, if a test was in progress, they picked up its telemetry too.

According to Karas, our largest ELINT satellites weighed between 2,000 and 4,400 pounds, and were launched between 1962 and 1970.[43] During that period they charted the locations, pulse frequencies, band widths, and other characteristics of air defense radars throughout the Soviet Union. From intercepted radio communications they also told us more than we had already learned from the cameras, radars, and multispectral scanners aboard our other spacecraft. While visual and radar imagery had given us the location of every Soviet military unit in the world, and revealed the numbers and kinds of weapons with which it was equipped, our ELINT and SIGINT satellites told us its unit designation, its organizational structure, its chain of command, and its training and maintenance schedules. They also provided valuable information about its level of readiness and its operational procedures.

Two months after we launched our first ELINT satellites, we launched the first of a series of much smaller satellites called *Ferrets*.[44] These were used for the next several years to confirm and update the information gathered by the larger spacecraft. Weighing only 120 pounds, the *Ferret* rode into space aboard a larger photographic satellite, was released, and then boosted itself into a somewhat higher orbit of about 300 miles. From that altitude, in "one day," reports Bamford, "as the satellite orbits north to south and the earth rotates east to west, the Ferret would come within receiving range of virtually all radars and high-frequency transmitters in the world."[45]

The first *Ferrets* were probably carried, in 1962, by Discoverer satellites. By 1966 they were being launched from SAMOS satellites; and by 1971, from Big Bird satellites.[46] While several *Ferrets* were in orbit at once, so that they repeatedly passed over Soviet missile test sites at frequent intervals, just as photographic satellites did, their coverage was not continuous. Intervals still existed. These were too short to prevent a photographic or radar satellite from observing a new missile undergoing launch preparations, however, since such preparations would take several hours. Jasani had pointed out that with just "one satellite the interval before the next observation" of any particular area "is 92 minutes," whereas "with two satellites this time would be reduced considerably."[47] He also showed that at any time, the United States usually had three photographic reconnaissance satellites in orbit.[48]

But the missile one or more of these satellites would have observed preparing for launch might easily be launched during just such an interval in similar coverage by ELINT satellites. The launch itself would take only a few minutes. It was just before, during, and after the moment of launch that a test missile transmitted its most important telemetry data. Our *Ferrets* and other ELINT craft might not be in a position to collect it. Nor might the Soviets be disinclined to time their test launches accordingly. For in the 1960s, the United States and the

Soviet Union had not yet agreed *not* to deny each other access to certain telemetry data.

What were needed were geosynchronous satellites, orbiting at a height of 22,300 miles above the earth, where their speed kept pace with the earth's rotation, so that each of them remained stationed over the same point on its surface, permanently in position to collect telemetry and all the other electromagnetic data they were equipped to provide.

Could satellites be placed in orbit at that height? They were placed at that height in May, 1960, when the first of our MIDAS (Missile Defense Alarm System) satellites was launched.[49] The MIDAS satellites, equipped with infrared sensors to detect missile launches from the heat of their exhaust plumes, took permanent station over the Indian and South Pacific Oceans, whence they could view almost all of the Soviet Union and China. Since that time, most of our communications and early warning satellites had been placed at geosynchronous altitudes.[50]

So it is not surprising that in June, 1970, we placed the first of our *Rhyolite* ELINT satellites at the same height.[51] In March, 1972, reports Bamford, a second *Rhyolite* "was placed into a geosynchronous orbit and parked above the Horn of Africa," where it could "intercept telemetry signals transmitted" from missiles launched from both Tyuratum and Plesetsk.[52] In May, 1977, a third *Rhyolite* was "positioned above Borneo," where it could "pick up telemetry intelligence from Soviet missiles that are fired from the eastern test ranges" as they "smash into the Kamchatka Peninsula impact zone or in the North Pacific."[53] Two additional *Rhyolites* were launched in December, 1977, and April, 1978, as spares.[54]

Each of these satellites, Lindsey notes, was developed "especially" to monitor "the eastern Soviet Union, China and Soviet missile test ranges,"[55] and "to intercept telemetry signals transmitted by Soviet missiles during test launchings."[56] Each "carried a battery of antennas capable of sucking foreign microwave signals from out of space like a vacuum cleaner."[57] Karas calls the *Rhyolite* system our "listening post" in space, whose "most important role is to intercept the telemetry from those Soviet ICBM tests."[58]

These were the satellites whose presence may have caused the Soviets to begin encrypting some of their telemetry. They had observed *Ferrets* passing over their test sites for years, but also knew that once these craft moved beyond the radio horizon, they could no longer receive telemetry. The *Rhyolites,* however, were continuously on station and missed nothing.

Bamford worried, though, that their altitude might place them beyond receiving range. The "laws of physics," he knew, "would prevent the telemetry signals reaching Rhyolite from being more than one-thousandth the magnitude of those that had been received in Iran."[59] True. But why did that make any difference? As long ago as 1957, "a simple type of coherent integration" had been developed at the Massachusetts Institute of Technology's Lincoln Laboratory, in order "to amplify weak signals occurring below the noise level of the receiver."[60] If this had not made signals from 22,300 miles away quite distinct, how could we receive signals from an 8-watt transmitter aboard Pioneer 10 at the outer reaches of Pluto, 2.7 *billion* miles away? We did.[61] Traveling at the speed of light, these signals still took 4 hours and 16 minutes to reach earth, "their strength reduced," John Noble Wilford reports, "to 20 billionths of a watt."[62] Be it a cry or a whisper, it is heard.

As a result, Lauran Paine observes, one of these satellites "could pick up, record, and transmit emanations from all land communications systems, including radio and microwave telephonic transmissions," and was "sensitive enough to do the work of the hundreds of listening posts the United States intelligence community had in such places as Turkey, Iran, and West Germany. It was capable of duplicating everything those listening posts could do."[63]

Not only, then, could we see everything in the Soviet Union. We could *hear* it too.

That is why, as Bamford acknowledges, "Rhyolite serves as one of America's chief 'national technical means of verification' of Soviet compliance with the strategic arms limitation agreement."[64] It is why the Carter administration, as Lindsey notes, knew perfectly well "that the United States would be able through other means to verify Soviet compliance" with SALT II. For when it announced the loss of the Iranian listening posts, it also knew that, aside from many other redundant means of collecting Soviet telemetry, "four Rhyolite satellites" were already "then in orbit."[65] When Burt reported that we would not have such satellites until 1983, we had already had the entire *Rhyolite* system for more than two years. When the Iranian listening posts were abandoned, the earliest of those satellites had already been duplicating their work for almost six years.

Thus, there was no significance at all to our loss of the Iranian listening posts. The claim that this left us unable to verify Soviet treaty compliance was a complete hoax.

The hoax, however, succeeded in expanding the opposition to SALT II. Despite initial efforts by the more loyal members of the Carter administration to keep the public informed of our comprehensive means of verification, key members of our military and intelligence establishments were among the most influential sources keeping the general media informed. Their claim that these means were inadequate became the official point of view, partly on the presumption that they had no reason to hide the truth and therefore must be telling it. It seems to have been forgotten that long before the Iranian revolution they had declared themselves determined opponents of SALT II, a treaty whose ratification would have delayed and in some cases prevented development and production of a variety of new strategic weapons already planned—whether or not they were needed. If the truth demonstrated that there was no reason to oppose SALT II, then these people had every reason to hide it.

45 A Comprehensive Test Ban

Similar has been Washington's reluctance to seek a comprehensive nuclear test ban, even though it placed itself under a permanent, binding commitment to do so when it signed the Limited Test Ban Treaty in 1963, which pledges its signatories "to achieve the discontinuance of all test explosions of nuclear weapons for all time," and "to continue negotiations to this end."[1] It repeated that pledge verbatim in 1968 when it signed the Nuclear Non-Proliferation Treaty,[2] whose signatories also committed themselves to the broader task of continuing "negotiations in good faith on effective measures relating to cessation of the nuclear arms race at an early date and to nuclear disarmament."[3]

Nothing would so quickly bring about a qualitative end to the nuclear arms race as a comprehensive test ban. Guidance systems, of course, might still be improved, and delivery systems made marginally more secure. But if new warheads could not be tested, their yields verified, and the reliability of their triggering mechanisms ensured, the importance of other improvements would steadily decline, for they could not suffice by themselves to ensure that a weapon, even if successfully placed on its target, would perform its intended task. Consequently, development of new nuclear weapons, and modernization of old ones, would soon cease.

In the same way, nothing would so quickly limit the further proliferation of nuclear weapons to the arsenals of other nations; nor would anything so surely erode confidence in the reliability of existing warheads. According to Herbert York, an arms control advisor to several administrations, the Joint Chiefs of Staff have repeatedly warned that "as long as the nation maintains a stockpile of nuclear weapons it will be necessary to conduct at least occasional tests to be confident that the weapons in the stockpile are still in working order."[4]

Critics of a test ban are quick to suggest that a loss of confidence in the reliability of our nuclear weapons is the same as a loss of faith in their deterrent power. By discussing only our own weapons, they imply that only our weapons would be affected by such a ban, placing us at a disadvantage, whereas in fact it would affect every other nation's nuclear weapons in exactly the same way. They also imply that deterrence depends only on faith in the reliability and survivability of a retaliatory force, when in fact it has always depended far more on a *lack* of faith in the reliability of an attacking force.

Deterrence has always been based on uncertainty. The largest uncertainty of all has been whether the weapons launched in a first strike would perform as planned. This uncertainty has always existed, because no nuclear weapons have ever been tested against the actual targets they were meant to destroy. We don't know, for example, how many of the missiles launched in a nuclear strike would actually clear their launch pads, how many would propel themselves to the proper altitude and follow their anticipated trajectories, or how many might later be thrown off course by malfunctioning guidance systems, polar magnetism, or the effects of earlier nuclear explosions in their paths. We don't know how many might be damaged in flight by such explosions, how many would arrive within effective range of their targets, or how many of those that did arrive would detonate. Such knowledge could only become available after it ceased to matter. It can never play a role in predicting the results of a nuclear attack.

By the late 1950s, just as soon as a second superpower had acquired the means to deliver its nuclear weapons, these several uncertainties produced a further uncertainty as to whether a first strike could ever be assured of eliminating retaliatory forces. Because this was no longer possible to ensure, it was impossible to know whether the retaliatory damage inflicted by the nation first struck—no matter how few its surviving weapons—might far outweigh the advantages sought by the nation that chose to strike first. If the damage might be unacceptable, then the risks of launching a first strike that might incur it were unacceptable.

These risks remain, because the uncertainties remain. The vast surfeit of nuclear weapons added to the arsenals of the superpowers since that time has done nothing to reduce those uncertainties. No amount of technological improvement will reduce them in the future. All the superpowers can do is refine their means of threatening retaliatory forces considered invulnerable today. Improved air defenses may place bomber forces at greater risk; improved antisubmarine warfare technology may pose a larger threat to submarines. But no nation contemplating a first strike will ever be sure it can eliminate all these forces before some are used.

We may continue theoretically to improve the accuracy and reliability of existing weapons, and we may measure the theoretical odds of reliability from extrapolated test data. But we will never be sure how accurate and reliable such systems are. Uncertainty thus preserves unacceptable risks for all parties to nuclear conflict. It can no more ensure that a particular nuclear strike will succeed than ensure that it will not.

In the same way, if existing warheads continued to age without occasional tests to confirm their reliability, doubts about their reliability, far from reducing faith in deterrence, would only increase uncertainties that are already irreducible, and on which deterrence is already based. Nor could these doubts increase one kind of uncertainty over another. Just as we could fear that a growing number of our weapons might not work, the Soviets would still have to fear that they might. Just as we could fear that Soviet weapons might continue to work, the Soviets would have to fear they might not.

Therefore, a comprehensive test ban, while bringing a halt to qualitative improvements in nuclear arms and so eliminating the larger threat they would pose, can neither eliminate the threat existing weapons pose nor, by the same token, revoke their deterrent power. Because deterrence requires less confidence in the reliability of weapons than first strike planning does, any erosion of confidence can only improve more than it can diminish global security. Together with a quantitative freeze on further production and deployment of existing warhead designs, a test ban would bring a complete halt to the nuclear arms race—a necessary precondition for steps toward our committed goal of nuclear disarmament.

Contrary to this commitment, and in direct violation of its pledge, the United States, after two decades of progress toward a comprehensive test ban treaty with the Soviet Union and Great Britain, and after what columnist Tom Wicker saw to be "unprecedented Soviet concessions,"[5] unilaterally suspended negotiations in 1980. And this despite the fact that all three nations, as Eugene Carroll notes, had already "formally agreed to the major elements" of such a treaty, "including on-site inspection and improved seismic sensors,"[6] a substantial number of which "the Russians indicated their willingness to accept," adds Herbert York, "on their territory."[7]

In July, 1982, President Reagan approved an interagency recommendation "not to resume negotiations on a comprehensive ban on nuclear testing," on the grounds that testing was "vital to the security of the United States."[8] No one in his administration offered to explain why a nation that was committed to "significant reductions" in the nuclear weapons stockpile, as the President had assured the world only two months earlier,[9] now suddenly found it vital to continue tests, in the absence of any need for them in order to maintain deterrence— unless the President really intended, contrary to his latest assurance, to increase the stockpile instead. Wicker concluded this was the case. "The Reagan buildup," he realized, "under which an estimated 17,000 new warheads are to be built, would be impossible if a comprehensive test ban were to be agreed upon."[10]

This, Carroll knew, made Reagan "the first President since Truman to refuse flatly to negotiate the most important arms-control measure of all: an end to all nuclear explosions." That refusal, he saw, "constituted a clear violation of the Limited Test Ban Treaty of 1963, in which the U.S. pledged to continue negotiations leading to an end to nuclear testing."[11]

In December, 1982, when the United Nations resolved by a vote of 111 to 1 that all further nuclear tests should be banned, the United States again violated its pledge by casting the only opposing vote, on the grounds, according to deputy representative Kenneth Adelman, that such a ban would not "reduce the threat implicit in the existing stockpile of nuclear weapons."[12] No one except his own colleagues had ever suggested it would. Now, contradicting them, he was admitting that a total ban could not revoke the deterrent power of existing weapons.

Yet the sole purpose of a total ban had always been to eliminate the larger threat of a stockpile that continued to increase. Nevertheless, because it planned to increase that threat with unprecedented increases in its own stockpile, rather than the reductions it had promised, the United States now refused to agree to the ban it had long pledged to seek.

At first, Reagan administration officials were reluctant to explain their newly developed antipathy toward a comprehensive test ban, and feared, as Judith Miller reported, that any attempt they made to explain the need for continued testing "would foster a perception that the Administration was not seriously committed to arms control initiatives."[13] Indeed. A better explanation had to be found for their refusal to complete twenty years of negotiations. The explanation finally adopted was a familiar one. Efforts to negotiate a comprehensive ban on nuclear tests would be set aside "until verification measures of existing testing treaties can be strengthened."[14]

The two existing treaties—the Threshold Test Ban Treaty, signed by Presidents Nixon and Brezhnev in 1974, and the Peaceful Nuclear Explosions Treaty, signed by Presidents Ford and Brezhnev in 1976—prohibit underground nuclear explosions, whether for military or ostensibly peaceful purposes, exceeding 150 kilotons in yield. Both were submitted to the Senate for ratification by the Presidents who signed them. Both remain on the Senate's Treaty Calendar, and may be ratified without further word from the executive branch. Though neither has been ratified, both superpowers have pledged themselves to abide by the limits they specify, just as they have agreed to honor SALT II. Neither has been ratified, because the Reagan administration claims that compliance with them cannot be verified. "Despite the intelligence community's assessment in 1977," Carl

Marcy recalls, "that both treaties could be verified,"[15] a Reagan administration official now said: "On several occasions seismic signals from the Soviet Union have been of sufficient magnitude to call into question Soviet compliance with the threshold of 150 kilotons."[16]

As a result, President Reagan claimed in March, 1983, that the treaties are "so restricted as to verification that we have reason to believe that there have been numerous violations. And yet, because of the lack of verification capability, we could not make such a charge and sustain it."[17] This raises the question of how, if it could not sustain such a charge, the administration could have sufficient "reason to believe" there is cause to make it.

It also fails to answer the question of why a comprehensive test ban should be avoided. If the only real grounds for delaying agreement on such a ban are that less comprehensive bans are more difficult to monitor, then why not agree on a total ban that would be easier to monitor? If difficulties truly exist in determining whether certain explosions exceed a specified limit of yield, then why not eliminate those difficulties by agreeing to eliminate all explosions? To refuse a complete solution because a partial one is said to be unsatisfactory is pure sophistry. Yet this was all the administration used to distract public attention away from the real issue of its refusal, on very different grounds, to complete a comprehensive test ban agreement.

Arguments that a comprehensive test ban would *not* be simpler to monitor have been thoroughly refuted. Aside from our High Altitude Sampling Program (HASP) to collect radioactive particles thrown into the upper atmosphere by tests, and from satellites bearing electromagnetic pulse meters and infrared, gamma ray, beta wave, and neutron detectors to locate and measure the yield of any nuclear detonation on the earth's surface or in the atmosphere almost immediately, sensors have been embedded, as York points out, at "seismic stations all over the world,"[18] including the ocean floor, and have made it virtually impossible for nuclear explosions of any significant size to go undetected.

Writing in *Scientific American,* Lynn Sykes, a Columbia University geologist who helped negotiate the Threshold Test Ban Treaty, and Jack Evernden, of the National Center for Earthquake Research, demonstrated that we have long since reached the point where "the state of knowledge of seismology and the techniques for monitoring seismic waves are sufficient to insure that a feasible network could soon detect a clandestine underground testing program involving explosions as small as one kiloton." Consequently, they conclude, "the technical capabilities needed to police a comprehensive test ban down to explosions of very small size unquestionably exist." The only "issues to be resolved," they feel, "are political."[19]

Nuclear explosions, Sykes and Evernden show, may be distinguished from earthquakes by several differences in their seismological patterns. Both types of disturbance produce short pressure waves moving through the earth; but while such waves emanating from quakes move in highly erratic patterns, those generated from nuclear explosions are perfectly symmetrical. Both generate shear waves through the earth. While such waves are always among the first shocks recorded from earthquakes, they are never among the first shocks recorded from nuclear explosions.

Short waves sent through the earth also produce two types of longer waves, known as Love waves and Rayleigh waves, which move across the earth's surface. Earthquakes generate both types of surface wave, whereas nuclear explosions produce no Love waves at all, and the Rayleigh waves they produce are of much lower magnitude than those resulting from earthquakes. Finally, the ratio of long surface waves to short body waves has also "been shown to be a reliable criterion for distinguishing the seismic waves of earthquakes from those of explosions."[20]

As for seismic records that "call into question" Soviet compliance with the Threshold Test Ban Treaty limit of 150 kilotons, Sykes and Evernden say these are "based on a miscalibration of one of the curves that relates measured seismic magnitude to explosive yield."[21] *New York Times* reporter Judith Miller notes that "the Administration and its critics disagree in part because they are using different formulas for assigning waves a specific magnitude," and that the formulas in question "can not be discussed in detail, because they are secret."[22] From that, one might conclude that the barrier of secrecy prevents the public from resolving this issue.

What is not secret, however, is that the administration's formula is based, as former government arms control specialists Anne Cahn and James Leonard note, "on seismographic data from the short waves that travel through the earth, rather than the long waves that travel along the surface," even though "most geologists believe that surface waves more accurately measure explosions."[23] Indeed, Sykes and Evernden show that "there is an essentially universal relation" between the magnitude of longer waves and the yield of nuclear explosions, whereas the curve relating the magnitude of shorter waves and yield "must be calibrated for each test site."[24]

The United States has developed formulas relating the seismic magnitude of both long and short waves to nuclear yield, derived from tests conducted at the Nevada Test Site (NTS). Sykes and Evernden point out that when estimates of the yield of nuclear explosions at many test sites around the world use the NTS formula based on the magnitude of longer waves, they "have invariably agreed with actual yields," whereas estimates using the NTS formula based on the magnitude of short waves "have sometimes been in drastic disagreement with the actual yield."[25]

Nevertheless, the Reagan administration has taken only its NTS formula based on *short* waves, and applied it, *without calibration,* to seismic magnitudes recorded from explosions monitored at the Soviet test site near Semipalatinsk, even though the resulting estimates of yield "are more than four times as great" as those based on the magnitude of longer waves.[26]

"When the correct calibration is employed," Sykes and Evernden find, "it is apparent that none of the Russian weapons tests exceeds 150 kilotons, although several come close to it."[27] Similarly, estimates of yield can simply be based on the magnitudes of long waves, with their "essentially universal relation" to yield"; for, as Cahn and Leonard note, "analyses of such waves do not confirm that Moscow has tested above the threshold."[28]

That is why Michael May, associate director of the Lawrence Livermore Laboratory, concluded that "there was no evidence that the Soviets had cheated on the Threshold Test Ban Treaty."[29] It is why Colorado's Senator Gary Hart reminded the administration that its professed doubts about Soviet compliance are simply "not shared by the majority of those in the scientific community."[30] Maryland's Senator Charles Mathias noted that the administration "has not produced any evidence" of Soviet violations of the two treaties still unratified by the Senate, and that the only real obstacle to their ratification "instead appears to be one of political will."[31] And Tom Wicker could only conclude that "opposition within the U.S. Government—in the Pentagon, in Congress, at the national nuclear laboratories—as well as in the 'military-industrial complex' and the press" is "a bigger obstacle than the Soviet Union to agreement on a comprehensive test ban."[32]

APPENDIXES

Contents

Appendix A

The Strategic Balance:
Author's Estimate

This appendix gives an independent estimate of the numbers of nuclear weapons American and Soviet strategic forces could deliver from 1979 through 1983. The estimate first compiles the numbers of warheads deliverable by American and Soviet land-based missiles, then the numbers of warheads deliverable by American and Soviet sea-based missiles, and finally the numbers of nuclear weapons deliverable by American and Soviet aircraft equipped and deployed as intercontinental bombers.

For each component of America's strategic arsenal, from land-based and sea-based missiles to bombers, the estimate first provides a chronology of critical changes in force structure, giving precise dates for the initial deployment of new systems and the retirement of older ones, so that the resulting changes in warhead inventory are reflected at the proper time.

Estimates of Soviet and American missile warheads are based on Defense Department figures as well as a range of additional estimates from competent sources offering breakdowns of missiles by type. Estimates for Soviet missile warheads are consistent with normal growth following the Defense Department's estimate of a total of 6,300 Soviet missile warheads in May, 1982.

Critical changes in Soviet force structure, especially the introduction of each new Soviet missile type, are based on the consensus of all these estimates, as are the numbers of new and old Soviet missiles deployed at any given time during the period under study.

This consensus, and the author's estimate based upon it, conflict with figures for Soviet missile warheads offered concurrently to the public by the Reagan administration. Those figures, which claimed 1,100 more Soviet missile warheads than the Defense Department substantiated in 1982, could only be obtained by assuming, first of all, that every Soviet missile deployed had been fitted with the maximum number of warheads allowed by SALT II, and secondly, that new Soviet missiles were being deployed more rapidly than any evidence could show.

An example of the latter assumption was the administration's suggestion that Soviet SS-N-20 missiles would be operationally deployed aboard the first *Typhoon* class submarine before the end of 1983. In the second edition of its booklet *Soviet Military Power,* the administration stated that "the first submarine of this type will be fully operational by the end of 1983."[1] Yet according to the Joint Chiefs of Staff, the *Typhoon* would not be deployed until "the mid-1980s" at the earliest.[2] And according to the International Institute for Strategic Studies, by the end of 1983 the SS-N-20 missile was still "under development."[3]

Nor did any evidence support the administration's first assumption. Most of the evidence contradicted it. Rather than reporting every Soviet SS-18 missile fitted with the maximum of ten warheads allowed by SALT II, only three sources reported any SS-18s of this type, and they reported only small numbers. All sources reported a preponderance of SS-18s with only eight warheads. The International Institute for Strategic Studies reported that "the bulk of SS-18" were of this latter type; it reported only half the number of Soviet sea-based SS-N-18 missiles deployed with seven warheads each, and the other half fitted with only three each.[4]

All sources reported many SS-N-18s with the lower number of warheads, and all reported substantial numbers of land-based SS-18s and SS-19s with a *single* warhead. The Defense Intelligence Agency even acknowledged in 1984 that a number of Soviet missiles capable of being fitted with multiple warheads "are still configured to carry single warheads."[5] An administration spokesman claimed that this information had been omitted from its annual editions of *Soviet Military Power* due to "space considerations."[6] All of this directly contradicted the assumption on which the administration had based its high figure for the number of Soviet missile warheads.

The author's estimate also examines the load capacities of American and Soviet bombers. For the normal operational loads carried by America's strategic bomber force, it bases its figures again on a consensus of available estimates giving the loads carried by each bomber type.

But America's bombers have a considerable capacity to carry additional weapons, and very large stocks of weapons to draw from. The estimate breaks down the different loads each bomber type normally carries by the number and types of weapons each load includes, the total weight of that load, and the percentage of maximum load capacity this weight represents. It then notes additional combinations of weapons whose weight does not exceed the percentage of load capacity normally used. Some of these combinations include much greater numbers of weapons, all of them independently targetable.

This leads to two estimates for America's bomber force: one of its normal operational loadings; and the other of its maximum deliverable weapons capacity. The two estimates show that during the period under study, America's strategic bombers could deliver a minimum of 2,400 weapons, or a maximum of more than 4,000. This high capacity has been noted by many sources. The International Institute for Strategic Studies, for example, estimated that if all of America's B-52G and B-52H bombers were fitted with the maximum number of SRAMs (Short-Range Attack Missiles) they could carry, "the U.S. bomber warhead total would exceed 5,000."[7]

By contrast, this study notes, the Soviet bomber force is capable of delivering no more than two hundred nuclear weapons. Nor could this force be enlarged with Tu-22M *Backfire* bombers, as the Reagan administration suggested. Evidence is cited here to show that the *Backfire* is neither equipped nor deployed as an intercontinental strategic bomber, lacks the range to carry out that mission, lacks tanker aircraft to refuel it,[8] and is incapable, as the majority of sources acknowledge, of carrying as many weapons as the administration assigned to it.

As the numbers of missiles, submarines, bombers, and bomber weapons of each type are estimated here, their performance characteristics and specifications are also compared. Throughout, sources are given for this information, as they are for all estimates, deployment dates, and other pertinent data cited.

The evolving balance of deliverable strategic warheads is then summarized at six-month intervals throughout the period under study, showing America's minimum totals as well as the maximum totals its strategic forces could deliver if its bombers were armed with all the weapons they could carry.

This information is used to recapitulate the composition of Soviet and American strategic forces as they existed in June, 1982, December, 1982, and June, 1983. It also illustrates the hypothetical composition of those forces as they *might* have existed in December, 1982, had all the missiles and bombers available to both nations really been loaded with nuclear weapons to the maximum extent allowed by SALT II. This only shows that had such maximum loads been achieved, the United States still would have held the lead in numbers of deliverable strategic warheads, and would have held it by an even larger margin than it already had throughout this period.

It should be kept in mind that if and when these maximum loads ever are achieved, the only result will be that the balance of warheads will favor the United States by the larger margin shown.

The estimate next calculates the proportions of warhead inventory, aggregate throwweight, and aggregate megatonnage delivered in selected years by each component of each nation's strategic forces.

The composition of Soviet and American strategic forces in 1984 and 1985 is subsequently given, based on rates of conversion and force modernization already established, but taking into account any evidence of changes in those rates, as well as evidence of the introduction of new or additional weapons, including the introduction of Soviet SS-N-20 SLBMs aboard the first *Typhoon* class submarines, the deployment of additional *Trident C-4* SLBMs aboard new *Trident* submarines, the deployment of increasing numbers of Air-Launched Cruise Missiles (ALCMs) assigned to additional squadrons of B-52G and B-52H bombers, and the introduction of *Pershing II* and *Tomahawk* Ground-Launched Cruise Missiles (GLCMs) in Europe, and *Tomahawk* Sea-Launched Cruise Missiles (SLCMs) with nuclear warheads on ships and submarines of the United States fleet.

Finally, the balance of deliverable strategic warheads is given from 1979 through 1985, showing the growth in numbers of such warheads in Soviet and American arsenals throughout this period.

This balance is given both with and without the addition of Euromissiles and SLCMs to America's strategic force capabilities. The official American position is that these additional missiles are not intended for use as strategic weapons, and therefore should not be included in the balance of deliverable strategic warheads. However, these weapons, like those that may be carried by America's nuclear-capable strike aircraft based in Europe or based on aircraft carriers within range of Europe, are capable of striking targets in the Soviet Union.

It should be kept in mind that the Soviet Union does not possess nuclear-capable strike aircraft based on carriers. Its YAK-36 *Forger* aircraft aboard the carriers *Kiev* and *Minsk* cannot deliver nuclear weapons.[9] The Soviet Union does not possess stable forward bases where it might place either missiles or nuclear-capable strike aircraft within closer range of targets in the United States. It does not possess long-range cruise missiles deliverable either by aircraft or by the submarine and surface combatants of its fleet.

The maximum range reported for any Soviet sea-launched cruise missile is 620 miles, possibly obtained by the SS-N-12.[10] The maximum range reported for any Soviet Air-Launched Cruise Missile is 400 miles, obtained by the AS-3.[11]

The Soviet Sea-Launched Cruise Missile that veered off course during naval exercises on December 28, 1984, did not travel the vast distances implied by Defense Secretary Weinberger when he told a Senate committee that it was "starting to work its way across

Norway and Finland."[12] It flew over no more than 80 miles of Norwegian territory, and probably traveled a total of no more than 200 miles before it crashed near Finland's Lake Inari. It could not have reached West Germany, as the London *Daily Express* reported.[13] According to Lieutenant Colonel Norbert Huebner of the West German Defense Ministry, the missile "was not capable of covering such a distance."[14]

America's Sea-Launched Cruise Missile, by contrast, has a range of 2,210 miles.[15] This missile is but one of several new types of nuclear weapons in America's arsenal, to which the Soviet Union has as yet no counterparts. Their range or their proximity to Soviet territory give them strategic capabilities. The United States has begun to deploy them in substantial quantities. If the Soviets had comparable weapons, American officials certainly would want to include their numbers in the balance of deliverable strategic warheads. Since the United States has such weapons, impartial observers feel their numbers should be included in the balance. If they are included, they only further raise the margin of America's continuing lead in numbers of deliverable strategic warheads.

The following estimate of the strategic balance is organized in four sections:

- United States and Soviet Strategic Land-Based Missiles
- United States and Soviet Strategic Sea-Based Missiles
- United States and Soviet Strategic Bomber Forces
- The Strategic Balance: Summary and Analysis

Notes

1. Department of Defense, *Soviet Military Power* (March, 1983), page 21.
2. Joint Chiefs of Staff, *Fiscal Year 1983 Military Posture Statement*, page 107.
3. IISS, *The Military Balance, 1982–1983,* page 113.
4. *Ibid.,* page 140, notes b and g.
5. William Arkin and Jeffrey Sands, "The Soviet Nuclear Stockpile," *Arms Control Today,* Volume 14, no. 5 (June, 1984), page 4.
6. *Ibid.*
7. IISS, *The Military Balance, 1976–1977,* page 106.
8. The United States has 24 KC-10A and 615 KC-135A and KC-135Q long-range tanker aircraft. The Soviet Union has 30 MYA-4 *Bison* long-range tanker aircraft. See IISS, *The Military Balance, 1984–1985,* pages 5 and 17.
9. Center for Defense Information, "U.S. Strategic Momentum," *The Defense Monitor,* Volume III, no. 4 (May, 1974), page 2. The YAK-36 was initially deployed the same year. IISS has not listed it under "Nuclear Delivery Systems" in any edition of *The Military Balance.* See the listings for Soviet tactical aircraft under that heading on pages 121 and 123 of *The Military Balance, 1983–1984,* and on pages 135 and 136 of *The Military Balance, 1984–1985.*
10. IISS, *The Military Balance, 1984–1985,* page 135.
11. IISS, *The Military Balance, 1983–1984,* page 121.
12. Bill Keller, "Weinberger, in Error, Says Soviet Downed Own Missile," *The New York Times,* February 1, 1985.
13. *Ibid.*
14. *Ibid.*
15. General Dynamics/Convair, the prime contractor for the SLCM, quoted by James Munves, "The War Museum," *The Nation* (September 3–10, 1983), page 165.

United States and Soviet Strategic Land-Based Missiles

TABLES IN THIS SECTION

- Chronology of Critical Changes in Minuteman Force Structure, 1970–83
- Author's Estimate of United States ICBM Warheads, 1979–83
- Available Estimates of Soviet ICBM Warheads, 1979–83, Broken Down by Missile Type
- Author's Estimate of Soviet ICBM Warheads, 1979–83
- Characteristics of United States and Soviet ICBMs Deployed from 1979 Through 1983

Chronology of Critical Changes in Minuteman Force Structure, 1970–83

Date	Event
Dec. 1970	The first squadron of 50 *Minuteman III* missiles is deployed with the 91st Strategic Missile Wing at Minot Air Force Base, North Dakota. Each *Minuteman III* is equipped with Mk 12 reentry vehicles and W-62 warheads, each warhead with a yield of 170 kilotons.
Mar. 1973	The last squadron of *Minuteman I* missiles of the 90th Strategic Missile Wing at Warren Air Force Base, Wyoming, is retired and replaced with *Minuteman IIs*.
Feb. 1975	A Silo Upgrade Program is completed for the first wing of *Minuteman* missiles at Minot Air Force Base. Ten inches of borated concrete are added to silo lids, and bins are added to catch rubble when silo lids slide open for missile launch. To reduce the effects of ground shock from nuclear explosions, missiles are removed from their shock-absorbent springs and placed in free suspension systems. To protect their guidance circuitry from the effects of electromagnetic pulse, missile nosecones are covered with titanium shrouds.
Feb. 1975	Installation of the Command Data Buffer System is completed on *Minuteman III* missiles at Minot Air Force Base, providing the capability for remote retargeting of these missiles by radio command.
July 1975	The last *Minuteman III* missiles originally planned for deployment become operational with the 341st Strategic Missile Wing at Malmstrom Air Force Base, Montana. The *Minuteman* force now comprises 450 *Minuteman IIs* and 550 *Minuteman IIIs*.
July 1976	The first flight test of the *Minuteman III* with INS-20 guidance.
Sept. 1977	The Silo Upgrade Program is completed for all *Minuteman III* silos. Formerly able to withstand overpressures of no more than 300 psi, they are now hardened sufficiently to resist up to 2000 psi.
Sept. 1978	Completion of program to install Command Data Buffer System on all 550 *Minuteman III* missiles. Any *Minuteman III* can now be retargeted in 25 minutes, and the entire force can be retargeted in 10 hours.
Sept. 1978	Completion of program to implement NS-20 guidance software improvements for all 550 *Minuteman IIIs*. Defense Secretary Harold Brown had earlier noted that "To some extent, the effects of the guidance improvement program have already been realized by the gradual refinement of NS-20 guidance software." The more perfected NS-20 guidance system gives the *Minuteman III* a CEP of 729 ft.
July 1979	Replacement of the NS-20 guidance system on the *Minuteman III* with the new INS-20 guidance system begins. This reduces the missile's CEP to 607 ft.
Jan. 1980	The Silo Upgrade Program is completed for all remaining *Minuteman* missiles. The entire *Minuteman* force is now protected against overpressures of up to 2000 psi. Total cost for the program is $1.4 billion. According to Congressman Les Aspin, this has "delayed *Minuteman* vulnerability for at least six years."
June 1980	First operational deployment of the Mk 12A reentry vehicle on the *Minuteman III*. The Mk 12A has a W-78 warhead with a yield of 335 kilotons, roughly doubling the yield of the weapon it replaces.

Date	Event
Mar. 1981	93 *Minuteman III* missiles have now been refitted with a total of 279 Mk 12A reentry vehicles.
Jan. 1982	Phase III implementation of the Airborne Launch Control System is completed for 200 *Minuteman III* missiles, providing jam-resistant secure data links from underground launch control centers to the E-4B Airborne National Command Post for direct launch control under National Command Authority, including encrypted rapid retargeting and almost instantaneous launch of this portion of the *Minuteman* force under attack conditions.
Dec. 1982	Installation of the new INS-20 guidance system is completed on all 550 *Minuteman IIIs,* providing the total of 1650 reentry vehicles deployed on them with a CEP of 607 ft.
Dec. 1982	Retrofit of the Mk 12A reentry vehicle is completed on 300 *Minuteman III* missiles.
Dec. 1983	50 *Minuteman II* missiles of the 341st Strategic Missile Wing at Malmstrom Air Force Base, Montana, are replaced with *Minuteman IIIs.* The *Minuteman* force now comprises 400 *Minuteman IIs* and 600 *Minuteman IIIs.*

Sources

Dec. 1970	Thomas B. Cochran, William M. Arkin, and Milton M. Hoenig, *Nuclear Weapons Databook: Volume I* (Cambridge, Mass.: Ballinger, 1984), page 118.
Mar. 1973	*Ibid.*
Feb. 1975	*Ibid.;* Les Aspin, "Judge Not by Numbers Alone," *Bulletin of the Atomic Scientists* (June, 1980), page 30.
Feb. 1975	Cochran, Arkin, and Hoenig, *op. cit.,* page 118.
July 1975	*Ibid.*
July 1976	*Ibid.*
Sept. 1977	Department of Defense, *Annual Report, Fiscal Year 1979,* Washington, D.C., February, 1978, page 108.
Sept. 1978	Anthony H. Cordesman, *Deterrence in the 1980s: Part I, American Strategic Forces and Extended Deterrence,* Adelphi Paper no. 175 (London: IISS, 1982), page 22; Cochran, Arkin, and Hoenig, *op. cit.,* page 118.
Sept. 1978	Department of Defense, *op. cit.* (February, 1978), page 108; Cochran, Arkin, and Hoenig, *op. cit.,* page 118; Paul H. Nitze, Prepared Statement Before the Senate Foreign Relations Committee, *The SALT II Treaty,* July 12, 1979, reprinted in *The Congressional Record,* July 20, 1979, page S10078.
July 1979	Arms Control and Disarmament Agency, *Fiscal Year 1982 Arms Control Impact Statement,* page 3; House Armed Services Committee, *Authorization Hearings, Fiscal Year 1979,* Part 3, Book 1, page 307; Cochran, Arkin, and Hoenig, *op. cit.,* page 118.

(continued)

Chronology of Critical Changes in Minuteman Force Structure, 1970–83 *(cont.)*

Jan. 1980   Arms Control and Disarmament Agency, *Fiscal Year 1983 Arms Control Impact Statement,* page 3; Aspin, *op. cit.,* page 30; Cochran, Arkin, and Hoenig, *op. cit.,* page 117.

June 1980   Cochran, Arkin, and Hoenig, *op. cit.,* pages 108 and 116; confirmed to author by Major Michael Greece, US Air Force, February 18, 1983.

Mar. 1981   House Appropriations Committee, *Department of Defense Appropriations, Fiscal Year 1982,* Part 2, page 225.

Mar. 1982   Arms Control and Disarmament Agency, *op. cit.,* FY 1982, page 3; House Armed Services Committee, *op. cit.,* FY 1979, Part 3, Book 1, page 307.

Jan. 1982   Arms Control and Disarmament Agency, *op. cit.,* FY 1982, pages 2 and 4; Cordesman, *op. cit.,* page 23; confirmed to author by Major Michael Greece, US Air Force, February 18, 1983.

Dec. 1982   Arms Control and Disarmament Agency, *op. cit.,* FY 1983, page 3.

Dec. 1982   Arms Control and Disarmament Agency, *op. cit.,* FY 1983, page 3; Clarence A. Robinson, Jr., "U.S. Upgrading Its Strategic Arsenal," *Aviation Week & Space Technology,* March 9, 1981, page 25; Cochran, Arkin, and Hoenig, *op. cit.,* page 108; confirmed to author by Major Michael Greece, US Air Force, February 18, 1983.

Dec. 1983   Joint Chiefs of Staff, *Fiscal Year 1983 Posture Statement,* page 72; Clarence A. Robinson, Jr., "Emphasis Grows on Nuclear Defense," *Aviation Week & Space Technology,* March 8, 1982, page 27.

Author's Estimate of United States Land-Based Intercontinental Ballistic Missile (ICBM) Warheads, 1979–83, Reflecting Critical Changes in Force Structure

ICBM Type/Number of Warheads Each	Total of ICBMs of Each Type/Total of Targetable Warheads by Missile Type							
	Dec. 79	June 80	Dec. 80	June 81	Dec. 81	June 82	Dec. 82	June 83
TITAN II (1 RV)	54/ 54	54/ 54	54/ 54	54/ 54	53/ 53	53/ 53	52/ 52	49/ 49
MINUTEMAN II (1 RV)	450/ 450	450/ 450	450/ 450	450/ 450	450/ 450	450/ 450	450/ 450	450/ 450
MINUTEMAN III (3 × Mk 12 RV)	550/1650	541/1623	500/1500	450/1350	350/1050	300/ 900	250/ 750	250/ 750
MINUTEMAN III (3 × Mk 12A RV)		9/ 27	50/ 150	100/ 300	200/ 600	250/ 750	300/ 900	300/ 900
TOTALS:	1054/2154	1054/2154	1054/2154	1054/2154	1053/2153	1053/2153	1052/2152	1049/2149

Sources

For the numbers of warheads of each type deployed, see *Chronology of Critical Changes in Minuteman Force Structure, 1970–83,* immediately preceding this table. For the numbers of *Titan II* missiles deployed, see Joint Chiefs of Staff, *Fiscal Year 1984 Posture Statement,* page 13. For the numbers of *Minuteman II* and *Minuteman III* missiles deployed, see Department of Defense, *Annual Report, Fiscal Year 1984,* page 333. For the numbers of *Minuteman II* missiles deployed, see Colin S. Gray, *The Future of Land-Based Missile Forces,* Adelphi Paper no. 140 (London: International Institute for Strategic Studies), page 33.

Available Estimates of Soviet Land-Based Intercontinental Ballistic Missile (ICBM) Warheads, Broken Down by Missile Type, 1979–83

ICBM Type/Number of Warheads Each	Collins Dec. 79	Kaplan Jan. 80	SIPRI Sept. 80	SIPRI Sept. 82	Forsberg Nov. 82	Cordesman Dec. 82	IISS 1982–1983	Cordesman Feb. 83
	Total of ICBMs of Each Type/Total of Targetable Warheads by Missile Type							
SS-9 (1 RV or 3 MRV)*	68/ 68	61/ 61	8/ 8					
SS-11 (1 RV or 3 MRV)*	650/ 650	639/ 639	580/ 580	520/ 520	580/ 580	518/ 518	570/ 570	570/ 570
SS-13 (1 RV)	60/ 60	60/ 60	60/ 60	60/ 60	60/ 60	60/ 60	60/ 60	60/ 60
SS-17 (1 RV)	20/ 20	20/ 20				32/ 32		
SS-17 (4 MIRV)	120/ 480	130/ 520	150/ 600	150/ 600	150/ 600	120/ 480	150/ 600	150/ 600
SS-18 (1 RV)	26/ 26	26/ 26	60/ 60		50/ 50	58/ 58	58/ 58	
SS-18 (8 MIRV)	214/1712	171/1368	240/1920	308/2464	258/2064	175/1400	250/2000	290/2320
SS-18 (10 MIRV)		50/ 500				75/ 750		18/ 180
SS-19 (1 RV)	30/ 30	30/ 30			50/ 50	60/ 60	60/ 60	72/ 72
SS-19 (6 MIRV)	210/1260	211/1266	300/1800	360/2160	250/1500	300/1800	250/1500	238/1428
TOTALS:	1398/4306	1398/4490	1398/5028	1398/5804	1398/4904	1398/5158	1398/4848	1398/5230

* See note below on distinction between MRV and MIRV.

Sources

John M. Collins, *U.S.-Soviet Military Balance: Concepts and Capabilities, 1960–1980* (New York: McGraw-Hill, 1980), pages 443–445; Fred M. Kaplan, *Dubious Specter* (Washington, D.C.: Institute for Policy Studies, 1980), page 90; Stockholm International Peace Research Institute (SIPRI), *World Arms and Disarmament Yearbook, 1980* (Stockholm: Almqvist & Wiksell, 1980), page xxvii; SIPRI, *The Arms Race and Arms Control* (London: Taylor & Francis, 1982), page 85; Randall Forsberg, "A Bilateral Nuclear-Weapon Freeze," *Scientific American* (November, 1982), page 54; Anthony H. Cordesman, Jr., "M-X and the Balance of Power: Reasserting America's Strengths," *Armed Forces Journal International* (December, 1982), page

exception to it, counting more than one MRV per missile in its 1980 edition, and counting every MRV as a separate warhead in its 1982 publication. This has produced higher warhead totals for both the Soviet Union and the United States, though it has chiefly inflated Soviet figures, since the Soviet Union deployed many more MRVs in 1980 and is the only superpower to retain them today.

The redundant MRVs SIPRI counts have been eliminated here throughout. In its 1980 edition SIPRI acknowledges, though only in footnotes, that MRVs from a single missile cannot hit separate targets, and then provides its estimates of the lower totals of missile warheads in Soviet and American

41: International Institute for Strategic Studies, *The Military Balance, 1982–1983*, pages 140 and 141; Anthony H. Cordesman, Jr., "Using a Strategy of Fear to Counter a Fear of Strategy," *Armed Forces Journal International* (February, 1983), page 60.

* MIRVs are Multiple Independently targetable Reentry Vehicles. MRVs are Multiple Reentry Vehicles that are not independently targetable. Consequently, almost every source counts the total of MRVs carried by a missile as a single warhead. That practice is followed here. SIPRI makes an arsenals which can. Those are the same totals shown here. The Soviet totals shown for 1982 would correspond to similar SIPRI totals were they provided. But SIPRI has not provided them, and has included no footnote in its 1982 publication explaining that the MRVs it counts are not independently targetable. Readers who do not know otherwise are naturally led to assume that each MRV is equivalent to a MIRV and should be counted accordingly.

Author's Estimate of Soviet Land-Based Intercontinental Ballistic Missile (ICBM) Warheads, 1979–83, Consistent with Initial Deployment Dates, Production, and Conversion Rates Demonstrated in Prior Years, and the Defense Department Estimate of May, 1982

ICBM Type/Number of Warheads Each	Total of ICBMs of Each Type/Total of Targetable Warheads by Missile Type							
	Dec. 79	June 80	Dec. 80	June 81	Dec. 81	June 82	Dec. 82	June 83
SS-9 (1 RV or 3 MRV)*	70/ 70	50/ 50	30/ 30	10/ 10	5/ 5			
SS-11 (1 RV or 3 MRV)*	650/ 650	630/ 630	620/ 620	610/ 610	600/ 600	590/ 590	580/ 580	570/ 570
SS-13 (1 RV)	60/ 60	60/ 60	60/ 60	60/ 60	60/ 60	60/ 60	60/ 60	60/ 60
SS-17 (1 RV)	20/ 20	20/ 20	20/ 20	10/ 10	10/ 10	10/ 10	10/ 10	10/ 10
SS-17 (4 MIRV)	120/ 480	130/ 520	130/ 520	140/ 560	140/ 560	140/ 560	140/ 560	140/ 560
SS-18 (1 RV)	30/ 30	30/ 30	30/ 30	30/ 30	30/ 30	30/ 30	30/ 30	30/ 30
SS-18 (8 MIRV)	188/1504	203/1624	213/1704	228/1824	228/1824	228/1824	223/1784	218/1744
SS-18 (1 RV)	20/ 20	25/ 25	30/ 30	30/ 30	30/ 30	30/ 30	30/ 30	30/ 30
SS-18 (10 MIRV)			5/ 50	10/ 100	15/ 150	20/ 200	25/ 250	30/ 300
SS-19 (1 RV)	60/ 60	60/ 60	60/ 60	60/ 60	60/ 60	60/ 60	60/ 60	60/ 60
SS-19 (6 RV)	180/1080	190/1140	200/1200	210/1260	220/1360	230/1380	240/1440	250/1500
TOTALS:	1398/3974	1398/4159	1398/4324	1398/4554	1398/4689	1398/4744	1398/4804	1398/4864

* *See earlier note on distinction between MRV and MIRV.*

Sources

See the discussion *The Strategic Balance: Author's Estimate*, on page 279, and Defense Department testimony to Congress in May, 1982, published by *The New York Times*, "U.S. and Soviet Strategic Arsenals," May 2, 1982.

Characteristics of United States and Soviet Intercontinental Ballistic Missiles Deployed from 1979 Through 1983

UNITED STATES

Missile Type	Year First Deployed	Total Deployed 1983	Weight (Tons)	Dimensions (ft/in) Length	Diameter	Throwweight (lbs)	Number of RVs	Yield of Each (KT/MT)	Range Statute Miles	CEP (ft) 1983	Type Propellant
TITAN II	1963	49	163.5	103'	10'	8300	1	9 MT	9322	3038	Liquid
MINUTEMAN II	1966	450	36.5	57'6"	5'7"	2500	1	1.2 MT	8000	1215	Solid
MINUTEMAN III with Mk 12	1970	250	39.0	60'	5'5"	2400	3	170 KT	8000	607	Solid
MINUTEMAN III with Mk 12A	1980	300	39.0	60'	5'5"	2435	3	335 KT	8000	607	Solid

SOVIET UNION

Missile Type	Year First Deployed	Total Deployed 1983	Weight (Tons)	Dimensions (ft/in) Length	Diameter	Throwweight (lbs)	Number of RVs	Yield of Each (KT/MT)	Range Statute Miles	CEP (ft) 1983	Type Propellant
SS-11 Mod 1	1966	110	52.8	64'	6'	2000	1	1 MT	6000	4617	Liquid
SS-11 Mod 3	1973	470	53.0	64'	6'	2500	3 MRV	300 KT	5500	3608	Liquid
SS-13 Mod 1	1968	60	38.5	65'7"	5'5"	1000	1	750 KT	5000	6561	Solid
SS-17 Mod 1	1975	140	72.7	80'	8'6"	6000	4	750 KT	5500	1640	Liquid
SS-17 Mod 2	1977	10	71.5	80'	8'6"	3600	1	3 MT	5700	1640	Liquid
SS-18 Mod 1	1975	30	241.9	120'	11'	16,500	1	25 MT	6000	1397	Liquid
SS-18 Mod 2	1977	218	242.0	120'	11'	16,700	8	750 KT	5500	1397	Liquid
SS-18 Mod 3	1979	30	241.7	120'	11'	16,000	1	20 MT	6500	1154	Liquid
SS-18 Mod 4	1980	30	242.0	120'	11'	16,700	10	500 KT	5500	850	Liquid
SS-19 Mod 1	1974	250	85.8	80'	8'6"	7525	6	550 KT	5000	850	Liquid
SS-19 Mod 2	1979	60	85.5	80'	8'6"	7000	1	1 MT	5500	1275	Liquid

RV: Reentry Vehicle

KT: Explosive power measured by the number of kilotons of TNT required to release an equivalent amount of energy.

MT: Explosive power measured by the number of megatons of TNT required to release an equivalent amount of energy. 1 megaton is 1000 kilotons.

CEP: Circular Error Probable, or the distance from a specific aimpoint within which half of the reentry vehicles of a specific type are expected to fall.

Sources

Sources for the more controversial information are as follows: The throwweight and range of the U.S. *Titan II* are from *The Military Balance, 1983–1984* (London: IISS, 1983), page 118, and its CEP is from Colin S. Gray, *The Future of Land-Based Missile Forces*, Adelphi Paper no. 140 (London: IISS), page 32. The throwweight of the U.S. *Minuteman II* is from William Schneider, Jr., and Francis P. Hoeber, *Arms, Men and Military Budgets: Issues for Fiscal Year 1977* (New York: Crane, Russak, 1978), page 27. Throwweight of the *Minuteman III* with Mk 12 RV is from the General Accounting Office, *The MX Weapon System, Issues and Challenges* (Washington, D.C.: GAO, February 17, 1981), page 34. Throwweight of the *Minuteman III* with Mk 12A RV is from Les Aspin, "Judge Not by Numbers Alone," *Bulletin of the Atomic Scientists* (June, 1980), page 29. Ranges of all *Minuteman* missiles are from John M. Collins, *U.S.–Soviet Military Balance, 1960–1980* (New York: McGraw-Hill, 1980), page 446. CEP of the *Minuteman II* is from Paul H. Nitze, Prepared Statement Before the Senate Foreign Relations Committee, *The SALT II Treaty*, July 12, 1979, reprinted in *Congressional Record*, July 20, 1979, page S10078. CEP of the *Minuteman III* is from the House Armed Services Committee, *Authorization Hearings, Fiscal Year 1979* (Washington, D.C.: United States Congress, Part 3, Book 1), page 307.

The dimensions of all but one Soviet missile are from *Aviation Week & Space Technology, Aerospace Forecast and Inventory*, "Soviet Missiles," March 14, 1983, page 153, and March 12, 1984, page 165. Dimensions of the SS-13, not given by *Aviation Week*, are from *Jane's Weapon Systems, Seventh Edition, 1976* (London: Macdonald and Jane's, 1975), page 19. Throwweights of all Soviet missiles except the SS-19 are from IISS, *op. cit., 1983–1984*, page 119. Throwweights of the SS-19 Mods 1 and 2 are from Collins, *op. cit.*, page 446. The range of the SS-18 Mod 3 is from IISS, *op. cit., 1983–1984*, page 119, while the ranges of all other Soviet missiles are from Collins, *op. cit.*, page 446. Yields of both modifications of the SS-11, the SS-13, the SS-17 Mod 1, and the SS-18 Mods 3 and 4 are from IISS, *op. cit., 1983–1984*, page 119. Yields of the SS-17 Mod 2 and the SS-18 Mod 2 are from Fred Kaplan, *Dubious Specter* (Washington, D.C.: Institute for Policy Studies, 1980), page 90. Yields of the SS-18 Mod 1 and the SS-19 Mod 1 are from Robert C. Aldridge, *First Strike!* (Boston: South End Press, 1983), pages 59 and 60. Yield of the SS-19 Mod 2 is from Randall Forsberg, "A Bilateral Nuclear-Weapon Freeze," *Scientific American* (November, 1982), page 54. CEPs of the SS-11 Mod 1 and the SS-18 Mods 1 and 2 are from the Congressional Budget Office, *Modernizing U.S. Strategic Offensive Forces* (May, 1983), page 90. CEPs of the SS-11 Mod 2, the SS-13, and the SS-18 Mod 3 are from IISS, *op. cit., 1983–1984*, page 119. The CEP of the SS-19 Mod 2, generally considered the less accurate of the two SS-19 modifications, is a composite estimate based on Kaplan, *op. cit.*, page 90, and Collins, *op. cit.*, page 446. All other CEPs are from Aldridge, *op. cit.*, pages 59 and 60.

United States and Soviet Strategic Sea-Based Missiles

TABLES IN THIS SECTION

- Available Estimates of United States SLBM Warheads, 1979–83, Broken Down by Missile Type
- Chronology of Critical Changes in United States Strategic Submarine Force Structure, 1979–83
- Author's Estimate of United States SLBM Warheads, 1979–83
- Available Estimates of Soviet SLBM Warheads, 1979–83, Broken Down by Missile Type
- Author's Estimate of Soviet Submarines and SLBMs, 1979–83
- Characteristics of American and Soviet Strategic Ballistic Missile Submarines Deployed from 1979 Through 1983
- Author's Estimate of Soviet SLBM Warheads, 1979–83
- Characteristics of United States and Soviet SLBMs Deployed from 1979 Through 1983

Available Estimates of United States Submarine-Launched Ballistic Missile (SLBM) Warheads, Broken Down by Missile Type, 1979–83

	Collins Dec. 79	Kaplan Jan. 80	SIPRI Sept. 80	SIPRI Sept. 82	Forsberg Nov. 82	Cordesman Dec. 82	IISS 1982–1983	Cordesman Feb. 83
Submarine Type/Number of Missile Tubes Each	Total of Submarines of Each Type/Total of SLBMs by Submarine Type							
POLARIS (16 × A-3)	10/ 160	10/ 160	10/ 160					
POSEIDON (16 × C-3)	30/ 480	30/ 480	31/ 496	20/ 320	19/ 304	19/ 304	19/ 304	19/ 304
POSEIDON with TRIDENT Retrofit (16 × C-4)	1/ 16	1/ 16		11/ 176	12/ 192	12/ 192	12/ 192	12/ 192
TRIDENT (24 × C-4)				1/ 24	1/ 24	2/ 48	1/ 24	1/ 24
TOTALS:	41/ 656	41/ 656	41/ 656	32/ 520	32/ 520	33/ 544	32/ 520	32/ 520
SLBM Type/Number of Warheads Each	Total of SLBMs of Each Type/Total of Targetable Warheads by Missile Type							
POLARIS A-3 (3 MRV)*	160/ 160	160/ 160	160/ 160					
POSEIDON C-3 (9 MIRV)		480/4320				304/2736		
POSEIDON C-3 (10 MIRV)	480/4800		496/4960	320/3200	304/3040		304/3040	304/3040
POSEIDON C-3 (14 MIRV)								
TRIDENT C-4 (8 MIRV)	16/ 160	16/ 128		200/1600	216/1728	240/1920	216/1728	216/1728
TRIDENT C-4 (10 MIRV)								
TOTALS:	656/5120	656/4608	656/5120	520/4800	520/4768	544/4656	520/4768	520/4768

* See earlier note on distinction between MRV and MIRV.

Sources

Collins, *op. cit.*, pages 448–449; Kaplan, *op. cit.*, page 88; SIPRI, 1980, page xxviii; SIPRI, page 85; Forsberg, *op. cit.*, November, 1982, page 54; Cordesman, *op. cit.*, December, 1982, page 41; IISS, *op. cit.*, 1982–1983, page 140: Cordesman, *op. cit.*, February, 1983, page 60.

Chronology of Critical Changes in United States Strategic Submarine Force Structure, 1979–83

Date	Event
Oct. 1979	First retrofit of *Trident C-4* missiles in *Poseidon* submarine, SSBN-457 *Francis Scott Key.* A total of 12 *Poseidon* submarines will have their *Poseidon C-3* missiles, each with 10 warheads, replaced by *Trident C-4* missiles, each with 8 warheads, over the next 40 months. This will result in a net reduction of 384 warheads in the US strategic missile fleet, but will extend the range of America's sea-based missiles from 3200 to 4870 statute miles.
Nov. 1979	Deployment of the first *Trident* submarine, SSBN-726 *Ohio,* equipped with 24 of the new *Trident C-4* missiles, adding 192 warheads to the US strategic missile fleet.
Mar. 1982	The final *Polaris* submarine, SSBN-601 *Robert E. Lee,* is phased out of service. 8 of the 10 retired *Polaris* boats are reclassified attack submarines. Their retirement removes 160 *Polaris A-3* missiles, each with 3 warheads, from active service. Because those 480 warheads are not independently targetable, their loss is equivalent to a reduction of only 160 targetable warheads. More than compensating for it, and for further reductions in warheads from the retrofit of *Trident C-4* missiles on 12 *Poseidon* submarines, the 304 *Poseidon C-3* missiles to be retained on 19 additional *Poseidon* submarines after the *Trident* retrofit are equipped with their maximum load of 14 W-68 warheads. This results in an increase of 1216 warheads in the US strategic missile fleet.
Sept. 1982	Deployment of the second *Trident* submarine, SSBN-727 *Michigan,* adding another 192 warheads to the US strategic missile fleet.
Mar. 1983	Retrofit of *Trident C-4* missiles is completed on SSBN-633 *Casimir Pulaski,* the twelfth and final *Poseidon* submarine scheduled to receive them.

Sources

Oct. 1979	Collins, *op. cit.,* page 450; *The New York Times,* October 23, 1979; Cochran, Arkin, and Hoenig, *op. cit.,* pages 105 and 137.
Nov. 1979	*United States Naval Institute Proceedings* (February, 1983), page 125; date confirmed to author by U.S. Navy, January 18, 1983.
Mar. 1982	Vice Admiral Robert L. Walters, Deputy Chief of Naval Operations, testimony to House Armed Services Committee, *Hearings,* March 4, 1982, page 5; House Appropriations Committee, *Hearings, Defense Department Appropriations, Fiscal Year 1982,* Part 7, page 544; House Armed Services Committee, *Authorization Hearings, FY 1982,* Part 3, page 156; SIPRI, *op. cit.,* 1982, pages 94–95; Aldridge, *op. cit.,* page 44; Cochran, Arkin, and Hoenig, *op. cit.,* pages 69–70 and 137; Associated Press, "U.S. Adds Warheads to Poseidon Submarine Missiles," *The New York Times,* October 30, 1980; facts and dates confirmed to author by Lieutenant Commander John Alexander, U.S. Navy, January 18, 1983.
Sept. 1982	*United States Naval Institute Proceedings* (February, 1983), page 125; date confirmed to author by U.S. Navy, January 18, 1983.
Mar. 1983	Cochran, Arkin, and Hoenig, *op. cit.,* pages 104 and 137.

Author's Estimate of United States Submarine-Launched Ballistic Missile (SLBM) Warheads, Reflecting Critical Changes in Strategic Submarine Force Structure, 1979–83

Submarine Type/Number of Missile Tubes Each	Dec. 79	June 80	Dec. 80	June 81	Dec. 81	June 82	Dec. 82	June 83
				Total of Submarines of Each Type/Total of SLBMs by Submarine Type				
POLARIS (16 × A-3)	10/ 160	10/ 160	7/ 112	5/ 80	5/ 80			
POSEIDON (16 × C-3)	30/ 480	28/ 448	27/ 432	26/ 416	22/ 352	20/ 320	20/ 320	19/ 304
POSEIDON with TRIDENT Retrofit (16 × C-4)	1/ 16	3/ 48	4/ 64	5/ 80	9/ 144	11/ 176	11/ 176	12/ 192
TRIDENT (24 × C-4)					1/ 24	1/ 24	2/ 48	2/ 48
TOTALS:	41/ 656	41/ 656	38/ 608	36/ 576	37/ 600	32/ 520	33/ 544	33/ 544
SLBM Type/Number of Warheads Each								
				Total of SLBMs of Each Type/Total of Targetable Warheads by Missile Type				
POLARIS A-3 (3 MRV)*	160/ 160	160/ 160	112/ 112	80/ 80	80/ 80			
POSEIDON C-3 (10 MIRV)	240/2400	224/2240	224/2240	208/2080	176/1760	320/4480	320/4480	304/4256
POSEIDON C-3 (14 MIRV)	240/3360	224/3136	208/2912	208/2912	176/2464			
TRIDENT C-4 (8 MIRV)	16/ 128	48/ 384	64/ 512	80/ 640	168/1344	200/1600	224/1792	240/1920
TOTALS:	656/6048	656/5920	608/5776	576/5712	600/5648	520/6080	544/6272	544/6176

* See earlier note on distinction between MRV and MIRV.

Sources

For the numbers of missiles and warheads of each type deployed, see *Chronology of Critical Changes in United States Strategic Submarine Force Structure, 1979–83*, immediately preceding this table.

Available Estimates of Soviet Submarine-Launched Ballistic Missile (SLBM) Warheads, Broken Down by Missile Type, 1979–83

Total of SLBMs of Each Type/Total of Targetable Warheads by Missile Type

SLBM Type/Number of Warheads Each	Collins Dec. 79	Kaplan Jan. 80	SIPRI Sept. 80	SIPRI Sept. 82	Forsberg Nov. 82	Cordesman Dec. 82	IISS 1982–1983	Cordesman Feb. 83
SS-N-4 (1 RV)	3/ 3							
SS-N-5 (1 RV)	57/ 57	18/ 18		18/ 18	18/ 18	18/ 18	57/ 57	57/ 57
SS-N-6 (1 RV or 3 MRV)*	468/ 468	468/ 468	464/ 464	374/ 374	374/ 374	352/ 352	400/ 400	400/ 400
SS-N-8 (1 RV)	289/ 289	289/ 289	326/ 326	290/ 290	290/ 290	292/ 292	292/ 292	292/ 292
SS-N-17 (1 RV)	12/ 12	12/ 12	16/ 16	12/ 12	12/ 12	12/ 12	12/ 12	12/ 12
SS-N-18 (3 MIRV)	160/ 480	160/ 480	144/ 432	256/ 768	192/ 576		104/ 312	104/ 312
SS-N-18 (7 MIRV)					32/ 224	240/1680	104/ 728	104/ 728
SS-N-20 (6–12 MIRV)						20/ 200		
TOTALS:	989/1309	947/1267	950/1238	950/1462	918/1494	934/2554	969/1801	969/1801

* See earlier note on distinction between MRV and MIRV.

Sources

Collins, *op. cit.*, pages 448–449; Kaplan, *op. cit.*, page 90; SIPRI, *op. cit.*, 1980, page xvii; SIPRI, *op. cit.*, 1982, page 85; Forsberg, *op. cit.*, November 1982, page 54; Cordesman, *op. cit.*, December, 1982, page 41; IISS, *op. cit.*, 1982–1983, page 140; Cordesman, *op. cit.*, February, 1983, page 60.

Author's Estimate of Soviet Submarines and Submarine-Launched Ballistic Missiles, 1979–83, Consistent with Initial Deployment Dates

Submarine Type/Number of Missile Tubes Each	Total of Submarines of Each Type/Total of SLBMs by Submarine Type							
	Dec. 79	June 80	Dec. 80	June 81	Dec. 81	June 82	Dec. 82	June 83
*GOLF II (3 × SS-N-5)	13/ 39	13/ 39	13/ 39	13/ 39	13/ 39	13/ 39	13/ 39	13/ 39
**HOTEL II (3 × SS-N-5)	6/ 18	6/ 18	6/ 18	6/ 18	6/ 18	6/ 18	6/ 18	6/ 18
YANKEE I (16 × SS-N-6)	25/400	25/400	25/400	25/400	25/400	25/400	25/400	25/400
*GOLF III (6 × SS-N-8)	1/ 6	1/ 6	1/ 6	1/ 6	1/ 6	1/ 6	1/ 6	1/ 6
**HOTEL III (6 × SS-N-8)	1/ 6	1/ 6	1/ 6	1/ 6	1/ 6	1/ 6	1/ 6	1/ 6
DELTA I (12 × SS-N-8)	18/216	18/216	18/216	18/216	18/216	18/216	18/216	18/216
DELTA II (16 × SS-N-8)	4/ 64	4/ 64	4/ 64	4/ 64	4/ 64	4/ 64	4/ 64	4/ 64
YANKEE II (12 × SS-N-17)	1/ 12	1/ 12	1/ 12	1/ 12	1/ 12	1/ 12	1/ 12	1/ 12
DELTA III (16 × SS-N-18)	11/176	12/192	13/208	13/208	13/208	13/208	13/208	13/208
	80/937	81/953	82/969	82/969	82/969	82/969	82/969	82/969

*These 13 submarines, and their 39 missiles, are not included under the SALT II Agreement. Six of the submarines are normally stationed in the Baltic Sea.

** These 8 submarines are not included under the SALT II Agreement, but their 30 missiles are.

Consequently, some estimates of these forces may list 69 submarines and 930 SLBMs, or 61 submarines and 930 SLBMs, in December, 1982.

Sources

See IISS, op. cit., 1982–1983, pages 13 and 140, and the table Available Estimates immediately preceding this one.

Characteristics of American and Soviet Strategic Ballistic Missile Submarines Deployed from 1979 Through 1983

UNITED STATES

Submarine Class/Type	Year First Deployed	Total Deployed 1983	Missiles Number/Type	Dimensions (ft) Length	Beam	Displacement (tons) Surf	Subm	Speed (knots) Surf	Subm	Power Plant	Crew	Patrol Period (days)	Readiness Rate (percent)
WASHINGTON	1959	0	16 POLARIS A-3	382	33	6000	6700	20	30	Nuclear	139	68	55%
ALLEN	1961	0	16 POLARIS A-3	410	33	6955	7900	20	30	Nuclear	141	68	55%
LAFAYETTE	1963	9	16 POSEIDON C-3	425	33	7250	8250	20	30	Nuclear	141	68	66%
MADISON	1965	10	16 POSEIDON C-3	425	33	7250	8250	20	30	Nuclear	141	68	66%
FRANKLIN	1965	12	16 TRIDENT C-4	425	33	7250	8250	20	30	Nuclear	141	68	66%
OHIO	1981	2	24 TRIDENT C-4	560	42	16,600	18,750	20	25	Nuclear	153	70	75%

SOVIET UNION

Submarine Class/Type	Year First Deployed	Total Deployed 1983	Missiles Number/Type	Dimensions (ft) Length	Beam	Displacement (tons) Surf	Subm	Speed (knots) Surf	Subm	Power Plant	Crew	Patrol Period (days)	Readiness Rate (percent)
HOTEL II	1958	6	3 SS-N-5	377	28	4400	5150	20	20	Nuclear	92		33%
GOLF II	1967	13	3 SS-N-5	320	25	2300	2800	14	17	Diesel	85		33%
YANKEE I	1967	25	16 SS-N-6	426	33	7800	9000	18	24	Nuclear	120		33%
GOLF III	1977	1	6 SS-N-8	360	25	2900	9000	14	17	Diesel	85		33%
HOTEL III	1979	1	6 SS-N-8	377	28	4750	5500	20	20	Nuclear	92		33%
DELTA I	1972	18	12 SS-N-8	446	38	8200	9700	20	25	Nuclear	130		33%
DELTA II	1973	4	16 SS-N-8	498	38	9700	11,300	20	25	Nuclear	130		33%
YANKEE II	1977	1	12 SS-N-17	426	33	7800	9000	20	26	Nuclear	100		33%
DELTA III	1977	13	16 SS-N-18	508	38	10,500	13,250	20	25	Nuclear	100		33%

Sources

Sources for the more controversial information are as follows: Deployment dates for all U.S. submarines are from Collins, op. cit., page 452. Dimensions and crew manning levels for the Ethan Allen and George Washington classes of Polaris submarine are from Norman Polmar, The Ships and Aircraft of the U.S. Fleet (12th ed., Annapolis, Md.: Naval Institute Press, 1983), pages 22 and 23, respectively, while their displacements and speeds the Congressional Budget Office, op. cit., May, 1983, page 95. Deployment dates for all but one type of Soviet submarine are from Collins. op. cit., page 452. The date for the Hotel III is the author's estimate. Dimensions of all Hotel and Golf classes of submarine are from Jane's, op. cit., 1976, pages 692 and 293, respectively, except that the greater length of the Golf III is from the Office of the Chief of Naval Operations, Under-are from *Jane's Fighting Ships, 1976–1977* (London: Macdonald and Jane's, 1976), pages 543 and 544, respectively. Patrol periods and readiness rates for submarines of this type are from Cochran, *op. cit.*, page 135. Dimensions, displacements, and crew-manning levels for the *Lafayette, James Madison,* and *Benjamin Franklin* classes of *Poseidon* submarine are from Polmar, *op. cit.*, page 20. Their speeds are from *Jane's, op. cit.*, 1976, page 541. Their patrol periods are from Cochran, *op. cit.*, page 135. Their readiness rates are from the Congressional Budget Office, *op. cit.*, May, 1983, page 95. Dimensions and manning levels for the *Ohio* class are from Polmar, *op. cit.*, page 17, while displacements are from Cochran, *op. cit.*, page 138. The submerged speed of the *Ohio* class of *Trident* submarine is from Gerhard Albrecht, *Weyer's Warships of the World, 1982–1983* (Annapolis, Md.: Nautical and Aviation Publishing, 1981), page 233. *Ohio* patrol days are from Cochran, *op. cit.*, page 139. The readiness rate for this class is from

standing Soviet Naval Developments (4th ed., Department of the Navy, January, 1981), page 92. Surface displacements of the *Golf III* and *Delta III* are from the same source, pages 92 and 89, respectively. Displacements of the *Hotel II*, and the submerged displacements of the *Yankee I* and *Yankee II*, are from *Jane's, op. cit.*, 1976, pages 692 and 691, respectively. All other displacements are from Albrecht, *op. cit.*, page 268. The surface speeds of all Soviet submarines, as well as the submerged speeds of *Yankee I, Yankee II,* and *Delta III*, are from the same source, page 269. Submerged speeds of the *Golf II* and *Golf III* are from Collins, *op. cit.*, page 452. Submerged speeds of the *Hotel II, Hotel III, Delta II,* and *Delta III* are from *Jane's, op. cit.*, 1976, pages 692 and 690, respectively. All crew-manning levels are from Albrecht, *op. cit.*, page 268. The readiness rates for all Soviet submarines are from the Congressional Budget Office, *op. cit.*, May, 1983, page 95.

Author's Estimate of Soviet Submarine-Launched Ballistic Missile (SLBM) Warheads, 1979–83, Consistent with Initial Deployment Dates, Production, and Conversion Rates Demonstrated in Prior Years, and the Defense Department Estimate of May, 1982

SLBM Type/Number of Warheads Each	Total of SLBMs of Each Type/Total of Targetable Warheads by Missile Type							
	Dec. 79	June 80	Dec. 80	June 81	Dec. 81	June 82	Dec. 82	June 83
SS-N-5 (1 RV)	57/ 57	57/ 57	57/ 57	57/ 57	57/ 57	57/ 57	57/ 57	57/ 57
SS-N-6 (1 RV or 3 MRV)*	400/ 400	400/ 400	400/ 400	400/ 400	400/ 400	400/ 400	400/ 400	400/ 400
SS-N-8 (1 RV)	292/ 292	292/ 292	292/ 292	292/ 292	292/ 292	292/ 292	292/ 292	292/ 292
SS-N-17 (1 RV)	12/ 12	12/ 12	12/ 12	12/ 12	12/ 12	12/ 12	12/ 12	12/ 12
SS-N-18 (3 MIRV)	176/ 528	192/ 576	208/ 624	192/ 576	176/ 528	160/ 480	144/ 432	128/ 384
SS-N-18 (7 MIRV)				16/ 112	32/ 224	48/ 336	64/ 448	80/ 560
TOTALS:	937/1289	953/1337	969/1385	969/1449	969/1513	969/1577	969/1641	969/1705

* See earlier note on distinction between MRV and MIRV.

Source

See the discussion *The Strategic Balance: Author's Estimate* on page 279, as well as Defense Department testimony to Congress in May, 1982, published by *The New York Times*, "U.S. and Soviet Strategic Arsenals," May 2, 1982.

Characteristics of United States and Soviet Submarine-Launched Ballistic Missiles Deployed from 1979 Through 1983

Missile Type	Year First Deployed	Total Deployed 1983	Weight (Tons)	Dimensions (ft/in) Length	Diameter	Throwweight (lbs)	Number of RVs	Yield of Each (KT/MT)	Range Statute Miles	CEP (ft) 1983	Type Propellant
UNITED STATES											
POLARIS A-3	1964	0	17.5	32'3"	4'6"	1835	3 MRV	200 KT	2880	2952	Solid
POSEIDON C-3	1971	0	31.7	34'1"	6'2"	3670	10	40 KT	3200	1519	Solid
POSEIDON C-3	1971	304	32.5	34'1"	6'2"	5152	14	40 KT	2880	1200	Solid
TRIDENT C-4	1979	240	36.5	34'1"	6'2"	2900	8	100 KT	4870	911	Solid
SOVIET UNION											
SS-N-5	1964	57		42'3"	4'7"	1500	1	1 MT	800	12,152	Liquid
SS-N-6 Mod 1	1968	96		31'7"	54"	1500	1	1 MT	1490	6076	Liquid
SS-N-6 Mod 3	1974	304		31'7"	54"	1500	3 MRV	350 KT	1860	6076	Liquid
SS-N-8	1972	292		42'5"	54"	1500	1	1 MT	4860	5103	Liquid
SS-N-17	1977	12		36'3"	5'5"	2500	1	1 MT	1960	3038	Solid
SS-N-18 Mod 2	1979	104		46'3"	5'10"	1500	3	200 KT	4600	4617	Solid
SS-N-18 Mod 3	1981	104		46'3"	5'10"	3500	7	200 KT	4000	4617	Solid

RV: Reentry Vehicle.

KT: Explosive power measured by the number of kilotons of TNT required to release an equivalent amount of energy.

MT: Explosive power measured by the number of megatons of TNT required to release an equivalent amount of energy. 1 megaton is 1000 kilotons.

CEP: Circular Error Probable, or the distance from a specific aimpoint within which half of the reentry vehicles of a specific type are expected to fall.

Sources

Sources for the more controversial information are as follows: Throwweights for both versions of the *Poseidon C-3*, that equipped with 10 RVs and that with 14, are estimates of minimum weight based on the 367lb weight of the W-68 warhead carried by each of the *Poseidon's* Mk 3 RVs, and given by Thomas B. Cochran, William M. Arkin, and Milton M.

Hoenig in *Nuclear Weapons Databook: Volume I* (Cambridge, Mass.: Ballinger, 1984), page 69. The resulting difference in weight between these two versions corresponds to the higher and lower launchweights of the complete missile given, respectively, by *Aviation Week & Space Technology, Aerospace Forecast and Inventory*, "U.S. Missiles," March 12, 1984, page 160, and

(continued)

Characteristics of United States and Soviet Submarine-Launched Ballistic Missiles Deployed from 1979 Through 1983 *(cont.)*

by Cochran, Arkin, and Hoenig (hereinafter referred to as Cochran), *op. cit.*, page 137. Throwweight for the *Polaris A-3* is a minimum estimate based on *Aviation Week's* observation, *op. cit.*, March 12, 1984, page 161, that the *Poseidon C-3* "has twice *Polaris A-3* payload." Throwweight for the *Trident C-4* is based on the 362.5lb weight given by Cochran, *op. cit.*, page 74, for the W-76 warhead carried by each of the *Trident's* Mk 4 RVs. Therefore, it is again a minimum possible throwweight. It matches the estimate given by Paul Nitze, *op. cit.*, July 12, 1979. Launchweights of the *Polaris* and *Trident* missiles are from *Aviation Week*, *op. cit.*, March 12, 1984, page 160, as are the dimensions of the *Polaris A-3*. Dimensions of the *Poseidon* and *Trident* missiles are from Cochran, *op. cit.*, pages 136 and 142.

The range of the *Polaris A-3* is from Robert C. Aldridge, *The Counterforce Syndrome* (Washington, D.C. and Amsterdam: Transnational Institute, 1978), page 57. It is further confirmed by Collins, *op. cit.*, page 453. The range of the *Poseidon C-3* with 10 RVs is from Admiral Jean Labayle Couhat, *Combat Fleets of the World, 1978–1979* (Annapolis, Md.: Naval Institute Press, 1978), and is further confirmed by *The World's Missile Systems*, 6th ed., page 328. Admiral Couhat points out, however, that increasing the *Poseidon's* payload to its full complement of 14 RVs reduces its range to 2880 miles, no better than that of the earlier *Polaris*. This lower range has recently been given for the *Poseidon* by numerous sources, including Collins, *op. cit.*, page 453, Cochran, *op. cit.*, page 137, and Anthony H. Cordesman, *Deterrence in the 1980s: Part I*, Adelphi Paper no. 175 (London: IISS, 1982), page 26. Sources which simultaneously cite the higher *Poseidon* launchweight and the lower *Poseidon* range—as *Aviation Week's Aerospace Forecast and Inventory* did in its issues of March 8, 1982, pages 142–143, March 14, 1983, pages 148–149, and March 12, 1984, pages 160–161—further confirm that the *Poseidon* has been equipped with its maximum number of 14 RVs. The range of the *Trident C-4* missile is from the Arms Control and Disarmament Agency, *Arms Control Impact Statement, Fiscal Year 1982*, page 82, and is further confirmed by Cordesman, *op. cit.*, 1982, page 26.

CEP of the *Polaris A-3* is from the Stockholm International Peace Research Institute (SIPRI), *World Arms and Disarmament Yearbook, 1980* (Stockholm: Almqvist & Wiksell, 1980), page XXIX. The original CEP for the *Poseidon C-3* is from Collins, *op. cit.*, page 453, and is further confirmed by Cordesman, *op. cit.*, 1982, page 26. CEP of the *Trident C-4* is from Collins, *op. cit.*, page 453. According to *Aviation Week*, June 16, 1980, page 91, *Trident C-4* accuracy may be further improved, reducing its CEP to 750 ft.

Deployment dates for all Soviet missiles except the SS-N-18 are from the IISS, *op. cit.*, 1983–1984, page 119. The date for the SS-N-18 Mod 2 is from *Jane's Weapon Systems, Twelfth Edition, 1981–1982* (London: Macdonald & Jane's, 1981), page 9. The date for the SS-N-18 Mod 3 is assumed to be the earliest possible date inasmuch as no source lists an earlier one and most sources before that time, including Collins, *op. cit.*, page 453 and Kaplan, *op. cit.*, page 90, do not list this version of the missile at all. Dimensions of all Soviet missiles are from *Jane's*, *op. cit.*, 1981, pages 7, 8, and 9. Yields for all but two Soviet missiles are from the IISS, *op. cit.*, 1983–1984, page 119. The yield of the MRVs carried by the SS-N-6 Mod 3 is from Aldridge, *op. cit.*, 1983, page 60, and that for the MIRVs carried by the SS-N-18 Mod 2 is from *Aviation Week*, *op. cit.*, March 14, 1983, page 153. Throwweights of both versions of the SS-N-6, as well as those for the SS-N-8 and the SS-N-17, are from the IISS, *op. cit.*, 1983–1984, page 119. These, together with known details of yield and range, are the basis for the author's estimates of all other throwweights of Soviet SLBMs. Ranges of the SS-N-5, SS-N-17, and SS-N-18 Mod 2 are from *Aviation Week*, *op. cit.*, March 12, 1984, page 165. The ranges of the SS-N-6 Mods 1 and 3 are from *Jane's*, *op. cit.*, 1981, page 8. The range of the SS-N-8 is from General George S. Brown, chairman of the Joint Chiefs of Staff, 1980, as quoted by *Jane's*, *op. cit.*, 1981, page 8. The range of the SS-N-18 Mod 3, lower than that for the Mod 2 version, reflecting its heavier payload with 7 RVs, is from the IISS, *op. cit.*, 1983–1984, page 119. CEPs of all Soviet missiles are from Aldridge, *op. cit.*, 1983, page 60.

United States and Soviet Strategic Bomber Forces

TABLES IN THIS SECTION

Available Estimates of United States Strategic Bomber Weapons, Broken Down by Bomber Type and Weapons Load, 1979–83

Total of Bombers of Each Type/Total of Bomber Weapons by Weapons Load

Bomber Type/Load	Kaplan Jan. 80	SIPRI Sept. 80	Forsberg Nov. 82	Cordesman Dec. 82	IISS 1982–1983	Cochran Jan. 83	CBO May 83	CDI Sept. 83
B-52D (4 NGB)	79/ 316	83/ 332	75/ 300		75/ 300	31/ 124		35/ 140
B-52D (2 SRAM 4 NGB)		107/ 428		75/ 450				
B-52G/H (4 NGB)							90/ 360	
B-52G/H (4 SRAM 4 NGB)	269/2152		255/2040	241/1928	241/1928	227/1816		90/ 720
B-52G/H (8 SRAM 4 NGB)		150/1800					105/1260	116/1392
B-52G/H (4 SRAM 4 NGB/12 ALCM)				16/ 320		14/ 280		
B-52G/H (8 SRAM 4 NGB/12 ALCM)							46/1104	
B-52G (12 ALCM)								32/ 384
FB-111A (2 NBG)					60/ 120			
FB-111A (2 SRAM 2 NGB)	66/ 264		60/ 240					
FB-111A (4 SRAM 2 NGB)						60/ 360	56/ 336	60/ 240
TOTALS:	414/2732	340/2560	390/2580	332/2698	376/2348	332/2580	297/3060	333/2876

NGB: Nuclear Gravity Bomb.
SRAM: Short-Range Attack Missile.
ALCM: Air-Launched Cruise Missile.

Sources

Kaplan, *op. cit.*, page 88; SIPRI, *op. cit.*, 1980, page xviii; Forsberg, *op. cit.*, November, 1982, page 54; Cordesman, *op. cit.*, December, 1982, page 41; IISS, *op. cit.*, 1982–1983, page 140; Cochran, Arkin, and Hoenig, *op. cit.*, page 102; Congressional Budget Office, *Modernizing U.S. Strategic Offensive Forces*, May, 1983, page 78; Center for Defense Information, *The Defense Monitor*, Volume XII, no. 7 (September, 1983), page 10.

Chronology of Critical Changes in United States
Strategic Bomber Force Structure, 1981–84

Date	Event
Sept. 1981	Initial operating capability of the ALCM-A Air-Launched Cruise Missile (AGM-86B Mod 1). One B-52G bomber of the 668th Bomb Squadron, Griffis Air Force Base, New York, placed on alert armed with 12 ALCMs.
Oct. 1982	Retirement of 3 squadrons of B-52D bombers, comprising 44 aircraft. These are placed in storage, joining 187 other B-52s, mostly B-52E and B-52F models, at Davis-Monthan Air Force Base, Arizona. The total of B-52s now in storage is 231; the total of B-52Ds remaining in service is now 31. Of the total of 744 B-52s of all models produced, 299 operational aircraft now remain in service.
Dec. 1982	Armed with 192 ALCMs, 16 B-52Gs of the 416th Bomb Wing at Griffis Air Force Base, New York, become the first Strategic Air Command squadron declared fully operational with the Cruise missile.
Apr. 1983	A second squadron of B-52s, of the 379th Bomb Wing, Wurtsmith Air Force Base, Michigan, becomes operational armed with ALCMs.
Oct. 1983	A third squadron of B-52s, of the 319th Bomb Wing, Grand Forks Air Force Base, North Dakota, becomes operational armed with ALCMs. This brings the total of ALCMs operationally deployed in 1983 to a minimum of 576.
Jan. 1984	A fourth squadron of B-52s, of the 28th Bomb Wing, Ellsworth Air Force Base, South Dakota, becomes operational armed with ALCMs.

Sources

Sept. 1981	Cochran, Arkin, and Hoenig, *op. cit.,* page 150.
Oct. 1982	Senate Armed Services Committee, *Authorization Hearings, Fiscal Year 1983, Department of Defense,* Part 7, page 4556; Cochran, Arkin, and Hoenig, *op. cit.,* pages 150–151.
Dec. 1982	*Aviation Week & Space Technology,* "News Digest," December 20, 1982, page 25; Samuel Freedman, "Nuclear Deterrence as Neighbor," *The New York Times,* December 27, 1982; Richard G. O'Lone, "ALCMs Delivered Ahead of Schedule," *Aviation Week & Space Technology,* January 17, 1983, page 101; Cochran, Arkin, and Hoenig, *op. cit.,* pages 150 and 175.
Apr. 1983	Department of Defense, *Selected Acquisitions Report,* June 30, 1982; O'Lone, *op. cit.,* January 17, 1983, page 101; Cochran, Arkin, and Hoenig, *op. cit.,* page 176; Chris Pocock and Colin Smith, *The USAF Today* (London: West London Aviation Group, 1975), pages 49–51.
Oct. 1983	O'Lone, *op. cit.,* January 17, 1983, page 101; Cochran, Arkin, and Hoenig, *op. cit.,* page 176; Pocock and Smith, *op. cit.,* pages 49–51.
Jan. 1984	Cochran, Arkin, and Hoenig, *op. cit.,* page 176; Pocock and Smith *op. cit.,* pages 49–51.

Normal Operational Loadings of United States Strategic Bombers, Broken Down by Load Type and Weight in Pounds

Bomber Type	Maximum Capacity	Load Type	Weight of Missiles		Total Weight with Bombs Added/Percent of Maximum Capacity				
			SRAMs 2240@	ALCMs 3300@	B-28 2540@	B-43 2060@	B-53 8850@	B-61 718@	B-83 2408@
FB-111A	37,500	2 SRAM/2 NGB	4480			8600/23%		5916/16%	9296/25%
FB-111A		4 SRAM/2 NGB	8960			13,080/35%		10,396/28%	13,776/37%
B-52D	60,000	4 NGB			10,160/17%	8240/14%	35,400/59%	2872/05%	9632/16%
B-52G/H	70,000	4 NGB			10,160/15%	8240/12%	35,400/51%	2872/04%	9632/14%
		4 SRAM/4 NGB	8960		19,120/27%	13,080/19%	44,360/63%	11,832/17%	18,592/26%
		8 SRAM/4 NGB	17,920		28,080/40%	26,160/37%	53,320/76%	20,792/30%	27,552/39%
		4 SRAM/4 NGB	8960		58,720/84%	56,800/81%		51,432/73%	58,192/83%
		12 ALCM		39,600					
		8 SRAM/4 NGB	17,920		67,680/96%	65,760/94%		60,392/86%	67,152/96%
		12 ALCM		39,600					

NGB: Nuclear Gravity Bomb.
SRAM: Short-Range Attack Missile.
ALCM: Air-Launched Cruise Missile.

Sources

Senate Appropriations Committee, *Hearings, Defense Department Appropriations, Fiscal Year 1981*, Part 5, page 1629; Congressional Budget Office, *Modernizing U.S. Strategic Offensive Forces*, May, 1983, page 86; John W. R. Taylor and Gordon Swanborough, *Military Aircraft of the World* (London: Ian Allan, 1975), page 23.

Additional Loadings Within the Capacity of United States Strategic Bombers, Broken Down by Load Type and Weight in Lbs

| Bomber Type | Maximum Capacity | Load Type | Weight of Missiles | | Total Weight/Percent of Maximum Capacity | | | | |
| | | | | | Total Weight with Bombs Added | | | | |
			SRAMs 2240@	ALCMs 3300@	B-28 2540@	B-43 2060@	B-53 8850@	B-61 718@	B-83 2408@
FB-111A	37,500	6 NGB				12,360/33%		4308/12%	14,448/38%
		6 SRAM	13,440/36%						
B-52G/H	70,000	12 NGB			30,480/44%	24,720/35%		8616/12%	28,896/41%
		12 SRAM							
		4 NGB	26,880		37,040/53%	35,120/50%	62,280/89%	29,752/43%	36,512/52%
		20 SRAM							
		4 NGB	44,800		54,960/78%	53,040/76%		47,672/68%	54,432/77%
		20 SRAM	44,800/64%						
		12 ALCM							
		4 NGB		39,600	49,760/71%	47,840/68%		42,472/61%	49,232/70%
		20 ALCM		66,000				68,872/98%	
		4 NGB							
		20 ALCM		66,000/94%					

NGB: Nuclear Gravity Bomb
SRAM: Short Range Attack Missile
ALCM: Air-Launched Cruise Missile

Sources

Senate Armed Services Committee, *Authorization Hearings, Fiscal Year 1982, Department of Defense*, Part 7, page 4329; Cochran, Arkin and Hoenig, *op. cit.*, 1984, page 106.

Operational Aircraft and Weapons Available to United States Strategic Air Command (SAC), 1979–1983

Bomber Type	Total of Operational Aircraft/Total of Aircraft Assigned to SAC Units as Primary Authorized Airvehicles							
	Dec 79	June 80	Dec 80	June 81	Dec 81	June 82	Dec 82	June 83
B-52D	80/ 75	80/ 75	80/ 75	79/ 75	79/ 75	75/ 75	31/ 31	31/ 31
B-52G	172/ 151	172/ 151	172/ 151	172/ 151	172/ 151	172/ 151	172/ 151	172/ 151
B-52H	96/ 90	96/ 90	96/ 90	96/ 90	96/ 90	96/ 90	96/ 90	96/ 90
TOTAL:	348/ 316	348/ 316	348/ 316	347/ 316	347/ 316	343/ 316	299/ 272	299/ 272
FB-111A	65/ 60	63/ 60	63/ 60	62/ 60	62/ 60	60/ 56	60/ 56	60/ 56
TOTALS:	413/ 376	411/ 376	411/ 376	409/ 376	409/ 376	403/ 372	359/ 328	359/ 328

Weapon Type	Total of Operational Weapons/Total Assigned to SAC Units (Total of Assigned Nuclear Gravity Bombs Unknown)							
SRAM	1396/1300	1396/1300	1383/1260	1374/1260	1374/1260	1300/1140	1300/1140	1300/1140
ALCM			10/	36/	70/ 12	150/ 60	320/ 192	560/ 384
B-28	1200/	1200/	1200/	1200/	1200/	1200/	1200/	1200/
B-43	2000/	2000/	2000/	2000/	2000/	2000/	2000/	2000/
B-53	150/	150/	150/	150/	150/	150/	150/	150/
B-61	3000/	3000/	3000/	3000/	3000/	3000/	3000/	3000/
TOTALS:	7746/	7733/	7743/	7760/	7794/	7800/	7970/	8210/

Sources

See sources listed for the two tables *Normal Operational Loadings* and *Additional Loadings* immediately preceding this one. See also Cochran, Arkin, and Hœnig, *op. cit.*, pages 42, 49, 58, 66, 101, 149 through 155, and 174 through 178.

Author's Estimate of Minimum Number of United States Strategic Bomber Weapons, Based on Normal Operational Loadings and Primary Authorized Air Vehicles Only, 1979–83

Bomber Type/Load	Total of Bombers of Each Type/Total of Bomber Weapons by Weapons Load							
	Dec. 79	June 80	Dec. 80	June 81	Dec. 81	June 82	Dec. 82	June 83
FB-111A (4 SRAM 2 NGB)	60/ 360	60/ 360	60/ 360	60/ 360	60/ 360	56/ 336	56/ 336	56/ 336
B-52D (4 NGB)	75/ 300	75/ 300	75/ 300	75/ 300	75/ 300	75/ 300	31/ 124	31/ 124
B-52G (4 NGB)	31/ 124	31/ 124	31/ 124	31/ 124	32/ 128	36/ 144	47/ 188	63/ 252
B-52G (4 SRAM 4 NGB)	120/ 960	120/ 960	120/ 960	120/ 960	118/ 944	110/ 880	88/ 704	56/ 448
B-52H (4 SRAM 4 NGB)	90/ 720	90/ 720	90/ 720	90/ 720	90/ 720	90/ 720	90/ 720	90/ 720
B-52G (8 SRAM 4 NGB/12 ALCM)					1/ 24	5/ 120	16/ 384	32/ 768
TOTALS:	376/2464	376/2464	376/2464	376/2464	376/2476	372/2500	328/2456	328/2648

NGB: Nuclear Gravity Bomb.
SRAM: Short-Range Attack Missile.
ALCM: Air-Launched Cruise Missile.

Sources

See the discussion *The Strategic Balance: Author's Estimate*, on page 279, as well as the sources listed for the chronology *Critical Changes in United States Strategic Bomber Force Structure, 1981–84*, on page 305, and for the three tables, *Normal Operational Loadings, Additional Loadings, and Operational Aircraft and Weapons Available to the United States Strategic Air Command*, immediately preceding this one.

Author's Estimate of Deliverable Weapons Capacity of United States Strategic Bombers, Based on All Available Operational Aircraft Not Retired or in Storage, and Utilizing Loadings That Do Not Exceed Weight of Normal Operational Loadings, 1979–83

Bomber Type/Load	Total of Bombers of Each Type/Total of Bomber Weapons by Weapons Load							
	Dec. 79	June 80	Dec. 80	June 81	Dec. 81	June 82	Dec. 82	June 83
FB-111A (4 SRAM 2 NGB)	30/ 180	30/ 180	30/ 180	30/ 180	30/ 180	30/ 180	30/ 180	30/ 180
FB-111A (6 NGB)	35/ 210	33/ 198	33/ 198	32/ 192	32/ 192	30/ 180	30/ 180	30/ 180
B-52D (4 NGB)	80/ 320	80/ 320	80/ 320	79/ 316	79/ 316	75/ 300	31/ 124	31/ 124
B-52G (12 NGB)	21/ 252	21/ 252	21/ 252	21/ 252	21/ 252	21/ 252	21/ 252	21/ 252
B-52G (8 SRAM 4 NGB)	151/1812	121/1812	151/1812	151/1812	150/1800	146/1752	135/1620	119/1428
B-52G (8 SRAM 4 NGB/12 ALCM)					1/ 24	5/ 120	16/ 384	32/ 768
B-52H (12 NGB)	96/1152	96/1152	96/1152	96/1152	96/1152	96/1152	96/1152	96/1152
TOTALS:	413/3926	411/3914	411/3914	409/3904	409/3916	403/3936	359/3892	359/4084

NGB: Nuclear Gravity Bomb.
SRAM: Short-Range Attack Missile.
ALCM: Air-Launched Cruise Missile.

Sources

See the discussion *The Strategic Balance: Author's Estimate*, on page 279, and all other sources listed for the table *Author's Estimate of Minimum Number of United States Strategic Bomber Weapons* immediately preceding this one.

**Load Capacities of Soviet Bombers Equipped with
Air-to-Surface Nuclear Standoff Missiles**

Bomber Type	Deployed in Strategic Role	Load Capacity	Missile Load	Load Weight	Percent of Capacity
Tu-95A *Bear*	Yes	25,000 lbs	1 × AS-3	24,200 lbs	96%
MYA-4 *Bison*	Yes	10,000 lbs	None		
Tu-22M *Backfire*	No	17,500 lbs	1 × AS-4	12,100 lbs	69%
			1 × AS-6	10,600 lbs	60%
Tu-22 *Blinder*	No	12,000 lbs	1 × AS-6	10,600 lbs	88%
Tu-16 *Badger*	No	20,000 lbs	1 × AS-4	12,100 lbs	60%
			1 × AS-6	10,600 lbs	53%

Sources

Load capacities of the Tu-95A *Bear* and MYA-4 *Bison* are taken from Norman Polmar, *World Combat Aircraft Directory* (London: Macdonald and Jane's, 1976), pages 237 and 238. They are further confirmed by John W. R. Taylor and Gordon Swanborough, *Military Aircraft of the World* (London: Ian Allan, 1975), pages 107 and 140, respectively. Load capacities for the Tu-22M *Backfire*, the Tu-22 *Blinder*, and the Tu-16 *Badger* are taken from the International Institute for Strategic Studies, *The Military Balance, 1982–1983*, page 115. They are further confirmed by Bill Gunston, *Modern Military Aircraft* (London: Salamander, 1977), pages 114, 128, and 126, respectively. Weights of all missiles are taken from James F. Dunnigan, *How to Make War* (New York: Morrow, 1982), pages 116–117.

Types of missiles and aircraft normally associated with each other are based on IISS, *op. cit., 1982–1983*, page 13; the Center for Defense Information, *The Defense Monitor*, Volume XII, no. 6 (September, 1983), page 7; and Bill Gunston, *An Illustrated Guide to Modern Airborne Missiles* (London: Salamander, 1983), pages 72–77.

The three air-to-surface missiles listed are probably all of the types armed with nuclear warheads available to Soviet forces. IISS, *op. cit., 1982–1983*, page 115, also lists the AS-2 missile with a nuclear warhead, though it gives no quantity availble, as it does of the other three missile types. But Gunston, *op. cit.*, 1977, page 72, observes that the warhead on the AS-2 is "generally believed to be conventional."

The weight of even a single one of any of these missiles exceeds the load capacity of the MYA-4 *Bison*, which therefore carries none. The weight of a single AS-3 missile exceeds the load capacity of all the other aircraft but the Tu-95A *Bear*. Consequently, the *Bear* is the only aircraft that can carry it, and when it does it carries only one. The weight of more than one AS-4 or AS-6 exceeds the load capacity of all the remaining aircraft. Consequently, these aircraft can carry only a single one of either kind. The *Bear* is the only aircraft capable of carrying two AS-4s or AS-6s. However, the missile normally associated with it is the AS-3, as noted by Gunston, *op. cit.*, 1977, pages 72–73, Taylor and Swanborough, *op. cit.*, page 140, and Norman Polmar, *World Combat Aircraft Directory* (London: Macdonald and Jane's 1976), page 237, who specifies that the *Bear* carries only one AS-3. This is further confirmed by Bill Sweetman, *The Presidio Concise Guide to Soviet Military Aircraft* (Novato, Calif.: Presidio, 1981), page 182. IISS, *op. cit., 1982–1983*, page 13, notes that "some 70 *Bear B* have AS-3 ASM."

Characteristics of United States and Soviet Aircraft Deployed as Intercontinental Strategic Bombers

Type	Load Capacity	Powerplant	Maximum Speed	Ceiling	Unrefueled Range in Statute Miles		First Deployed	Number Produced	Operating 1982–83	Other Missions
					Combat Range	Combat Radius				
USA										
FB-111A	37,500 lbs	Turbofan Jet 2 × PW TF 30-P-7	1650 mph	60,000 ft	4700	2350	1956	76	60	6 in storage.
B-52D	60,000 lbs	Turbojet 8 × J57-P-19W	634 mph	50,000 ft	7600	3800	1956	170	31	44 in storage.*
B-52G	70,000 lbs	Turbojet 8 × PW J57-P43WB	636 mph	50,000 ft	7960	3980	1958	193	172	
B-52H	70,000 lbs	Turbofan Jet 8 × PW TF 33-P-3	639 mph	50,000 ft	8950	4477	1961	102	96	
USSR										
Tu-95A Bear	25,000 lbs	Propeller 4 × NK-12MV	515 mph	45,000 ft	7800	3900	1956	120	100	
MYA-4 Bison	10,000 lbs	Turbojet 4 × AM-3D	560 mph		6050	3025	1956	85	35	50 converted as tankers, of which 35 operational.
Aircraft Not Equipped or Deployed as Intercontinental Strategic Bombers										
USSR										
Tu-22M Backfire	17,500 lbs	Turbojet 2 × NK-144	1265 mph		3600	1800	1975	180	180	80 assigned to Navy, 100 to Warsaw Pact.
Tu-95A Bear D	22,000 lbs	Propeller 4 × NK-12MV	515 mph	45,000 ft	7800	3900	1956	45	45	45 assigned to Navy.

* These aircraft are now in inactive reserve, together with at least 221 additional B-52s of earlier types in storage.

Sources

Sources for the more controversial information are as follows: load capacities of all United States aircraft and of the Soviet Tu-22M Backfire are taken from IISS, The Military Balance, 1983–1984, pages 120 and 121. Load capacities of the Soviet Tu-95A Bear and MYA-4 Bison are taken from Polmar, World Combat Aircraft Directory, pages 237 and 238. The range of the FB-111A is taken from Kosta Tsipis, Arsenal: Understanding Weapons in the Nuclear Age (New York: Simon & Schuster, 1983), page 152, and is further confirmed by Bernard Weinraub, "Air Force Urges Revival of FB-111 as a Long-Range Bomber," The New York Times, September 7, 1977. Speeds and ranges of all models of B-52 are taken from Ray Wagner, American Combat Planes (Garden City, N.Y.: Doubleday, 1967). pages 152 and 153. The figures for all B-52s produced and operational are taken from Cochran, Arkin, and Hoenig, op. cit., pages 150 and 151. The figure for B-52s in storage is from the Department of Defense, Annual Report, Fiscal Year 1982, January, 1981, page 53.

The ranges of all Soviet aircraft are taken from IISS, The Military Balance, 1975–1976, page 72; this includes the range of the Tu-22M Backfire. Ranges of up to 7200 miles, or precisely double the IISS figure of 3600 miles, were first quoted for this aircraft by the Defense Department in 1976, in an unsuccessful effort to require its inclusion among heavy bombers counted under the limit of 2400 strategic delivery vehicles agreed upon in the SALT negotiations at Vladivostok. The IISS figure is based on a McDonnell Douglas study commissioned by the CIA in 1975. Its accuracy was confirmed by the White House in 1976. See Aviation Week & Space Technology, September 13, 1976, page 13. It is more recently confirmed by Bill Sweetman, The Presidio Concise Guide to Soviet Military Aircraft (Novato, Calif.: Presidio Press, 1981), page 177, who gives the Backfire a combat range of 1650 miles at sea level, a maximum combat range of 3200 miles, and an unarmed ferry range of 5000 miles. IISS now quotes the last of these figures, which is susceptible of misinterpretation as a combat range. Quotations of much higher figures naturally persist.

The speed of the Tu-22M Backfire is taken from Understanding Soviet Naval Developments, Office of the Chief of Naval Operations, Department of the Navy, Washington, D.C., 1981, page 122. Deployment figures for the Soviet Tu-95A Bear and MYA-4 Bison, both of which ceased production in the early 1960s, are taken from IISS, The Military Balance, 1978–1979, page 83. Deployment figures for the Tu-22M Backfire, which continues in production, are taken from IISS, The Military Balance, 1982–1983, pages 13, 16, 115, 118, and 136. The disposition and capabilities of the Tu-95A Bear D have never been in dispute, but those of the Tu-22M Backfire have. They are clearly defined by our State Department, however, as limited to the "theater and anti-ship role" in Verification of the SALT II Agreement, United States Department of State, Bureau of Public Affairs, Special Report No. 56, Washington, D.C., August, 1979, page 5. The Backfire, in short, is neither equipped nor deployed as an intercontinental strategic bomber. The United States knows this because it has the capability to know it, as well as the capability to verify "with confidence" any change in the bomber's deployment, as the State Department points out, ibid., page 5.

Nuclear Weapons Deliverable by United States Strategic Bombers

Weapon Type and Designation	Weight (lbs)	Speed (mph)	Range (miles)	Guidance and Accuracy (ft)	Warhead			Number Produced/Operational in 1982/Bomber Type
					Type	Weight (lbs)	Yield	
AGM-69A SRAM	2240	2310	136	Inertial with radar altimeter 300	W-69	300	170–200 KT	1500 produced. 1300 operational.
AGM-86B Mod 1 ALCM-A	3300	500	1841	Inertial with TERCOM 100	W-80	270	200–250 KT	1547 produced. 1499 operational.
AGM-86B Mod 2 ALCM-B	3300	500	2473	Inertial with TERCOM 100	W-80	270	200–250 KT	2849 planned, with production beginning in 1984.
ASALM		2310	2991	Inertial with TERCOM 100				SCRAMJET engine with Shelldyne-H Fuel. Planned for 1987.
Nuclear Gravity Bombs								
B-28	2540			600			350 KT/1.5 MT	1200 produced. 1200 operational.
B-43	2060			600			1 MT	2000 produced. 2000 operational.
B-53	8850			600			9 MT	150 produced. 150 operational.
B-61-1	718			600			100–500 KT	3000 produced. 3000 operational.
B-83	2408			600			1 MT	2500 planned, with production beginning in 1984.

Nuclear Weapons Deliverable by Soviet Strategic Bombers

Weapon Type and Designation	Weight (lbs)	Speed (mph)	Range (miles)	Guidance and Accuracy (ft)	Warhead			Number Produced/Operational in 1982/Bomber Type
					Type	Weight (lbs)	Yield	
AS-3 Kangaroo	24,200	1188	400	Radio command			800 KT	70 deployed. Carried by Tu-95A.
AS-4 Kitchen	12,100	2310	185	Inertial with radar homing			200 KT	135 deployed. Carried by Tu-22M.
AS-6 Kingfish	10,600	1790	155	Inertial with radar homing			200 KT	65 Deployed. Carried by Tu-16 and Tu-22M
Nuclear Gravity Bomb	2000			1215			1 MT	130 Deployed. Carried by Tu-95A and MYA-4.

Sources

Sources for the more controversial information are as follows: weights of all U.S. bombs and missiles, their warhead yields, and the numbers of each produced, deployed, or planned for production are from Thomas B. Cochran, William M. Arkin, and Milton M. Hoenig, *Nuclear Weapons Databook* (Cambridge, Mass.: Ballinger, 1984). The ranges of the ALCM-A and ALCM-B are from the same source, page 178. The range of the ASALM (Advanced Strategic Air-Launched Cruise Missile) is from Robert C. Aldridge, *First Strike!* (Boston: South End Press, 1983), page 151. The speed of the ASALM is from Bill Gunston, *Modern Airborne Missiles* (London: Salamander, 1983), page 88. The accuracy of the Cruise missile with TERCOM guidance is from *Analysis of Arms Control Impact Statement Submitted in Connection with the Fiscal Year 1978 Budget Request*, a joint publication of the House International Relations and Senate Foreign Relations Committees, April, 1977, page 83. The accuracy of the Cruise missile is further confirmed by the Congressional Budget Office, *Modernizing U.S. Strategic Offensive Forces*, May, 1983, page 86. The weights of Soviet missiles are from James F. Dunnigan, *How to Make War* (New York: William Morrow, 1982), pages 116–117. The speed of the AS-6 is also from Dunnigan, page 116, while the speeds of the AS-3 and AS-4 are from Gunston, *op. cit.*, pages 72–74. Guidance features of Soviet missiles are also taken from Gunston, pages 72–77. The warhead yields of the AS-3 and AS-4 are taken from *Jane's Weapon Systems, 1981–82* (London: Macdonald and Jane's, 1981), page 162, while the warhead yield of the AS-6, as well as the ranges and deployment numbers of all three Soviet missiles, are taken from IISS, *The Military Balance 1981–1982*, page 107. The accuracy and one probable yield of the Soviet nuclear gravity bomb is taken from Fred Kaplan, *Dubious Specter* (Washington, D.C.: Institute for Policy Studies, 1980), page 90. The accuracy of American gravity bombs is taken from Kaplan, *ibid.*, page 88, and from *Aerospace Daily*, December 28, 1978, page 263.

Author's Estimate of Deliverable Weapons Capacity of Soviet Aircraft Equipped and Deployed as Intercontinental Strategic Bombers, 1979–83

Bomber Type	Load	Number of Bombers Deployed	Total of Weapons
Tu-95A *Bear*	1 × AS-3	70	70
Tu-95A *Bear*	2 × NGB	30	60
MYA-4 *Bison*	2 × NGB	35	70
	Totals:	135	200

Sources

The numbers of bombers deployed are from the International Institute for Strategic Studies, *The Military Balance, 1978–1979,* page 83. The Tu-22M *Backfire* is not included, because it is not equipped or deployed as an intercontinental strategic bomber. See *Verification of the SALT II Agreement,* U.S. Department of State, Special Report No. 56, August, 1979, page 5. Due to their own load limitations and the weights of available air-to-surface missiles, the MYA-4 *Bison* can carry none of these weapons, and the Tu-95A *Bear* can carry only one AS-3. See the separate table, *Load Capacities of Soviet Bombers Equipped with Air-to-Surface Nuclear Standoff Missiles,* and its sources. The number of *Bears* equipped with the AS-3 missile is taken from IISS, *The Military Balance, 1981–1982,* page 11, and again from IISS, *The Military Balance, 1982–1983,* page 13. The large majority of sources agree that remaining aircraft carry a maximum of two nuclear gravity bombs each. See Les Aspin, "The Verification of the SALT Agreement," *Scientific American* (February, 1979), page 41, and Fred M. Kaplan, *Dubious Specter* (Washington, D.C.: Institute for Policy Studies, 1980, rev. 1982), page 90. Also see the table, *Soviet Strategic Bombers and Bomber Weapons: An Analysis of Sources, 1979–83,* in Appendix B: The Strategic Balance: A Chronology of Estimates, which counts fourteen out of nineteen sources reporting all Soviet strategic aircraft armed with a maximum of no more than two nuclear weapons each.

Appendix A

Summary and Analysis

TABLES IN THIS SECTION

- Summary: Author's Estimates of United States Strategic Warheads, 1979–83
- Summary: Author's Estimates of Soviet Strategic Warheads, 1979–83
- Recapitulation: Composition of American and Soviet Strategic Forces, June, 1982
- Recapitulation: Composition of American and Soviet Strategic Forces, December, 1982
- Recapitulation: Composition of American and Soviet Strategic Forces, June, 1983
- Hypothetical Composition of American and Soviet Strategic Forces, December, 1982, with Maximum Loads Allowed by SALT II
- Weapons, Delivery Vehicles, Aggregate Throwweight, and Megatonnage of United States Strategic Forces—December, 1981, and December, 1982
- Weapons, Delivery Vehicles, Aggregate Throwweight, and Megatonnage of Soviet Strategic Forces—December, 1981 and December, 1982
- Comparative Measures of Strategic Power: Soviet and American Strategic Forces—December, 1981, to December, 1982
- Deployment Schedule: BGM-109 *Tomahawk* GLCM and *Pershing II* MRBM
- Deployment Schedule: BGM-109 T-ALM/N *Tomahawk* SLCM
- Estimated Composition of American and Soviet Strategic Forces, 1984
- Estimated Composition of American and Soviet Strategic Forces, 1985
- Recapitulation: The Balance of Strategic Warheads, Missile Warheads Only, 1979–85
- Recapitulation: The Balance of Deliverable Strategic Warheads, Including Aircraft Weapons, 1979–85

Summary: Author's Estimates of United States Strategic Warheads, 1979–83

					Total of Missiles/Total of Warheads			
Missile Type	Dec. 79	June 80	Dec. 80	June 81	Dec. 81	June 82	Dec. 82	June 83
ICBMs	1054/2154	1054/2154	1054/2154	1054/2154	1053/2153	1053/2153	1052/2152	1049/2149
SLBMs	656/6048	656/5920	608/5776	576/5712	600/5648	520/6080	544/6272	544/6176
TOTALS:	1710/8202	1710/8074	1662/7930	1630/7866	1653/7801	1573/8233	1596/8424	1593/8325

Adding Minimum Number of United States Strategic Bomber Weapons

					Total of Launchers/Total of Warheads			
Launcher Type	Dec. 79	June 80	Dec. 80	June 81	Dec. 81	June 82	Dec. 82	June 83
Missiles	1710/ 8202	1710/ 8074	1662/ 7930	1630/ 7866	1653/ 7801	1573/ 8233	1596/ 8424	1593/ 8325
Bombers	376/ 2464	376/ 2464	376/ 2464	376/ 2464	376/ 2476	372/ 2500	328/ 2456	328/ 2648
TOTALS:	2086/10,666	2086/10,538	2038/10,394	2006/10,330	2029/10,277	1945/10,733	1924/10,880	1921/10,973

Adding Total of Weapons Deliverable by United States Strategic Bombers

					Total of Launchers/Total of Weapons			
Launcher Type	Dec. 79	June 80	Dec. 80	June 81	Dec. 81	June 82	Dec. 82	June 83
Missiles	1710/ 8202	1710/ 8074	1662/ 7930	1630/ 7866	1653/ 7801	1573/ 8233	1596/ 8424	1593/ 8325
Bombers	413/ 3926	411/ 3914	411/ 3914	409/ 3904	409/ 3916	403/ 3936	359/ 3892	359/ 4084
TOTALS:	2123/12,128	2121/11,988	2073/11,844	2039/11,770	2062/11,717	1976/12,169	1955/12,316	1952/12,409

Summary: Author's Estimates of Soviet Strategic Warheads, 1979–83

Summary of Estimates of Soviet ICBM and SLBM Warheads, Consistent with the Defense Department Estimate of May, 1982

Missile Type	Total of Missiles/Total of Warheads							
	Dec. 79	June 80	Dec. 80	June 81	Dec. 81	June 82	Dec. 82	June 83
ICBMs	1398/3974	1398/4159	1398/4324	1398/4554	1398/4689	1398/4744	1398/4804	1398/4864
SLBMs	937/1289	953/1337	969/1385	969/1449	969/1513	969/1577	969/1641	969/1705
TOTALS:	2335/5263	2351/5496	2367/5709	2367/6003	2367/6202	2367/6321	2367/6445	2367/6569

Summary of Soviet Strategic Warheads, 1979–83, Including Weapons Deliverable by Aircraft Deployed as Strategic Bombers

Launcher Type	Total of Launchers/Total of Warheads							
	Dec. 79	June 80	Dec. 80	June 81	Dec. 81	June 82	Dec. 82	June 83
Missiles	2335/5263	2351/5496	2367/5709	2367/6003	2367/6202	2367/6321	2367/6445	2367/6569
Bombers	135/ 200	135/ 200	135/ 200	135/ 200	135/ 200	135/ 200	135/ 200	135/ 200
TOTALS:	2470/5463	2486/5696	2502/5909	2502/6203	2502/6402	2502/6521	2502/6645	2502/6769

Recapitulation: Composition of American and Soviet Strategic Forces—June, 1982

Soviet Union				United States			
Missile or Aircraft Type	Number	Warheads on Each	Total Warheads	Missile or Aircraft Type	Number	Warheads on Each	Total Warheads
SS-11	590	1	590	Titan II	53	1	53
SS-13	60	1	60	Minuteman II	450	1	450
SS-17 Mod 1	140	4	560	Minuteman III	550	3	1650
SS-17 Mod 2	10	1	10	Poseidon C-3	320	14	4480
SS-18 Mod 1	30	1	30	Trident C-4	200	8	1600
SS-18 Mod 2	228	8	1824	FB-111A			
SS-18 Mod 3	30	1	30	4 × SRAM			
SS-18 Mod 4	20	10	200	and 2 × B-61	56	6	336
SS-19 Mod 1	230	6	1380	B-52D			
SS-19 Mod 2	60	1	60	4 × NGB	75	4	300
SS-N-5	57	1	57	B-52G			
SS-N-6	400	1	400	4 × NGB	36	4	144
SS-N-8	292	1	292	B-52G			
SS-N-17	12	1	12	4 × SRAM			
SS-N-18 Mod 1	160	3	480	and 4 × NGB	110	8	880
SS-N-18 Mod 3	48	7	336	B-52G			
Tu-95A				12 × ALCM			
1 × AS-3	70	1	70	8 × SRAM			
Tu-95A				and 4 × B-61	5	24	120
2 × NGB	30	2	60	B-52H			
MYA-4				4 × SRAM			
2 × NGB	35	2	70	and 4 × NGB	90	8	720
		TOTAL:	6521			TOTAL:	10,733

NGB: Nuclear Gravity Bomb.
SRAM: Short-Range Attack Missile.
ALCM: Air-Launched Cruise Missile.

Recapitulation: Composition of American and Soviet Strategic Forces—December, 1982

Soviet Union				United States			
Missile or Aircraft Type	Number	Warheads on Each	Total Warheads	Missile or Aircraft Type	Number	Warheads on Each	Total Warheads
SS-11	580	1	580	*Titan II*	52	1	52
SS-13	60	1	60	*Minuteman II*	450	1	450
SS-17 Mod 1	140	4	560	*Minuteman III*	550	3	1650
SS-17 Mod 2	10	1	10	*Poseidon C-3*	320	14	4480
SS-18 Mod 1	30	1	30	*Trident C-4*	224	8	1792
SS-18 Mod 2	223	8	1784	FB-111A			
SS-18 Mod 3	30	1	30	*4 × SRAM*			
SS-18 Mod 4	25	10	250	*and 2 × B-61*	56	6	336
SS-19 Mod 1	240	6	1440	B-52D			
SS-19 Mod 2	60	1	60	*4 × NGB*	31	4	124
SS-N-5	57	1	57	B-52G			
SS-N-6	400	1	400	*4 × NGB*	47	4	188
SS-N-8	292	1	292	B-52G			
SS-N-17	12	1	12	*4 × SRAM*			
SS-N-18 Mod 1	144	3	432	*and 4 × NGB*	88	8	704
SS-N-18 Mod 3	64	7	448	B-52G			
Tu-95A				*12 × ALCM*			
1 × AS-3	70	1	70	*8 × SRAM*			
Tu-95A				*and 4 × B-61*	16	24	384
2 × NGB	30	2	60	B-52H			
MYA-4				*4 × SRAM*			
2 × NGB	35	2	70	*and 4 × NGB*	90	8	720
		TOTAL:	6645			TOTAL:	10,880

NGB: Nuclear Gravity Bomb.
SRAM: Short-Range Attack Missile.
ALCM: Air-Launched Cruise Missile.

Recapitulation: Composition of American and Soviet Strategic Forces—June, 1983

Soviet Union				United States			
Missile or Aircraft Type	Number	Warheads on Each	Total Warheads	Missile or Aircraft Type	Number	Warheads on Each	Total Warheads
SS-11	570	1	570	Titan II	49	1	49
SS-13	60	1	60	Minuteman II	450	1	450
SS-17 Mod 1	140	1	560	Minuteman III	550	3	1650
SS-17 Mod 2	10	1	10	Poseidon C-3	304	14	4256
SS-18 Mod 1	30	1	30	Trident C-4	240	8	1920
SS-18 Mod 2	218	8	1744	FB-111A			
SS-18 Mod 3	30	1	30	4 × SRAM			
SS-18 Mod 4	30	10	300	and 2 × B-61	56	6	336
SS-19 Mod 1	250	6	1500	B-52D			
SS-19 Mod 2	60	1	60	4 × NGB	31	4	124
SS-N-5	57	1	57	B-52G			
SS-N-6	400	1	400	4 × NGB	63	4	252
SS-N-8	292	1	292	B-52G			
SS-N-17	12	1	12	4 × SRAM			
SS-N-18 Mod 1	128	3	384	and 4 × NGB	56	8	448
SS-N-18 Mod 3	80	7	560	B-52G			
Tu-95A				12 × ALCM			
1 × AS-3	70	1	70	8 × SRAM			
Tu-95A				and 4 × B-61	32	24	768
2 × NGB	30	2	60	B-52H			
MYA-4				4 × SRAM			
2 × NGB	35	2	70	and 4 × NGB	90	8	720
		TOTAL:	6769			TOTAL:	10,973

NGB: Nuclear Gravity Bomb.
SRAM: Short-Range Attack Missile.
ALCM: Air-Launched Cruise Missile.

Sources

The changing composition of Soviet and American strategic forces shown here from June, 1982, through June, 1983, recapitulates information developed in the three preceding sections estimating the strategic balance, and is based entirely on sources provided for the tables in those sections. It reflects the consensus those sources reach on the following points:

• That no fewer Soviet ICBMs than shown here remained fitted with a single warhead.
• That conversion of the Soviet SS-11 ICBM with a single warhead to the Mod 1 version of the SS-19 with 6 warheads proceeded no more quickly than at the rate shown.
• That conversion of the Soviet SS-18 Mod 2 ICBM with 8 warheads to the Mod 4 version of the SS-18 with 10 warheads proceeded no more quickly than at the rate shown.
• That conversion of the Soviet SS-N-18 Mod 1 SLBM with 3 warheads to the Mod 3 version of the SS-N-18 with 7 warheads proceeded no more quickly than at the rate shown.
• That the Soviet SS-N-20 SLBM was not deployed in this period.
• That Soviet Tu-22M Backfire aircraft are neither equipped nor deployed as intercontinental strategic bombers.

- That Soviet aircraft deployed as intercontinental strategic bombers, but not fitted with the AS-3 air-to-surface missile, carry no more than 2 nuclear gravity bombs each.
- That the count of America's aircraft equipped and deployed as intercontinental strategic bombers should be limited to Primary Authorized Airvehicles of the Strategic Air Command, rather than including all operational B-52 and FB-111A aircraft available.
- That the count of weapons carried by America's strategic bombers should be limited to the normal operational loadings shown, rather than reflecting their full deliverable weapons capacity.

Sources cited in the three preceding sections have also documented the following changes in America's strategic force structure:

- The initial stage of retirement of 52 remaining *Titan II* missiles from the ICBM force.
- The retirement of SSBN-601 *Robert E. Lee,* the last of 10 *Polaris* submarines whose withdrawal reduced the SLBM arsenal by the equivalent of 160 warheads, in March, 1982.
- The retrofit of *Trident C-4* missiles on SSBN-663 *Casimir Pulaski,* completing the scheduled retrofit of 192 *Trident C-4* missiles with 1536 warheads on 12 *Poseidon* submarines, in March, 1983.
- The addition of 4 more warheads to the 10 already carried by each of the 304 *Poseidon C-3* missiles that would remain on 19 *Poseidon* submarines after the *Trident C-4* retrofit was completed, raising the total of *Poseidon* warheads carried by the SLBM force from 3040 to 4256 between 1980 and 1982.
- The addition to the fleet of the first 2 *Trident* submarines, SSBN-726 *Ohio* in November, 1979, and SSBN-272 *Michigan* in September, 1982, adding 48 *Trident C-4* missiles and 384 warheads to the SLBM force.
- Limited deployment of the AGM-86B ALCM (Air-Launched Cruise Missile) on B-52Gs of the 668th Bomb Squadron at Griffis Air Force Base, New York, in September, 1981.
- The retirement of 3 squadrons of B-52D bombers, comprising 44 aircraft, in October, 1982.
- Full deployment of ALCMs on B-52Gs of the 668th Bomb Squadron, 416th Bomb Wing at Griffis Air Force Base, New York, in December, 1982, and on B-52Gs of the 524th Bomb Squadron, 379th Bomb Wing, Wurtsmith Air Force Base, Michigan, in April, 1983.

Hypothetical Composition of American and Soviet Strategic Forces—December, 1982— If All Operational Aircraft Were Used and Loaded to Maximum Capacity, and If All Missiles Were Fitted with the Maximum Number of Warheads Specified by SALT II as the Limit of Their Flight-Tested Operational Capability, or with Any Higher Number Already Deployed

Soviet Union				United States			
Missile or Aircraft Type	Number	Warheads on Each	Total Warheads	Missile or Aircraft Type	Number	Warheads on Each	Total Warheads
SS-11	580	1	580	Titan II	52	1	52
SS-13	60	1	60	Minuteman II	450	1	450
SS-17 Mod 1	150	4	600	Minuteman III	550	7	3850
SS-18 Mod 4	308	10	3080	Poseidon C-3	320	14	4480
SS-19 Mod 1	300	6	1800	Trident C-4	224	8	1792
SS-N-5	57	1	57	TOTAL MISSILES:			10,624
SS-N-6	400	1	400				
SS-N-8	292	1	292	FB-111A	60	6	360
SS-N-17	12	1	12	B-52D	31	4	124
SS-N-18 Mod 3	208	7	1456	B-52G	156	12	1872
TOTAL MISSILES:			8337	B-52G	16	24	384
				B-52H	96	12	1152
Tu-95A	100	2	200	GRAND TOTAL:			14,516
MYA-4	35	2	70				
GRAND TOTAL:			8607				

Sources

For the maximum number of warheads which SALT II allows each nation to fit on each type of ballistic missile it deploys, see *SALT II Agreement, Vienna, June 18, 1979,* Article IV, Paragraphs 10 and 12, U.S. Department of State, Selected Documents No. 12A, pages 35 and 36. With one exception, the figures above reflect these limitations. The exception is the *Trident C-4* missile, which SALT II limits to a maximum of 7 warheads. To confirm that the *Trident C-4* is fitted with 8 warheads, see Joint Chiefs of Staff, *Fiscal Year 1984 Posture Statement,* page 16. This is an unambiguous violation of SALT II. For an assessment of America's ability to detect Soviet violations of SALT II, and of the likelihood that America publicly would have accused the Soviet Union of comparable violations if any had ever occurred, see the sections *Violations of SALT II, Verification, On-Site Inspection,* and *Telemetry* in the main text, and *United States Military Satellite Systems* in *Appendix I.*

Independently Targetable Nuclear Weapons Deployed by United States Strategic Forces, December, 1981, Compared with Their Delivery Vehicles, Aggregate Throwweight, and Aggregate Megatonnage

ICBMs	Load	Total Weight (lbs)	Total Yield (MT)	Vehicles Deployed 1981	Aggregate Throwweight	Aggregate Megatons	Total of Targetable Weapons
TITAN II	1 × RV	8,300	9	53	439,900	477	53
MINUTEMAN II	1 × RV	2,500	1.2	450	1,125,000	540	450
MINUTEMAN III	3 × MIRV	2,400	.51	350	840,000	178.5	1,050
MINUTEMAN III	3 × MIRV	2,435	1.005	200	487,000	201	600
				1,053	2,891,900	1,396.5	2,153
SLBMs							
POLARIS A-3	3 × MRV	1,835	.6	80	146,800	48	80
POSEIDON C-3	10 × MIRV	3,670	.4	176	645,920	70.4	1,760
POSEIDON C-3	14 × MIRV	5,152	.56	176	906,752	98.6	2,464
TRIDENT C-4	8 × MIRV	2,900	.8	168	487,200	134.4	1,344
				600	2,186,672	351.4	5,648
Bombers							
FB-111A	4 × SRAM						
	2 × B-61	10,396	2	60	623,760	120	60
B-52D	4 × B-28	10,160	4	75	762,000	300	300
B-52G	4 × B-53	35,400	36	32	1,132,800	1,152	128
B-52G	4 × SRAM						
	4 × B-61	11,832	2.8	118	1,396,176	330.4	944
B-52H	4 × SRAM						
	4 × B-61	11,832	2.8	90	1,064,880	252	720
B-52G	8 × SRAM						
	4 × B-61						
	12 × ALCM	60,392	6.6	1	60,392	6.6	24
				376	5,040,008	2,161	2,476
Totals:				2,029	10,118,580	3,908.9	10,277

Independently Targetable Nuclear Weapons Deployed by United States Strategic Forces, December, 1982, Compared with Their Delivery Vehicles, Aggregate Throwweight, and Aggregate Megatonnage

ICBMs	Load	Total Weight (lbs)	Total Yield (MT)	Vehicles Deployed 1982	Aggregate Throwweight	Aggregate Megatons	Total of Targetable Weapons
TITAN II	1 × RV	8,300	9	52	431,600	468	52
MINUTEMAN II	1 × RV	2,500	1.2	450	1,125,000	540	450
MINUTEMAN III	3 × MIRV	2,400	.51	250	600,000	127.5	750
MINUTEMAN III	3 × MIRV	2,435	1.005	300	730,500	301.5	900
				1,052	2,887,100	1,437	2,152
SLBMs							
POSEIDON C-3	14 × MIRV	5,152	.56	320	1,648,640	179.2	4,480
TRIDENT C-4	8 × MIRV	2,900	.8	224	649,600	179.2	1,792
				544	2,298,240	358.4	6,272
Bombers							
FB-111A	4 × SRAM						
	2 × B-61	10,396	2	56	582,176	112	336
B-52D	4 × B-28	10,160	4	31	314,960	124	124
B-52G	4 × B-28	10,160	4	15	152,400	60	60
B-52G	4 × B-53	35,400	36	32	1,132,800	1,152	128
B-52G	4 × SRAM						
	4 × B-61	11,832	2.8	88	1,041,216	246.4	704
B-52H	4 × SRAM						
	4 × B-61	11,832	2.8	90	1,064,880	252	720
B-52G	8 × SRAM						
	4 × B-61						
	12 × ALCM	60,392	6.6	16	966,272	105.6	384
				328	5,254,704	2,052	2,456
Totals:				1,924	10,440,044	3,847.4	10,880

Independently Targetable Nuclear Weapons Deployed by Soviet Strategic Forces, December, 1981, Compared with Their Delivery Vehicles, Aggregate Throwweight, and Aggregate Megatonnage

ICBMs	Load	Total Weight (lbs)	Total Yield (MT)	Vehicles Deployed 1981	Aggregate Throwweight	Aggregate Megatons	Total of Targetable Weapons
SS-11	3 × MRV	2,500	.9	600	1,500,000	540	600
SS-13	1 × RV	1,000	.75	60	60,000	45	60
SS-17	1 × RV	3,600	3	10	36,000	30	10
SS-17	4 × MIRV	6,000	3	140	840,000	420	560
SS-18	1 × RV	16,500	25	30	495,000	750	30
SS-18	8 × MIRV	16,700	6	228	3,807,600	1,368	1,824
SS-18	1 × RV	16,000	20	30	480,000	600	30
SS-18	10 × MIRV	16,700	5	15	250,000	75	150
SS-19	1 × RV	7,000	1	60	420,000	60	60
SS-19	6 × MIRV	7,525	3.3	220	1,655,500	726	1,360
				1,398	9,544,600	4,614	4,689
SLBMs							
SS-N-5	1 × RV	1,500	1	57	85,500	57	57
SS-N-6	3 × MRV	1,500	1.05	400	600,000	420	400
SS-N-8	1 × RV	1,500	1	292	438,000	292	292
SS-N-17	1 × RV	2,500	1	12	30,000	12	12
SS-N-18	3 × MIRV	1,500	.6	176	264,000	105.6	528
SS-N-18	7 × MIRV	3,500	1.4	32	112,000	44.8	224
				969	1,529,500	931.4	1,513
Bombers							
Tu-95A	1 × AS-3	24,200	.8	70	1,694,000	56	70
Tu-95A	2 × NGB	4,000	2	30	120,000	60	60
MYA-4	2 × NGB	4,000	2	35	140,000	70	70
				135	1,954,000	186	200
Totals:				2,502	13,028,100	5,731.4	6,402

Independently Targetable Nuclear Weapons Deployed by Soviet Strategic Forces, December, 1982, Compared with Their Delivery Vehicles, Aggregate Throwweight, and Aggregate Megatonnage

ICBMs	Load	Total Weight (lbs)	Total Yield (MT)	Vehicles Deployed 1982	Aggregate Throwweight	Aggregate Megatons	Total of Targetable Weapons
SS-11	3 × MRV	2,500	.9	580	1,450,000	522	580
SS-13	1 × RV	1,000	.75	60	60,000	45	60
SS-17	1 × RV	3,600	3	10	36,000	30	10
SS-17	4 × MIRV	6,000	3	140	840,000	420	560
SS-18	1 × RV	16,500	25	30	495,000	750	30
SS-18	8 × MIRV	16,700	6	223	3,724,100	1,338	1,784
SS-18	1 × RV	16,000	20	30	480,000	600	30
SS-18	10 × MIRV	16,700	5	25	417,500	125	250
SS-19	1 × RV	7,000	1	60	420,000	60	60
SS-19	6 × MIRV	7,525	3.3	240	1,806,000	792	1,440
				1,398	9,728,600	4,682	4,804
SLBMs							
SS-N-5	1 × RV	1,500	1	57	85,500	57	57
SS-N-6	3 × MRV	1,500	1.05	400	600,000	420	400
SS-N-8	1 × RV	1,500	1	292	438,000	292	292
SS-N-17	1 × RV	2,500	1	12	30,000	12	12
SS-N-18	3 × MIRV	1,500	.6	144	216,000	86.4	432
SS-N-18	7 × MIRV	3,500	1.4	64	224,000	89.6	448
				969	1,593,500	957	1,641
Bombers							
Tu-95A	1 × AS-3	24,200	.8	70	1,694,000	56	70
Tu-95A	2 × NGB	4,000	2	30	120,000	60	60
MYA-4	2 × NGB	4,000	2	35	140,000	70	70
				135	1,954,000	186	200
Totals:				2,502	13,276,100	5,825	6,645

Comparative Measures of Strategic Power: Independently Targetable Nuclear Weapons, Delivery Vehicles, Aggregate Throwweight,* and Aggregate Megatonnage of Soviet and American Strategic Forces—December, 1981, to December, 1982

December, 1981

	USA				USSR			
	Throwweight % of Total	Megatons % of Total	Vehicles % of Total	Weapons % of Total	Throwweight % of Total	Megatons % of Total	Vehicles % of Total	Weapons % of Total
ICBMs	2.892 (28)	1396.5 (36)	1053 (52)	2153 (21)	9.545 (73)	4614 (81)	1398 (56)	4689 (73)
SLBMs	2.187 (22)	351.4 (09)	600 (30)	5648 (55)	1.529 (12)	931.4 (16)	969 (39)	1513 (24)
Bombers	5.040 (50)	2161 (55)	376 (18)	2476 (24)	1.954 (15)	186 (03)	135 (05)	200 (03)
	10.119	3908.9	2029	10,277	13.028	5731.4	2502	6402

December, 1982

	USA				USSR			
	Throwweight % of Total	Megatons % of Total	Vehicles % of Total	Weapons % of Total	Throwweight % of Total	Megatons % of Total	Vehicles % of Total	Weapons % of Total
ICBMs	2.887 (28)	1437 (37)	1052 (55)	2152 (20)	9.729 (73)	4682 (81)	1398 (56)	4804 (72)
SLBMs	2.298 (22)	358.4 (09)	544 (28)	6272 (58)	1.593 (12)	957 (16)	969 (39)	1641 (25)
Bombers	5.255 (50)	2052 (54)	328 (17)	2456 (20)	1.954 (15)	186 (03)	135 (05)	200 (03)
	10.440	3847.4	1924	10,880	13.276	5825	2502	6645

* Throwweight is given in millions of lbs.

Deployment Schedule and Minimum Deployment Capacity: BGM-109 Tomahawk GLCM (Ground-Launched Cruise Missile) with 1 × W-84 Nuclear Warhead, and Pershing II MRBM (Medium-Range Ballistic Missile) with 1 × W-85 Nuclear Warhead

Missile Type	Missiles per Launcher	1983 Launchers	1983 Missiles	1983 Total	1984 Launchers	1984 Missiles	1984 Total	1985 Launchers	1985 Missiles	1985 Total	1988 Launchers	1988 Missiles	1988 Total
Tomahawk GLCM	4	8	32	32	24	96	96	40	160	160	116	464	464
Pershing II	1	9	9	9	36	36	36	48	48	48	108	108	108
Deployed Warhead Totals:				41			132			208			572

Sources

Dates for initial deployment of both missile types are from the Department of Defense, *Fiscal Year 1983, Program of Research, Development and Acquisition,* page VII-13, and are further confirmed by the Senate Armed Services Committee, *Authorization Hearings, Fiscal Year 1982, Department of Defense,* Part 7, page 3803. The date for completion of *Tomahawk* GLCM deployment is from the House Armed Services Committee, *Authorization Hearings, Fiscal Year 1982, Department of Energy,* page 45. According to the Department of Defense, *op. cit.,* page VII-13, deployment of 108 *Pershing II* missiles will be completed by 1986.

Figures given here are for the *minimum* numbers of missiles that may be fired as first rounds from available launchers. Larger numbers of both missile types are being produced, some of them to serve as reloads. According to the House Appropriations Committee, *Hearings, Defense De-*

partment Appropriations, Fiscal Year 1982, Part 3, page 592, a total of 565 *Tomahawk* GLCMs will be produced. According to the House Armed Services Committee, *Authorization Hearings, Fiscal Year 1983, Department of Defense,* Part 3, pages 762 and 764, a total of 384 *Pershing IIs* will be produced, 228 of them as first rounds, reloads, and spares. According to the House Appropriations Committee *Hearings, Defense Department Appropriations, Fiscal Year 1983,* Part 4, page 431, the 9 launchers in each *Pershing II* battery will be supplied with a minimum of 13 missiles. In that case, at least 156 *Pershing II* missiles, and possibly as many as 228, will accompany the 108 launchers comprising the 12 batteries of the 56th Field Artillery Brigade stationed in West Germany.

Tomahawk GLCM and *Pershing II* launchers have been planned for deployment at the following locations:

Tomahawk GLCM

Country	Base Location	Launchers	Missiles
West Germany	Wueschein	24	96
United Kingdom	RAF Greenham Common	24	96
United Kingdom	RAF Molesworth	16	64
Italy	Comiso	28	112
Belgium	Florennes	12	48
Netherlands	Woensdrecht	12	48
	Totals:	116	464

Pershing II

Country	Base Location	Launchers	Missiles
West Germany	Swaebisch Gmuend	36	36
West Germany	Neckars Ulm	36	36
West Germany	Neu Ulm	36	36
	Totals:	108	108

Deployment Schedule and Minimum Deployment Capacity
BGM-109 T-ALM/N (*Tomahawk* Land-Attack Missile/Nuclear) SLCM (*Sea-Launched Cruise Missile*) with 1 × W-80 Nuclear Warhead

Vessel Type and Class	Launch System (Number)	Minimum T-ALM/Ns per Launcher	1984			1985			1990		
			Vessels Fitted	T-ALM/Ns Each Vessel	Total	Vessels Fitted	T-ALM/Ns Each Vessel	Total	Vessels Fitted	T-ALM/Ns Each Vessel	Total
Submarines											
SSN-594 *Permit*	Torpedo Tubes (8)	1				13	8	104	13	8	104
SSN-637 *Sturgeon*	Torpedo Tubes (8)	1	1	8	8						
SSN-637 *Sturgeon*	Torpedo Tubes (8) and Vertical Launch System (1)	1									
		12				22	20	440	22	20	440
SSN-688 *Los Angeles*	Torpedo Tubes (8)	1	22	8	176	3	8	24	25	8	200
SSN-688 *Los Angeles*	Torpedo Tubes (8) and Vertical Launch System (1)	1									
		12	1	20	20	31	20	620	31	20	620
Battleships											
BB-61 *Iowa*	Armored Box Launcher (8)	4	2	32	64	2	32	64			
BB-61 *Iowa*	Ex41 Vertical Launch System (1)	8				1	8	8	4	8	32
Cruisers											
CGN-9 *Long Beach*	Armored Box Launcher (4)	4	1	16	16	1	16	16	1	16	16

(continued)

Deployment Schedule and Minimum Deployment Capacity
BGM-109 T-ALM/N (Tomahawk Land-Attack Missile/Nuclear) SLCM (Sea-Launched Cruise Missile) with 1 × W-80 Nuclear Warhead (cont.)

Vessel Type and Class	Launch System (Number)	Minimum T-ALM/Ns per Launcher	1984			1985			1990		
				T-ALM/Ns			T-ALM/Ns			T-ALM/Ns	
			Vessels Fitted	Each Vessel	Total	Vessels Fitted	Each Vessel	Total	Vessels Fitted	Each Vessel	Total
Cruisers											
CGN-36 California	Ex41 Vertical Launch System (2)	8				2	16	32	2	16	32
CGN-38 Virginia	Ex41 Vertical Launch System (2)	8							4	16	64
CG-47 Ticonderoga	Ex41 Vertical Launch System (3)	8							20	24	480
Destroyers											
DD-963 Spruance	Armored Box Launcher (1)	4	1	4	4						
DD-963 Spruance	Ex41 Vertical Launch System (2)	8				24	16	384	31	16	496
DDG-51 Burke	Ex41 Vertical Launch System (1)	8							60	8	480
Minimum Total T-ALM/N Launch Capacity:					288			1692			2964

Sources and Method

Date for the initial deployment of T-ALM/Ns in June, 1984, is from the Senate Armed Services Committee, *Authorization Hearings, Fiscal Year 1983, Department of Defense*, Part 7, page 4517, and Department of Defense, *Fiscal Year 1983 Program of Research, Development and Acquisition*, page VII-8. Initial T-ALM/N deployment on that date in torpedo tubes of *Los Angeles* class attack submarines and in armored box launchers aboard *Iowa* class battleships is confirmed by the Senate Armed Services Committee, *Authorization Hearings, Fiscal Year 1982, Department of Defense*, Part 7, page 4088; by the Department of Defense, *Fiscal Year 1984 Annual Report*, page 144; by Thomas B. Cochran, William M. Arkin, and Milton M. Hoenig, *Nuclear Weapons Databook:* Volume I (Cambridge, Mass.: Ballinger, 1984), pages 185–186, 245–246, 247, 249, and 256; by Wayne Biddle, "Amid Congress Debate, Navy Gets Cruise Missiles," *The New York Times*, June 28, 1964; and by Michael A. Lerner, Mary Lord, and Ron LaBrecque, "The Cruise Makes Its Debut," *Newsweek*, January 3, 1983, page 13.

A total of 4086 *Tomahawk* SLCMs is planned for production (see Cochran, Arkin, and Hoenig, *op. cit.*, page 186). According to Michael Getler in *The Washington Post*, January 19, 1983, a total of 1000 of these will be T-ALM/Ns with nuclear warheads. According to *The Philadelphia Inquirer*, December 4, 1981, a total of 384 T-ALM/Ns is planned for deployment. According to *The Philadelphia Inquirer*, December 4, 1981, a total of 384 T-ALM/Ns is planned for deployment. If these figures are correct, then by 1985 the capacity to launch T-ALM/Ns estimated here already exceeded the number of T-ALM/Ns actually planned for deployment. The excess capacity would accommodate the large number of SLCMs that is certainly also being deployed armed with conventional, nonnuclear warheads.

The launch capacity for T-ALM/Ns estimated here is a *minimum* launch capacity, based not on the total of T-ALM/Ns which the United States fleet theoretically could carry, but on the much smaller number of such missiles its vessels would most likely be able to fire as first rounds. Aside from torpedoes, attack submarines may carry a variety of missiles that can be fired from torpedo tubes, including SUBROCs and *Harpoons* as well as SLCMs. Some might carry more than 20 SLCMs, but 20 are all that even

a submarine fitted with vertical launch tubes could fire as first rounds, using all available launch and torpedo tubes. Aboard surface combatants, armored box launchers accommodate 8 missiles as first rounds, and the Ex-41 Vertical Launch System now being fitted accommodates 61. These ships can carry many more missiles as reloads. *Aviation Week & Space Technology*, March 2, 1981, page 15, estimates that battleships could carry as many as 320 to 400 missiles. But these missiles, whether stored or ready for launch, are a mix of several types, all compatible with the same launchers, including ASROCs, *Harpoons*, *Standard-2s*, and *Tomahawk* SLCMs. According to Cochran, Arkin, and Hoenig, *op. cit.*, page 186, the normal operational mix of missiles loaded in the Ex-41 Vertical Launch System would include 8 SLCMs. According to the House Armed Services Committee, *Authorization Hearings, Fiscal Year 1982, Department of Defense*, Part 3, page 107, the normal operational loadings on each of the 8 armored box launchers fitted aboard an *Iowa* class battleship would include 4 SLCMs. These parameters are followed here, and applied to all classes of naval vessels.

It must further be kept in mind that not all of the SLCMs assumed here as normal operational loadings are necessarily T-ALM/Ns. Yet they *may* be. By 1985, then, the United States fleet was already able to launch as first rounds either 384 T-ALM/Ns, if that figure is accepted as the maximum number ever to be deployed, or 1000 T-ALM/Ns, if that figure is accepted as the maximum number ever to be produced and consequently deployed, or 1692 T-ALM/Ns, if both those assumptions are discarded and the number of deliverable T-ALM/Ns is assumed to be limited only by the capacity to deliver them shown here.

Though there are 37 boats in the SSN-637 *Sturgeon* class of attack submarine, T-ALM/Ns will be deployed in vertical launch systems aboard only 22 of them, according to the Senate Armed Services Committee, *Authorization Hearings, Fiscal Year 1983, Department of Defense*, Part 6, page 4043, and Cochran, Arkin, and Hoenig, *op. cit.*, page 186, table 6.6, note 6. One of these, SSN-665 *USS Guitarro*, was a test platform for SLCMs in 1983, as was a single *Spruance* class destroyer, DD-976 *USS Merrill*, using an armored box launcher. (See Cochran, Arkin, and Hoenig, *op. cit.*, page

(continued)

Deployment Schedule and Minimum Deployment Capacity
BGM-109 T-ALM/N (*Tomahawk* Land-Attack Missile/Nuclear) SLCM (Sea-Launched Cruise Missile) with 1 × W-80 Nuclear Warhead *(cont.)*

185, and Norman Polmar, *The Ships and Aircraft of the U.S. Fleet* [12th ed., Annapolis, Md.: Naval Institute Press, 1983], page 92.) The first *Los Angeles* class attack submarine fitted with vertical launch tubes was SSN-719 *USS Providence*, commissioned in August, 1984 (see *United States Naval Institute Proceedings* [January 1985], page 140, and Senate Armed Services Committee, *Authorization Hearings, Fiscal Year 1983, Department of Defense,* Part 2, page 1063). Though 56 boats are planned in this class (Senate Armed Services Committee, *op. cit., Fiscal Year 1983,* Part 6, page 4043), only 31 will be fitted with vertical launch tubes, including SSN-719 and all boats constructed thereafter (Department of Defense, *Fiscal Year 1984 Annual Report,* page 144), as well as six earlier boats retrofitted.

Battleships initially deployed in 1984 with T-ALM/Ns in armored box launchers are BB-61 *Iowa* and BB-62 *New Jersey*. They will eventually be refitted with the Ex-41 Vertical Launch System, as will be BB-63 *Missouri* and BB-64 *Wisconsin*. According to Norman Polmar, *op. cit.*, 1983, page 92, CGN-9 *Long Beach*, "after her modernization in the early 1980s," has been fitted with "*Tomahawk* launchers aft." According to *Weyer's Warships of the World, 1982–1983* (Annapolis, Md.: Nautical and Aviation Publishing, 1981), page 535, the *Long Beach* has been fitted with 4 launchers for the *Standard ER* missile. The *Tomahawk* and *Standard* launchers must then be the same box launchers compatible with both missiles. The capacity to launch T-ALM/Ns from 4 armored box launchers on the *Long Beach* is accordingly reflected here.

The *California* and *Virginia* class cruisers being fitted with 2 Ex-41 Vertical Launch Systems each are CGN-36 *California,* CGN-37 *South Carolina,* CGN-38 *Virginia,* CGN-39 *Texas,* CGN-40 *Mississippi,* and CGN-41 *Arkansas* (see Polmar, *op cit.,* 1983, pages 75 and 77; and Cochran, Arkin, and Hoenig, *op. cit.,* pages 185 and 186). The first five CG-47 *Ticonderoga* class cruisers will not be fitted with Ex-41 Vertical Launch Systems (see Department of Defense, *Fiscal Year 1984 Annual Report,* page 144), but all those constructed thereafter will be fitted with 3 such launch systems each (see Cochran, Arkin, and Hoenig, *op. cit.,* page 186, table 6.6). The keel for the first of these, CG-52, was laid by Ingalls in January, 1984 (*United States Naval Institute Proceedings* [January, 1985], page 140), and it is expected to be in service by 1988.

All DD-963 *Spruance* class destroyers are being retrofitted with 2 Ex-41 Vertical Launch Systems each (see Polmar, *op. cit.,* 1983, page 104, and Department of Defense, *Fiscal Year 1984 Annual Report,* page 144). All DDG-51 *Burke* class destroyers will be fitted with one Ex-41 Vertical Launch System, providing 61 launch tubes, and possibly a smaller system with 29 launch tubes aft as well (see Polmar, *op. cit.,* 1983, page 93, and Department of Defense, *Fiscal Year 1984 Annual Report,* page 144). The minimum capacity expected is reflected here.

Estimated Composition of American and Soviet Strategic Forces—1984

Soviet Union				United States			
Missile or Aircraft Type	Number	Warheads on Each	Total Warheads	Missile or Aircraft Type	Number	Warheads on Each	Total Warheads
SS-11	520	1	520	*Titan II*	49	1	49
SS-13	60	1	60	*Minuteman II*	400	1	400
SS-17 Mod 1	140	4	560	*Minuteman III*	600	3	1800
SS-17 Mod 2	10	1	10	*Poseidon C-3*	304	14	4256
SS-18 Mod 1	30	1	30	*Trident C-4*	264	8	2112
SS-18 Mod 2	208	8	1664	FB-111A			
SS-18 Mod 3	30	1	30	*4 × SRAM*			
SS-18 Mod 4	40	10	400	*and 2 × B-61*	56	6	336
SS-19 Mod 1	300	6	1800	B-52D			
SS-19 Mod 2	60	1	60	*4 × NGB*	31	4	124
SS-N-5	48	1	48	B-52G			
SS-N-6	384	1	384	*4 × NGB*	77	4	308
SS-N-8	292	1	292	B-52G			
SS-N-17	12	1	12	*4 × SRAM*			
SS-N-18 Mod 1	112	3	336	*and 4 × NGB*	42	8	336
SS-N-18 Mod 3	112	7	784	B-52G			
SS-N-20	20	9	180	*12 × ALCM*			
Tu-95A				*8 × SRAM*			
1 × AS-3	70	1	70	*and 4 × B-61*	32	24	768
Tu-95A				B-52H			
2 × NGB	30	2	60	*12 × ALCM*			
MYA-4				*8 × SRAM*			
2 × NGB	35	2	70	*and 4 × B-61*	28	24	672
				B-52H			
				4 × SRAM			
				and 4 × NGB	62	8	496
						TOTAL:	11,657
				Pershing II	36	1	36
				Tomahawk GLCM	96	1	96
				Tomahawk SLCM	288	1	288
		TOTAL:	7370			GRAND TOTAL	12,077

NGB: Nuclear Gravity Bomb.
SRAM: Short-Range Attack Missile.
ALCM: Air-Launched Cruise Missile.
GLCM: Ground-Launched Cruise Missile.
SLCM: Sea-Launched Cruise Missile.

Estimated Composition of American and Soviet Strategic Forces—1985

Soviet Union				United States			
Missile or Aircraft Type	Number	Warheads on Each	Total Warheads	Missile or Aircraft Type	Number	Warheads on Each	Total Warheads
SS-11	470	1	470	Titan II	37	1	37
SS-13	60	1	60	Minuteman II	400	1	400
SS-17 Mod 1	140	4	560	Minuteman III	600	3	1800
SS-17 Mod 2	10	1	10	Poseidon C-3	304	14	4256
SS-18 Mod 1	30	1	30	Trident C-4	288	8	2304
SS-18 Mod 2	198	8	1584	FB-111A			
SS-18 Mod 3	30	1	30	4 × SRAM			
SS-18 Mod 4	50	10	500	and 2 × B-61	56	6	336
SS-19 Mod 1	350	6	2100	B-52G			
SS-19 Mod 2	60	1	60	4 × NGB	29	4	116
SS-N-5	45	1	45	B-52G			
SS-N-6	368	1	368	12 × ALCM			
SS-N-8	292	1	292	8 × SRAM			
SS-N-17	12	1	12	and 4 × B-61	60	24	1440
SS-N-18 Mod 1	96	3	288	B-52H			
SS-N-18 Mod 3	128	7	896	12 × ALCM			
SS-N-20	40	9	360	8 × SRAM			
Tu-95A				and 4 × B-61	28	24	672
1 × AS-3	70	1	70	B-52H			
Tu-95A				4 × SRAM			
2 × NGB	30	2	60	and 4 × NGB	62	8	496
MYA-4							
2 × NGB	35	2	70			TOTAL:	11,857
				Pershing II	48	1	48
				Tomahawk GLCM	160	1	160
				Tomahawk SLCM	384	1	384
		TOTAL:	7865			GRAND TOTAL:	12,449

NGB: Nuclear Gravity Bomb.
SRAM: Short-range Attack Missile.
ALCM: Air-Launched Cruise Missile.
GLCM: Ground-Launched Cruise Missile.
SLCM: Sea-Launched Cruise Missile.

Sources

The changing composition of Soviet and American strategic forces shown here in 1984 and 1985 is based on rates of conversion and force modernization established in the three preceding sections estimating the strategic balance from 1979 through 1983. For the most part, it is confirmed by sources provided for the tables in those sections, and reflects the consensus those sources reach on the following points:

- That no fewer Soviet ICBMs than shown here remained fitted with a single warhead.
- That conversion of the Soviet SS-18 Mod 2 ICBM with 8 warheads to the Mod 4 version of the SS-18 with 10 warheads proceeded no more quickly than at the rate shown.
- That conversion of the Soviet SS-N-18 Mod 1 SLBM with 3 warheads to the Mod 3 version of the SS-N-18 with 7 warheads proceeded no more quickly than at the rate shown.
- That Soviet Tu-22M *Backfire* aircraft are neither equipped nor deployed as intercontinental strategic bombers.
- That Soviet aircraft deployed as intercontinental strategic bombers, but not fitted with the AS-3 air-to-surface missile, carry no more than 2 nuclear gravity bombs each.
- That the count of America's aircraft equipped and deployed as intercontinental strategic bombers should be limited to Primary Authorized Airvehicles of the Strategic Air Command, rather than including all operational B-52 and FB-111A aircraft available.
- That the count of weapons carried by America's strategic bombers should be limited to the normal operational loadings shown, rather than reflecting their full deliverable weapons capacity.

However, the following changes in Soviet strategic force structure are documented by the new sources shown:

- Conversion of the Soviet SS-11 ICBM with a single warhead to the Mod 1 version of the SS-19 with 6 warheads is proceeding more rapidly than at previous rates. For the numbers of SS-11s and SS-19s deployed in 1984, see the International Institute for Strategic Studies (IISS), *The Military Balance, 1984–1985,* page 133. The same higher rate of conversion is assumed for 1985.
- Some Soviet SS-N-5 and SS-N-6 SLBMs have been withdrawn, with the retirement of one *Yankee I* and one *Hotel II* class submarine. For the numbers of SS-N-5 and SS-N-6 missiles remaining deployed at the end of 1984, see IISS, *op. cit.,* 1984–1985, page 134.
- Soviet SS-N-20 SLBMs are now deployed, with the introduction of the first *Typhoon* class submarine at the end of 1983, and of another in 1984. For the number of SS-N-20 missiles deployed at the end of 1984, see IISS, *op. cit.,* 1984–1985, pages 17 and 134.

The following changes in America's strategic force structure are documented by the new sources shown:

- The introduction of two more *Trident* submarines, SSBN-729 *Georgia* in February, 1984, and SSBN-730 *Henry M. Jackson* in October, 1984, adding 48 more *Trident C-4* missiles with 384 warheads to the SLBM force. See *United States Naval Institute Proceedings* (January, 1985), page 140.
- Deployment of ALCMs on B-52H bombers of the 46th Bomb Squadron, 319th Bomb Wing, Grand Forks Air Force Base, North Dakota, 1983, and on B-52Hs of the 77th Bomb Squadron, 28th Bomb Wing, Ellsworth Air Force Base, South Dakota, in January, 1984. See Cochran, Arkin, and Hoenig, *Nuclear Weapons Databook: Volume I* (Cambridge, Mass.: Ballinger, 1984), pages 86 and 176; and Chris Pocock and Colin Smith, *The USAF Today* (London: West London Aviation Group, 1975), pages 49 to 51.
- Deployment of ALCMs on B-52G bombers of the 340th Bomb Squadron, 97th Bomb Wing, Blytheville Air Force Base, Arkansas, and on B-52Gs of the 92nd Bomb Squadron, 92nd Bomb Wing, Fairchild Air Force Base, Washington, D.C., in late 1984. See Senate Armed Services Committee, *Authorization Hearings, Fiscal Year 1982, Department of Defense,* Part 7, page 4291; Cochran, Arkin, and Hoenig, *op. cit.,* pages 86 and 176; and Pocock and Smith, *op. cit.,* pages 49 to 51.
- The replacement of 50 *Minuteman II* missiles of the 341st Strategic Missile Wing, Malmstrom Air Force Base, Montana, with 50 *Minuteman IIIs* in December, 1983, reducing the *Minuteman II* force to 400 missiles and raising the *Minuteman III* force to 600 missiles, with a net increase of 100 warheads to the ICBM force. See Joint Chiefs of Staff, *Fiscal Year 1983 Posture Statement,*

Estimated Composition of American and Soviet Strategic Forces—1985 *(cont.)*

page 72; and Clarence A. Robinson, Jr., "Emphasis Grows on Nuclear Defense," *Aviation Week & Space Technology,* March 8, 1982, page 27.

- The introduction of *Pershing II* and *Tomahawk* GLCMs (Ground-Launched Cruise Missiles) in Europe in December, 1983, and the continuing deployment of those missiles in 1984 and 1985. See sources for the preceding table, *Deployment Schedule and Minimum Deployment Capacity, BGM-109* Tomahawk *GLCM and* Pershing II *MRBM.*
- The introduction of *Tomahawk* SLCMs (Sea-Launched Cruise Missiles) on battleships and nuclear attack submarines of America's fleet in June 1984, and the continuing deployment of those missiles and of launchers accommodating them in 1985. See sources for the preceding table, *Deployment Schedule and Minimum Deployment Capacity, BGM-109 T-ALM/N (Tomahawk Land-Attack Missile/Nuclear)/SLCM.*

Recapitulation: The Balance of Strategic Warheads,
Missile Warheads Only, 1979–85

Date	Soviet Union			United States		
	ICBMs	SLBMs	Total	ICBMs	SLBMs	Total
December 1979	3974	1289	5263	2154	6048	8202
June 1980	4159	1337	5496	2154	5920	8074
December 1980	4324	1385	5709	2154	5776	7930
June 1981	4554	1449	6003	2154	5712	7866
December 1981	4689	1513	6202	2153	5648	7801
June 1982	4744	1577	6321	2153	6080	8233
December 1982	4804	1641	6445	2152	6272	8424
June 1983	4864	1705	6569	2149	6176	8325
August 1984	5134	2036	7170	2249	6368	8617
August 1985	5404	2261	7665	2237	6560	8797

Recapitulation: The Balance of Deliverable Strategic Warheads,
Including Aircraft Weapons, 1979–85

Date	Soviet Union			United States				
	Missiles	Aircraft	Maximum Total	Missiles	Aircraft	Minimum Total	Adding SLCMs and Euro-missiles	Adding Maximum Aircraft Loads
December 1979	5263	200	5463	8202	2464	10,666		12,128
June 1980	5496	200	5696	8074	2464	10,538		11,988
December 1980	5709	200	5909	7930	2464	10,394		11,844
June 1981	6003	200	6203	7866	2464	10,330		11,770
December 1981	6202	200	6402	7801	2476	10,277		11,717
June 1982	6321	200	6521	8233	2500	10,733		12,169
December 1982	6445	200	6645	8424	2456	10,880		12,316
June 1983	6569	200	6769	8325	2648	10,973		12,409
August 1984	7170	200	7370	8617	3040	11,657	12,077	13,513
August 1985	7665	200	7865	8797	3060	11,857	12,449	13,761

Appendix B

The Strategic Balance:
A Chronology of Estimates

This appendix contains a collection of estimates made of Soviet and American land-based and sea-based missile warheads, bombers, and bomber weapons from 1979 through 1983. These estimates have been drawn from a variety of sources, some of them official and many in the private sector. Of those in the private sector, some were research institutes specializing in military affairs. Others were independent authorities. Many were news media. All were influential in shaping public opinion.

Sources are abbreviated in the following tables, but fully identified at the end of this section.

These estimates are also compared with the author's estimates for concurrent inventory levels, arrived at by the methods shown in the previous section. Substantial differences between the author's estimates and those cited here are frequently apparent. These discrepancies are fully examined, and their principal causes identified, in Part I of this book, *The Myth of Soviet Strategic Superiority.*

It is apparent, from a sequential review of the estimates quoted, how quickly and frequently official estimates were repeated by other sources. It is also apparent which sources regularly took the lead in repeating official estimates. For example, after the Reagan administration raised the official count of Soviet missile warheads from 6,300 to 7,500 within the space of a single week in May, 1982, *The New York Times,* which had reported the lower figure on May 2, reported the higher figure on May 16, and quoted the higher figure thereafter. So did NBC. When the administration reduced the official count of America's missile warheads to 7,100 in November, 1982, without offering any explanation for the reduction, *The New York Times* and *The Washington Post* immediately reported the new figure without challenging it.

These estimates are followed by a longer chronology of estimates of the balance of deliverable strategic warheads since 1950.

TABLES IN THIS SECTION

- Chronology of Estimates of United States Missile Warheads, 1979–83
- Chronology of Estimates of Soviet Missile Warheads, 1979–83
- Chronology of Comparative Estimates of American and Soviet Missile Warheads, 1979–83
- Chronology of Estimates of United States Strategic Bombers, 1979–83
- Chronology of Estimates of United States Strategic Bomber Weapons, 1979–83
- United States Strategic Bombers: Analysis of Sources, 1979–83
- Chronology of Estimates of Soviet Strategic Bombers and Bomber Weapons, 1979–83
- Soviet Strategic Bombers and Bomber Weapons: Analysis of Sources, 1979–83
- Chronology of Comparative Estimates of American and Soviet Strategic Warheads, Including Aircraft Weapons, 1979–83
- Sources for Estimates of Warheads and Delivery Vehicles Quoted, 1979–83
- A Chronology of Estimates of the Balance of Deliverable Strategic Warheads, 1950–85

Chronology of Estimates of United States Missile Warheads, 1979–83

Date	Source	Estimate			Author's Total at Time of Estimate	Discrepancy
		On ICBMs	On SLBMs	Total		
Feb. 1979	Aspin	2154	5120	7274	8202	(−) 928
July 1979	JCS	2152	4600	6752	8202	(−) 1450
Dec. 1979	Collins	2154	5120	7274	8202	(−) 928
Jan. 1980	Kaplan	2154	4608	6762	8202	(−) 1440
Jan. 1980	DOD	2152	4600	6752	8202	(−) 1450
Sept. 1980	SIPRI	2152	5120	7272	7930	(−) 658
Dec. 1980	IISS			7301	7930	(−) 629
Jan. 1981	Pincus	2152	4656	6808	7930	(−) 1122
Mar. 1981	Heylin	2152	4880	7032	7930	(−) 898
June 1981	CBS-TV (B)	2152	4448	6600	7866	(−) 1266
June 1981	CBS-TV (T)	2152	4000	6152	7866	(−) 1714
Mar. 1982	*NY Times*	2152	4750	6902	8233	(−) 1331
Apr. 1982	*NY Times*	2152	4750	6902	8233	(−) 1331
May 1982	DOD/*NY Times*	2150	5050	7200	8233	(−) 1033
May 1982	Reagan admin	2150	5300	7450	8233	(−) 783
May 1982	*NY Times*	2100	5400	7500	8233	(−) 733
June 1982	*NY Times*	2100	5400	7500	8233	(−) 733
June 1982	NBC-TV	2150	5300	7450	8233	(−) 783
June 1982	SIPRI	2152	4800	6952	8233	(−) 1281
Nov. 1982	Forsberg	2152	4768	6920	8424	(−) 1504
Nov. 1982	*Wash. Post*	2100	5000	7100	8424	(−) 1324
Nov. 1982	*NY Times*	2100	5000	7100	8424	(−) 1324
Dec. 1982	*NY Times*			7100	8424	(−) 1324
Dec. 1982	Cordesman	2152	4656	6808	8424	(−) 1616
Dec. 1982	IISS	2152	4768	6920	8424	(−) 1504
Jan. 1983	*Newsweek*			7200	8424	(−) 1224
Jan. 1983	Cochran	2152	4960	7112	8424	(−) 1312
Feb. 1983	Cordesman	2152	4768	6920	8424	(−) 1504
July 1983	Harvard	2150	5000	7150	8325	(−) 1175

Sources

For sources, see page 349.

Chronology of Estimates of Soviet Missile Warheads, 1979–83

Date	Source	Estimate			Author's Total at Time of Estimate			Discrepancy
		On ICBMs	On SLBMs	Total	On ICBMs	On SLBMs	Total	
Feb. 1979	Aspin	3310	926	4236	3974	1289	5263	(−) 1027
July 1979	JCS	3500	1250	4750	3974	1289	5263	(−) 513
Dec. 1979	Collins	4306	1309	5615	3974	1289	5263	(+) 352
Jan. 1980	Kaplan	4490	1267	5757	3974	1289	5263	(+) 494
Jan. 1980	DOD	4500	1200	5700	3974	1289	5263	(+) 437
Sept. 1980	SIPRI	5028	1238	6266	4324	1385	5709	(+) 557
Dec. 1980	IISS			6000			5709	(+) 291
Jan. 1981	Pincus	5354	1334	6688	4324	1385	5709	(+) 979
Mar. 1981	Heylin	5500	1334	6834	4324	1385	5709	(+) 1125
June 1981	CBS-TV (B)	5000	700	5700	4554	1449	6003	(−) 303
June 1981	CBS-TV (T)	5000	1000	6000	4554	1449	6003	(−) 3
Mar. 1982	NY Times	5500	1900	7400	4744	1577	6321	(+) 1079
Apr. 1982	NY Times	5500	1900	7400	4744	1577	6321	(+) 1079
May 1982	DOD/NY Times			6300			6321	(−) 21
May 1982	Reagan admin	5500	1900	7400	4744		6321	(+) 1079
May 1982	NY Times	5100	2400	7500	4744	1577	6321	(+) 1179
June 1982	NY Times	5100	2400	7500	4744	1577	6321	(+) 1179
June 1982	NBC-TV	5500	1900	7400	4744	1577	6321	(+) 1079
June 1982	SIPRI	5804	1462	7266	4744	1577	6321	(+) 945
Nov. 1982	Forsberg	4904	1498	6398	4804	1641	6445	(−) 47
Nov. 1982	Wash. Post	6000	1500	7500	4804	1641	6445	(+) 1055
Nov. 1982	NY Times	6000	1500	7500	4804	1641	6445	(+) 1055
Dec. 1982	Cordesman	5158	2554	7712	4804	1641	6445	(+) 1267
Dec. 1982	IISS	5230	1809	7039	4804	1641	6445	(+) 594
Jan. 1983	Newsweek			7500			6445	(+) 1055
Feb. 1983	Cordesman	5230	1809	7039	4804	1641	6445	(+) 594
Apr. 1983	Reagan			8700			6569	(+) 2131
July 1983	Harvard	5900	1600	7500	4864	1705	6569	(+) 931

Sources

For sources, see page 349.

Chronology of Comparative Estimates of American and Soviet Missile Warheads, 1979–83

Date	Source	USA	USSR	US Lead	Soviet Lead	USA	USSR	US Lead
		Estimate				Author's Total at Time of Estimate		
Feb. 1979	Aspin	7274	4236	3038		8202	5263	2929
July 1979	JCS	6752	4750	2002		8202	5263	2929
Dec. 1979	Collins	7274	5615	1659		8202	5263	2929
Jan. 1980	Kaplan	6762	5757	1005		8202	5263	2929
Jan. 1980	DOD	6752	5700	1052		8202	5263	2929
Sept. 1980	SIPRI	7272	6266	1006		7930	5709	2221
Dec. 1980	IISS	7301	6000	1301		7930	5709	2221
Jan. 1981	Pincus	6808	6688	120		7930	5709	2221
Mar. 1981	Heylin	7032	6834	198		7930	5709	2221
June 1981	CBS-TV (B)	6600	5700	900		7866	6003	1863
June 1981	CBS-TV (T)	6152	6000	152		7866	6003	1863
Mar. 1982	*NY Times*	6902	7400		498	8233	6321	1912
Apr. 1982	*NY Times*	6902	7400		498	8233	6321	1912
May 1982	DOD/*NY Times*	7200	6300	900		8233	6321	1912
May 1982	Reagan admin	7450	7500		50	8233	6321	1912
May 1982	*NY Times*	7500	7500			8233	6321	1912
June 1982	*NY Times*	7500	7500			8233	6321	1912
June 1982	NBC-TV	7450	7400	50		8233	6321	1912
June 1982	SIPRI	6952	7266		314	8233	6321	1912
Nov. 1982	Forsberg	6920	6398	522		8424	6445	1979
Nov. 1982	*Wash. Post*	7100	7500		400	8424	6445	1979
Nov. 1982	*NY Times*	7100	7500		400	8424	6445	1979
Dec. 1982	Cordesman	6808	7712		1104	8424	6445	1979
Dec. 1982	IISS	6920	7039		119	8424	6445	1979
Jan. 1983	*Newsweek*	7200	7500		300	8424	6445	1979
Feb. 1983	Cordesman	6920	7039		119	8424	6445	1979
July 1983	Harvard	7150	7500		350	8325	6569	1756

Sources

For sources, see page 349.

Chronology of Estimates of United States Strategic Bombers, 1979–83

Date	Source	Estimate			Remarks on Method
		B-52	FB-111A	Total	
Feb. 1979	Aspin	348	0	348	Counts operational B-52s but excludes FB-111As.
Dec. 1979	Collins	316	60	376	Includes FB-111As but counts only authorized aircraft.
Jan. 1980	Kaplan	348	66	414	Overcounts FB-111As by 1.
Sept. 1980	SIPRI	340	0	340	Excludes FB-111As and undercounts operational B-52s by 8.
Jan. 1981	Pincus			345	Excludes FB-111As and undercounts operational B-52s by 3.
June 1981	CBS-TV			350	Excludes FB-111As and overcounts operational B-52s, whose number had dropped to 347.
Mar. 1982	*NY Times*			316	Excludes FB-111As, and counts only authorized B-52s.
Apr. 1982	*NY Times*	316	60	376	Now adds FB-111As but still counts only authorized B-52s.
May 1982	DOD			400	Counts all but 3 operational aircraft, 28 more than authorized at that time. Includes FB-111As.
June 1982	*NY Times*			400	Follows DOD count of all operational aircraft.
June 1982	SIPRI	347	0	347	Excludes FB-111As and overcounts operational B-52s, whose number had dropped from 347 to 343.
Nov. 1982	Forsberg	330	60	390	Does not yet reflect retirement of 44 B-52Ds, and undercounts remaining operational aircraft by 13.
Nov. 1982	*Wash. Post*	347	63	410	Does not yet reflect retirement of 44 B-52Ds, and overcounts remaining operational B-52s by 4, FB-111As by 3.
Dec. 1982	Cordesman	332	0	332	Excludes FB-111As. Does not yet reflect retirement of 44 B-52Ds, and undercounts remaining operational B-52s by 11.
Dec. 1982	IISS	316	60	376	Includes FB-111As but counts only authorized B-52s. Does not yet reflect retirement of 44 B-52Ds.
Jan. 1983	Cochran	272	60	332	Counts only authorized B-52s.

Date	Source	Estimate B-52	Estimate FB-111A	Estimate Total	Remarks on Method
Feb. 1983	Cordesman	316	60	376	Now includes FB-111As, following IISS count.
May 1983	CBO	241	56	297	Excludes remaining 31 B-52Ds and counts only authorized aircraft.

Sources   For sources, see page 349.

Chronology of Estimates of United States Strategic Bomber Weapons, 1979–83

Date	Source	Estimate	Author's Estimated Capacity at Time of Estimate Minimum	Author's Estimated Capacity at Time of Estimate / Deliverable	Discrepancies from Capacity From Minimum	Discrepancies from Capacity From Deliverable
Feb. 1979	Aspin	2892	2464	3926	(+) 428	(−) 1034
July 1979	JCS	2392	2464	3926	(−) 72	(−) 1534
Dec. 1979	Collins	1926	2464	3926	(−) 538	(−) 2000
Jan. 1980	Kaplan	2732	2464	3926	(+) 268	(−) 1194
Jan. 1980	DOD	2392	2464	3926	(−) 72	(−) 1534
Sept. 1980	SIPRI	2560	2464	3914	(+) 96	(−) 1354
Jan. 1981	Pincus	2192	2464	3914	(−) 272	(−) 1722
May 1981	Heylin	1926	2464	3904	(−) 538	(−) 1978
June 1981	CBS-TV	2400	2464	3904	(−) 64	(−) 1504
Mar. 1982	*NY Times*	2500	2464	3904	(+) 36	(−) 1404
May 1982	DOD/*NY Times*	2100	2500	3936	(−) 400	(−) 1836
June 1982	*NY Times*	1500	2500	3936	(−) 1000	(−) 2436
June 1982	NBC-TV	1500	2500	3936	(−) 1000	(−) 2436
June 1982	SIPRI	2588	2500	3936	(+) 88	(−) 1348
Nov. 1982	Forsberg	2580	2456	3892	(+) 124	(−) 1312
Dec. 1982	Cordesman	2698	2456	3892	(+) 242	(−) 1194
Dec. 1982	IISS	2348	2456	3892	(−) 108	(−) 1544
Jan. 1983	Cochran	2580	2456	3892	(+) 124	(−) 1312
May 1983	CBO	3060	2584	4080	(+) 476	(−) 1020
July 1983	Harvard	2750	2584	4080	(+) 166	(−) 1330
Sept. 1983	CDI	2876	2584	4080	(+) 292	(−) 1204

Sources   For sources, see page 349.

United States Strategic Bombers: Analysis of Sources, 1979–83

Sources Reviewed	Sources Including FB-111A in Count	Sources Excluding FB-111A from Count
18	11	7
	Sources Offering a Count of All Operational Aircraft	Sources Offering a Count of Only Authorized Aircraft
	12	6

Chronology of Estimates of Soviet Strategic Bombers and Bomber Weapons, 1979–83

Date	Source	Tu-95A Bear	MYA-4 Bison	Tu-22M Backfire	Total	Total Weapons	Remarks on Method
Feb. 1979	Aspin	100	40	0	140	280	2 weapons to each aircraft.
July 1979	JCS					250	
Dec. 1979	Collins	100	40	60	200	260	Retains similar weapons load and introduces *Backfire* with 2 weapons each by reducing load of other bombers to 1 weapon each.
Jan. 1980	Kaplan	113	43	0	156	312	2 weapons to each aircraft.
Jan. 1980	DOD					300	
Jan. 1981	Pincus			0	156	312	2 weapons to each aircraft.
May 1981	Heylin	100	49	0	149	260	Less than 2 weapons each aircraft.
June 1981	CBS-TV					300	
Mar. 1982	*NY Times*			0	150	600	Would require 4 weapons each aircraft.
May 1982	DOD			(200)	350	900	Must include 200 *Backfire*. Even so, and with 2 weapons to each aircraft, still an excess of 200 weapons.
June 1982	*NY Times*			(200)	350	1000	Follows DOD aircraft count. Could achieve weapons total by giving each *Backfire* 2 weapons, and giving other bombers 4 each, as in March precedent.

Date	Source	Estimate					Remarks on Method
		Tu-95A *Bear*	MYA-4 *Bison*	Tu-22M *Backfire*	Total	Total Weapons	
June 1982	NBC-TV					700	Probably follows DOD aircraft count, but with 2 weapons to each aircraft.
June 1982	SIPRI	100	56	0	156	412	2 weapons to each *Bison*, 3 to each *Bear*.
Nov. 1982	Forsberg	105	49	0	149	259	1 weapon to each *Bison*, 2 to each *Bear*.
Nov. 1982	*Wash. Post*	100	45	200	345		First official inclusion of *Backfire* by statement rather than implication.
Dec. 1982	Cordesman	113	43	0	156	313	1 weapon each to 75 *Bears,* but 4 each to remaining 38. 2 to each *Bison.*
Dec. 1982	IISS	105	45	0	150	300	2 weapons to each aircraft.
Feb. 1983	Cordesman	105	45	0	150	300	Now follows IISS count.
Sept. 1983	CDI	100	45	0	145	290	2 weapons to each aircraft. Notes that including 100 *Backfires* would add 200 weapons.

Sources

For sources, see page 349.

Soviet Strategic Bombers and Bomber Weapons: Analysis of Sources, 1979–83

Sources Reviewed	Sources Reporting Tu-95A *Bear* and MYA-4 *Bison* Only	Sources Reporting Tu-22M *Backfire*
19	14	5
	Sources Reporting 2 Weapons or Less per Aircraft	Sources Reporting over 2 Weapons per Aircraft
	14	5

Chronology of Comparative Estimates of American and Soviet Strategic Warheads, Including Aircraft Weapons, 1979–83

Date	Source	Estimate				Author's Total at Time of Estimate		
		USA	USSR	US Lead	Soviet Lead	USA	USSR	US Lead
Feb. 1979	Aspin	10,166	4500	5666		10,666	5463	5203
July 1979	JCS	9200	5000	4200		10,666	5463	5203
Dec. 1979	Collins	9200	5975	3225		10,666	5463	5203
Jan. 1980	Kaplan	9494	6069	3425		10,666	5463	5203
Jan. 1980	DOD	9200	6000	3200		10,666	5463	5203
Sept. 1980	SIPRI	9200	6000	3200		10,394	5909	4485
Jan. 1981	Pincus	9000	7000	2000		10,394	5909	4485
Mar. 1981	Heylin	10,458	7094	3364		10,394	5909	4485
June 1981	CBS-TV (B)	9000	6000	3000		10,330	6203	4127
June 1981	CBS-TV (T)	8552	6300	2252		10,330	6203	4127
Mar. 1982	*NY Times*	9402	8000	1402		10,733	6521	4212
May 1982	DOD/*NY Times*	9300	7200	2100		10,733	6521	4212
May 1982	*NY Times*	9000	8500	500		10,733	6521	4212
June 1982	NBC-TV	9000	8100	900		10,733	6521	4212
June 1982	SIPRI	9540	7678	1862		10,733	6521	4212
Nov. 1982	Forsberg	9500	6657	2843		10,880	6645	4235
Dec. 1982	Cordesman	9516	8041	1475		10,880	6645	4235
Dec. 1982	*NY Times*	9100	10,000		900	10,880	6645	4235
Dec. 1982	IISS	9268	7300	1968		10,880	6645	4235
Feb. 1983	Cordesman	9268	7300	1968		10,880	6645	4235
July 1983	Harvard	9900	7800	2100		10,973	6769	4204
Sept. 1983	CDI	10,173	7742	2431		10,973	6769	4204

Sources for Estimates of Warheads and Delivery Vehicles Quoted, 1979–83

Date	Source
Oct. 1978	Philip Morrison and Paul F. Walker, "A New Strategy for Military Spending," *Scientific American* (October, 1978), page 54.
Feb. 1979	Representative Les Aspin, "The Verification of the SALT II Agreement," *Scientific American* (February 1979), pages 40 and 41.
July 1979	Chairman of the Joint Chiefs of Staff General David C. Jones, July 11, 1979, in testimony before Congress. Reprinted in *SALT II Senate Testimony, July 9–11, 1979*, Current Policy Bulletin No. 72A, United States Department of State, Bureau of Public Affairs, Washington, D.C., 1979, page 34.
Dec. 1979	John M. Collins, *U.S.-Soviet Military Balance: Concepts and Capabilities, 1960–1980* (New York: McGraw-Hill, 1980), pages 444, 449, 454, 459, and 460.
Jan. 1980	Fred M. Kaplan, *Dubious Specter* (Washington, D.C.: Institute for Policy Studies, 1980), pages 88 and 90.
Jan. 1980	Department of Defense, *Annual Report, Fiscal Year 1981*, Washington, D.C., January 29, 1980, page 89.
Sept. 1980	Stockholm International Peace Research Institute, *World Arms and Disarmament Yearbook, 1980* (Stockholm: Almqvist & Wiksell, 1980), page xxvii.
Sept. 1980	United Nations General Assembly, Thirty-Fifth Session, *General and Complete Disarmament: Comprehensive Study on Nuclear Weapons*, Report of the Secretary General A/35/392, New York, United Nations, 12 September 1980, pages 21–26.
Dec. 1980	International Institute for Strategic Studies, *The Military Balance, 1980–1981* (London: IISS, 1980), pages 3 and 4.
Jan. 1981	Walter Pincus, "The Pincus Plan: Limit Warheads Dramatically," *The Washington Post*, March 21, 1982.
Jan. 1981	Department of Defense, *Annual Report, Fiscal Year 1982*, January, 1981, page 53.
Mar. 1981	Michael Heylin, "Nuclear Arms Race Gearing for Speedup," *Chemical and Engineering News*, March 16, 1981, page 28.
June 1981	CBS-TV, *The Defense of the United States*, June 14, 1981.
June 1981	CBS-TV, *The Defense of the United States*, transcript published September, 1981, pages 10 and 11.
Oct. 1981	Leslie H. Gelb, "Vulnerability Assumes the Soviets Will Strike First," *The New York Times*, October 18, 1981. Source given: Department of Defense.
Mar. 1982	*The New York Times*, "Three Ways to Measure Nuclear Forces," March 21, 1982. Sources given: International Institute for Strategic Studies, United States Air Force, and Defense Department, Center for Defense Information.
Apr. 1982	*The New York Times*, "The Arms Race: United States vs. the Soviet Union in Strategic Weapons," April 2, 1982. No sources given.
May 1982	Defense Department, in testimony before Congress. Published by *The New York Times* in "U.S. and Soviet Strategic Arsenals," May 2, 1982, and reported

(continued)

Sources for Estimates of Warheads and Delivery Vehicles Quoted, 1979–83 *(cont.)*

Date	Source
	again by the *Times* in "Precise Arms Figures Difficult to Pin Down," May 10, 1982. Sources given on May 2: "Pentagon publications, Congressional testimony." Sources given on May 10: "Pentagon Testimony and reports by the International Institute of Strategic Studies."
May 1982	Reagan administration officials, in a briefing before the President's address to the graduating class of Eureka College, Ill., May 9, 1982. Reported by Howell Raines, "President Wants Moscow to Begin Negotiations by the End of June," *The New York Times,* May 10, 1982.
May 1982	*The New York Times,* "Measuring Strategic Arsenals," May 16, 1982. Sources given: "Official U.S. Briefings."
June 1982	*The New York Times,* "The Arms Race: A Balance Sheet," June 29, 1982. Sources listed: "Official U.S. Briefings."
June 1982	NBC-TV, June 10, 1982.
June 1982	Stockholm International Peace Research Institute, *The Arms Race and Arms Control* (London: Taylor & Francis, 1982), page 85.
Nov. 1982	Randall Forsberg, "A Bilateral Nuclear-Weapon Freeze," *Scientific American* (November, 1982), page 54.
Nov. 1982	*The Washington Post,* "Strategic Nuclear Forces as of June 30, 1982," November 24, 1982. Sources listed: "U.S. Government Unclassified Sources."
Nov. 1982	Leslie H. Gelb, "Emphasis Is Likely to Be on Arms, Not Arms Control," *The New York Times,* November 28, 1982. Source given: "U.S. Government Estimates."
Dec. 1982	Anthony H. Cordesman, Jr., "M-X and the Balance of Power: Reasserting America's Strengths," *Armed Forces Journal International* (December, 1982), page 41. Sources given: Estimate by the office of Senator Albert Gore, Jr., August 10, 1982, and IISS, *The Military Balance, 1982–1983,* pages 112–115.
Dec. 1982	International Institute for Strategic Studies, *The Military Balance, 1982–1983,* pages 140 and 141.
Dec. 1982	*The New York Times,* "Nuclear Missiles and Bombers: A Balance Sheet," December 22, 1982. Sources given: International Institute for Strategic Studies, U.S. State Department, and Defense Department.
Jan. 1983	*Newsweek,* "The Negotiating Scorecard," January 31, 1983, page 18. Sources given: International Institute for Strategic Studies, *Jane's Weapon Systems, 1982–1983* (London: 1982).
Jan. 1983	Thomas B. Cochran, William M. Arkin, and Milton M. Hoenig, *Nuclear Weapons Databook: U. S. Nuclear Forces and Capabilities* (Cambridge, Mass.: Ballinger, 1984), page 102.
Feb. 1983	Anthony H. Cordesman, Jr., "Using a Strategy of Fear to Counter a Fear of Strategy," *Armed Forces Journal International* (February, 1983), page 60. Sources given: IISS, *The Military Balance, 1982–1983,* page 140, and *The New York Times,* December 23, 1982.
Apr. 1983	Ronald Reagan, statement on the Report of the President's Commission on Strategic Forces, April 19, 1983. Transcript published by *The New York Times* on April 20, 1983.

Date	Source
May 1983	Congressional Budget Office, *Modernizing U.S. Strategic Offensive Forces,* May, 1983, pages 84, 85, 90, and 91.
July 1983	Harvard Nuclear Study Group, *Living with Nuclear Weapons* (New York: Bantam Books, 1983), page 120.
Sept. 1983	Center for Defense Information, *The Defense Monitor,* Volume XII, No. 7 (September, 1983), page 10.

A Chronology of Estimates of the Balance of Deliverable Strategic Warheads, 1950–85

Year	USA	USSR	Source
1950	1000		*The New York Times,* May 7, 1950.
1951		80	*The New York Times,* June 7, 1951. Maximum figure for USSR.
1953	1000	200	*The New York Times,* December 10, 1953. Maximum figure for USSR.
1954	2000	300	*The New York Times,* February 13, 1954.
1954	3000	400	*The New York Times,* February 13, 1954.
1954	5000	300	Sidney Lens, *The Day Before Doomsday* (1977), page 71.
1955	5000	500	*The New York Times,* February 13, 1955.
1956	7000	2000	*Air Force Magazine,* "Weapons," Volume 40, no. 8 (August, 1957), page 353.
1960	60	100	John M. Collins, *U.S.-Soviet Military Balance,* 1980, page 37. Figures are for missile warheads only. Maximum figure for USSR.
1960	6500	300	SALT II Testimony, Ground Zero, *Nuclear War: What's In It for You,* 1982, page 267.
1961	1830	310	Seymour Melman, *The Permament War Economy* (1974), page 165.
1962	7400	400	SALT II Testimony, *op. cit.,* 1982, page 267.
1964	6800	500	*Ibid.*
1966	5000	550	*Ibid.*
1967	4500	1000	DOD, *Annual Report, FY 1968,* January, 1967.
1967	4000	1000	Robert S. McNamara, *Life* magazine, September 2, 1967, page 28B.
1967	5000	900	Murray Polner, ed., *The Disarmament Catalogue,* 1982, page 15.
1968	4200	1100	DOD, *Annual Report, FY 1969,* January, 1968.
1968	3800	1100	Melman, *op. cit.,* page 165.

(continued)

A Chronology of Estimates of the Balance of Deliverable Strategic Warheads, 1950–85 (*cont.*)

Year	USA	USSR	Source
1968	4200	1200	Sanford Gottlieb, *Ramparts Magazine* (May, 1975), page 20.
1968	4500	850	SALT II Testimony, *op. cit.*, 1982, page 267.
1969	4200	1350	DOD, *Annual Report, FY 1970*, January, 1969.
1969	2600		Herbert Scoville, Jr., *The New Republic*, March 4, 1972.
1969	3950	1659	Les Aspin, *Bulletin of the Atomic Scientists* (June, 1980), page 28.
1969	3950	1659	Anthony H. Cordesman, Jr., *Deterrence in the 1980s: Part I* Adelphi Paper no. 175, 1982, page 48.
1969	4200	1300	Daniel Ford, Henry Kendall, and Steven Nadis, *Beyond the Freeze*, 1982, page 29.
1970	4000	1800	DOD, *Annual Report, FY 1971*, January, 1970.
1970	2500	1700	Ralph E. Lapp, *The New York Times Magazine*, February 1, 1970, page 40.
1970	4200		Steve d'Arazien, *The Nation*, November 16, 1970, page 500.
1970	4000	1800	Center for Defense Information, *The Defense Monitor*, Volume VI, no. 4 (May, 1977), page 7.
1970	4100	1856	John M. Collins, *American and Soviet Military Trends Since the Cuban Missile Crisis*, 1978, page 114.
1970	4000	1800	Stockholm International Peace Research Institute, *World Arms and Disarmament Yearbook, 1979*, page 422.
1970	3900	1800	SALT II Testimony, *op. cit.*, 1982, page 267.
1970	4710		John Edwards, *Super Weapon: The Making of MX*, Norton, 1982, page 89.
1971	4600	2100	DOD, *Annual Report, FY 1972*, January, 1971.
1971	6000	2000	International Institute for Strategic Studies, *The Military Balance, 1970–1971*.
1971	4700	2030	Collins, *op. cit.*, page 114.
1972	5700	2500	DOD, *Annual Report, FY 1973*, January 1972.
1972	4000		Herbert Scoville, Jr., *The New Republic*, May 20, 1972.
1972	5700	2500	Erwin Knoll, *The Progressive* (August, 1972), page 16.
1972	5760	2200	Center for Defense Information, *The Defense Monitor*, Volume III, no. 7, page 1.
1972	5888	2220	J. William Fulbright, *The Progressive* (September, 1974), page 23.

Year	USA	USSR	Source
1972	5700	2500	Melman, *op. cit.,* page 165.
1972	5700	2164	Collins, *op. cit.,* page 114.
1972	4000		Herbert Scoville, Jr., *The Nation,* May 27, 1978.
1972	6500	2200	Roy and Zhores Medvedev, *The Nation,* January, 1982.
1972	5700	2500	*Time* magazine, March 29, 1982.
1972	5800	2100	SALT II Testimony, *op. cit.,* 1982, page 267.
1972	6000	2300	Polner, *op. cit.,* page 15.
1973	6784	2200	DOD, *Annual Report, FY 1974,* January 1973.
1973	6000	2500	C. Robert Zelnick, *Washington Monthly* (May, 1973).
1973	6784	2200	Center for Defense Information, *The Defense Monitor,* Volume IV, no. 2 (February, 1975), page 12.
1973	6784	2256	Collins, *op. cit.,* page 114.
1974	7940	2600	DOD, *Annual Report, FY 1975,* January, 1974.
1974	7100	2300	*Time* magazine, February 11, 1974, page 18.
1974	7100	2300	*Time* magazine, July 1, 1974, page 25.
1974	7940		*Newsweek,* July 8, 1974, page 24.
1974	7940	2600	Center for Defense Information, *The Defense Monitor,* Volume III, no. 7 (August, 1974), page 1.
1974	7200	2200	*Newsweek,* September 23, 1974, page 62.
1974	7888	2620	J. William Fulbright, *The Progressive* (September, 1974), page 23.
1974	5500	2200	*Newsweek,* December 9, 1974, page 46.
1974	7650	2500	DOD, *Annual Report, FY 1976,* January, 1975.
1974	7650	2396	Collins, *op. cit.,* page 114.
1974	8400	2400	SALT II Testimony, *op. cit.,* 1982, page 267.
1975	8500	2500	DOD, *Annual Report, FY 1976,* January, 1975.
1975	8000	2600	Sanford Gottlieb, *Ramparts Magazine* (May, 1975), page 20.
1975	8500	2500	Center for Defense Information, *The Defense Monitor,* Volume V, no. 3 (May, 1976), page 6.
1975	8500	2800	Lens, *op. cit.,* 1977, page 27.
1975	8500	2829	Collins, *op. cit.,* page 114.
1976	8900	3500	DOD, *Annual Report, FY 1977,* January, 1976, page 44.
1976	8500	2800	Dave Johnson of the Center for Defense Information, quoted by Sidney Lens, *The Progressive* (February, 1976), page 22.

(continued)

A Chronology of Estimates of the Balance of Deliverable Strategic Warheads, 1950–85 *(cont.)*

Year	USA	USSR	Source
1976	9000		John Holum, *The Nation,* March 20, 1976, page 329.
1976	8530	3250	International Institute for Strategic Studies, *The Military Balance, 1976–1977,* page 106.
1976	8400	3300	DOD, *Annual Report, FY 1978,* January, 1977, pge 58.
1976	8530	3250	David Gompert, Michael Mandelbaum, Richard L. Garwin, and John Barton, *Nuclear Weapons and World Politics,* 1977, page 348.
1976	8900	3115	Collins, *op. cit.,* 1978, page 114.
1976	8900	3123	Collins, *U. S. Soviet Military Balance, 1960–1980,* 1980, page 460.
1976	7200	1900	Ford, Kendall, and Nadis, *op. cit.,* 1982, page 31.
1976	9400	3200	SALT II Testimony, *op. cit.,* page 267.
1976	9000		Edwards, *op. cit.,* 1982, page 89.
1977	8500	4000	DOD, *Annual Report, FY 1978,* January, 1977, page 58.
1977	8500	4000	Center for Defense Information, *The Defense Monitor,* Volume VI, no. 4 (May, 1977), page 3.
1977	8500		George McGovern, *The Progressive* (May, 1977), page 19.
1977	8500	3500	*Time* magazine, May 23, 1977.
1977	9000	3500	Lens, *op. cit.,* 1977, page 63.
1977	9000	3500	Richard Barnet, *The Giants: Russia and America,* Simon & Schuster, 1977, page 99.
1977	8500	4000	Center for Defense Information, *The Defense Monitor,* Volume VII, no. 6 (July, 1978), page 1.
1977	9308	3633	Collins, *op. cit.,* 1978, page 114.
1977	9308	3907	Collins, *op. cit.,* 1980, page 460.
1978	9000	4500	DOD, *Annual Report, FY 1979,* February, 1978, page 47.
1978	9000	4500	Herbert Scoville, Jr., *The Nation,* May 27, 1978.
1978	9200	4500	Center for Defense Information, *The Defense Monitor,* Volume VII, no. 6 (July, 1978), page 1.
1978	11,500	3900	Philip Morrison and Paul F. Walker, *Scientific American* (October, 1978), page 54.
1978	11,000	4500	International Institute for Strategic Studies, *The Military Balance, 1978–1979,* pages 3–4.
1978	11,894	4398	Stockholm International Peace Research Institute, *World Arms and Disarmament Yearbook, 1978,* pages 438–439.

Year	USA	USSR	Source
1978	9200	5091	Collins, *op. cit.*, 1980, page 460.
1978	9800	5200	SALT II Testimony, *op. cit.*, 1982, page 267.
1979	9200	5000	DOD, *Annual Report, FY 1980*, January, 1979.
1979	9500	5000	Center for Defense Information, *The Defense Monitor*, Volume VIII, no. 2 (February, 1979), page 4.
1979	10,166	4500	Les Aspin, *Scientific American* (February, 1979), pages 40–41.
1979	9200	5000	Sanford Gottlieb, *Newsweek,* March 26, 1979, page 19.
1979	9200	5000	J. David Singer, *The New York Times,* March 28, 1979.
1979	9200	5000	*The New York Times,* May 11, 1979.
1979	9000	4000	Tom Wicker, *The New York Times,* May, 1979.
1979	10,000		Robert C. Johansen, *Harper's Magazine* (May, 1979).
1979	9200	5000	General David C. Jones, Chairman of the Joint Chiefs of Staff, SALT II Testimony, July 11, 1979.
1979	9200	5100	Fred Kaplan, *The New York Times Magazine,* July 15, 1979.
1979	9200	5000	*Inquiry Magazine,* August 6 and 20, 1979.
1979	9994		Center for Defense Information, *The Defense Monitor*, Volume VIII, no. 5, page 7.
1979	10,000		Henry Kendall, *Bulletin of the Atomic Scientists* (September, 1979).
1979	11,000	5000	International Institute for Strategic Studies, *The Military Balance, 1979–1980,* pages 3–4.
1979	9200	5975	Collins, *op. cit.*, 1980, page 460.
1979	9200	5000	Polner, *op. cit.*, page 15.
1979	9000	4000	Sidney Lens, *The Bomb,* 1982, page 112.
1980	9200	6000	DOD, *Annual Report, FY 1981*, January, 1980, pages 77 and 89.
1980	9200	6000	Les Aspin, *Bulletin of the Atomic Scientists* (June, 1980), page 28.
1980	9000	6000	United Nations, *Comprehensive Study on Nuclear Weapons*, Report of the Secretary General A/35/392, 12 September 1980, page 31.
1980	11,000	7500	United Nations, *op. cit.*, 1980, page 31.
1980	9582	6000	*Newsweek,* October 27, 1980.
1980	7301	6000	International Institute for Strategic Studies, *The Military Balance, 1980–1981,* pages 3–4.

(continued)

A Chronology of Estimates of the Balance of Deliverable Strategic Warheads, 1950–85 (*cont.*)

Year	USA	USSR	Source
1980	7301	6000	*The New York Times,* December 7, 1980.
1980	9200	6000	Stockholm International Peace Research Institute, *World Arms and Disarmament Yearbook, 1981,* page 273.
1980	8946	7273	*Aviation Week & Space Technology,* April 12, 1982.
1980	10,000	6000	SALT II Testimony, *op. cit.,* 1982, page 267.
1981	9000	7000	DOD, *Annual Report, FY 1982,* January, 1981, page 53.
1981	9200	6000	Herbert Scoville, Jr., January, 1981.
1981	10,458	7094	Michael Heylin, *Chemical & Engineering News,* March 16, 1981.
1981	9000	6000	CBS-TV, *The Defense of the United States,* June 14, 1981.
1981	8552	6300	CBS-TV, *op. cit.,* transcript, June, 1981.
1981		7000	DOD, *Soviet Military Power* (September, 1981), page 3.
1981	9000	7000	*The New York Times,* October, 1981.
1981	9000	7000	International Institute for Strategic Studies, *The Military Balance, 1981–1982,* pages 3–4.
1981	9200	6000	Lieutenant Colonel D. M. O. Miller, *The Balance of Military Power,* 1981, page 16.
1981	9000	7000	Walter Pincus, *The Washington Post,* March 21, 1982.
1981	9200	6000	Fred Halliday, *The Making of the Second Cold War,* 1983, page 72.
1982	9000	7000	Jonathan Schell, *The Fate of the Earth,* Knopf, 1982, page 54.
1982	12,000	8000	Center for Defense Information, *The Defense Monitor,* Volume XI, no. 1, page 5.
1982	10,000		Union of Soviet Socialist Republics, *Whence the Threat to Peace?* (March, 1982), page 8.
1982	9402	8000	*The New York Times,* March 21, 1982.
1982	9480	8040	*Time* magazine, March 29, 1982.
1982		6512	Joint Chiefs of Staff, *FY 1983 Posture Statement,* May, 1982.
1982	9300	7200	DOD, Congressional testimony, May, 1982.
1982	9300	7200	*The New York Times,* May 2, 1982.
1982	9000	8500	*The New York Times,* May 16, 1982.
1982	9000	8100	NBC-TV, June 10, 1982.
1982	9400	8000	Alexander Cockburn and James Ridgeway, *The Village Voice,* June 15, 1982.

Year	USA	USSR	Source
1982	9000	8500	*The New York Times,* June 29, 1982.
1982	9540	7678	Stockholm International Peace Research Institute, *The Arms Race and Arms Control,* 1982, page 85.
1982	9775	7226	Center for Defense Information, *Force Level Calculator,* 1982.
1982	11,154	7051	James Dunnigan, *How to Make War,* Morrow, 1982, pages 298, 304, and 305.
1982	10,000	7000	Paul Warnke, 1982.
1982	11,000	8000	SALT II Testimony, *op. cit.,* 1982, page 267.
1982	10,000	7400	Ruth Leger Sivard, *World Military and Social Expenditures,* 1982.
1982	9970		Council for a Livable World, July, 1982.
1982	9000		Anthony H. Cordesman, Jr., *op. cit.,* 1982, page 29.
1982	9704	7730	Andrew Cockburn, *Mother Jones,* September 10, 1982.
1982	9536	7800	Center for Defense Information, *The Defense Monitor,* Volume XI, no. 6, page 3.
1982	9200	8000	SANE, 1982.
1982	9500	6657	Randall Forsberg, *Scientific American* (November, 1982), page 54.
1982	7100	7500	*The Washington Post,* November 24, 1982.
1982	7100	7500	*The New York Times,* November 28, 1982.
1982	9000	8500	*The New York Times,* December 5, 1982.
1982	9100	10,000	*The New York Times,* December 22, 1982.
1982	9516	8041	Anthony H. Cordesman, Jr., *Armed Forces Journal International* (December, 1982), page 41.
1982	9268	7300	International Institute for Strategic Studies, *The Military Balance, 1982–1983,* page 140.
1983	9268	7300	Anthony H. Cordesman, Jr., *Armed Forces Journal International* (February, 1983), page 60.
1983	9000	7000	Sidney Drell, March 19, 1983.
1983	9268	7339	Senator Daniel K. Inouye, quoted in *The New York Times,* March 24, 1983.
1983	9200	8200	Robert S. McNamara, CBS-TV, March 30, 1983.
1983	9500	7700	Union of Concerned Scientists, 1983.
1983	9900	7800	Harvard Nuclear Study Group, Living with Nuclear Weapons, 1983, page 120.
1983	8506	5981	Cambridge University Disarmament Seminar, *Defended to Death,* 1983, page 296.

(continued)

A Chronology of Estimates of the Balance of Deliverable Strategic Warheads, 1950–85 *(cont.)*

Year	USA	USSR	Source
1983	10,100	7360	Operation Dismantle, Ottawa, August, 1983.
1983	9300	7300	SANE, *Deadly Standoff*, 1983.
1983	10,173	7742	Center for Defense Information, *The Defense Monitor*, Volume XII, no. 7 (September, 1983), page 10.
1983	"Dead Even"		ABC-TV, *The Soviet Military Threat*, November 15, 1983.
1983	9689		Thomas B. Cochran, William M. Arkin, and Milton M. Hoenig, *Nuclear Weapons Databook, Volume I*, 1984, page 102.
1984	9575	8072	*Common Cause, Up in Arms*, 1984, page 51.
1984	11,190	8420	Center for Defense Information, *The Defense Monitor*, Volume XIII, no. 6 (September, 1984), page 3.
1984	11,030	9710	*Newsweek*, October 1, 1984, page 29.
1985	15,000	15,000	Henry Kissinger, ABC-TV, *Nightline*, January, 1985.
1985	10,848	8744	*The New York Times*, January 7, 1985.
1985	13,748	19,114	William M. Arkin and Richard W. Fieldhouse, *Nuclear Battlefields: Global Links in the Arms Race*, June, 1985, pages 45 and 46. Figures given only for stockpiled, not deliverable, weapons. Maximum figure for USSR.
1985	13,748	9032	William M. Arkin and Richard W. Fieldhouse, *Nuclear Battlefields: Global Links in the Arms Race*, June, 1985, pages 45 and 46. Figures given only for stockpiled, not deliverable, weapons. Minimum figure for USSR.
1985	11,400	8300	Center for Defense Information, *Force Level Calculator, 1985*. Figures for deliverable strategic nuclear weapons.
1985	13,000	9000	Center for Defense Information, *Force Level Calculator, 1985*. Figures for all weapons deliverable on opponent's territory, including some tactical weapons delivered by aircraft.
1985	30,000	23,000	Center for Defense Information, *Force Level Calculator, 1985*. Figures for all nuclear weapons of all types stockpiled.
1985		8500	Missile warheads only. David Sullivan, aide to Senator James McClure, interviewed by *The New York Times*, "Missile Strength in Soviet Disputed," March 23, 1985.
1985		9000	Bill Keller, "Soviet Reported to Build Up Nuclear Arsenal," *The New York Times*, June 26, 1985.
1985	11,466	9208	Center for Defense Information, *The Defense Monitor*, Volume XIV, No. 6, page 5.

Year	USA	USSR	Source
1985	7500	7900	Missile warheads only. William Safire, "The New Summitry," *The New York Times*, September 5, 1985.
1985	12,000	10,000	Soviet count of U.S. weapons, and U.S. count of Soviet weapons, according to Hedrick Smith, "U.S. Officials Say Soviet Arms Plan is Not Balanced," *The New York Times*, October 1, 1985.
1985	8000	9000	Missile warheads only. Leslie H. Gelb, "Arms Offer: Gap Narrows," *The New York Times*, November 1, 1985.
1985	8000	9000	Missile warheads only. Bernard Weinraub, "U.S. Will Present New Arms Offer in Geneva Today," *The New York Times*, November 1, 1985.
1985	8000	9000	Missile warheads only. *The New York Times*, "Tass Dismisses U.S. Arms Plan," November 2, 1985.
1985	9857	9700	*Time* magazine, "Reagan Makes a New Offer," November 11, 1985, page 19.
1985	11,134	9750	Ted Koppel, ABC-TV World News, November 11, 1985.
1985	8682	9030	*The New York Times*, "The Arms Proposals: A Balance Sheet," November 13, 1985. Includes cruise missile warheads but exempts nuclear gravity bombs. Source listed: House Committee on Foreign Affairs.
1985	11,085	10,064	William Arkin, The Today Show, NBC-TV, November 15, 1985. Using Arkin's verbal figures for bomber warheads.
1985	11,206	9684	William Arkin, The Today Show, NBC-TV, November 15, 1985. Using chart graphics for bomber warheads.
1985	10,786	9460	*The New York Times*, "Global Arsenals: The Balance Now," November 18, 1985. Includes nuclear gravity bombs among bomber warheads.

Appendix C

Missile Accuracy: A Chronology of Estimates

This appendix contains a collection of estimates of Soviet and American missile accuracy during a period of growing American superiority in precision guidance, from 1978 through 1983. It evaluates the relative influence each estimate exerted on public opinion.

At the beginning of this period, the most accurate American systems operationally deployed, the Mk 12 and Mk 12A reentry vehicles fitted with an improved INS-20 guidance system aboard our *Minuteman IIIs,* were capable of striking within 600 feet of their aimpoints.[1] Further guidance improvements were being made to enable them to strike within 490 feet.[2] The most accurate Soviet systems operationally deployed during this period, the reentry vehicles on the Soviet SS-18 Mod 4 and SS-19 Mod 1 missiles, could strike no closer than within 850 feet of their aimpoints.[3]

Nevertheless, the majority of official and unofficial reports throughout this period suggested a trend in which American missile accuracy seemed to decline and Soviet accuracy rapidly to improve. Confirmation of superior American accuracy grew more difficult to obtain, and gained only limited circulation, while claims of superior Soviet accuracy achieved much wider dissemination through the major news media.

In 1978, the International Institute for Strategic Studies (IISS) claimed that the "reported accuracy" of the leading Soviet systems was 600 feet.[4] It said this again in 1979.[5] In 1980, it said that the accuracy of the Soviet SS-18 was "about 600 ft," and at the same time promised that when deployment of the new Mk 12A reentry vehicle was "completed" in 1981, this "will reduce" the CEP of the *Minuteman III* to 600 feet. Meanwhile, IISS claimed, the *Minuteman's* CEP was 900 feet.[6]

Not until 1982 did IISS acknowledge that Soviet missiles did not have the accuracy it had earlier claimed. It now said that the most accurate Soviet missile had a CEP of 984 feet.[7] Though it had earlier promised the *Minuteman III* a CEP of 600 feet, IISS now gave it a CEP of 721 feet.[8]

Those who relied on IISS—and there were many who did—would have had no idea that the *Minuteman III* had been capable of CEPs of 600 feet for the previous three years. This capability first achieved operational status in July, 1979, with the initial installation of an improved INS-20 guidance system on operational missiles.[9] By the end of 1982, this guidance upgrade was completed.[10] It gave a CEP of 600 feet to all of the 1,650 Mk 12 and Mk 12A reentry vehicles we had deployed at that time on 550 *Minuteman IIIs.*

This pattern of reporting culminated in journalist Theodore White's announcement, in the pages of *The New York Times Magazine* early in 1983, that Soviet missiles were capable of striking within 450 feet of their aimpoints.[11] The Pentagon official in charge of Research and Engineering who gave White this figure certainly knew that it represented the level of accuracy which *America's* missiles, not the Soviet Union's, were then approaching. It was a characteristic reversal of the truth in which those who exaggerate Soviet capabilities frequently delight. What better way to support Reagan administration claims of superior Soviet accuracy than to suggest that Soviet missiles were as accurate as ours?

Notes

1. House Armed Services Committee, *Authorization Hearings, Fiscal Year 1979,* Part 3, Book 1, page 307.
2. Clarence A. Robinson, Jr., "MX Basing Delay Threatens SALT Ratification," *Aviation Week & Space Technology,* November 20, 1978, page 22.
3. James Miller, Head, Defense Intelligence Agency Weapons and Systems Division, Senate Appropriations Committee Hearings, 1981, quoted by Joe Room and Kosta Tsipis, *Analysis of Dense Pack Vulnerabilities,* MIT Program in Science and Technology for International Security, Report no. 8, November, 1982, note 17.
4. IISS, *The Military Balance, 1978–1979,* page 81.
5. IISS, *The Military Balance, 1979–1980,* page 87.
6. IISS, *The Military Balance, 1980–1981,* pages 3 and 89.
7. IISS, *The Military Balance, 1982–1983,* page 113.
8. *Ibid.,* page 112.
9. Arms Control and Disarmament Agency, *Fiscal Year 1982 Arms Control Impact Statement,* page 3; House Armed Services Committee, *Authorization Hearings, Fiscal Year 1979,* Part 3, Book 1, page 307.
10. Arms Control and Disarmament Agency, *Fiscal Year 1983 Arms Control Impact Statement,* page 3.
11. Theodore H. White, "Weinberger on the Ramparts," *The New York Times Magazine,* February 6, 1983, page 17.

TABLES IN THIS SECTION

- Estimates of *Minuteman III* Accuracy, 1979–83
- Chronology of Estimates of Soviet Missile Accuracy, 1975–83
- Comparative Chronology of Estimates of United States and Soviet Missile Accuracy During a Period of Growing American Superiority in Precision Guidance, 1979–83

Estimates of Minuteman III Accuracy, 1979–83, After Replacement of NS-20 with INS-20 Guidance System in 1979

Date	Source	Current CEP (ft) with Mk 12 RV	Current CEP (ft) with Mk 12A RV	Future CEP (ft) with Mk 12A RV	Future CEP (ft) with Improved Guidance	Initial Date of Improvement/Comments/Implications
Mar. 1978	HASC				600	Result of initial deployment of INS-20 with Mk 12 in 1979. Old CEPs were 1215 ft with NS-17, and 900 ft with NS-20 guidance.
Nov. 1978	AW&ST				486	"Current U.S. advanced technology capability."
Jan. 1979	Aspin	607		607		Initial deployment of Mk 12A in 1980. Mk 12A will not improve CEP beyond level already attained by INS-20 refinements.
June 1979	Galen			600		U.S. "will begin" refitting with Mk 12A. Does not say when. This "will increase" accuracy to 600 ft. Acknowledges INS-20 improvements "already completed." Thus, implies new CEP only achieved by INS-20 guidance "in combination" with Mk 12A.
July 1979	Nitze	729		729		Best CEP with INS-20. Initial deployment of Mk 12A in 1980. Mk 12A will not further improve CEP.
July 1979	Kaplan	600				Initial deployment of Mk 12A in 1980.
Sept. 1979	SIPRI	656		656		Initial deployment of Mk 12A in October, 1979. Mk 12A will not further improve CEP.
Jan. 1980	Kaplan	607	607			Initial deployment of Mk 12A in December, 1979. Mk 12A does not further improve CEP.
June 1980	AW&ST		729			Best CEP. Acknowledges current deployment of Mk 12A.
June 1980	Aspin	600			490	Further improvements in guidance will achieve "theoretical peak of accuracy" for purely ballistic RVs by 1985. Mk 12A does not further improve current CEP.
July 1980	Collins	729				Best CEP with INS-20 guidance. Specifically asserts that CEP of 600 ft "has not been attained." Mk 12A "scheduled" for deployment "during the first half of this decade." Due to its higher yield, Mk 12A "will improve" lethality.
Sept. 1980	SIPRI	984			656	Acknowledges no current deployment of Mk 12A. Same CEP for both Mk 12 and Mk 12A after guidance improvements in 1985. Thus, Mk 12A does not improve CEP. Poor current CEP suggests INS-20 refinements not yet installed. Anticipated improvement could therefore be taken either as initial installation or further improvement of INS-20.
Sept. 1980	UN	984	984			Acknowledges current deployment of Mk 12A. Neither Mk 12A nor INS-20 appears to improve CEP over level of earlier NS-20.

Date	Source				Comments
Dec. 1980	IISS	900	600		Deployment of Mk 12A "should be completed" by end of 1981. This "will reduce" CEP to 600 ft at that time. Poor current CEP implies INS-20 improvements have not already achieved 600 ft or have not yet been installed and are only a part of Mk 12A upgrade.
May 1981	Heylin	1215	607		Initial deployment of Mk 12A in 1981. Mk 12A appears to improve CEP. CEP without Mk 12A is now same as with old NS-17. This suggests NS-20 guidance ineffective, and INS-20 improvements ineffective too or not installed until deployment of Mk 12A.
Sept. 1981	SIPRI	656	656		Mk 12A does not improve CEP.
Dec. 1981	Jane's	1312	1312		Initial deployment of Mk 12A in December, 1979. CEP is now worse than with old NS-17. NS-20 "improvements are scheduled." This could mean either installation of INS-20 or installation of NS-20 as an improvement over NS-17. Either interpretation, taken with indicated CEP, implies INS-20 changes not yet made.
Mar. 1982	AW&ST	900+	900+	500	Future CEP attributed to "further improvements to the INS-20 guidance system." This acknowledges original INS-20 refinements already made, but creates impression they have not achieved better CEP thus far. Mk 12A does not improve CEP.
Aug. 1982	Cordesman	1312	1312	656	Current CEP is worse than with old NS-17. Yet acknowledges NS-17 "already replaced" by NS-20. This implies NS-17 worse than it was and NS-20 ineffective. Acknowledges improved NS-20 guidance "is further reducing" CEP to 656 ft. Does not say when this reduction will have been attained. Mk 12A improves lethality but not CEP.
Nov. 1982	Aldridge	607	607		Mk 12A does not improve CEP.
Dec. 1982	IISS	918	721		Implies either that Mk 12A improves CEP, or that INS-20 guidance improvements made only on Mk 12A but not on Mk 12 RVs.
Feb. 1983	Middleton	630	630		All *Minuteman IIIs*, and therefore presumably Mk 12 and Mk 12A RVs.
May 1983	CBO	729	729		Mk 12A does not improve CEP.
Dec. 1983	IISS	918	721		Implies either that Mk 12A improves CEP, or that INS-20 guidance improvements made only on Mk 12A but not on Mk 12 RVs.

RV: Reentry Vehicle.

CEP: Circular Error Probable, or the distance from a specific aimpoint within which half of the reentry vehicles of a specific type are expected to fall.

Note: small differences, for example between 600 and 607 ft, or between 721 and 729 ft, are the result of conversion to linear feet from meters in one case, or from fractions of a nautical mile in another.

Sources for Estimates of Minuteman III Accuracy and Lethality, 1978–83

Date	Source
Mar. 1978	House Armed Services Committee, *Authorization Hearings, FY 1979,* United States Congress (Washington, D.C.: U.S. Government Printing Office, Part 3, Book 1), page 307.
Nov. 1978	Clarence A. Robinson, Jr., "MX Basing Delay Threatens SALT Ratification," *Aviation Week & Space Technology,* November 20, 1978, page 22.
Jan. 1979	Les Aspin, "The Mineshaft Gap Revisited," *Congressional Record,* January 15, 1979, page E30.
June 1979	Justin Galen, "The Party Line: Taking the FY80 Force Plans at Face Value," *Armed Forces Journal International* (June, 1979), page 36.
July 1979	Paul H. Nitze, Prepared Statement Before Senate Foreign Relations Committee, *The SALT II Treaty,* July 12, 1979, reprinted in *Congressional Record,* July 20, 1979, page S10078.
July 1979	Fred Kaplan, "The Arms of Armageddon," *Washington Post Magazine,* July 15, 1979.
Sept.1979	Stockholm International Peace Research Institute, *World Arms and Disarmament Yearbook, 1979* (Stockholm: Almqvist & Wiksell: 1979), page 12.
Jan. 1980	Fred Kaplan, *Dubious Specter* (Washington, D.C.: Institute for Policy Studies, 1980), pages 88 and 89.
June 1980	Jeffrey M. Lenorovitz, "ALCM to Enter Inventory Next Year," *Aviation Week & Space Technology,* June 16, 1980, page 177.
June 1980	Les Aspin, "Judge Not by Numbers Alone," *Bulletin of the Atomic Scientists* (June, 1980), pages 28 and 29.
July 1980	John M. Collins, *U.S.-Soviet Military Balance: Concepts and Capabilities, 1960–1980* (New York: McGraw-Hill, 1980), pages 133, 135, 413, and 446.
Sept.1980	Stockholm International Peace Research Institute, *World Arms and Disarmament Yearbook, 1980* (Stockholm: Almqvist & Wiksell, 1980), page XIXX.
Sept.1980	United Nations Secretary General, *General and Complete Disarmament: Comprehensive Study on Nuclear Weapons,* A/35/392, September 12, 1980, page 26.
Dec. 1980	International Institute for Strategic Studies, *The Military Balance, 1980–1981* (London: IISS, 1980), page 3.
May 1981	Michael Heylin, "Nuclear Arms Race Gearing for Speedup," *Chemical and Engineering News,* March 16, 1981, page 29.
Sept.1981	Stockholm International Peace Research Institute, *World Arms and Disarmament Yearbook, 1981* (Stockholm: Almqvist & Wiksell, 1981).
Dec. 1981	*Jane's Weapon Systems, 1981–1982* (London: Macdonald & Jane's, 1981), page 13.
Mar. 1982	Clarence A. Robinson, Jr., "Congress Questioning Viability of MX ICBM," *Aviation Week & Space Technology,* March 22, 1982, page 18.
Aug. 1982	Anthony H. Cordesman, Jr., *Deterrence in the 1980s: Part I,* Adelphi Paper no. 175 (London: IISS, 1982), pages 24 and 25.

Date	Source
Nov. 1982	Robert C. Aldridge, *First Strike! The Pentagon's Strategy for Nuclear War* (Boston: South End Press, 1983), page 59.
Dec. 1982	International Institute for Strategic Studies, *The Military Balance, 1982–1983* (London: IISS, 1983), page 112.
May 1983	Congressional Budget Office, *Modernizing U.S. Strategic Offensive Forces,* United States Congress, Washington, D.C., May, 1983, pages 84 and 85.
Dec. 1983	International Institute for Strategic Studies, *The Military Balance, 1983–1984* (London: IISS, 1984), page 118.
Feb. 1983	Drew Middleton, "Fundamental Question: 'Triad' Nuclear Defense," *The New York Times,* February 15, 1983.

Chronology of Estimates of Soviet Missile Accuracy, 1975–83

Date	Source	Lowest Current CEP (ft)	Missile Type/Future Improvements/Qualifications
Nov. 1975	Schlesinger	1519	Between 1519 and 2005 ft.
Mar. 1977	USAF	1822	
Oct. 1977	Aldridge		SS-18 "will have" CEP of 1500 ft. Notes that *Minuteman III* now has CEP of 1200 ft.
Aug. 1978	*Business Wk*	600	
Dec. 1978	*NY Times*	600	CEP is "about" 600 ft.
Dec. 1978	IISS	600	CEP is "reported accuracy."
July 1979	Nitze	897	For SS-18 Mod 4 and SS-19 Mod 3.
Aug. 1979	Gallois	2829	Between 2829 and 3279 ft.
Dec. 1979	Collins	850	For SS-18 Mod 4 and SS-19 Mod 3 (Mod 2 at that time). Notes that reported CEPs of 600 ft for Soviet ICBMs "were premature."
Dec. 1979	IISS	600	CEP is "reported accuracy."
Jan. 1980	Kaplan	911	For SS-18 Mod 4 and SS-19 Mod 3.
Feb. 1980	*AW&ST*	600	Between 600 and 900 ft.
Aug. 1980	Lee	600	Between 600 and 900 ft.
Aug. 1980	Lee	364	Between 364 and 607 ft. Misquotes *AW&ST* of Feb. 1980.
Sept. 1980	SIPRI	984	Between 984 and 1476 ft for SS-19.
Sept. 1980	UN	984	Between 984 and 1476 ft for SS-19.
Oct. 1980	Powers	1519	For SS-18.
Dec. 1980	IISS	600	CEP for SS-18 is "about 600 ft."
May 1981	Heylin	1215	For SS-18 and SS-19.
Sept. 1981	SIPRI		CEP "comparable to that of the Minuteman III has been attributed to the Soviet SS-18."
Dec. 1981	IISS	600	CEP for SS-18 is "about 600 ft."
1981	Koenig	1033	Soviet ICBMs will improve CEP to 721 ft by 1985.
1981	DIA	850	Best CEP "credited" to Soviet ICBMs.
June 1982	*AW&ST*	1387	Quoting "Pentagon official."
Aug. 1982	Cordesman	911	For SS-19. Will improve to 486 ft by 1985.
Nov. 1982	*AW&ST*	800	For SS-18. CEPs of 600 ft for Soviet ICBMs are "expected in the late 1980s."
Nov. 1982	Aldridge	850	For SS-18 Mod 4 and SS-19 Mods 1 and 2.
Dec. 1982	IISS	984	For SS-18 Mod 4 and SS-19 Mods 2 and 3.
1982	Lens	1500	For SS-18.

Date	Source	Lowest Current CEP (ft)	Missile Type/Future Improvements/Qualifications
Feb. 1983	White	450	CEP of "about 450 ft." According to editor, White's notes show that "Richard DeLauer told him that verbally."
Mar. 1983	*AW&ST*	600	For SS-18.
May 1983	CBO	911	For SS-18 and SS-19. These ICBMs will achieve CEPs of 729 ft by 1990, 486 ft by 1996.
Dec. 1983	IISS	984	For SS-18 Mod 4 and SS-19 Mods 2 and 3.

Sources for Chronology of Estimates of Soviet Missile Accuracy, 1975–83

Date	Source
Nov. 1975	Clarence A. Robinson, Jr., "Cabinet Shifts May Speed SALT," *Aviation Week & Space Technology,* November 10, 1975, page 12.
Mar. 1977	*Air Force Magazine* (March, 1977).
Oct. 1977	Robert C. Aldridge, *The Counterforce Syndrome* (Washington, D.C. and Amsterdam: 1978), page 60.
Aug. 1978	"The Budget Choice SALT Puts to the Pentagon," *Business Week,* April 14, 1978, page 68.
Dec. 1978	Drew Middleton, "Study Says Soviet Has Gained Nuclear Superiority," *The New York Times,* December 1, 1978.
Dec. 1978	International Institute for Strategic Studies, *The Military Balance, 1978–1979* (London: IISS, 1978), page 81.
July 1979	Paul H. Nitze, Prepared Statement Before Senate Foreign Relations Committee, *The Salt II Treaty,* July 12, 1979, page 458.
Aug. 1979	General Pierre M. Gallois, "The Future of France's Force de Disuasion," *Strategic Review* (Summer, 1979), page 35.
Dec. 1979	Collins, *op. cit.,* pages 136 and 446.
Dec. 1979	International Institute for Strategic Studies, *The Military Balance, 1979–1980* (London: IISS, 1979), page 87.
Jan. 1980	Kaplan, *op. cit.,* pages 90 and 91.
Feb. 1980	"Pressure for New Bomber Rises in Congress," *Aviation Week & Space Technology,* February 11, 1980, page 12.
Aug. 1980	William T. Lee, "Debate Over U.S. Strategic Forecasts: A Poor Record," *Strategic Review* (Summer, 1979), page 49.
Aug. 1980	Lee, *op. cit.,* page 56, note 13.
Sept. 1980	SIPRI, *op. cit.,* 1980, page XVIII.
Sept. 1980	United Nations Secretary General, *op. cit.,* 12 September, 1980, page 26.

(continued)

Sources for Chronology of Estimates of Soviet Missile Accuracy, 1975–83 *(cont.)*

Date	Source
Oct. 1980	Thomas Powers, "Crossing the Nuclear Threshold," first published in *Commonweal,* October 10, 1980, and reprinted in *Thinking About the Next War* (New York: Knopf, 1982), page 85.
Dec. 1980	IISS, *op. cit., 1980–1981,* page 89.
May 1981	Heylin, *op. cit.,* March 16, 1981, page 29.
Sept. 1981	SIPRI, *op. cit.,* 1981, page 22.
Dec. 1981	IISS, *op. cit., 1981–1982,* page 105.
1981	William J. Koenig, *Weapons of World War 3* (London: Bison Books, 1981), page 104.
1981	James Miller, Head, Defense Intelligence Agency Weapons and Systems Division, Senate Appropriations Committee Hearings, 1981, quoted by Joe Room and Kosta Tsipis, *Analysis of Dense Pack Vulnerabilities,* Massachusetts Institute of Technology Program in Science and Technology for International Security, Report No. 8, November, 1982, note 17.
June 1982	"MX Basing Plan Readied for Delivery to Congress," *Aviation Week & Space Technology,* June 28, 1982, page 23.
Aug. 1982	Cordesman, *op. cit.,* Adelphi Paper no. 175 (London: IISS, 1982), page 31.
Nov. 1982	"President Gets Defense Department MX Basing Options, Recommendations," *Aviation Week & Space Technology,* November 22, 1982, page 19.
Nov. 1982	Aldridge, *op. cit.,* (Boston: South End Press, 1983), page 60.
Dec. 1982	IISS, *op. cit., 1982–1983,* page 113.
1982	Sidney Lens, *The Bomb* (New York: Lodestar/E. P. Dutton, 1982), page 94.
Feb. 1983	Theodore H. White, "Weinberger on the Ramparts," *The New York Times Magazine,* February 6, 1983, page 17.
Mar. 1983	"Aerospace Forecast & Inventory," *Aviation Week & Space Technology,* March 14, 1983, Specifications Tables, Soviet Missiles, page 153.
May 1983	Congressional Budget Office, *op. cit.,* May, 1983, pages 90 and 91. As sources, it cites *Aviation Week & Space Technology, op. cit.,* June 16, 1980; Nitze, *op. cit.,* July 12, 1979; Aspin, *op. cit.,* June, 1980; and Collins and Glakas, *US/Soviet Military Balance, Statistical Trends, 1970–1981,* Congressional Research Report No. 82-162S, October, 1981, revised September, 1982.
Dec. 1983	IISS, *op. cit., 1983–1984,* page 119.
July 1985	CIA announces new estimate lowering accuracy of SS-19 to CEP of 1305 feet. Reported by Bill Keller, "Imperfect Science, Important Conclusions," The New York Times, July 28, 1985.

Comparative Chronology of Estimates of United States and Soviet Missile Accuracy During a Period of Growing American Superiority in Precision Guidance, 1979–83

Date	Soviet CEP (ft)	American CEP (ft)	Source	Dissemination	Impression Created
Mar. 1978		600	HASC	Limited/Influential	Official acknowledgment of U.S. capability.
Aug. 1978	600		Bus. Wk	Broad	Equal to rumored U.S. CEP. Suggests Soviet parity.
Dec. 1978	600		NY Times	Very broad	Equal to rumored U.S. CEP. Suggests Soviet parity.
Dec. 1978	600		IISS	Broad/Influential	Equal to rumored U.S. CEP. Suggests Soviet parity.
Jan. 1979		600	Aspin	Limited/Influential	Confirms officially acknowledged U.S. CEP.
June 1979		600	Galen	Broad	Confirms officially acknowledged U.S. CEP but suggests not yet attained.
July 1979	897	729	Nitze	Limited/Influential	Casts doubt on officially acknowledged U.S. CEP. Confirms but narrows U.S. lead, suggesting dangerous trend.
July 1979		600	Kaplan	Very Broad	Confirms officially acknowledged U.S. CEP for wider public.
Sept. 1979		656	SIPRI	Limited	Confirms officially acknowledged U.S. CEP.
Dec. 1979	850	729	Collins	Limited/Influential	Follows Nitze, further narrowing U.S. lead. Renounces 1978 reports of lower Soviet CEP. This lends further credibility to claim of higher U.S. CEP.
Dec. 1979	600		IISS	Broad/Influential	Reinforces impression of lower Soviet CEP.
Jan. 1980	911	607	Kaplan	Limited	Reconfirms officially acknowledged U.S. CEP. Quote of Soviet CEP is closer than Collins to original Nitze statement.
Feb. 1980	600		AW&ST	Broad/Influential	Reinforces impression of lower Soviet CEP, but takes into account semi-official acknowledgment of higher one by placing range between 600 and 900 ft. Thus appears "balanced."
June 1980		729	AW&ST	Broad/Influential	Reinforces impression of higher U.S. CEP. Taken together, February and June statements suggest possible Soviet lead.
June 1980		600	Aspin	Limited/Influential	Reconfirms officially acknowledged U.S. CEP.
July 1980		729	Collins	Limited/Influential	Reinforces impression of higher U.S. CEP, directly confronting reports of lower one and denying their validity.

(continued)

Comparative Chronology of Estimates of United States and Soviet Missile Accuracy During a Period of Growing American Superiority in Precision Guidance, 1979–83 (cont.)

Date	Soviet CEP (ft)	American CEP (ft)	Source	Dissemination	Impression Created
Aug. 1980	600		Lee	Limited	Follows *Aviation Week*'s February statement, placing range of CEP between 600 and 900 ft.
Aug. 1980	364		Lee	Limited	Attributes but misquotes *Aviation Week*'s February statement in footnote. Suggests Soviet CEP may be far lower than reported.
Sept. 1980	984	984	SIPRI	Limited	Places Soviet CEP within range between 984 and 1476 ft. Thus, suggests parity with possible U.S. lead.
Sept. 1980	984	984	UN	Broad	Follows SIPRI statement.
Oct. 1980	1519		Powers	Limited	Follows lowest of Schlesinger estimates given in 1975. Suggests reports of lower Soviet CEPs are exaggerated.
Dec. 1980	600	900	IISS	Broad/Influential	Suggests current Soviet superiority, and no more for U.S. than parity in the immediate future.
May 1981	1215	607	Heylin	Limited	Suggests U.S. superiority.
Sept. 1981		656	SIPRI	Limited	With statement that "comparable" CEP has been attributed to Soviet missiles, suggests parity.
Dec. 1981		1312	*Jane's*	Broad/Influential	Taken with other reports of Soviet CEPs lower than this one, suggests Soviet superiority.
Dec. 1981	600		IISS	Broad/Influential	Reinforces impression of lower Soviet CEP. Avoids confirming whether U.S. has achieved the same CEP, as anticipated in previous year's report. Thus, suggests possible continuing Soviet lead, or parity at best.
1981	1033	1148	Koenig	Limited	Suggests poorer CEPs than generally reported, and slight Soviet lead continuing through 1985 with CEP of 721 ft against U.S. CEP of 738 ft.
1981	850		DIA	Limited/Influential	Official assertion of Soviet capability.
Mar. 1982		900+	AW&ST	Broad/Influential	Reinforces impression of higher U.S. CEP created by 1980 reports from IISS, SIPRI, and UN,

Date			Source	Category	Description
June 1982	1387		AW&ST	Broad/Influential	May be unauthorized leak of true Soviet capability. Taken together with March statement, suggests poorer CEPs than generally reported—but with U.S. lead.
Aug. 1982	911	1312	Cordesman	Limited/Influential	Acknowledges U.S. CEP will soon be 656 ft, but suggests Soviet superiority meanwhile.
Nov. 1982	800		AW&ST	Broad/Influential	Taken together with March statement, now suggests Soviet lead.
Nov. 1982	850	600	Aldridge	Limited/Influential	Reconfirms official statements acknowledging U.S. superiority.
Dec. 1982	984	721	IISS	Broad/Influential	Now suggests U.S. superiority, but with higher than officially acknowledged CEPs, returning U.S. CEP to Nitze level.
Feb. 1983		630	Middleton	Very Broad	Reconfirms officially acknowledged U.S. CEP.
Feb. 1983	450		White	Very Broad	Stunning exaggeration of Soviet capability. Appears to have been officially planted. Taken together with Middleton statement, suggests significant Soviet lead.
Mar. 1983	600		AW&ST	Broad/Influential	Reinforces impression of Soviet CEP substantially lower than officially acknowledged.
May 1983	911	729	CBO	Limited/Influential	Returns CEPs to Nitze levels. Indicates expected improvement in Soviet CEPs, but not in U.S. CEPs.
Dec. 1983	984	721	IISS	Broad/Influential	Continues to acknowledge U.S. superiority, but with higher than officially acknowledged CEPs.

CEP: Circular Error Probable, or the distance from a specific aimpoint within which half of the reentry vehicles of a specific type are expected to fall.

Note: small differences, for example between 600 and 607 ft, or between 721 and 729 ft, are the result of conversion to linear feet from meters in one case, or from fractions of a nautical mile in another.

Appendix D

The Quest for Certainty: The Future of Nuclear Weapons

The study in this appendix examines the proven capabilities of nuclear weapons, and the continuing effort to increase their accuracy and lethality, in order to increase the likelihood that they will destroy whatever targets they attack. It examines weapons in current inventory as well as those now in development, and demonstrates that the lethality of a nuclear weapon depends more on its accuracy than on its explosive yield.

The study also demonstrates that even though increasing levels of lethality can be offset partially by hardening their intended targets to resist greater levels of blast overpressure, there is a limit not only to the degree to which structures may be hardened but also to how much difference hardening them will finally make. Once a weapon has become so accurate that its probable radius of error is *smaller* than its radius of lethal destruction, no amount of hardening will protect its target. It will detonate within such close proximity to that target that it will either excavate and vaporize whatever is there or bury it under tons of rubble.

Weapons with this degree of accuracy have reached what analysts call a level of maximum lethality. This study notes that a number of America's weapons have either reached that level of accuracy or are closer to it than those the Soviet Union now possesses. Taking the most accurate weapons now deployed or soon to gain operational status, it compares the probable radius of error of each to the radius of its lethal blast overpressures, the radius and depth of the crater it will dig, first in rock, then in soil, and the larger radius of the debris it will throw up around the lip of its crater. This provides a number of graphic examples of maximum lethality.

But this study also notes that no matter how far these improvements progress, and despite the inevitability of a time when the Soviets will match them, improved lethality can never *guarantee* that every target a nation attacks will be destroyed. The only successful first strike is one which renders the nation first struck incapable of retaliating. Any retaliatory action may inflict unacceptable damage upon the attacker. Because success will always remain uncertain, and there is no guarantee of preventing retaliation, the risks of failure will always remain too high.

Through a series of hypothetical first strike and survivability scenarios, this study examines the effects of probability on operational planning for the offensive use of strategic weapons. Probability is everywhere. It is expressed in the very definition of missile accuracy. The Circular Error Probable of a specific type of reentry vehicle is defined as the distance from its aimpoint within which only half the reentry vehicles of that type are expected to fall. The other half are anticipated to fall *beyond* that distance, most probably with no military effect.

Planners consider probability when they acknowledge that many weapons may not perform as expected, and may not survive long enough in a nuclear combat environment to carry out their missions. They express these probabilities by assigning each weapon system percentage rates of reliability and survivability. Almost all of these rates fall well below 100 percent. To the degree that they do so, they reflect a corresponding degree of uncertainty about the outcome of their use. Yet even the smallest uncertainty immediately involves an unacceptable level of risk.

According to these scenarios, a maximum first strike effort against 1,737 military targets in the United States would still leave at least 847 targets untouched, even though the attack came without warning, and even though the United States chose not to launch its land-based missiles under attack but to ride out the attack instead. Or that same attack *might* leave as many as 5,316 targets untouched. A maximum American first strike effort against 1,848 military targets in the Soviet Union might leave as few as six targets undestroyed, if that attack, too, came without warning and if the Soviet Union also chose to ride it out and not launch its own land-based missiles. Or the attack might leave as many as 601 targets undestroyed. Any or all of these could be silos holding missiles American planners had hoped to eliminate.

Even theoretically, then, the success of a nuclear attack is in doubt. These theoretical results are but the beginning of uncertainty. The uncertainties they already express are dangerous enough. But many further uncertainties cannot be expressed at all in theoretical formulas. Formulas for the probable accuracy, reliability, and survivability of nuclear weapons cannot begin to take them into account.

Nuclear weapons, and an attack utilizing them, can never be fully tested except in war itself. No amount of extrapolation from limited test data can ever assure that every missile whose fuel is ignited will launch, that it will follow its intended trajectory, that atmospheric conditions or variable shifts in polar magnetism, impossible to predict in advance, will not throw it off course, that it will release its reentry vehicles at the proper time and place, that these will fall toward their intended targets, that all of them will detonate, that all will achieve their anticipated yield, and that the effects of their explosions will not blow other reentry vehicles off course or destroy them before they can detonate themselves.

These are but a few of the random and systematic uncertainties that will always make it impossible to predict the outcome of a nuclear attack. Those uncertainties are beyond the scope of these scenarios, or of any other scenarios devised by governments. Such uncertainties continue to pose unacceptable risks. Thus, while all of our efforts to improve the lethality of our weapons are only attempts to gain certainty and eliminate risk, certainty never can be achieved.

Appendix D is divided into two sections:

Accuracy and Lethality. This section documents the theoretical levels of accuracy that have now been achieved and will soon be achieved for nuclear weapons of various types, and illustrates the extent to which improvements in accuracy have increased the theoretical lethality of such weapons against hardened targets.

Warfighting Scenarios: Probability and Strategic Offensive Operations. This section demonstrates that no matter how lethal individual nuclear weapons theoretically have become, their combined operational use is governed by uncertainties which cannot be eliminated or even reduced to proportions that guarantee against failure, the risks of which will always be too high.

Accuracy and Lethality

TABLES IN THIS SECTION

Nuclear Warhead Lethality Depends More on Accuracy than on Yield: Illustrations

Comparable Accuracy, with a Ten-Fold Increase in Yield

RV Type	Yield (KT)	CEP (ft)	Target Destruction Probability	
			SSKP	TSKP
SS-N-18 Mod 1 (USSR)	200	4617	.9%	1%
SS-11 Mod 2 (USSR)	2000	4253	4%	10%

Comparable Yield, with a Ten-Fold Increase in Accuracy

RV Type	Yield (KT)	CEP (ft)	Target Destruction Probability	
			SSKP	TSKP
SS-N-6-Mod 3 (USSR)	350	6076	1%	3%
Minuteman III (USA) with Mk 12A	335	607	55%	83%

RV: Reentry Vehicle.

KT: Explosive power measured by the number of kilotons of TNT required to release an equivalent amount of energy.

CEP: Circular Error Probable, or the distance from a specific aimpoint within which half of the reentry vehicles of a specific type are expected to fall.

SSKP: Single-Shot Kill Probability, or the likelihood that a single warhead will destroy its intended target.

TSKP: Two-Shot Kill Probability, or the likelihood that two warheads aimed at the same target will destroy it.

Sources and Method

Kill probabilities are computed on the assumption that Soviet missile silos are hardened to resist 3000 psi of atmospheric overpressure, while American silos are hardened to resist 2000 psi. Computations are based on formulas provided by Kosta Tsipis, *Offensive Missiles: Stockholm Paper 5,* Stockholm International Peace Research Institute (Stockholm: Almqvist & Wiksell, 1974), page 18. Kill probabilities are shown here assuming 100% system reliability. Yields and CEPs of weapons compared are drawn from Robert C. Aldridge, *First Strike! The Pentagon's Strategy for Nuclear War* (Boston: South End Press, 1983), pages 59–60.

Increasing Resistance to Blast Overpressures: Its Effects on Probable Warhead Lethality

RV Type	Yield (KT)	CEP (ft)	SSKP Against Soviet Missile Silos Hardened to Resist:			
			450 psi	1000 psi	2500 psi	3000 psi
Minuteman III						
with Mk 12	170	607	86%	75%	55%	38%
with Mk 12A	335	607	97%	88%	70%	55%

RV: Reentry Vehicle.

KT: Explosive power measured by the number of kilotons of TNT required to release an equivalent amount of energy.

CEP: Circular Error Probable, or the distance from a specific aimpoint within which half of the reentry vehicles of a specific type are expected to fall.

SSKP: Single-Shot Kill Probability, or the likelihood that a single warhead will destroy its intended target.

Sources

Kill probabilities are computed on the basis of formulas provided by Tsipis, *op. cit.*, page 18. CEPs are from the House Armed Services Committee, *Authorization Hearings, FY 1979*, Part 3, Book 1, page 307.

Estimates of the Resistance of Hardened Missile Silos to Blast Overpressures, 1978–83

Date	Source	Resistance Measured in psi			Comments
		USSR	USA	Future	
May 1978	Aldridge				USA "has always been ahead" in "target hardening."
Dec. 1979	Collins	1000			
June 1980	Aspin	2500	2000		"We have very nearly reached the limit of silo hardness."
Feb. 1981	HAC		2000		
Sept. 1981	SIPRI	1000			
Dec. 1981	Powers	2000 to 4000	2000 to 4000		Estimates cited in professional literature.
1981	Scoville	3000	2000		3000 psi is maximum hardness "believed possible" for silos.
Jan. 1982	*AW&ST*			5000	Option exists to harden silos to this level "if Congress approves."
Jan. 1982	Townes				Raised questions on the "levels of hardness possible" and on the "survivability" of MX.
Mar. 1982	*AW&ST*			5000	"Inherent hardness" of MX Dense Pack *capsule.*
May 1982	*AW&ST*			10,000	Hardness of MX *silo* against airburst. Hardness of silo against ground shock now 5000 to 6000 psi.
June 1982	*AW&ST*			5000 to 10,000	Hardness of MX *capsule.* Could be hardened to "levels several times higher."
June 1982	Hall				"Requisite levels of hardness can be achieved" for MX.
June 1982	Agbabian				"We have good confidence in theoretical ability" to achieve higher levels of hardness.
Aug. 1982	Cordesman	3500 to 4000	2000		
Aug. 1982	*AW&ST*			15,000	Hardness of "vertical shelters" against airburst.
Nov. 1982	*NY Times*		2000		

(*continued*)

Estimates of the Resistance of Hardened Missile Silos to Blast Overpressures, 1978–83 (*cont.*)

Date	Source	Resistance Measured in psi			Comments
		USSR	USA	Future	
Nov. 1982	USAF			10,000	Intended hardness of MX silo against airburst. Hardness against ground shocks up to 5000 psi.
Nov. 1982	USAF			100,000	Possible hardness of silos.
Nov. 1982	*Air Force Mag.*			130,000	Possible hardness of silos.
Nov. 1982	*NY Times*			100,000	Possible hardness of silos.
Nov. 1982	Townes				Expresses "skepticism" that MX silos "could be hardened enough" to withstand blast of "all-out" Soviet attack.
1983	Cambridge Univ.	450			
Jan. 1983	*AW&ST*	7200			Hardness of "some" Soviet silos as a result of "recent improvements by the USSR."
May 1983	DeLauer			25,000	*Minuteman* silos could be hardened to "nearly thirteen times" their current hardness.

Sources

May 1978   Robert Aldridge, "The Missile Shell Game," *The Nation,* May 13, 1978, page 562.

Dec. 1979   John M. Collins, *op. cit.,* 1980, page 136.

June 1980   Les Aspin, *op. cit.* (June, 1980), page 30.

Feb. 1981   House Appropriations Committee, *Hearings, Department of Defense Appropriations, Fiscal Year 1982,* Part 2, page 499.

Sept. 1981   SIPRI, *op. cit.,* 1981, page 12.

Dec. 1981   Thomas Powers, "How Accurate Is Accurate?" *Commonweal,* December 4, 1981, reprinted in Powers, *Thinking About the Next War,* 1982, page 77.

1981   Herbert Scoville, *MX: Prescription for Disaster* (Cambridge, Mass.: MIT Press, 1981), pages 15–16.

Jan. 1982   *Aviation Week & Space Technology,* January 11, 1982, page 21.

Jan. 1982   Charles H. Townes, head of Defense Department commission to study MX basing, quoted in *Aviation Week & Space Technology,* January 22, 1982, page 18.

Mar. 1982   *Aviation Week & Space Technology,* March 29, 1982, page 21.

May 1982   *Aviation Week & Space Technology,* May 3, 1982, page 14.

June 1982   *Aviation Week & Space Technology,* June 28, 1982, page 22.

June 1982   William T. Hall, Department of Civil Engineering, University of Illinois at Urbana, and member of Townes Commission, interview with author, June 18, 1982.

June 1982   Mihran Agbabian, Agbabian Associates, Los Angeles, and Member of Townes Commission, interview with author, June 18, 1982.

Aug. 1982   Anthony H. Cordesman, *op. cit.,* 1982, page 25.

Aug. 1982   *Aviation Week & Space Technology,* August 9, 1982, page 18.

Nov. 1982   Charles Mohr, "Credibility of Basing System for MX Affects Military, Money and Politics," *The New York Times,* November 24, 1982.

Nov. 1982   United States Air Force, quoted by Mohr, *op. cit.,* November 24, 1982.

Nov. 1982   United States Air Force, quoted by Mohr, *op. cit.,* November 24, 1982.

Nov. 1982   *Air Force Magazine,* quoted by Mohr, *op. cit.,* November 24, 1982.

Nov. 1982   Richard Halloran, "President Urges Support for Dense Pack Deployment of MX Missile," *The New York Times,* November 23, 1982.

Nov. 1982   Charles Townes, quoted by Halloran, *op. cit.,* November 23, 1982. The Townes Commission concluded that the United States "has not been able to achieve" necessary silo hardness to withstand Soviet attack.

1983   Cambridge University Disarmament Seminar, *Defended to Death* (Harmondsworth, Middlesex: Penguin, 1983), page 302.

Jan. 1983   *Aviation Week & Space Technology,* "Navy to Develop New Trident Warhead," January 17, 1983, page 26.

May 1983   Richard DeLauer, Under Secretary of Defense for Research and Engineering, in testimony before the House Defense Appropriations Subcommittee, May 3, 1983.

Comparative Estimate of the Lethality of the Most Accurate ICBMs in American and Soviet Arsenals, 1979–83

USA RV Type	Number of RVs Deployed December, 1982	Against Soviet Missile Silos Hardened to Resist 3000 psi			
		Yield (KT)	CEP (ft)	SSKP	TSKP
Minuteman III					
with Mk 12	750	170	607	38%	63%
with MK 12A	900	335	607	55%	83%
USSR RV Type	Probable Number of RVs Deployed December, 1982	Against American Missile Silos Hardened ro Resist 2000 psi			
		Yield (KT)	CEP (ft)	SSKP	TSKP
SS-18 Mod 4	250	500	850	40%	65%
SS-19 Mod 1	1440	550	850	42%	68%

RV: Reentry Vehicle.

KT: Explosive power measured by the number of kilotons of TNT required to release an equiva-lent amount of energy.

CEP: Circular Error Probable, or the distance from a specific aimpoint within which half of the reen-try vehicles of a specific type are expected to fall.

SSKP: Single-Shot Kill Probability, or the likelihood that a single warhead will destroy its intended tar-get.

TSKP: Two-Shot Kill Probability, or the likelihood that two warheads aimed at the same target will destroy it.

Sources and Method

Kill probabilities are computed on the basis of formulas provided by Tsipis, *op. cit.*, 1974, page 18, and are shown here assuming 100% system reliability. RV yields and CEPs are drawn from Aldridge, *op. cit.*, 1983, pages 59 and 60. The numbers of Mk 12 and Mk 12A RVs deployed by December, 1982, are taken from Cochran, *op. cit.*, pages 102, 108, and 117. Probable numbers of Soviet SS-18 Mod 4 and SS-19 Mod 1 RVs deployed by December, 1982, are taken from the table, *Composition of American and Soviet Strategic Forces— December, 1982*, in Appendix A: The Strategic Balance: Author's Estimate, Summary and Analysis, and are based entirely on sources provided in that appendix.

Comparative Estimate of Additional Strategic Weapons of Very High Lethality in Soviet and American Arsenals, 1979–83

| USA | Number | Against Soviet Missile Silos Hardened to Resist 3000 psi | | | |
| | Deployed | Yield | CEP | | |
Weapon Type	December, 1982	(KT)	(ft)	SSKP	TSKP
AGM-69A SRAM	1300	200	300	99%	99%
AGM-86B ALCM	192	250	100	99%	99%
B-28 NGB	500	1500	600	99%	99%
B-43 NGB	1000	1000	600	94%	99%
B-61 NGB	1000	500	600	87%	99%
B-53 NGB	150	9000	600	99%	99%

USSR	Probable	Against American Missile Silos Hardened to Resist 2000 psi			
	Number				
RV or Weapon	Deployed	Yield	CEP		
Type	December, 1982	(KT)	(ft)	SSKP	TSKP
SS-18 Mod 1	30	25,000	1519	97%	99%
SS-18 Mod 2	1784	750	1519	34%	56%
SS-18 Mod 3	30	20,000	1519	97%	99%
SS-19 Mod 2	60	1000	1275	51%	76%
NGB	200	1000	1215	52%	77%

RV: Reentry Vehicle.

KT: Explosive power measured by the number of kilotons of TNT required to release an equivalent amount of energy.

CEP: Circular Error Probable, or the distance from a specific aimpoint within which half of the reentry vehicles of a specific type are expected to fall.

SSKP: Single-Shot Kill Probability, or the likelihood that a single warhead will destroy its intended target.

TSKP: Two-Shot Kill Probability, or the likelihood that two warheads aimed at the same target will destroy it.

Sources and Method

Kill probabilities are computed on the basis of formulas provided by Tsipis, *op. cit.*, 1974, page 18, and are shown here assuming 100% system reliability. Yields of all American weapons are from Cochran, *op. cit.*, 1984, pages 42, 49, 58, 65, 154, and 177. The CEP of the ALCM is from House International Relations and Senate Foreign Relations Committees, *Analysis of Arms Control Impact Statement Submitted in Connection with the Fiscal Year 1978 Budget Request*, United States Congress, April, 1977, page 83, and is further confirmed by the Congressional Budget Office, *Modernizing U.S. Strategic Forces*, May, 1983, pages 86–87. The CEP of the B-61 is from *Aerospace Daily*, December 28, 1978, page 263. The CEPs of other American nuclear gravity bombs are from Kaplan, *op. cit.*, 1980, page 88. Yields and CEPs of Soviet weapons are based on Kaplan, *op. cit.*, 1980, page 90, with the following exceptions: the higher yield of the SS-18 Mod 1 is from Aldridge, *op. cit.*, 1983, page 59; the lower yield of the SS-19 Mod 2 is from Randall Forsberg, "A Bilateral Nuclear-

Weapon Freeze," *Scientific American* (November, 1982), page 54. The numbers of all Soviet and American weapons deployed are from the table, *Composition of American and Soviet Strategic Forces—December, 1982,* in Appendix A, The Strategic Balance: Author's Estimate, Summary and Analysis, and are based entirely on sources provided in that appendix.

Additional American Weapons of Very High Lethality Under Development or Now Being Deployed and Available for Strategic Use

Weapon Type	Probable Number Deployed December 1990	Against Soviet Missile Silos Hardened to Resist 3000 psi			
		Yield (KT)	CEP (ft)	SSKP	TSKP
BGM-109 GLCM	464	50	100	99%	99%
BGM-109 SLCM	384	250	100	99%	99%
Pershing II	108	50	100	99%	99%
Mk 4/Improved Trident I C-4	3072	100	303	99%	99%
Mk 21/ABRV/MX	1000	300	303	99%	99%
Mk 600 PGRV Trident II D-5	816	75	30	99%	99%
B-83 NGB	2500	1000	600	99%	99%

RV: Reentry Vehicle.

KT: Explosive Power measured by the number of kilotons of TNT required to release an equivalent amount of energy.

CEP: Circular Error Probable, or the distance from a specific aimpoint within which half of the reentry vehicles of a specific type are expected to fall.

SSKP: Single-Shot Kill Probability, or the likelihood that a single warhead will destroy its intended target.

TSKP: Two-Shot Kill Probability, or the likelihood that two warheads aimed at the same target will destroy it.

Sources and Method

Kill probabilities are computed on the basis of formulas provided by Tsipis, *op. cit.,* 1974, page 18, and are shown here assuming 100% system reliability. Yields of all weapons are from Cochran, *op. cit.,* 1984, pages 125, 126, 142, 179, 185, 200, and 294, except that the yield of the Mk 600 PGRV is from Aldridge, *op. cit.,* 1983, page 96. CEPs for all weapons are from sources noted in the table, *The Present and Future of Accuracy: Current and Scheduled Improvements in American Strategic Missile Guidance Systems.* Probable numbers of weapons deployed by 1990 are based on figures planned for production and deployment, and noted in the same entries in Cochran, *op. cit.,* 1984.

The Destructive Effects of Increasing Thermonuclear Yields

Warhead Type/RV/Weapon System	Nation	Maximum Yield (KT/MT)	Radius of Atmospheric Overpressure (ft)			Crater Size (ft)		
			10,000 psi	5000 psi	2000 psi	Depth Rock/Soil	Radius Rock/Soil	Radius of Debris Rock/Soil
W-68/Mk 3/Poseidon C-3	USA	40 KT	280	370	500	80/ 95	160/ 195	315/ 400
W-84/GLCM and W-85/Pershing II	USA	50 KT	285	375	520	85/105	175/ 210	345/ 420
Mk 600 PGRV/Trident II D-5	USA	75 KT	295	390	550	95/115	200/ 245	395/ 485
W-76/Mk 4/Trident I C-4	USA	100 KT	300	400	560	105/135	210/ 265	420/ 525
W-62/Mk 12/Minuteman III	USA	170 KT	375	470	675	125/150	240/ 315	500/ 655
W-69/SRAM	USA	200 KT	400	520	750	135/160	265/ 345	550/ 665
W-80/ALCM and SLCM	USA	250 KT	440	560	790	140/185	290/ 370	635/ 775
W-78/Mk 12A/Minuteman III	USA	335 KT	480	610	840	155/195	315/ 400	660/ 790
SS-18 Mod 4	USSR	500 KT	560	680	960	175/210	340/ 435	740/ 815
SS-19 Mod 1	USSR	550 KT	570	700	1000	180/215	370/ 445	765/ 825
SS-18 Mod 2	USSR	750 KT	640	800	1450	205/255	420/ 530	810/1050
		900 KT	660	840	1480	210/265	455/ 610	820/1205
W-56/Mk 11C/Minuteman II	USA	1 MT	690	880	1510	225/275	475/ 635	825/1240
		5 MT	1360	1740	2450	380/475	800/ 840	1665/2085
W-53/Mk 6/Titan II	USA	9 MT	1590	2100	2830	465/635	835/1270	2030/2590
		10 MT	1730	2150	2900	480/665	845/1315	2110/2640
SS-18 Mod 1	USSR	25 MT	2200	2800	3380	715/800	1400/1820	2930/3695

The Present and Future of Accuracy: Current and Scheduled Improvements in American Strategic Missile Guidance Systems

		CEP (Ft)									
Warhead/RV	Weapon System	with INS-20 1984	1985	with Northrop AIRS	with Mk 6 SIG	with Radar Alt	with NAVSTAR/ GPS	with TERCOM	with RADAG	with Terminal Homing	with Terminal Homing & NAVSTAR/GPS
Currently Deployed											
W-78/Mk 12A	*Minuteman III*	607	490			300	303				
W-69	SRAM										
W-80	ALCM/SLCM							100			
W-84	GLCM							100			
W-85	*Pershing II*								100		
In Advanced Development											
W-87/Mk 21	MX			400			303				
ABRV											
W-76/Mk 4	*Trident I C-4*						303				
W-87/Mk 5	*Trident II D-5*				400		303				
Mk 600 PGRV	*Trident II D-5*									100	30

Glossary of Acronyms

RV: Reentry Vehicle

AIRS: Advanced Inertial Reference Sphere

SIG: Stellar Inertial Guidance

GPS: Global Positioning System

ABRV: Advanced Ballistic Reentry Vehicle

PGRV: Precision Guided Reentry Vehicle

TERCOM: Terrain Contour Mapping

RADAG: Radar Area Correlation Guidance

CEP: Circular Error Probable, the distance from a specific aimpoint within which half of the reentry vehicles of a specific type are expected to fall.

NAVSTAR: Navigational System using Timing and Ranging. NAVSTAR/GPS satellites, six of which are now operational, will provide mid-course guidance corrections for RVs to within 10 ft in three dimensions.

385

Sources

CEP of *Minuteman III* in 1984 and 1985: see sources for the numerous citations given in the table. *Estimates of Minuteman III Accuracy, 1979–83.* CEP of *Minuteman III* with NAVSTAR/GPS: *interview with General Brent Scowcroft, NBC-TV, April 22, 1983. Comparing the potential accuracy of Minuteman III* with MX, Scowcroft said: "Warhead for warhead, you could make them virtually as accurate" as the MX, once mid-course corrections from NAVSTAR/GPS satellites were provided for both. CEP of ALCM and SLCM: House International Relations and Senate Foreign Relations Committees, *op. cit.*, April, 1977, page 83. CEP of GLCM: Cochran, *op. cit.*, 1984, page 187. This is under the entry for the *Tomahawk* SLCM. The GLCM entry, which gives no CEP, notes that "GLCM is a version of the

Tomahawk BGM-109 cruise missile [the Navy's SLCM]." CEP of *Pershing II:* Arms Control and Disarmament Agency, *Arms Control Impact Statement, Fiscal Year 1979*, page 115, and IISS, *The Military Balance, 1982–1983,* page 112. CEP of the MX missile's Mk 21 ABRV with Northrop AIRS: *Aviation Week & Space Technology,* "Congress Questioning Viability of MX ICBM," March 22, 1982, pages 18–19. CEP of the MX with NAVSTAR/GPS: Eliot Marshal, "A Question of Accuracy," *Science* (September, 1981), page 1231. CEP of Mk 4 on *Trident I* with improved accuracy: Robert C. Aldridge, *op. cit.*, 1983, page 96. CEP of Mk 5 for *Trident II:* Aldridge, *op. cit.*, 1983, page 96. CEP of Mk 600 PGRV: Aldridge, *op. cit.*, 1983, pages 93 and 96.

Maximum Lethality: When the Radius of Assured Destruction Equals or Exceeds the Probable Radius of Error

Warhead Type/RV/Weapon System	Maximum Yield (KT/MT)	CEP (ft)	Radius of Atmospheric Overpressure (ft)			Crater Size (ft)	
			10,000 psi	5000 psi	2000 psi	Radius Rock/Soil	Radius of Debris Rock/Soil
Current American Weapons							
W-84/GLCM and W-85/Pershing II	50 KT	100	285	375	520	175/ 210	345/ 420
W-62/Mk 12/Minuteman III	170 KT	607			675		/ 655
W-69/SRAM	200 KT	300	400	520	750	265/ 345	550/ 655
W-80 ALCM	250 KT	100	440	560	790	290/ 370	635/ 775
W-78/Mk 12A/Minuteman III	335 KT	607		610	840		660/ 790
B-61 NGB	500 KT	600		680	960		740/ 815
W-56/Mk 11C/Minuteman II	1 MT	1215			1510		/1240
B-43 and B-83 NGB	1 MT	600	690	880	1510	/ 635	825/1240
B-53 NGB	9 MT	600	1590	2100	2830	835/1270	2030/2590
Current Soviet Weapons							
SS-18 Mod 4	500 KT	850			960		
SS-19 Mod 1	550 KT	850			1000		
SS-19 Mod 2	1 MT	1275			1510		/1240
NGB	1 MT	1215			1510		/1240
SS-18 Mod 3	20 MT	1519	2010	2660	3240	/1770	2820/3530
SS-18 Mod 1	25 MT	1519	2200	2800	3380	/1820	2930/3695
Future American Weapons							
Mk 600 PGRV/Trident II D-5	75 KT	30	295	390	550	200/ 245	395/ 485
W-76/Mk 4/Trident I C-4	100 KT	303	300	400	560	210/ 265	420/ 525
W-80/SLCM	250 KT	100	440	560	790	290/ 370	635/ 775
W-78/Mk 12A/Minuteman III	335 KT	490	480	610	840		660/ 790
Mk 12A with NAVSTAR/GPS	335 KT	303	480	610	840	315/ 400	660/ 790
W-87/Mk 21 ABRV/MX	300 KT	303	480	610	840	315/ 400	660/ 790
W-87/Mk 5/Trident II D-5	300 KT	303	480	610	840	315/ 400	660/ 790
W-87 Upgrade	475 KT	303	540	670	945	335/ 425	725/ 805

Notes

With mid-course corrections from NAVSTAR/GPS satellites, the accuracy of the Mk 12A reentry vehicle can be improved, reducing its CEP from 490 ft to 300 ft, and further increasing its lethal effects as shown. NAVSTAR/GPS guidance will be used to achieve the same level of accuracy, as shown, for the Mk 21 and Mk 5 reentry vehicles. The yield of the W-87 warhead used on the Mk 21 and Mk 5 reentry vehicles may be upgraded to 475 kilotons, producing the greater lethal effects shown.

RV: Reentry Vehicle.

KT: Explosive power measured by the number of kilotons of TNT required to release an equivalent amount of energy.

MT: Explosive power measured by the number of megatons of TNT required to release an equivalent amount of energy. 1 megaton is equal to 1000 kilotons.

CEP: Circular Error Probable, or the distance from a specific aimpoint within which half of the reentry vehicles of a specific type are expected to fall.

psi: Pounds per Square Inch of transient atmospheric overpressure, induced by the force of energy released. A force of 10,000 psi, believed to be the maximum overpressure produced by a thermonuclear explosion, will be generated nearest to its point of detonation. Lesser forces will radiate further from that point.

Interpretation

According to Herbert Scoville, the greatest strength "believed possible" for missile silos or other subsurface structures adjoining ground surfaces will resist a maximum of 3000 psi (see Scoville, MX: Prescription for Disaster [Cambridge: MIT Press, 1981], pages 15–16). Higher forces may then be expected to destroy any such hardened structure. Targets within a radius of overpressures of 5000 psi or more will certainly be destroyed. Even if targets within a radius of 2000 psi of overpressure have been hardened to resist that level of force, they may still be destroyed or rendered inoperable by a variety of other effects not considered here. These include, for example, the effects of ground acceleration, thermal radiation, and electromagnetic pulse, all of which vary according to the limited options possible for protection against them, local geologic conditions, unlimited variations in atmospheric conditions, and such additional random factors as the degree of efficiency with which a weapon's fissile materials achieve their anticipated yield.

There have been many recent claims, especially in connection with efforts to gain public and congressional approval of Dense Pack basing of the MX missile, that targets may be hardened to withstand much greater forces than 3000 psi. The truth of such claims becomes irrelevant when targets are within the radius of the crater excavated by a nuclear explosion or buried by the tons of debris of the crater which form its lip. The depth of a crater, its radius, and the larger radius of its debris, as well as the areas subject to lethal blast overpressures, all increase with the magnitude of the explosion that produces them. These variations are shown in the tables, ranked by increases in explosive yield. If the probable radius of error attributed to a bomb or reentry vehicle in striking the center of its aimpoint becomes smaller than the crater it digs, the debris it throws out, or the area it subjects to lethal overpressures, then that weapon is said to approach maximum lethality.

Sources and Method

Radii of atmospheric overpressure are derived from formulas provided by Kosta Tsipis, Nuclear Explosion Effects on Missile Silos (Cambridge, Mass.: MIT Center for International Studies, 1978) pages 20 and 23. They assume surface bursts to optimize peak overpressures at 100 feet above ground level. Crater depths and radii are computed for sea-level conditions by the Lovelace Foundation's "Nuclear Bomb Effects Computer," rev. ed., 1962, based on data from Samuel Glasstone, ed., The Effects of Nuclear Weapons (Washington, D.C.: United States Department of Defense and United States Atomic Energy Commission, 1962), chapter VI.

Possible Composition of American Strategic Forces—December, 1990

Missile or Aircraft Type	Number	Warheads on Each	Total Warheads	RV and Warhead Type	Yield (KT)	CEP (ft)	SSKP	TSKP
Minuteman II	400	1	400	Mk 11C/W-56	1200	1215	31%	52%
Minuteman III	600	3	1800	Mk 12A/W-78	335	303	94%	99%
MX	100	10	1000	Mk 21/W-87	300	303	99%	99%
Poseidon C-3	304	14	4256	Mk 3/W-68	40	1200	10%	19%
Trident C-4	384	8	3072	Mk 4/W-76	100	303	99%	99%
Trident D-5	48	17	816	Mk 600 PGRV	75	30	99%	99%
FB-111A	56	6	336					
B-52G	90	12	1080	B-83 NGB	1000	600	99%	99%
B-52H	90	12	1080	SRAM/W-69	200	300	99%	99%
B-1	90	22	1980	ALCM/W-80	250	100	99%	99%
T-ALM/N								
SLCM	384	1	384	W-80	250	100	99%	99%
GLCM	464	1	464	W-84	50	100	99%	99%
Pershing II	108	1	108	W-85	50	100	99%	99%
Warhead Total:			16,776					

Sources

Kill probabilities are computed on the basis of formulas provided by Tsipis, *op. cit.*, 1974, page 18, and are shown here assuming 100% system reliability. Yields of all weapons are from Cochran, *op. cit.*, 1984, pages 62, 69, 71, 74, 75, 79, 113, 116, 126, 137, 142, 154, 179, 185, 200, and 294, except that the yield of the Mk 600 PGRV is from Aldridge, *op. cit.*, 1983, page 96. CEPs for all weapons are from the sources noted in the preceding table. *The Present and Future of Accuracy: Current and Scheduled Improvements in American Strategic Missile Guidance Systems*. The probable numbers of weapons deployed by 1990 are based on figures planned for production and deployment, and noted in the same entries in Cochran, *op. cit.*, 1984. Operational bomber loadings are from the Congressional Budget Office, *Modernizing U.S. Strategic Forces*, May, 1983, page 86.

Warfighting Scenarios
Probability and Strategic Offensive Operations

TABLES IN THIS SECTION

- Possible Results of a Soviet First Strike, December, 1982
  —Limited First Strike, Targeting Each ICBM Silo with One RV
  —Limited First Strike, Cross-Targeting with Two RVs per ICBM Silo
  —Maximum First Strike Effort
- Possible Results of a U.S. First Strike, December, 1982
  —Limited First Strike, Cross-Targeting with Two RVs per ICBM Silo
  —Maximum First Strike Effort
- Soviet Retaliatory Capability After a Maximum U.S. First Strike Effort, December, 1982
- United States Retaliatory Capability After a Maximum Soviet First Strike Effort, December, 1982
- Summary of United States and Soviet First Strike and Retaliatory Capabilities, December, 1982

The Effects of Probability on Strategic Offensive Operations: Possible Results of a Soviet First Strike—December, 1982

First Scenario: A Limited First Strike on 825 U.S. ICBM Silos. *Targets:* 550 *Minuteman III* and 275 *Minuteman II* Silos.
Operational Plan: Target Each ICBM Silo with One RV, Using Most Accurate RVs Available.

Type of Weapon Used	Yield (KT)	CEP (ft)	Number of RVs Used in Attack	System Reliability Rate	Max. Probable Number of Operational RVs on Target	Max. Possible Number of Targets	Target Destruction Probability (SSKP)	U.S. ICBMs Destroyed	
								If in Silos	If Already Launched
SS-19 Mod 1	550	850	825	75%	618	618	42%	259	0

Second Scenario: A Limited First Strike on 825 U.S. ICBM Silos. *Targets:* 550 *Minuteman III* and 275 *Minuteman II* Silos.
Operational Plan: Cross-Targeting with Two RVs per ICBM Silo, Using Most Accurate RVs Available.

Types of Weapon Used	Yield (KT)	CEP (ft)	Number of RVs Used in Attack	System Reliability Rate	Max. Probable Number of Operational RVs on Target	Max. Possible Number of Targets	Target Destruction Probability (TSKP)	U.S ICBMs Destroyed	
								If in Silos	If Already Launched
SS-18 Mod 4	500	850	210	75%	158	79	65%	51	0
SS-19 Mod 1	550	850	1440	75%	1080	540	68%	367	0
						Total of U.S. ICBMs Destroyed:		418	0
						Total of U.S. ICBMs Intact:		407	825

See Note on Assumptions, page 393.

Third Scenario: A Maximum Soviet Effort to Destroy All U.S. ICBMs and Other Military Targets.

Targets: 1052 U.S. ICBM Silos, and 685 Other Hardened Targets, including Command and Communications Centers.*

Operational Plan: Cross-Targeting with Two RVs per Target, Using All Accurate RVs Available, Single Targeting of Additional Targets with High-Yield RVs, and Bomber Strikes.

Types of Weapon Used	Yield (KT)	CEP (ft)	Number of Weapons Used in Attack	System Reliability Rate	Max. Probable Number of Operational Weapons on Target	Max. Possible Number of Targets	Target Destruction Probability (TSKP)	U.S. Targets Destroyed: ICBMs and All Other Targets	If ICBMs Already Launched
SS-18 Mod 2	750	1519	1784	75%	1338	669	56%	374	
SS-18 Mod 4	500	850	250	75%	188	94	65%	61	
SS-19 Mod 1	550	850	1440	75%	1080	540	68%	367	
							(SSKP)		
SS-18 Mod 1	25,000	1519	30	75%	23	23	97%	22	
SS-18 Mod 3	20,000	1519	30	75%	23	23	97%	22	
SS-19 Mod 2	1000	1275	60	75%	45	45	51%	23	
				Bomber Survivability Rate			(SSKP)		
Nuclear Gravity Bomb	1000	1215	200	20%	40	40	52%	21	
								890	1052
								162	
								847	

Total of Targets Attacked: 1737   Total of U.S. Targets Destroyed: 890
If All Targets Destroyed Were ICBMs, Total of U.S. ICBMs Intact: 162
If All Undestroyed Targets Were ICBMs, Possible Total of U.S. ICBMs Intact: 847

* U.S. airfields, radar installations, and submarine bases could be targeted with the less accurate remaining Soviet ICBMs and with SLBMs. See Note on Assumptions, page 393.

The Effects of Probability on Strategic Offensive Operations: Possible Results of a U.S. First Strike—December, 1982

Fourth Scenario: A Limited First Strike on 825 Soviet ICBM Silos. *Targets:* 308 SS-18 Silos, 300 SS-19 Silos, 150 SS-17 Silos, 60 SS-13 Silos, and 7 SS-11 Silos.*
Operational Plan: Cross-Targeting with Two RVs per ICBM Silo.

Types of Weapon Used	Yield (KT)	CEP (ft)	Number of RVs Used in Attack	System Reliability Rate	Max. Probable Number of Operational RVs on Target	Max. Possible Number of Targets	Target Destruction Probability (TSKP)	Soviet ICBMs Destroyed	
								If in Silos	If Already Launched
Minuteman III									
with Mk 12	170	607	750	98%	735	367	63%	231	0
with Mk 12A	335	607	900	98%	882	441	83%	366	0
Total of Soviet ICBMs Destroyed:								597	0
Total of Soviet ICBMs Intact:								228	825

* Of the 1398 Soviet ICBM silos, this includes all but 573 SS-11 silos.
See Note on Assumptions, page 393.

Fifth Scenario: A Maximum Effort to Destroy All Soviet ICBMs and Other Military Targets.
Targets: 1398 Soviet ICBM Silos, and 450 Other Hardened Targets, including Command and Communications Centers.*
Operational Plan: Cross-Targeting with Two RVs per Target, using All Accurate RVs Available, Combined with Bomber Strikes.

Types of Weapon Used	Yield (KT)	CEP (ft)	Number of Weapons Used in Attack	System Reliability Rate	Maximum Probable Number of Operational Weapons on Target	Max. Possible Number of Targets	Target Destruction Probability (TSKP)	Soviet Targets Destroyed	
								ICBMs and All Other Targets	If ICBMs Already Launched
Mk 12	170	607	750	98%	735	367	63%	231	
Mk 12A	335	607	900	98%	882	441	83%	366	

						Bomber Survivability Rate		(SSKP)	
SRAM	200	300	224	(FB-111A)	168	75%	168	99%	166
B-61	500	600	112	(FB-111A)	84	75%	84	87%	73
SRAM	200	300	840	(B-52G/H)	420	50%	420	99%	415
ALCM	250	100	192	(B-52G)	96	50%	96	99%	95
B-43	1000	600	664	(B-52D/G/H)	332	50%	332	94%	312
B-61	500	600	424	(B-52G/H)	212	50%	212	87%	184
							1842		1398
							6		

Total of Soviet Targets Attacked: 1848   Total of Soviet Targets Destroyed: 1842
If All Undestroyed Targets Were ICBMs, Possible Total of Soviet ICBMs Intact: 6

* Soviet airfields, radar installations, and submarine bases could be targeted with the less accurate remaining U.S. ICBMs and with SLBMs. See Note on Assumptions, below.

First Strike Scenarios—A Note on Assumptions

(1) Soviet ICBM silos are assumed to be hardened to resist 3000 lbs per square inch (psi) of transient atmospheric overpressure. According to Herbert Scoville, this is the maximum hardness "believed possible" for missile silos (see Scoville, *MX: Prescription for Disaster*, pages 15–16). Consequently, this is a worst-case assumption. It is probably a good deal worse than the actual case, given the number of estimates, even from sources intent on maximizing the Soviet threat, which place the strength of Soviet silos at levels able to resist between 450 and 1000 psi.

(2) United States silos are assumed to be hardened to resist 2000 psi. This is confirmed as the actual strength of all *Minuteman* silos by the House Appropriations Committee, *Hearings, Department of Defense Appropriations, Fiscal Year 1982*, Part 2, page 499. It is further reported by Aspin, *op. cit.*, 1980, page 30, and Cordesman, *op. cit.*, 1982, page 24. Remaining *Titan II* silos are hardened to resist only 300 psi. (See House Appropriations Committee, *op. cit., Military Construction, Fiscal Year 1982*, Part 6, page 275.) *Titan II* silos comprise less than 5% of America's ICBM force. *Minuteman* silos therefore comprise more than 95%.

(3) Operational planning for cross-targeting, to expose a single target to the energy of two warheads, presupposes the use of atomic clocks for precision timing and synchronized detonation to avoid the prompt fractricidal effects of one warhead upon another. This technology is available, and its operational use is well within current Soviet as well as American capabilities. (See Kosta Tsipis and Joe Room, *Analysis of Dense Pack Vulnerabilities* [Cambridge, Mass.: MIT Department of Physics], November, 1982.)

(4) The reliability rates shown for Soviet systems are the most optimistic, those for American systems probably below standard. All but that for the *Minuteman III* are drawn from Robert Aldridge, *op. cit.*, 1983, page 56. The very high reliability rate for *Minuteman III* is confirmed by the Senate Armed Services Committee, *Hearings, Department of Defense, Fiscal Year 1981*, part 2, page 549.

(5) In scenarios involving the use of bombers, the survivability rates for all U.S. bombers are drawn from the Congressional Budget Office, *op. cit.*, May, 1983, page 61. The survivability rate for the small and vulnerable Soviet bomber force, the major portion of which is propeller-driven, is optimistic.

(6) In scenarios involving cross-targeting, the remaining number of reentry

(continued)

The Effects of Probability on Strategic Offensive Operations: Possible Results of a U.S. First Strike—December, 1982 (cont.)

vehicles performing reliably, after reductions have been made for probable system failures, has been assumed to distribute itself evenly among all possible targets. This assumption is made in order to maximize the higher lethality of cross-targeting, and to present what seems the worst case of maximum possible losses. In reality, some silos might not be hit at all, while others might be hit with far more destructive force than needed to destroy them. Formulas for kill probabilities attempt to compensate for these random results, as well as for the expectation that only *half* the reentry vehicles with a given CEP will fall within it. To the extent that they fail to reflect these conditions, however, the results they are utilized to predict become even more theoretical than they already were to begin with.

(7) Operational planning for first strikes will always be subject to a variety of additional uncertainties, both random and systematic, which remain impossible to resolve, and which are discussed at several points in the text. Also see Kosta Tsipis, *Arsenal: Understanding Weapons in the Nuclear Age* (New York: Simon & Schuster, 1983), "The Calculus of Counterforce," and Appendixes D, E, F, G, and H.

Based on the foregoing assumptions, the first strike scenarios provided

here are merely the product of a series of informed estimates of probability. They are the best that theory can do. That is not good enough, because it falls short of certainty. A first strike may be more successful than these assumptions suggest. It also may be less so.

As the accuracy and reliability of weapons improve, the result of their use seems to grow more predictable. But it never becomes certain. Improvements may reduce some uncertainties, but they do not eliminate them. Nor do they even address other uncertainties. In planning the use of nuclear weapons, even the smallest uncertainty immediately involves an unacceptable level of risk. The only successful first strike is one which renders the nation first struck incapable of retaliating. Any retaliatory action may inflict unacceptable damage upon the attacker. There is no certainty that any first strike will be able to prevent this.

If uncertainty cannot be eliminated, it cannot be treated as a marginal problem. It is fundamental and immutable. Strategic planning which ignores uncertainty is irrational. Public declarations of strategic policy which appear to ignore it are either irrational or insincere.

Soviet Retaliatory Capability After a Maximum U.S. First Strike Effort—December, 1982

Attack Without Warning (Peacetime Alert)

Bomber Forces

Bomber Warheads	Readiness		Surviving Attack	
	Bomber Rate	Warheads	Bomber Rate	Warheads
200	30%	60	90%	54

Submarine Forces

SLBM Warheads	Surviving Attack	
	Boats on Patrol	Warheads
1641	33%	541

ICBM Forces

ICBM Warheads	Readiness Rate	Surviving Attack	
		Launch Under Attack	Ride Out Attack
4804	30%	1441	6
Total of Surviving Warheads in Triad:		2036	601
*Maximum Possible Total of Surviving Hard-Target Warheads:		1495	60

Attack With Warning (Generated Alert)

Bomber Forces

Bomber Warheads	Readiness		Surviving Attack	
	Bomber Rate	Warheads	Bomber Rate	Warheads
200	95%	190	85%	161

Submarine Forces

SLBM Warheads	Surviving Attack	
	Boats on Patrol	Warheads
1641	66%	1083

ICBM Forces

ICBM Warheads	Readiness Rate	Surviving Attack	
		Launch Under Attack	Ride Out Attack
4804	98%	4707	6
Total of Surviving Warheads in Triad:		5951	1279
*Maximum Possible Total of Surviving Hard-Target Warheads:		3755	196

* Includes surviving bomber warheads, and assumes that all surviving ICBM warheads are those capable of destroying hard targets. The latter figure, however, cannot exceed the total of 3594 such warheads Soviet ICBM forces initially possess. This is reflected in the total of hard target warheads surviving if the Soviets were to launch all ICBMs under attack after a generated alert. Totals are also presented here before deductions are made for lack of 100% system reliability.

United States Retaliatory Capability After a Maximum Soviet First Strike Effort—December, 1982

Attack Without Warning (Peacetime Alert)

Bomber Forces

Bomber Warheads	Readiness		Surviving Attack	
	Bomber Rate	Warheads	Bomber Rate	Warheads
2456	30%	736	94%	691

Submarine Forces

SLBM Warheads	Surviving Attack	
	Boats on Patrol	Warheads
6272	66%	4139

ICBM Forces

ICBM Warheads	Surviving Attack		
	Readiness Rate	Launch Under Attack	Ride Out Attack
2152	98%	2108	486
Total of Surviving Warheads in Triad:		6938	5316
*Maximum Possible Total of Surviving Hard-Target Warheads:		1177	

Attack With Warning (Generated Alert)

Bomber Forces

Bomber Warheads	Readiness		Surviving Attack	
	Bomber Rate	Warheads	Bomber Rate	Warheads
2456	95%	2333	85%	1983

Submarine Forces

SLBM Warheads	Surviving Attack	
	Boats on Patrol	Warheads
6272	66%	4139

ICBM Forces

ICBM Warheads	Surviving Attack		
	Readiness Rate	Launch Under Attack	Ride Out Attack
2152	98%	2108	486
Total of Surviving Warheads in Triad:		8230	6608
*Maximum Possible Total of Surviving Hard-Target Warheads:		3633	2468

* Includes surviving bomber warheads, and assumes that all surviving ICBM warheads are those capable of destroying hard targets. The latter figure, however, cannot exceed the total of 1650 such warheads U.S. ICBM forces initially possess. This is reflected in the total of hard-target warheads surviving if the U.S. were to launch all ICBMs under attack. Totals are also presented here before deductions are made for lack of 100% system reliability.

Summary of United States and Soviet First Strike and Retaliatory Capabilities—December, 1982

| | Warheads Available for a First Strike | | Warheads Surviving if ICBM Force Launches Under Attack | | | | Warheads Surviving if ICBM Force Rides Out Attack | | | |
| | | | After Attack with Prior Warning | | After Attack Without Warning | | After Attack with Prior Warning | | After Attack Without Warning | |
	Total	Hard Target	Total	Hard Target	Total	*Hard Target	Total	*Hard Target	Total	*Hard Target
USA	10880	4106	8230	3633	6938	2341	6608	2468	5316	1177
USSR	6645	3794	5951	3794	2036	1495	1279	196	601	60

* This is the maximum possible number of hard-target warheads surviving. It assumes all targets left undestroyed after a first strike are ICBM silos, and that all the ICBMs left intact, moreover, are equipped with warheads of a type capable of destroying hard targets. The degree to which the totals shown would be lowered by chance and a variety of other agents, including varying rates of system reliability, is wholly unknown. See Note on Assumptions.

The figures shown here for surviving warheads are also based on the worst-case assumption of a maximum first strike effort. The mere computation of surviving hard-target warheads after such an effort also assumes there remains some purpose in having such a force at hand, and that it may still be used against hard targets in the attacker's homeland because those targets still hold military potential. This assumption is absurd, but it is the only basis given for expanding efforts to increase the number and survivability of such warheads, and for the nuclear war fighting strategies predicated on their use.

Sources

Readiness rates of all United States forces, and of Soviet submarine forces, are drawn from the Congressional Budget Office, op. cit., May, 1983, page 95. The survivability rates for U.S. bombers under both generated and peacetime alerts are from the same source, pages 104 and 105. Readiness and survivability rates for Soviet bombers are assumed comparable to those for U.S. bombers. The assumption is generous, as is the further assumption that Soviet submarine and ICBM forces under a generated alert will be brought to a state of readiness matching that of corresponding U.S.

forces. Submarines in port are assumed destroyed. ICBMs ready to launch under attack are assumed intact. The readiness rate of 30% for Soviet ICBMs under peacetime conditions is from Clarence A. Robinson, Jr., "SALT May Allow 3 New Soviet Missiles," *Aviation Week & Space Technology*, June 25, 1979, page 22. It is used here in favor of even lower estimates— for example, that of 25% given by William J. Koenig, *Weapons of World War 3* (London: Bison Books, 1981), page 104.

Appendix E

The Strategic Arms Race:
The Record Since 1945

This appendix provides a historical record of significant initiatives in the strategic arms race up to the present time. It demonstrates that contrary to the impressions carefully cultivated by the Reagan administration, it is America which has taken almost every new step in the arms race. America first announced its planning for nuclear war in 1961. America first moved war into space. It began testing antisatellite weapons in 1961, while the Soviets did not begin testing them until 1968. America had an operational antisatellite weapon at Johnston Island and Kwajalein Atoll in the Pacific by 1964. The first such Soviet weapon, of limited capability and low reliability, did not appear until 1981.

It is America which introduced the first multiple warheads on a single missile, and the first long-range Cruise missile. As it did with multiple warheads, the Soviet Union will inevitably follow our initiative by deploying long-range cruise missiles of its own. Those who would deny our larger responsibility in this cycle of action and reaction like to point out that the Soviets had begun *development* of multiple warheads and Cruise missiles before America's systems were operationally deployed. They neglect to mention, of course, that in order to deploy our systems first, we began their development first. Time after time, it was this activity which began each cycle of action and reaction.

This section also provides a record of the operational deployment of strategic weapons of every kind, weapon by weapon, year by year, from 1945 to 1983. This record includes the very large number of American bombers that were capable, at one time or another, of striking targets in the Soviet Union from bases either in Europe or in the United States. It demonstrates that the United States has been able to deliver nuclear weapons to targets in the Soviet Union since 1945, when hundreds of its medium-range bombers were already stationed at forward positions overseas, whereas the Soviet Union, lacking stable forward positions where it might place bombers of comparable range, had no permanent, assured means of delivering nuclear weapons to targets in the United States until 1954, when the first of its bombers of intercontinental range appeared.

TABLES IN THIS SECTION

- Chronology of Initiatives in the Strategic Arms Race
- Deliverable United States Strategic Warheads, 1945–83
- Deliverable Soviet Strategic Warheads, 1945–83
- Operational Deployment of United States Strategic Bombers, 1945–83
- The Strategic Arms Race: Operational Deployment of Strategic Weapons, 1945–83
- Deliverable Strategic Nuclear Weapons of the Superpowers, 1945–90

Chronology of Initiatives in the Strategic Arms Race

Event	First Achieved by		Next Achieved by	
	Nation	Date	Nation	Date
Nuclear Chain Reaction	USA	1942	USSR	1946
Atomic Bomb Test	USA	1945	USSR	1949
Atomic Bomb Use	USA	1945	USSR	Not to Date
Forward-Based Strategic Bomber	USA	1945	USSR	Not to Date
Intercontinental Strategic Bomber	USA	1948	USSR	1954
European Military Alliance	USA	1949	USSR	1955
Carrier-Based Nuclear-Capable Aircraft	USA	1950	USSR	Not to Date
Hydrogen Bomb Test	USA	1952	USSR	1953
Tactical Nuclear Weapons in Europe[a]	USA	1952	USSR	1957
Submarine Cruise Missile[b]	USA	1952	USSR	1962
Nuclear-Powered Submarine	USA	1955	USSR	1959
Strategic Reconnaissance Aircraft Overflights[c]	USA	1956	USSR	Not to Date
Intercontinental Ballistic Missile (ICBM) Test	USSR	1957	USA	1958
Nuclear-Capable Fighter-Bomber Based in Europe[d]	USA	1958	USSR	1970
Forward Land-Based Missile[e]	USA	1958	USSR	1962
Low-Penetration Bomber	USA	1959	USSR	Not to Date
Supersonic Bomber	USA	1960	USSR	1975
Strategic Reconnaissance Satellite[f]	USA	1960	USSR	1962
Operational ICBM[g]	USA	1959	USSR	1960
Operational Submarine-Launched Ballistic Missile (SLBM)[h]	USA	1960	USSR	1968
High-Speed Reentry Vehicle[i]	USA	1960	USSR	1975
Missile Guidance by Onboard Computer	USA	1960	USSR	1968
Solid Propellant for ICBMs	USA	1960	USSR	1968
Forward-Based Strategic Submarine	USA	1961	USSR	Not to Date
Accelerated Buildup of ICBMs	USA	1961	USSR	1967
Test of Antisatellite (ASAT) System[j]	USA	1961	USSR	1968
Operational ASAT System[k]	USA	1964	USSR	1981
Synchronous Orbit Satellite	USA	1963	USSR	1974
Test of Multiple Reentry Vehicle (MRV)	USA	1963	USSR	1968
Chaff and Decoys on Missiles	USA	1963	USSR	Not to Date
Operational MRV[l]	USA	1964	USSR	1969
Antiballistic Missile (ABM) System[m]	USSR	1968	USA	1974
Test of Multiple Independently Targetable Reentry Vehicle (MIRV) on ICBM	USA	1968	USSR	1973
Test of MIRV on SLBM	USA	1968	USSR	1977
Operational MIRV on ICBM[n]	USA	1970	USSR	1975
Operational MIRV on SLBM[o]	USA	1971	USSR	1978
Test of Maneuvering Reentry Vehicle (MARV)	USA	1975	USSR	Not to Date
Operational Neutron Bomb	USA	1981	USSR	Not to Date
Operational Long-Range Cruise Missile	USA	1982	USSR	Not to Date

Notes and Sources

Except as noted below, the dates shown are derived from information provided by the Center for Defense Information, "U.S. Strategic Momentum" (*The Defense Monitor*, Volume III, no. 4 [May, 1974], page 2); Les Aspin, "Debate Over U.S. Strategic Forecasts: A Mixed Record" (Strategic Review [Summer, 1980], pages 29–43); and the International Institute for Strategic Studies, *The Military Balance,* annual editions from 1974 through 1984. Notes on the more controversial information, or on information unavailable from the foregoing sources, follows:

(a) The first nuclear-capable weapon system deployed in Europe by the USA was the 280 mm artillery gun with Mk 19 nuclear projectile, in 1952. The *Corporal* and *Honest John* missiles followed in 1953 and 1954, respectively. The first nuclear-capable weapon system deployed in Europe by the USSR, in 1957, was the Scud 1B missile.

(b) The *Regulus I* missile was deployed by the USA in 1952, the SS-N-3 *Shaddock* by the USSR in 1962. The *Shaddock* remains operational. *Regulus II* missiles were withdrawn from service in 1964. However, the US Navy plans to begin deployment of its *Tomahawk* Sea-Launched Cruise Missile (SLCM) on 95 attack submarines, among other vessels, in 1984. *Regulus* had a range of 500 miles. The effective range of the *Shaddock,* still the longest range attainable by any Soviet Cruise missile deployed to date, is 290 miles. Maximum range of the SLCM, burning Shelldyne-H fuel, will be 2,880 miles. (Source: Robert C. Aldridge, "The Cruise—Salt-Free and Deadly, *The Nation,* April 14, 1979, pages 402 and 403.) This capability should come as no surprise. The *Snark,* an earlier Cruise missile deployed by the USA from 1957 to 1965, had a range of more than 6000 miles. (Source: Bernard Fitzsimons, Bill Gunston, Ian V. Hogg, and Antony Preston, *The Illustrated Encyclopaedia of 20th Century Weapons and Warfare* [London: Purnell & Sons, 1967–78], Vol. 22, page 2359.)

(c) By the time the U-2 aircraft piloted by Francis Gary Powers was shot down over the USSR in 1960, it had already been making such overflights for four years. (Sources: Francis Gary Powers, *Operation Overflight* [New York: Holt Rinehart & Winston, 1970], page 374, and Thomas Karas, *The New High Ground* [New York: Simon & Schuster, 1983], page 98.)

(d) The Lockheed F-104 *Starfighter* was first deployed in Europe by the USA in 1958, the MiG-21 by the USSR in 1970.

(e) The USA deployed 60 *Thor* missiles in England in 1958, and followed them with 45 *Jupiter* missiles in Turkey and Italy. It did not withdraw them until 1963. (Source: Fitzsimons, Guston, Hogg, and Preston, *op. cit.,* Vol. 14, pages 1531–1532, and Vol. 23, pages 2488–2489.) In 1962 the USSR briefly deployed 42 T-1 missiles in Cuba. With a range of 400 miles, they threatened SAC bombers then stationed at Eglin Air Force Base and other bases in Florida. They were withdrawn the same year. At the time, their range was commonly misreported as more than 1100 miles, sufficient to threaten Washington, D.C. (Sources: *Aviation Week,* "Soviets Study Military Aspects of Space," March 9, 1959, page 314. Robert Hotz, "What Was the Threat?" *Aviation Week,* November 12, 1962, page 21. James Trainor, "Cuba Missile Threat Detailed," *Missiles and Rockets,* October 29, 1962, pages 12–14 and 47. *Jane's All the World's Aircraft, 1963-1964* [New York: McGraw-Hill, 1963], pages 421–423. Willy Ley, *Rockets, Missiles and Men in Space,* [New York: Viking Press, 1968], pages 474–475.)

(f) Source for the first successful US satellite reconnaissance mission: John Prados, *The Soviet Estimate* [New York: Dial Press, 1982], page 109. For the USSR: Karas, *op. cit.,* 1983, page 99.

(g) The first operational ICBM deployed by the USA was the *Atlas,* 129 of which were organized in 13 squadrons, and not withdrawn until 1966. (Source: Fitzsimons, Gunston,

Hogg, and Preston, *op. cit.,* Vol. 2, pages 190–192.) The first ICBM deployed by the USSR was the SS-6, no more than 4 of which were operational through 1960, when the USA had 72 Atlas ICBMs operational. (Sources: Fred Kaplan, *The Wizards of Armageddon* [New York: Simon & Schuster, 1983], page 286. Daniel Ellsberg, "First Strike," *Inquiry Magazine,* April 13, 1981, page 15.)

(h) Though the USSR had short-range SLBMs operational as early as 1960, with deployment of the SS-N-4 on its diesel-powered *Golf* class submarines, it was not until 1968 that it deployed its first *Yankee* class submarine with the SS-N-6 missile, whose range of 1490 miles was sufficient to classify it as strategic. The SS-N-4 and SS-N-5 SLBMs before it had maximum ranges of 350 and 850 miles, respectively.

(i) According to the Center for Defense Information, the USSR first *tested* high-speed reentry vehicles in 1973, but did not deploy them until 1975. (Source: *The Defense Monitor,* Volume III, no. 4 [May, 1974], page 2.)

(j) The first ASAT system tested by the USA was developed in the US Navy's Project Blackeye in 1961. (Source: Robert C. Aldridge, "First Strike: The Pentagon's Secret Strategy," *The Progressive* [May, 1978], page 19.) Aldridge lists several subsequent projects. Several more are listed by Karas, *op. cit.,* 1982, pages 148–149. Source for the first Soviet test: Karas, *op. cit.,* 1982, page 149.

(k) The first ASAT system deployed by the USA was the Army's *Nike-Zeus* "interim" system, operational from 1964 through 1967. (Source: Karas, *op. cit.,* 1982, page 148.) The next system, operational from 1967 through 1975, utilized *Thor* launchers located at Johnston Island and Kwajalein Atoll in the Pacific. (Sources: Karas, *op. cit.,* 1982, page 149, and Aldridge, *op. cit.,* May, 1978, page 19.) A new ASAT system, the Vought MHIV (Miniature Homing Intercept Vehicle), is currently being tested in the USA and is scheduled for deployment in 1985. For a description of why it is vastly superior to anything the Soviets have, see Karas, *op. cit.,* 1982, pages 149–153. For an evaluation of the effectiveness of Soviet ASAT systems, see Robert C. Aldridge, *First Strike! The Pentagon's Strategy for Nuclear War* (Boston: South End Press, 1983), pages 221–225.

(l) The earliest deployment of MRVs on a Soviet ICBM was 1971, on the SS-9 Mod 4. (Sources: Michael J. H. Taylor and John W. R. Taylor, *Missiles of the World* [London: Ian Allan, 1976], page 135. *Jane's Weapon Systems,* 1976 [London: Macdonald and Jane's, 1975], page 14.) The earliest deployment of MRVs on a Soviet SLBM, however, was 1969, on the SS-N-6 Mod 3. (Source: IISS, *op. cit., 1981–1982,* page 105.) The earlier date is given here.

(m) The *Safeguard* ABM system deployed by the USA at Grand Forks, North Dakota, in 1974 was deactivated the following year when it became clear that ABMs were tactically obsolete because an attacker could always add MIRVs and decoys to overwhelm such a defense more rapidly and economically than the defensive system itself could be expanded. It had incorporated the *Nike X* long-range exoatmospheric interceptor, renamed *Spartan,* and a short-range endoatmospheric *Sprint* missile. *Nike X,* a development of the *Nike-Zeus,* had been operational since 1969, and its use had been authorized that year for an earlier ABM system named *Sentinel.* But the *Sentinel* system, so far as is now known, was never activated.

(n) The first deployment of MIRV warheads on a Soviet ICBM was in 1975, on the SS-19 Mod 1, as noted in IISS, *op. cit., 1975–1976,* page 71. Subsequent editions of *The Military Balance,* however, have changed the date to 1974. This change does not take place until the edition of 1982–83. The date originally given, and kept for seven years, is therefore used here.

(o) IISS, *op. cit., 1981–1982,* page 105, gives the earliest date of MIRV deployment on a Soviet SLBM as 1978, on the SS-N-18.

Deliverable United States Strategic Warheads, 1945–83

Year	Estimate — Based on SALT II Testimony	Author's Figures	DOD Figures
1945		2	
1946		9	
1947		13	
1948		50	
1949		250	
1950		450	
1951		650	
1952		1000	
1953		1800	
1954		3600	
1955		4750	
1956		5400	
1957		6092	
1958		5544	
1959		5559	
1960	6500	5437	
1961	6950	5428	
1962	7400	5415	
1963	7100	5625	
1964	6800	5386	
1965	5900	4862	
1966	5000	4648	
1967	4750	4706	4500
1968	4500	4918	4200
1969	4200	5018	4200
1970	3900	5522	4000
1971	4850	6624	4600
1972	5800	7244	5700
1973	7100	8160	6784
1974	8400	8950	7940
1975	8900	9744	8500
1976	9400	10,201	8900
1977	9600	10,774	8500
1978	9800	10,742	9000
1979	9900	10,666	9200
1980	10,000	10,394	9200
1981	10,500	10,277	9000
1982	11,000	10,880	9300
1983		10,973	

Sources and Method

For every year but 1982, official Defense Department figures are taken from the Department's *Annual Report* issued that year for the following fiscal year. Figures for two years, 1974 and 1976, were retroactively reduced in subsequent *Annual Reports*; the original figures are used here. After its *Annual Report, Fiscal Year 1982*, which gave figures for 1981, the Defense Department ceased publishing such data. The figure for 1982 is taken from congressional testimony by Defense Department officials in May of that year, as reported by *The New York Times* on May 2.

Figures based on SALT II testimony, which for recent years match the author's estimates far more closely than do the Defense Department's published figures, are taken from "official U.S. estimates provided in Congressional testimony on the SALT II Treaty," published for every even year by former Defense Department arms control specialist Roger Molander, a staff member of the National Security Council under the Carter administration,

(continued)

Deliverable United States Strategic Warheads, 1945–83 *(cont.)*

and the Ground Zero organization in *Nuclear War: What's In It for You* (New York: Pocket Books, 1982), Appendix C, page 267.

Author's estimates of increases and fluctuations in the number of deliverable strategic warheads are based on the following considerations:

- The number of aircraft and missiles available each year to deliver American nuclear weapons to targets in the Soviet Union.

- The number of nuclear warheads or bombs known to be carried by each of these systems.

- The number of nuclear weapons available for use by these systems, based on the size of America's nuclear weapons stockpile, which until 1956 fell short of America's available delivery capacity but thereafter rapidly exceeded it. For the years 1945 through 1956, this stockpile estimate is based on David Alan Rosenberg, "U.S. Nuclear Stockpile, 1945–1950," *Bulletin of the Atomic Scientists* (May, 1982); Thomas B. Cochran, William M. Arkin, and Milton M. Hoenig, "U.S. Nuclear Weapons Stockpile," in *Nuclear Weapons Databook: Volume I*, (Cambridge, Mass.: Ballinger, 1984), page 15; and figures substantially higher than those provided by Cochran and his associates, volunteered to *The New York Times* by Defense Department officials and published by the *Times* on February 13, 1954, and February 13, 1955.

- The availability, at the end of World War II, of more than 3900 bombers, most of them B-29s at forward positions based overseas, where they were able to reach Soviet targets with nuclear weapons from the moment the United States first possessed such weapons.

- The gradual retirement of this force, and its replacement by a somewhat smaller but more capable force of B-47s and other jet-engined aircraft between 1948 and 1958.

- The simultaneous creation of a long-range bomber force, beginning in 1948 with the B-36, capable of attacking Soviet targets from bases in the United States.

- The introduction in 1954 of the B-52 bomber, capable of carrying a greater number of nuclear weapons at longer ranges.

- The introduction of *Thor* and *Jupiter* medium-range ballistic missiles at forward positions based overseas in 1959 and 1960.

- The withdrawal of *Thor* and *Jupiter* missiles in 1963.

- The introduction of 1,300 AGM-28 *Hound Dog* missiles to the Strategic

- The simultaneous addition of 4 warheads to each of the 304 *Poseidon C-3* missiles remaining after the *Trident C-4* retrofit, providing the SLBM force with a net increase of 1216 warheads between 1980 and 1982.

- The introduction of the AGM-68A Air-Launched Cruise Missile (ALCM) to the Strategic Air Command in 1982, increasing by 192 the number of weapons carried by the bomber force that year, but promising a minimum increase of 2880 warheads in the bomber force by 1990.

Initial dates for the operational deployment of all aircraft, and dates of withdrawal from service, are from Ray Wagner, *American Combat Planes* (Garden City, N.Y.: Doubleday, 1968, and Bernard Fitzsimons, *et al.*, *The Illustrated Encyclopaedia of 20th Century Weapons and Warfare* (London: Purnell & Sons, 1967–78). Initial dates for the operational deployment of all ballistic missiles are from the Center for Defense Information, "U.S. Strategic Momentum," *The Defense Monitor*, Volume III, no. 4 (May, 1974), page 2. These dates are further confirmed by the International Institute for Strategic Studies, *The Military Balance, 1975–1976*, page 73, *The Military Balance, 1980–1981*, pages 90–91, *The Military Balance, 1982–1983*, page 140, *The Military Balance, 1983–1984*, page 121, and John M. Collins, *U.S.-Soviet Military Balance: Concepts and Capabilities, 1960–1980* (New York: McGraw-Hill, 1980). Those sources also provide the numbers of missiles and aircraft in service in any given year with the exception of ICBMs in 1961. The number of ICBMs in service in 1961 is from *U.S. News and World Report*, February 27, 1961.

Dates of deployment and withdrawal of *Thor* and *Jupiter* forward-based IRBMs, as well as the numbers of these missiles in service, are from Fitzsimons, *op. cit.*, Vol. 14, pages 1531–1532, and Vol. 23, pages 2488–2489. Dates of deployment and withdrawal from service of the AGM-28 *Hound Dog* air-to-surface missile are from the same source, Vol. 13, pages 1369–1370, and are further confirmed by Michael and John Taylor, *Missiles of the World*, page 55. Date of deployment of the AGM-69A SRAM air-to-surface missile, as well as the number of missiles delivered, is also from Taylor and Taylor, *op. cit.*, page 132. Date of deployment of the B-61 nuclear gravity bomb is from Thomas B. Cochran, William M. Arkin, and Milton M. Hoenig, *Nuclear Weapons Databook: Volume I* (Cambridge, Mass.: Ballinger, 1984), page 66. Date of deployment of the AGM-86B Air-Launched Cruise Missile is from *Aviation Week & Space Technology*, "News Digest," De-

Air Command in 1960.

• The introduction from 1960 through 1963 of the B-52G and B-52H bombers, capable of carrying even greater numbers of nuclear weapons at long ranges.

• The growth of an ICBM force from 9 missiles to 1054 between 1959 and 1967.

• The growth of an SLBM force from 48 missiles in 1960 to 656 in 1967.

• The retirement of the B-47 bomber in 1966, and with it the end of deployment of forward-based aircraft officially defined as "strategic."

• The introduction in 1968 of the lightweight B-61 nuclear gravity bomb, expanding to 12 the number of nuclear bombs each B-52G and B-52H bomber could deliver to Soviet targets.

• The retirement of the B-58 *Hustler* bomber in 1969, marginally reducing the size of the long-range bomber force.

• The introduction in 1969 of the FB-111 bomber, marginally increasing the number of weapons carried by the strategic bomber force, but greatly increasing its capabilities for low-level strikes at very high speeds.

• The addition of multiple independently targetable (MIRV) warheads to *Minuteman III* missiles, providing a net increase of 1100 warheads in the ICBM force between 1970 and 1975.

• The conversion of 31 *Polaris* submarines to accept the *Poseidon C-3* missile, 496 of which, with a minimum of 10 warheads each, provided the SLBM force with a net increase of 4464 warheads between 1971 and 1977.

• The introduction of 1500 AGM-69A Short-Range Attack Missiles (SRAM) to the Strategic Air Command in 1972, increasing the possible number of weapons carried by the FB-111 bomber to 6, and the possible number carried by the B-52 to 20.

• The retrofit of 192 *Trident C-4* missiles, each with a minimum of 8 warheads, on 12 *Poseidon* submarines, producing a net reduction of 384 warheads in the SLBM force between 1980 and 1982.

• The retirement of 10 *Polaris* submarines, and with them 160 *Polaris A-3* missiles, producing an additional net reduction of 160 warheads in the SLBM force between 1980 and 1982.

• The addition to the fleet of two *Trident* submarines, whose 48 missiles, each with a minimum of 8 warheads, produced a net increase of 384 warheads in the SLBM force between 1981 and 1982, and also greatly extended the range of America's sea-based missiles from 3200 statute miles, achieved by the *Poseidon C-3* with 10 warheads, to 4870 miles.

cember 20, 1982, page 25, and is further confirmed by Cochran, Arkin, and Hoenig, *op. cit.*, 1984, pages 150 and 175. The numbers of Air-Launched Cruise Missiles deployed and planned for deployment are from the same source, pages 150 and 175. Dates of deployment of the first two *Trident* class submarines are from the *United States Naval Institute Proceedings* (February, 1983), page 125. Dates for the retrofit of *Trident* missiles on *Poseidon* submarines are from Cochran, Arkin, and Hoenig, *op. cit.*, 1984, pages 104 and 137.

The numbers of warheads on each missile type are from sources noted in the tables, *Characteristics of United States and Soviet Intercontinental Ballistic Missiles Deployed from 1979 Through 1983* and *Characteristics of United States and Soviet Submarine-Launched Ballistic Missiles Deployed from 1979 Through 1983* (see pages 291 and 301). The numbers of nuclear weapons carried by each bomber type are dependent on the load capacities of each bomber type and the weights of the weapons, confirmed, respectively, by sources noted in the tables *Characteristics of United States and Soviet Aircraft Deployed as Intercontinental Strategic Bombers and Nuclear Weapons Deliverable by United States Bombers* (see pages 313 and 315). Normal and potential operational loadings of the B-52 and FB-111 bombers, respectively, are from Cochran, Arkin, and Hoenig, *op. cit.*, 1984, pages 106 and 153, and are further confirmed by the Congressional Budget Office, *Modernizing U.S. Strategic Offensive Forces*, May, 1983, page 86.

Carrier-based nuclear-capable aircraft were first introduced by the United States in 1950. Nuclear-capable fighter bombers, presumably for no other mission but Europe's defense, were first based on European soil by the United States in 1958. These weapon systems have always been capable of striking targets in the Soviet Union. They consequently comprise an additional strategic force, whether or not they are intended to be one, and whether or not this intention is acknowledged. Because the Defense Department has not defined the nuclear weapons they carry as "strategic," and therefore has not included them in its official totals of strategic weapons, for purposes of exact comparison with those totals neither have such weapons been included in the author's estimates.

The addition of MIRV warheads to the ICBM and SLBM forces added a minimum of 5564 warheads to America's strategic arsenal between 1970 and 1977. Official Defense Department figures show a net increase of only 4500 warheads through this period. The discrepancy has never been explained, and subsequent adjustments in official figures have only marginally compensated for it.

Year	Estimate Based on SALT II Testimony	Author's Figures	DOD Figures
1945			
1946			
1947			
1948			
1949			
1950			
1951			
1952			
1953			
1954		4	
1955		20	
1956		60	
1957		120	

Year	Estimate Based on SALT II Testimony	Author's Figures	DOD Figures
1958		180	
1959		280	
1960	300	327	
1961	350	399	
1962	400	536	
1963	450	528	
1964	500	637	
1965	525	716	
1966	550	772	
1967	700	955	1000
1968	850	1207	1100
1969	1325	1562	1350
1970	1800	1914	1800

Year	Estimate Based on SALT II Testimony	Author's Figures	DOD Figures
1971	1950	2251	2100
1972	2100	2366	2500
1973	2250	2475	2200
1974	2400	2567	2600
1975	2800	2830	2500
1976	3200	3147	3500
1977	4200	3862	4000
1978	5200	4730	4500
1979	5600	5463	5000
1980	6000	5909	6000
1981	7000	6402	7000
1982	8000	6645	7000
1983	8666	6769	7200

Sources and Method

For every year but 1982, official Defense Department figures are taken from the Department's *Annual Report* issued that year for the following fiscal year. Figures for two years, 1974 and 1976, were retroactively reduced in subsequent *Annual Reports*; the original figures are used here. After its *Annual Report, Fiscal Year 1982*, which gave figures for 1981, the Defense Department ceased publishing such data. The figure for 1982 is taken from congressional testimony by Defense Department officials in May of that year, as reported by *The New York Times* on May 2.

For every year but 1983, figures based on SALT II testimony are taken from "official U.S. estimates provided in Congressional testimony on the SALT II Treaty," published for every even year by former Defense Department arms control specialist Roger Molander, a staff member of the National Security Council under the Carter administration, and the Ground Zero organization in *Nuclear War: What's In It for You* (New York: Pocket Books, 1982), Appendix C, page 267. The figure for 1983 is based on "extrapo-

- The initial deployment of 4 liquid-fueled SS-6 missiles, the first operational Soviet ICBMs, at Plesetsk in 1960.
- Deployment in 1960 of the first Soviet diesel-powered *Golf* class submarine, whose three SS-N-4 ballistic missiles had a maximum range of 350 statute miles.
- The gradual buildup of a force of SS-N-4 and SS-N-5 missiles, the latter with a maximum range of 850 statute miles, reaching a maximum inventory of 105 short-range SLBMs of both kinds in 1972, aboard Soviet *Golf* and *Hotel* class submarines.
- Deployment in 1968 of the first *Yankee* class Soviet nuclear-powered submarine, whose SS-N-6 missiles, with a range of 1490 statute miles, were the first comparable in range to the earliest American SLBM, the *Polaris A-1*, already replaced by that time with the *Polaris A-3*, with a range of 2880 statute miles.
- The continuing buildup of longer-range Soviet SLBMs, including the

- SS-N-8 with a reported range of 4860 statute miles, reaching an inventory of 912 SLBMs of various types by 1980.

- A decline in the number of Soviet short-range SLBMs to 57 by 1979.

- A decline in the number of Soviet long-range aircraft to 140 in 1974, and a subsequent marginal increase in that number with refurbished aircraft.

- The buildup of the Soviet ICBM force to a maximum strength of 1618 missiles in 1974, and its subsequent reduction to 1398 missiles by 1979.

- The introduction of multiple independently targetable (MIRV) warheads on the Soviet SS-17 missile, creating the SS-17 Mod 1 with 4 warheads each, and providing a net increase to the Soviet ICBM force of 420 warheads on 140 such missiles between 1975 and 1983.

- The introduction of MIRV warheads on the Soviet SS-19 missile, creating the SS-19 Mod 1 with 6 warheads each, and providing a net increase to the Soviet ICBM force of 1250 warheads on 250 such missiles between 1975 and 1983.

- The introduction of MIRV warheads on the Soviet SS-18 missile, creating the SS-18 Mod 2 with 8 warheads each and the SS-18 Mod 4 with 10 warheads each, and providing a net increase to the Soviet ICBM force of 1526 warheads on 218 SS-18 Mod 2 missiles between 1977 and 1983, and another 270 warheads on 30 SS-18 Mod 4 missiles between 1980 and 1983.

- The introduction of MIRV warheads on the Soviet SS-N-18 missile, creating the SS-N-18 Mod 2 with 3 warheads each and the SS-N-18 Mod 3 with 7 warheads each, and providing a net increase to the Soviet submarine fleet of 256 warheads on 128 SS-N-18 Mod 2 missiles between 1978 and 1980, and another 480 warheads on 80 SS-N-18 Mod 3 missiles between 1981 and 1983.

- The acknowledgment by all sources that no addition of MIRV warheads to any type of Soviet ICBM or SLBM began at an earlier date, and the consensus among official and semiofficial sources that no type of MIRV conversion described progressed at a more rapid rate than shown.

Initial dates for the operational deployment of all aircraft and missile types are from the Center for Defense Information, "U.S. Strategic Momentum," *The Defense Monitor*, Volume III, no. 4 (May, 1974), page 2, and Les Aspin, "Debate over U.S. Strategic Forecasts: A Mixed Record," *Strategic Review* (Summer, 1980), pages 29–43. With the exception of the first operational Soviet ICBM, the SS-6, these dates are further confirmed by

lations of official U.S. estimates" by the same source for future years.

Author's estimates of increases and fluctuations in the number of deliverable strategic warheads are based on the following considerations:

- The unavailability of any Soviet aircraft or missiles with sufficient range to deliver nuclear weapons to targets in the United States from bases in the Soviet Union until at least 1954, even though Soviet production of nuclear weapons may have begun four years earlier.

- The continuing unavailability to the Soviet Union of stable forward bases from which Soviet aircraft or missiles with less than intercontinental range could deliver nuclear weapons to targets in the United States.

- The instability of Cuba as such a base for Soviet nuclear weapons, after the temporary introduction there of 42 T-1 MRBMs, and their withdrawal in the same year.

- The initial appearance in 1954 of the Soviet long-range MYA-4 *Bison* bomber, the first means available for the delivery of nuclear weapons from bases in the Soviet Union to targets in the United States.

- The subsequent buildup of a small force of Soviet MYA-4 and Tu-95A long-range bombers, reaching its maximum inventory of 210 aircraft in 1967.

- The inability of such bombers, based on their known load capacities and the known weights of Soviet nuclear-armed air-to-surface missiles, to carry more than one such missile to intercontinental ranges.

- The remote likelihood that such bombers, based on their known load capacities, the reported yield of Soviet nuclear gravity bombs, and the continuing Soviet inability to match the United States in miniaturization of the mechanical components of nuclear weapons, and therefore to build bombs lighter than American bombs of comparable yield, could carry more than 2 such weapons each to intercontinental ranges.

- The inability of the Soviet force of long-range aerial tankers, comprising only 35 aircraft today compared with America's 615, to provide a significant aerial refueling capability for any additional Soviet bombers, including the Tu-22M *Backfire*, all of which are acknowledged to have insufficient range on internal fuel for intercontinental strategic bombing missions.

- The acknowledged absence of any Tu-22M *Backfire* bombers deployed in the intercontinental strategic role, and the acknowledged ability of the United States to verify any change in deployment of the Tu-22M or any other Soviet bomber.

(continued)

Deliverable Soviet Strategic Warheads, 1945–83 (cont.)

the International Institute for Strategic Studies, The Military Balance, 1975–1976, page 73, The Military Balance, 1980–1981, pages 90–91, The Military Balance, 1982–1983, page 140, The Military Balance, 1983–1984, page 121, and John M. Collins, U.S.-Soviet Military Balance: Concepts and Capabilities, 1960–1980 (New York: McGraw-Hill, 1980), page 449. Those sources also provide the numbers of aircraft and missiles in service in any given year. The date of the first operational Soviet ICBM is from Daniel Ellsberg, "First Strike," Inquiry Magazine, April 13, 1981, page 15, and is further confirmed by Fred M. Kaplan, The Wizards of Armageddon (New York: Simon & Schuster, 1983), page 286.

Dates of deployment and withdrawal from service of Soviet forward-based MRBMs in Cuba, as well as the number and type of missiles deployed, are from Robert B. Hotz, "What Was the Threat?" Aviation Week, November 12, 1962, page 21; James Trainor, "Cuba Missile Threat Detailed," Missiles and Rockets, October 29, 1962, pages 12–14 and 27; and Jane's All the World's Aircraft, 1963–1964 (New York: McGraw-Hill, 1963), pages 421–423. The earliest date of deployment of multiple independently targetable (MIRV) warheads on Soviet ICBMs is from the International Institute for Strategic Studies, The Military Balance, 1975–1976, page 71. The earliest date of deployment of MIRV warheads on Soviet SLBMs is from The Military Balance, 1981–1982, page 105. The numbers of warheads on each missile type are from sources noted in the tables Characteristics of United States and Soviet Intercontinental Ballistic Missiles Deployed from 1979 Through 1983 and Characteristics of United States and Soviet Submarine-Launched Ballistic Missiles Deployed from 1979 Through 1983 (see pages 291 and 301). The numbers of nuclear weapons carried by each bomber type are dependent on the load capacities of each bomber type and the weights of the weapons, confirmed, respectively, by sources noted in the tables, Characteristics of United States and Soviet Aircraft Deployed as Intercontinental Strategic Bombers and Nuclear Weapons Deliverable by Soviet Strategic Bombers (see pages 313 and 315). The TU-22M Backfire is not included among strategic bombers, because it is neither equipped nor deployed as an intercontinental strategic bomber. See Verification of the SALT II Agreement, U.S. Department of State, Special Report No. 56, August, 1979, page 5. Due to their own load limitations and the weights of available air-to-surface missiles, the MYA-4 Bison can carry none of these weapons and the Tu-95A Bear can carry only 1 AS-3. The number of Bears equipped with the AS-3 missile is from the International Institute for Strategic Studies, The Military Balance, 1981–1982, page 11, and again from the same source, The Military Balance, 1982–1983, page 13. The large majority of sources agree that remaining Soviet strategic aircraft carry a maximum of 2 nuclear gravity bombs each. See Les Aspin, "The Verification of the SALT Agreement," Scientific American (February, 1979), page 41, and Fred M. Kaplan, Dubious Specter (Washington, D.C.: Institute for Policy Studies, 1980), revised 1982, page 90. The number of strategic warheads deliverable by the Soviet bomber force has been estimated accordingly.

Operational Deployment of United States Strategic Bombers, 1945–83

Year	Medium-Range Bombers							Long-Range Bombers					GRAND TOTAL
	B-29	B-32	B-45	B-47	B-50	B-66	Total	B-36	B-52	B-58	FB-111	Total	
1945	3873	115					3988						3988
1946	3352	48					3400						3400
1947	2830						2830						2830
1948	2309		96		80		2485	95				95	2580
1949	2048		106		125		2279	170				170	2449
1950	1787		106		347		2240	170				170	2410
1951	1467		106	405	342		2320	248				248	2568
1952	1147		106	405	270	217	2145	248				248	2393
1953	504		102	1722	126	217	2671	364				364	3035
1954	216		102	1722	54	217	2311	385	3			388	2699
1955	206		78	1722		216	2222	385	28			413	2635
1956			78	1716		144	1938	383	188			571	2509
1957			72	1702		144	1918	256	308			564	2482
1958			72	1644		62	1778	96	356	30		482	2260
1959				1486			1486	96	452	74		622	2108
1960				1296			1296		543	112		655	1951
1961				1152			1152		591	112		703	1855
1962				1008			1008		648	66		714	1722
1963				864			864		720	66		786	1650
1964				504			504		720	62		782	1286
1965				288			288		672	62		734	1022
1966				144			144		656	60		716	860
1967									600	56		656	656
1968									600	56		656	656
1969									560	56	24	640	640
1970									550		50	600	600
1971									505		76	581	581
1972									455		75	530	530
1973									442		73	515	515
1974									437		70	507	507
1975									432		68	500	500

(continued)

Operational Deployment of United States Strategic Bombers, 1945–83 (cont.)

Year	Medium-Range Bombers							Long-Range Bombers					GRAND TOTAL
	B-29	B-32	B-45	B-47	B-50	B-66	Total	B-36	B-52	B-58	FB-111	Total	
1976									387		68	455	455
1977									373		66	439	439
1978									366		65	431	431
1979									348		65	413	413
1980									348		63	411	411
1981									347		62	409	409
1982									299		60	359	359
1983									299		60	359	359

Notes and Sources

Figures shown here are for all operational aircraft. On average, the numbers of aircraft assigned to Strategic Air Command units as Primary Authorized Airvehicles are 10% lower. On the other hand, the totals of aircraft produced are substantially higher. The figures shown here are for bomber versions only, and do not include aircraft built or later converted for reconnaissance, inflight refueling, and other missions. The total production figures are as follows:

B-29	B-32	B-45	B-47	B-50	B-66	B-36	B-52	B-58	FB-111	Total
3960	115	203	2012	371	289	461	744	116	76	8347

Approximate numbers of these aircraft currently in inactive storage at Davis-Monthan Air Force Base, Arizona, are as follows:

B-29	B-32	B-45	B-47	B-50	B-66	B-36	B-52	B-58	FB-111	Total
2900	77	94	1062	268	112	306	224	109		5152

Under the terms of SALT II, its ratification would require that the United States destroy its 224 B-52 aircraft now in storage.

Production figures, initial dates of deliveries to the Strategic Air Command, and dates of withdrawal from service, are from Ray Wagner, *American Combat Planes* (Garden City, N.Y.: Doubleday, 1968), and Bernard Fitzsimons, et al., *The Illustrated Encyclopaedia of 20th Century Weapons and Warfare* (London: Purnell & Sons, 1967–69). Numbers of aircraft in service in any specific year are further confirmed by a variety of official and semiofficial sources. In 1957, General Thomas Power, Chief of Strategic Air Command, told *The New York Times* that the United States had 2500 jet-engined aircraft able to carry out nuclear strikes against targets in the Soviet Union from 32 bases in the United States and 27 bases overseas (see *The New York Times*, September 27, 1957). The estimate here is of 2482 aircraft operationally deployed that year. In 1962, the International Institute for Strategic Studies estimated that the United States had 1000 B-47 medium-range bombers and 650 long-range B-52s in service (see IISS, *The Military Balance, 1962–1963*, page 5). The estimate here is of 1008 B-47s and 648 B-52s that year.

Figures shown here do not include nuclear-capable carrier-based aircraft deployed by the United States since 1950, or nuclear-capable fighter bombers deployed by the United States in Europe since 1958 but not officially defined as "strategic."

The Strategic Arms Race: Operational Deployment of Strategic Weapons, 1945–83

Year	USA						USSR						
	ICBM	SLBM	Forward-Based MRBM	Long-Range Bomber	Forward-Based Bomber	Deliverable Warheads	ICBM	SLBM	Short-Range SLBM	Forward-Based MRBM	Long-Range Bomber	Forward-Based Bomber	Deliverable Warheads
1945					3988	2							
1946					3400	9							
1947					2830	13							
1948				95	2485	50							
1949				170	2279	250							
1950				170	2240	450							
1951				248	2320	650							
1952				248	2145	1000							
1953				364	2671	1800							
1954				388	2311	3600					2		4
1955				413	2222	4750					10		20
1956				571	1938	5400					30		60
1957				564	1918	6092					60		120
1958			60	482	1778	5544					90		180
1959	9		90	622	1486	5559					140		280
1960	72	48	105	655	1296	5437	4		3		160		327
1961	127	80	105	703	1152	5428	10		9		190		399
1962	294	144	105	714	1008	5415	75		39	42	190		536
1963	424	224	105	786	864	5625	100		48		190		528
1964	834	416		782	504	5386	200		57		190		637
1965	854	496		734	288	4862	270		66		190		716
1966	904	592		716	144	4648	300		72		200		772
1967	1054	656		656		4706	460		75		210		955
1968	1054	656		656		4918	800	32	75		150		1207
1969	1054	656		640		5018	1050	128	84		150		1562
1970	1054	656		600		5522	1300	224	90		150		1914
1971	1054	656		581		6624	1510	336	105		150		2251
1972	1054	656		530		7244	1527	444	105		145		2366

(continued)

The Strategic Arms Race: Operational Deployment of Strategic Weapons, 1945–83 *(cont.)*

| | USA | | | | | | USSR | | | | | | |
Year	ICBM	SLBM	Forward-Based MRBM	Long-Range Bomber	Forward-Based Bomber	Deliverable Warheads	ICBM	SLBM	Short-Range SLBM	Forward-Based MRBM	Long-Range Bomber	Forward-Based Bomber	Deliverable Warheads
1973	1054	656		515		8160	1575	508	102		145		2475
1974	1054	656		507		8950	1618	588	81		140		2567
1975	1054	656		500		9744	1527	660	81		140		2830
1976	1054	656		455		10,201	1477	748	78		140		3147
1977	1054	656		439		10,774	1350	816	72		140		3862
1978	1054	656		431		10,742	1400	864	60		140		4730
1979	1054	656		413		10,666	1398	880	57		150		5463
1980	1054	608		411		10,394	1398	912	57		150		5909
1981	1053	600		409		10,277	1398	912	57		150		6402
1982	1052	544		359		10,880	1398	912	57		150		6645
1983	1049	544	41	359		10,973	1398	912	57		150		6769

Sources and Method

Initial dates for operational deployment of all aircraft and missiles are from sources listed for the separate table *Initiatives in the Arms Race*. Numbers of United States aircraft in service in any given year are from sources listed for the separate table *Operational Deployment of United States Strategic Bombers, 1945–83*. The number of United States ICBMs in service in 1961 is from *U.S. News and World Report*, February 27, 1961. The numbers of all other United States missiles, Soviet missiles, and Soviet aircraft in service in any given year are from IISS, *The Military Balance, 1975–1976*, page 73, *The Military Balance, 1980–1981*, pages 90–91, *The Military Bal-*

ance, 1982–1983, page 140, *The Military Balance, 1983–1984*, page 121, and John M. Collins, *U.S.-Soviet Military Balance: Concepts and Capabilities, 1960–1980* (New York: McGraw-Hill, 1980), page 449. Initial dates for the availability of deliverable nuclear warheads, and for the numbers of nuclear warheads deliverable by each nation in any given year, are author's estimates, based on sources and derived by methods indicated for the separate tables *Deliverable United States Strategic Warheads, 1945–83*, and *Deliverable Soviet Strategic Warheads, 1945–83*.

Deliverable Strategic Nuclear Weapons of the Superpowers, 1945–90

Type of Delivery Vehicle	Nation	Year and Number of Weapons									
		1945	1950	1955	1960	1965	1970	1975	1980	1985	1990
Land-Based Missiles	USSR				4	270	1300	1527	4324	5404	6420
	USA				72	854	1054	2154	2154	2445	3772
Sea-Based Missiles	USSR						224	660	1385	2261	3240
	USA				48	496	656	5120	5776	6944	8448
Bombers	USSR			20	320	380	300	200	200	200	400
	USA	2	450	4750	5317	3512	3842	2470	2464	3060	4860
All Delivery Vehicles	USSR			20	324	650	1824	2387	5909	7865	10,060
	USA	2	450	4750	5437	4862	5552	9744	10,394	12,449	17,080

Notes

Force levels for weapons carried by land-based missiles include warheads mounted in forward-based United States *Atlas*, *Thor*, *Pershing II*, and Ground-Launched Cruise Missiles in their respective years of deployment. All of these weapon systems have been capable of striking targets in the Soviet Union. Force levels for weapons carried by sea-based missiles do not include those on early United States *Regulus* Cruise missiles, or on short-range Soviet ballistic missiles not capable of striking targets in the United States. But they do include long-range United States Sea-Launched Cruise Missiles mounting nuclear warheads, deployed since 1984.

Force levels for weapons carried by United States bombers include those carried in the late 1940s, the 1950s, and the early 1960s by forward-based medium-range B-29s, B-32s, B-45s, B-47s, B-50s, and B-66s, and those carried in the 1950s and 1960s by long-range B-36s and B-58 *Hustlers*. A decline in the bomber weapons inventory after 1960 reflects the withdrawal of medium-range bombers from forward bases. A further decline after 1970 reflects reductions in the size of the long-range bomber force, which now comprises only B-52s and FB-111As. An increase after 1980 reflects the deployment of Air-Launched Cruise Missiles, which began in 1982.

Force levels for weapons carried by Soviet bombers do not include those carried by medium-range bombers, which have never had forward bases from which to deploy, and consequently cannot deliver weapons to targets in the United States. This applies to the Tu-22M *Backfire* bomber, which our State Department acknowledged is neither equipped nor deployed as an intercontinental strategic bomber, and which has a range of only 3600 statute miles. The Soviets also lack the capacity to refuel it in flight, with an aerial tanker force of but 35 aircraft, compared with the United States force of 615. A decline in Soviet long-range bomber weapons after 1965 reflects a reduction in numbers of Tu-95A *Bear* and MYA-4 *Bison* aircraft deployed.

United States force-level projections for 1990 presume the deployment of 100 MX missiles and 90 B-1 bombers, completion of deployment of *Pershing II* and Ground-Launched Cruise Missiles in Europe, continued deployment of Air-Launched Cruise Missiles and *Trident* submarines, and the retrofit of *Trident D-5* missiles on the first two of these submarines. Soviet

(continued)

Deliverable Strategic Nuclear Weapons of the Superpowers, 1945–90 (*cont.*)

force-level projections for 1990 presume continued conversion of land-based and sea-based missiles with multiple warheads at current rates, to the maximum levels allowable within the constraints of SALT II, continued deployment of *Typhoon* submarines, and an improved capability to miniaturize the mechanical components of nuclear gravity bombs, so that long-range bombers might carry 4 weapons each rather than 2.

A sharp rise in the number of strategic warheads deployed by United States forces between 1970 and 1975 reflects the introduction of multiple warheads in that period. A similar rise in Soviet force levels five years later reflects the same development. Alarmists were correct in pointing to this as a rapid expansion of Soviet strategic capabilities. They merely neglected to mention that the United States had already undertaken the same expansion itself five years earlier.

United States fighter-bombers based on aircraft carriers and in Europe, and capable of delivering nuclear weapons to targets in the Soviet Union, are not included in the force levels shown, since they are presumably assigned to no other mission but Europe's defense.

Appendix F

Nuclear Weapons Stockpiled and Deployed by the Superpowers

United States Nuclear Weapons Stockpiled and Deployed, 1982–84

Warhead Type	Weapon System/In U.S. Service or Service Abroad	1982		1983		1984	
		Total in Stockpile	of Which Deployed	Total in Stockpile	of Which Deployed	Total in Stockpile	of Which Deployed
W-25	AIR-2A *Genie* Air-to-Air Missile. Carried by Canadian CF-101 and U.S. F-101, F-106, F-4D, and F-15 interceptor aircraft.	800	400	800	400	800	400
W-28	B-28 Nuclear Gravity Bomb. Carried by U.S. B-52, A-7, and F-4 aircraft, and by NATO F-4, F-100, and F-104 aircraft.	1200	1200	1200	1200	1200	1200
W-31	MGR-1B *Honest John* Surface-to-Surface Missile. Deployed by NATO and South Korean field artillery battalions.	800	300	800	300	800	300
W-31	MiM-14 *Nike-Hercules* Surface-to-Air or Surface-to-Surface Missile. Deployed by NATO and South Korean air defense artillery batteries.	1250	750	1250	750	1250	750
W-33	M-422 203 mm Artillery-Fired Atomic Projectile. 1000 stored in Europe. Deployed by U.S. and NATO howitzer battalions.	1800	564	1800	564	1800	564
W-43	B-43 Nuclear Gravity Bomb. Carried by U.S. B-52, FB-111A, F-111, A-4, A-6, A-7, and F-4 aircraft, and by NATO F-4, F-100, and F-104 aircraft.	2000	2000	2000	2000	2000	2000
W-44	Mk 17 Nuclear Depth Bomb fitted to the RUR-5A ASROC Anti-Submarine Rocket. Carried by 28 cruisers, 78 destroyers, and 65 frigates in U.S. Navy.	1700	850	1700	855	1700	855

W-45	RIM-2D *Terrier* Surface-to-Air Missile. Carried by 21 cruisers, 10 destroyers, and 3 aircraft carriers in U.S. Navy.	600	340	600	340	340
W-45	M-167, M-172, or M-175 Medium Atomic Demolition Munition (MADM). 279 deployed by U.S. Army in Europe, and 21 in Guam and South Korea.	300	300	300	300	300
W-48	M-454 155 mm Artillery-Fired Atomic Projectile. 3000 stored in Europe. Deployed by U.S. and NATO field artillery battalions.	3300	1670	3300	1670	1670
W-50	MGM-31A/B *Pershing I* Surface-to-Surface Missile. 108 deployed by U.S. Army and 72 by West German Luftwaffe in Europe.	410	180	410	171	144
W-53	B-53 Nuclear Gravity Bomb. Carried by US B-52 aircraft.	150	150	150	150	150
W-53	Mk 6 Reentry Vehicle on U.S. *Titan II* ICBM.	65	53	64	52	49
W-54	M-129 and M-159 Special Atomic Demolition Munition (SADM). 93 deployed by U.S. Army in Europe, and 215 stored in USA.	308	93	308	93	93
W-55	Mk 57 Nuclear Depth Bomb fitted to the UUM-44A SUBROC Submarine Rocket. Deployed by 73 attack submarines in U.S. Navy.	800	400	800	440	440
W-56	Mk 11 Reentry Vehicle on *Minuteman II* ICBM.	540	450	540	450	400
W-57	B-57 Nuclear Gravity Bomb. Carried by U.S. B-52, FB-111A, F-111, A-4, A-6, A-7, AV-8B, F-4, F-15, F-16, and F-18					

(continued)

United States Nuclear Weapons Stockpiled and Deployed, 1982–84 (cont.)

Warhead Type	Weapon System/In U.S. Service or Service Abroad	1982		1983		1984	
		Total in Stockpile	of Which Deployed	Total in Stockpile	of Which Deployed	Total in Stockpile	of Which Deployed
	aircraft, and by NATO F-4, F-100, F-104, and *Tornado* aircraft.	1000	1000	1000	1000	1000	800
W-57	B-57 Nuclear Depth Bomb. Carried by P-3, S-3, SH-3, and SH-60F aircraft in U.S. Navy.	400	112	400	112	400	112
W-61	B-61 Nuclear Gravity Bomb. Carried by U.S. B-52, FB-111A, F-111, A-4, A-6, A-7, AV-8B, F-4, F-15, F-16, and F-18 aircraft, and by NATO F-4, F-100, F-104, and *Tornado* aircraft. Total of 4000 planned.	3000	3000	3000	3000	3500	3200
W-62	Mk 12 Reentry Vehicle on *Minuteman III* ICBM.	1650	750	1650	750	1650	750
W-68	Mk 3 Reentry Vehicle on *Poseidon C-3* SLBM.	4960	4480	4960	4256	4960	4256
W-69	AGM-69A Short-Range Attack Missile (SRAM). Carried by US B-52G/H and FB-111A aircraft.	1500	1140	1500	1140	1500	1140
W-70	MGM-52 *Lance* Surface-to-Surface Missile. Deployed by U.S. and NATO field artillery battalions. 360 stored in Europe. 380 Enhanced Radiation warheads (W-70 Mod 3) stored in USA.	565	126	945	126	945	126
W-76	Mk 4 Reentry Vehicle on *Trident I C-4* SLBM. Total of 3600 planned.	1860	1792	2028	1920	2640	2112
W-78	Mk 12A Reentry Vehicle on *Minuteman III* ICBM.	1083	900	1083	900	1083	1050

Desig.	Description						
W-79	M-753 203 mm Artillery-Fired Atomic Projectile. Enhanced Radiation weapons for use by U.S. and NATO howitzer battalions. 800 planned. All stored in USA.	50					460
W-80	AGM-86B Air-Launched Cruise Missile (ALCM). Carried by US B-52 and B-1 aircraft. 4348 planned, including 2849 advanced ALCMs.	320	120		576	1470	960
W-80	BGM-109A Sea-Launched Cruise Missile (SLCM). 1000 nuclear versions planned, initially for 41 surface combatants and 91 attack submarines in U.S. Navy.	192	800				288
W-83	B-83 Nuclear Gravity Bomb. Carried by U.S. B-1B, B-52, FB-111A, F-111, A-4, A-6, A-7, F-4, F-15, F-16, and F-18 aircraft, and by NATO F-4 and F-104 aircraft. 2500 planned.	88	208			530	
W-84	BGM-109 *Tomahawk* Ground-Launched Cruise Missile (GLCM). 565 planned, 464 for deployment at 6 bases in Europe.		500			1000	300
W-85	*Pershing II* Surface-to-Surface Missile. Deployed by 1 U.S. Army field artillery brigade in Europe. 384 planned, 108 for deployment in Europe.	65	149	32		269	96
		21	112	9		228	36
TOTALS:		32,585	23,119	34,477	23,556	37,657	24,783

Method and Sources

Weapons in the stockpile include all of those stored for reloads at forward positions, and those available for replenishment at sea, as well as those planned for retirement or replacement. Weapons deployed include only those which may be launched or fired as first rounds from available gun tubes and launchers, and those which may be delivered in a single sortie from available aircraft. This criterion is based on the probability, higher than any other, that despite the fact that provision is always made for reloads, in a nuclear war few aircraft, surface ships, missile silos, mobile launchers, or artillery pieces will survive long enough to be reloaded, and few surviving command centers will have the information needed to redirect such forces to remaining secondary targets, let alone the means to communicate with them.

(continued)

United States Nuclear Weapons Stockpiled and Deployed, 1982–84 *(cont.)*

Figures for the numbers of W-25 and W-31 warheads deployed, respectively, with *Genie* and *Nike-Hercules* missiles, and for the total number of W-48 warheads stockpiled, are from the Center for Defense Information, *The Defense Monitor*, Volume X, no. 8 (1982), pages 12 and 13. Figures for the numbers of all other warheads stockpiled and deployed are based on Thomas B. Cochran, William M. Arkin, and Milton M. Hoenig, "U.S. Nuclear Weapons Stockpile (1983)," in *Nuclear Weapons Databook: Volume I* (Cambridge, Mass.: Ballinger, 1984), page 39, but with the following revisions:

The figure for W-31 warheads deployed with *Honest John* missiles has been raised from 200 to 300, because the missiles remain not only in Turkey and Greece but also in South Korea, where the final *US Honest John* batallion was turned over to South Korean forces in 1979, with warheads remaining under U.S. control. See House Appropriations Committee, *Hearings, Defense Department Appropriations, Fiscal Year 1980*, Part 1, page 740, and House Armed Services Committee, *Authorization Hearings, Fiscal Year 1981*, Part 1, page 931.

Figures for the numbers of W-33, W-48, and W-70 warheads actively deployed have been reduced, respectively, from 1800 to 564, 3300 to 1670, and 945 to 126, reflecting the numbers of 203 mm and 155 mm howitzers, and the number of *Lance* missile launchers available to U.S. and NATO forces to fire first rounds without reloads. For the number of *Lance* missile launchers, and the types of artillery pieces available to U.S. and NATO forces, see Cochran, Arkin, and Hoenig, *op. cit.*, pages 73 and 301. For the number of artillery pieces available to U.S. forces in Europe, see the International Institute for Strategic Studies, *The Military Balance, 1983–1984*, page 120. For the numbers of nuclear-capable artillery pieces available to NATO forces, see Tom Gervasi, *Arsenal of Democracy II* (New York: Grove Press, 1981), pages 239 through 243.

The figure for W-44 warheads deployed with ASROC launchers has been raised from 850 to 855 in 1983 and 1984, due to the addition to the fleet of CG-47 *USS Ticonderoga*, equipped with ASROC launchers, in January, 1983. See Cochran, Arkin, and Hoenig, *op. cit.*, pages 258 and 260.

The figure for W-45 warheads deployed with *Terrier* launchers has been raised from 310 to 340, because these launchers and missiles are carried not only aboard 21 cruisers and 10 destroyers, as the Center for Defense

missiles reflects the minimum once required, and therefore certainly produced, to arm the 496 such missiles once deployed with 10 warheads each, prior to the replacement of 192 of those missiles with *Trident C-4* missiles on 12 *Poseidon* submarines. 10 warheads each was in fact the average. See Joint Chiefs of Staff, *Fiscal Year 1984 Posture Statement*, page 16.

The Center for Defense Information notes (*op. cit.*, page 12) that after the *Trident* missile retrofit, and the simultaneous retirement of *Polaris* submarines, the number of W-68 warheads on the remaining 304 *Poseidon* missiles was "selectively increased." Cochran, Arkin, and Hoenig note (*op. cit.*, page 137) that this increase "was announced" in October, 1980, raising the number of warheads on each missile "to 14." They further note (page 69) that "as many as 4256 warheads" of this type may consequently be deployed. Yet the Center for Defense Information does not list 4256 W-68 warheads in service; it lists only 3480. This is an average of 11 per missile. Cochran, Arkin, and Hoenig, despite the evidence they cite for the higher figure, simply quote the Center's lower figure in their warhead estimate on page 39.

Nor does that estimate, which gives warheads deployed and stockpiled in a single figure, take account of the W-68 warheads retired with the *Trident* retrofit, even though its authors acknowledge, on page 70, that this "probably results in a large number of warheads in the stockpile," which they estimate to be "circa 2000 warheads." They may have excluded them, of course, because they regard them to be "pending continued retirement."

Yet only 784 of those warheads could be retired, because the remaining 1216 would have been used to increase the complement of warheads on each of the remaining 304 *Poseidon* missiles from 10 to 14. On October 29, 1980, the Defense Department announced it was increasing the number of warheads carried by each *Poseidon* missile "to 14 from 10," and that such an increase "more than offsets the effect" of retiring 10 older *Polaris* submarines over the subsequent 14 months. See Associated Press, "U.S. Adds Warheads to Poseidon Submarine Missiles," *The New York Times*, October 30, 1980. The Stockholm International Peace Research Institute (SIPRI) noted that this increase "will add a total of 1216 warheads to the US SLBM force in the early 1980s." See SIPRI, *The Arms Race and Arms Control* (London: Taylor & Francis, 1982), page 95.

Former missile systems engineer Robert Aldridge notes that "*Poseidon*

Information notes (op. cit., page 12), but also aboard 3 aircraft carriers. See Senate Armed Services Committee, Authorization Hearings, Fiscal Year 1981, Part 4, page 2518. Center for Defense Information estimates 10 warheads per ship armed with Terriers. Cochran, Arkin, and Hoenig note that 3 aircraft carriers are so armed—pages 251, 252, and 273—but have not correspondingly raised their estimate of warheads on page 39.

The figure for W-50 warheads deployed with Pershing I missiles has been reduced from 410 to 180, reflecting the number of launchers available to fire first rounds, and has been further reduced in 1982 and 1983 to reflect replacements by Pershing II missiles. See Cochran, Arkin, and Hoenig, op. cit., page 292.

The figure for W-54 warheads deployed with M-129 and M-159 Special Atomic Demolition Munitions has been reduced from 308 to 93, because 215 of these weapons are stored not in Europe but in the United States.

The figure for W-55 warheads deployed with SUBROC depth bombs has been raised from 400 to 440 in 1983 and 1984, because SUBROC is no longer deployed with only 66 attack submarines, as the Center for Defense Information noted in 1982 (op. cit., page 12), but with 73. Cochran, Arkin, and Hoenig note the higher number of submarines so armed (page 269), but have not raised their estimate for warheads on page 39.

The figure for W-56 warheads deployed with the Mk 11 reentry vehicle on Minuteman II ICBMs has been reduced from 540 to 450 to reflect the actual number of warheads deployed, and further reduced to 400 in 1984, reflecting the replacement of 50 Minuteman II missiles of the 341st Strategic Missile Wing at Malmstrom Air Force Base, Montana, with Minuteman IIIs in December, 1983. See Joint Chiefs of Staff, Fiscal Year 1983 Posture Statement, page 72, and Clarence A Robinson, Jr., "Emphasis Grows on Nuclear Defense," Aviation Week & Space Technology, March 8, 1982, page 27.

The figure for W-78 warheads deployed with the Mk 12A reentry vehicle on Minuteman III ICBMs has been increased from 900 in 1983 to 1050 in 1984.

While Cochran, Arkin, and Hoenig note (op. cit., page 63) that the B-57 is intended for antisubmarine warfare (ASW) as well as for land warfare, and estimate "approximately 1000" B-57's available "for tactical (non ASW) use" in 1983, they have included none for ASW use in their warhead estimate on page 39. 400 for ASW use have been added, with 112 actively deployed.

The figure of 4960 W-68 warheads in the stockpile for Poseidon C-3 missiles were originally deployed with two warhead 'mixes': the full load of 14 on some missiles to reach targets within 2,500 nautical miles, and a reduced load of 10 warheads on others to achieve greater range for destroying targets farther away. Since the longer range Trident I missiles have been backfitted into twelve Poseidon submarines and can cover the farther targets, it seems logical that the remaining nineteen Poseidon submarines would carry a full load"—First Strike! (Boston: South End Press, 1983), page 44. The increase in Poseidon warheads is further confirmed by Vice Admiral Robert L. Walters, Deputy Chief of Naval Operations, in testimony to the House Armed Services Committee, Hearings, March 4, 1982, page 5; by the House Appropriations Committee, Hearings, Defense Department Appropriations, Fiscal Year 1982, Part 7, page 544; and by the House Armed Services Committee, Authorization Hearings, Fiscal Year 1982, Part 3, page 156. The figure for W-68 warheads deployed on Poseidon missiles has accordingly been raised here from 3480 to 4256.

While Cochran, Arkin, and Hoenig note (page 71) that the number of W-69 warheads available in the stockpile for Short-Range Attack Missiles (SRAMs) is "probably more" than the 1140 authorized for use, they give only the authorized figure in their "stockpile" estimate on page 39. But on page 155 of their own book, as on page 168 of Jane's Weapon Systems, 1981–1982 (London: Jane's Publishing, 1981), and on page 132 of Michael J. H. Taylor and John W. R. Taylor, Missiles of the World (London: Ian Allan, 1976), the figure of 1500 is given for the total number of SRAMs so armed and delivered to the U.S. Air Force. Since the SRAM remains one of America's most lethal strategic weapons, it may be safely assumed that the additional 360 SRAMs not actively deployed remain in the stockpile. That assumption is reflected here.

The figure for W-76 warheads deployed with the Mk 4 reentry vehicle on Trident I C-4 SLBMs has been reduced from 2028 to 1920, reflecting the number actually deployed in 1983 by submarines on active patrol. It has been increased to 2112 in 1984 to reflect the addition to the U.S. fleet of SSBN-728 USS Florida. See Cochran, Arkin, and Hoenig, op. cit., page 140, and International Institute for Strategic Studies, The Military Balance, 1983–1984, pages 3 and 4.

Stockpile figures have been increased in 1984 for W-61, W-76, W-79, and W-80 warheads, and added in 1984 for W-83, W-84, and W-85 warheads, reflecting continued production which Cochran, Arkin, and Hoenig document themselves on pages 16, 66, 77 through 80, 142 and 143, 174

(continued)

United States Nuclear Weapons Stockpiled and Deployed, 1982–84 (cont.)

through 187, 200 and 201, and 292 through 297 of their book. Those pages also document figures included here, but not included in the warhead estimate given on page 39 of that book, for W-80 warheads deployed with Air-Launched and Sea-Launched Cruise Missiles (ALCMs and SLCMs), W-84 warheads deployed with Tomahawk Ground-Launched Cruise Missiles (GLCMs), and W-85 warheads deployed with Pershing II missiles.

Initial ALCM deployments are also documented by the Department of Defense, Selected Acquisition Report, June 30, 1982; by Samuel Freedman, "Nuclear Deterrence as Neighbor," The New York Times, December 27, 1982; and by Aviation Week & Space Technology, January 17, 1983, page 101. Initial SLCM deployments are documented by the Senate Armed Services Committee, Authorization Hearings, Fiscal Year 1982, Department of Defense, Part 7, page 4088; and by Wayne Biddle, "Amid Congress Debate, Navy Gets Cruise Missiles," The New York Times, June 28, 1984. Initial Tomahawk and Pershing II deployments are documented by the Department of Defense, Program of Research, Development and Acquisition, Fiscal Year 1983, page VII-13.

Some earlier warheads, including the W-25 arming the Genie, the W-31 arming both the Honest John and Nike-Hercules, and the W-44 and W-45, arming the ASROC and Terrier missiles respectively, were produced in great quantities. As many as 10,000 Genie missiles may have been built. See Bernard Fitzsimons, Bill Gunston, Ian V. Hogg, and Antony Preston, The Illustrated Encyclopaedia of 20th Century Weapons and Warfare (London: Purnell & Sons, 1967–69), Vol. 11, page 1122. Over 20,000 ASROC missiles were produced. See Norman Polmar, The Ships and Aircraft of the U.S. Fleet (12th ed., Annapolis, Md.: U.S. Naval Institute Press, 1981), page 332. In 1963, 134 Nike-Hercules air defense batteries were deployed across the United States, with another 80 in 9 NATO nations and 3 others abroad. The Honest John missile equipped 16 U.S. Army field artillery battalions and another 26 battalions serving 10 NATO nations and 2 others abroad. This placed in active service 2568 Nike-Hercules and 1134 Honest John launchers, or a total of 3702 launchers of both types, with the same total of missiles of both types available as first rounds. Many more of both would have been available as reloads. See Fitzsimons, et al., op. cit., Vol. 18, page 1998, and the International Institute for Strategic Studies, The Military Balance, 1974–1975, pages 6, 7, 18 through 26, and 53 through 56.

As long as such missiles remain in service, it is not unreasonable to assume that now, as before, a greater quantity of operational missiles will remain stockpiled as reloads than will be available as deployed first rounds. Genie, ASROC, Nike-Hercules, and Terrier missiles will all remain in service until new missile types are available to replace them. 1000 W-31 warheads for Honest John and Nike-Hercules missiles were recently returned to the United States from Europe. See House Armed Services Committee, Authorization Hearings, Fiscal Year 1982, Department of Energy, page 104. But 300 Honest John and 750 Nike-Hercules missiles remain deployed. W-31 warheads for them will remain in inventory until 1992. See House Appropriations Committee, Hearings, Department of Energy Appropriations, Fiscal Year 1982, Part 7, page 279. Consequently, an additional quantity of W-31 warheads, sufficient at least for resupply, will remain in inventory too. as will comparable quantities of warheads to resupply Genie, ASROC, and Terrier launchers as long as they remain in service. The stockpile figures given here, representing only small portions of the numbers of such warheads originally produced, reflect this fact.

Stockpile figures for warheads arming nuclear gravity bombs are the minimum figures on which all sources agree, and represent a sufficient capacity for resupply, given normal operational loadings. However, the full supply of all such bombs could easily be delivered in a single sortie by the available strategic and tactical aircraft certified to carry them. Soviet planners could not fail to take this into account. Therefore, with the exceptions of the B-83 bomb entering service for the first time in 1984, and of newly produced B-61s not yet allocated to designated commands, the figures for weapons deployed account for the possibility of full deployment by matching the figures for weapons stockpiled.

Cochran, Arkin, and Hoenig also note (op. cit., page 3) that stocks of two warheads, those for the W-66 Sprint and W-71 Spartan missiles, are "in active storage and being retired," and further note (page 9) that dismantling of the missiles themselves "began in FY 1983." Since Sprint and Spartan were, respectively, the terminal intercept and high-altitude missiles comprising our Safeguard antiballistic missile site at Grand Forks, North Dakota, a site dismantled in 1975 when it first became evident that antiballistic missile defense was unfeasible, this is an indication of how long warheads may remain in the stockpile when there is no longer any ostensible intent to deploy them.

Soviet Nuclear Weapons Stockpiled and Deployed, 1982–84

Weapon System Type/Number of Warheads Each	1982		1983		1984	
	Total in Stockpile	of Which Deployed	Total in Stockpile	of Which Deployed	Total in Stockpile	of Which Deployed
Intercontinental Ballistic Missiles						
SS-11 Mod 1. 1 × 1 MT.	140	120	140	110	140	100
SS-11 Mod 3. 3 × 300 KT MRV. Each set of 3 counts as 1 warhead, because they are not independently targetable.	560	470	560	460	500	420
SS-13 Mod 1. 1 × 750 KT.	100	60	100	60	100	60
SS-17 Mod 1. 4 × 170 KT MIRV.	670	560	670	560	670	560
SS-17 Mod 2. 1 × 3 MT.	20	10	20	10	20	10
SS-18 Mod 1. 1 × 25 MT.	40	30	40	30	40	30
SS-18 Mod 2. 8 × 750 KT MIRV.	2000	1824	2000	1744	1800	1664
SS-18 Mod 3. 1 × 20 MT.	40	30	40	30	40	30
SS-18 Mod 4. 10 × 500 KT MIRV.	250	200	360	300	480	400
SS-19 Mod 1. 6 × 550 KT MIRV.	1600	1380	1800	1500	2100	1800
SS-19 Mod 2. 1 × 1 MT.	72	60	72	60	72	60
Submarine-Launched Ballistic Missiles						
SS-N-5. 1 × 1 MT.	65	57	65	57	65	48
SS-N-6 Mod 1. 1 × 1 MT	110	96	110	96	110	80
SS-N-6 Mod 3. 3 × 350 KT MRV. Each set of 3 counts as 1 warhead, because they are not independently targetable.	350	304	350	304	350	304
SS-N-8 Mod 1. 1 × 1 MT	350	292	350	292	350	292
SS-N-17. 1 × 1 MT.	15	12	15	12	15	12
SS-N-18 Mod 2. 3 × 200 KT MIRV.	550	480	550	384	500	336
SS-N-18 Mod 3. 7 × 200 KT MIRV.	400	336	650	560	950	784
SS-N-20. 9 × 200 KT MIRV.	50		100		200	180
Intermediate-Range Ballistic Missiles						
SS-4. 1 × 1 MT. Being withdrawn from deployment in Europe. Range: 1200 miles.	400	340	350	275	300	223

(continued)

Soviet Nuclear Weapons Stockpiled and Deployed, 1982–84 (cont.)

Weapon System Type/Number of Warheads Each	1982 Total in Stockpile	1982 of Which Deployed	1983 Total in Stockpile	1983 of Which Deployed	1984 Total in Stockpile	1984 of Which Deployed
SS-5. 1 × 1 MT. Now completing withdrawal from deployment in Europe. Range: 2300 miles.	50	40	40	16	30	16
SS-20 Mod 2. 3 × 150 KT MIRV. In production to replace SS-4 and SS-5. Warheads deployed in Europe: 450 in 1982, 630 in 1983, 720 in 1984. Range: 2300 miles.	830	690	1130	945	1300	1080
Short-Range Ballistic Missiles						
SS-1b SCUD A and SS-1c SCUD B. 1 × 40 to 100 KT. Deployed in Europe: 140 in 1982, 150 in 1983, 150 in 1984. Range: 185 miles.	500	410	540	450	540	440
SS-23. 1 × 40 to 100 KT. Replacement for SS-1b and SS-1c. None deployed in Europe. Range: 310 miles.			20	10	20	10
FROG 7. 1 × 25 to 40 KT. Deployed in Europe: 80 in 1982, 80 in 1983, 72 in 1984. Range: 43 miles.	580	482	580	482	740	620
SS-21. 1 × 40 to 100 KT. Replacement for FROG 7. None deployed in Europe. Range: 75 miles.			20	10	75	62
SS-12 *Scaleboard.* 1 × 200 KT. Deployed in Europe: 60 in 1982, 70 in 1983, 70 in 1984. Range: 300 miles.	80	65	85	70	150	120
SS-22. 1 × 500 KT. Replacement for SS-12. None deployed in Europe. Range: 560 miles.			125	100	125	100
SS-C-1b Ground-Launched Cruise Missile. 1 × 350 KT. Range: 280 miles. None deployed in Europe.	120	100	120	100	120	100
Sea-Launched Antiship Cruise Missiles						
SS-N-3. 1 × 350 KT. Range: 280 miles.	390	324	430	356	400	316
SS-N-7. 1 × 200 KT. Range: 27 miles.	165	138	185	154	185	144
SS-N-9. 1 × 200 KT. Range: 170 miles.	155	130	165	136	185	154
SS-N-12. 1 × 350 KT. Range: 340–620 miles.	70	56	80	62	100	80
SS-N-19. 1 × 350 KT. Range: 285 miles.	50	40	60	44	60	44
SS-N-22. 1 × 200 KT. Range: 300 miles.					30	20

Antisubmarine Warfare Weapons

SS-N-14. 1 × 40 KT. Range: 35 miles.	64	292	350	350	288
SUW-N-1. 1 × 25 KT. Range: 22 miles.				15	12

Surface-to-Air Missiles

ABM-1B *Galosh*. 1 × 1 MT. Range: 185 miles.		32	64	64	32
SA-N-6. 1 × 5 KT. Range: 23 miles.				30	20

Artillery Projectiles

SAU-152 self-propelled howitzer. Deployed at Division level in Europe.	700	558	1000	1000	558
M-1978 152 mm towed artillery gun. Deployed at Army level in Europe.		72	200	400	144
SU M-1975 self-propelled 203 mm howitzer. Deployed at Front level in Europe.		90	200	400	180

Strategic Air Weapons

AS-3 air-to-surface missile. 1 × 800 KT. Range: 400 miles. Carried by Tu-95A.	85	70	85	85	70
Nuclear gravity bomb. 1 MT. Two carried by Tu-95A and MYA-4 aircraft each.	200	130	200	200	130

Tactical and Naval Aviation Weapons

AS-4 air-to-surface missile. 1 × 200 KT. Range: 185 miles. Carried by Tu-22M *Backfire*. Deployed against Europe: 32 in 1982, 50 in 1983, 55 in 1984. Deployed by Naval Aviation: 35 in 1982, 40 in 1983, 50 in 1984.	135	67	180	210	105
AS-6 air-to-surface missile. 1 × 200 KT. Range: 155 miles. Carried by Tu-16. Deployed against Europe: 65 in 1982, 65 in 1983, 110 in 1984. Deployed by Naval Aviation: 110 in 1984.	90	65	120	440	220
Nuclear gravity bomb. 1 MT. Two carried by Tu-16, Tu-22, and Su-25 aircraft each. One carried by MiG-21, MiG-27, Su-7, Su-17/20, and					

(continued)

Soviet Nuclear Weapons Stockpiled and Deployed, 1982–84 (cont.)

Weapon System Type/Number of Warheads Each	1982		1983		1984	
	Total in Stockpile	of Which Deployed	Total in Stockpile	of Which Deployed	Total in Stockpile	of Which Deployed
Su-19/24 aircraft each. Deployed against Europe. 332 in 1982, 358 in 1983, 268 in 1984.	1600	1327	1600	1177	1600	757
TOTALS:	13,646	11,179	15,921	12,355	17,656	13,215

Method and Sources

Weapons in the stockpile include all of those stored for reloads at forward positions, and those available for replenishment at sea, as well as those planned for retirement or replacement. Weapons deployed include only those which may be launched or fired as first rounds from available gun tubes and launchers, and those which may be delivered in a single sortie from available aircraft. This criterion is based on the probability, higher than any other, that despite the fact that provision is always made for reloads, in a nuclear war few aircraft, surface ships, missile silos, mobile launchers, or artillery pieces will survive long enough to be reloaded, and few surviving command centers will have the information needed to redirect such forces to remaining secondary targets, let alone the means to communicate with them.

The distinction between weapons stockpiled and weapons deployed is essential to maintain in comparing Soviet and American nuclear arsenals. It prevents all the weapons in one nation's stockpile, many of which could never be delivered to their targets, from being compared with just those weapons the other nation deploys and could deliver. It helps to prevent a variety of assumptions from inflating the size of one nation's stockpile over the other's, and so misrepresenting the balance of warheads between them. One of these is that reload weapons, so far as they exist, should be considered deployed weapons. Another is that the Soviet Union has many more reload weapons than the United States has, though Soviet planners could not have thought it any more sensible than American planners have to build

suming all Soviet missiles had been fitted with multiple warheads to the maximum extent allowed by SALT II, even though Defense Intelligence Agency officials told Arkin and Sands that some "are still configured to carry single warheads," and that "current force loading is actually below" Wagner's estimate, "taking into consideration actual single warhead deployments." The Defense Department, they note, explained that this information was omitted from its annual editions of *Soviet Military Power* due to "space considerations."

The Soviet stockpile is further inflated in Wagner's estimate by its assumption that large numbers of nuclear gravity bombs would have been built to arm every Soviet aircraft deemed capable of carrying them, though the Soviets could not have assigned a much larger portion of their available strike aircraft to nuclear weapons delivery than the United States has assigned of its own, without leaving the many other missions aircraft must perform in serious neglect.

In the European theater, for example, NATO itself, in its publication *NATO and Warsaw Pact Force Comparisons*, 1983, page 15, concedes that "the majority" of Soviet strike aircraft assigned to the Warsaw Pact's defense "would likely be used in a conventional role." The International Institute for Strategic Studies, in *The Military Balance, 1981–1982*, page 129, note d, notes that only "about 25 percent" of the 2,595 nuclear-capable Soviet strike aircraft in existence are "generally deployed" in eastern Europe, and that only "some 25 percent" of *those* are "retained in nuclear role," together large numbers of reload weapons whose prospects for use are so poor.

The most notorious example of an estimate which makes this assumption, among a number of others, is that presented by Assistant Secretary of Defense for Atomic Affairs Richard L. Wagner to the House Appropriations Committee on March 14, 1984, *Energy and Water Development Appropriations, Fiscal Year 1985*, Part 6, page 118. Wagner produced an estimate of 34,000 nuclear warheads in the Soviet stockpile. If this estimate was accurate, *New York Times* correspondent Richard Halloran noted, then the Soviet Union had "moved ahead of the United States in numbers of nuclear warheads," because "the United States, by comparison, has 26,000 warheads" (see Halloran, "Soviet Said to Lead U.S. by 8,000 Warheads," *The New York Times*, June 18, 1984). Halloran's figure was close to the number of *deployed* American warheads, but did not include another 12,874 warheads in America's *stockpile*.

In fact, if deployed weapons are compared, it is the United States which leads by 11,568 warheads. If stockpiled weapons are compared, then the United States leads again, this time by 20,001 warheads. Assistant Secretary Wagner had almost *doubled* the figure for warheads in the Soviet stockpile.

Through articles like Halloran's, this estimate created the public impression of what researchers William Arkin and Jeffrey Sands called a "Warhead Gap." Writing in the June, 1984, issue of *Arms Control Today*, "The Soviet Nuclear Stockpile," Volume 14, no. 5, pages 1 and 4 through 7, they found Wagner's estimate no less "contrived" than "past misrepresentations" that appeared to show a Soviet lead. They recalled that only a month before Wagner had presented his estimate, the Joint Chiefs of Staff, in their *Fiscal Year 1985 Posture Statement*, had reiterated that "the United States has more warheads."

Arkin and Sands noted that Wagner's estimate "necessarily depends on an assumed high level of reloads," even though the Strategic Air Command had noted that Soviet reload missiles would not be "compatible with existing silo launchers," the Defense Department had acknowledged that "reloading a significant fraction of the ICBM force" might take the Soviets "up to several weeks," and the Defense Intelligence Agency had informed them that reloading missiles at sea, too, was "unlikely, if not impossible, during a nuclear war."

Wagner's estimate also inflated the size of the Soviet stockpile by as-

with "some 50 percent" of the 365 Soviet medium-range bombers stationed in the western Soviet Union. In that case, the total of all such aircraft held by the Soviet Union for nuclear strike missions against European targets that year was only 344. In view of their load capacities, the types of weapons they normally carried, and the weights of those weapons, they could have deployed no more than 429 nuclear weapons against NATO. Wagner instead assumes enough nuclear weapons are available to load *all* Soviet strike aircraft, wherever they are stationed, frequently beyond their load capacities.

Arkin and Sands conclude that a more realistic estimate—no longer based on more reloads than the Soviets would have any reason, let alone the resources, to build, or on the assumption that all Soviet missiles are fitted with the maximum number of warheads allowable under SALT II, when the Defense Department has acknowledged this is not the case—could produce a Soviet stockpile estimate "as small as 18,000." That is close to the stockpile estimate provided here.

Stockpile figures in this estimate average 20% over the figures for warheads deployed, based on a similar average for most American warhead types, and on the assumption that this will provide sufficient spares to maintain the deployment levels shown. Greater numbers of weapons for reloads are likely to have been provided only for air-launched and artillery-fired systems. That likelihood, too, is reflected in this estimate, though the likelihood of opportunities for the use of such weapons is barely more plausible than it is for nuclear reloads of any other kind. High figures for some systems now being withdrawn reflect the author's assumption that the Soviets may be as slow as the Americans are in retiring warheads for systems no longer deployed.

The explosive yields of both modifications of the SS-11, the SS-13, the SS-17 Mod 1, and the SS-18 Mods 3 and 4 are from the International Institute for Strategic Studies, *The Military Balance, 1983–1984*, page 119. Yields of the SS-17 Mod 2 and the SS-18 Mod 2 are from Fred Kaplan, *Dubious Specter* (Washington, D.C.: Institute for Policy Studies, 1980), page 90. Yields of the SS-18 Mod 1 and the SS-19 Mod 1 are from Robert C. Aldridge, *First Strike!* (Boston: South End Press, 1983), pages 59 and 60. Yield of the SS-19 Mod 2 is from Randall Forsberg, "A Bilateral Nuclear-Weapon Freeze," *Scientific American* (November, 1982), page 54.

Yields for all but two Soviet submarine-launched ballistic missiles are

(continued)

Soviet Nuclear Weapons Stockpiled and Deployed, 1982–84 (cont.)

from IISS, op. cit., 1983–1984, page 119. The yield of the the MRVs carried by the SS-N-6 Mod 3 is from Aldridge, op. cit., page 60, and that for the MIRVs carried by the SS-N-18 is from Aviation Week & Space Technology, March 14, 1983, page 153. Yields of the FROG 7, SCUD B, and SS-12 Scaleboard Short-Range Ballistic Missiles are from David C. Isby, Weapons and Tactics of the Soviet Army (London: Jane's, 1981), page 211. All other yields are from IISS, op. cit., 1983–1984, page 119, as are all the ranges shown for Intermediate- and Short-Range Ballistic Missiles and Sea-Launched Cruise Missiles, with the exception of the SS-20 Mod 2, whose range is from Jane's Weapon Systems, 1981–1982 (London: Jane's, 1981), page 7. Yields of the AS-3 and AS-4 are also from Jane's, op. cit., 1981, page 162, while the yield of the AS-6, as well as the ranges and deployment numbers of all three Soviet air-to-surface missiles, are from IISS, The Military Balance, 1981–1982, page 107. The probable yields of Soviet nuclear gravity bombs are from Kaplan, op. cit., 1980, page 90.

Estimates of the numbers of ICBMs not fitted with multiple warheads but still carrying a single one are consistent with normal growth following the Defense Department's estimate of 6300 Soviet missile warheads in May, 1982. This was 1100 fewer than the number concurrently offered in press briefings by the Reagan administration. The Defense Department's estimate was given by DOD officials in testimony to Congress, and published by The New York Times, "U.S. and Soviet Strategic Arsenals," May 2, 1982. The Defense Department's estimate is also consistent with the following sources, on which the estimates given here of ICBMs with single warheads are also based: John M. Collins, U.S.-Soviet Military Balance: Concepts and Capabilities, 1960–1980 (New York: McGraw-Hill, 1980), pages 443–445 and 448–449; Fred Kaplan, op. cit., 1980, page 90; Stockholm International Peace Research Institute (SIPRI), World Arms and Disarmament Yearbook, 1980 (Stockholm: Almqvist & Wiksell, 1980), page xxvii; SIPRI, The Arms Race and Arms Control (London: Taylor & Francis, 1982), page 85; Randall Forsberg, op. cit., November, 1982, page 54; An-

thony H. Cordesman, Jr., "M-X and the Balance of Power," Armed Forces Journal International (December, 1982), page 41; IISS, The Military Balance, 1982–1983, pages 140–141; and Anthony H. Cordesman, Jr., "Using a Strategy of Fear to Counter a Fear of Strategy," Armed Forces Journal International (February, 1983), page 60.

Six of these sources report SS-18s with a single warhead, and half of them report the same number shown here or 2 missiles fewer. Six of these sources report SS-19s with a single warhead, and half report the same number shown here or 2 missiles more. Only 3 report SS-18s with the maximum of 10 warheads each allowed by SALT II, but they do not report many. IISS, on page 140, note b, bases its estimate "on the assumption that the bulk of SS-18 are Mod 2," with 8 warheads each. Only 4 report SS-N-18s with 7 warheads, and the final 2 sources, including IISS, report only half of the SS-N-18s deployed with 7 warheads, while they report the other half with only 3 warheads each. It therefore does not appear that the maximum multiple warhead capacity of Soviet missiles has been utilized any more quickly than shown here, or any more fully than would be expected following the Defense Department's estimate of May, 1982.

The numbers of Intermediate-Range and Short-Range Ballistic Missiles, and of Sea-Launched Cruise Missiles given here are taken for each year shown from IISS, The Military Balance, 1981–1982, page 105; 1982–1983, pages 113 and 115; and 1983–1984, page 119. Numbers and types of nuclear-capable Soviet artillery are based on David C. Isby, Weapons and Tactics of the Soviet Army (London: Macdonald and Jane's, 1981), pages 176–177 and 199–202. Numbers of tactical air weapons are based on the load capacities of aircraft assigned to the nuclear strike role. Those numbers, in turn, are based on the proportions IISS estimates, as noted earlier, in The Military Balance, 1981–1982, page 129, note d. The total numbers of available Soviet strike aircraft from which those proportions are taken may be found for the years shown in IISS, The Military Balance, 1981–1982, pages 11 and 14; 1982–1983, pages 13 and 16; and 1983–1984, pages 15 and 18.

Appendix G

Theater Nuclear Weapons in Europe

Weapons Carried by Nuclear Strike Aircraft in Europe, 1981–82: NATO

Nuclear-Capable Aircraft Type	Load Capacity (lbs)	Number Available in Europe	Number Assigned to Nuclear Strike Role	Weapons on Each	Total Weapons
USA					
F-111	28,000	156	78	3	234
F-4 *Phantom*	16,000	312	94	3	282
A-6 *Intruder*	18,000	60	30	3	90
A-7 *Corsair*	20,000	144	72	4	288
Total USA:		672	274		894
Other NATO					
F-4 *Phantom*	16,000	332	100	3	300
F-100	6000	68	34	1	34
F-104	4000	441	132	1	132
F-16	20,000	74	37	3	111
A-7 *Corsair*	20,000	60	30	4	120
Vulcan	21,000	57	57	2	114
Tornado	18,000	16	8	2	16
Buccaneer	16,000	74	37	2	74
Super Etendard	16,000	36	18	2	36
Mirage IVA	16,000	33	33	1	33
Mirage IIIE	19,000	30	15	2	30
Jaguar	10,000	143	41	1	71
Total:		1364	572		1071
GRAND TOTAL:		2036	846		1965

Sources and Method

The number of NATO aircraft assigned to the nuclear strike role is based on calculations by the International Institute for Strategic Studies, in *The Military Balance, 1981–1982,* page 129, "Utilization" column, that all *Vulcan* and *Mirage IVA* aircraft, a third of all F-4s and F-104s, and half the aircraft of all other types available to NATO will be assigned that role, and is also based on the total of 2036 such nuclear-capable NATO strike aircraft available in Europe. This total is taken from pages 8 to 10, 27 to 39, and 44 of the same publication.

The total of available NATO aircraft includes 672 American aircraft, of which 348 are within range of European targets from 6 carriers in the Atlantic and Mediterranean, as IISS assumes on pages 106 and 110, note e. It includes 1364 other NATO aircraft. Though all of these are listed on pages 27 to 39 and 44, only a portion are listed in the "Inventory" column on page 129. All of NATO's newly delivered F-16s, *Jaguars* and *Tornados,* nuclear-capable Danish and Turkish F-100s, and Greek A-7s have been eliminated from that column.

But the F-16s and *Tornados,* along with the Greek A-7s, are listed by the Stockholm International Peace Research Institute in *The Arms Race and Arms Control* (London: Taylor & Francis, 1982), pages 151–152. The Center for Defense Information lists F-100s among NATO's nuclear-capable strike aircraft in *The Defense Monitor,* Volume XII, no. 6 (September,

1983), page 6. And Anthony H. Cordesman, Jr., in "France's New Defense: The Economics of Going Nuclear," *Armed Forces Journal International* (February, 1983), page 21, lists "three squadrons of *Jaguar* and two of *Mirage IIIE* carrying 20 KT AN-52 bombs to provide a forward deterrent." Accordingly, all of these aircraft have been restored here to NATO's inventory, providing the basis for reductions from 2036 available NATO nuclear-capable aircraft to 846 such aircraft assigned to the nuclear strike role.

Load capacities for all aircraft but the F-16, *Buccaneer,* and *Tornado* are taken from the same IISS publication, pages 106 to 109. Those for the F-16 and *Tornado* are taken from IISS, *The Military Balance, 1983–1984,* page 122, and that for the *Buccaneer* is from Norman Polmar, *World Combat Aircraft Directory* (London: Macdonald and Jane's, 1976), page 183.

Several NATO aircraft are assigned higher nuclear weapons loads here than they are by IISS in the "Weapons per System" column on page 129 of *The Military Balance, 1981–1982,* though certainly the higher loads are more compatible with the high load capacities IISS acknowledges these aircraft possess. Standard nuclear weapons loads for the A-6 *Intruder,* the A-7 *Corsair,* the F-4 *Phantom,* the F-16, and the F-111 are taken from Thomas B. Cochran, William M. Arkin, and Milton M. Hoenig, *Nuclear Weapons Databook: Volume I* (Cambridge, Mass.: Ballinger, 1984), pages 208, 210, 216, 221, and 223, respectively. The weapons load for the French *Mirage IIIE* is taken from Normal Polmar, *op. cit.,* page 148.

In most cases, IISS will later list the same higher loads taken from these other sources and shown here, though it will not do so until three years later, in *The Military Balance, 1984–1985,* pages 131 and 132, as shown below:

Number of Nuclear Weapons Assigned

Aircraft Type	By IISS *Military Balance* *1981–1982*	By *Databook*	By Polmar	By IISS *Military Balance* *1984–1985*
A-6 *Intruder*	2	3		3
A-7 *Corsair*	2	4		4
F-4 *Phantom*	1	3		1
F-16		3		1–2
F-111	2	3		3
Mirage IIIE	1		2	2

These differences account for a much higher total of nuclear weapons deliverable by NATO aircraft assigned to the nuclear strike role than IISS had originally suggested in *The Military Balance, 1981–1982.*

Weapons Carried by Nuclear Strike Aircraft in Europe, 1981–82: Warsaw Pact

Nuclear-Capable Aircraft Type	Load Capacity (lbs)	Number Available in Europe	Number Assigned to Nuclear Strike Role	Weapons on Each	Total Weapons
USSR Bombers					
Tu-16 *Badger*	20,000	50	25	2	50
Tu-16 *Badger* with 1 × AS-6		130	65	1	65
Tu-22 *Blinder*	12,000	120	60	2	120
Tu-22M *Backfire* with 1 × AS-4	17,500	64	32	1	32
Total:		364	182		267
USSR Strike					
MiG-21 *Fishbed*	2000	187	47	1	47
MiG-27 *Flogger*	7500	125	31	1	31
Su-7 *Fitter*	5500	41	10	1	10
Su-17/20 *Fitter*	11,000	175	44	1	44
Su-19/24 *Fencer*	8000	120	30	1	30
Total:		648	162		162
GRAND TOTAL:		1013	344		429

Sources and Method

The number of Warsaw Pact aircraft assigned to the nuclear strike role is based on the full inventory of 2595 nuclear-capable Soviet strike aircraft listed by the International Institute for Strategic Studies (IISS) on page 14, and again on page 128, of *The Military Balance, 1981–1982;* on calculations by IISS on page 129, note d, of the same publication that "about 25 percent" of these, or 648 such aircraft, are "generally deployed in East" with Soviet Tactical Air Armies in Europe; on the observation by IISS on page 11 that 365 Soviet medium bombers are "in Western USSR" within range of European targets, so that a total of 1013 of both types of nuclear-capable Soviet aircraft are available for combat in Europe; and on the further calculation by IISS, on page 129, note d, that "some 50 percent" of the 365 available bombers, or 182 such aircraft, and "some 25 percent" of the 648 available tactical strike aircraft, or 162 such aircraft, will be "retained in nuclear role," so that a total of 344 aircraft of both types would be assigned such a role.

As IISS notes on page 110, note o, all Warsaw Pact nuclear warheads are "held in Soviet custody." On page 128, its lists no other Warsaw Pact aircraft but Soviet aircraft available for the nuclear strike role.

In its "Utilization" column on page 128, IISS does not follow the guidelines it specifies on page 129, note d, for determining the number of available Soviet aircraft assigned to the nuclear strike role. It assumes that only 40%, rather than 50%, of Soviet medium bombers and MiG-27s, and only 20%, rather than 25%, of all remaining Soviet aircraft are assigned to the nuclear strike role. However, it does not take these smaller percentages from the 365 Soviet bombers and 648 Soviet tactical strike aircraft available for combat in Europe.

It takes them from the entire inventory of 500 medium bombers possessed by the Soviet Air Force, and of 2595 tactical strike aircraft existing throughout the Soviet Union. Consequently, the "Utilization" column produces a higher total of 819 Soviet aircraft assigned to the nuclear strike role, rather than 344.

Since only a portion of the entire inventory of nuclear-capable Soviet aircraft is available for combat in Europe; since the higher total produced from that full inventory in the "Utilization" column ignores guidelines IISS specifies itself; and since the lower total more closely approximates estimates of the number of Soviet aircraft assigned to the nuclear strike role provided by other sources, including the estimate of only 201 such aircraft on "nuclear withhold" given by Phillip A. Petersen, Assistant for Europe in the Policy Support Program of the Deputy Under Secretary of Defense for Policy, in *Armed Forces Journal International* (August, 1984), page 52, the lower IISS total of 344 aircraft, produced by following its own guidelines, is used here.

The number of Soviet bombers of each type shown here available for combat in Europe is based on the assumption that a very high proportion of most modern types will be assigned to Europe. Accordingly, of the total of 365 bombers of all types which IISS, on page 11, places "in Western USSR" within reach of Europe, 64 of the 65 available Tu-22M *Backfires* it lists there, and 120 of the 125 available Tu-22 *Blinders* it lists there, are assumed to be assigned to Europe, with the remainder of this total made up of 180 Tu-16 *Badgers*.

Since IISS estimates that "some 50 percent" of these bombers are "retained in nuclear role," 32 of the *Backfires*, 60 of the *Blinders*, and 90 of the *Badgers* are assumed to be assigned to the nuclear strike role in Europe.

Load capacities for all Soviet aircraft are taken from page 107 of the same IISS publication. *Types* of loads carried by Soviet aircraft are taken from page 11 of that publication, which notes that the Tu-22M *Backfire* carries the "AS-4 *Kitchen* ASM"; from the Center for Defense Information, *The Defense Monitor*, Volume XII, no. 6 (September, 1983), page 7, which also associates the Tu-22M *Backfire* with the AS-4, and the Tu-16 *Badger* with the AS-6; and from aviation historian Bill Gunston, who again associates the Tu-22M *Backfire* with the AS-4, noting in *An Illustrated Guide to Modern Airborne Missiles* (London: Salamander, 1983), page 75, that the AS-4 has "frequently" been seen carried by the Tu-22M *Backfire*, "whereas," he continues, "the later AS-6 has been seen more often on aged Tu-16 *Badgers*."

On pages 74 and 75 of his book, Gunston provides two photographs of a single AS-4 missile mounted beneath a *Backfire*'s weapons bay, and on page 77, he provides a photograph of a Tu-16 *Badger* carrying one AS-6. On page 29 of *Soviet Military Power* (1984), the Department of Defense also published a photograph of a single AS-4 mounted beneath a *Backfire*'s weapons bay.

Accordingly, all 32 of the Tu-22M *Backfire* bombers shown here assigned to the nuclear strike role in Europe are assumed to be armed with the AS-4, and 65 of the 90 Tu-16 *Badger* bombers shown here assigned to that role are assumed to be armed with the AS-6, since IISS estimates, on page 107, that only 65 such missiles exist at the time. The remaining 25 *Badgers*, and all 60 Tu-22 *Blinders* assigned to the nuclear strike role, are assumed to carry 2 nuclear gravity bombs each, as IISS itself assumes in its "Weapons per System" column on page 128.

The maximum number of bombers assigned to the nuclear strike role have been assumed here to carry AS-4 and AS-6 air-to-surface missiles because IISS assumes, on page 129, note o, that "this would improve the penetration" of these weapons "substantially." Consequently, there is a military preference for the use of these weapons, rather than gravity bombs, whenever possible.

However, those bombers which carry air-to-surface missiles can carry only one each, since the weight of the AS-4 is 12,100 lbs and the weight of the AS-6 is 10,600 lbs, according to James F. Dunnigan in *How to Make War* (New York: Morrow, 1982), pages 116 and 117, and more than one of either of these missiles would exceed the load capacity IISS acknowledges for either of the aircraft, the Tu-22M *Backfire* or Tu-16 *Badger,* known to carry them.

This is further confirmed by aerospace analyst Bill Sweetman, who notes of the AS-6 missile, in *The Presidio Concise Guide to Soviet Military Aircraft* (Novato, Calif.: Presidio Press, 1981), page 175, that "the weapon appears to be larger than first reported, and is more suited to a single installation, like that of the AS-4 on the Tu-22." He concludes that "armament of the *Backfire* is likely to comprise a single AS-4 or AS-6."

In its "Weapons per System" column on page 128, however, IISS has assigned the *Backfire* 4 weapons each. it will not be until three years later, in its edition of *The Military Balance, 1984–1985,* page 135, that IISS will assign this aircraft only "1 or 2" weapons each.

All the remaining Soviet aircraft assigned to the nuclear strike role are shown here carrying a single nuclear gravity bomb each. In its "Weapons per System" column on page 128, IISS gives a single such weapon to all of the same aircraft excepting the Su-19/24 *Fencer,* to which it gives 2 bombs. Yet it earlier acknowledged, on page 107, that the *Fencer* had a load capacity of only 8000 lbs. On that same page, it gave the Tu-16 *Badger* a load capacity of 20,000 lbs, but on page 128 it assigned the *Badger* only 2 weapons. If a Soviet aircraft with 20,000 lbs of load capacity can carry only 2 weapons, then it is unlikely that another with but 8000 lbs of load capacity could carry more than 1. Accordingly, the *Fencer* here has been assigned 1 weapon.

NATO and Warsaw Pact Theater Nuclear Weapons Stockpiled and Deployed, 1982–84: Long-Range Systems

NATO Long-Range Theater Nuclear Forces

Delivery System	Warheads					
	1982		1983		1984	
	Stockpiled	Deployed	Stockpiled	Deployed	Stockpiled	Deployed
Aircraft	3000	1965	3200	2305	3200	2087
Poseidon (USA)	896	896	896	896	896	896
Polaris (UK)	200	64	630	210	1000	384
M-20 (Fr)	100	80	100	80	100	80
SSBS-2/3 (Fr)	60	18	60	18	60	18
Pershing II			27	9	108	36
Tomahawk GLCM			32	32	96	96
TOTAL:	4256	3023	4945	3550	5460	3597

Warsaw Pact Long-Range Theater Nuclear Forces

Delivery System	Warheads					
	1982		1983		1984	
	Stockpiled	Deployed	Stockpiled	Deployed	Stockpiled	Deployed
Aircraft	700	429	700	473	600	433
SS-20 Mod 2	900	450	1260	630	1440	720
SS-4	340	340	275	275	223	223
SS-5	40	40	16	16	16	16
SS-N-5	57	57	57	57	48	48
TOTAL:	2037	1316	2308	1451	2327	1440

Sources

Numbers of all weapons stockpiled and deployed in the years shown are from sources for the separate tables, *Weapons Carried by Nuclear Strike Aircraft in Europe, 1981–82*, *United States Nuclear Weapons Stockpiled and Deployed, 1982–84*, *Soviet Nuclear Weapons Stockpiled and Deployed, 1982–84*, and *Characteristics of NATO and Warsaw Pact Long- and Medium-Range Ballistic Missiles Deployed Against European Theater Targets from 1978 Through 1983*.

NATO and Warsaw Pact Theater Nuclear Weapons Stockpiled and Deployed, 1982–84: Shorter-Range Systems

NATO Shorter-Range Theater Nuclear Forces

Delivery System	Warheads 1982		Warheads 1983		Warheads 1984	
	Stockpiled	Deployed	Stockpiled	Deployed	Stockpiled	Deployed
Pershing 1A	410	180	410	171	410	144
Honest John	600	200	600	200	600	200
Nike-Hercules	1000	600	1000	600	1000	600
Pluton (Fr)	100	42	100	42	100	42
203 mm Howitzer	1000	564	1000	564	1000	564
155 mm Howitzer	3000	1670	3000	1670	3000	1670
Lance	360	126	360	126	360	126
Medium ADM	279	279	279	279	279	279
Special ADM	93	93	93	93	93	93
TOTAL:	6842	3754	6842	3745	6842	3718

Warsaw Pact Shorter-Range Theater Nuclear Forces

Delivery System	Warheads 1982		Warheads 1983		Warheads 1984	
	Stockpiled	Deployed	Stockpiled	Deployed	Stockpiled	Deployed
SCUD A/B (USSR)	280	140	300	150	300	150
SCUD A/B (WTO)	280	143	280	143	280	137
SS-12/22	120	60	140	70	140	70
FROG 7 (USSR)	200	80	200	80	200	72
FROG 7 (WTO)	410	205	410	205	410	198
M-1973 152 mm	700	352	1000	558	1000	558
M-1975 203 mm			200	90	400	180
M-1978 152 mm			200	72	400	144
TOTAL:	1990	980	2730	1368	3130	1509

Sources:

Numbers of Soviet SCUD A/B, SS-12/22, and FROG 7 missiles *deployed* in Europe are from David C. Isby, *Weapons and Tactics of the Soviet Army* (London: Macdonald and Jane's, 1981), page 211. All numbers of other weapons stockpiled and deployed in the years shown are from sources listed for long-range systems.

**Summary of NATO and Warsaw Pact Theater Nuclear Weapons
Stockpiled and Deployed, 1982–84**

	Long-Range Theater Nuclear Forces			
	NATO		Warsaw Pact	
Year	Stockpiled	Deployed	Stockpiled	Deployed
1982	4256	3023	2037	1316
1983	4945	3550	2308	1451
1984	5460	3597	2327	1440

	Shorter-Range Theater Nuclear Forces			
	NATO		Warsaw Pact	
Year	Stockpiled	Deployed	Stockpiled	Deployed
1982	6842	3754	1990	980
1983	6842	3745	2730	1368
1984	6842	3718	3130	1509

	All Theater Nuclear Forces			
	NATO		Warsaw Pact	
Year	Stockpiled	Deployed	Stockpiled	Deployed
1982	11,098	6777	4027	2296
1983	11,787	7295	5038	2819
1984	12,302	7315	5457	2949

Characteristics of NATO and Warsaw Pact Long- and Medium-Range Ballistic Missiles Deployed Against European Theater Targets from 1979 Through 1983

NATO Missile Type	Year First Deployed	Total Deployed 1983	Weight (Tons)	Dimensions (ft/in)		Throwweight (lbs)	Number of RVs 1983	Yield of Each (KT/MT)	Range Statute Miles	CEP (ft) 1983	Type Propellant
				Length	Diameter						
France											
SSBS S-3	1980	18	28.4	45'10"	4'11"	2180	1	1 MT	2174	2952	Solid
MSBS M-20	1977	80	22	34'1"	4'11"	2004	1	1 MT	1864	3038	Solid
UK											
Polaris A-3	1967	64	17.5	32'3"	4'6"	2202	6	40 KT	2860	1200	Solid
US											
Poseidon C-3	1971	64	32.5	34'1"	6'2"	5152	14	40 KT	2880	1200	Solid
Pershing II	1983	9	8.2	34'6"	3'3"	1470	1	50 KT	1242	100	Solid
BGM-109 GLCM	1983	32	1.3	18'3"	1'8"	270	1	50 KT	1864	100	Solid
WARSAW PACT											
USSR											
SS-4	1959	275	29.7	73'4"	5'5"	3000	1	1 MT	1200	7545	Liquid
SS-5	1961	16		80'	8'	3500	1	1 MT	2300	3608	Liquid
SS-20 Mod 2	1977	210		55'	6'6"	1590	3	150 KT	2300	1312	Solid
SS-N-5	1964	57		42'3"	47"	1500	1	1 MT	800	12,152	Liquid

Sources

Sources for the more controversial information are as follows: Ranges of French and British missiles are from IISS, *The Military Balance, 1983–1984*, page 122. Range of the *Pershing II* is from Anthony H. Cordesman, Jr., *Deterrence in the 1980s: Part I*, Adelphi Paper no. 175 (London: IISS, 1982), page 51. Range of the BGM-109 Ground-Launched Cruise Missile (GLCM) is from Cochran, Arkin, and Hoenig, *op. cit.*, 1984, page 178, note

miles for the press, or else they imply a lower range by giving their figures in nautical rather than statute miles.

CEP of the French MSBS M-20 is from James Dunnigan, *How to Make War* (New York: Morrow, 1982), page 298. CEP of the *Poseidon C-3* is from Collins, *op. cit.*, 1980, page 453, and is further confirmed by Cordesman, *op. cit.*, 1982, page 26. CEP of the *Pershing II* is from the United States

2, and page 179. These researchers note on page 179 that the GLCM has achieved this range "in tests." On page 178, they note that while the "system operational range" of the Air-Launched Cruise Missile (ALCM) is 1553 miles, Williams Research has produced a new engine which adds 345 miles to that range, for a total of 1898 miles. They also note that the second-generation ALCM, now in production, will add 920 miles to its original operational range, for a total of 2473 miles. The range given for the strategic version of the Sea-Launched Cruise Missile (SLCM) by its prime contractor, General Dynamics/Convair, is 2210 miles (see James Munves, "The War Museum," *The Nation*, September 3–10, 1983, page 165). What is important to note is that Williams Research makes the engine for *all* versions of the Cruise missile, the ALCM, GLCM, and SLCM (see Cochran, Arkin, and Hoenig, *op. cit.*, 1984, pages 173 and 176: "Major Tomahawk Cruise Missile Contractors" and "Major ALCM Subcontractors"). That is probably why the May, 1984, issue of *Defense Electronics*, page 50, gives the *same* range of 1726 miles for all three types of missile. The House Appropriations Committee, *Defense Department Appropriations, Fiscal Year 1982*, Part 9, page 246, gives 1841 miles for the current range of the ALCM. Former missile systems engineer Aldridge gives the same range of 1841 miles for the GLCM (see Aldridge, *First Strike!* [Boston: South End Press, 1983], page 155), and notes (*op. cit.*, page 151) that by 1987 the Advanced Strategic Air-Launched Cruise Missile (ASALM) will have a range of 2991 miles. From all of this, it seems reasonable to conclude that the original range of all Cruise missiles was close to 1800 miles, that their current range is close to 2500 miles, and that they will very soon have a range close to 3000 miles. Officials meanwhile continue to quote a lower current range of 1500

Arms Control and Disarmament Agency, *Fiscal Year 1979 Arms Control Impact Statement*, page 115. The CEP of the BGM-109 GLCM is from Cochran, Arkin, and Hoenig, *op. cit.*, 1984, page 180. Yield of the *Chevaline* warhead on the British *Polaris A-3* is from *Jane's Weapon Systems, 1981–1982* (London: Jane's, 1981), page 10. The British Ministry of Defence *White Paper* of April, 1981, noted that the *Chevaline* had a "manoeuvrable payload," so its CEP may be more accurate than estimated here.

Yields and CEPs of all Soviet systems are from IISS, *op. cit., 1983–1984*, page 119. Ranges of the SS-4 and SS-5 are from the same source, but the range of the SS-20 Mod 2 is from *Jane's, op. cit.*, 1981, page 7. The longer range usually given for the SS-20 is given by *Jane's* only for those versions carrying a single warhead. NATO insists that all SS-20s confronting western Europe are of the Mod 2 variety, with 3 warheads. Dunnigan, *op. cit.*, page 305, further confirms a lower range for this version of the SS-20, giving 2672 miles, rather than the ranges of 4000 and 4600 miles commonly cited by the press for all versions of the SS-20.

The number of SS-20s deployed in 1983 is taken from IISS, *The Military Balance, 1982–1983*, with special note of the comment made by *Jane's, op. cit.*, 1981, page 7, that "perhaps two thirds of this total deployed for maximum effect in the European theatre," and the comment made by IISS in the following year's edition of *The Military Balance, 1983–1984*, page 123, note f, that an "estimated two thirds of SS-20 within range of Europe." By both these reckonings, then, of the total of 315 SS-20s IISS listed as deployed by the Soviet Union in 1983, 210 were deployed against Europe, and of the total of 360 it listed in 1984, 240 were deployed against Europe.

Ground Forces and Conventional Weapons in Europe

This estimate of the conventional balance between NATO and the Warsaw Pact focuses on the critical region of central Europe, where NATO is claimed to be weakest. It first determines the numbers and types of units deployed in peacetime by both alliances, and the strengths of each unit, both before and after alert and mobilization, based on a consensus of the best evidence available from public sources.

The estimate next schedules the stages of mobilization and reinforcement available to each alliance for the central European theater, and determines the time reinforcing units at each stage would need to reach the zone of combat. It also determines the proportion of each alliance's troops in major combat units, and the proportion that accompanies major combat units as combat support or noncombat troops.

Figures for ground forces reserves are quoted, and the total tank holdings of all nations of NATO and the Warsaw Pact are estimated. What the reinforcement and mobilization schedules make clear, however, is that reserves in countries distant from the zone of combat will take time to mobilize and reach the central European front, and that a larger proportion of NATO's reserves is more likely to be used than that of the Warsaw Pact's reserves. One reason for this is that the Pact's reserves, compared with NATO's, are judged to be at a much lower state of readiness. But the primary reason is that the Warsaw Pact is presumed to be the only aggressor, and that consequently only NATO nations will have a full incentive to mobilize reserves in defense of their homelands. Accordingly, Warsaw Pact reinforcement schedules are shown reaching, but rarely exceeding, the level of each nation's active ground forces, including the entire Soviet Army, while the schedules for many NATO nations in central Europe are shown utilizing reserves that well exceed the level of their active ground forces.

The reinforcement schedules also demonstrate that, while both alliances have large numbers of main battle tanks, neither can bring all the tanks it has into battle in central Europe. The numbers of tanks are limited by the numbers of personnel trained to operate them, and by the numbers of formations into which they may be organized. They are also limited by the available frontage in which armored combat can take place.

Though the Warsaw Pact can bring more tanks into battle than NATO can, tables included here also demonstrate that NATO enjoys a very large qualitative lead. More of its tanks are better armed and more maneuverable than those of the Warsaw Pact, carry more ammunition, and fire it with greater effect.

The estimate finally compares the total manpower and tank strengths of NATO and Warsaw Pact forces available for the central European front after successive stages of reinforcement have been completed. It demonstrates that there would never be a time when NATO didn't already have more troops, and more troops in major combat units, than the Warsaw Pact could bring to oppose them.

A final table summarizes the balance of manpower, tanks, combat aircraft, helicopters, major surface warships, and attack submarines between NATO and the Warsaw Pact in all theaters of Europe.

TABLES IN THIS SECTION

- NATO Ground Forces Central Europe, Order of Battle, 1981–85: Manpower in Combat Units and Main Battle Tanks
- United States Ground Forces in Europe: Reinforcement Schedule, 1981–85
- USAREUR (United States Army Europe) Combat and Support Units in Position, 1981–85
- Summary: United States Ground Forces in Europe, 1981–85—Manpower in Place and Reinforcement Schedule
- NATO Main Battle Tank Holdings, 1981–85
- NATO Ground Forces Central Europe—Mobilization and Reinforcement Schedule, 1981–85
- NATO Ground Forces Central Europe—Mobilization and Reinforcement Schedule, 1981–85, Summary
- NATO Ground Forces Central Europe—Mobilization and Reinforcement Schedule, 1981–85, Summary: Totals
- Warsaw Pact Ground Forces Central Europe, Order of Battle, 1981–85: Manpower in Combat Units and Main Battle Tanks
- Warsaw Pact Ground Forces Reinforcement Schedule, Central Europe, 1981–85
- Warsaw Pact Main Battle Tank Holdings, 1981–85
- Key Operational Capabilities of Leading Current Tank Types and Tank Guns—1981–85
- Major Tank Ammunition Types in Current Service with NATO and the Warsaw Pact—1981–85
- Warsaw Pact Ground Forces Central Europe—Mobilization and Reinforcement Schedule, 1981–85
- Warsaw Pact Ground Forces Central Europe—Mobilization and Reinforcement Schedule, 1981–85, Summary
- Warsaw Pact Ground Forces Central Europe—Mobilization and Reinforcement Schedule, 1981–85, Summary: Totals
- Ground Forces in Central Europe, 1981–85: A Comparison of NATO and Warsaw Pact Strengths at Progressive Stages of Reinforcement
- NATO and the Warsaw Pact—All Theaters: The Balance on Land, in the Air, and at Sea, 1981–85

NATO Ground Forces Central Europe, Order of Battle, 1981–85: Manpower in Combat Units and Main Battle Tanks

AFCENT (Allied Forces Central Europe) HQ Brunssum, Netherlands

NORTHAG (Northern Army Group) HQ Mönchen-Gladbach, West Germany

Nation	Unit Designation	Unit Type	HQ Location	Current Strength in Place	Strength within 24 Hours	Tanks
Denmark	Jýtland Division	Mech Div	Aabenraa	11,500	11,500	120
Denmark	1st Brigade/Sjaelland Div	Mech Brig	Roskilde	3,800	3,800	44
Denmark	2nd Brigade/Sjaelland Div	Mech Brig	Vordinborg	3,800	3,800	44
West Germany	13th Heimatschutzkommando	Mech Brig	Eutin	3,730	3,730	66
West Germany	6th Panzer Division	Armd Div	Neumunster	17,000	17,000	300
Netherlands	1st Armored Recon Battalion	Armd Bn	Apeldoorn	860	860	59
Netherlands	1st Corps Artillery Brigade	Atty Brig	Apeldoorn	1,960	1,960	
Netherlands	1st Mechanized Division	Mech Div	Schaarsbergen/Arnhem	16,500	16,500	242
Netherlands	2nd Mechanized Division	Mech Div	Hardewijk	16,500	16,500	242
Netherlands	Marine Commando Battalion	Inf Bn	Kootwijk	640	640	
Netherlands	Marine Commando Battalion	Inf Bn	Het Loo	640	640	
Netherlands	103rd Armored Recon Battalion	Armd Bn	Bergen-Hohne	860	860	59
West Germany	1st Corps Artillery Brigade	Atty Brig	Münster	2,100	2,100	
West Germany	1st PanzerGrenadier Division	Mech Div	Hannover	17,500	17,500	250
West Germany	3rd Panzer Division	Armd Div	Buxtehude	17,000	17,000	300
West Germany	7th Panzer Division	Armd Div	Westfalen	17,000	17,000	300
West Germany	11th PanzerGrenadier Div	Mech Div	Oldenburg	17,500	17,500	250
West Germany	27th Luftlande Brigade	Airb Brig	Lippstadt	3,000	3,000	
United States	3rd Brigade/2nd Armored Div	Armd Brig	Carlstedt/Bremen	6,850	6,850	180*
United Kingdom	1st Corps Artillery Brigade	Atty Brig	Hildesheim	1,920	1,920	
United Kingdom	1st Armored Division	Armd Div	Verden	8,326	11,202	148
United Kingdom	2nd Armored Division	Armd Div	Lübeck	8,326	11,202	148
United Kingdom	3rd Armored Division	Armd Div	Münster	8,326	11,202	148
United Kingdom	4th Armored Division	Armd Div	Herford/Westfalen	8,326	11,202	148
United Kingdom	5th Field Force	Mech Brig	Mönchen-Gladbach	4,617	4,617	74
United Kingdom	6th Field Force	Mech Brig	Aldershot/Hampshire	4,617	4,617	74***

Country	Unit	Type	Location		Strength	
United Kingdom	7th Field Force	Mech Brig	Colchester/Essex		4,617	74***
United Kingdom	3rd Airmobile Division	Airb Div	Buford		9,300	
United Kingdom	16th Parachute Brigade	Airb Brig	Aldershot/Hampshire		4,900	
United Kingdom	3rd Commando, Royal Marines	Inf Bn	Portsmouth		300	
Belgium	16th Mechanized Division	Mech Div	Neuheim/Westfalen	11,108	11,108	162
Belgium	1st/2nd/3rd Armored Recon Bns	Mech Regt	Ludenscheid/Siegburg	1,710	1,710	
Belgium	6th Independent Tank Bn	Armd Bn	Berg Gladbach	432	432	54
Belgium	1st Mechanized Division	Mech Div	Leopoldsburg		10,714	54
Belgium	10th Mechanized Division	Mech Brig	Zonhoven		4,250	54
Belgium	12th Infantry Brigade	Inf Brig	Liege		4,856	
Belgium	1st ParaCommando Battalion	Inf Bn	Florennes/Namur		862	
Belgium	2nd ParaCommando Battalion	Inf Bn	Lombartzide		862	

2 ATAF (Second Allied Tactical Air Force) Ramstein Air Force Base (1,152 Aircraft)

CENTAG (Central Army Group) HQ Seckenheim, West Germany

Country	Unit	Type	Location		Strength	
West Germany	IInd Corps Artillery Brigade	Atty Brig	Ulm/Württemberg	2,100	2,100	
West Germany	2nd PanzerGrenadier Division	Mech Div	Marburg	17,500	17,500	250
West Germany	5th Panzer Division	Armd Div	Diez	17,000	17,000	300
West Germany	26th Luftlande Brigade	Airb Brig	Zweibrücken/Saarlouis	3,000	3,000	
United States	41st Field Artillery Brigade	Atty Brig	Darmstadt	2,300	2,300	
United States	42nd Field Artillery Brigade	Atty Brig	Giessen	2,300	2,300	
United States	3rd Armored Division	Armd Div	Frankfurt	18,900	18,900	360
United States	8th Infantry Division	Mech Div	Bad Kreuznach	19,872	19,872	360**
United States	11th Armored Cavalry Regt	Mech Brig	Fulda	3,834	3,834	159
United States	3rd Brigade/4th Infantry Div	Mech Brig	Wiesbaden	6,191	6,191	108*
United States	1st Armored Division	Armd Div	Ansbach	18,900	18,900	360
United States	3rd Infantry Division	Mech Div	Würzburg	18,500	18,500	324
United States	2nd Armored Cavalry Regt	Mech Brig	Nuremberg	3,834	3,834	159
United States	3rd Brigade/1st Infantry Div	Mech Brig	Göppingen	6,191	6,191	108
United States	72nd Field Artillery Brigade	Atty Brig	Aschaffenburg	2,300	2,300	
United States	210th Field Artillery Brigade	Atty Brig	Herzogenaurach	2,300	2,300	
United States	1st Bn/10th Special Forces	Inf Bn	Bad Tölz	250	250	
West Germany	12th Panzer Division	Armd Div	Veitshochheim	17,000	17,000	300
West Germany	10th Panzer Division	Armd Div	Sigmaringen	17,000	17,000	300
West Germany	4th Jaeger Division	Mech Div	Regensburg	17,500	17,500	250

(continued)

NATO Ground Forces Central Europe, Order of Battle, 1981–85: Manpower in Combat Units and Main Battle Tanks (cont.)

AFCENT (Allied Forces Central Europe) HQ Brunssum, Netherlands

CENTAG (Central Army Group) HQ Seckenheim, West Germany

Nation	Unit Designation	Unit Type	HQ Location	Current Strength in Place	Strength within 24 Hours	Tanks
West Germany	1st Gebirgsjaeger Division	Inf Div	Garmisch	9,000	9,000	
West Germany	25th Luftlande Brigade	Airb Brig	Calw/Württemberg	3,000	3,000	
West Germany	IIIrd Corps Artillery Brigade	Atty Brig	Koblenz	2,100	2,100	
West Germany	14th Heimatschutzkommando	Mech Brig	Neuberg/Donau	3,730	3,730	66
West Germany	15th Heimatschutzkommando	Mech Brig	Unna-Koenigsborn	3,730	3,730	66
West Germany	16th Heimatschutzkommando	Mech Brig	Landshut	3,730	3,730	66
West Germany	17th Heimatschutzkommando	Mech Brig	Karlsruhe	3,730	3,730	66
West Germany	18th Heimatschutzkommando	Mech Brig	Freiburg	3,730	3,730	66
Canada	4th Mechanized Brigade	Mech Brig	Lahr	3,400	5,400	59
United States	1st Brigade/1st Infantry Div	Mech Brig	Ft Riley/Kansas		6,191	108***
United States	2nd Brigage/1st Infantry Div	Mech Brig	Ft Riley/Kansas		6,191	108**
United States	3rd Air Cavalry Regiment	Mech Brig	Ft Bliss/Texas		4,522	54***
United States	1st Brigade/2nd Armored Div	Armd Brig	Ft Hood/Texas		6,100	120***
United States	2nd Brigade/2nd Armored Div	Armd Brig	Ft Hood/Texas		6,100	120***
United States	4th Brigade/2nd Armored Div	Armd Brig	Ft Hood/Texas		6,100	120***
United States	1st Brigade/4th Infantry Div	Mech Brig	Ft Carson/Colorado		6,191	108***
United States	2nd Brigade/4th Infantry Div	Mech Brig	Ft Carson/Colorado		6,191	108***
United States	4th Brigade/4th Infantry Div	Mech Brig	Ft Carson/Colorado		6,191	108***
United States	212th Field Artillery Brigade	Atty Brig	Ft Sill/Oklahoma		2,300	
United States	2nd Marine Division	Inf Div	Camp LeJeune/N Carolina		16,512	70***
United States	2nd/3rd/4th Bns/10th Spec Forces	Inf Regt	Ft Devens/Massachusetts		750	
United States	1st Bn/75th Special Forces	Inf Bn	Ft Devens/Massachusetts		250	
France	IInd Corps Artillery Brigade	Atty Brig	Baden-Oos	1,800	1,800	

Country	Unit	Type	Location			
France	1st Armored Division	Armd Div	Trier/Pfalz	7,000	7,000	202
France	3rd Armored Division	Armd Div	Freiburg	7,000	7,000	202
France	5th Armored Division	Armd Div	Mannheim	7,000	7,000	202
France	110th Airportable Inf Regiment	Inf Regt	Donaueschingen	1,350	1,350	
France	1st Armored Recon Battalion	Mech Bn	Erbach	560	560	
France	2nd Armored Recon Battalion	Mech Bn	Tuttlingen	560	560	
France	Ist Corps Artillery Brigade	Atty Brig	Nancy		1,920	
France	4th Armored Division	Armd Div	Verdun		7,000	202
France	6th Armored Division	Armd Div	Metz		7,000	202
France	7th Armored Division	Armd Div	Mulhouse		7,000	202
France	8th Armored Division	Armd Div	Compiègne		7,000	202
France	10th Armored Division	Armd Div	Soissons		7,000	202
France	11th Airborne Division	Airb Div	Pau		12,800	48
France	9th Marine Brigade	Mech Brig	St. Malo		2,700	52
France	17th Alpine Brigade	Mech Brig	Gap		2,796	52
France	27th Alpine Brigade	Inf Brig	Grenoble		3,270	
France	13th Infantry Division	Inf Div	Strasbourg		6,900	52
France	14th Infantry Division	Inf Div	Chambery		6,900	52
France	15th Infantry Division	Inf Div	Valence		6,900	52
France	16th Infantry Division	Inf Div	Spinal		6,900	52
Multinational	ACE Mobile Force	Mech Brig	Schenlen		8,640	30
	4 ATAF (Fourth Allied Tactical Air Force)		Ramstein AFB (2,304 Aircraft)			
Totals:	55 Divs/4 Regts/12 Bns		(3,456 Aircraft)	470,023	697,120	10,351

Key

Mech: Mechanized	Inf: Infantry	Div: Division	Bn: Battalion
Armd: Armored	Atty: Artillery	Brig: Brigade	
Airb: Airborne	Recon: Reconnaisance	Regt: Regiment	

Notes

Unlike the Warsaw Pact, the NATO alliance organizes its forces into a variety of formations, some of them smaller and some of them larger than Warsaw Pact divisions. The strengths of these formations vary from country to country. A battalion may include from 250 to 1000 troops, a regiment

(continued)

NATO Ground Forces Central Europe, Order of Battle, 1981–85: Manpower in Combat Units and Main Battle Tanks (cont.)

from 1300 to 3600, a brigade from 3000 to 6200, and a division from 6900 to more than 18,900. The total number of divisions given here in NATO's order of battle is the total of divisions and division equivalents the alliance can place in West Germany within 24 hours. To determine division equivalents, a ratio of three brigades per division has been used. This ratio is followed by all leading sources. See, for example, IISS, The Military Balance, 1980–1981, page 110, note b. Formations smaller than brigades have been counted separately, and have not been included in the count of division equivalents.

* These brigades belong to divisions of exceptional size. Unlike other divisions in the United States Army, which have three brigades each, the 2nd Armored and 4th Infantry Divisions have four brigades each. The remaining three brigades of the 2nd Armored Division are stationed at Fort Hood, Texas, and those of the 4th Infantry Division are stationed at Fort Carson, Colorado. All are kept ready as immediate reinforcements for NATO forces in central Europe. They constitute by themselves the equivalent strengths of a full armored and a full mechanized division. When they are joined with their extra brigades already deployed in West Germany, these divisions have much higher personnel and tank strengths than normal divisions of their respective types. Moreover, the 3rd Brigade of the 2nd Armored Division is organized as an independent armored brigade with five tank battalions. This further raises the Division's tank strength to the equivalent strength of one and a half standard armored divisions. See William P. Mako, U.S. Ground Forces and the Defense of Central Europe (Washington, D.C.: Brookings Institution, 1983), page 51, footnote h, and Charles Kamps, Jr., "Orders of Battle: North Atlantic Treaty Organization," in The Next War (New York: Simulations Publications, 1978), page 30.

** The 8th Infantry Division is "unique as a division," Stephen B. Patrick notes in "Red Star, White Star," Strategy & Tactics, (October 1975), page 26, because its 1st Brigade "is a fully airborne brigade," and because its two remaining brigades have "an unusually large tank strength" with five tank battalions each. This gives the division the same number of tanks as a standard American armored division.

*** Heavy equipment, including tanks, for all of these units has been pre-positioned in West Germany. Pre-positioning of British equipment is con-

here, as well as subsequent stages, and for the sources which confirm that number, see the separate table, United States Ground Forces in Europe: Reinforcement Schedule, 1981–85.

Only personnel in major combat units are included in this order of battle. Excluded are personnel in higher than divisional formations, in signals, engineer, transport, and other noncombat units, in aviation battalions, air defense artillery groups, and other formations that serve ground forces in a support role, in units whose mission is primarily strategic rather than tactical ground support, like that of America's 56th Field Artillery Brigade at Schwaebish-Gmuend, equipped with Pershing II missiles, and in formations assigned to areas outside central Europe, like the Southern European Task Force, an American airmobile brigade stationed at Vicenza. For a list of all American army units assigned to Europe during this period, see the separate table, USAREUR (United States Army Europe) Combat and Support Units in Position, 1981–85.

It should be kept in mind, as well, that many personnel within the divisional, brigade, and regimental formations listed here serve in noncombat and support roles. Nevertheless, the number of personnel in major combat units is widely accepted as a more accurate measure of ground combat capability than the total of all personnel assigned to ground forces. See Robert Lucas Fisher, Defending the Central Front: The Balance of Forces, Adelphi Paper no. 27 (London: IISS, 1976), pages 7 and 15, and Pat Hillier, Strengthening NATO: POMCUS and Other Approaches (Washington, D.C.: Congressional Budget Office, 1979), page 54.

Also excluded from the order of battle given here are NATO units in West Berlin, which is assumed to be isolated in a general war across the central European front. These units include an American infantry brigade of 4400, a British infantry brigade of 3100, a French infantry regiment of 1450 and a French armored regiment of 1250.

Composition of the ACE (Allied Command Europe) Mobile Force varies from year to year, but in recent years has included all of the following national contributions: United Kingdom (2 Troops Royal Tank Regiment, 2 Troops 9th/12th Lancers, 2 Troops 15th/19th Lancers), Belgium (3rd Battalion, ParaCommando Regiment, 3 Troops 1st Jagers te Paard, 3 Troops 4th Chasseurs), West Germany (1st and 2nd Panzeraufklärungs Battalions, 6 firmed by Diego A. Ruiz Palmer, "The Front Line in Europe: National Contributions," *Armed Forces Journal International* (May, 1984), page 54. Pre-positioning of American equipment is confirmed by the same source, page 74, and by the Department of Defense, *Annual Report, Fiscal Year 1985*, page 182. For the number of main battle tanks pre-positioned in Europe by the United States to equip the immediate stage of reinforcement shown

artillery batteries, 1 airborne infantry battalion), United States (1 airborne infantry battalion), Canada (1 infantry battalion), Portugal (1 infantry battalion), and Italy (1 infantry battalion and 1 artillery battalion). Generally attached, also, are 2 helicopter companies and 2 tactical fighter squadrons. See IISS, *The Military Balance, 1981–1982*, page 25.

large force that would be airlifted into position or ferried across the English Channel immediately from Great Britain. According to Deborah G. Meyer, "The British Army of the Rhine: New Tactics, Same Commitment," *Armed Forces Journal International* (May, 1983), page 56, "with over 55,000 British army troops stationed in West Germany," Great Britain has "another 150,000 or more regular army, reserve army, or territorial army troops ready to be there within hours in a time of crisis." According to *Strategy & Defense*, "Autumn Forge: The Biggest Landing Since D-Day," Dun Laoghaire, Ireland (February, 1985), page 7, in NATO's annual maneuvers scheduled for 1985, "over 130,000 British troops will be ferried across to Belgium and Holland, to later regroup in Lower Saxony."

Most sources agree that the French Army, as constituted throughout this period, has maintained three armored divisions in West Germany, with another five armored divisions and four mechanized divisions available as immediate reinforcements. See IISS, *The Military Balance, 1984–1985*, page 39; Diego A. Ruiz Palmer, "The Front Line in Europe: National Contributions," *Armed Forces Journal International* (May, 1984), page 61; Mako, *op. cit.*, page 50; and Major J. A. English, "Central Army Group: Pillar of NATO Defence," *Jane's 1982–1983 Military Review* (London: Jane's, 1982), page 113. The U.S. Army War College, *op. cit.*, 1981, lists all eight French armored divisions in the order of battle, and Kamps, *op. cit.*, page 28, lists additional French units available as immediate reinforcements.

Most sources agree on the numbers and types of West German regular army units in position in central Europe. See U.S. Army War College, *op. cit.*, 1981; Ruiz Palmer, *op. cit.*, page 65; Kamps, *op. cit.*, page 29; Mako, *op. cit.*, page 51; and IISS *op. cit.*, *1984–1985*, page 40. Kamps does not list the six Home Defense brigades of the West German Territorial Army,

Sources

Sources for all units included in this order of battle, and for most of their locations as well, are the United States Army War College, *NATO Data Base*, Carlisle Barracks, Pa., January 31, 1981; Lt. Col. Donald B. Vought and Lt. Col. J. R. Angolia, "United States Army," in *The U.S. War Machine* ed. by Ray Bonds (London: Salamander, 1978), pages 71–79; and Charles Kamps, Jr., "Orders of Battle: North Atlantic Treaty Organization," in *The Next War*, pages 27 to 30. Source for the location of Home Defense brigades (Heimatschutzkommando) of the West German Territorial Army is *International Defense Business*, "Defense Organization: Composition of the West German Armed Forces (Bundeswehr)," Washington, D.C., IMD International (June, 1972), pages 9–23.

All sources agree on the numbers and types of American units in position in West Germany, as well as on the numbers and types of American units allocated as immediate reinforcements for NATO's central European front. In addition to the above sources, see also IISS, *The Military Balance, 1981–1982*, page 7, and *The Military Balance, 1984–1985*, page 7, as well as William P. Mako, *U.S. Ground Forces and the Defense of Central Europe*, pages 50–51.

While IISS, *op. cit.*, *1984–1985*, page 35, lists only three British armored divisions in West Germany, the U.S. Army War College, *op. cit.*, 1981, lists four. Kamps, *op. cit.*, page 29, lists four. Mako *op. cit.*, page 50, lists four. While most sources agree that only one British Field Force, the equivalent of a brigade, is deployed in West Germany, they also agree that two more are available as immediate reinforcements for the British Army of the Rhine (BAOR). See Mako, *op. cit.*, page 50, and Kamps, *op. cit.*, page 29. Other British units designated to round out and reinforce the BAOR are listed by Kamps. They are only a portion of the

(continued)

NATO Ground Forces Central Europe, Order of Battle, 1981–85: Manpower in Combat Units and Main Battle Tanks *(cont.)*

but all of the other sources cited here do. The U.S. Army War College gives their unit designations, as does *International Defense Business, op. cit.* (June, 1972), pages 9–23. John M. Collins, in *American and Soviet Military Trends Since the Cuban Missile Crisis* (Georgetown, D.C.: Center for Strategic and International Studies, 1978), page 362, does not include them. The reason for excluding them has usually been that they would not operate under direct NATO control. But the West German Ministry of Defense, *White Paper, 1975–1976*, page 113, has committed them for possible use in NATO's forward defense, as well as for the defense of NATO command centers and strategic stockpiles. See also West German Ministry of Defense, *White Paper, 1979: The Security of the Federal Republic of Germany and the Development of the Federal Armed Forces*, pages 154–156, and Robert Lucas Fisher, *Defending the Central Front: The Balance of Forces*, Adelphi Paper no. 127 (London: IISS, 1976), pages 17–19. These brigades are consequently included here in NATO's order of battle in central Europe.

These brigades are but a part of a powerful West German Territorial Army that would quickly mobilize a far more significant combat capability in time of war. According to Chris Holshek, "The New German Army," *Armed Forces Journal International* (May, 1984), page 102, the Territorial Army would mobilize 6 more brigades, 15 regiments, 150 companies, and 324 independent security platoons, with a total of 450,000 troops. According to Ruiz Palmer, *op. cit.*, page 65, the Territorial Army would add 1200 more main battle tanks to the 3400 main battle tanks that already equip the West German Field Army, and could mobilize in 96 hours. According to Milton Leitenberg, "The Numbers Game or 'Who's on First?' " *Bulletin of the Atomic Scientists* (June–July, 1982), page 32, West Germany has "the ability to mobilize 1.2 million men in 60 hours in an acute crisis." See also James Blaker and Andrew Hamilton, *Assessing the NATO/Warsaw Pact Military Balance* (Washington, D.C.: Congressional Budget Office, 1977), page 16, and IISS, *op. cit.*, 1984–1985, page 40.

Personnel strengths of American armored and mechanized divisions and brigades are from IISS, *op. cit.*, 1981–1982, page vii, and 1984–1985, page vii. Tank strengths of American independent armored and mechanized brigades are from the same source, but the tank strength of an American armored division is from Kamps, *op. cit.*, page 31, and is further confirmed

of an American armored cavalry regiment is from Drew Middleton, "U.S. Army in Germany Confident It Is in Fighting Form," *The New York Times*, May 15, 1978. Tank strength of an American armored cavalry regiment is from Kamps, *op. cit.*, page 31. Personnel strengths of American Special Forces units are from Charles M. Simpson III, *Inside the Green Berets: The First Thirty Years* (Novato, Calif.: Presidio Press, 1983), page 209.

Personnel and tank strengths of West German armored and mechanized divisions are from IISS, *op. cit.*, 1981–1982, page vii, and 1984–1985, page vii. Personnel and tank strength of an independent West German mechanized brigade is from IISS, *The Military Balance, 1979–1980*, page vii, note e, and is further confirmed by Kamps, *op. cit.*, page 33.

Personnel and tank strengths of British armored divisions, both before and after full mobilization, are from Charles Kamps, Jr., "BAOR: The Thin Red Line in the 1980s," *Strategy & Tactics* (October, 1981), page 9, and are further confirmed by IISS, *op. cit.*, 1981–1982, page vii, note d, and 1984–1985, page vii, note d. Personnel and tank strength of a British Field Force is from Kamps, *op cit.* (October, 1981), page 9, and is further confirmed by IISS, *op. cit.*, 1979–1980, page vii, note d. Personnel strength of a British Royal Marine Commando is from Mark Herman, "Raid: Commando Operations in the 20th Century," *Strategy & Tactics* (October 1977), page 14. Personnel strengths of British Special Air Service units are from Tony Geraghty, *This is the SAS* (London: Arms and Armour Press, 1982).

Personnel strengths of French armored and infantry divisions are from IISS, *The Military Balance, 1980–1981*, pages 98–99. Personnel strengths of the French airborne, Alpine, and marine divisions are from IISS, *The Military Balance, 1984–1985*, page 38. Tank strengths of all French formations are from Kamps, *op. cit.*, 1978, pages 33 and 34. Kamps reports 202 tanks in each French armored division, 52 in each French infantry division, 52 in the French Alpine division, and 48 in the French airborne division. IISS, *op. cit.*, 1980–1981, pages 98–99, lists only 148 tanks in a French armored division, and none in a French infantry division.

IISS identifies the French tanks it lists as AMX-30s. The number of AMX-30s it reports roughly corresponds to the 150 AMX-30s Kamps identifies in French armored divisions. The remaining tanks Kamps reports in these divisions, and all of the tanks he reports in all other French formations, he by Col. Ernest O. Agee, "Submarine Tank Carrier," *Proceedings of the United States Naval Institute* (December, 1984), page 170, while the tank strength of an American mechanized division is from Drew Middleton, "Army Plans to Bolster Divisions to Counter a Buildup by Soviet," *The New York Times*, May 18, 1977. These sources report 324 tanks in American mechanized divisions and 360 tanks in American armored divisions.

By contrast, IISS, *op. cit.*, *1981–1982*, page vii, listed only 216 tanks in American mechanized divisions, and only 324 in American armored divisions. It has continued, *op. cit.*, *1984–1985*, to list these lower numbers. The last time IISS acknowledged such divisions had higher numbers of tanks was in *The Military Balance, 1977–1978*, pages 92–93, when it reported 270 tanks in American mechanized divisions, and from 351 to 378 tanks in American armored divisions. It specified, however, that all of the tanks contributing to these higher totals were "light" tanks. At that time, the United States still deployed the M-551 *Sheridan* tank in armored cavalry squadrons and other reconnaissance units. The *Sheridan* was considered a "light" tank, even though the caliber of its 152 mm gun was twice as heavy as that of the Soviet PT-76 "light" tank. If the *Sheridans* then present in these divisions were subtracted from the tank totals they fielded, the remaining balances of "main battle tanks" in each division type would indeed correspond to the numbers IISS has reported ever since. Presumably, this is the explanation IISS would offer, if asked why it reports fewer tanks in these formations than other sources do.

But according to Cols. Vought and Angolia, *op. cit.*, page 73, the *Sheridans* were already "being replaced" at that time "with the M-60A1s to simplify maintenance and resupply problems." Kamps, *op. cit.*, page 31, shows this replacement completed by 1980. There is unanimity among sources that the M-60A1 is a "main battle tank." Consequently, since at least 1980, the numbers of main battle tanks in these divisions have corresponded to the higher totals reported by Middleton, Agee, and Kamps. Accordingly, they are used here. IISS has continued to report the lower totals of such tanks as though new ones had never been added to replace the *Sheridans*.

Personnel and tank strengths of American armored and mechanized infantry battalions, and the personnel strength of American artillery brigades, are from Cols. Vought and Angolia, *op. cit.*, pages 71–75. Personnel strength

(continued)

identifies as AMX-13s. IISS lists none of these. Thus, when IISS notes, on page 112, *op. cit.*, *1980–1981*, that "450 tanks should be added to the NATO total" if the three French armored divisions stationed in West Germany "are taken into account," and that "a further 750 should be added" if the "divisions stationed in eastern France are also counted," it acknowledges that five armored divisions in France are available as immediate reinforcements, but counts only their AMX-30s.

In addition to the 1200 AMX-30s that all eight French armored divisions deploy, they also deploy 416 AMX-13s. In addition to those AMX-13s, 360 more AMX-13s equip other French units available as immediate reinforcements. That is a total of 776 tanks which IISS does not recommend be "added to the NATO total."

Presumably, IISS has excluded the AMX-13 from its count because it considers it a "light" tank, just as it considers the Soviet PT-76 and the British FV 101 *Scorpion*. For so it describes each of the three, on pages 25, 10, and 21, respectively (*op. cit.*, *1980–1981*). The Soviet PT-76 is equipped with a 76.2 mm gun, and the British *Scorpion* with a 76 mm gun (see Christopher Foss, *Jane's World Armoured Fighting Vehicles* (London: Macdonald & Jane's, 1976), pages 64 and 146. The AMX-13 was originally equipped with a 75 mm gun (Foss, *ibid.*, page 20). Guns of this caliber are considered too light to engage heavy armor. Foss (page 21) has this to say of the French 75 mm tank gun: "During the 1966 Six Day War the Israelis found that this weapon would not penetrate the front of a T-54/T-55 tank."

But the French do not use this gun on most of their AMX-13s. During the 1960s, according to Pierangelo Caiti, *Modern Armour: A Comprehensive Guide* (Parma, Italy: Delta Editrice, 1978), page 29, the French replaced the 75 mm gun on most of their AMX-13s with a 90 mm gun. This is further confirmed by Foss, *op. cit.*, page 20. Caiti (page 151) lists 1,120 AMX-13s in French inventory; of these he notes (page 30) that the French Army has "about 1,000 mounting the 90 mm gun."

High-velocity armor-piercing (HVAP) ammunition fired from the French 90 mm gun, and far more lethal than high-explosive antitank (HEAT) ammunition with shaped charges, is capable of penetrating 320 mm of armor at ranges of more than 1000 yards (see Caiti, page 156). The heaviest armor on the turret front of the T-54/T-55 tank is 170 mm thick (see Foss,

NATO Ground Forces Central Europe, Order of Battle, 1981–85: Manpower in Combat Units and Main Battle Tanks *(cont.)*

page 67). According to David C. Isby, *Weapons and Tactics of the Soviet Army* (London: Jane's, 1981), pages 90 and 101, the heaviest armor on the newer Soviet T-62 tank is 200 mm thick, and the heaviest armor on the newest Soviet T-72/T-80 tank is 210 mm thick. The armor protecting turret sides, hull front, and hull sides of all Soviet tanks, the areas next most prominently exposed to hostile fire, are from 80 mm to 130 mm thick.

French AMX-13s have accordingly been restored here to NATO's tank inventory.

The Netherlands, moreover, have refitted 198 AMX-13s, which they hold in reserve, with a 105 mm gun (see Caiti, page 151). The 105 mm gun is the standard NATO tank gun (see Foss, page 21). These AMX-13s have accordingly been restored to NATO's tank inventory in the separate table, *NATO Tank Holdings, 1981–85*.

Excluded from that table and this one is the British *Scorpion* tank, em-

ployed in considerable numbers by British and Belgian forces, because HVAP ammunition fired from its 76 mm gun cannot penetrate the heaviest Soviet armor. Similarly, because HVAP ammunition fired from the 76.2 mm gun on the Soviet PT-76 tank can penetrate (according to Foss, page 65) no more than 58 mm of armor at 1000 yards, the PT-76 has also been excluded from major tank holdings in the Warsaw Pact inventory.

Strength of the Canadian 4th Mechanized Brigade, both before and after full mobilization, is from the Canadian Ministry of Defence, Ottawa. Mako, *op. cit.*, pages 106–107, interprets IISS tables to imply that the strengths of Belgian, Dutch, and Danish divisions "would be similar to those for West German divisions." In fact, they are somewhat smaller than West German divisions. Personnel and tank strengths of Belgian, Dutch, and Danish formations given here have been supplied by their respective governments.

United States Ground Forces in Europe: Reinforcement Schedule, 1981–85

Immediate Reinforcements for AFCENT (Alllied Forces Central Europe)

Unit Designation	Manpower in Combat Units	Main Battle Tanks Pre-Positioned
3rd Air Cavalry Regiment	4,522	54
1st/2nd/4th Brigades/2nd Armored Division	18,300	360
1st/2nd/4th Brigades/4th Infantry Division	18,573	324
1st/2nd Brigades/1st Infantry Division	12,382	216
212th Field Artillery Brigade	2,300	
2nd Marine Division	16,512	70
2nd/3rd/4th Battalions/10th Special Forces	750	
1st Battalion/75th Special Forces	250	
Total for AFCENT:	73,589	1,024

Immediate Reinforcements for AFNORTH (Allied Forces Northern Europe)

7th Marine Amphibious Brigade	15,000	17
Total for AFCENT and AFNORTH:	88,589	1,041

Reinforcements for AFCENT Within Ten Days

6th Air Cavalry Combat Brigade	4,800	54
1st Cavalry Division	18,300	360
5th Infantry Division	18,500	324
256th Infantry Brigade	6,191	108
82nd Airborne Division	16,800	54
101st Air Assault Division	18,000	12
Total for AFCENT:	82,591	912

Cumulative Total for AFCENT:	156,180	1,936

Cumulative Total for AFCENT and AFNORTH:	171,180	1,953

Sources

Allocation of the 7th Marine Amphibious Brigade to reinforce AFNORTH is confirmed by Richard Sale, "The Ambiguous Flanks," *Defense & Foreign Affairs* (April, 1982), page 26. Pre-positioning of its equipment in Norway is confirmed by the same source, as well as by Reuters, "Norway Approves U.S. Plan to Store Arms for Marines," published in *The New York Times,* January 14, 1981. Combat strengths of all U.S. Marine Corps units, as well as the numbers of main battle tanks they field, are from Carl White, "Seapower, Marines," in *Almanac of Sea Power, 1983* (Arlington, Va: Navy League of the United States, 1983), pages 174–177.

Units designated to reinforce AFCENT are from the United States Army War College, *NATO Data Base,* Carlisle Barracks, Pa., January 31, 1981; Lt. Col. Donald B. Vought and Lt. Col. J. R. Angolia, "United States Army," in *The U.S. War Machine,* ed. by Ray Bonds (London: Salamander, 1978), page 79; and Charles Kamps, Jr., "Orders of Battle; North Atlantic Treaty Organization," in *The Next War* (New York: Simulations Publications, 1978), page 30. The numbers and types of units allocated or available to reinforce AFCENT are also confirmed by the International Institute for Strategic Studies (IISS), *The Military Balance, 1981–1982*, page 7, and *The Military Balance, 1984–1985*, page 7, as well as by William P. Mako, *U.S. Ground Forces and the Defense of Central Europe* (Washington, D.C.: Brookings Institution, 1983), pages 50–51.

Combat strengths of the 82nd Airborne and 101st Air Assault Divisions, as well as the numbers of main battle tanks they field, are from John M. Collins, *U.S.-Soviet Military Balance: Concepts and Capabilities, 1960–1980* (New York: McGraw-Hill, 1980), page 210, and are further confirmed by IISS, *op. cit., 1984–1985*, page vii, and by Mako, *op. cit.*, page 113. According to Collins (*op. cit.*, page 210), airborne divisions were equipped with the M-551 *Sheridan* tank, considered to be a "light" tank. But according to Cols. Vought and Angolia, the *Sheridans* were already "being replaced" at that time "with the M-60A1s to simplify maintenance and resupply problems." There is unanimity among sources that the M-60A1 is a "main battle tank." Accordingly, the number of M-60A1s fielded by these divisions since at least 1980 has been included in the total of main battle tanks counted here.

Personnel strengths of all other units are from IISS, *op. cit., 1984–1985*, page vii; Cols. Vought and Angolia, *op. cit.*, pages 71–75; and Drew Middleton, "U.S. Army in Germany Confident It Is in Fighting Form," *The New York Times*, May 15, 1978. Tank strengths of armored divisions and armored cavalry regiments are from Kamps, *op. cit.*, 1978, page 31. Tank strength of a mechanized division is from Drew Middleton, "Army Plans to Bolster Divisions to Counter a Buildup by Soviet," *The New York Times*, May 18, 1977. Tank strengths of armored and mechanized brigades are from IISS, *op. cit., 1984–1985*, page vii.

America's commitment, and its ability, to transport to Europe all of the units listed here or their equivalent strength within 10 days is confirmed by the Department of Defense, *Annual Report, Fiscal Year 1984*, page 209; by Drew Middleton, "U.S. Tells NATO It Will Double Army in Europe in Event of Crisis," *The New York Times*, May 19, 1980; by Robert W. Komer, "The Rejuvenation of the Seventh Army," *Armed Forces Journal International* (May, 1983), page 54; and by Diego A. Ruiz Palmer, "The Front Line in Europe: National Contributions," *Armed Forces Journal International* (May, 1984), page 71.

Since 1976, in *The Military Balance, 1976–1977*, page 6, IISS has reported that only two American Divisions and one armored cavalry regiment "have heavy equipment stockpiled in West Germany." In *The Military Balance, 1984–1985*, page 7, IISS continued to report that only this amount of equipment had been pre-positioned. But according to the Department of Defense, *Annual Report, Fiscal Year 1984*, page 215, complete sets of heavy equipment, including main battle tanks, "for three divisions" of reinforcements had already been "pre-positioned in the 1960s" in Europe. In its *Annual Report, Fiscal Year 1985*, page 182, the Defense Department acknowledged that "we have stored heavy equipment for four Army divisions and supporting units in Europe," and "will provide equipment for two more divisions." According to Mako, *op. cit.*, page 68: "By the end of 1981, equipment had been prepositioned for five divisions, an armored cavalry regiment, and other corps-level support units based in the United States." According to Ruiz Palmer, *op. cit.* (May, 1984), page 74, equipment for all six divisions and for separate brigades and armored cavalry regiments will have been pre-positioned in Europe by 1986.

In 1983, in *The Military Balance, 1983–1984*, page 9, IISS acknowledged that United States forces in Europe have 5000 main battle tanks. That is enough to equip all units currently deployed in Europe, together with nine, rather than six, additional divisions and supporting units, equal to all of the units listed here in both stages of reinforcement, and to a third stage of reinforcement of equivalent strength.

USAREUR (United States Army Europe) Combat and Support Units in Position, 1981–85

Headquarters Units

HQ United States Army Europe
HQ United States Army Element Central Army Group
HQ Seventh Army
HQ Fifth Corps
HQ Seventh Corps

Armoured and Mechanized Units

2nd Armored Cavalry Regiment*
11th Armored Cavalry Regiment*
1st Armored Division*
3rd Armored Division*
3rd Brigade/2nd Armored Division*
3rd Infantry Division*
8th Infantry Division*
3rd Brigade/1st Infantry Division*
3rd Brigade/4th Infantry Division*

Infantry Units

1st Battalion/10th Special Forces*
United States Army Berlin Brigade
United States Army Southern European Task Force (SETAF)

Aviation Units

11th Aviation Group
3rd Combat Aviation Battalion
11th Aviation Battalion
223rd Aviation Battalion

Field Artillery Units

17th Field Artillery Brigade
56th Field Artillery Brigade
41st Field Artillery Brigade*
42nd Field Artillery Brigade*
72nd Field Artillery Brigade*
210th Field Artillery Brigade*

Air Defense Artillery Units

32nd Army Air Defense Command
10th Air Defense Artillery Group
69th Air Defense Artillery Group
94th Air Defense Artillery Group
108th Air Defense Artillery Group

Support Units

1st Personnel Command
2nd Support Command
3rd Support Command
21st Support Command
4th Transportation Command
7th Medical Command
18th Engineer Brigade
22nd Signal Brigade
59th Ordnance Brigade

Notes and Sources

This is a complete list of all United States Army units currently assigned to Europe and stationed there. Only units marked with an asterisk are included in the separate table, *NATO Ground Forces Central Europe, Order of Battle, 1981–85: Manpower in Combat Units and Main Battle Tanks.* Most of the other units listed here are noncombat units. Some, like the aviation battalions and air defense artillery groups, are combat units but serve ground forces in a support role. The mission of others, like that of the 56th Field Artillery Brigade, equipped with *Pershing II* missiles, is primarily strategic rather than tactical ground support. One combat unit, the Southern European Task Force, an airmobile battalion at Vicenza, is stationed outside the central European area. Another, the Berlin Brigade, is assumed to be isolated in a general war across the central European front.

To obtain the full total of all United States Army personnel in Europe, the strengths given for combat units in the *Order of Battle* table must be added to the strengths of all other

(continued)

USAREUR (United States Army Europe) Combat and Support Units in Position, 1981–85 (*cont.*)

units listed here. For totals of United States Army and United States Marine Corps personnel throughout Europe, both in combat and noncombat units, see the table, *Summary: United States Ground Forces in Europe, 1981–85, Manpower in Place and Reinforcement Schedule.*

Sources for all units listed here are Lt. Col. Donald B. Vought and Lt. Col. J. R. Angolia, "United States Army," in *The U.S. War Machine,* ed. by Ray Bonds (London: Salamander, 1978), pages 71, 72, 75, and 79; Charles Kamps, Jr., "Orders of Battle: North Atlantic Treaty Organization," in *The Next War* (New York: Simulations Publications, 1978), page 30; and "U.S. Army Units Assigned to NATO," in *National Defense* magazine (January, 1985), page 12.

Summary: United States Ground Forces in Europe 1981–85— Manpower in Place and Reinforcement Schedule

Manpower in Place Central Europe	Major Combat Units	Combat Support and Noncombat Units	All Units
Army	112,522	100,373	212,895
USMC		473	473
Total:	112,522	100,846	213,368
Immediate Reinforcements Central Europe			
Army	57,077	48,973	106,050
USMC	16,512	3,600	20,112
Total:	73,589	52,573	126,162
Cumulative Total:	186,111	153,419	339,530
Immediate Reinforcements Northern Europe			
USMC	15,000	3,020	18,020
Cumulative Total:	201,111	156,439	357,550
Reinforcements Within 10 Days Central Europe			
Army	82,591	70,909	153,500
Cumulative Total:	283,702	227,348	511,150
Total in Central Europe:	268,702	224,328	493,030

Notes and Sources

The total of United States Army and Marine Corps personnel in place in central Europe is from the Department of Defense, Armed Forces Information Service, *Defense 81,* Arlington

Va. (September, 1981), page 22. Comparable figures are widely reported by other prominent sources, and have changed little from year to year. In *The Military Balance, 1981–1982,* page 9, the IISS reported a total of 212,400 United States Army personnel in central Europe, including Berlin. In *The Military Balance, 1983–1984,* page 9, the IISS reported a total of 213,100 such personnel in central Europe and Berlin.

Totals of personnel in major combat units in place in central Europe and available as immediate reinforcements are from the table, *NATO Ground Forces Central Europe, Order of Battle, 1981–85.* Totals of personnel in major combat units available as immediate reinforcements and available within 10 days are from the table, *United States Ground Forces in Europe: Reinforcement Schedule, 1981–85.*

Personnel in major combat units in place in central Europe comprise 52% of the total of personnel reported by the Department of Defense; the remainder are personnel in combat support and noncombat units. For a full list of Army combat and noncombat units deployed in Europe, see the table, *USAREUR (United States Army Europe) Combat and Support Units in Position, 1981–85.*

According to William P. Mako, *U.S. Ground Forces and the Defense of Central Europe* (Washington, D.C.: Brookings Institution, 1983), pages 80–81 and page 81, note 52, an Army reorganization completed in 1976 increased the proportion of personnel in major combat units from 48% of all Army personnel to between 52 and 56%. Thus, for every combat division averaging 18,500 troops, where the Army had earlier fielded an additional 19,500 combat support and noncombat troops, it thereafter fielded, on average, an additional 15,000. Mako (*op. cit.,* page 79) fixes the current average number of such personnel proportionate to each combat division of this size at 16,100. In that case, personnel in major combat units currently comprise, on average, 53% of all Army personnel.

This average has been adhered to in calculating the number of noncombat personnel accompanying personnel in major combat units in each stage of reinforcement shown here. Cumulative totals show an increase of 1% in the proportion of combat personnel, reflecting the inclusion of Marine Corps units with very different proportions of support personnel.

Strengths of personnel in Marine Corps combat units are from Carl White, "Seapower: Marines," in *The Almanac of Seapower, 1983* (Arlington, Va.: Navy League of the United States, 1983), pages 174–177. Numbers of Marine Corps support personnel are estimates. They probably underestimate substantially the number of support personnel that would actually accompany combat units. They are based on White, *op. cit.,* pages 176–177; on Alan Ned Sabrosky, "The United States Marine Corps," in *The U.S. War Machine,* ed. by Ray Bonds (London: Salamander, 1978), pages 210–212; and on J. Robert Moskin, *The U.S. Marine Corps Story* (New York: McGraw-Hill, 1977), pages 898 and 926.

NATO Main Battle Tank Holdings, 1981–85

Nation	Number	Type	Gun Caliber
Denmark	120	*Leopard I*	105 mm
	200	*Centurion Mk 13*	105 mm
	320	Total	
Netherlands	135	*Leopard II*	120 mm
	485	*Leopard I*	105 mm
	400	*Centurion Mk 13*	105 mm
	198	AMX-13	105 mm
	1,218	Total	
United Kingdom	70	*Challenger*	120 mm
	960	*Chieftain*	120 mm
	476	*Centurion*	105 mm
	1,506	Total	
Belgium	334	*Leopard I*	105 mm
	124	M-47	105 mm
	458	Total	
West Germany	1,000	*Leopard II*	120 mm
	2,437	*Leopard I*	105 mm
	1,400	M-48	105 mm
	4,837	Total	
Canada	114	*Leopard I*	105 mm
	300	*Centurion Mk 13*	105 mm
	444	Total	
France	1,120	AMX-30	105 mm
	1,220	AMX-13	90 mm
	2,340	Total	
United States	1,483	M-1 *Abrams*	105 mm
	2,695	M-60A3	105 mm
	540	M-60A2	152 mm
	4,580	M-60A1	105 mm
	1,535	M-60	105 mm
	1,825	M-48A5	105 mm
	12,658	Total	
Greece	106	*Leopard I*	105 mm
	285	AMX-30	105 mm
	350	M-47	105 mm

Nation	Number	Type	Gun Caliber
	818	M-48	90 mm
	200	M-24	90 mm
	1,759	Total	
Italy	1,000	*Leopard I*	105 mm
	350	M-60A1	105 mm
	1,800	M-47	105 mm
	3,150	Total	
Norway	78	*Leopard I*	105 mm
	38	M-48	90 mm
	72	M-24/NM-116	90 mm
	188	Total	
Spain	399	AMX-30	105 mm
	130	M-48	105 mm
	390	M-47	90 mm
	919	Total	
Portugal	23	M-48	105 mm
	100	M-47	90 mm
	60	M-24	90 mm
	183	Total	
Turkey	77	*Leopard I*	105 mm
	500	M-47	105 mm
	950	M-48	105 mm
	2,050	M-48	90 mm
	3,577	Total	
	33,557	Total All NATO Nations	

Sources

Except as noted below, figures for all NATO tank holdings are from Pierangelo Caiti, *Modern Armour: A Comprehensive Guide* (Parma, Italy: Delta Editrice, 1978), pages 150–152, and are further confirmed by various editions of IISS, *The Military Balance*.

The figure for Dutch *Centurions* is from IISS, *op. cit.*, 1974–1975, page 24, which also confirms Caiti's figure for Dutch *Leopard Is*. Caiti's figures for Canada's *Centurions*, all Belgian tanks, and Greek and Portuguese M-24s are confirmed by IISS, *op. cit.*, *1975–1976*, pages 20, 18, 23, and 25, respectively. Caiti's figures for French AMX-13s and Portuguese M-47s are confirmed by IISS, *op. cit.*, *1977–1978*, pages 23 and 27, respectively. Caiti's figures for all Danish tanks, Canada's *Leopard Is*, and France's AMX-30s are confirmed by IISS, *op. cit.*, *1980–1981*, pages 24, 23, and 25, respectively.

The figures for Greek M-47s, M-48s, and AMX-30s, Italian M-60A1s, Spanish M-48s, and Turkish M-47s and M-48s are from IISS, *op. cit., 1982–1983,* pages 38, 39, 42, and 44, respectively. The figures for British *Chieftains* and *Challengers,* and for Turkish *Leopard Is,* are from IISS, *op. cit., 1983–1984,* pages 27 and 42, respectively. The figures for Dutch *Leopard IIs,* and for West German and Greek *Leopard Is,* are from IISS, *op. cit., 1984–1985,* pages 44, 40, and 42, respectively. The figure for West German *Leopard IIs* is from Diego A. Ruiz Palmer, "The Front Line in Europe: National Contributions," *Armed Forces Journal International* (May, 1984), page 65.

The figure for United States M-48A5s is from IISS, *op. cit., 1981–1982,* page 6. Figures for United States M-60s, M-60A2s, M-60A3s, and M-1s are from IISS, *op. cit., 1984–1985,* page 6. The figures for United States M-60A1s is based on the number of these tanks reported by the IISS, *op. cit, 1981–1982,* page 6, and on the increase in the number of conversions from M-60A1 to M-60A3 standard reported in *1984–1985,* page 6. In the latter edition, IISS reports 373 fewer of both types of tank. That quantity has been restored here, and is presumed to comprise M-60A1s, not additional M-60As.

The potential lethality of NATO's 90 mm tank guns against Warsaw Pact armor is confirmed by sources for the separate table, *NATO Ground Forces Central Europe, Order of Battle, 1981–85.* NATO tanks with 90 mm armament are accordingly included here.

NATO Ground Forces Central Europe—Mobilization and Reinforcement Schedule, 1981–85

Nation	Active Ground Forces	Ground Forces Reserves	Total Ground Forces	Total Tanks
Denmark	19,300	126,500	145,800	320

Time Deployed after First Alert	Numbers and Types of Formations	Manpower			
		Combat Units	Noncombat and Support Units	All Units	Tanks
Within 24 Hrs	1 Mech Div 2 Mech Brig	19,100	16,400	35,500	208
Within 72 Hrs	1 Recon Bn 1 Mech Brig	4,600	4,000	8,600	44
	Total 72 Hrs	23,700		44,100	252
Within 7 Days	3 Mech Brig	11,400	10,100	21,500	68
	Total 7 Days	35,100		65,600	320
Within 10 Days	5 Regt Combat Team (Brig)	24,000	21,000	45,000	
	Total 10 Days	59,100		110,600	320
Within 30 Days	7 Inf Brig	18,600	16,600	35,200	
	Total 30 Days	77,000		145,800	320

Nation	Active Ground Forces	Ground Forces Reserves	Total Ground Forces	Total Tanks
Netherlands	67,000	145,000	212,000	1,218

Time Deployed after First Alert	Numbers and Types of Formations	Manpower			
		Combat Units	Noncombat and Support Units	All Units	Tanks
Within 24 Hrs	2 Mech Div 2 Recon Bn 2 Inf Bn 1 Atty Brig	37,960	33,540	71,500	602
Within 72 Hrs	1 Mech Div 2 Armd Brig 4 Inf Brig	39,300	34,700	74,000	362

(*continued*)

NATO Ground Forces Central Europe—Mobilization and Reinforcement Schedule, 1981–85 (cont.)

Time Deployed after First Alert	Numbers and Types of Formations	Manpower			Tanks
		Combat Units	Noncombat and Support Units	All Units	
	Total 72 Hrs	77,260		145,500	964
Within 7 Days	4 Armd Regt	6,840	5,860	12,700	254
	Total 7 Days	84,100		158,200	1,218
Within 10 Days	6 Inf Brig	28,500	25,300	53,800	
	Total 10 Days	112,600		212,000	1,218

Nation	Active Ground Forces	Ground Forces Reserves	Total Ground Forces	Total Tanks
United Kingdom	176,248	206,500	382,748	1,506

Time Deployed after First Alert	Numbers and Types of Formations	Manpower			Tanks
		Combat Units	Noncombat and Support Units	All Units	
Within 24 Hrs	4 Armd Div 4 Mech Brig 1 Atty Brig 1 Airb Brig 1 Inf Bn	75,079	64,924	140,000	814
Within 72 Hrs	4 Inf Brig	19,600	17,400	37,000	
	Total 72 Hrs	94,679		177,000	814
Within 7 Days	2 Armd Brig 6 Armd Recon Regt	13,040	11,460	24,500	148
	Total 7 Days	107,719		201,500	962
Within 10 Days	8 Inf Brig*	39,200	32,300	71,500	
	Total 10 Days	146,919		273,000	962
Within 30 Days	6 Inf Brig*	29,400	25,600	55,000	
	Total 30 Days	176,319		328,000	962
Within 60 Days	6 Inf Brig*	29,400	25,348	54,748	
	Total 60 Days	205,719		382,748	962

* These are brigade equivalents. Many British units, including infantry, armored, and paratroop units, are formed into separate regiments and battalions.

Nation	Active Ground Forces	Ground Forces Reserves	Total Ground Forces	Total Tanks
Belgium	65,000	133,000	198,000	458

Time Deployed after First Alert	Numbers and Types of Formations	Manpower			Tanks
		Combat Units	Noncombat and Support Units	All Units	
Within 24 Hrs	2 Mech Div 2 Mech Brig 1 Armd Bn 3 Recon Bn 2 Para Bn	34,794	30,206	65,000	324
Within 72 Hrs	1 Mech Brig 4 Inf Bns	7,960	6,800	14,490	54
	Total 72 Hrs	42,484		79,490	378
Within 7 Days	2 Mech Regt	3,420	2,980	6,400	80
	Total 7 Days	45,904		85,890	458
Within 10 Days	11 Inf Brig	59,400	52,710	112,110	
	Total 10 Days	105,304		198,000	458

Nation	Active Ground Forces	Ground Forces Reserves	Total Ground Forces	Total Tanks
West Germany	340,000	450,000	790,000	4,837

Time Deployed after First Alert	Numbers and Types of Formations	Manpower			Tanks
		Combat Units	Noncombat and Support Units	All Units	
Within 24 Hrs	6 Armd Div 4 Mech Div 1 Inf Div 3 Arib Brig 3 Atty Brig 6 Mech Brig	218,680	191,320	410,000	3,196
Within 72 Hrs	6 Mech Brig 15 Mech Regt 150 Mech Coy 324 Inf Plat	105,720	90,280	196,000	1,386
	Total 72 Hrs	324,400		606,000	4,582

(continued)

NATO Ground Forces Central Europe—Mobilization and Reinforcement Schedule, 1981–85 (cont.)

Time Deployed after First Alert	Numbers and Types of Formations	Manpower			
		Combat Units	Noncombat and Support Units	All Units	Tanks
Within 7 Days	5 Inf Div*				
	2 Inf Brig*	97,520	86,840	184,000	255
	Total 7 Days	421,920		790,000	4,837

* These are division and brigagde equivalents, utilizing remaining Territorial Army reserve personnel and tanks.

Nation	Active Ground Forces	Ground Forces Reserves	Total Ground Forces	Total Tanks
Canada	13,000	15,500	28,500	444

Time Deployed after First Alert	Numbers and Types of Formations	Manpower			
		Combat Units	Noncombat and Support Units	All Units	Tanks
Within 24 Hrs	1 Brig Group	5,400	4,700	10,100	59
Within 72 Hrs	1 Airb Regt	1,350	1,170	2,520	
	Total 72 Hrs	6,750		12,620	59
Within 7 Days	1 Brig Group	4,200	3,740	7,940	55
	Total 7 Days	10,950		20,560	114
Within 10 Days	1 Brig Group	4,200	3,740	7,940	
	Total 10 Days	15,150		28,500	114

Nation	Active Ground Forces	Ground Forces Reserves	Total Ground Forces	Total Tanks
France	321,230	280,000	601,320	2,340

Time Deployed after First Alert	Numbers and Types of Formations	Manpower			
		Combat Units	Noncombat and Support Units	All Units	Tanks
Within 24 Hrs	8 Armd Div				
	4 Mech Div				
	2 Mech Brig				
	2 Atty Brig				
	1 Airb Div				
	1 Inf Brig				
	1 Inf Regt				
	2 Mech Bn	111,356	98,644	210,000	1,976

Time Deployed after First Alert	Numbers and Types of Formations	Manpower			Tanks
		Combat Units	Noncombat and Support Units	All Units	
Within 72 Hrs	1 Light Armd Div				
	1 Airmobile Div				
	3 Inf Brig				
	6 Inf Regt	33,396	28,604	62,000	104
	Total 72 Hrs	144,752		272,000	2,080
Within 7 Days	4 Inf Div				
	2 Inf Brig	33,192	28,303	61,500	
	Total 7 Days	177,944		333,500	2,080
Within 10 Days	4 Inf Div				
	4 Inf Brig				
	25 Inf Regt	58,192	50,808	109,000	
	Total 10 Days	236,136		442,500	2,080
Within 60 Days	12 Inf Div*				
	1 Inf Brig*	84,174	74,646	158,820	
	Total 60 Days	320,310		601,320	2,080

* These are division and brigade equivalents, utilizing remaining French Army reserve personnel.

Nation	Active Ground Forces	Ground Forces Reserves	Total Ground Forces	Total Tanks
United States	775,000	605,400	1,380,400	12,658

Time Deployed after First Alert	Numbers and Types of Formations	Manpower			Tanks
		Combat Units	Noncombat and Support Units	All Units	
Within 24 Hrs	2 Armd Div				
	2 Mech Div				
	4 Armd Brig				
	7 Mech Brig				
	2 Armd Cav Regt				
	1 Air Cav Regt				
	1 Inf Div				
	5 Inf Bn				
	5 Atty Brig	186,111	153,419	339,530	3,142
Within 10 Days	1 Armd Div				
	1 Airmobile Div				
	1 Airb Div				
	1 Mech Div				
	1 Air Cav Brig				

(continued)

NATO Ground Forces Central Europe—Mobilization and Reinforcement Schedule, 1981–85 (*cont.*)

Time Deployed after First Alert	Numbers and Types of Formations	Manpower			
		Combat Units	Noncombat and Support Units	All Units	Tanks
	1 Mech Brig	82,591	70,909	153,500	912
	Total 10 Days	268,702		493,030	4,054
Within 30 Days	1 Armd Div				
	2 Mech Div				
	1 Armd Brig				
	1 Inf Div	81,100	69,600	151,000	1,512
	Total 30 Days	349,802		644,030	5,566
120 Days	2 Armd Div				
	1 Mech Div				
	5 Inf Div				
	4 Armd Brig				
	9 Mech Brig				
	12 Inf Brig				
	4 Armd Cav Regt	252,000	223,000	475,000	3,132
	Total 30 Days	601,802		1,119,030	8,698

NATO Ground Forces Central Europe—Mobilization and Reinforcement Schedule, 1981–85, Summary

Time Deployed After First Alert

| Nation | 24 Hours | | | 10 Days | | | 30 Days | | | 120 Days | | |
| | Manpower | | | Manpower | | | Manpower | | | Manpower | | |
	Combat Units	Total	Tanks	Combat Units	Total	Tanks	Combat Units	Total	Tanks	Combat Units	Total	Tanks
Denmark	19,100	35,000	208	59,100	110,600	320	77,000	145,800	320	77,000	145,800	320
Netherlands	37,960	71,500	602	112,600	212,000	1,218	112,600	212,000	1,218	112,600	212,000	1,218
UK	75,079	140,000	814	146,919	273,000	962	176,319	328,000	962	205,719	382,748	962
Belgium	34,794	65,000	324	105,304	198,000	458	105,304	198,000	458	105,304	198,000	458
FRG	218,680	410,000	3,196	421,920	790,000	4,837	421,920	790,000	4,837	421,920	790,000	4,837
Canada	5,400	10,100	59	15,150	28,500	114	15,150	28,500	114	15,150	28,500	114
France	111,356	210,000	1,976	236,136	442,500	2,080	236,136	442,500	2,080	320,310	601,320	2,080
USA	186,111	339,530	3,142	268,702	493,030	4,054	349,802	644,030	5,566	601,802	1,119,030	8,698
*Multi	8,640	16,250	30	8,640	16,250	30	8,640	16,250	30	8,640	16,250	30
Total	697,120	1,297,380	10,351	1,374,471	2,563,880	14,073	1,502,871	2,805,080	15,585	1,868,445	3,493,648	18,717

* ACE Mobile Force

NATO Ground Forces Central Europe—Mobilization and Reinforcement Schedule, 1981–85, Summary: Totals

Time Deployed after First Alert	Manpower		Tanks
	Combat Units	Total	
Within 24 Hrs	697,120	1,297,380	10,351
Within 10 Days	1,374,471	2,563,880	14,073
Within 30 Days	1,502,871	2,805,080	15,585
Within 120 Days	1,868,445	3,493,648	18,717

Sources and Method

With the exception of West German forces, figures for active ground forces and army reserves are from IISS, *The Military Balance, 1981–1982*, pages 6, 7, 27, 28, 29, 30, 31, 32, and 37. The figure for West Germany's active ground forces is from Diego A. Ruiz Palmer, "The Front Line in Europe: National Contributions," *Armed Forces Journal International* (May, 1984), page 65. The figure for West Germany's Army reserves is from Chris Holshek, "The New German Army," *Armed Forces Journal International* (May, 1984), page 102. It should be noted that William P. Mako, in *U.S. Ground Forces and the Defense of Europe* (Brookings, 1983), page 89, estimates West German Army reserves at 590,000, a figure 140,000 higher than that used here.

Figures for total tank holdings are from sources given for the separate table, *NATO Main Battle Tank Holdings, 1981–85.*

NATO planning for war invariably involves the assumption that the Warsaw Pact will be the aggressor, and that combat will take place on NATO soil. Since NATO presumably has no other reason to exist except to defend itself against this contingency, the same assumption is followed here. A consequence of this is the further assumption that, whether or not the Warsaw Pact uses all its reserves and equipment, those NATO countries in which combat is actually taking place will certainly use all of theirs. Full mobilization of all West German, Belgian, Danish, and Dutch reserves is accordingly shown. The inclusion here of forces from each of these nations is based on sources for the separate table, *NATO Ground Forces Central Europe, Order of Battle, 1981–85.*

These forces would probably mobilize more quickly than shown, not less so. As Milton Leitenberg points out, in "The Numbers Game or 'Who's on First?' " *Bulletin of the Atomic Scientists* (June–July, 1982), page 32, West Germany alone has "the ability to mobilize 1.2 million men in 60 hours in an acute crisis."

British and French capabilities for rapid mobilization of reserves, and for continuous reinforcement of NATO's central European front, are also confirmed by sources for the separate table, *NATO Ground Forces Central Europe, Order of Battle, 1981–85.* Warsaw Pact planners must presume that each stage of mobilization and reinforcement shown here would occur.

After they had completed their initial stages of reinforcement, however, Britain and France would take somewhat longer than NATO's other central European nations would to bring their remaining troops into battle. It would also be as difficult for them as it would be for most Warsaw Pact nations to bring all their remaining tanks and other heavy equipment into position. These circumstances are reflected here, in the assumption that many British and French reserve tanks could never be brought into battle.

The same, of course, is true for United States and Canadian reinforcements, whose later stages would take even longer to complete. Both nations, however, are perfectly capable of bringing the numbers of troops and tanks shown into battle in Europe within the time shown. Mako (*op. cit.*, page 133) acknowledges this of United States forces when he points out that "Reserve component forces, excluding round-out brigades, would contribute another 246,000 men in major combat units and weapons equivalent to over 13 armoured divisions."

While the initial waves of United States reinforcements for Europe would use pre-positioned equipment, it should be noted that the United States has a substantial sealift and airlift capacity to bring in heavy equipment for subsequent waves. According to Michael T. Klare, in *Beyond the Vietnam Syndrome* (Institute for Policy Studies, 1982), page 128, "the total displacement of U.S. amphibious vessels is 944,000 tons, compared to 175,000 tons for Soviet vessels." He adds, (*ibid.*, page 116) that United States airlift capabilities include "70 C-5A Galaxy heavy transports, 234 C-141 Starlifter medium transports, and 324 C-130 Hercules tactical transports," and that "the C-5As and C-141s can carry 16,000 tons of cargo or 60,000 fully-equipped soldiers over distances of 3,000 miles or more." Colonel Ernest O. Agee, in *Proceedings of the United States Naval Institute* (December, 1984), page 170, notes that by itself "the present 70 C-5 PAA force in a ten-day deployment to the Persian Gulf could make 359 sorties and airlift 518 tanks."

It should be kept in mind, as well, that according to IISS, *The Military Balance, 1984–1985,* page 10, the United States already has 5000 main battle tanks in Europe, equipping active forces or pre-positioned for the earliest reinforcements to arrive.

Warsaw Pact Ground Forces Central Europe, Order of Battle, 1981–85: Manpower in Combat Units and Main Battle Tanks

Nation	Unit Designation	Unit Type	HQ Location	Current Strength in Place	Strength within 24 Hours	Tanks
	Soviet Northern Group of Forces		Legnica			
Soviet Union	20th Tank Division	Armd Div	Borne, Pomerania	7,092	9,456	325
Soviet Union	38th Tank Division	Armd Div	Swietoszow, Silesia	7,092	9,456	325
Poland	2nd Motor Rifle Division	Mech Div	Leszno	8,250	11,000	219
Poland	16th Armoured Division	Armd Div	Poznan	6,750	9,000	316
Poland	4th Motor Rifle Division	Mech Div	Legnica	8,250	11,000	219
Poland	5th Tank Division	Armd Div	Wroclaw	6,750	9,000	316
Poland	10th Tank Division	Armd Div	Lodz	6,750	9,000	316
Poland	11th Tank Division	Armd Div	Czestochowa	6,750	9,000	316
Poland	12th Motor Rifle Division	Mech Div	Szczecinek	8,250	11,000	219
Poland	20th Tank Division	Armd Div	Wloclawek	6,750	9,000	316
East Germany	1st Motor Rifle Division	Mech Div	Potsdam	9,000	12,000	188
East Germany	8th Motor Rifle Division	Mech Div	Schwerin	9,000	12,000	188
East Germany	9th Tank Division	Armd Div	Eggesin	6,750	9,000	316
	Group of Soviet Forces Germany		Zossen-Wunstorf			
Soviet Union	9th Guards Tank Division	Armd Div	Neustrelitz	7,092	9,456	325
Soviet Union	32nd Guards Motor Rifle Division	Mech Div	Perleberg/Prignitz	9,853	13,138	255
Soviet Union	94th Guards Motor Rifle Division	Mech Div	Schwerin	9,853	13,138	255
Soviet Union	25th Tank Division	Armd Div	Templin	7,092	9,456	325
Soviet Union	12th Guards Tank Division	Armd Div	Neuruppin	7,092	9,456	325
Soviet Union	10th Guards Tank Division	Armd Div	Krampnitz	7,092	9,456	325
Soviet Union	47th Guards Tank Division	Armd Div	Hillersleben	7,092	9,456	325
Soviet Union	207th Motor Rifle Division	Mech Div	Stendal	9,853	13,138	255
Soviet Union	7th Guards Tank Division	Armd Div	Dessau/Rosslau	7,092	9,456	325
Soviet Union	9th Tank Division	Armd Div	Riesa/Sachsen-Zeithain	7,092	9,456	325
Soviet Union	11th Guards Tank Division	Armd Div	Dresden	7,092	9,456	325
Soviet Union	27th Guards Motor Rifle Division	Mech Div	Halle	9,853	13,138	255
Soviet Union	20th Guards Tank Division	Armd Div	Jena	7,092	9,456	325
Soviet Union	20th Guards Motor Rifle Division	Mech Div	Grimma	9,853	13,138	255
Soviet Union	39th Guards Motor Rifle Division	Mech Div	Ohrdruf	9,853	13,138	255
Soviet Union	57th Guards Motor Rifle Division	Mech Div	Naumburg/Saale	9,853	13,138	255
Soviet Union	6th Guards Motor Rifle Division	Mech Div	Bernau	9,853	13,138	255

Soviet Union	14th Guards Motor Rifle Division	Mech Div	Juterborg	9,853	12,138	255
Soviet Union	19th Motor Rifle Division	Mech Div	Dobertiz, Potsdam	9,853	13,138	255
Soviet Union	34th Guards Artillery Division	Atty Div	Dazu, Potsdam	15,066	20,088	
East Germany	4th Motor Rifle Division	Mech Div	Erfurt	9,000	12,000	188
East Germany	11th Motor Rifle Division	Mech Div	Halle/Sachsen-Anhalt	9,000	12,000	188
East Germany	7th Tank Division	Armd Div	Dresden	6,750	9,000	316
	Central Group of Soviet Forces		Milovice			
Soviet Union	18th Guards Motor Rifle Division	Mech Div	Mlada-Boleslav	9,853	13,138	255
Soviet Union	31st Tank Division	Armd Div	Milovice	7,092	9,456	325
Soviet Union	51st Tank Division	Armd Div	Bruntal	7,092	9,456	325
Soviet Union	48th Guards Motor Rifle Division	Mech Div	Vysoke Myto	9,853	13,138	255
Soviet Union	30th Guards Motor Rifle Division	Mech Div	Zvolen	9,853	13,138	255
Czechoslovakia	2nd Motor Rifle Division	Mech Div	Mlada Boleslav	9,000	12,000	219
Czechoslovakia	19th Motor Rifle Division	Mech Div	Jihlava	9,000	12,000	219
Czechoslovakia	1st Tank Division	Armd Div	Kladno	6,750	9,000	316
Czechoslovakia	3rd Motor Rifle Division	Mech Div	Plzen	9,000	12,000	219
Czechoslovakia	4th Tank Division	Armd Div	Pisek	6,750	9,000	316
Czechoslovakia	9th Tank Division	Armd Div	Vychodocesky	6,750	9,000	316
	(2,960 tactical aircraft, including 1,425 in 3 Soviet Air Armies)					
Totals:	47 Divs	(2,960 Aircraft)		390,607	520,810	12,766

Key

Armd: Armoured   Atty: Artillery
Mech: Mechanized   Div: Division

Notes

Only personnel in major combat units are included in this order of battle. Excluded are personnel in higher than divisional formations, in signals, engineers, transport, and other noncombat units, in aviation battalions, air defense artillery groups, and other formations that serve ground forces in a support role, in units whose mission is primarily strategic rather than tactical ground support, and in formations assigned to areas outside central Europe.

It should be kept in mind, as well, that many personnel within the divisional formations listed here serve in noncombat and support roles. Nevertheless, the number of personnel in major combat units is widely accepted as a more accurate measure of ground combat capability than the total of all personnel assigned to ground forces. See Robert Lucas Fisher, *Defending the Central Front: The Balance of Forces*, Adelphi Paper no. 27 (London: IISS, 1976), pages 7 and 15, and Pat Hillier, *Strengthening NATO: POMCUS and Other Approaches* (Washington, D.C.: Congressional Budget Office, 1979), page 54.

(continued)

Warsaw Pact Ground Forces Central Europe, Order of Battle, 1981–85: Manpower in Combat Units and Main Battle Tanks (*cont.*)

Sources

Sources for all units included in this order of battle, and for most of their locations as well, are David C. Isby, *Weapons and Tactics of the Soviet Army* (London: Jane's, 1981), pages 24–26; William J. Lewis, *The Warsaw Pact: Arms, Doctrine, and Strategy*, (New York: McGraw-Hill, 1982), pages 144, 155, 164, 182–183, 197, and 200; United States Army War College, *NATO Data Base*, Carlisle Barracks, Pa., January 31, 1981; and Charles Kamps, Jr., "Orders of Battle: Warsaw Pact," in *The Next War* (New York: Simulations Publications, 1978), pages 25–26.

All of these sources list many additional Soviet, Polish, and Czech formations which would eventually become available to reinforce the Warsaw Pact's central European front. But these units would not become available immediately. Most are in lower categories of readiness, and would take time to mobilize. All sources agree that Soviet and Warsaw Pact ground formations are in three categories of readiness, the highest being Category I. Isby (*op. cit.*, page 28) notes that while Category I units are kept, as shown here, at 75% of strength or higher, and could rapidly come to full strength, Category II units, kept at an average of "slightly more than 50 percent" strength, are only "deployable within 30 days of mobilization," and Category III units, "manned at 10–33 percent personnel strength," are "not deployable until between 90 and 120 days of mobilization." Only those Category I units stationed in East Europe, then, would be available immediately for combat. According to IISS, *The Military Balance, 1980–1981*, page 110, those Warsaw Pact forces "available without mobilization" for combat in central Europe "include all Category I divisions of East Germany (2 tank, 4 mechanized) Czechoslovakia (3 tank, 3 mechanized) and Poland (5 tank, 3 mechanized), and Soviet divisions deployed in those countries in peacetime." Accordingly, those are the units listed here.

Isby (*op cit.*, page 24) lists a total of 28 Soviet divisions stationed in East Germany, Poland, and Czechoslovakia. Kamps (*op. cit.*, page 25) lists the same number. Both sources include in their count the Soviet 6th Guards Tank Division. Isby, however, notes (page 28) that "elements" of this division, "and possibly the HQ, were redeployed to the Soviet Union and Czecho-slovakia in 1979–80." Lewis (*op. cit.*, page 187) recalls that "in October 1979, Brezhnev announced a unilateral withdrawal of 20,000 troops and

withdrawal. Lewis adds that according to the same intelligence officials, the Soviets "had simultaneously begun to strengthen their remaining forces in Eastern Europe" (page 187). His report nevertheless confirms that the Soviet forces remaining in eastern Europe number not 28 divisions but 27. IISS (*op. cit., 1980–1981*, page 12) reports 27 Soviet divisions in eastern Europe. IISS has reported the same total of 27 Soviet divisions in eastern Europe ever since (see *op. cit., 1982–1983*, page 14; *1983–1984*, page 16, and *1984–1985*, page 19). Consequently, a total of 27 Soviet divisions stationed in eastern Europe is listed in the order of battle shown here.

According to the United States Army, FM 30-40, *Handbook on Soviet Ground Forces*, 30 June 1975, pages A-10 and A-3, Soviet armored and mechanized divisions at full strength then had 9,000 and 11,000 personnel respectively. By 1980, however, John M. Collins reported, in *U.S.-Soviet Military Balance: Concepts and Capabilities, 1960–1980* (New York: McGraw-Hill, 1980), page 212, that each Soviet armored division had gained "1,000 more men than in 1970," and that Soviet mechanized divisions "have been bolstered by 2,000 troops." He placed the new strengths of Soviet armored and mechanized divisions at 9,500 and 12,000 respectively (page 211). Lewis (*op. cit.*, page 43) gives the strengths of Soviet armored and mechanized divisions as 9,000 and 12,000 respectively. He gives man-power strengths for the formations of no other Warsaw Pact nation but Poland, whose armored divisions he assigns the equivalent Soviet strength but whose mechanized divisions he estimates (page 199) average only 11,000 personnel.

It would appear from all of this that, with the exception of Polish mech-anized divisions, 9,000 and 12,000 continue to be the respective armored and mechanized division strengths of all Category I units of the Warsaw Pact. However, IISS, *The Military Balance, 1978–1979*, reported the man-power strengths of Soviet armored and mechanized divisions at 11,000 and 13,000 respectively. William P. Mako, in *U.S. Ground Forces and the Defense of Europe* (Brookings, 1983), page 107, gives the same estimates for all Warsaw Pact divisions of both types. In much more detail, Isby (*op. cit.*, pages 80 and 111) gives ranges of from 8,615 to a maximum of 9,456 personnel in Soviet armored divisions, and from 12,771 to a maximum of

1,000 tanks from the Group of Soviet Forces, Germany, back to the Soviet homeland," and notes that "by June 1980, American intelligence officials agreed that the Soviets had lived up to their pledge," and completed this 13,138 personnel in Soviet mechanized divisions. These estimates are summarized in the following table.

			Source				
Division Type	U.S. Army 1975	IISS 1978–1979	Collins 1980	Isby Low 1981	Isby Max. 1981	Lewis 1982	Mako 1983
Armd	9,000	11,000	9,500	8,615	9,456	9,000	11,000
Mech	11,000	13,000	12,000	12,771	13,138	12,000	13,000

Given the preponderance of estimates from different sources which place the maximum of personnel in Warsaw Pact armored divisions in the range of 9,000, and which place the maximum of personnel in Warsaw Pact mechanized divisions in the range of from 12,000 to 13,000, those ranges are used in the order of battle shown here. Bearing in mind the assertions of American intelligence officials reported by Lewis, indicating the Soviets had taken special steps to raise the strengths of their divisions in eastern Europe beyond standard levels, this order of battle assumes that the manpower strengths of Soviet divisions in eastern Europe correspond to Isby's maximum estimates, that the strengths of the few remaining Soviet Category I units stationed elsewhere correspond to Isby's maximum estimate for armored divisions and to his lower estimate for mechanized divisions, and that the manpower strengths of all Category I units of all other Warsaw Pact nations, with the exception already noted of Polish mechanized divisions, correspond to Lewis's estimate.

According to the United States Army (op. cit., 30 June 1975, pages A-10 and A-3), the main battle tank strengths of Soviet armored and mech-anized divisions were 316 and 188 respectively. Collins (op. cit., page 211) gives the same figures. Lewis (op. cit., pages 37 and 31, respectively) gives Soviet armored divisions 322 such tanks and mechanized divisions 266. IISS (op. cit., 1978–1979, page vii) gives Soviet armored divisions 325 such tanks and mechanized divisions 266, but notes that these figures are only "for Soviet divisions in Eastern Europe; other Soviet divisions have fewer." Isby (op. cit., pages 80 and 111) gives Soviet armored divisions 325 main battle tanks and mechanized divisions from 212 to 263, according to whether they have an attached independent tank battalion and what the size of that battalion is. He notes (page 80) that "at least some divisional independent tank battalions use the 40-tank organization," rather than the larger unit estimated by Lewis (op. cit., page 31). Mako (op. cit., pages 121 and 122) gives Soviet armored and mechanized divisions 325 and 215 tanks, respectively. William Koenig and Peter Scofield, in Soviet Military Power (Greenwich, Conn.: Bison, 1983), page 217, give Soviet armored divisions 316 tanks and Soviet mechanized divisions 219.

These estimates are summarized in the following table.

Division Type	U.S. Army 1975	IISS 1978–1979	Collins 1980	Isby Low 1981	Isby Max. 1981	Lewis 1982	Mako 1983	Koenig 1983
Armd	316	325	316	325	325	322	325	316
Mech	188	266	188	212	263	266	215	219

Given the number of estimates which assign Soviet divisions lower numbers of main battle tanks than IISS does, and given the acknowledgment by IISS that its high estimates are only "for Soviet divisions in Eastern Europe," this order of battle assumes that only Soviet armored divisions in

(continued)

Warsaw Pact Ground Forces Central Europe, Order of Battle, 1981–85: Manpower in Combat Units and Main Battle Tanks *(cont.)*

eastern Europe have 325 such tanks, while all remaining Soviet Category I armored divisions, and the Category I armored divisions of all other Warsaw Pact nations, have 316. On the same basis, it assumes that only Soviet mechanized divisions in eastern Europe have 266 tanks, while all the remaining Soviet Category I mechanized divisions, and the Category I divisions of all other Warsaw Pact nations, with one exception, have 219.

The exception is East Germany, each of whose mechanized divisions IISS, *The Military Balance, 1981–1981*, page 19, has taken care to point out have "1 tank, 3 motor rifle regiments." In each edition of *The Military Balance* since that time, IISS has specified that this is the composition of East German mechanized divisions (see *1982–1983*, page 21; *1983–1984*, page 21; and *1984–1985*, page 25). IISS does not specify the number of tank and motor rifle regiments in the divisions of any other Warsaw Pact nation. Yet 1 tank and 3 motor rifle regiments are the normal complement of Soviet and Warsaw Pact mechanized divisions, whose tank strength, as Isby notes (*op. cit.*, page 111), are included entirely in these four units and, if the division is Category I, in an independent tank battalion as well. IISS does not include an independent tank battalion among the units it specifies in East German mechanized divisions, even though it calls them Category I divisions. Presumably, then, this is IISS's way of letting us know that East German mechanized divisions do not have independent tank battalions attached. The number of main battle tanks in an East German mechanized division has accordingly been reduced here to 188. This figure is confirmed by Pierangelo Caiti, *Modern Armour* (Parma, Italy: Delta, 1978), page 151.

Isby (*op. cit.*, page 177), reports two basic types of artillery division in the Soviet Army: one comprising 162 guns, 18 antitank guns, and 9,696 officers and men, the other 72 guns, 18 antitank guns, and 4,247 officers and men. He notes (page 178) that the Soviet 34th Guards Artillery Division at Potsdam is reported to be "three times the strength of a standard artillery division." The strength of that division has been derived here accordingly, based on the larger of the two standard divisional strengths.

The numbers of combat aircraft cited here include 975 tactical aircraft with the Group of Soviet Forces, Germany, 350 with the Soviet Northern Group of Forces in Poland, 100 with the Soviet Central Group of Forces in Czechoslovakia, 471 Czech aircraft, 359 East German aircraft, and 705 Polish aircraft.

Numbers of Soviet aircraft are from Isby, *op. cit.*, 1981, page 24. Lewis, *op. cit.*, page 71, notes that "the largest of the tactical air armies" the Soviets have stationed in eastern Europe "is the 16th Tactical Air Army deployed with the Group of Soviet Forces, Germany," whose "1,000 aircraft represent almost one-fourth of the whole tactical air force." This figure is close to Isby's. The total of aircraft in all three Soviet Tactical Air Armies included in this order of battle is 1,425. IISS, *op. cit., 1981–1982*, page 14, places a total of 2,000 Soviet aircraft in eastern Europe. However, it places them in not three but "four Tactical Air Armies," the fourth being that stationed in Hungary, as Lewis (*op. cit.*, page 71) confirms. In this order of battle, as in every source upon which it is based, forces stationed in Hungary, air and ground alike, are assumed to be reserved for the Southern Front. Consequently, Soviet aircraft stationed in Hungary are no more included here than Italian aircraft are on NATO's side. When these aircraft are subtracted from the total IISS gives, the remaining number of aircraft roughly corresponds to the total Isby provides for the three Soviet air armies assigned to central Europe.

Nor does this total appear to have changed, despite continuing emphasis by Western governments on the number of aircraft the Soviet Union has the *capacity* to produce. IISS continues to count just 2,000 aircraft in all four Soviet tactical air armies in eastern Europe (see *op. cit., 1983–1984*, page 18; and *1984–1985*, page 21).

Numbers of Czech, East German, and Polish aircraft are from IISS, *op. cit., 1981–1982*, pages 18, 19, and 20. In *The Military Balance, 1983–1984*, pages 20, 21, and 23. IISS continues to list exactly the same number of combat aircraft available to each of these three Warsaw Pact nations.

Warsaw Pact Ground Forces Reinforcement Schedule, Central Europe, 1981–85

Reinforcement from Category I Units Within 72 Hours

Nation	Unit & Location	Manpower in Combat Units	Tanks
Soviet Union	6th Guards Tank Division, Milovice	9,456	316
Soviet Union	120th Rogachev Guards Motor Rifle Division, Minsk	13,138	219
Soviet Union	76th Guards Airborne Division, Pskov	8,473	
Soviet Union	7th Guards Airborne Division, Kaunas	8,473	
Soviet Union	103rd Guards Airborne Division, Vitebsk	8,473	
Soviet Union	106th Guards Airborne Division, Tula-Ryazan	8,473	
Soviet Union	102nd Guards Airborne Division, Kishinev	8,473	
Soviet Union	104th Guards Airborne Division, Kirovabad	8,473	
Soviet Union	105th Guards Airborne Division, Fergona	8,473	
Soviet Union	6th Guards Airborne Division, Belogorsk	8,473	
	Total Within 72 Hours	90,378	535

Reinforcement from Category II Units Within 96 Hours

Poland	6th Airborne Division, Krakow	8,473	
Czechoslovakia	22nd Airborne Regiment, Prostejov	2,000	
	Total	10,473	
	Total Within 96 Hours	100,851	535

Reinforcement from Category I Units Within 10 Days

Nation	Unit & Location	Manpower in Combat Units	Tanks
Soviet Union	15th "Iron" Guards Motor Rifle Division, Vladimir-Volinski	13,138	219
Soviet Union	37th Guards Motor Rifle Division, Pargolova	13,138	219
Soviet Union	8th Guards Tank Division, Marina-Gorka	9,456	316

(continued)

Warsaw Pact Ground Forces Reinforcement Schedule, Central Europe, 1981–85 *(cont.)*

Reinforcement from Category I Units Within 72 Hours

Nation	Unit & Location	Manpower in Combat Units	Tanks
Soviet Union	23rd Tank Division, Ovruch	9,456	316
Soviet Union	2nd Taman Guards Motor Rifle Division, Alabino	13,138	219
	Total	58,326	1,289
	Total Within 10 Days	159,177	1,824

Reinforcement from Category II Units Within 15 Days

Nation	Unit & Location	Manpower in Combat Units	Tanks
Poland	15th Motor Rifle Division, Grudziadz	11,000	188
Poland	8th Motor Rifle Division, Chojnice	11,000	188
	Total	22,000	376
	Total Within 15 Days	181,177	2,200

Reinforcement from Category II Units Within 30 Days

Nation	Unit & Location	Manpower in Combat Units	Tanks
Soviet Union	1st Tank Division, Kaliningrad	8,615	316
Soviet Union	1st Guards Motor Rifle Division, Kaliningrad	12,771	188
Soviet Union	8th Tank Division, Slonim	8,615	316
Soviet Union	29th Tank Division, Slutsk	8,615	316
Soviet Union	50th Guards Motor Rifle Division, Brest	12,771	188
Soviet Union	72nd Guards Motor Rifle Division, Belaya	12,771	188
Soviet Union	29th Guards Motor Rifle Division, Lubny	12,771	188
Soviet Union	4th Motor Rifle Division, Lugansk/Vorishilovgrad	12,771	188
Soviet Union	23rd Guards Motor Rifle Division, Klaipeda	12,771	188
Soviet Union	18th Motor Rifle Division, Borisov	12,771	188

		Manpower in Combat Units	Tanks
Total		115,242	2,264
Total Within 30 Days		296,419	4,464

Reinforcement from Category III Units Within 90 Days

Nation	Unit & Location	Manpower in Combat Units	Tanks
Poland	1st Motor Rifle Division, Ostrow	11,000	75
Poland	3rd Motor Rifle Division, Lublin	11,000	75
Poland	9th Motor Rifle Division, Tarnow	11,000	75
Czechoslovakia	20th Motor Rifle Division, Brno	11,000	75
Czechoslovakia	15th Motor Rifle Division, Svitavy	11,000	75
Czechoslovakia	13th Tank Division, Bratislava	8,615	158
Czechoslovakia	14th Tank Division, Kosice	8,615	158
	Total	72,230	691
	Total Within 90 Days	368,649	5,155

Reinforcement from Category III Units Within 120 Days

Nation	Unit & Location	Manpower in Combat Units	Tanks
Soviet Union	19 Armored Divisions	163,685	3,002
Soviet Union	48 Motor Rifle Divisions	528,000	3,600
	Total	691,685	6,602
	Total Within 120 Days	1,060,334	11,757

Sources

Sources for all units listed here, and for most of their locations as well, are David C. Isby, *Weapons and Tactics of the Soviet Army* (London: Jane's, 1981), pages 24–26; William J. Lewis, *The Warsaw Pact: Arms, Doctrine, and Strategy* (New York: McGraw-Hill, 1982), pages 144, 164, and 200; United States Army War College, *NATO Data Base*, Carlisle Barracks, Pa., January 31, 1981; and Charles Kamps, Jr., "Orders of Battle: Warsaw Pact," in *The Next War* (New York: Simulations Publications, 1978), pages 25–26.

The number of Soviet, Polish, Czech, and East German formations of each type available to reinforce the Warsaw Pact's central European front, or to reinforce any other theater of war, and the readiness category of each formation, are from IISS, *The Military Balance, 1980–1981*, page 111; and

(continued)

Warsaw Pact Ground Forces Reinforcement Schedule, Central Europe, 1981–85 (cont.)

Isby, op. cit., pages 24–26. Isby identifies each Soviet division by readiness category, and confirms the small number of Soviet armored and mechanized divisions, apart from those already stationed in eastern Europe, that are maintained in readiness Category I. He identifies just seven such divisions, together with eight airborne divisions, in this category. Aside from the same eight airborne divisions, IISS (op. cit., 1980–1981) counts only two additional Soviet divisions in Category I.

The two such divisions likely to be nearest the central European front, one of them possibly in Czechoslovakia, are therefore listed here, together with the Soviet Army's eight airborne divisions, as the first units available to reinforce that theater. The airborne divisions could be mobilized and transported rapidly. Except as elite infantry, however, airborne units have no significant function in modern war. The highly increased lethality of modern air defenses has created unacceptable risks for airdrops behind enemy lines. Armored and mechanized units in the Soviet Union would take more time to reach the front. Even the Soviet 28th Corps, headquartered, as Isby notes (op. cit., page 25), at Grodno in Byelorussia, is 1800 kilometers by road from Fulda. Armored units fielded by 28th Corps would take at least three days to cover that distance and deploy in battle order. These contraints are reflected in this reinforcement schedule.

Since they are airborne units, the Polish 6th Airborne Division and the Czech 22nd Airborne Regiment are here assumed capable of mobilizing and reaching the zone of combat within four days, even though IISS (op. cit., 1980–1981, page 111) lists them only in readiness Category II.

IISS (loc. cit.) counts as available for reinforcement a total of fifteen Soviet armored and mechanized divisions in readiness Category II. Isby (op. cit., page 28) notes that Category II units are not deployable until "within 30 days of mobilization." But five of the Soviet divisions IISS places in Category II Isby places in Category I (pages 24–25). Consequently, those five are here assumed to be capable of reaching the central European front within 10 days, while the remaining 10 divisions IISS counts are assumed unavailable until 30 days have elapsed.

Isby notes (op. cit., page 28) that Category III units of the Soviet Army are "not deployable until between 90 and 120 days after mobilization." IISS (op. cit., 1980–1981, page 111), counts a total of 3 Polish, 4 Czech, and 67 Soviet divisions available for reinforcement in readiness Category III. Since the Polish and Czech divisions would be much closer to the zone of

combat, it is here assumed that they would be available within 90 days, while the Soviet divisions in this category would not be available until after 120 days.

Any major effort to increase the readiness of any Soviet divisions, or to increase their number in eastern Europe, would more than likely trigger the NATO mobilization process. As IISS notes in The Military Balance, 1977– 1978 page 105, should the Soviet Union begin to mobilize, "it would be impossible to conceal it on any scale."

The personnel and tank strengths of all Category I armored and mechanized divisions listed here are based on sources to the separate table, Warsaw Pact Ground Forces Central Europe, Order of Battle, 1981–85. The personnel strength of a Soviet airborne division is from Isby (op. cit., page 289). The personnel strength of the Polish 6th Airborne Division is assumed here to be the same as that of a Soviet airborne division. The personnel strength of the Czech 22nd Airborne Regiment is from William P. Mako, U.S. Ground Forces and the Defense of Europe (Washington, D.C.: Brookings, 1983), page 107. Personnel strengths of all Category II and III armored divisions of the Warsaw Pact are based on the lower of the two figures Isby supplies (op. cit., page 80) for the manpower of a Soviet armored division. Personnel strengths of all Category II and III mechanized divisions of the Warsaw Pact are based on the figure given by the United States Army, FM 30-40, Handbook on Soviet Ground Forces, 30 June 1975, page A-3, for the manpower of a Category I mechanized division at that time, and on the assumption that Category II and III divisions of this type will have a lower manpower strength because their tank strength is lower.

Isby notes (op. cit., page 111) that "none" of the mechanized divisions in readiness Categories II and III in the Soviet Army has an independent tank battalion. Accordingly, while the tank strength of Category II armored divisions of the Warsaw Pact has been kept here at 316, the tank strength of Category II mechanized divisions has been reduced from 219 to 188. Isby further notes (page 28) that Category III units of the Soviet Army "usually have only 33–50 percent of their required equipment." Accordingly, the tank strength of all Category III armored divisions of the Warsaw Pact has been reduced here by 50%, from 316 to 158, and the tank strength of all mechanized divisions of the Warsaw Pact has been reduced by 40%, from 188 to 75.

Warsaw Pact Main Battle Tank Holdings, 1981–85

Nation	Number	Type	Gun Caliber
Bulgaria	300	T-34	85 mm
	1,000	T-54/55	100 mm
	60	T-72	125 mm
	1,360	Total	
Czechoslovakia	3,100	T-54/55	100 mm
	400	T-72	125 mm
	3,500	Total	
East Germany	1,500	T-54/55	100 mm
	830	T-72	125 mm
	2,330	Total	
Hungary	1,200	T-54/55	100 mm
	60	T-72	125 mm
	1,260	Total	
Poland	3,400	T-54/55	100 mm
	50	T-72	125 mm
	3,450	Total	
Romania	200	T-34	85 mm
	1,000	T-54/55	100 mm
	30	T-72	125 mm
	1,230	Total	
Soviet Union	23,322	T-54/55	100 mm
	14,085	T-62	115 mm
	7,500	T-64	125 mm
	4,500	T-72/80	125 mm
	49,407	Total	
	62,537	Total All Warsaw Pact Nations	

Notes and Sources

The Soviet PT-76 light reconnaissance tank, with 76 mm armament, has been excluded from this list of main battle tank holdings, just as the British *Scorpion* light tank with 76 mm armament, and other NATO tanks with 76 mm armament or less, have been excluded from the corresponding list of NATO's main battle tank holdings.

The T-62 is here shown in service only with the Soviet Army. According to David Isby, *Weapons and Tactics of the Soviet Army*, page 108, "T-62s were received and evaluated by most Warsaw Pact armies," but "with the possible exception of Bulgaria," they "never entered large-scale service with any of these armies." IISS, *The Military Balance, 1983–1984*, pages 20–23, lists no T-62s in service with any of these armies, including Bulgaria's.

The source for all Bulgarian, Czech, Hungarian, Polish, and Romanian tank holdings shown is IISS, *op. cit., 1983–1984*, pages 20–23. The source for the total of East German tank holdings is Pierangelo Caiti, *Modern Armour* (Parma, Italy: Delta Editrice, 1978), page 151. IISS, *op. cit., 1983–1984*, page 21, notes that 1,500 of East Germany's tanks are T-54/55s. The remainder are here presumed to be T-72s.

The source for the number of T-54/55s and T-62s in service or stored by the Soviet Army is Isby, *op. cit.*, page 29. The T-64 was still in production at the time of Isby's writing, and he lists only 3,871 of these tanks in Soviet service. IISS, *op. cit., 1983–1984*, page 16, lists 7,500 T-64s. The higher figure is used here.

IISS, *op. cit., 1983–1984*, page 16, gives the Soviet Union a total holding of 50,000 tanks, including 35,000 T-54/55s and T-62s, 7,500 T-64s, and 7,500 T-72/80s and PT-76s. According to Caiti (*op. cit.*, page 63), a total of 3,000 PT-76s equip Soviet reconnaissance battalions and reconnaissance companies. The remaining 4,000 tanks are here presumed to be T-72/80s.

Isby (*op. cit.*, page 29) gives the Soviet Union a total of 48,403 tanks of all types, but notes that 3,051 of these are in storage.

Key Operational Capabilities of Leading Current Tank Types and Tank Guns—1981–85

Tank	Speed	Unrefueled Range	Turret Rotation Speed	Gun Caliber & Type	Gun Elevation Depression	Maximum Rate of Fire	Rounds of Ammunition Stored
M-60A1/A3	30 mph	310 miles	24° p/sec	105 mm M-68	+20°–10°	10 rpm	63 rds
M-48A5	30 mph	285 miles	24° p/sec	105 mm M-68	+20°– 9°	10 rpm	57 rds
M-1 Abrams	43 mph	279 miles	24° p/sec	105 mm M-68	+19°– 9°	10 rpm	55 rds
Centurion Mk 10	21 mph	114 miles	14° p/sec	105 mm L7A2	+20°–10°	10 rpm	64 rds
Leopard I	40 mph	372 miles	24° p/sec	105 mm L7A3	+20°– 9°	10 rpm	60 rds
AMX-30	40 mph	404 miles	30° p/sec	105 mm DEFA F1	+20°– 8°	8 rpm	50 rds
Leopard II	44 mph	341 miles	24° p/sec	120 mm RMTL SB	+20°– 8°	8 rpm	42 rds
Chieftain Mk 5	30 mph	310 miles	20° p/sec	120 mm L11A5	+20°–10°	8 rpm	64 rds
T-55	19 mph	260 miles	17° p/sec	100 mm D-10T2S	+17°– 4°	5 rpm	43 rds
T-62	31 mph	298 miles	17° p/sec	115 mm U-5TS	+15°– 3°	4 rpm	40 rds
T-72/T-80	37 mph	310 miles	17° p/sec	125 mm DBL-12T	+18°– 5°	2 rpm	40 rds

Note

A figure of 6 rounds per minute is frequently given as the rate of fire of the 125 mm gun on the Soviet T-72. This is the theoretical rate of fire the gun would achieve with use of its automatic loading system. Several serious injuries, however, have been suffered by Soviet crewmen attempting to use the loading system, whose power rammer tends to load the gunner's arm into the gun breech. Consequently, Soviet crews have not used the automatic loader since 1979. The gun must be manually loaded, and would be so loaded in combat. This reduces its rate of fire to the maximum of 2 rounds per minute shown.

Sources

Pierangelo Caiti, *Modern Armour: A Comprehensive Guide* (Parma, Italy: Delta Editrice, 1978); David C. Isby, *Weapons and Tactics of the Soviet Army* (London: Jane's 1981); and Christopher F. Foss, *Jane's World Armoured Fighting Vehicles* (London: Macdonald & Jane's, 1976).

Major Tank Ammunition Types in Current Service with NATO and the Warsaw Pact—1981–85

Designation	Type	Caliber	Produced by	Used by	Muzzle Velocity	Maximum Effective Range
M-393A2	HEP	105 mm	USA	NATO	4,208 fps	2,185 yds
M-456A1E2	HEAT	105 mm	USA	NATO	4,348 fps	2,185 yds
M-392A2	APDS	105 mm	USA	NATO	5,467 fps	3,250 yds
M-111	APFSDS	105 mm	Israel	NATO	5,612 fps	3,755 yds
M-735A1	APFSDS	105 mm	USA	NATO	5,875 fps	3,545 yds
M-774	*APFSDS	105 mm	USA	NATO	5,910 fps	3,345 yds
M-833	*APFSDS	105 mm	USA	NATO	6,127 fps	3,640 yds
L52	APFSDS	105 mm	UK	NATO	5,540 fps	1,965 yds
L64	APFSDS	105 mm	UK	NATO	5,622 fps	3,250 yds
OE-61	HE	105 mm	France	NATO	4,524 fps	3,825 yds
OCC-61	HEAT	105 mm	France	NATO	3,093 fps	3,280 yds
L86	HESH	120 mm	UK	UK	2,198 fps	8,744 yds
L90	APFSDS	120 mm	UK	UK	4,494 fps	3,270 yds
AFAC	APFSDS	120 mm	FRG	FRG	5,576 fps	3,835 yds
BR-412D	AP	100 mm	USSR	WPO	3,034 fps	1,115 yds
BR-354P	AP	100 mm	USSR	WPO	3,168 fps	1,350 yds
BK-5M	HEAT	100 mm	USSR	WPO	2,952 fps	1,640 yds
BM-6	APDS	100 mm	USSR	WPO	4,642 fps	1,750 yds
BK-4M	HEAT	115 mm	USSR	USSR	2,559 fps	1,640 yds
BR-5	APFSDS	115 mm	USSR	USSR	4,921 fps	2,060 yds
BR-11	APFSDS	125 mm	USSR	WPO	5,298 fps	2,185 yds

Notes

The maximum effective ranges given here are those at which the probability of penetrating 225 mm of armor is at least 33%. A thickness of 225 mm exceeds that on any part of any tank now in active service with the Warsaw Pact, or on any tank likely to be in service with the Warsaw Pact within the next decade. The armor on some current NATO tanks, however, is thicker.

HEAT (High Explosive Anti-Tank) ammunition rounds achieve lower muzzle velocities than do kinetic energy projectiles. The explosive charge within the HEAT warhead is shaped into an inverse cone and lined with copper. Its shape concentrates its explosive pressures at a single point at the base of the cone, making up in convergent energy for what the projectile lacked in kinetic force, and producing a jet of molten copper moving at 27,000 feet per second (fps), whose effects on the target material are best understood in hydrodynamic terms, for at its point of impact the molybdenum, nickel, and chrome of armored plate is reduced to a perfect fluid. So precise is the focus of energy, however, that this penetrating stream of molten alloys can be too narrow to cause sufficient devastation. Compound armor reduces the effectiveness of HEAT rounds.

The warheads of HEP (High Explosive Plastic) and HESH (High Explosive Squash Head) ammunition rounds are filled with a malleable explosive material which spreads to form a blob on impact with the target. Its detonation generates a shock wave through the armor, leaving only a dent externally, but knocking chunks of metal off compartment walls within. These travel through the compartment at speeds of 2800 to 3100 feet per second. Spaced armor can greatly reduce the effectiveness of these rounds.

APDS (Armor-Piercing Discarding Sabot) ammunition employs a large-caliber cartridge case with high propellant force and a projectile of equal diameter, most of which, however, fragments as it clears the gun barrel, leaving only a dense inner core, usually composed of tungsten carbide, whose lighter weight and minimal aerodynamic drag do not reduce its muzzle velocity as much as does the mass of a full-sized projectile. It thus retains high kinetic energy on impact with the target.

As rifled barrels came into use, providing projectiles with spin in order to flatten their trajectories and so increase accuracy of fire, it was found that the motion of spin increased aerodynamic drag, somewhat reducing forward velocity and losing kinetic energy. APFSDS (Armor-Piercing Fin-Stabilized Discarding Sabot) ammunition was consequently developed to permit spin while at the same time stabilizing pitch and yaw. This substantially reduced aerodynamic drag, restoring most of the forward velocity previously lost by spin, while also retaining a flat trajectory. The combination of greater accuracy and very high kinetic energy, reflected in the muzzle velocities shown, gives APFSDS rounds the greatest penetrating power against most armored targets.

*M-774 and M-833 105 mm rounds use depleted uranium cores. These are of an even more dense material than tungsten carbide, and retain much of the very high muzzle velocities shown.

Muzzle velocities of 5249 and 5511 fps are frequently claimed by NATO for the Soviet BR-5 and BR-11 APFSDS rounds, respectively. No evidence exists to support these claims. Even were their velocities as claimed, they would still fall short of those achieved by several NATO rounds shown in the table. Nor do they match the effective ranges of many NATO projectiles.

Additionally, an APFSDS round is said to have been developed for the D-10T2S 100 mm gun used on the Soviet T-55. This would imply higher muzzle velocities, and hence greater penetrating power, for that gun when it fired such ammunition, suggesting, in turn, that the T-55 ought still to be considered a threat to NATO. The D-10T2S gun has a rifled barrel. By the time APFSDS ammunition came into existence, the Soviets were already designing guns of larger caliber, and all of these were smoothbore weapons. Fin-stabilized ammunition, when fired from a smoothbore gun, does not require driving bands, but cannot be fired from a rifled barrel without them. These bands, composed of insoluble polymer materials similar to Teflon, are the product of a highly sophisticated technology which the Soviets neither possess nor have had any need to pursue, throughout the past 15 years, while developing APFSDS ammunition which did not require it. To have pursued it more recently, on behalf of a gun of lower caliber that is fast becoming obsolete, on a tank which eventually will be replaced and, whether or not it could fire APFSDS ammunition, in too many other respects is no longer a match for anything NATO can field, would seem prodigal.

Sources

Pierangelo Caiti, *Modern Armour: A Comprehensive Guide* (Parma, Italy: Delta Editrice, 1978); David C. Isby, *Weapons and Tactics of the Soviet Army* (London: Jane's, 1981); Christopher F. Foss, *Jane's World Armoured Fighting Vehicles* (London: Macdonald & Jane's, 1976); Donald R. Kennedy, "The Infantryman vs the MBT," *National Defense* (March, 1985), pages 27–34, and "The Infantryman vs the MBT Part II," *National Defense* (April, 1985), pages 45–49.

Warsaw Pact Ground Forces Central Europe—Mobilization and Reinforcement Schedule, 1981–85

Nation	Active Ground Forces	Ground Forces Reserves	Total Ground Forces	Total Tanks
Czechoslovakia	140,000	295,000	435,000	3,500

Time Deployed after First Alert	Numbers & Types of Formations	Manpower			Tanks
		Combat Units	Noncombat & Support Units	All Units	
Within 24 Hrs	3 Armd Div 2 Mech Div	63,000	29,647	92,647	1,605
Within 96 Hrs	1 Airb Regt	2,000	941	2,941	
	Total 96 Hrs	65,000	30,588	95,588	1,605
Within 90 Days	2 Armd Div 2 Mech Div	39,230	18,461	57,691	466
	Total 90 Days	104,230	49,049	153,279	2,071

Nation	Active Ground Forces	Ground Forces Reserves	Total Ground Forces	Total Tanks
East Germany	113,000	250,000	363,000	2,330

Time Deployed after First Alert	Numbers & Types of Formations	Manpower			Tanks
		Combat Units	Noncombat & Support Units	All Units	
Within 24 Hrs	2 Armd Div 4 Mech Div	66,000	31,058	97,058	1,384
	Total 24 Hrs	66,000	31,058	97,058	1,384

Nation	Active Ground Forces	Ground Forces Reserves	Total Ground Forces	Total Tanks
Poland	210,000	500,000	710,000	3,450

Time Deployed after First Alert	Numbers & Types of Formations	Manpower			Tanks
		Combat Units	Noncombat & Support Units	All Units	
Within 24 Hrs	5 Armd Div 3 Mech Div	78,000	36,705	114,705	2,237

Time Deployed after First Alert	Numbers & Types of Formations	Manpower			Tanks
		Combat Units	Noncombat & Support Units	All Units	
Within 96 Hrs	1 Airb Div	8,473	3,987	12,460	
	Total 96 Hrs	86,473	40,692	127,165	2,237
Within 15 Days	2 Mech Div	22,000	10,352	32,352	376
	Total 15 Days	108,473	51,044	159,517	2,613
Within 90 Days	3 Mech Div	33,000	15,529	48,529	225
	Total 90 Days	141,473	66,573	208,046	2,838

Nation	Active Ground Forces	Ground Forces Reserves	Total Ground Forces	Total Tanks
Soviet Union	1,825,000	2,000,000	2,825,000	49,407

Time Deployed after First Alert	Numbers & Types of Formations	Manpower			Tanks
		Combat Units	Noncombat & Support Units	All Units	
Within 24 Hrs	13 Armd Div 13 Mech Div 1 Atty Div	313,810	147,675	461,485	7,540
Within 96 Hrs	1 Armd Div 1 Mech Div 8 Airb Div	90,378	42,530	132,908	535
	Total 96 Hrs	404,188	190,205	594,393	8,075
Within 10 Days	2 Armd Div 3 Mech Div	58,326	27,447	85,773	1,289
	Total 10 Days	462,514	217,652	680,166	9,364
Within 30 Days	3 Armd Div 7 Mech Div	115,242	54,231	169,473	2,264
	Total 30 Days	577,756	271,883	849,639	11,628
Within 120 Days	19 Armd Div 48 Mech Div	691,685	325,498	1,017,183	6,602
	Total 120 Days	1,269,441	597,381	1,866,822	18,230

Warsaw Pact Ground Forces Central Europe—Mobilization and Reinforcement Schedule, 1981–85, Summary

Time Deployed After First Alert

Nation	24 Hours Manpower Combat Units	Total	Tanks	10 Days Manpower Combat Units	Total	Tanks	30 Days Manpower Combat Units	Total	Tanks	120 Days Manpower Combat Units	Total	Tanks
Czechoslovakia	63,000	92,647	1,605	65,000	95,588	1,605	65,000	95,588	1,605	104,230	153,279	2,071
GDR	66,000	97,058	1,384	66,000	97,058	1,384	66,000	97,058	1,384	66,000	97,058	1,384
Poland	78,000	114,705	2,237	86,473	127,165	2,237	108,473	159,517	2,613	141,473	208,046	2,838
USSR	313,810	461,485	7,540	462,514	680,166	9,364	577,756	849,639	11,628	1,269,441	1,866,822	18,230
Total	520,810			679,987			817,229			1,581,144		
Total		765,895			999,977			1,201,802			2,325,205	
Total			12,766			14,590			17,230			24,523

Warsaw Pact Ground Forces Central Europe—Mobilization and Reinforcement Schedule, 1981–85, Summary: Totals

Time Deployed after First Alert	Manpower		Tanks
	Combat Units	Total	
Within 24 Hrs	520,810	765,895	12,766
Within 10 Days	679,987	999,977	14,590
Within 30 Days	817,229	1,201,802	17,230
Within 120 Days	1,581,144	2,325,205	24,523

Sources and Method

Figures for active ground forces are from IISS, *The Military Balance, 1981–1982*, pages 11, 18, 19, and 20. Figures for Czech and East German ground forces reserves are from the same source, but those for Polish and Soviet ground forces reserves are from William J. Lewis, *The Warsaw Pact: Arms, Doctrine, and Strategy* (New York: McGraw-Hill, 1982), pages 205 and 43, respectively. Figures for total tank holdings are from sources for the separate table, *Warsaw Pact Main Battle Tank Holdings, 1981–85.*

Little confidence can be placed in the figures for reserves. Lewis (*op. cit.,* page 205), calls the Polish reserves "the Voluntary Reserve of the Citizens' Militia." IISS (*op. cit., 1981–1982*, page 19) counts "350,000 Citizen's Militia, 'League for National Defence' (some 200,000 active)," and refers the reader to a note (page 18) advising: "May be non-operational." Estimates vary widely. While Lewis (*op. cit.,* page 43) reports that the Soviet Army is "backed up by over 2,000,000 trained reservists," IISS (*op. cit., 1981–1982*, page 14) asserts that "total reserves" for all Soviet military services "could be 25,000,000, of which some 5,000,000 have served in the last five years."

Nor can much confidence be placed in the ability of any Warsaw Pact nation, including the Soviet Union, to mobilize its reserves. David Isby, in *Weapons and Tactics of the Soviet Army* (London: Jane's 1981), page 28, notes that "the Soviets have no reserve units that meet for regular peacetime training, as does the U.S. National Guard, except for some small specialist units." He estimates that designated reserve units of the Soviet Army, "which have no peacetime existence," comprise at most 50 formations, and that no more than 20 of these have cadres of more than 300 men. Equipment for these units, he adds, "will come from national strategic reserve stocks, and civilian trucks or BTR-152s will probably be issued to motorized rifle units. Tanks will be T-54s (or maybe even T-34s), and artillery will be wartime vintage as well." Such formations, he concludes, "are unlikely to be deployable even for second-line duties before 180 days after mobilization."

Reserves, in any case, are most likely to be mobilized in defense of the homeland. The mobilization and reinforcement schedule shown here, and the corresponding schedule for NATO, proceed on the assumption, invariably followed by all NATO planners, that only the Warsaw Pact will be the aggressor, and only NATO's homelands must be defended. Consequently, full mobilization of NATO'S central European reserves is anticipated, but mobilization of the Warsaw Pact's reserves is not. Both schedules reflect this assumption.

According to William P. Mako, in *U.S. Ground Forces and the Defense of Central Europe* (Washington, D.C.: Brookings, 1983), page 79, for every Soviet division deployed in Eastern Europe, whose average personnel strength is 12,000, an additional 5,500 combat support and noncombat troops are deployed, producing an aggregate "division slice" of 17,500 troops of all types per division. In that case, personnel in major Soviet combat units comprise, on average, 68% of all deployed Soviet Army personnel. Lothar Ruehl, in *MBFR: Lessons and Problems,* Adelphi Paper no. 176 (London: IISS, 1982), page 29, estimates that "65 percent of Soviet soldiers are front-line troops," serving in combat and combat support units.

Based on these estimates, an average of 68% of all Warsaw Pact army personnel is here assumed to be in major combat units. This average has been adhered to in calculating the number of combat support and noncombat personnel accompanying major combat units in each stage of reinforcement shown.

Ruehl (*op. cit.*, page 24) quotes NATO's own total of 476,000 Soviet ground forces personnel, in both combat and noncombat units, stationed in East Germany, Czechoslovakia, and Poland. That is reasonably close to the total of 461,485 such personnel shown here.

Ground Forces in Central Europe, 1981–85: A Comparison of NATO and Warsaw Pact Strengths at Progressive Stages of Reinforcement

| | Manpower | | | | Tanks | |
| | Combat Units | | Total | | | |
Time Deployed After First Alert	NATO	Warsaw Pact	NATO	Warsaw Pact	NATO	Warsaw Pact
Within 24 Hours	697,120	520,810	1,297,380	765,895	10,351	12,766
Within 10 Days	1,374,471	697,987	2,563,880	999,977	14,073	14,590
Within 30 Days	1,502,871	817,229	2,805,080	1,201,802	15,585	17,230
Within 120 Days	1,868,445	1,581,144	3,493,648	2,325,205	18,717	24,523

NATO and the Warsaw Pact—All Theaters: The Balance on Land, in the Air, and at Sea, 1981–85

	NATO	Warsaw Pact
Active Personnel	5,900,000	4,800,000
Main Battle Tanks	33,557	62,537
Combat Aircraft	12,000	12,000
Helicopters	12,400	4,500
Major Surface Warships	490	295
Attack Submarines	242	279

Sources

Figures for main battle tanks are from sources for the separate tables, *NATO Main Battle Tank Holdings, 1981–85* and *Warsaw Pact Main Battle Tank Holdings, 1981–85.* All other figures are from the Center for Defense Information, Washington, D.C., *Force Level Calculator,* 1982.

Appendix I

Verification: United States Military Satellite Systems

United States Military Satellite Systems

Designation & Program Code	First Orbit	Function/Equipment/Orbiting Altitude/Lifetime/Weight & Size/Program History Other Known Launches/Number Orbited or Planned/Significant Features
RECONNAISSANCE: VISUAL IMAGERY SYSTEMS		
Discoverer	Feb. 59	Photographic. Telescopic lenses and ejectable film capsules. 6,200 frames per capsule. 115 square miles per frame. Orbit at 567 miles. 38 launched. 26 orbited. 23 capsules ejected. 12 capsules recovered, the first in August, 1960. Discoverer 33 launched in July, 1966. Ground resolution of film in 1960: 36 inches.
TIROS (Television and Infra-Red Observation Satellite)	Apr. 60	Electro-optical scanning. Vidicon tubes and photoelectric cells sensitive to visible and infrared light. Over 2,000 scanning lines. First use of electron beam conversion to transmit imagery to ground terminals. TIROS 1 produced 22,852 images. Orbit from 429 to 468 miles. Lifetime: 78 days. Weight: 290 lbs. TIROS 10 launched in July, 1965. Ground resolution of imagery in 1960: about 6 feet.
WS-117L Sentry/SAMOS (Satellite and Missile Observation System)	Jan. 61	Primarily photographic. Ejectable film capsules. Some models equipped with photoelectric cells for electro-optical scanning in both the visible light and infrared spectrums. Some also equipped with VHF receiving antennas for ELINT and SIGINT collection. Some orbits were near-polar at 300 miles. Some were from 100 to 120 miles. Lifetime of SAMOS 2: 7 days. Weight: 2 tons. Length: 22 ft. Diam: 5 ft. Over 60 were launched. Ground resolution of film in 1964: 16 to 20 inches.
KH-4 Corona	Mar. 62	Photographic. Orbit from 157 to 423 miles. Ground resolution in 1962: 12 inches.
KH-8 Close-Look	July 66	Photographic for high-resolution search, with ejectable film capsules, and multispectral scanning with photoelectric sensors for area surveillance. Early orbits from 83 to 249 miles. Current orbits from 77 to 221 miles. Lifetime in 1966: 7 days. Current lifetime: from 70 to 80 days. Two or three launched per year. One launched on July 31, 1983. Weight: 3.5 tons. Length: 26 ft. Diam: 5 ft. Ground resolution of film in 1983: probably less than 1 inch.
KH-9 Big Bird Code 467	June 71	Photographic for high-resolution search, with 4 separate ejectable film capsules, and multispectral scanning with photoelectric sensors for area surveillance. VHF and UHF receiving antennas probably included for secondary ELINT/SIGINT mission. Early orbits from 95 to 177 miles. Current orbits from 101 to 155 miles. Early lifetime was 109 days. Average lifetime is 180 days, but Big Bird 52A, launched in June, 1980, remained in orbit for 261 days. Weight: 12.5 tons. Length: 50 ft. Diam: 10 ft. Second Big Bird was launched in January, 1972. At least 2 launched every year until the advent of KH-11. One launched per year thereafter. One launched on June 20, 1983. Ground resolution of film in 1983: less than 6 inches.
KH-11 Code 1010 Keyhole II	Dec. 76	Multispectral scanning. Microminiaturized photoelectric sensor arrays and RBV (Return Beam Vidicon) tube with over 6,000 scanning lines for high definition. Refined sensitivity to infrared spectrum. Electron beam conversion from charge-coupled cells for instantaneous digital transmission of imagery to ground terminals. VHF and UHF receiving antennas probably included. Early orbits from 150 to ˜ 80 miles. Current orbits from 155 to 329 miles. Average lifetime is 2 years,

but KH-11 60A, launched in June, 1978, had a lifetime of 3 years and 19 days. Weight: 14 tons. Length: 64 ft. Diam: 6.5 ft. One launched every other year. Thus at least 2 are always in orbit. Known launches: 125A in December, 1976; 60A in June, 1978; 10A in February, 1980; 85A in September, 1981. One launched in November, 1982. Ground resolution of imagery: less than 1 inch.

NOSS (Naval Ocean Surveillance Satellite)	Dec. 77	Active imaging radar. Holographic conversion of radar signal returns by laser light. Digital transmission of imagery to ground terminals. Orbit from 656 to 693 miles. Weight: 2.5 tons. Ground resolution of imagery: probably less than 12 inches.
RORSAT (Radar Ocean Reconnaissance Satellite)	Apr. 83	Active imaging radar. Holographic conversion of radar signal returns by laser light. Digital transmission of imagery to ground terminals. Weight: probably more than 3 tons. Ground resolution of imagery: probably less than 6 inches.
TEAL RUBY Code 649	Nov. 83	Electro-optical scanning and tracking. Infrared and ultraviolet measurement of radiation to identify bomber and missile targets in flight. Space sextant to measure target ranges and determine speed and bearing of each. Principal component of Integrated High Altitude Large Optics System. Tested aboard the space shuttle Columbia in June, 1982. Now operational. Orbit at 460 miles.
KH-12 (DRM-4)	Jan. 86	Improved KH-11. Orbit at 150 miles. Weight: 16 tons.
ITSS (Integrated Tactical Surveillance System)	1986	Active imaging radar. Planned replacement for Clipper Bow program cancelled in 1980.

RECONNAISSANCE: ELINT AND SIGINT SYSTEMS

ELINT Code 343	Mar. 62	VHF and UHF receiving antennas, amplifiers, and recorders to collect full spectrum of radio, radar, and other microwave signals. Transmission on command or at periodic intervals to relay satellites or ground terminals. Various types placed at a variety of altitudes through 1974. Early orbits were near-polar at 300 miles. Later orbits from 884 to 912 miles. Most recent orbits from 488 to 515 miles. Lifetimes vary from 2 to 10,000 years. ELINT Sat 20B, launched in April, 1974, has an expected lifetime of 90 years. Weights from 1 to 2.5 tons. Over 30 launched.
Ferret/Code 711	May 62	VHF and UHF receiving antennas and associated equipment to collect, record, and transmit full spectrum of radio, radar, and other microwave signals. Early orbits from 180 to 401 miles with lifetime of 3 years. Current orbits from 302 to 332 miles with lifetime of 6 years. Launched aboard photographic satellites. Ferret 85C, for example, was launched aboard Big Bird 51A in June, 1975. Weight: 125 lbs. Diam: 3 ft. Second generation Ferret, Code 711, will probably weigh about 500 lbs. About 3 launched per year until ELINT and SIGINT collection was duplicated by equipment on photographic and multispectral scanning satellites, as well as by geosynchronous satellites at higher altitudes. Since 1976, about 1 launched per year. Over 50 launched.
Rhyolite	June 70	VHF and UHF receiving antennas, coherent integration amplifiers, recorders, and high-power transmitters to collect full spectrum of radio, radar, and other microwave signals, including telemetry from Soviet and Chinese missile tests, and

(continued)

United States Military Satellite Systems *(cont.)*

Designation & Program Code	First Orbit	Function/Equipment/Orbiting Altitude/Lifetime/Weight & Size/Program History Other Known Launches/Number Orbited or Planned/Significant Features
		provide periodic or continuous transmission to relay satellites or ground terminals. Prototype placed in geosynchronous orbit at 22,300 miles over the Horn of Africa. Second launch in March, 1973, to geosynchronous orbit over the Indian Ocean. Third launch in May, 1977, to geosynchronous orbit over Borneo in South Pacific. Two spares launched in December 1977 and April, 1978. Lifetimes between 10 and 20 years. Weight: 1,540 lbs.
White Cloud EORSAT (ELINT Ocean Reconnaissance Satellite)	Dec. 71	Passive infrared scanners, millimeter-wave radiometers, VHF and UHF receiving antennas and associated equipment to collect, record, and transmit full spectrum of radio, radar, and other microwave signals. Orbits at 700 miles. Weight: 1.5 tons. Launched in clusters of 4. Five additional clusters launched: in April, 1976; December, 1977; March, 1980; February, 1983; and June 1983.
Chalet	June 78	VHF and UHF receiving antennas. Orbit at 22,300 miles. Additional launches in October, 1979, and October, 1981.
ARGUS	Jan. 85	Advanced *Rhyolite*. Orbit at 22,300 miles. First satellite placed in orbit by space shuttle Discovery on January 25, 1985.
EARLY WARNING SYSTEMS		
MIDAS (Missile Defense Alarm System)	May 60	Infrared sensor arrays to detect missile launches from rocket exhaust plumes. Geosynchronous orbit at 22,300 miles. Lifetime: 10 to 15 years. Weight: 2 tons. 10 orbited, the last 2 in 1966.
Vela Hotel	Oct. 63	X-ray, gamma ray, neutron, and radioactive particle detectors, and electromagnetic pulse meters, to detect and measure radioactivity from surface or atmospheric nuclear detonations, as well as from solar flares or other radioactive sources within a range of 100 million miles. Orbits from 69,106 to 69,796 miles. Lifetime: 10 to 18 years. Weight: 571 lbs. Length: 4 ft. Diam: 4 ft. 12 orbited, the last 2 in 1970.
DSP 949	Aug. 68	An array of 2,000 VLS (Visible Light Sensor) elements operating in the 2 to 5 micron region to detect missile launches from rocket exhaust plumes. Geosynchronous orbit at 22,300 miles over Singapore, but inclined at 9.9 degrees to shift south over India and back over South China Sea. Second satellite launched in April, 1969, to track north at same altitude while the first moves south, keeping all areas of Soviet Union and China under continuous surveillance. Weight: 1 ton. Length: 10 ft. Only 2 launched.
DSP 647 IMEWS (Integrated Missile Early Warning Satellite)	May 71	An array of 80,000 VLS elements operating in the 2 to 5 micron region to detect missile launches from rocket exhaust plumes. X-ray, gamma ray, neutron, and radioactive particle detectors to locate and measure radioactivity from surface or atmospheric nuclear detonations. VHF and UHF receiving antennas for ELINT/SIGINT collection. First IMEWS placed in geosynchronous orbit at 22,300 miles over Indian Ocean. Second launched in March, 1972, and placed at same altitude over Panama Canal. Weight: 1 ton. Length: 22 ft. Diam. 5 ft. 14 launched to date.

Name	Date	Description
IONDS (Integrated Operational Nuclear Detection System)	83	Advanced VLS arrays, X-ray, gamma ray, and neutron detectors, and electromagnetic pulse meters, to locate and measure the yield of a nuclear detonation within several miles of its point of detonation anywhere on the surface of the earth on in the atmosphere, almost instantaneously. Digital transmission of data on the number, scale, and locations of all detonations to relay satellites or ground or airborne terminals, within one millionth of a second. This provides capability for instantaneous damage assessment in the event of nuclear war, and guides most efficient reallocation of remaining forces. Operational aboard 4 NAVSTAR/GPS (Global Positioning System) Block 1 satellites launched to subsynchronous orbits at 12,500 miles in 1983.

COMMUNICATIONS SYSTEMS

Name	Date	Description
Score/Echo	May 58	Aluminized plastic (Mylar) balloon. Score carried tape recorder and transmitter. Echo, launched in August, 1960, carried passive HF and VHF receiving antennas. Orbit from 1,018 to 1,160 miles. Diam: 100 ft.
Courier	Oct. 60	HF and VHF receiving antennas, amplifiers, and transmitters. First active signal transponder in space. Orbit from 500 to 745 miles. At least 9 launched through 1964.
Relay	Dec. 62	HF and VHF receiving antennas, amplifiers, and transmitters. At least 2 launched, the second in January, 1964.
Early Bird SYNCOM (Synchronous Orbit and Communications)	Feb. 63	First geosynchronous orbit of signal transponder at 22,300 miles. 12 channels. Equipment did not perform reliably until fourth launch, in April, 1965. 12 channels, with maximum load of 4,000 simultaneous data relays. At least 25 launched for military use through 1960. Another 12 launched in the same period as INTELSATS (International Telecommunications Satellites) managed by COMSAT (Communications Satellite Corporation) for commercial use.
IDSCS (Initial Defense Satellite Communications System)	June 66	UHF and VHF channels. Geosynchronous orbit at 20,900 miles. Lifetime: 2 years. Weight: 100 lbs. Length: 3 ft. Diam: 2.6 ft. Total of 26 launched through June, 1968. 13 were still operational in 1973.
SDS (Satellite Data System)	Mar. 71	UHF communications for AFSATCOM (Air Force Satellite Communications System) and SAC (Strategic Air Command). Includes SIGINT equipment. Elliptical polar orbits from 200 to 24,000 miles for polar communications and relay from reconnaissance and early warning satellites. Weight: 500 lbs. Length: 6 ft. Diam: 3 ft. Second SDS launched in August, 1973, the third in March, 1975, and the fourth in May, 1977.
DSCS II	Nov. 71	SHF channels for use by WWMCCS (Worldwide Military Command and Control System) and NCA (National Command Authority). Spot beam antennas and 1,300 channels. Geosynchronous orbits at 23,230 miles over the Indian, Atlantic, and West Pacific Oceans. Weight: 1,245 lbs. Length: 13 ft. Diam: 9 ft. 8 launched, including spares. DSCS 7 and DSCS 8 were launched in May, 1977.
NATO III	Apr. 76	UHF communications for NATO forces between 12 ground terminals. Geosynchronous orbit over Atlantic Ocean at 22,200 miles. Weight: 1,545 lbs. Length: 5.2 ft. Diam.: 4.5 ft. Second launched January, 1977, and the third November, 1978. A fourth launched to serve as a spare in October, 1983.
FLTSATCOM (Fleet Satellite Communications)	Feb. 78	UHF and SHF communications for USN, USAF, and SIOP (Strategic Integrated Operating Plan) forces. 23 channels, 10 for USN, 12 for AFSATCOM, and 1 for NCA. Geosynchronous orbit at 22,250 miles. Weight: 4,100 lbs. Length: 8 ft.

(continued)

United States Military Satellite Systems (cont.)

Designation & Program Code	First Orbit	Function/Equipment/Orbiting Altitude/Lifetime/Weight & Size/Program History Other Known Launches/Number Orbited or Planned/Significant Features
		Diam: 4.3 ft. Second FLTSATCOM launched in May, 1979, the third in January, 1980, the fourth in October, 1980, and the fifth in August, 1981. 3 more are planned. All have been hardened against EMP (Electromagnetic Pulse) from nuclear detonation.
DSCS III	Oct. 82	UHF and SHF communications for WWMCCS and NCA. Multibeam spot antennas to focus transmissions into beams as narrow as 70 miles in diameter, difficult to locate and jam. 2,600 channels. Single-channel AFSATCOM downlink for EAM (Emergency Action Message). Solid-state uninterruptible power system. Hardened against EMP. Axis-stabilized. Geosynchronous orbits over the Atlantic, Eastern Pacific, Western Pacific, and Indian Oceans at 22,300 miles. Orbits may be repositioned by command from ground terminals. Weight: 1,876 lbs. Length: 8.8 ft. Diam: 6.7 ft. Second launched in March, 1983. Total of 14 planned.
LEASAT (Leased Satellite)	84	UHF communications leased by USN from Hughes Communications Services to supplement FLTSATCOM. 4 geosynchronous satellites with 13 channels each. USN will have 1,100 terminals by 1988. USN currently uses 400 terminals for 6 leased channels on each of 3 MARISAT (Maritime Communications Satellite) craft operated by COMSAT.
MILSTAR (Military Strategic Tactical and Relay System)	due 87	UHF, SHF, and EHF communications for SIOP forces. EHF (Extremely High Frequency) band width is between 55 and 65 gigahertz, providing high volume, jam-resistant transmission. Hardened against EMP. Laser communications link between satellites. Instantaneous worldwide coverage. 3 operational satellites in elliptical polar orbits from 200 to 24,000 miles, and 4 operational satellites and 1 spare in geosynchronous orbits at 22,300 miles. Full-scale development funding approved in fiscal year 1983 budget.
NAVIGATIONAL SYSTEMS		
Transit/Nova	Apr. 60	Floated gas-bearing gyrocompass, electronic accelerometer, and gyrostabilizers to measure velocity, pitch, and yaw of satellite and determine its position. Clock and transmitters with crystal oscillators for position broadcasts at 2-minute intervals. Simultaneous broadcasts at 150 and 400 megahertz. By measuring time lapse between transmission of both signals and receipt of each, receiver may determine its own position in 2 dimensions to within 300 ft. Polar orbit at 600 miles. Lifetime: 6 years. Weight: 301 lbs. 4 or 5 in orbit at any time. At least 38 launched, the most recent one in May, 1981.
NAVSTAR/GPS (Navigation System using Timing and Ranging) (Global Positioning System)	May 77	Atomic clock with rubidium-atom oscillator, accurate to within one millionth of a second. Synchronized time and position broadcasts from all NAVSTAR/GPS satellites on a single UHF frequency whose signal speed is the speed of light. Receiver may measure its range from each satellite by measuring time lapse between transmission and receipt of signal. By triangulating its range from 3 such satellites simultaneously, the receiver may determine its own position in 3 dimen-

sions to within 10 ft, and its own velocity to within one tenth of one mile per hour. GPS receivers on reconnaissance satellites enable them to determine their own position so that they may precisely determine the positions of targets observed. USAF will have 12,000 receivers, USN from 1,400 to 4,700, and Army from 1,600 to 13,000. Subsynchronous orbits at 12,540 miles. Weight: 1,636 lbs. 6 satellites now operational. IONDS (Integrated Operational Nuclear Detection System) carried on 4 Block 1 satellites.

METEOROLOGICAL SYSTEMS

TIROS (Television and Infra-Red Observation Satellite) — Apr. 60

Electro-optical scanning along sun-synchronous orbits at 500 miles to provide near-term weather forecasting for aircraft and naval units twice daily. Infrared radiometer for vertical measurement of temperatures and atmospheric vapor content. Ultraviolet sensor to measure atmospheric density at altitudes orbited by reconnaissance satellites, from 60 to 150 miles. Ionospheric sounder to measure density of ionosphere and determine strength of reflected signals for surface ELINT/SIGINT collection. Visual imagery of cloud-cover patterns used to guide orbital routes of reconnaissance satellites. Weight: 310 lbs. Similar to models used for visual reconnaissance during this period. More than 60 launched through 1976.

DMSP (Defense Meteorological Satellite Program) Block 5D-1 — Sept. 76

Multispectral scanning, with refinement of technology used by earlier TIROS models. Infrared radiometer, ultraviolet sensor, and ionospheric sounder, similar to those used by TIROS. Microwave temperature sounder to measure vertical temperatures up to 18 miles in any weather. Ion and gamma ray sensors. Electron spectrometer to predict radiotransmission interference from star radiation. APT (Automatic Picture Transmission) to provide visual imagery of near-term weather conditions to ground or airborne terminals, or to terminals at sea. Near-polar sun-synchronous orbit at 500 miles. Weight: 1,131 lbs. Length: 17 ft. Diam: 5 ft. 13 launched. Some provide secondary photomapping and aerial survey function. Long-term weather forecasting provided by TIROS-N satellites of NOAA (National Oceanographic and Atmospheric Administration) in geosynchronous orbits at 22,250 miles.

DMSP Block 5D-2 — Dec. 82

Upgrade of Block 5D-1, with microwave imager to provide visual images of surface and near-surface conditions, including soil moisture, formation of sea ice, density of rain and wind speeds, in all weather conditions, including heavy cloud cover. Weight: 1,650 lbs. Length: 14 ft. Diam: 5 ft. Funds for 2 additional Block 5D-2 satellites were included in the fiscal year 1983 budget.

Sources

Willy Ley, *Rockets, Missiles, and Men in Space* (rev. and expanded, New York: The Viking Press, 1968). John W. R. Taylor and David Mondey, *Spies in the Sky* (London: Ian Allan, 1972). Sandra Hochman and Sybil Wong, *Satellite Spies* (Indianapolis and New York: Bobbs-Merrill, 1976). James Bamford, *The Puzzle Palace* (Boston: Houghton Mifflin, 1982). Thomas Karas, *The New High Ground* (New York: Simon & Schuster, 1983). James Canan, *War in Space* (New York: Harper & Row, 1982). James F. Dunnigan, "The War in Space," in *How to Make War* (New York: Morrow, 1982). Brassey's and The Royal United Services Institute for Defence Studies, "Reconnaissance Satellites," in *International Weapons Developments* (3rd rev. ed., London: Brassey's, 1979). Bhupendra Jasani, "Military Use of Outer Space," in *The Arms Race and Arms Control*, Stockholm International (continued)

United States Military Satellite Systems (cont.)

Peace Research Institute (SIPRI) (London: Taylor & Francis, 1982). Bhupendra Jasani, "Reconnaissance Satellites," *World Armaments and Disarmament Yearbook, 1976 through 1983* (Stockholm: Almqvist & Wiksell, 1976–83). Congressional Budget Office, *Strategic Command, Control and Communications: Alternative Approaches for Modernization* (Washington, D.C.: CBO, October, 1981). Commander Cecil B. Jones, USN, "Photographic Reconnaissance Satellites," *Proceedings of the United States Naval Institute* (June, 1980). Deborah G. Meyer, "Strategic Satellites: Our Eyes in the Sky," *Armed Forces Journal International* (February, 1983). Specifications tables, "Aerospace Forecast and Inventory," *Aviation Week & Space Technology,* March 14, 1983. "Industry Observer," *Aviation Week & Space Technology* (December 14, 1962); "Washington Round-Up," *Aviation Week & Space Technology* (June 4, 1979); Clarence Robinson, "Soviet Push Telemetry Bypass," *Aviation Week & Space Technology* (April 16, 1979); "Navy Will Develop All-Weather Ocean Monitor Satellite," *Aviation Week & Space Technology* (October 6, 1980); "New Payload Could Boost Shuttle Cost," *Aviation Week & Space Technology* (August 14, 1978); "Space Reconnaissance Dwindles," *Aviation Week & Space Technology* (October 6, 1980); Philip J. Klass, "U.S. Monitoring Capability Impaired," *Aviation Week & Space Technology* (May 14, 1978); Philip J. Klass, *Secret Sentries in Space* (New York: Random House, 1971); Gerald L. Borrowman, "Recent Trends in Orbital Reconnaissance," *Spaceflight* (January 1, 1982); Anthony Kenden, "U.S. Reconnaissance Satellite Programs," *Spaceflight,* Volume 20, no. 2 (1978); James Fusca, "Space Surveillance," *Space/Aeronautics* (June, 1984); "Big Bird: America's Spy in Space," *Flight International* (January 27, 1977); Anthony Kenden, "U.S. Military Activities in Space, 1983," *Journal of the British Interplanetary Society;* King-Hele et alii, *The RAE Table of Earth Satellites, 1957–1980;* John Noble Wifford, "Spy Satellite Reportedly Aided in Shuttle Flight," *The New York Times* (October 20, 1981); John Pike, "Reagan Prepares for War in Outer Space," *CounterSpy* (September–November, 1982); U.S. Congress, House Committee on Foreign Affairs, *The Role of Intelligence in the Foreign Policy Process* (Washington, D.C.: U.S. Government Printing Office, 1980); Robert Lindsey, *The Falcon and the Snowman* (New York: Simon & Schuster, 1979); Jeffrey T. Richelson, "Technical Collection and Arms Control," in William C. Potter, ed., *Verification and Arms Control* (Lexington, Mass: Lexington Books, 1985); Jeffrey T. Richelson, "Imaging and Signals Intelligence" and "Ocean Surveillance, Space Surveillance, and Nuclear Detonation Monitoring," in Richelson, *The U.S. Intelligence Community* (Cambridge: Ballinger, 1985).

Notes

1. Expanding America's Defense

1. Ronald Reagan, televised address to the nation on military spending and a new defense, March 23, 1983, transcript published by *The New York Times,* March 24, 1983. Ronald Reagan, quoted by Bernard Gwertzman, "Reagan Foresees Offering to Share Antimissile Arms," *The New York Times,* March 30, 1983.
2. Bill Keller, "U.S. Arms Official, in Geneva, Voices Hope on the Talks," *The New York Times,* March 10, 1985.
3. Ronald Reagan, quoted by Bernard Gwertzman, "U.S. Says Its Team in Talks on Arms Has Wide Latitude," *The New York Times,* March 9, 1985.
4. Edward Teller, debate with McGeorge Bundy, Loeb Student Center, New York University, March 18, 1985.
5. Union of Concerned Scientists, *The Fallacy of Star Wars: Why Space Weapons Can't Protect Us* (New York: Vintage Books, 1984), page 40.
6. *Ibid.,* pages 48 and 86–87.
7. *Ibid.,* pages 48, 88–89, and 97–98.
8. *Ibid.,* page 102.
9. *Ibid.,* pages 60 and 62.
10. *Ibid.,* page 100.
11. George Keyworth, quoted by William Safire, "Degrading Gracefully," *The New York Times,* March 21, 1985.
12. Union of Concerned Scientists, *op. cit.,* page 100.
13. *Ibid.*
14. *Ibid.,* pages 95 and 100.
15. *Ibid.,* page 108.
16. *Ibid.,* pages 108–109.
17. *Ibid.,* pages 48 and 101–102.
18. David E. Sanger, "A Debate About 'Star Wars': Can Software Be Designed?," *The New York Times,* October 23, 1985.
19. David E. Sanger, "Pentagon and Critics Dispute Roles of Space Arms Designers," *The New York Times,* November 5, 1985.
20. Sanger, *op. cit., The New York Times,* October 23, 1985.
21. *Scientific American,* July, 1985; and William E. Broad, "Space Weapon Test Failure Reported," *The New York Times,* November 1, 1985.
22. *Science* magazine, November 8, 1985; and Broad, *op. cit., The New York Times,* November 1, 1985.
23. Associated Press, "Expert on Space Shield Quits," *The New York Times,* November 2, 1985.
24. Union of Concerned Scientists, *op. cit.,* pages 120 and 127.
25. *Ibid.,* page 98; and Charles Mohr, "Army Test Missile Is Said to Destroy a Dummy Warhead," *The New York Times,* June 12, 1984.

26. Mohr, *op. cit.,* June 12, 1984.
27. Sir Geoffrey Howe, quoted by R. W. Apple, Jr., "Britain Questions 'Star Wars' Plan," *The New York Times,* March 16, 1985.
28. Lieutenant General Daniel O. Graham, USAF, "A New Age of Deterrence," letter to *The New York Times,* March 8, 1985, published by the *Times* on March 24, 1985.

2. Strengthening Deterrence

1. A. G. B. Metcalf, "The Minuteman Vulnerability Myth and the MX," editorial, *Strategic Review* (Spring, 1983), page 8.
2. A. G. B. Metcalf, editorial, *Strategic Review* (Spring, 1981).
3. Major General Warren E. Moore, USAF, former vice-director, NORAD, quoted by CBS Reports, "Ground Zero," in the series *The Defense of the United States,* June 14, 1981, transcript published by CBS News, 1981, pages 13–16; Department of Defense, *Annual Report, Fiscal Year 1979,* page 106, and *Annual Report, Fiscal Year 1981,* page 142; and Anthony H. Cordesman, Jr., "Deterrence in the 1980s: Part I," Adelphi Paper no. 175 (London: International Institute for Strategic Studies [IISS], 1982), page 23.
4. Office of Technology Assessment, *The Effects of Nuclear War,* Congress of the United States, Washington, D.C., 1979, page 44.
5. Ashton B. Carter and David N. Schwartz, eds., *Ballistic Missile Defense* (Washington, D.C.: Brookings Institution, 1984), page 163.
6. Peter Pringle and William Arkin, *S.I.O.P. The Secret U.S. Plan for Nuclear War* (New York: Norton, 1983), page 186.
7. *Strategic Review, 1980–1981* (London: IISS, 1981), page 15. For the number of weapons, see Appendix A: The Strategic Balance: Summary and Analysis.
8. *Ibid.* For the number of weapons, see Appendix A: The Strategic Balance: Summary and Analysis.
9. *Ibid.* For the number of weapons, see Appendix A: The Strategic Balance: Summary and Analysis.
10. William Safire, "Degrading Gracefully," *The New York Times,* March 21, 1985.
11. Kosta Tsipis, *Arsenal: Understanding Weapons in the Nuclear Age* (New York, Simon & Schuster, 1983), pages 212–239.
12. *Ibid.,* pages 238–239.
13. Congressional Budget Office, *Modernizing U.S. Strategic Offensive Forces,* Washington, D.C., May, 1983, pages 61 and 104–105.
14. Report of the President's Commission on Strategic Forces, quoted by Leslie H. Gelb, "MX Report: Dogma Ends," *The New York Times,* April 12, 1983.
15. Coalition for Peace Through Strength, Position Paper, excerpts published by *The New York Times,* April 12, 1979.
16. Joyce E. Larson and William C. Bodie, *The Intelligent Layperson's Guide to the Nuclear Freeze and Peace Debate* (New York: National Strategy Information Center, 1983), page 16.
17. Zbigniew Brzezinski, Robert Jastrow, and Max Kampelman, "Defense in Space Is Not 'Star Wars,' " *The New York Times Magazine,* January 27, 1985, page 29.
18. Ronald Reagan, quoted by Robert Scheer in *With Enough Shovels* (New York: Random House, 1982), page 241.
19. Brzezinski, Jastrow, and Kampelman, *op. cit.,* January 27, 1985, page 29.
20. Center for Defense Information, *The Defense Monitor,* Volume IX, no. 8 (1980), page 6.
21. Robert McNamara, quoted by Robert E. Kuenne in *The Polaris Missile Strike* (Columbus, Ohio: Ohio State University Press, 1966), page 20.
22. Brzezinski, Jastrow, and Kampelman, *op. cit.,* January 27, 1985, page 28.
23. Thomas J. Downey, letter to *The New York Times Magazine,* published March 10, 1985, page 118.
24. Center for Defense Information, *The Defense Monitor,* Volume IX, no. 8 (1980), page 4.
25. See the separate table, *Characteristics of United States and Soviet Submarine-Launched Ballistic Missiles,* in Appendix A: The Strategic Balance. See also John M. Collins, *U.S.-Soviet Military*

Balance, 1960–1980 (New York: McGraw-Hill, 1980), page 453; and *Aviation Week & Space Technology,* June 16, 1980, page 91.

26. See the separate table, *Characteristics of United States and Soviet Intercontinental Ballistic Missiles,* in Appendix A: The Strategic Balance. See also the Congressional Budget Office, *op. cit.,* May, 1983, page 90; Fred Kaplan, *Dubious Specter* (Washington, D.C.: Institute for Policy Studies, 1980), page 90; and Robert Aldridge, *First Strike!* (Boston: South End Press, 1983), pages 59 and 60.

27. House Armed Services Committee, *Authorization Hearings, Fiscal Year 1979* (Washington, D.C.: United States Congress, Part 3, Book 1), page 307. See also George Wilson, *The Washington Post,* April 17, 1982.

28. See the separate table, *Nuclear Weapons Deliverable by United States Strategic Bombers,* in Appendix A: The Strategic Balance. See also the Congressional Budget Office, *op. cit.,* May, 1983, page 86.

29. *Ibid.* See also House International Relations and Senate Foreign Relations Committees, *Analysis of Arms Control Impact Statement Submitted in Connection with the Fiscal Year 1978 Budget Request,* a joint publication (Washington, D.C.: United States Congress, April, 1977), page 83.

30. See the separate table, *Maximum Lethality,* in Appendix D: The Quest for Certainty: The Future of Nuclear Weapons.

31. Downey, letter to the *The New York Times Magazine,* March 10, 1985.

32. Sidney Lens, *The Day Before Doomsday* (Boston: Beacon Press, 1978), page 204.

33. William Safire, "The New Strategic Reality: MAD is Dead," *The New York Times,* March 11, 1985.

34. Center for Defense Information, *The Defense Monitor,* Volume X, no. 1 (1981), page 6.

35. Union of Concerned Scientists, *Space-Based Missile Defense* (Cambridge, Mass.: March, 1984), page 3.

36. Bill Keller, "Weinberger Backs Antimissile Plan," *The New York Times,* April 12, 1985.

37. Wayne Biddle, "Pentagon Scientist Backtracked at Secret Hearing on Space Arms," *The New York Times,* December 22, 1984.

38. Hedrick Smith, "U.S. Presses Soviet for Big Reduction in Its ICBM Force," *The New York Times,* June 22, 1983; and Serge Scheman, "Soviet Asserts U.S. Seeks Edge in Arms," *The New York Times,* July 12, 1983.

39. Leslie H. Gelb, "Soviet General Amplifies Offer of 25% Arms Cut," *The New York Times,* July 10, 1985.

40. Bernard Gwertzman, "Soviet Plan: U.S. Reacts," *The New York Times,* October 5, 1985; and *Time* magazine, "Reagan Makes a New Offer," November 11, 1985, page 19.

41. Seth Mydans, "Soviet to Stop Atomic Tests; It Bids U.S. Do Same," *The New York Times,* July 30, 1985.

42. *The New York Times,* "U.S. Officials Say 2 Key Projects Require More Atomic Tests," July 30, 1985.

43. *Treaty Banning Nuclear Weapons Tests in the Atmosphere, in Outer Space and Under Water,* Article I, Paragraph 2; and *Treaty on Principles Governing the Activities of States in the Exploration and Use of Outer Space, Including the Moon and Other Celestial Bodies,* Article V, in United States Arms Control and Disarmament Agency, *Arms Control and Disarmament Agreements, 1982 Edition,* Washington, D.C., 1982, pages 41 and 52.

44. *Treaty Between the United States of America and the Union of Soviet Socialist Republics on the Limitation of Anti-Ballistic Missile Systems,* Article V, United States Arms Control and Disarmament Agency, *op. cit.,* 1982, page 140.

45. Bernard Gwertzman, "Shultz Faults Moscow Arms Plan But Calls 'Real Progress' Possible, *The New York Times,* October 15, 1985; and *The New York Times,* "ABM Treaty: What It Says," October 16, 1985.

46. ABM Treaty, Articles XIII and XIV and Agreed Statement D, United States Arms Control and Disarmament Agency, *op. cit.,* 1982, pages 141–143.

47. Ronald Reagan, interview with Genrikh Borovik, Stanislav Kondrashov, Vsevolod Ovchinnikov

and Gennadi Shishkin, Washington, D.C., October 31, 1985; transcript published by *The New York Times,* November 5, 1985.

48. *Time* magazine, "Reagan Makes a New Offer," November 11, 1985, page 19.
49. Leslie H. Gelb, "Arms Accord: Elusive Goal," *The New York Times,* November 17, 1983.
50. *Time* magazine, *op. cit.,* November 11, 1985, page 19.
51. Gwertzman, *op. cit., The New York Times,* October 15, 1985.
52. William Safire, "Shield-Sharing," *The New York Times,* November 14, 1985.
53. *Ibid.*
54. *Ibid.*
55. Ronald Reagan, Voice of America radio address, November 9, 1985; transcript published by *The New York Times,* November 10, 1985.

3. Limiting the Framework of Debate

1. Gordon Adams and Laura Weiss, "Military Spending Boosts the Deficit," *Bulletin of the Atomic Scientists* (April, 1985), pages 26–27.
2. Office of Management and the Budget, *Historical Tables, Budget of the US Government, FY 1986,* reprinted by the Defense Budget Project, *The Fiscal Year 1986 Defense Budget: The Weapons Buildup Continues* (Washington, D.C.: Center on Budget and Policy Priorities, April, 1985), page 49.
3. Adams and Weiss, *op. cit.,* page 26.
4. Keith Sinzinger, *In These Times,* February 20, 1985.
5. Jim Wright, quoted by James Reston, "What's 'Security' Anyway?" *The New York Times,* March 24, 1985.
6. Tom Wicker, "A Riverboat Gamble," *The New York Times,* April 9, 1985.
7. Congressional Budget Office, figures quoted by Ed Glennon, "Battle of the Budget Begins," *Sane World Newsletter* (January, 1984), page 3; and Adams and Weiss, *op. cit.,* page 26.
8. Anthony Lewis, "In the Emerald City," *The New York Times,* March 24, 1985.
9. William Greider, "The Education of David Stockman," *The Atlantic Monthly* (December, 1981).

4. Rearming America

1. George W. S. Kuhn, quoted by William Greider, "Arms for the Poor," *Rolling Stone,* March 3, 1983, page 9.
2. Richard Halloran, "Contractor Penalties Harsher," *The New York Times,* March 29, 1985.
3. Jeff Gerth, "Inefficiency Laid to Weapon Makers," *The New York Times,* March 24, 1985.
4. Report of the President's Private Sector Survey on Cost Control, Washington, D.C., June 30, 1983, quoted by B. Drummond Ayres, Jr., "Panel Offers Government a Plan on Saving $137 Billion in Outlays," *The New York Times,* July 1, 1983. See also Jonathan Alter and Mary Lord, "Cutting Waste at the Pentagon," *Newsweek,* July 11, 1983, pages 24–25; and J. Peter Grace, "How to Cut $100 Billion from Defense" in *Burning Money: The Waste of Your Tax Dollars* (New York: Macmillan, 1984), pages 88–102.
5. A. Ernest Fitzgerald, quoted by Charles Mohr, "Subpoenaed Official Aide Assails Pentagon on High Military Costs," *The New York Times,* June 26, 1984.
6. Halloran, *op. cit.,* March 29, 1985.
7. Jonathan Fuerbringer, "Senate Committee Votes for Ceiling on Military Funds," *The New York Times,* March 6, 1985.
8. Associated Press, "Pentagon Announces Record Rise of $114 Billion in Weapons Costs," published by *The New York Times,* March 20, 1982.
9. Murray L. Weidenbaum "The Cynics Were Right: Reagan Still Can't Hold Spending Down," *The New York Times,* February 6, 1983.

10. Joseph Sherick, quoted by Richard Halloran, *op. cit.,* March 29, 1985.
11. Defense Budget Project, *Weapons vs. Readiness* (Washington, D.C.: Center for Budget and Policy Priorities, October 4, 1983).
12. David Stockman, quoted by William Greider, *op. cit.*
13. See the separate table, *The Balance of Deliverable Strategic Warheads, 1979–85,* in Appendix A: The Strategic Balance.
14. Center for Defense Information, *The Defense Monitor,* Volume IX, no. 8 (1980), page 10.
15. National Security Decision Directive 84 on Safeguarding National Security Information, signed by President Reagan on March 11, 1983.
16. Representative Jack Brooks, chairman, House Committee on Government Operations, interview with author, December 19, 1984.
17. Frank C. Conahan, "Polygraph and Prepublication Review Policies of Federal Agencies" (GAO/ NSIAD-84-134), a report submitted to Representative Jack Brooks by the Director, General Accounting Office, National Security and International Affairs Division, Washington, D.C., June 11, 1984, pages 2 and 7.
18. *Ibid.*

5. Exploiting Conventional Wisdom

1. William Arkin, address to the Boston Roundtable on "Security, the War System and Peace Mobilization," Boston, August, 1984, transcribed by The Nation Institute, New York.
2. *Ibid.*
3. Richard L. Garwin, interviewed on "This Week with David Brinkley," ABC-TV, March 10, 1985.
4. See the separate table, *Chronology of Initiatives in the Strategic Arms Race,* in Appendix E: The Strategic Arms Race: The Record Since 1945.
5. See *ibid.*
6. Garwin, *ref. cit.,* March 10, 1985.

6. Ignoring the Real Danger

1. Admiral Noel Gayler, "The Way Out: A General Nuclear Settlement," in *The Nuclear Crisis Reader* (New York: Vintage Books, 1984), page 235.
2. See the separate table, *Chronology of Initiatives in the Strategic Arms Race,* in Appendix E: The Strategic Arms Race: The Record Since 1945.
3. See *ibid.* Also *Aviation Week & Space Technology,* "News Digest," December 20, 1982, page 25; Samuel Freedman, "Nuclear Deterrence as Neighbor," *The New York Times,* December 17, 1982; and Richard G. O'Lone, "ALCMs Delivered Ahead of Schedule," *Aviation Week & Space Technology,* January 17, 1983, page 101.
4. Arthur Macy Cox, "End the War Game," *The New York Times,* November 8, 1983.
5. Carl Sagan, "Nuclear War and Climatic Catastrophe: Some Policy Implications," *Foreign Affairs,* Volume 62, no. 2 (Winter, 1983–84), page 292. Sagan writes: "There is a real danger of the extinction of humanity." Also see Paul R. Ehrlich, Carl Sagan, Donald Kennedy, and Walter Orr Roberts, *The Cold and the Dark* (New York: Norton, 1984), pages 22–23, 166–167, and 188, note 2.
6. Daniel Ford, "The Button—II: A Reporter At Large," *The New Yorker,* April 8, 1985, pages 63, 89.
7. *Ibid.,* page 59.
8. Paul Bracken, *The Command and Control of Nuclear Forces* (New Haven, Conn.: Yale University Press, 1983), pages 236–237.
9. *Ibid.*
10. *Ibid.,* page 237.

11. Daniel Ellsberg, "First Strike," *Inquiry Magazine*, April 13, 1981, page 14.
12. General Curtis E. LeMay, quoted by D. A. Rosenberg, "A Smoking Radiating Ruin at the End of Two Hours," *International Security* (Winter, 1981–82), page 27.
13. Defense Secretary Donald Rumsfeld, *Annual Report, Fiscal Year 1978*, Department of Defense, January 17, 1977, pages 76–79.
14. Ford, *op. cit.*, April 8, 1985, page 53.
15. *Ibid.*, page 49.
16. *Ibid.*, page 63.

7. The Dynamics of the Arms Race

1. John Kenneth Galbraith, "The Military Power," in *The Nuclear Crisis Reader*, page 199.
2. Jeff Gerth, "Contract Savings by U.S. Questioned," *The New York Times*, May 2, 1985.
3. *Ibid.*
4. Jeff Gerth, "U.S. Weapons Makers Ring Up Healthy Profits," *The New York Times*, April 9, 1985.
5. *Ibid.*
6. Morris Amchan, "Congress Should Act on Weapons Profiteering," letter to *The New York Times*, April 1, 1985, published April 9, 1985.
7. *Ibid.*
8. Weidenbaum, *op. cit.*, February 6, 1983.
9. Wayne Biddle, "Records Released in Dynamics Case," *The New York Times*, July 26, 1984.
10. Jeff Gerth, "Pentagon Barring General Electric from Future Jobs," *The New York Times*, March 29, 1985.
11. Halloran, *op. cit.*, March 19, 1985.
12. Wayne Biddle, "45 of 100 Biggest Contractors Being Investigated, U.S. Says," *The New York Times*, April 25, 1985.
13. Halloran, *op. cit.*, March 29, 1985; and Gerth, *op. cit.*, May 2, 1985.

8. Enforcing Political Consensus

1. Congressional Budget Office, *Defense Spending and the Economy*, February, 1983, page 4.
2. Coalition for a New Foreign and Military Policy, figures quoted by J. J. Joseph, "The Economic Impact of Military Spending," in Paul Joseph and Simon Rosenblum, eds., *Search for Sanity: The Politics of Nuclear Weapons and Disarmament* (Boston: South End Press, 1984), page 254.
3. American Forces Information Service, "Top Defense Contractors," in *Defense 81* and *Defense 82*, Arlington, Va. (September, 1981) and (September, 1982).
4. *Mother Jones* (September–October, 1982), page 12.
5. Employment Research Associates, Lansing, Mich., figures quoted by Thomas C. Hayes, "Pentagon Spends More in Fewer Districts, Researcher Says," *The New York Times*, August 13, 1984.
6. Bureau of Labor Statistics, Washington, D.C., February 4, 1983.
7. Donna A. Demac, *Keeping America Uninformed: Government Secrecy in the 1980s* (New York: Pilgrim Press, 1984).

9. Exploiting the Myth in America

1. Howell Raines, "President Wants Moscow to Begin Negotiations by the End of June," *The New York Times*, May 10, 1982.
2. Defense Department Congressional testimony, figures quoted by *The New York Times* in "U.S. and Soviet Strategic Arsenals," May 2, 1982.
3. Center for Defense Information, *The Defense Monitor*, Volume X, no. 1 (1981), page 6.

10. Exploiting the Myth in Europe

1. See the separate table, *Chronology of Initiatives in the Strategic Arms Race,* in Appendix E: The Strategic Arms Race: The Record Since 1945.
2. Department of State, *Bulletin,* Volume 47, no. 1220, November 12, 1962, pages 741–743. See also Roger Hilsman, *To Move a Nation* (Garden City, N.Y.: Doubleday, 1967), page 220.
3. Graham T. Allison, *Essence of Decision: Explaining the Cuban Missile Crisis* (Boston: Little Brown, 1971), page 142.
4. Mikhail S. Gorbachev, address to the Communist Party Central Committee, April 23, 1985, distributed in translation by Tass and published as "Excerpts from Gorbachev Remarks to Central Committee," by *The New York Times,* April 24, 1985.
5. *Defense Electronics,* "International Report" (August, 1983), page 19.
6. Helmut Schmidt, the 1977 Alistair Buchan Memorial Lecture, London, October 28, 1977, reprinted in *Survival* (January–February, 1978), by the International Institute for Strategic Studies, London, pages 2 through 10.
7. Comptroller General of the United States, *Report to Congress: Comparison of the Pershing II with the Acquisition Plan Recommended by the Commission on Government Procurement,* PSAD-77-51 (Washington, D.C.: General Accounting Office, January 24, 1977), pages 16 and 17.
8. McGeorge Bundy, George F. Kennan, Robert S. McNamara, and Gerard Smith, "Nuclear Weapons and the Atlantic Alliance," *Foreign Affairs,* Volume 60, no. 4 (Spring, 1982), pages 753–768.

11. Disseminating the Myth

1. Raines, *op. cit.,* May 10, 1982.
2. Defense Department Congressional testimony, figures quoted by *The New York Times* in "U.S. and Soviet Strategic Arsenals," May 2, 1982.
3. François Mitterand, quoted by James Markham, "Mitterand, on Bonn Visit, Warns Against Efforts to Divide the West," *The New York Times,* January 21, 1983.

14. The Machinery of Coercion

1. Representative Les Aspin, "Judge Not by Numbers Alone," *Bulletin of the Atomic Scientists* (June, 1980), page 31; House Armed Services Committee, *Defense Department Appropriations, Fiscal Year 1981,* Part 4, Book 2, pages 1886–1887; Senate Appropriations Committee, *Defense Department Appropriations, Fiscal Year 1981,* Part 5, pages 1657–1658; and *Aviation Week & Space Technology,* November 30, 1981, page 54.
2. Congressional Budget Office, *Modernizing U.S. Strategic Offensive Forces,* May, 1983, page 61.
3. Ben H. Bagdikian, *The Media Monopoly* (Boston: Beacon Press, 1983).
4. On page 197 of Edward S. Herman's *The Real Terror Network,* the author shows that over a period of five and a half years, from the beginning of 1976 through the middle of 1981, *The New York Times* reported human rights abuses suffered by five prominent dissidents in the Soviet Union and Poland no fewer than 580 times, while it reported abuses suffered by eight dissidents of no lesser prominence in five countries outside the Soviet sphere of influence just 64 times. Abuses suffered by six additional dissidents of equal prominence in five other countries outside the Soviet sphere were not mentioned at all by the *Times* in this period. The five dissidents in the Soviet sphere were Alexander Ginzburg, Yuri Orlov, Andrei Sakharov, Anatoly Scharansky and Lech Walesa. Two of the fourteen dissidents in ten countries outside the Soviet sphere, El Salvador's Archbishop Oscar Romero and Guatemala's Father Stanley Rother, were murdered. Four more, El Salvador's Enrique Alvarez Cordova, Bolivia's Father Luis Espinel, Guatemala's Father Carlos Galvez and Uruguay's Zelmar Michelini, were both tortured and murdered.

16. Announcing the Myth

1. Ronald Reagan, news conference, Washington, D.C., March 31, 1982, text reprinted by *The New York Times,* April 1, 1982.
2. David Stockman, quoted by William Greider, "The Education of David Stockman," *The Atlantic Monthly* (December, 1981).
3. Robert Aldridge, "The Ultimate First Strike Weapon," *The Nation,* February 4, 1978, page 113.
4. Department of Defense, *Annual Report, Fiscal Year 1982,* January, 1981, page 53.
5. Anthony H. Cordesman and Benjamin F. Schemmer, "The Failure to Defend Defense," *Armed Forces Journal International* (March, 1983), pages 32 and 44.
6. Caspar Weinberger, quoted by Richard Halloran, "Weinberger Says the US Military Has 'Begun to Catch Up' to Soviet," *The New York Times,* March 10, 1983.
7. Department of Defense, *Soviet Military Power* (September, 1981), page 3.
8. Edward Teller, "Dangerous Myths About Nuclear Arms," *Reader's Digest* (November, 1982), page 139.

17. Misrepresenting the Balance of Strategic Power

1. Ronald Reagan, televised address, November 22, 1982, text reprinted by *The New York Times,* "Address to the Nation on Nuclear Strategy," November 23, 1982.
2. Ronald Reagan, address to the Veterans of Foreign Wars Convention, Chicago, August 18, 1980, quoted by Howell Raines, "Reagan Calls Arms Race Essential to Avoid a 'Surrender or Defeat,' " *The New York Times,* August 19, 1980.
3. Leslie H. Gelb, "Reagan and Military Balance: His Numbers Are Right But Nearly Irrelevant," *The New York Times,* November 24, 1982.
4. See the separate table, *The Strategic Arms Race: Operational Deployment of Strategic Weapons, 1945–83,* on pages 411–412.
5. Daniel O. Graham, letter on behalf of United States Defense Committee, February 15, 1983.
6. "Excerpts from Report of the Commission on Strategic Forces," *The New York Times,* April 12, 1983.
7. Hedrick Smith, "U.S. Presses Soviet for Big Reduction in Its ICBM Force," *The New York Times,* June 22, 1983; and Serge Scheman, "Soviet Asserts U.S. Seeks Edge in Arms," *The New York Times,* July 16, 1983.
8. Robert Aldridge, *First Strike!* (Boston: South End Press, 1983), page 96; and Thomas Cochran, William Arkin, and Milton Hoenig, *Nuclear Weapons Databook: Volume I* (Cambridge, Mass.: Ballinger, 1984), page 110.
9. Aldridge, *op. cit.,* page 126.
10. David Baker, *The Shape of Wars to Come* (New York: Stein & Day, 1981), page 48.
11. Bernard Fitzsimons, Bill Gunston, and Ian V. Hogg, *Illustrated Encyclopaedia of 20th Century Weapons and Warfare* (London: Purnell & Sons, 1967–78), Vol. 2, pages 190–192.
12. J. J. DiCerto, *Missile Base Beneath the Sea: The Story of Polaris* (New York: St. Martin's Press, 1967), page 7.
13. *SALT II Agreement,* Vienna, June 18, 1979, Article IV, Paragraph 9, Second Agreed Statement, U.S. Department of State, Selected Documents No. 12A, 1979, page 34.
14. *Ibid.,* Article IV, Paragraph 10, First Agreed Statement, and Paragraph 12, First Agreed Statement, U.S. Department of State, *op. cit.,* pages 35 and 36.
15. Cyrus R. Vance, letter to President Jimmy Carter, June 21, 1979, U.S. Department of State, *op. cit.,* page 7.
16. *SALT II Agreement,* Vienna, June 18, 1979, Article IV, Paragraph 10, First Agreed Statement, and Paragraph 12, First Agreed Statement, U.S. Department of State, *op. cit.,* pages 35 and 36.
17. *Ibid.,* pages 35 and 36.

18. Lieutenant Commander John Alexander, U.S. Navy, interview with author, January 18, 1983.
19. *SALT II Agreement,* Vienna, June 18, 1979, Article IV, Paragraph 10, First Agreed Statement, and Paragraph 12, First Agreed Statement, U.S. Department of State, *op. cit.,* pages 35 and 36.
20. Lieutenant General Alton D. Slay, quoted by Drew Middleton, *The New York Times,* October 10, 1977.
21. *Compliance with SALT I Agreements,* U.S. Department of State, Special Report No. 55, July, 1979, page 4.
22. Les Aspin, "The Verification of the SALT II Agreement," *Scientific American* (February, 1979), pages 38 and 43.
23. For a detailed discussion of how well our "national technical means" perform to monitor the Soviet Union's compliance with arms control agreements, and of how the Reagan administration has tried to minimize or obscure their performance, see the later sections in this book on *Violations of SALT II, Verification, On-Site Inspection, Telemetry, A Comprehensive Test Ban,* and *United States Military Satellite Systems.*
24. Harold Brown, "SALT II and the National Defense," address before the Council on Foreign Relations, New York, April 5, 1979, reprinted by U.S. Department of State, *SALT II: Two Views,* Current Policy No. 62, April, 1979, page 11.
25. Daniel O. Graham, "America's Strategy Gap," letter to *The New York Times,* published October 16, 1980.
26. See the later table, *Comparative Measures of Strategic Power: Independently Targetable Nuclear Weapons, Delivery Vehicles, Aggregate Throwweight and Aggregate Megatonnage of Soviet and American Strategic Forces—December, 1981 to December, 1982,* on page 329.
27. Paul Warnke, discussion with Eugene Rostow before the Association of the Bar of the City of New York, March, 1982, excerpts published by *The New York Times,* March 31, 1982.
28. See the later table, *Recapitulation: The Balance of Strategic Warheads, 1979–85,* on page 338.

18. Misrepresenting the Balance of Strategic Warheads

1. See the later table, *Comparative Measures of Strategic Power: Independently Targetable Nuclear Weapons, Delivery Vehicles, Aggregate Throwweight and Aggregate Megatonnage of Soviet and American Strategic Forces—December, 1981 to December, 1982,* on page 329.
2. Ronald Reagan, address to the Los Angeles World Affairs Council, Beverly Hills, March 30, 1983, reprinted by *The New York Times,* April 1, 1983.
3. Les Aspin, "Judge Not by Numbers Alone," *Bulletin of the Atomic Scientists* (June, 1980), page 31.
4. Cochran, Arkin, and Hoenig, *op. cit.,* page 151.
5. Congressional Budget Office, *Modernizing U.S. Strategic Offensive Forces,* May, 1983, page 61.
6. See the separate table, *Comparative Estimate of the Lethality of the Most Accurate ICBMs in American and Soviet Arsenals, 1979–83,* on page 380.
7. See *ibid.*
8. Fred Kaplan, *Dubious Specter* (Washington, D.C.: Institute for Policy Studies, 1980), page 88.
9. See the separate table, *Comparative Estimate of Additional Strategic Weapons of Very High Lethality in American and Soviet Arsenals, 1979–83,* on page 381.
10. House International Relations Committee and Senate Foreign Relations Committee, *Analysis of Arms Control Impact Statement Submitted in Connection with Fiscal Year 1978 Budget Request,* April, 1977, page 83.
11. See the separate table, *Summary: Author's Estimates of United States Strategic Warheads, 1979–83,* on page 318. For comparison, IISS, *The Military Balance, 1982–1983,* page 140, gives America's bomber force 2,348 weapons. Cochran, Arkin, and Hoenig, *op. cit.,* page 102, give the bomber force 2,580 weapons.

12. See the separate table, *Recapitulation: The Balance of Strategic Warheads, 1979–85,* on page 338.
13. Joint Chiefs of Staff, *Fiscal Year 1984 Military Posture Statement,* page 16.
14. *Ibid.*
15. Associated Press, "U.S. Adds Warheads to Poseidon Submarine Missiles," *The New York Times,* October 30, 1980.
16. Aldridge, *op. cit.,* page 44.
17. See sources for the separate table, *Characteristics of United States and Soviet Submarine-Launched Ballistic Missiles Deployed from 1979 Through 1983,* on page 301.
18. SIPRI, *The Arms Race and Arms Control* (London: Taylor & Francis, 1982), page 95.
19. Vice Admiral Robert L. Walters, Deputy Chief of Naval Operations, in testimony to the House Armed Services Committee, *Hearings,* March 4, 1982, page 5.
20. House Appropriations Committee, *Hearings, Defense Department Appropriations, Fiscal Year 1982,* Part 7, page 544.
21. House Armed Services Committee, *Authorization Hearings, Fiscal Year 1982,* Part 3, page 156.
22. See the separate table, *Chronology of Estimates of United States Missile Warheads, 1979–83,* on page 341.
23. Reagan administration officials, in a briefing before the President's address to the graduating class of Eureka College, Illinois, May 9, 1982. Reported by Howell Raines, "President Wants Moscow to Begin Negotiations by the End of June," *The New York Times,* May 10, 1982, and again by the *Times* in "Precise Arms Figures Difficult to Pin Down," May 10, 1982.
24. *The New York Times,* "Precise Arms Figures Difficult to Pin Down," May 10, 1982.
25. Les Aspin, "The Verification of the SALT II Agreement," *Scientific American* (February, 1979), page 41.
26. U.S. Department of State, *Verification of the SALT II Agreement,* Special Report No. 56, August, 1979, page 5.
27. Department of Defense, "U.S. and Soviet Strategic Arsenals," published by *The New York Times,* May 2, 1982, and again by the *Times* in "Precise Arms Figures Difficult to Pin Down," May 10, 1982. Sources given by the *Times* on May 2: "Pentagon publications, Congressional testimony." Sources given on May 10: "Pentagon Testimony and reports by the International Institute of Strategic Studies."
28. See the separate table, *Recapitulation: The Balance of Strategic Warheads, 1979–85,* on page 338.
29. Ronald Reagan, statement on the Report of the President's Commission on Strategic Forces, reprinted by *The New York Times,* April 20, 1983.
30. See the section, *Estimating the Strategic Balance: Missiles at Sea,* pages 296–300.
31. IISS, *The Military Balance, 1982–1983,* page 140.
32. See the section, *Estimating the Strategic Balance: Land-Based Missiles,* pages 288–289.
33. IISS, *The Military Balance, 1982–1983,* page 140, note b.
34. See the section, *Estimating the Strategic Balance: Land-Based Missiles.*
35. See the separate table, *Characteristics of Soviet and American Intercontinental Ballistic Missiles Deployed from 1979 Through 1983,* on page 290.
36. See *ibid.*
37. William M. Arkin and Jeffrey I. Sands, "The Soviet Nuclear Stockpile," *Arms Control Today,* Volume 14, no. 5 (June, 1984), pages 4 and 7.
38. *Ibid.,* page 4.
39. Department of Defense, *Soviet Military Power,* 1984, page 30.
40. Cochran, Arkin, and Hoenig, *op. cit.,* page 178, note 2.
41. Aldridge, *op. cit.,* page 151.
42. Department of Defense, *Soviet Military Power,* 1984, page 30.
43. Cochran, Arkin, and Hoenig, *op. cit.,* page 178, note 2.
44. IISS, *The Military Balance, 1983–1984,* page 119, gives 1,000 kilometers, the equivalent of 620 statute miles, as the maximum range for the Soviet SS-N-12 antiship cruise missile.

45. See the separate table, *Chronology of Estimates of United States Strategic Bomber Weapons, 1979–83,* on page 345.
46. See the author's estimates, *Minimum Number of United States Strategic Bomber Weapons,* and *Deliverable Weapons Capacity of United States Strategic Bombers,* in the section, *Estimating the Strategic Balance: Bombers,* on pages 309–310.
47. Department of Defense, *Soviet Military Power,* 1984, page 29.
48. James F. Dunnigan, *How to Make War* (New York: Morrow, 1982), page 116.
49. IISS, *The Military Balance, 1982–1983,* page 115.
50. See sources for the separate table, *Load Capacities of Soviet Bombers Equipped with Air-to-Surface Nuclear Standoff Missiles,* on page 311.
51. Bill Sweetman, *The Presidio Concise Guide to Soviet Military Aircraft* (Novato, Calif.: Presidio Press, 1981), page 175.
52. See the separate table, *Chronology of Estimates of Soviet Strategic Bombers and Bomber Weapons, 1979–83,* on page 346.
53. *Ibid.*
54. See the separate table, *Author's Estimate of Deliverable Weapons Capacity of Soviet Aircraft Equipped and Deployed as Intercontinental Strategic Bombers, 1979–83,* on page 316.
55. IISS, *The Military Balance, 1982–1983,* page 13.
56. *Jane's Pocket Book of Missiles,* edited by Ronald Pretty (New York: Macmillan, 1975), page 109.
57. William J. Koenig and Peter Scofield, *Soviet Military Power* (London: Bison, 1983), page 109.
58. Dunnigan, *op. cit.,* page 116.
59. See the separate table, *Load Capacities of Soviet Bombers Equipped with Air-to-Surface Nuclear Standoff Missiles,* on page 311.
60. SIPRI, *op. cit.,* 1982, page 95.
61. *Aviation Week & Space Technology,* September 13, 1976, page 13.
62. See the accompanying table, *Manipulating Perceptions of the Strategic Balance, 1975–83: The Reinterpretation of Range Characteristics to Qualify the Soviet Tu-22M Backfire as a Strategic Bomber, and to Disqualify the American FB-111A,* on page 106.
63. See the separate table, *Characteristics of United States and Soviet Aircraft Deployed as Intercontinental Strategic Bombers, 1979–83,* on page 312.
64. Cochran, Arkin, and Hoenig, *op. cit.,* page 153.
65. Department of Defense, *Annual Report, Fiscal Year 1979,* February, 1978, page 118, and IISS, *The Military Balance, 1983–1984,* page 4.
66. IISS, *op. cit., 1983–1984,* page 15.
67. House Appropriations Committee, *Energy and Water Development Appropriations, Fiscal Year 1985,* March 14, 1984, Part 6, page 118.
68. *Ibid.*
69. Rick Atkinson, "Soviets Leading in Warheads, Pentagon Claims in Reversal," *The Washington Post,* June 18, 1984.
70. Richard Halloran, "Soviets Said to Lead U.S. by 8,000 Warheads," *The New York Times,* June 18, 1984.
71. *Ibid.*
72. See separate tables, *United States Nuclear Weapons Stockpiled and Deployed, 1982–84,* and *Soviet Nuclear Weapons Stockpiled and Deployed, 1982–84,* on pages 416–428.
73. Arkin and Sands, *op. cit.,* page 1.
74. *Ibid.,* page 4.
75. *Ibid.,* page 5.

19. Disseminating the Myth

1. Ariela Gross, quoted in "President and a Student Indirectly Debate Arms," *The New York Times,* June 17, 1983.

2. Arkin and Sands, *op. cit.,* page 4.
3. Ronald Reagan, news conference, Washington, D.C., May 17, 1983, transcript published by *The New York Times,* May 18, 1983.
4. Milton Leitenberg, "The Numbers Game or 'Who's on First?' " *Bulletin of the Atomic Scientists* (June–July, 1982), page 28.
5. IISS, *The Military Balance, 1978–1979,* pages 3 and 4.
6. IISS, *The Military Balance, 1979–1980,* pages 3 and 4.
7. IISS, *The Military Balance, 1980–1981,* pages 3 and 4.
8. IISS, *The Military Balance, 1981–1982,* page 4.
9. *Ibid.,* page 3.
10. IISS, *The Military Balance, 1982–1983,* pages 3 and 140.
11. *Ibid.,* pages 11 and 140.
12. IISS, *The Military Balance, 1983–1984,* pages 3 and 4.
13. *The New York Times,* "Three Ways to Measure Nuclear Forces," March 21, 1982; "U.S. and Soviet Strategic Arsenals," May 2, 1982; "The Arms Race: A Nuclear Balance Sheet," June 29, 1982.
14. *The New York Times,* "Nuclear Missiles and Bombers: A Balance Sheet," December 22, 1982.
15. *The New York Times,* "Three Ways to Measure Nuclear Forces," March 21, 1982; "The Arms Race: A Nuclear Balance Sheet," June 29, 1982; "The Nuclear Balance Without MX," November 18, 1982.
16. *The New York Times,* "Precise Arms Figures Difficult to Pin Down," May 10, 1982.
17. *Ibid.*
18. Steven R. Weisman, "Cuing In the Press for a Big Speech," *The New York Times,* April 29, 1983.
19. Mark Hertsgaard, "How Reagan Seduced Us," *The Village Voice,* September 18, 1984, page 16.
20. Sally Bedell Smith, "Rather Cites White House Criticism," *The New York Times,* November 18, 1983.
21. *Ibid.*
22. *The Washington Post,* "Strategic Forces as of June 30, 1982," November 24, 1982.
23. Paul Newman, "Missile Count," letter published by *Newsweek,* March 14, 1983.
24. *Newsweek,* "The Negotiating Scorecard," January 31, 1983, pages 18 and 19.
25. *Ibid.*

20. The Myth of Soviet Missile Accuracy

1. Caspar W. Weinberger, press conference, Washington, D.C., April 14, 1982, quoted by *The New York Times,* April 15, 1982.
2. Anthony H. Cordesman, *Deterrence in the 1980s: Part I,* Adelphi Paper no. 175 (London: IISS, 1982), pages 24 and 25.
3. Michael Heylin, "Nuclear Arms Race Gearing for Speedup," *Chemical and Engineering News,* March 16, 1981, page 29.
4. Theodore H. White, "Weinberger on the Ramparts," *The New York Times Magazine,* February 6, 1983, page 17.
5. Clarence A. Robinson, Jr., "MX Basing Delay Threatens SALT Ratification," *Aviation Week & Space Technology,* November 20, 1978, page 22.
6. House Armed Services Committee, *Authorization Hearings, Fiscal Year 1979* (Washington, D.C.: United States Congress, Part 3, Book 1), page 307.
7. See the separate table, *Comparative Estimate of the Lethality of the Most Accurate ICBMs in American and Soviet Arsenals, 1979–83,* on page 380.
8. James Miller, Head, Defense Intelligence Agency Weapons and Systems Division, Senate Appropriations Committee Hearings, 1981, quoted by Joe Room and Kosta Tsipis, *Analysis of*

Dense Pack Vulnerabilities, MIT Program in Science and Technology for International Security, Report no. 8, November, 1982, note 17.

9. George Wilson, *The Washington Post,* April 17, 1982.
10. Herbert Scoville, Jr., *MX: Prescription for Disaster* (Cambridge, Mass.: MIT, 1981), page 15.
11. See the separate table, *Maximum Lethality: When the Radius of Assured Destruction Equals or Exceeds the Probable Radius of Error,* on page 386.
12. Eliot Marshal, "A Question of Accuracy," *Science* (September, 1981), page 1231.
13. See the separate table, *Maximum Lethality: When the Radius of Assured Destruction Equals or Exceeds the Probable Radius of Error,* on page 386.
14. See the separate table, *Chronology of Initiatives in the Strategic Arms Race,* on page 400.
15. Henry A. Kissinger, *Years of Upheaval* (Boston: Little Brown, 1982), page 1003.
16. Hans A. Bethe, Richard L. Garwin, Kurt Gottfried, and Henry W. Kendall, "Space-Based Ballistic-Missile Defense," *Scientific American* (October, 1984), page 49.
17. Ashton B. Carter, "Directed Energy Missile Defense in Space," Office of Technology Assessment, Washington, D.C., 1984.
18. George Rathjens, interview, CBS-TV News, March 30, 1983.

22. Contradictions in Declared Policy

1. "Excerpts from Report of the Commission on Strategic Forces," *The New York Times,* April 12, 1983.
2. Paul Nitze, quoted by Desmond Ball, "U.S. Strategic Forces: How Would They be Used?" *International Security,* Volume 17, no. 3 (Winter, 1982–83), pages 32–33. See also Robert Aldridge, "First Strike: The Pentagon's Secret Strategy," *The Nation* (May, 1978), page 16.

23. Extending Deterrence to Europe

1. Christoph Bertram, *America's Security in the 1980s: Part I,* Adelphi Paper no. 173 (London: IISS, 1982), page 3.
2. Earl C. Ravenal, "The Case for a Withdrawal of Our Forces," *The New York Times Magazine,* March 6, 1983, page 60.
3. *Report to Congress: Comparison of the Pershing II with the Acquisition Plan Recommended by the Commission on Government Procurement,* Comptroller General of the United States, PSAD-77-51, January 24, 1977 (Washington, D.C.: General Accounting Office), page 16.
4. *Ibid.,* page 17.
5. *Ibid.*
6. Arms Control and Disarmament Agency, *Fiscal Year 1979 Arms Control Impact Statement,* page 115.
7. International Report, *Defense Electronics* (August, 1983), page 19.
8. *Ibid.*
9. The Public Agenda Foundation and the Center for Foreign Policy Development, *Voter Options on Nuclear Arms Policy* (New York and Providence: Brown University, 1984), pages 22, 24, 34, and 36.
10. Ronald Reagan, debate with Walter Mondale, Kansas City, October 21, 1984, transcript published by *The New York Times,* October 22, 1984.
11. Sidney Lens, *The Day Before Doomsday* (Boston: Beacon Press, 1978), page 204.
12. Robert Aldridge, *First Strike!* (Boston: South End Press, 1983), page 143.

24. Justifying Deployment of the Cruise and *Pershing II*

1. David Whitman, *The Press and the Neutron Bomb,* Harvard College, Kennedy School of Government, Report no. C94-84-595, 1983, page 144.

2. *Ibid.,* pages 144–145.
3. Flora Lewis, "Deadline for NATO," *The New York Times,* March 4, 1983.
4. Department of State, "U.S. Program for Peace and Arms Control," Current Policy No. 346, Bureau of Public Affairs, November 18, 1981, page 5.
5. North Atlantic Treaty Organization, "NATO and the Warsaw Pact: Force Comparisons," 1982, page 55.
6. IISS, *The Military Balance, 1983–1984,* page 118.
7. *Time* magazine, January 31, 1983; *Newsweek,* January 31, 1983.
8. Anthony H. Cordesman, Jr., *Deterrence in the 1980s: Part I,* Adelphi Paper no. 175 (London: IISS, 1982), page 51.
9. Strobe Talbott, *Deadly Gambits: The Reagan Administration and the Stalemate in Nuclear Arms Control* (New York: Knopf, 1984), page 59.
10. Caspar Weinberger, letter to Theodore Draper, November 6, 1984, published in "Journalism, History and Journalistic History—An Exchange," *The New York Times Book Review,* December 16, 1984.
11. Helmut Schmidt, the 1977 Alastair Buchan Memorial Lecture, London, IISS, October 28, 1977, reprinted by IISS in *Survival* (January–February, 1978), page 4.
12. John Newhouse, "Arms and Allies: A Reporter At Large," *The New Yorker,* February 28, 1983, page 66.
13. *Ibid.*
14. Helmut Schmidt, quoted by Theodore Stanger, "A Talk with Schmidt," *Newsweek,* May 30, 1983, page 68.
15. Ronald Reagan, news conference, Washington, D.C., February 16, 1983, transcript published by *The New York Times,* February 17, 1983.
16. James Reston, "The Two Dangers," *The New York Times,* February 13, 1983.
17. Stephen J. Solarz, "NATO Must Be Ready to Deploy the Missiles," *The New York Times,* January 9, 1983.
18. See the table, *Chronology of Initiatives in the Nuclear Arms Race,* in Appendix E: The Strategic Arms Race.
19. *The New York Times,* "Euromissile Facts and Feints," editorial, February 27, 1983.
20. Alexander Cockburn, "Lunchtime O'Perle," Press Clips, *The Village Voice,* June 14, 1983. See also Fred Kaplan, *The Boston Globe,* June 2, 1983.
21. Richard Burt, "West Is Considering Missile for Europe Able to Hit Soviet," *The New York Times,* January 20, 1979.
22. Bernard Gwertzman, "Reagan Offers 4-Point Plan for U.S.-Soviet Missile Curbs and Force Limits in Europe," *The New York Times,* November 19, 1981.
23. Gwertzman, *ibid.*

25. Refining Declared Policy

1. Department of State, "Arms Control and NATO INF Modernization," Gist, Bureau of Public Affairs, July, 1982.
2. Ronald Reagan, address to the National Press Club, Washington, D.C., November 18, 1981, text reprinted by *The New York Times,* November 19, 1981.
3. IISS, *The Military Balance, 1983–1984,* page 119.
4. Department of State, *op. cit.,* July, 1982.
5. *Ibid.*
6. Ronald Reagan, address to the National Press Club, Washington, D.C., November 18, 1981, text reprinted by *The New York Times,* November 19, 1981.
7. Department of State, "U.S. Program for Peace and Arms Control," Current Policy No. 346, Bureau of Public Affairs, November 18, 1981, page 5.

8. Richard Halloran, "U.S. Says Soviet Plans to Increase Warheads Aimed at West Europe," *The New York Times,* October 15, 1979.

9. Anthony H. Cordesman, Jr., *Deterrence in the 1980s: Part I,* Adelphi Paper no. 175 (London: IISS, 1982), page 51; James F. Dunnigan, *How to Make War* (New York: Morrow, 1982), page 305.

10. *Jane's Weapon Systems, 1981–1982* (London: Jane's, 1981), page 7.

11. John M. Collins, *U.S.-Soviet Military Balance: Concepts and Capabilities, 1960–1980* (New York: McGraw-Hill, 1980), page 461.

12. *Jane's, op. cit.,* page 7.

13. Department of Defense, *Soviet Military Power* (September, 1981), page 31, and (March, 1983), page 35; North Atlantic Treaty Organization, "NATO and the Warsaw Pact: Force Comparisons," 1982, page 49; and Gunther Gillesen, "Countering Soviet Nuclear Supremacy in Europe," *NATO Review,* 1982, page 21.

14. SIPRI, *The Arms Race and Arms Control* (London: Taylor & Francis, 1982), page 144; Carnegie Panel on U.S. Security and the Future of Arms Control, *Challenges for U.S. National Security,* "Nuclear Strategy Issues for the 1980s: Theatre Nuclear Forces, A Third Report," Carnegie Endowment for International Peace, 1982, page 145.

15. *The New York Times,* "Theater Nuclear Weapons in Europe," November 30, 1981; *Time* magazine, "A Trio to Tax Any Negotiations," January 31, 1983, page 12; *Newsweek,* "Europe's Nuclear Imbalance," May 16, 1983, page 27; and "The Nuclear Landscape," October 24, 1983, page 38.

16. *The New York Times,* "Theater Nuclear Weapons in Europe," November 30, 1981.

17. *Jane's Weapon Systems, 1983–1984* (London: Jane's, 1983), page 25.

18. Collins, *op. cit.,* page 461.

19. IISS, *The Military Balance, 1981–1982,* page 105.

20. IISS, *The Military Balance, 1982–1983,* page 113; *The Military Balance, 1983–1984,* page 119.

21. IISS, *The Military Balance, 1983–1984,* page 119.

22. *Ibid.*

23. Ronald Reagan, address to the National Press Club, Washington, D.C., November 18, 1981, transcript published by *The New York Times,* November 19, 1981.

24. Bernard Fitzsimons, Bill Gunston, and Ian V. Hogg, *Illustrated Encyclopaedia of 20th Century Weapons and Warfare* (London: Purnell & Sons, 1967–78), Vol. 14, pages 1531–1532, and Vol. 23, pages 2488–2489.

25. Joint Committee on Atomic Energy, *The Study of US and NATO Nuclear Arrangements,* February 11, 1961, quoted by Defense Secretary Robert S. McNamara in testimony before Senate Committee on Armed Services, and published by the Committee in *Military Procurement Authorization, Fiscal Year 1964,* 88th Congress, 1st Session, 1963, page 7.

26. Fitzsimons, Gunston, and Hogg, *op. cit.,* Vol. 14, pages 1531–1532.

27. *Ibid.,* Vol. 23, pages 2488–2489.

28. Union of Concerned Scientists, "Euromissiles: The Military Flaws," *Braking Point,* Volume 2, no. 1 (Fall, 1983), page 2.

29. Randall Forsberg, "A Bilateral Nuclear-Weapon Freeze," *Scientific American* (November, 1982), page 59.

30. IISS, *The Military Balance, 1979–1980,* page 115.

31. *Ibid.*

32. Joint Chiefs of Staff, *Fiscal Year 1984 Military Posture Statement,* page 16.

33. Forsberg, *op. cit.,* page 59.

34. Vice Admiral Robert L. Walters, Deputy Chief of Naval Operations, in testimony to the House Armed Services Committee, *Hearings,* March 4, 1982, page 5; House Appropriations Committee, *Hearings, Defense Department Appropriations, Fiscal Year 1982,* Part 7, page 544; House Armed Services Committee, *Authorization Hearings, Fiscal Year 1982,* Part 3, page 156.

35. Department of Defense, *Annual Report, Fiscal Year 1979,* page 133.

36. IISS, *The Military Balance, 1981–1982,* page 129, note u, and *1982–1983,* page 137, note u.
37. Carnegie Panel on U.S. Security and the Future of Arms Control, *Challenges for U.S. National Security,* "Nuclear Strategy Issues for the 1980s: Theatre Nuclear Forces, A Third Report," Carnegie Endowment for International Peace, 1982, page 141.
38. Frank Blackaby, "World Arsenals, 1982," *Bulletin of the Atomic Scientists* (June–July, 1982), page 24; SIPRI, *op. cit.,* 1982, pages 144 and 243.
39. *The New York Times,* "Two Views of Theater Nuclear Forces in Europe," November 22, 1981; "Theater Nuclear Weapons in Europe," November 30, 1981; "Theater Arms: A Nuclear Balance Sheet," December 12, 1982.
40. Strobe Talbott, "Playing Nuclear Poker," *Time* magazine, January 31, 1983, pages 9–23.
41. *The New York Times,* "Theater Nuclear Weapons in Europe," November 30, 1981; and "Theater Arms: A Nuclear Balance Sheet," December 12, 1982.
42. *Newsweek,* "Europe's Nuclear Imbalance," May 16, 1983, page 27.
43. *Newsweek,* "European Theater Nuclear Arms," October 24, 1983, page 38.
44. François Mitterand, quoted by James Markham, "Mitterand, on Bonn Visit, Warns Against Efforts to Divide the West," *The New York Times,* January 21, 1983.
45. *Ibid.*
46. IISS, *The Military Balance, 1981–1982,* page 128, and *The Military Balance, 1982–1983,* page 136.
47. *Newsweek,* "European Theater Nuclear Arms," October 24, 1983, page 38.
48. *The New York Times,* "Theater Nuclear Weapons in Europe," November 30, 1981; and "Theater Arms: A Nuclear Balance Sheet," December 12, 1982.
49. *The New York Times,* "Theater Nuclear Weapons in Europe," November 30, 1981; "The Arms Race: A Nuclear Balance Sheet," June 29, 1982; and "Theater Arms: A Nuclear Balance Sheet," December 12, 1982.
50. Drew Middleton, "Wide Range of Arms Likely to Be Involved in the Negotiations," *The New York Times,* November 30, 1981.
51. Leslie H. Gelb, "Moscow Indicates Easing of Stance on Cuts in Missiles," *The New York Times,* December 12, 1982.
52. See the separate table, *Characteristics of NATO and Warsaw Pact Long- and Medium-Range Ballistic Missiles Deployed Against European Theater Targets from 1979 Through 1983,* on page 438.
53. Department of State, "U.S. Program for Peace and Arms Control," Current Policy No. 346, Bureau of Public Affairs, November 18, 1981, page 5.
54. Gillesen, *op. cit.,* page 21.
55. See the separate table, *NATO and Warsaw Pact Theater Nuclear Weapons Stockpiled and Deployed, 1982–84,* on page 437.
56. Department of State, *op. cit.,* Current Policy No. 346, November 18, 1981, page 5; IISS, *The Military Balance, 1981–1982,* pages 105 and 128.
57. IISS, *op. cit., 1981–1982,* page 129.
58. *Jane's Weapon Systems, 1981–1982,* page 7.
59. IISS, *The Military Balance, 1983–1984,* page 123.
60. Richard Halloran, "Weinberger Says the U.S. Military Has 'Begun to Catch Up' to Soviet," *The New York Times,* March 10, 1983.
61. IISS, *The Military Balance, 1982–1983,* page 113.
62. House Armed Services Committee, *Authorization Hearings, Department of Defense, Fiscal Year 1983,* Part 3, pages 762 and 764.
63. *Ibid.,* Part 3, pages 762 and 764.
64. Department of Defense, *Fiscal Year 1980 Program of Research, Development and Acquisition,* page VII-8.
65. *Ibid.*
66. Department of Defense, *Annual Report, Fiscal Year 1980,* page 137; Arms Control and Disarmament Agency, *Fiscal Year 1982 Arms Control Impact Statement;* and see also sources for separate table, *United States Nuclear Weapons Stockpiled and Deployed, 1982–84.*

67. See the separate table, *NATO and Warsaw Pact Theater Nuclear Weapons Stockpiled and Deployed, 1982–84*, on page 437.

68. IISS, *The Military Balance, 1983–1984*, page 122.

69. *Jane's Weapon Systems, 1981–1982*, page 10.

70. *Ibid.*

71. Anthony H. Cordesman, Jr., "France's New Defense: The Economics of Going Nuclear," *Armed Forces Journal International* (February, 1983), pages 21–24; *Defense and Foreign Affairs*, "En Clair" (April, 1982); and John Vinocur, "France Deploys 9 New Nuclear Missiles," *The New York Times*, January 29, 1983.

72. Joint Chiefs of Staff, *Fiscal Year 1982 Military Posture Statement*, page 78.

73. See the separate table, *Characteristics of NATO and Warsaw Pact Long- and Medium-Range Ballistic Missiles Deployed Against European Theater Targets from 1979 Through 1983*, on page 438.

74. SIPRI, *op. cit.*, 1982, page 150.

75. IISS, *The Military Balance, 1981–1982*, pages 13 and 128.

76. *Ibid.*, pages 11 and 128.

77. *Ibid.*, page 11.

78. *Ibid.*, page 13.

79. J. Erickson, "Soviet Theatre Warfare Capability," in L. L. Whetten, ed., *The Future of Soviet Military Power*, quoted by David Hazel in "The Sudden Attack Debate: Arguments and Alternatives," *Journal of the Royal United Services Institute* (December, 1978).

80. Collins, *op. cit.*, pages 540, 550, and 552.

81. William J. Lewis, *The Warsaw Pact: Arms, Doctrine, and Strategy* (New York: McGraw-Hill, 1982), pages 67 and 71.

82. *Ibid.*, page 71.

83. Collins, *op. cit.*, pages 540, 550, and 552.

84. IISS, *The Military Balance, 1981–1982*, page 129, note d.

85. *Ibid.*

86. Phillip A. Petersen, Assistant for Europe, Policy Support Program, Office of the Deputy Under Secretary of Defense for Policy, in *Armed Forces Journal International* (August, 1984), page 52.

87. IISS, *The Military Balance, 1981–1982*, pages 108 and 107; *Ibid.*, pages 128–129, "Warheads per System" column.

88. *Ibid.*, pages 107 and 108; *Ibid.*, pages 128–129, "Warheads per System" column.

89. *Ibid.*, page 129, "Warheads per System" column; and Thomas B. Cochran, William M. Arkin, and Milton M. Hoenig, *Nuclear Weapons Databook: Volume I* (Cambridge, Mass.: Ballinger, 1984), page 216.

90. IISS, *The Military Balance, 1984–1985*, page 132; *Ibid.*, page 131; IISS, *The Military Balance, 1981–1982*, pages 128–129, "Warheads per System" column.

91. IISS, *The Military Balance, 1984–1985*, page 135.

92. IISS, *The Military Balance, 1981–1982*, page 129, note d; *Ibid.*, page 128, "Inventory" and "Utilization" columns.

93. *Ibid.*, page 129, "Inventory" column and "Air-delivered weapon sub-totals," and pages 10, 27, through 39, and 44.

94. *Ibid.*, page 129, note s; *Ibid.*, pages 106, and 110, note e.

95. *Ibid.*, page 8.

96. *Ibid.*, page 129, "Utilization" column.

97. *Ibid.*, pages 128–129, "Inventory," "Warheads per System," and "Utilization" columns.

98. See sources for the separate tables, *Weapons Carried by Nuclear Strike Aircraft in Europe, 1981–82*, on pages 430–434.

99. See the separate tables, *Weapons Carried by Nuclear Strike Aircraft in Europe, 1981–82*, on pages 430–434, and *NATO and Warsaw Pact Theater Nuclear Weapons Stockpiled and Deployed, 1982–84*, on page 437.

100. IISS, *The Military Balance, 1981–1982,* page 128, "Inventory" column and "Air-delivered weapon sub-totals."
101. *Ibid.,* pages 10, 27 through 39, and 44; and page 129, "Inventory" column and "Air-delivered weapon sub-totals."
102. *Ibid.,* page 128, "Utilization" column.
103. IISS, *The Military Balance, 1982–1983,* pages 136–137.
104. See the separate table, *NATO and Warsaw Pact Theater Nuclear Weapons Stockpiled and Deployed, 1982–84,* on page 437.
105. See *ibid.*
106. Department of Defense, *Annual Report, Fiscal Year 1979,* page 133.
107. Department of Defense, *Soviet Military Power, 1984,* page 75.
108. Anthony H. Cordesman, Jr., "Whence the Threat to Peace? The Soviet View of the Threat," *Armed Forces Journal International* (April, 1983).
109. *The New York Times,* "Theater Nuclear Weapons in Europe," November 30, 1981; *The New York Times,* "Theater Arms: A Nuclear Balance Sheet," December 12, 1982.
110. *Newsweek,* "Europe's Nuclear Imbalance," May 16, 1983, page 27.
111. *Newsweek,* "European Theater Nuclear Arms," October 24, 1983, page 38.
112. William J. Koenig, *Weapons of World War 3* (London: Bison, 1981), page 114.
113. Department of Defense, *Soviet Military Power, 1984,* page 53.
114. *Ibid.,* page 75.
115. IISS, *The Military Balance, 1982–1983,* page 115, and *The Military Balance, 1983–1984,* page 121; and David C. Isby, *Weapons and Tactics of the Soviet Army* (London: Jane's, 1981), pages 176–177 and 199–202.
116. See sources for the separate table, *United States Nuclear Weapons Stockpiled and Deployed, 1982–84,* on pages 416–422.
117. See sources for the separate tables, *NATO and Warsaw Pact Theater Nuclear Weapons Stockpiled and Deployed, 1982–84,* on pages 435–437, and *United States Nuclear Weapons Stockpiled and Deployed, 1982–84,* on pages 416–422.
118. See the separate table, *NATO and Warsaw Pact Theater Nuclear Weapons Stockpiled and Deployed, 1982–84,* on page 437.

26. The Balance of Ground Forces in Europe

1. Gordon Adams and Laura Weiss, "Military Spending Boosts the Deficit," *Bulletin of the Atomic Scientists* (April, 1985), pages 26–27.
2. Sam Nunn, John D. Warner, J. James Exon, William L. Armstrong, Bill Chappell, Les Aspin, Ike Skelton, and Newt Gingrich, in the Foreword to John M. Collins, *U.S.-Soviet Military Balance 1980–1985* (McLean, Va.: Pergamon-Brassey's, 1985), page xvii.
3. *Ibid.,* page xvii.
4. *The New York Times,* "Soviet Found Ahead in Arms," July 28, 1985.
5. NATO Information Service, *NATO and the Warsaw Pact: Force Comparisons,* Brussels, 1982, page 9.
6. *Ibid.,* page 68.
7. David C. Isby, *Weapons and Tactics of the Soviet Army* (London: Jane's, 1981), page 27.
8. Department of Defense, *Soviet Military Power* (March, 1983), page 37.
9. NATO Information Service, *NATO and the Warsaw Pact: Force Comparisons,* Brussels, 1984, page 7. On page 49, NATO notes: "The information presented in this publication is as of the end of 1983."
10. *Ibid.,* page 49.
11. *Ibid.,* page 50.
12. Isby, *op. cit.,* page 27.
13. Reuters, "NATO Cuts Soviet Bloc Estimate," *The New York Times,* June 22, 1984.

14. Isby, *op. cit.*, pages 80 and 111; and sources for the separate tables, *NATO Ground Forces, Central Europe, Order of Battle, 1981–85* and *Warsaw Pact Ground Forces, Central Europe, Order of Battle, 1981–85*, in Appendix H: Ground Forces and Conventional Weapons in Europe.
15. Collins, *op. cit.*, page xviii.
16. *Ibid.*, page 128.
17. *Ibid.*, page 261.
18. Isby, *op. cit.*, page 28.
19. Collins, *op. cit.*, page 261.
20. IISS, *The Military Balance, 1981–1982*, page vii.
21. Isby, *op. cit.*, page 80.
22. U.S. Department of State, *Atlas of U.S. Foreign Relations: U.S. National Security*, Washington, D.C., July, 1982, page 4.
23. *Ibid.*, page 4.
24. *Ibid.*, page 4. Also see Seth S. King, "Spain Enters NATO as First Country to Join Since 1955," *The New York Times*, May 31, 1982.
25. William P. Mako, *U.S. Ground Forces and the Defense of Europe* (Washington, D.C.: The Brookings Institution, 1983), page 131.
26. Drew Middleton, "France's Forces Quietly Renewing Ties for NATO," *The New York Times*, May 21, 1978.
27. Robert Lucas Fischer, *Defending the Central European Front: The Balance of Forces*, Adelphi Paper no. 127 (London: IISS, 1976), page 7.
28. West German Ministry of Defense, *White Paper, 1979: The Security of the Federal Republic of Germany and the Development of the Federal Armed Forces, 1979*, page 118.
29. Robert W. Komer, interview with *Newsweek*, December 20, 1982, page 35.
30. IISS, *op. cit.*, *1981–1982*, pages 31–33.
31. *Ibid.*, pages 43–44.
32. U.S. Department of State, *Atlas of U.S. Foreign Relations*, page 4.
33. NATO, *op. cit.*, 1982, page 7.
34. *Ibid.*, page 7.
35. *Ibid.*, page 68.
36. NATO, *op. cit.*, 1984, page 4. On page 49, NATO notes: "The information presented in this publication is as of the end of 1983."
37. *Ibid.*, pages 49–50.
38. *Ibid.*, Foreword by Secretary General Joseph M. A. H. Luns.
39. *Ibid.*, Contents page and page 50.
40. *Ibid.*
41. IISS, *The Military Balance, 1981–1982*, pages 5, 9, 10–14, 18–21, 27–39, and 43–44.
42. *Ibid.*, pages 5, 9, 10–14, 18–21, 27–39, and 43–44; see also table on page 124, which includes all NATO forces but Spain's.
43. *Ibid.*, pages 9, 10, and 30.
44. IISS, *The Military Balance, 1975–1976*, page 102.
45. Lothar Ruehl, *MBFR: Lessons and Problems*, Adelphi Paper no. 176 (London: IISS, 1982), page 24.
46. IISS, *The Military Balance, 1984–1985*, page 19.
47. Isby, *op. cit.*, page 24; Ruehl, *op. cit.*, page 24.
48. IISS, *The Military Balance, 1981–1982*, page 11.
49. *Ibid.*, page 33.
50. IISS, *The Military Balance, 1977–1978*, page 105; Chris Holshek, "The New German Army," *Armed Forces Journal International* (May, 1984), page 102.
51. Milton Leitenberg, "The Numbers Game or 'Who's on First?' " *Bulletin of the Atomic Scientists* (June–July, 1982), page 32.
52. Center for Defense Information, *Force Level Calculator*, Washington, D.C., 1982.

53. William J. Lewis, *The Warsaw Pact: Arms, Doctrine, and Strategy* (New York: McGraw-Hill, 1982), page 43.
54. IISS, *The Military Balance, 1981–1982,* page 14.
55. Isby, *op. cit.,* page 28.
56. Lewis, *op. cit.,* page 43; and IISS, *The Military Balance, 1981–1982,* pages 5–10, 18–21, 27–39, and 43–44.
57. IISS, *The Military Balance, 1977–1978,* pages 105–106.
58. Steven Rattner, "West Discloses New Plan for Troop Cuts," *The New York Times,* July 9, 1982.
59. U.S. Department of State, *Gist—Arms Control: MBFR Talks,* October, 1982; *The New York Times,* "Proposals for Reductions Of Troops Levels in Europe," July 9, 1982.
60. USSR Ministry of Defense, *Whence the Threat to Peace,* Moscow, 1982, page 70.
61. IISS, *The Military Balance, 1975–1976,* page 102; *Ibid.,* page 96.
62. *Ibid.,* page 97.
63. *Ibid.*
64. *Ibid.,* pages 102 and 96.
65. U.S. Department of State, *Gist—Arms Control.*
66. IISS, *The Military Balance, 1978–1979,* page 109.
67. *Ibid.,* page 109.
68. *Time* magazine, "I Can Move Damned Fast," December 11, 1978, page 41.
69. Jeffrey Record, "France 1940 and the NATO Center 1980: A Disquieting Comparison," *Strategic Review* (Summer, 1980), page 69.
70. *Ibid.*
71. IISS, *The Military Balance, 1979–1980,* page 110.
72. Record, *op. cit.,* page 69.
73. See the separate tables, *NATO Ground Forces Central Europe—Mobilization and Reinforcement Schedule, 1981–85* and *Warsaw Pact Ground Forces Central Europe—Mobilization and Reinforcement Schedule, 1981–85,* in Appendix H: Ground Forces and Conventional Weapons in Europe.
74. IISS, *The Military Balance, 1977–1978,* page 106.
75. *Ibid.,* page 105.
76. Drew Middleton, "Haig Lifts Estimate of NATO Alert Time," *The New York Times,* September 15, 1977.
77. IISS, *The Military Balance, 1977–1978,* page 106.
78. Mako, *op. cit.,* page 68.
79. Drew Middleton, "U.S. Tells NATO It Will Double Army in Europe in Event of Crisis," *The New York Times,* May 19, 1980.
80. Deborah Meyer, "The British Army of the Rhine: New Tactics, Same Commitment," *Armed Forces Journal International* (May, 1983), page 56.
81. Diego A. Ruiz Palmer, "The Front Line in Europe: National Contributions," *Armed Forces Journal International* (May, 1984), page 61: and Mako, *op. cit.,* page 50.
82. Stephen Canby, "Symposium on Military Strategy in Western Europe: Rejoinder," *Armed Forces and Society* (Fall, 1980), page 38.
83. See *Order of Battle* and *Mobilization and Reinforcement Schedules* in Appendix H.
84. See *ibid.*
85. IISS, *The Military Balance, 1980–1981,* page 111.
86. Isby, *op. cit.,* pages 24–26.
87. IISS, *The Military Balance, 1980–1981,* page 111.
88. Isby, *op. cit.,* page 28.
89. IISS, *The Military Balance, 1980–1981,* page 111.

90. Anthony H. Cordesman, Jr., "Whence the Threat to Peace? The Soviet View of the Threat," *Armed Forces Journal International* (August, 1983), page 92.

27. The Balance of Tanks

1. Department of Defense, *Soviet Military Power* (September, 1981), page 12.
2. Department of Defense, *Soviet Military Power* (March, 1983), page 80.
3. Department of Defense, *Fiscal Year 1981 Annual Report,* January 29, 1980, page 37.
4. General Accounting Office, "Selecting Production Site for Army's New Main Battle Tank," PSAD-77-107, Washington, D.C., May 11, 1977, pages 2 and 35.
5. *Ibid.,* page 13.
6. Department of Defense, *Soviet Military Power* (September, 1981), page 11.
7. *Ibid.*
8. General Accounting Office, *op. cit.,* PSAD-77-107, May 11, 1977, page 6.
9. *Ibid.,* pages 14–24.
10. *Ibid.,* page 45.
11. *Ibid.,* page 25.
12. Drew Middleton, "Haig LIfts Estimate of NATO Alert Time," *The New York Times,* September 15, 1977.
13. *Ibid.*
14. See the separate tables for *NATO Ground Forces, Central Europe—Mobilization and Reinforcement Schedule, 1981–85* and *Warsaw Pact Ground Forces Central Europe—Mobilization and Reinforcement Schedule, 1981–85* in Appendix H.
15. See the separate tables for *NATO Main Battle Tank Holdings, 1981–85* and *Warsaw Pact Main Battle Tank Holdings, 1981–85* in Appendix H.
16. Center for Defense Information, *The Defense Monitor,* Volume IV, no. 10 (December, 1975), page 6.
17. Center for Defense Information, *The Defense Monitor,* Volume XI, no. 1 (1982), page 2.
18. IISS, *The Military Balance, 1979–1980,* page 110.
19. See the separate table for *Key Operational Capabilities of Leading Current Tank Types, 1981–85* in Appendix H.
20. Department of Defense, *Soviet Military Power* (March, 1983), pages 38–39.
21. Steven J. Zaloga, *Soviet Tanks Today* (London: Arms and Armour Press, 1983), page 12.
22. See the separate tables for *Key Operational Capabilities of Leading Current Tank Types, 1981–85* and *Major Tank Ammunition Types in Current Service with NATO and the Warsaw Pact, 1981–85* in Appendix H.
23. Isby, *op. cit.,* pages 78 and 101.
24. Center for International Security, advertisement, *The New York Times,* February 27, 1983. See also Bernard Gwertzman, "Israelis to Share Lessons of War with Pentagon," *The New York Times,* March 22, 1983.
25. Center for Defense Information, *The Defense Monitor,* Volume XI, no. 6 (1982), page 4.

28. The Balance in the Air and at Sea

1. IISS, *The Military Balance, 1983–1984,* pages 10 and 26–42.
2. *Ibid.,* pages 18 and 20–24.
3. Drew Middleton, "U.S. Tells NATO It Will Double Army in Europe in Event of Crisis," *The New York Times,* May 19, 1980.
4. Center for Defense Information, *Force Level Calculator,* Washington, D.C. 1982.

5. Center for Defense Information, *The Defense Monitor,* Volume IX, no. 5 (June, 1980), page 4.
6. Anthony H. Cordesman and Benjamin E. Schemmer, "The Failure to Defend Defense," *Armed Forces Journal International* (March, 1983), page 32.

29. Renewing the Soviet Threat

1. Richard Halloran, "Criticism Rises on Reagan's Plan for 5-Year Growth of the Military," *The New York Times,* March 22, 1982.
2. *Time* magazine, "The Coming Defense Bonanza," April 20, 1981.
3. *Newsweek,* "Reagan's Arms Buildup," June 8, 1981.
4. Roger Morris, "Reporting for Duty: The Pentagon and the Press," *Columbia Journalism Review* (July–August, 1980), page 28.
5. Hodding Carter, "Dateline Moscow," Inside Story, Press and the Public Workshop, Public Television Network, April 14, 1983.
6. William E. Colby, "Understanding the Realities," a review of Andrew Cockburn's *The Threat: Inside the Soviet Military Machine, The New York Times Book Review,* June 26, 1983.

30. Soviet Military Spending

1. Central Intelligence Agency, National Foreign Assessment Center, "Soviet and US Defense Activities, 1970–79: A Dollar Cost Comparison," CIA, SR 80-10005, January, 1980, page 1.
2. John M. Collins, *U.S.-Soviet Military Balance, 1960–1980: Concepts and Capabilities* (New York: McGraw-Hill, 1980), page 87.
3. *Ibid.*
4. *Ibid.,* page 86.
5. Franklyn D. Holzman, "A Gap? Another?" *The New York Times,* March 9, 1983.
6. *The Military Balance, 1979–1980* (London: IISS, 1979), page 9.
7. Central Intelligence Agency, "Estimated Soviet Defense Spending in Rubles," CIA, SR 78-10121, June, 1978.
8. United States Air Force, *Soviet Aerospace Handbook,* USAF Pamphlet 200-21, Department of the Air Force, May, 1978, page 134.
9. CIA, *op. cit.,* SR 80-10005, January, 1980, page 3.
10. IISS, *The Military Balance, 1978–1979,* page 5.
11. Figures for 1979, and the CIA's "dollar cost" estimate of Soviet military spending in 1980, are from sources previously cited. The U.S. military budget for 1980 is from IISS, *The Military Balance, 1980–1981,* page. 5. The CIA's ruble estmate of real Soviet military spending in 1980 is from Joint Economic Committee, Congress of the United States, *USSR: Measures of Economic Growth and Development, 1950–1980,* December 8, 1982, page 123, "Estimated Soviet Defense Expenditures, 1951–1980." In both 1979 and 1980, the CIA's ruble estimates of real Soviet military spending do give an upper and lower range, and the lower figures are used here. However, the higher figures, 64 billion rubles in 1979 and 79 billion rubles in 1980, are equivalent only to $92.8 billion in 1979 and $114.5 billion in 1980. That is still well short of America's defense spending in both years.
12. CIA, *op. cit.,* SR 80-10005, January, 1980, page 3.
13. IISS, *The Military Balance, 1980–1981,* page 13.
14. Captain G. Roger Villar, DSC, *Jane's Weapon Systems, 1981–1982* (London: Jane's, 1981), Commentary, page 91.
15. Joint Economic Committee, Congress of the United States, *USSR: Measures of Economic Growth and Development, 1950–1980,* December 8, 1982, page 123, "Estimated Soviet Defense Expenditures, 1951–1980."

16. Leslie H. Gelb and Richard Halloran, "C.I.A. Analysts Now Said to Find U.S. Overstated Soviet Arms Rise," *The New York Times,* March 3, 1983.
17. *The Economist,* "Soviet Defense Spending: Slowing Down," November 26, 1983.
18. Holzman, *op. cit.,* March 9, 1983.

31. The Common Wisdom

1. Charles Mohr, "For the U.S., A Hard-Liner," *The New York Times,* December 1, 1981.
2. *Ibid.*
3. Fred Kaplan, *The Wizards of Armageddon* (New York: Simon & Schuster, 1983), page 139.
4. Dean Acheson and Louis Johnson, "A Report to the National Security Council by the Executive Secretary on United States Objectives and Programs for National Security," NSC-68, April 14, 1950, NSC File, FR: 1950, I, pages 234–292, President's Secretary's File, Harry S. Truman Library.
5. Kaplan, *op. cit.,* pages 140–141.
6. John Lewis Gaddis, *Strategies of Containment* (New York: Oxford University Press, 1982), page 93. On page 377, Gaddis cites the source for Bradley's testimony before the House Armed Services Committee on October 19, 1949.
7. Kaplan, *op. cit.,* page 141.
8. Albert Wohlstetter and Fred Hoffman, "Protectng U.S. Power to Strike Back in the 1950s and 1960s," RAND Report No. R-290, September 1, 1956.
9. National Intelligence Estimates NIE 11-12-57 and NIE 2-9-60, in Lawrence McQuade to Paul Nitze, "But Where Did the Missile Gap Go," memorandum, May 31, 1963, declassified July 25, 1979, pages 7–12, National Security File Box 298, "Missile Gap: February–May, 1963," John F. Kennedy Library.
10. Central Intelligence Agency, NIE 11-4-57, "Main Trends in Soviet Capabilities and Policies, 1957–1962," November 12, 1957, declassified April 24, 1978, page 6.
11. National Security Council, "Deterrence and Survival in the Nuclear Age," Report of the Security Resources Panel (Rowan Gaither Report), November 7, 1957, declassified January 10, 1973, page 14.
12. Kaplan, *op. cit.,* pages 152–154.
13. Chalmers Roberts, "Enormous Arms Outlay Is Held Vital to Survival," *The Washington Post,* December 20, 1957. Less prominent stories had appeared earlier, but Kaplan believes (*op. cit.,* page 153) that the Roberts story was primarily responsible for the congressional and public concern that followed. John Prados agrees. (See John Prados, *The Soviet Estimate: U.S. Intelligence Analysis and Russian Military Strength* [New York: The Dial Press, 1982], page 74.)
14. Henry A. Kissinger, *The Necessity for Choice* (New York: Harper & Brothers, 1961), page 15.
15. Prados, *op. cit.,* page 109.
16. Kaplan, *op. cit.,* page 286.
17. Ellsberg, *op. cit.,* April 13, 1981, page 15.
18. Kaplan, *op. cit.,* page 289.
19. Mohr, *op. cit.,* December 1, 1981.
20. John Foster Dulles, interview, *U.S. News & World Report* (March, 1949).
21. Bertram, *op. cit.,* page 2.
22. Roy Gutman, "The Nay-Sayer of Arms Control," *Newsday,* February 18, 1983.
23. G. Stigler and C. Friedland, "Profits of Defense Contractors," *American Economic Review* (September, 1971).
24. Parenti, *op. cit.,* July, 1980, page 27.
25. Gordon Adams, *The Iron Triangle* (New York: Council on Economic Priorities, 1981), page 283.
26. *Who's Who in America* (38th ed., Chicago: Marquis Who's Who, 1974–75), page 2295.
27. Subcommittee on Reports, Accounting and Management, Senate Committee on Governmental

Affairs, *Interlocking Directorates Among the Major U.S. Corporations,* 95th Congress, 2nd Session, Document No. 95-107, June 15, 1978, pages 713–718. Nitze had left the board of Northwestern Mutual Life before 1976, the year whose interlocks the Senate investigation studied. But most of the firm's other directors listed in that study are listed in earlier years, together with their other affiliations, at the same time Nitze is. He lists himself on its board, for example, in the same edition of *Who's Who* which lists Catherine Cleary as a trustee of Northwestern Mutual Life and director of General Motors and AT&T (*op. cit.,* page 580).

28. Armed Forces Information Service, *Defense '76,* Arlington, Va., 1976.

29. Mohr, *op. cit.,* December 1, 1981, and *Who's Who* (see note 26 supra).

30. Ferdinand Lundberg, *The Rich and the Super-Rich* (New York: Lyle Stuart, 1968), pages 648–649.

31. Armed Forces Information Service, *op. cit.,* 1976.

32. Bernard Gwertzman, "Nitze Is Appointed Adviser to Shultz in Gromyko Talks," *The New York Times,* December 6, 1984.

33. Gwertzman, *op. cit.,* December 6, 1984.

34. Strobe Talbott, *Deadly Gambits: The Reagan Administration and the Stalemate in Nuclear Arms Control* (New York: Knopf, 1984).

35. Theodore Draper, "Journalism, History and Journalistic History," a review of *Deadly Gambits, The New York Times Book Review,* December 9, 1984.

36. Theodore Draper, "Journalism, History and Journalistic History—An Exchange," letters published in *The New York Times Book Review,* December 16, 1984.

37. Talbott, *op. cit.,* page xiii.

38. Draper, *op. cit.,* December 9, 1984.

39. *Ibid.*

40. Paule Nitze, letter to Theodore Draper, November 7, 1984, published in "Journalism, History and Journalistic History—An Exchange," *The New York Times Book Review,* December 16, 1984.

41. Mohr, *op. cit.,* December 1, 1981.

42. Norman Podhoretz, *The Present Danger* (New York: Simon & Schuster, 1980), page 12.

43. Judith Miller and Jeff Gerth, "Navy Secretary Said to Keep Ties to Company Aiding Arms Makers," *The New York Times,* December 27, 1982; and Jeff Gerth, "Aide Urged Pentagon to Consider Weapons Made by Former Client," *The New York Times,* April 17, 1983.

44. Senate Subcommittee on Reports, Accounting and Management, *op. cit.,* page 808.

45. *Ibid.,* page 277. Pages 651–663 of the same volume show how Laird's affiliation with Metropolitan Life Insurance Company kept him in regular contact with directors of AVCO Corporation, Atlantic Richfield, Eastman Kodak, EXXON, General Motors, Goodyear Tire & Rubber, IBM, North American Phillips, Procter & Gamble, Raytheon, RCA, and Sperry Rand—all leading defense contractors.

46. David Shribman, "Group Goes from Exile to Influence," *The New York Times,* November 23, 1981. Additional members of the Committee on the Present Danger, including Frank Barnett, Melvin Laird, and David Packer, are listed by Robert Sherrill, "Gene Rostow's Propaganda Club," *The Nation,* August 11–18, 1979, cover and pages 107–110.

47. Karen Rothmyer, "Scaife's Seed Money Helps New Right Blossom," *Common Cause* magazine (August, 1981), page 15.

48. Bernard Weinraub, "Foundations Assist Conservative Cause," *The New York Times,* January 20, 1981.

49. Rothmyer, *op. cit.,* August, 1981, page 15.

50. Weinraub, *op. cit.,* January 20, 1981.

51. A partial listing of the Coalition's membership includes the Association of Former Intelligence Officers, the Citizens Committee for the Right to Keep and Bear Arms, Citizens for Freedom, Inc., College Republican National Committee, the Council Against Communist Aggression, the Council for Inter-American Security, the John Paul Jones Foundation, the National Com-

mittee for Responsible Patriotism, the National Security Political Action Committee, the Reserve Officers Association, the Solzhenitsyn Society, Young Americans for Freedom, and the Young Republican National Federation.

52. Senate Subcommittee on Reports, Accounting and Management, *op. cit.,* page 350, and Armed Forces Information Service, *op. cit.,* 1976.

53. Senate Subcommittee on Reports, Accounting and Management, *op. cit.,* page 271, and Armed Forces Information Service, *op. cit.,* 1976.

54. American Security Council, "President's Report," 1980, ASC, Boston, Va.

55. General Accounting Office, letter from J. K. Fasick, Director, to Senator Barry M. Goldwater, August 27, 1979, page 1.

32. The Concept of Linkage

1. Charles Mohr, "Kissinger Suggests Senate Link Treaty to More Arms Funds," *The New York Times,* August 1, 1979.

2. Henry Kissinger, "Secretary Kissinger's News Conference of April 22," *Department of State Bulletin,* May 17, 1976, Department of State, Washington, D.C., page 617.

3. *Ibid.*

4. Associated Press, "Excerpts from Kissinger's Testimony on Arms Pact," *The New York Times,* August 1, 1979.

5. Bernard Weinraub, "President Urges Soviet to Resolve Wars in 5 Nations," *The New York Times,* October 25, 1985.

6. Ronald Reagan, address to the United Nations General Assembly, October 24, 1985, quoted by Weinraub, *op. cit., The New York Times,* October 25, 1985.

7. Center for Military Research and Analysis, *Open Use of Force Abroad by United States Military Personnel to Impose or Restore Favorable Political Conditions,* and *United States Covert Action Abroad to Impose or Restore Favorable Political Conditions,* New York, 1984.

8. *Ibid.*

9. Leslie H. Gelb, "Your Move: An Offer From Reagan Raises Hopes for Geneva," *The New York Times,* November 3, 1985.

10. Weinraub, *op. cit., The New York Times,* October 25, 1985.

11. John Chancellor, NBC-TV News, October 24, 1985.

12. Weinraub, *op. cit., The New York Times,* October 25, 1985.

13. Ronald Reagan, televised address to the American people, November 14, 1985; transcript published by *The New York Times,* November 15, 1985.

14. Karen Cowgill, letter to *The New York Times,* October 15, 1985; published by the *Times* on October 26, 1985.

33. An Adverse Imbalance of Power

1. Joseph Alsop, "Losing the Balance of Power," *Newsweek,* November 13, 1978, page 35.

2. *Foreign Policy Perspectives,* "The Quiet War," advertisement, *The New York Times,* January 21, 1979.

3. Bernard Weinraub, "U.S. Military Strength Dwindling, Republicans Say," *The New York Times,* March 2, 1979.

4. Coalition for Peace Through Strength, "Excerpts from Criticism of Arms Pact," *The New York Times,* April 12, 1979.

5. Bernard Weinraub, "Army Chief Sees Soviet Surpassing U.S. Strategic Capability in the 1980s," *The New York Times,* June 16, 1979.

6. Ben J. Wattenberg, "It's Time to Stop America's Retreat," *The New York Times Magazine,* July 22, 1979.

7. George F. Will, "The Defense Gap," *Newsweek,* October 1, 1979, page 84.

8. Elizabeth Drew, "1980: Reagan," A Reporter At Large, *The New Yorker,* March 24, 1980.

9. Howell Raines, "Reagan Calls Arms Race Essential to Avoid a 'Surrender' or 'Defeat,' " *The New York Times,* August 19, 1980. (Raines quotes from Reagan's address to the Veterans of Foreign Wars Convention in Chicago on August 18, 1980.)

10. Drew Middleton, "U.S. General Says Soviet Nuclear Forces Hold Lead," *The New York Times,* March 9, 1980.

11. Jack Maury, "Where Are We Going, Militarily?" *The Washington Post,* August 19, 1980.

12. Center for Defense Information, "Pentagon Rebuts Charges of U.S. Military Weakness," *The Defense Monitor,* Volume IX, no. 8 (1980), pages 3 and 11.

13. Edward N. Luttwak, "A New Arms Race?" *Commentary* (September, 1980), page 27.

14. Leslie H. Gelb, "Soviet Might: A U.S. View," *The New York Times,* September 27, 1981.

15. To defeat Adlai Stevenson in the 1956 presidential campaign, President Eisenhower broke off arms limitation talks with the Soviet Union, charging that an arms agreement with the Soviets at that time, which Stevenson urged, would leave them with a "clear strategic lead." After Eisenhower won reelection, the talks, which he had initiated himself, were resumed. To defeat Richard Nixon in the 1960 campaign, John F. Kennedy, armed with Paul Nitze's report for the Gaither Committee (see note 11, Chapter 31, supra), charged that the Republicans had "allowed the nation to fall hostage" to Soviet missiles. After he was elected, Kennedy announced he was relieved to find no missile gap existed (see Gervasi, *op. cit.,* page 23).

16. Ronald Reagan, news conference, Washington, D.C., March 30, 1982, as recorded by *The New York Times,* "President's News Conference on Foreign and Domestic Matters," April 1, 1982.

17. Hanrahan, *op. cit., Common Cause* magazine (May–June, 1983), page 49.

18. Caspar Weinberger, news conference, Washington, D.C., March 9, 1983, as recorded by Richard Halloran, "Weinberger Says the U.S. Military Has 'Begun to Catch Up' to Soviet," *The New York Times,* March 10, 1983.

19. Halloran, *ibid.*

20. Richard Halloran, "Criticism Rises on Reagan's Plan for 5-Year Growth of the Military," *The New York Times,* March 22, 1983.

34. "A Window of Vulnerability"

1. American Security Council, "The SALT Syndrome," transcript quoted in *The Defense Monitor,* Volume IX, no. 8 (1980), page 10.

2. Patrick J. Buchanan, "Not Quite a Whiz at the Spy Biz," *The New York Daily News,* October 14, 1979.

3. Ronald Reagan, news conference, Washington, D.C., March 30, 1982. See note 16 supra.

4. Center for Defense Information, *The Defense Monitor,* Volume IX, no. 8 (1980), page 10.

5. Coalition for Peace Through Strength, *op. cit.,* April 12, 1979.

6. Center for Defense Information, *op. cit.,* Volume IX, no. 8 (1980), page 6.

7. *Ibid.,* page 10.

8. Coalition for Peace Through Strength, *op. cit.,* April 12, 1979.

35. Strategic Modernization

1. Drew, *op. cit.,* March 24, 1980.

2. Raines, *op. cit.,* August 19, 1980.

3. White House transcript, presidential address of November 22, 1982, reprinted in *The New York Times,* "Reagan's Address to Nation on Nuclear Strategy Toward the Soviet Union," November 23, 1982.

4. White House transcript, President's news conference of January 14, 1983, reprinted in *The New York Times,* January 15, 1983.

5. Kenneth W. Dam, "Ensuring Security in the Nuclear Age," Denver, Col., March 8, 1983,

reprinted by the U.S. Department of State, Bureau of Public Affairs, Current Policy No. 466, page 2.

6. Ronald Reagan, address to the Los Angeles World Affairs Council, Beverly Hills, March 30, 1983, reprinted by *The New York Times,* April 1, 1983.

7. Representative Les Aspin, "Judge Not by Numbers Alone," *Bulletin of the Atomic Scientists* (June, 1980), page 31.

8. American Security Council, *op. cit.,* quoted in *The Defense Monitor, op. cit.,* page 3.

9. Jed C. Snyder, "A Freeze Rewards Moscow," *The New York Times,* Op-Ed page, March 15, 1983.

10. Center for Defense Information, *The Defense Monitor,* Volume XI, no. 1 (1982), page 6.

11. Aspin, *op. cit.,* pages 28 and 30.

12. Snyder, *op. cit.,* March 15, 1983.

13. Raines, *op. cit.,* August 19, 1980; Ronald Reagan, address to the United Nations, New York, June 17, 1982, reprinted by *The New York Times,* June 18, 1982; Daniel O. Graham, Lieutenant General USA, Ret., solicitation letter on behalf of the United States Defense Committee, Fairfax, Va., February 15, 1983.

14. Coalition for Peace Through Strength, *op. cit.,* April 12, 1979; Daniel O. Graham, Lieutenant General USA, Ret., "America's Strategy Gap," letter, *The New York Times,* October 16, 1980; *Ibid.*

15. American Security Council, *op. cit.,* quoted in *The Defense Monitor, op. cit.,* page 7; Coalition for Peace Through Strength, *op. cit.,* April 12, 1979; Frank R. Barnett, letter to Victor Navasky, reprinted in *The Nation,* August 11–18, 1979, page 110.

36. Soviet Intentions

1. Morton Kondracke, "Ronnie's for Real," *The New Republic,* April 5, 1980.

2. Drew, *op. cit.,* March 24, 1980.

3. Michael Kramer, "$1.5 Trillion for Defense?" *New York* magazine, June 22, 1981, page 18.

4. Ronald Reagan, address to the National Association of Evangelicals, Orlando, Fla., March 8, 1983, transcript excerpts reprinted by *The New York Times,* March 9, 1983.

5. *Ibid.*

6. Ronald Reagan, news conference, Washington, D.C., January 20, 1983, transcript reprinted by *The New York Times,* January 21, 1983.

7. Steven R. Weisman, "Reagan Misstatements Getting Less Attention," *The New York Times,* February 1, 1983. Deputy White House Press Secretary Lyndon K. Allin is the source quoted here.

8. Zahid Mahmood, " '10 Commandments' of Dubious Origin," letter, *The New York Times,* February 3, 1983.

37. Soviet Expansionism

1. Kondracke, *op. cit.,* April 5, 1980.

2. Center for Military Research and Analysis, *Open Use of Force Abroad by United States Military Personnel to Impose or Restore Favorable Political Conditions,* and *United States Covert Action Abroad to Impose or Restore Favorable Political Conditions,* New York, 1984. In addition to its list of eighty-three covert operations, the Center has documented fifty open military interventions since 1800. A partial list of forty-three covert operations documented by the Center since 1963 was published by *Harper's Magazine,* "Black Ops, 1963–1983," (April, 1984), pages 17–20. The Center's full list of covert operations is published in Darrell Garwood, *Undercover: Thirty-Five Years of CIA Deception* (New York: Grove/Dell, 1985).

3. *The Washington Post,* "Brezhnev," editorial, November 11, 1982.

4. Morris, *op. cit.,* page 27.

5. Ronald Reagan, address to the National Association of Evangelicals, Orlando, Fla., March 8, 1983.
6. *Time* magazine, "Sinking Deeper into a Quagmire," November 22, 1982, page 28.
7. *The Wall Street Journal,* "Meeting the Challenge," editorial, December 8, 1982.
8. William A. Dorman, "The Image of the Soviet Union in the American News Media: Coverage of Brezhnev, Andropov and MX," Conference on War, Peace and the News Media, New York University, March 19, 1983, page 9.
9. Joint Economic Committee, Congress of the United States, "USSR: Measures of Economic Growth and Development, 1950–1980," 97th Congress, 2nd Session, Washington, D.C., December 8, 1982, page 15.
10. Bernard Gwertzman, "U.S. Survey Shows a Steady Growth in Soviet's G.N.P.," *The New York Times,* December 26, 1982.
11. *Newsweek,* "The Soviet Economy: Down But Not Out," January 10, 1983, page 62.
12. Joint Economic Committee, *op. cit.,* page 19.
13. Ronald Reagan, address to the Los Angeles World Affairs Council, Beverly Hills, March 30, 1983.
14. Ronald Reagan, address to the National Association of Evangelicals, Orlando, Fla., March 8, 1983.

38. Soviet Planning for Nuclear War

1. Amoretta H. Hoeber and Joseph D. Douglass, Jr., *Soviet Strategy for Nuclear War* (Stanford, Calif.: Hoover Institution Press, 1979), page 2. Douglass is also the author of *The Soviet Theater Nuclear Offensive,* Volume 1 of the U.S. Air Force series *Studies in Communist Affairs.*
2. *Ibid.,* page 10.
3. *Ibid.,* page 3.
4. *Ibid.,* page 214.
5. Department of Defense, *Annual Report, Fiscal Year 1975,* "U.S. and U.S.S.R. Strategic Force Levels" (Washington, D.C.: U.S. Government Printing Office, 1974). Also quoted in Stockholm International Peace Research Institute (SIPRI), *World Armaments and Disarmament Yearbook, 1976* (Stockholm: Almqvist & Wiksell, 1976), page 25, and by John M. Collins, *American and Soviet Military Trends Since the Cuban Missile Crisis* (Washington, D.C.: Center for Strategic and International Studies, Georgetown University, 1978), page 114.
6. Hoeber and Douglass, *op. cit.,* page 124.
7. Department of Defense, *Annual Report, Fiscal Year 1969,* "U.S. and U.S.S.R. Strategic Force Levels" (Washington, D.C.: U.S. Government Printing Office, 1968); SIPRI, *op. cit.,* 1976, page 25, and Collins, *op. cit.,* page 114.
8. Wieseltier, *op. cit.,* January 10 and 17, 1983, page 16.
9. U.S. Army Field Manual FM-287, *The Tank and Mechanized Infantry Combat Team,* February, 1980, quoted by Cockburn, *op. cit.,* pages 11 and 213, and earlier quoted by Cockburn, "Sure, But What About the Russkies?" *Mother Jones* (September–October, 1982), page 26, and by Fred Kaplan, "Russian and American Intentions," *The Atlantic,* July, 1982.
10. Wieseltier, *op. cit.,* January 10 and 17, 1983, page 24.
11. Robert McNamara, University of Michigan, Ann Arbor, Mich., June 16, 1962, in a revised version of an address to NATO Foreign Ministers, Athens, May 5, 1962. Quoted by Robert E. Kuenne, *The Polaris Missile Strike* (Ohio State University Press, 1966), page 20; by Kaplan, *op. cit.,* page 284; and by Cockburn, *op. cit.,* page 213.
12. U.S. Army Field Manual FM 7-11, *Rifle Company, Infantry, Airborne, and Mechanized,* Headquarters, Department of the Army, April, 1965, page 61.
13. Leon Goure and Michael J. Deane, "The Soviet Strategic View," *Strategic Review* (Winter, 1981), page 74.

39. Arms Control: The Soviet Record

1. Ronald Reagan, address to the Los Angeles World Affairs Council, Beverly Hills, March 30, 1983.
2. Sidney Lens, *The Day Before Doomsday* (Boston: Beacon Press, 1978), page 204.
3. Reagan, *loc. cit.,* Beverly Hills, March 30, 1983.
4. Alva Myrdal, *The Game of Disarmament* (New York: Pantheon, 1982), pages 81–82.
5. Sidney Lens, *The Bomb* (New York: Lodestar/Dutton, 1982), pages 49–50.
6. Myrdal, *op. cit.,* page 82.
7. Lens, *The Bomb,* page 50.
8. Myrdal, *op. cit.,* page 82.
9. United Nations, *The United Nations and Disarmament, 1949–1970,* page 58.
10. David Wise and Thomas B. Ross, *The U-2 Affair* (New York: Random House, 1962), page 16.
11. *Ibid.,* page 16.
12. See the separate table *Chronology of Initiatives in the Strategic Arms Race* on page 400.
13. Ronald Reagan, address to the United Nations, June 17, 1982, transcript reprinted in *The New York Times,* June 18, 1982, and Reagan, *loc. cit.,* Beverly Hills, March 30, 1983.
14. See Department of State, Bureau of Public Affairs, "US Arms Control Policy," Gist, July, 1982, and Department of State, Bureau of Public Affairs, "Nuclear Arms Control and the Future of U.S.-Soviet Relations," address by Eugene V. Rostow to the Los Angeles World Affairs Council, September 10, 1982, Current Policy No. 425, page 3.

40. Chemical and Toxin Warfare

1. Reagan, address to the United Nations, June 17, 1982.
2. *The New York Times,* "Afghan Rebels Say the Russians Have Already Used Gas in Some Attacks," December 29, 1979.
3. United Press International, "U.S. Is Told Soviet Uses Poison Gas on Afghans," *The New York Times,* January 24, 1980.
4. Alexander Cockburn, "Gas in Afghanistan: Atrocity Journalism," Press Clips, *The Village Voice,* May 14, 1980.
5. Gwynne Roberts, "The Campaign of Misinformation," *New Statesman,* April 4, 1980.
6. Richard Burt, "Use of Chemical Weapons in Asia," statement to the Senate Foreign Relations Subcommittee on Arms Control, Oceans, International Operations and Environment, November 10, 1981, Bureau of Public Affairs, Department of State, Current Policy No. 342, page 2.
7. Walter J. Stoessel, Jr., "Afghanistan Day: March 21," statement to the Senate Foreign Relations Committee, March 8, 1982, Bureau of Public Affairs, Department of State, Current Policy No. 375, page 2.
8. *The New York Times,* March 14, 1982.
9. Alexander M. Haig, Jr., "Chemical Warfare in Southeast Asia and Afghanistan," Department of State, Special Report No. 98, March 22, 1982.
10. *Ibid.,* page 6; *Ibid.,* page 15.
11. Philip Taubman, "U.S. Offers Report on Use of Toxins by Soviet Forces," *The New York Times,* March 23, 1982.
12. Haig, *op. cit.,* March 22, 1982, page 6.
13. *Ibid.,* pages 6, 8, and 11.
14. *Bangkok World,* March 8, 1980.
15. George P. Shultz, "Chemical Warfare in Southeast Asia and Afghanistan: An Update," Department of State, Special Report No. 104, November, 1982, page 3.
16. *Ibid.,* page 4.
17. *Ibid.*
18. Philip M. Boffey, "Are the Russians Using 'Yellow Rain' in Asia? Experts Debate the Data," *The New York Times,* November 23, 1981; *Ibid.*

19. Philip M. Boffey, "Some Are Swayed on Chemical War," *The New York Times,* April 2, 1982.
20. Taubman, *op. cit.,* March 23, 1982.
21. Boffey, *op. cit.,* November 23, 1981.
22. Richard Bernstein, "Afghans, in New York, Tell of a Massacre by Russians," *The New York Times,* January 28, 1983.
23. Lawrence S. Eagleburger, "Yellow Rain: The Arms Control Implications," address to Senate Foreign Relations Subcommittee on Arms Control, Oceans, International Operations and Environment, February 24, 1983, Bureau of Public Affairs, Department of State, Current Policy No. 458, pages 1 and 2.
24. Philip M. Boffey, "Bee Waste Is Suspected as 'Yellow Rain' Source," *The New York Times,* June 1, 1983.
25. Philip M. Boffey, "U.S. Dismisses Bee Theory as 'Yellow Rain' Source," *The New York Times,* June 2, 1983.
26. Shultz, *op. cit.,* November, 1982, letter to Congress and Member States of the United Nations.
27. Boffey, *op. cit.,* June 1, 1983.
28. Boffey, *op. cit.,* November 23, 1981.
29. Bill Schaap, "U.S. Biological Warfare: The 1981 Cuba Dengue Epidemic," *Covert Action Information Bulletin,* no. 17 (Summer, 1982), page 28.
30. Stockholm International Peace Research Institute, *World Arms and Disarmament Yearbook, 1976,* pages 470 and 472.
31. Arnaud de Borchgrave, "Bum Tips and Spies," *The New York Times,* Op-Ed page, August 12, 1981.
32. Peter Hall, "Nerve Gas Politics," *The Progressive* (September, 1980), page 43.
33. A. O. Sulzberger, Jr., "Chemical Weapons Out of the Bottle Again," *The New York Times,* September 21, 1980.
34. Wayne Biddle, "Restocking the Chemical Arsenal," *The New York Times Magazine,* May 24, 1981, page 48. Biddle reports that officials at the Denver Rocky Mountain Arsenal "confirmed that minute quantities" of the nerve gas GB "had been detected in the void spaces of the airtight shipping containers of 70 Weteyes," a Navy chemical bomb. "By minute," he continues, "they meant between .00003 and .0001 milligrams of nerve gas per cubic meter of space. Such 'leaks' are not like a drippy faucet. Because of microscopic weld defects around the bomb filler caps, vapor seeps out through a tortuous path. The limit for acceptable leakage, set by the Defense Department and accepted by the United States Public Health Service, is .2 milligrams per cubic meter, or 2,000 times greater than the worst case detailed." The Weteyes figured prominently in publicizing leaks.

41. Violations of SALT II

1. Reagan, *loc. cit.,* Beverly Hills, March 31, 1983.
2. Hedrick Smith, "U.S. Report Said to Accuse Soviet on Arms Treaty," *The New York Times,* April 3, 1983.
3. *Newsweek,* "Who's Cheating on SALT?" May 9, 1983, page 23.
4. Hedrick Smith, "Panel Tells Reagan the Russians Seem to Have Broken Arms Pact," *The New York Times,* April 21, 1983.
5. Smith, *op. cit.,* April 3, 1983.
6. Hedrick Smith, "U.S. Sees New Soviet Arms Violation," *The New York Times,* May 12, 1983.
7. *Ibid.*
8. SALT II Agreement, Article IV, Paragraph 9, First Agreed Statement and First and Third Common Understandings, Vienna, June 18, 1979, Department of State, Selected Documents, No. 12A, page 34.
9. Richard Burt, "Arms Treaty: How to Verify Moscow's Compliance," *The New York Times,* March 21, 1979.

10. SALT II Agreement, Article IV, Paragraph 10 and First Agreed Statement, and Paragraph 12 and First Agreed Statement, June 18, 1979, *op. cit.,* pages 35 and 36.
11. Smith, *op. cit.,* May 12, 1983.
12. Smith, *op. cit.,* April 21, 1983.
13. Smith, *op. cit.,* May 12, 1983.
14. Ronald Reagan, news conference, Washington, D.C., May 17, 1983, transcript published in *The New York Times,* May 18, 1983.
15. Tom Wicker, "Cheating on SALT," *The New York Times,* May 3, 1983.
16. Charles Mohr, "U.S. Says Soviet Violates Treaty With a Missile," *The New York Times,* October 16, 1985.
17. *Ibid.;* and *Treaty Between the United States and the Union of Soviet Socialist Republics on the Limitation of Anti-Ballistic Missile Systems,* Article VI, Paragraph (b), United States Arms Control and Disarmament Agency, *Arms Control and Disarmament Agreements,* 1982 Edition, Washington, D.C., 1982, page 141.
18. Michael R. Gordon, "CIA Is Skeptical that New Soviet Radar Is Part of an ABM Defense System," *National Journal,* March 9, 1985, pages 523–526.
19. Central Intelligence Agency, "Implications of a New Soviet Phased-Array Radar," 1984, quoted by Gordon, *op. cit.,* March 9, 1985, pages 523–524.
20. Cabinet Joint Intelligence Committee, "Soviet Union: the Abalakovo Radar," United Kingdom, January 25, 1985, quoted by Gordon, *op. cit.,* March 9, 1985, page 524.
21. Leslie H. Gelb, "Moscow Proposes To End A Dispute On Siberia Radar," *The New York Times,* October 29, 1985.
22. Reagan, *op. cit.,* May 17, 1983.
23. *Ibid.*
24. Smith, *op. cit.,* April 21, 1983.

42. Verification

1. Kaplan, *op. cit.,* page 286. According to Kaplan, Discoverer 13 was launched in August, 1960. According to John Taylor and David Mondey, TIROS (Television and Infra-red Observation Satellite) had already been launched in April of that year. Its electron beam conversion technology clearly presaged the development of the Landsat and KH-11 series, the latter first launched sixteen years later (see note 14 below). By their account, TIROS already had some limited ability to transmit its signals "direct to ground receivers." They add that "scientists expressed themselves as being shocked" at its "highly detailed photographs of the Soviet Union and Communist China," in which "aircraft runways and missile sites could be identified easily." While they say "we may never know" whether TIROS was simply a meteorological satellite, as the public had been told, or also a reconnaissance satellite, in view of what it was photographing, it should be safe to assume that while it certainly performed the former mission, as it continues to do, it also performed the latter. However, they give no estimate of the quality of its ground resolution. Because its technology was then still in a very early stage of development, Discoverer photographs probably offered finer ground resolution than TIROS imagery at that time. (See John W. R. Taylor and David Mondey, *Spies in the Sky* [London: Ian Allan, 1972], page 112.)
2. James A. Fusca, *Space/Aeronautics* (June, 1964). The first SAMOS satellite was launched in January, 1961 (see Taylor and Mondey, *op. cit.,* page 113).
3. Richard Burt, "Technology Is Essential to Arms Verification," *The New York Times,* August 14, 1979.
4. Bhupendra Jasani, "Reconnaissance Satellites," *World Armaments and Disarmament Yearbook, 1975,* Stockholm International Peace Research Institute (SIPRI) (Stockholm: Almqvist & Wiksell, 1975), pages 391–394.
5. John Noble Wilford, "Eyes in the Sky: Satellites' Uses Growing with Capabilities," *The New York Times,* March 29, 1983.

6. Jasani, *op. cit.,* page 394.
7. Wayne Hill and Werner Frank, "The KA-102A LOROP Camera," *Proceedings of the Society of Photo-Optical Instrumentation Engineers,* Volume 79, *Aerial Reconnaissance Systems,* SPIE, Palos Verdes Estates, Calif., 1976, page 160.
8. James Bamford, *The Puzzle Palace* (Boston: Houghton-Mifflin, 1982), page 201.
9. *Ibid.*
10. Jasani, *op. cit.,* page 394.
11. Thomas Karas, *The New High Ground: Strategies and Weapons of Space-Age War* (New York: Simon & Schuster, 1983), page 105.
12. Bhupendra Jasani, "Reconnaissance Satellites," *World Armaments and Disarmament Yearbook 1976,* SIPRI (Stockholm: Almqvist & Wiksell, 1976), page 107.
13. Philip J. Klass, "U.S. Scrutinizing New Soviet Radar," *Aviation Week & Space Technology,* August 22, 1983, page 19.
14. Bamford, *op. cit.,* page 202. Though Karas gives this date as December, 1978, two years later (see Karas, *op. cit.,* page 107), there is a good deal of evidence confirming the earlier date. See, for example, Bhupendra Jasani, "Military Uses of Outer Space," *The Arms Race and Arms Control,* SIPRI (London: Taylor & Francis, 1982), page 99, and *Aviation Week & Space Technology,* "Aerospace Forecast and Inventory," March 14, 1983, page 142.
15. Wilford, *op. cit.,* March 29, 1983.
16. *Ibid.*
17. John Noble Wilford, "Satellite Map Images Found Vastly Improved," *The New York Times,* February 9, 1983.
18. *Ibid.*
19. John Noble Wilford, "Mapping in the Space Age," *The New York Times Magazine,* June 5, 1983, pages 48 and 55.
20. Karas, *op. cit.,* page 107.
21. Bamford, *op. cit.,* page 201.
22. Wilford, *op. cit.,* June 5, 1983, page 50.
23. *Ibid.*
24. See note 1 supra.
25. Harry V. Martin, "Electronics Remains Keystone to U.S. Intelligence Mission," *Defense Electronics* (December, 1981), page 74.
26. Wilford, *op. cit.,* June 5, 1983, page 50.
27. Center for Defense Information, *The Defense Monitor,* Volume XI, no. 1 (1982), page 3.
28. Jasani, "Military Uses of Outer Space," *op. cit.,* 1982, page 99.
29. Benjamin F. Schemmer, " 'Electronic Cameras' with Instantaneous Ground Read-Out Now Make Real-Time, Precision Tactical Targeting Operationally Feasible," *Armed Forces Journal International* (November, 1982), page 70.
30. Karas, *op. cit.,* page 109.
31. Schemmer, *op. cit.,* November, 1982, page 70.
32. *Jane's Weapon Systems, 1981–1982* (12th ed., London: Jane's, 1981), page 596.
33. Jim Meacham, "Defense Technology Survey," *The Economist,* May 21, 1983, page 28.
34. Wilford, *op. cit.,* June 5, 1983, page 56.
35. L. C. Graham, "Exploitation of Synthetic Aperture Radar Imagery," *Proceedings of the Society of Photo-Optical Instrumentation Engineers, Aerial Reconnaissance Systems,* Volume 79, *Aerial Reconnaissance Systems,* SPIE, Palos Verdes Estates, Calif., 1976, page 107.
36. Wilford, *op. cit.,* June 5, 1983, page 56.
37. James Canan, *War in Space* (New York: Harper & Row, 1982), page 99.
38. Jim Meacham, "Marching Forward," *The Economist,* May 21, 1983, page 28.
39. *Aviation Week,* "How U.S. Taps Soviet Missile Secrets," October 21, 1957, page 26.
40. There are two Plesetsks. The other is in the Volgograd region, 125 miles south of the port of Archangelsk and 500 miles northeast of Moscow.

41. *Jane's Weapon Systems* (7th ed., London: Macdonald & Jane's, 1976), page 582.

42. *Ibid.,* page 574.

43. *Ibid.,* page 574.

44. *Ibid.,* pages 574–575.

45. *Jane's Weapon Systems* (12th ed., 1981), page 497.

46. Canan, *op. cit.,* page 100.

47. Those in current service, with their hull numbers, are the *Wheeling* (AGM-8), *General H. H. Arnold* (AGM-9), *General Hoyt S. Vandenberg* (AGM-10), *Vanguard* (AGM-19), *Redstone* (AGM-20), *Range Sentinel* (AGM-22), *Observation Island* (AGM-23), *Compass Island* (AG-153), and *Kingsport* (AG-164). Those listed as stricken from the Naval Vessel Register, transferred to the custody of the Maritime Administration, or otherwise disposed of are the *Valcour* (AGF-1), *Range Tracker* (AGM-1), *Range Recoverer* (AGM-2), *Longview* (AGM-3), *Richfield* (AGM-4), *Sunnyvale* (AGM-5), *Watertown* (AGM-6), *Huntsville* (AGM-7), *Twin Falls* (AGM-11), *American Mariner* (AGM-12), *Sword Knot* (AGM-13), *Rose Knot* (AGM-14), *Coastal Sentry* (AGM-15), *Timber Hitch* (AGM-17), *Sampan Hitch* (AGM-18), *Mercury* (AGM-21), and *Shelburne* (AGM-22). That a vessel has been stricken seems to mean little. According to Samuel L. Morison, the *Redstone* and *Vanguard,* both now in active service, had been stricken no fewer than three times from the Register before they were reacquired for conversion. (See Samuel L. Morison, *The Ships and Aircraft of the U.S. Fleet* [10th ed., Annapolis, Md.: Naval Institute Press, 1965], page 88). Nor do sources always agree on what has happened to some of these vessels. According to one, the *Coastal Sentry* (AGM-15, formerly AK-212) was scrapped in 1968. (See *Jane's Fighting Ships, 1970–1971* [New York: McGraw-Hill, 1970], page 543.) According to another, it was not even stricken from the Register until 1971. (See Norman Polmar, *The Ships and Aircraft of the U.S. Fleet* [12th ed., Annapolis, Md.: Naval Institute Press, 1981], page 401.)

48. Polmar, *op. cit.,* page 187.

49. "Cobra Judy Goes to Sea," *Proceedings of the United States Naval Institute* (October, 1981), page 131.

50. Canan, *op. cit.,* page 101.

51. Roy Varner and Wayne Collier, *A Matter of Risk* (New York: Random House, 1978), pages 26–27.

52. Bamford, *op. cit.,* page 201.

53. *Ibid.,* page 159. These are some of the stations that would have intercepted communications between Soviet interceptor aircraft and their ground controllers when Korean Air Lines Flight 7 was intercepted in Soviet air space on September 1, 1983.

54. ELINT information from satellites is received at the Merino Station in Pine Gap, near Alice Springs, Australia, and at Harrogate and Menwith Hill stations in England, and then relayed to National Security Agency headquarters at Fort Meade, Md. Visual imagery from KH-11 and other satellites is received at the Casino Station in Nurrungar, Australia, 600 miles southeast of Alice Springs, and at Cheltenham in England, and relayed to Buckley Air National Guard Base in Aurora, near Denver, Col., and to Fort Meade. (See Bamford, *op. cit.,* pages 207–211, and Meacham, *op. cit.,* May 21, 1983, page 28.)

55. David Shribman, "Side Effect: Peek at U.S. Intelligence Activities," *The New York Times,* September 2, 1983. Bamford (*op. cit.,* page 161) confirms the number of intercept stations in the NSA's worldwide network.

56. Those listed in active service today are seven oceanographic research ships in the *Robert D. Conrad* class (AGOR-3), along with the *Eltanin* (AGOR-8), *Mizar* (AGOR-11), *Melville* (AGOR-14), *Knorr* (AGOR-15), *Gyre* (AGOR-21), and *Moana Wave* (AGOR-22); four surveying ships in the *Silas Bent* class (AGS-26), two in the *Chauvenet* class (AGS-29), two in the *Bowditch* class (AGS-21), and the *Coastal Crusader* (AGS-36) and *H. H. Hess* (AGS-38); three command ships, the *La Salle* (AGF-3), *Blue Ridge* (LCC-19), and *Mount Whitney* (LCC-20); and two ships classed as cargo vessels, the *Mirfak* (AK-271) and *Lt. James R. Robinson* (AK-274), the

latter of which served in "special project work," according to Norman Polmar (*op. cit.,* page 206) as AG-170 in 1963 and 1964. The *Mizar* located and photographed the wreckage of the American submarines *Thresher,* in May, 1964, and *Scorpion,* in May, 1968, as well as the Soviet submarine later raised by the *Glomar Explorer* (AG-193). Again, the current disposition of more than seventy inactive vessels in these several classes is not clear. The former aircraft carriers are the communications relay ships *Annapolis* (AGMR-1), formerly the *Gilbert Islands* (CVE-107), and *Arlington* (AGMR-2), formerly the *Saipan* (CVL-48). These and most of the others are listed as stricken from the Register, but again, there are conflicting reports. For example, according to *Jane's,* the *Kellar* (AGS-25) was sunk in a hurricane in September, 1965 (see *Jane's, op. cit., 1970–71,* page 547). But according to Norman Polmar, it was sold to Portugal seven years later (Polmar, *op. cit.,* page 401). Additional ships are sometimes pressed into service for surveillance. The *LST Fairfax County* (LST-1193), for example, was sent to the Barents Sea in March, 1981, to observe Russian naval exercises.

57. *Jane's, op. cit., 1970–71,* page 547.
58. Trevor Armbrister, *A Matter of Accountability: The True Story of the Pueblo Affair* (New York: Coward-McCann, 1970), pages 82–83.
59. *Jane's, op. cit., 1970–71.* page 543. See also Armbrister, *op. cit.,* pages 86–88.
60. Clyde W. Burleson, *The Jennifer Project* (Englewood Cliffs, N.J.: Prentice-Hall, 1977), pages 111–114. The official version of the Jennifer Project attempted both to improve the image of the CIA and deny the Soviets the opportunity to make formal complaints. It did this by officially refusing to acknowledge the project existed, while hinting off the record that it may only partially have succeeded. For an analysis of this version, see Burleson, pages 149–151, and William Colby, *Honorable Men: My Life in the CIA* (New York: Simon & Schuster, 1978), pages 413–418. For the official version itself, see Roy Varner and Wayne Collier, *A Matter of Risk.*
61. Richard Halloran, "25 Take Lie Detector Tests as Pentagon Seeks Disclosure Source," *The New York Times,* January 24, 1982. The *Backfire* bomber photo appears on page 61 of *Soviet Military Power,* published by the Department of Defense on October 1, 1981.
62. Les Aspin, "The Verification of the SALT II Agreement," *Scientific American* (February, 1979), page 40.
63. *Ibid.,* page 38.
64. Karas, *op. cit.,* page 108.
65. Aspin, *op. cit.,* page 39.
66. Dr. William J. Perry, July 18, 1979, quoted in *The Defense Monitor,* Volume XI, no. 7 (1982), Center for Defense Information, Washington, D.C., page 4.
67. Taylor and Mondey, *op. cit.,* page 123.
68. Aspin, *op. cit.,* February, 1979, page 38.
69. Dr. Ray S. Cline, "The U.S. Intelligence Machine," *The U.S. War Machine* (New York: Crown, 1978), page 53.
70. Senate Intelligence Committee, "Test of Senate Committee's Findings on Ability of U.S. to Monitor Nuclear Pact," *The New York Times,* October 6, 1979.
71. George M. Seignious, "SALT II Senate Testimony," July 10, 1979, U.S. Department of State, Bureau of Public Affairs, Current Policy No. 72A, page 24.
72. Harold Brown, "SALT II: Two Views," April 5, 1979, U.S. Department of State, Bureau of Public Affairs, Current Policy No. 62, April, 1979, page 11.
73. Aspin, *op. cit.,* page 45.
74. Edward P. Boland, *Congressional Record,* January 5, 1981, page E19.
75. Reagan, *loc. cit.,* Orlando, Fla., March 8, 1983.
76. *Time* magazine, "Freeze No, Deployment Yes," April 18, 1983.
77. Edward M. Kennedy, Letter to *Time* magazine, published on May 9, 1983.
78. William Colby, "Reagan Should Turn from 'Appeasement' to a Freeze," *The Washington Post,* Op-Ed page, April 10, 1983.
79. William Colby, May 13, 1982, quoted in *The Defense Monitor,* Volume XI, no. 7 (1982), Center for Defense Information, page 4. Italics are mine.

43. On-Site Inspection

1. Reagan, *loc. cit.,* Orlando, Fla., March 8, 1983.
2. Richard Burt, "Arms Treaty: How to Verify Moscow's Compliance," *The New York Times,* March 21, 1979.
3. *Ibid.*
4. Wilford, *op. cit.,* June 5, 1983, page 50.
5. *Ibid.,* page 48.
6. Article V, Paragraph 2, Interim Agreement Between the United States of America and the Union of Soviet Socialist Republics on Certain Measures with Respect to the Limitation of Strategic Offensive Arms, Moscow, May 26, 1972, *Arms Control and Disarmament Agreements, 1982 Edition* (Washington, D.C.: United States Arms Control and Disarmament Agency), page 151.
7. Article XV, Paragraph 2, SALT II Agreement, Vienna, June 18, 1979, U.S. Department of State, Bureau of Public Affairs, Selected Documents No. 12A, page 43.
8. *Aviation Week, op. cit.,* October 21, 1957, page 26.
9. Joel Wit, "Verifying Weapons Accords," *The New York Times,* Op-Ed page, April 5, 1983.
10. Myrdal, *op. cit.,* page 82.
11. Fox Butterfield, "Anatomy of the Nuclear Protest," *The New York Times Magazine,* July 11, 1982, page 17.
12. *Ibid.*
13. Joel Wit, *op. cit.,* April 5, 1983.
14. Christopher Paine, "The Freeze and the United Nations," *Bulletin of the Atomic Scientists* (June–July, 1982), page 12.
15. Eugene J. Carroll, Jr., "A Freeze *Can* Be Verified," *The New York Times,* Op-Ed page, June 3, 1982.
16. Paragraph 19, Tripartite Report to the United Nations on a Comprehensive Test Ban Treaty, July 31, 1980, quoted by Carroll, *op. cit.,* June 3, 1982.
17. See note 74, Chapter 42, supra.
18. *Time* magazine, "Arrows Amid the Olive Branches," June 14, 1982, page 22.
19. *Ibid.*
20. Bernard D. Nossiter, "Soviet Wants to Open Some A-Plants to U.N.," *The New York Times,* February 12, 1983.
21. William Safire, "Site Unseen," *The New York Times,* January 10, 1983.

44. Telemetry

1. *Jane's Weapon Systems, Seventh Edition, 1976* (London: Macdonald & Jane's, 1975), page 19.
2. See note 15, Chapter 42, supra.
3. See note 14, Chapter 41, supra.
4. Charles Mohr, "MX Panel Urged to Alter Arms Treaty Plan," *The New York Times,* August 30, 1983.
5. Varner and Collier, *op. cit.,* page 26.
6. *The Military Balance, 1982–1983* (London: IISS, 1982), page 113.
7. See note 63, Chapter 42, supra.
8. Karas, *op. cit.,* page 111.
9. Smith, *op. cit.,* April 21, 1983.
10. SALT II Agreement, Article XV, Paragraph 3, Second Common Understanding, Vienna, June 18, 1979, U.S. Department of State, Bureau of Public Affairs, Selected Documents No. 12A, page 44.
11. Tom Wicker, "Cheating on SALT," *The New York Times,* May 3, 1983.
12. Ronald Reagan, May 31, 1982, quoted by Wicker, *ibid.*
13. Hedrick Smith, "U.S. Seeking Soviet Parley on Arms Violation Issues," *The New York Times,* August 12, 1983.

14. SALT II Agreement, *op. cit.,* page 44.
15. Richard Burt, *op. cit.,* March 21, 1979.
16. Smith, *op. cit.,* April 21, 1983.
17. Smith, *op. cit.,* May 12, 1983.
18. Hedrick Smith, "Reagan Is Urged Not to Publicize Arms Accusations Against Soviet," *The New York Times,* April 22, 1983.
19. Smith, *op. cit.,* April 21, 1983.
20. Robert Lindsey, "Soviet Spies Got Data on Satellites to Be Used for Monitoring Missiles," *The New York Times,* April 29, 1979.
21. Robert Lindsey, "Alleged Spy for Soviet Linked to C.I.A. Contractor," *The New York Times,* April 13, 1977.
22. Bamford, *op. cit.,* page 198; Tad Szulc, "Deciphering the Russians," *The New Republic,* February 21, 1981, page 13.
23. Burt, *op. cit.,* August 14, 1979.
24. Lindsey, *op. cit.,* April 29, 1979.
25. Robert Lindsey, "Californian Is Given 40 Years for Spying," *The New York Times,* September 13, 1977.
26. *The New York Times,* "Comment from the C.I.A.," April 29, 1979.
27. Lindsey, *op. cit.,* September 13, 1977.
28. Burt, *op. cit.,* August 14, 1979.
29. Szulc, *op. cit.,* February 21, 1981, page 13.
30. Burt, *op. cit.,* August 14, 1979.
31. Bamford, *op. cit.,* page 101.
32. Kosta Tsipis, interview with the author, March, 1981. Our discussion dealt with the use of computers in high-speed signal processing to locate and track submarines from their acoustic signatures. Tsipis described the Soviet inability to build for this purpose a computer comparable to our ILLIAC IV. This kind of technology has equally significant applications to cryptoanalysis. As long ago as 1970, the ILLIAC IV could already "carry out as many as 200 million instructions per second," according to Douglas Star (see Star, "The Computer Museum," *Technology Illustrated* [September, 1983], page 33). According to James Bamford, in 1976 the National Security Agency's CRAY-1 could process "up to 320 million words per second," and the Agency is currently reaching for the capacity to perform one million *billion* calculations per second (see Bamford, *op. cit.,* page 102).
33. Hedrick Smith, "Turner Sees a Gap in Verifying Treaty," *The New York Times,* April 17, 1979.
34. *Ibid.*
35. Burt, *op. cit.,* August 14, 1979.
36. Daniel O. Graham, quoted in *Aviation Week & Space Technology,* "Administration's Verification Claims Hit," April 26, 1979, page 16.
37. Szulc, *op. cit.,* February 21, 1981. Brown referred to some four hundred aircraft which perform photomapping, radar intelligence (RADINT), telemetry intelligence (TELINT), signals intelligence (SIGINT), and electronic intelligence (ELINT) missions for the Defense Department and National Security Agency. These include about 40 Lockheed U-2C, U-2D, and U-2R aircraft of the type Gary Powers flew, together with the first few of 25 new U-2R aircraft reequipped and redesignated TR-1, about 32 Lockheed SR-71A strategic reconnaissance aircraft, more than 240 Beech RU-21 and RU-21J aircraft flown by the Army Security Agency, about 20 Lockheed EC-121S, EC-121R, and NC-121K aircraft, the last type flown by the Navy for ELINT missions, and 47 Boeing RC-135B and RC-135C ELINT aircraft, EC-135G SIGINT aircraft, and RC-135A photographic reconnaissance aircraft flown by the Air Force. The RC-135A appears to be the type whose flight path crossed that of KAL Flight 7 on September 1, 1983, possibly leading to Soviet misidentification of the Korean aircraft and raising suspicions about why Flight 7 was so far off course.
38. Burt, *op. cit.,* March 21, 1979.

39. Burt, *op. cit.,* August 14, 1979.
40. "Uncle Sam and His 40,000 Snoopers," *National Review* (Australia), October 5–11, 1973, page 1612.
41. Burt, *op. cit.,* August 14, 1979.
42. Richard Burt, "U.S. Plans New Way to Check Soviet Missile Tests," *The New York Times,* June 29, 1979.
43. Karas, *op. cit.,* page 109.
44. *Ibid.*
45. Bamford, *op. cit.,* page 196.
46. Karas, *op. cit.,* page 110.
47. Jasani, "Military Uses of Outer Space," *op. cit.,* 1982, page 99.
48. *Ibid.,* pages 100–101.
49. Taylor and Mondey, *op. cit.,* page 112.
50. See section on *United States Military Satellite Systems* below, pages 488–494.
51. Jeffrey T. Richelson, *The U.S. Intelligence Community* (Cambridge: Ballinger, 1985), page 121.
52. Bamford, *op. cit.,* page 197.
53. *Ibid.*
54. *Ibid.*
55. Robert Lindsey, *The Falcon and the Snowman* (New York: Simon & Schuster, 1979), page 57.
56. Lindsey, *op. cit.,* April 29, 1979.
57. Lindsey, *The Falcon and the Snowman,* page 57.
58. Karas, *op. cit.,* pages 111 and 112.
59. Bamford, *op. cit.,* page 198.
60. *Aviation Week,* "How U.S. Taps Soviet Missile Secrets," October 21, 1957, page 26.
61. John Noble Wilford, "Pioneer 10 Pushes Beyond Goals, into the Unknown," *The New York Times,* April 26, 1983.
62. *Ibid.*
63. Lauran Paine, quoted by Desmond Ball in *A Suitable Piece of Real Estate: The American Installations in Australia* (Sydney: Hale & Tremonger, 1980), page 70.
64. Bamford, *op. cit.,* page 197.
65. Lindsey, *The Falcon and the Snowman,* page 347.

45. A Comprehensive Test Ban

1. Treaty Banning Nuclear Weapon Tests in the Atmosphere, in Outer Space and Under Water, Moscow, August 5, 1963, *Arms Control and Disarmament Agreements, 1982 Edition* (Washington, D.C.: U.S. Arms Control and Disarmament Agency, 1982, page 41.
2. Treaty on the Non-Proliferation of Nuclear Weapons, Washington, London and Moscow, July 1, 1968, U.S. Arms Control and Disarmament Agency, *op. cit.,* page 91.
3. *Ibid.,* Article VI, page 93.
4. Herbert F. York, "Bilateral Negotiations and the Arms Race," *Scientific American* (October, 1983), page 150.
5. Tom Wicker, "Small Risk for Big Gains," *The New York Times,* December 12, 1982.
6. Eugene J. Carroll, Jr., "Ignored Prerequisite to Real Arms Control," letter, *The New York Times,* April 12, 1983.
7. York, *op. cit.,* page 150.
8. Judith Miller, "U.S. Said to Decide Against New Talks to Ban All A-Tests," *The New York Times,* July 20, 1982.
9. Ronald Reagan, address at Eureka College, Eureka, Ill., May 9, 1982, text published by *The New York Times,* May 10, 1982.
10. Tom Wicker, "After MX, Why Not CTB?" *The New York Times,* December 10, 1982.
11. Carroll, *op. cit.,* April 12, 1983.

12. Kenneth L. Adelman, quoted by Tom Wicker, *op. cit.*, December 12, 1982.
13. Judith Miller, *op. cit.*, July 20, 1982.
14. Judith Miller, "U.S. Confirms a Plan to Halt Talks on a Nuclear Test Ban," *The New York Times*, July 21, 1982.
15. Carl Marcy, "Two Nuclear Treaties: Just Sitting There," letter, *The New York Times*, December 23, 1982.
16. Miller, *op. cit.*, July 21, 1982.
17. Ronald Reagan, interview, Washington, D.C., March 29, 1983, transcript published by *The New York Times*, March 30, 1983.
18. York, *op. cit.*, page 160.
19. Lynn R. Sykes and Jack F. Evernden, "The Verification of a Comprehensive Nuclear Test Ban," *Scientific American* (October, 1982), page 47.
20. *Ibid.*, page 52.
21. *Ibid.*, page 54.
22. Judith Miller, "Debate Over Nuclear Ban: Can U.S. Spot Cheats?" *The New York Times*, March 8, 1983.
23. Anne H. Cahn and James F. Leonard, "Don't Accuse Moscow," *The New York Times*, Op-Ed page, April 26, 1983.
24. Sykes and Evernden, *op. cit.*, page 55.
25. *Ibid.*
26. *Ibid.*
27. *Ibid.*, page 54.
28. Cahn and Leonard, *op. cit.*, April 26, 1983.
29. Michael May, quoted by Judith Miller, *op. cit.*, March 8, 1983.
30. Gary Hart, quoted by Judith Miller, *op. cit.*, July 21, 1982.
31. Charles McC. Mathias, Jr., "Two Nuclear Treaties Ready for the Senate," letter, *The New York Times*, February 23, 1983.
32. Tom Wicker, "Tale of Two Treaties," *The New York Times*, October 7, 1983.

Index